ANCIENT AND MEDIEVAL EUROPE
To 1500

PROBLEMS IN EUROPEAN HISTORY
Norman F. Cantor & Samuel Berner, EDITORS

Volume I
ANCIENT AND MEDIEVAL EUROPE, to 1500

Volume II
EARLY MODERN EUROPE, 1500–1815

Volume III
THE MODERN ERA, 1815 to the present

ANCIENT AND MEDIEVAL EUROPE

To 1500

edited by NORMAN F. CANTOR
BRANDEIS UNIVERSITY

& SAMUEL BERNER
UNIVERSITY OF VIRGINIA

Thomas Y. Crowell Company
NEW YORK   ESTABLISHED 1834

COPYRIGHT © 1970 by Thomas Y. Crowell Company, Inc.

All Rights Reserved

Except for use in a review, the reproduction or utilization
of this work in any form or by any electronic, mechanical,
or other means, now known or hereafter invented,
including photocopying and recording,
and in any information storage and retrieval system
is forbidden without the written permission of the publisher.

L. C. Card Number 70-101941

DESIGNED BY JUDITH WORACEK BARRY

Manufactured in the United States of America

ACKNOWLEDGMENTS

The editors wish to thank the following publishers and individuals for permission to reprint extracts from the books and articles listed below. Where no permission credit is given, the work cited is in the public domain.

1. Heinrich Graetz, *History of the Jews*, 6 vols. (Philadelphia: The Jewish Publication Society of America, 1891), vol. I, 10–15. Reprinted by permission of the publisher.

2. Julius Wellhausen, *Sketch of the History of Israel and Judah* (London: Adam & Charles Black, 1891), pp. 17–23, 108–9, 114–16. Reprinted by permission of the publisher.

3. William F. Albright, "The Biblical Period," in *The Jews: Their History, Culture, and Religion*, ed. Louis Finkelstein, 2 vols., 3d ed. (New York: Harper & Row, 1960), vol. I, 11–12. Copyright © 1949, 1955, 1960 by Louis Finkelstein. Reprinted by permission of Harper & Row, Publishers.

4. William F. Albright, *From the Stone Age to Christianity* (Baltimore: The Johns Hopkins Press, 1946; 2d ed., 1957), pp. 196, 205–7. Reprinted by permission of Harper & Row, Publishers.

5. Yehezkel Kaufmann, *The Religion of Israel*, trans. Moshe Greenberg (Chicago: The University of Chicago Press, 1960), pp. 223–25. Copyright © 1960 by The University of Chicago. Reprinted by permission of Moshe Greenberg and the publisher.

6. William C. Graham, *The Prophets and Israel's Culture* (Chicago: The University of Chicago Press, 1934), pp. 95–96.

7. H. H. Rowley, *The Faith of Israel* (London: Student Christian Movement Press Ltd., 1956; Philadelphia: The Westminster Press, 1957), pp. 71–73. Used by permission of the publishers. H. H. Rowley, *Men of God* (Lon-

Acknowledgments

don: Thomas Nelson & Sons Ltd., 1963), pp. 35–36. Reprinted by permission of the publisher.

8. John Bright, *A History of Israel* (Philadelphia: The Westminster Press, 1959), pp. 92–93, 317–19. Copyright © 1959 by W. L. Jenkins, The Westminster Press. Reprinted by permission of the publisher.

9. R. B. Y. Scott, *The Relevance of the Prophets* (New York: The Macmillan Company, 1954), pp. 40–41, 59–62, 105–6. Copyright 1944 by The Macmillan Company. Reprinted with permission of The Macmillan Company.

10. Sigmund Freud, *Moses and Monotheism*, trans. Katharine Jones (New York: Alfred A. Knopf, Inc., Vintage Books, 1955), pp. 133–36, 171–73. Copyright 1939 by Sigmund Freud; renewed © 1967 by Ernest L. Freud and Anna Freud. Reprinted by permission of Alfred A. Knopf, Inc.

11. George Grote, *Greece*, 12 vols. (New York: Peter Fenelon Collier, 1899), vol. I, 463; vol. IV, 100–1.

12. Mikhail Rostovtzeff, *A History of the Ancient World*, 2 vols. (Oxford: Clarendon Press, 1926; 2d ed., 1930), vol. I, 229–41. Reprinted by permission of the Clarendon Press, Oxford.

13. Victor Ehrenberg, *The Greek State* (Oxford: Basil Blackwell, 1940), pp. 5–9. Reprinted by permission of the publisher.

14. C. M. Bowra, *The Greek Experience* (Cleveland: The World Publishing Company, 1957), pp. 3–13, 20–21, 40–41. Reprinted by permission of the publisher.

15. Arnold J. Toynbee, *Hellenism: The History of a Civilization* (New York: Oxford University Press, 1959), pp. 9–15. Copyright © 1959 by Oxford University Press. Reprinted by permission of the publisher.

16. Werner Jaeger, *Paideia: The Ideals of Greek Culture*, 3 vols., 2d ed. (New York: Oxford University Press, 1945), vol. I, 5–14. Copyright 1939, 1945, renewed © 1967 by Oxford University Press, Inc. Reprinted by permission of Oxford University Press and Basil Blackwell Ltd.

17. Bruno Snell, *The Discovery of the Mind* (New York: Harper & Row, 1960), pp. 39–42. Reprinted by permission of Harvard University Press and Basil Blackwell Ltd.

18. Chester G. Starr, *The Origins of Greek Civilization* (New York: Alfred A. Knopf, Inc., 1961), pp. 381–85. Copyright © 1961 by Chester G. Starr. Reprinted by permission of Alfred A. Knopf, Inc.

19. H. D. F. Kitto, *The Greeks* (Baltimore: Penguin Books, 1960), pp. 26–28. Reprinted by permission of the publisher.

20. Finley Hooper, *Greek Realities* (New York: Charles Scribner's Sons, 1967), pp. 124–25. Copyright © 1967 by Finley Hooper. Reprinted with the permission of Charles Scribner's Sons.

21. Theodor Mommsen, *The History of Rome*, 5 vols. (New York: Charles Scribner's Sons, 1911), vol. V, 305–15.

22. Ronald Syme, *The Roman Revolution* (Oxford: Clarendon Press, 1939), pp. 12–18. Reprinted by permission of the Clarendon Press, Oxford.

23. Léon Homo, *Roman Political Institutions* (London: Kegan Paul, Trench, Trubner & Co., Ltd., 1929), pp. 147–56, 202–4. Reprinted by permission of Routledge & Kegan Paul Ltd. and Barnes & Noble, Inc.

24. H. H. Scullard, *From the Gracchi to Nero: A History of Rome from 133 B.C. to A.D. 68* (New York: Barnes & Noble, Inc., 1964), pp. 13–16, 19–22. Reprinted by permission of Methuen & Company, Ltd., London.

25. F. R. Cowell, *Cicero and the Roman Republic* (London: Sir Isaac Pitman & Sons Ltd., 1948), pp. 288–94. Reprinted by permission of Sir Isaac Pitman & Sons Ltd.

26. Richard E. Smith, *The Failure of the Roman Republic* (Cambridge: Cambridge University Press, 1955), pp. 163–66. Reprinted by permission of the author and the publisher.

27. Mikhail Rostovtzeff, *A History of the Ancient World*, 2 vols. (Oxford: Clarendon Press, 1927), vol. II, 158–61, 363–64. Reprinted by permission of the Clarendon Press, Oxford.

28. Ernest Renan, *The Life of Jesus* (London: Trubner & Company, 1864), pp. 300–7.

29. Albert Schweitzer, *The Quest of the Historical Jesus* (New York: The Macmillan Company, 1959; London: A. & C. Black Ltd.), pp. 398–403. Reprinted by permission of A. & C. Black Ltd.

30. Adolf Harnack, *The Mission and Expansion of Christianity* (New York: Harper & Row, Publishers, 1962), pp. 36–43.

31. Shirley Jackson Case, *The Social Origins of Christianity* (Chicago: University of Chicago Press, 1923), pp. 38–39, 53–57. Copyright 1923 by The University of Chicago. Reprinted by permission of the University of Chicago Press.

32. Jules Lebreton and Jacques Zeiller, *The History of the Primitive Church*, 2 vols. (New York: The Macmillan Company, 1949), vol. I, 83–86, 91–93, 105–9. Copyright 1949 by The Macmillan Company. Reprinted with permission of The Macmillan Company and Burns & Oates Ltd.

33. Joseph Klausner, *From Jesus to Paul* (New York: The Macmillan Company, 1943), pp. 3–6, 588–90. Copyright 1943 by The Macmillan Company. Reprinted with permission of The Macmillan Company.

34. Charles Guignebert, *The Jewish World in the Time of Jesus* (London: Kegan Paul, Trench, Trubner & Co., Ltd., 1939), pp. 258–61. Reprinted by permission of Routledge & Kegan Paul Ltd.

35. Rudolf Bultmann, *Primitive Christianity* (Cleveland: The World Publishing Company, Meridian Books, 1956), pp. 86–93, 175–79. Reprinted by permission of Thames and Hudson Ltd.

36. Edward Gibbon, *The Decline and Fall of the Roman Empire*, abridged by D. M. Low (New York: Harcourt, Brace & World, 1960), pp. 523–29. Copyright © 1960 by Chatto & Windus Ltd. Reprinted by permission of D. M. Low, Chatto & Windus Ltd. and Harcourt, Brace & World.

37. Tenney Frank, *A History of Rome* (New York: Henry Holt and Company, 1923), pp. 566–68, 574. Copyright 1923 by Holt, Rinehart and Winston, Inc. Copyright 1951 by Grace Frank. Reprinted by permission of Holt, Rinehart and Winston.

38. Mikhail Rostovtzeff, *The Social and Economic History of the Roman Empire*, 2 vols., 2d ed. trans. by P. M. Fraser (Oxford: Clarendon Press, 1926; 2d ed., 1957), vol. I, 477–81, 486–87. Reprinted by permission of the Clarendon Press, Oxford.

39. Charles Norris Cochrane, *Christianity and Classical Culture*, 2d ed. (New York: Oxford University Press, 1944), pp. 155–62. Copyright 1944 by Oxford University Press. Reprinted by permission of the publisher.

40. Frank W. Walbank, *The Decline of the Roman Empire in the West* (New York: Abelard-Schuman Ltd., 1953), pp. 66–69. Copyright 1953 by

Acknowledgments

Abelard-Schuman Ltd. All Rights Reserved. Reprinted by permission of the publisher.

41. Joseph Vogt, *The Decline of Rome*, trans. Janet Sondheimer (New York: New American Library, 1967), pp. 50–51, 60–62, 183–84. Copyright © 1965 by Joseph Vogt; English translation copyright © 1967 by George Weidenfeld & Nicolson Ltd. Reprinted by permission of The World Publishing Company and Weidenfeld & Nicolson Ltd.

42. A. H. M. Jones, *The Later Roman Empire*, 4 vols. (Oxford: Basil Blackwell, 1964), vol. II, 1026–31, 1062–68. Reprinted by permission of the publisher.

43. F. Oertel, "The Economic Life of the Empire," *The Cambridge Ancient History*, 12 vols. (Cambridge: Cambridge University Press, 1939), vol. XII, 249–55, 262–70. Reprinted by permission of the publisher.

44. James Bryce, *The Holy Roman Empire* (New York: The Macmillan Company, 1923), pp. 23–33, 68–75. Reprinted by permission of Miss Margaret V. Bryce, Executrix of the late Viscountess Bryce.

45. R. R. Bolgar, *The Classical Heritage and Its Beneficiaries* (Cambridge: Cambridge University Press, 1954), pp. 91–92, 95, 116–17, 127–29. Reprinted by permission of the publisher.

46. Henri Pirenne, *Mohammed and Charlemagne* (London: George Allen & Unwin Ltd., 1958), pp. 140–44, 284–85. Reprinted by permission of George Allen & Unwin Ltd. and Barnes & Noble, Inc.

47. Robert Latouche, *The Birth of Western Economy*, trans. E. M. Wilkinson (London: Methuen & Company, Ltd., 1961), pp. 117–25. Reprinted by permission of the publisher.

48. Alfons Dopsch, *The Economic and Social Foundations of European Civilization* (London: Kegan Paul, Trench, Trubner & Co., Ltd., 1937; New York: Howard Fertig, Inc., 1969), pp. 384–90. Reprinted by permission of Howard Fertig, Inc.

49. Ferdinand Lot, *The End of the Ancient World* (New York: Barnes & Noble, Inc., 1953), pp. 183–86, 403–7. Reprinted by permission of Barnes & Noble, Inc., and Routledge & Kegan Paul Ltd.

50. Heinrich Fichtenau, *The Carolingian Empire* (Oxford: Basil Blackwell, 1957), pp. 5–10, 46. Reprinted by permission of the publisher.

51. C. Delisle Burns, *The First Europe* (New York: W. W. Norton & Company, Inc., 1948), pp. 221–28, 609–11. Copyright 1948. All Rights Reserved by W. W. Norton & Company, Inc. Reprinted by permission of W. W. Norton & Company, Inc. and George Allen & Unwin Ltd.

52. O. M. Dalton, *Gregory of Tours, The History of the Franks*, 2 vols. (Oxford: Clarendon Press, 1927), vol. I, 191–94, 237. Reprinted by permission of the Clarendon Press, Oxford.

53. Rushton Coulburn, *Feudalism in History* (Princeton, N.J.: Princeton University Press, 1956), pp. 189–94. Reprinted by permission of Princeton University Press.

54. Carl Stephenson, *Mediaeval Institutions* (Ithaca, N.Y.: Cornell University Press, 1954), pp. 216–18, 224–30. Copyright 1954 by Cornell University. Reprinted by permission of Cornell University Press.

55. François L. Ganshof, *Feudalism*, trans. Philip Grierson (London: Longmans, Green & Co., Ltd., 1952), pp. xv–xvii, 3–4, 15, 52–56, 59–62. Reprinted by permission of the publisher.

56. Marc Bloch, *Feudal Society* (Chicago: The University of Chicago Press, 1961), pp. 59–61, 441–47, 450–52. Copyright © 1961 by The University of Chicago. Reprinted by permission of the publisher.

57. Joseph R. Strayer, *Feudalism* (Princeton, N.J.: D. Van Nostrand Co., Inc., 1965), pp. 11–14. Reprinted courtesy of D. Van Nostrand Company, Inc.

58. Georges Duby and Robert Mandrou, *A History of French Civilization*, trans. James Blakeley Atkinson (New York: Random House, 1964), pp. 32–33, 38–41. Copyright © 1964 by Random House, Inc. Reprinted by permission of the publisher.

59. Bryce D. Lyon, *From Fief to Indenture: The Transition from Feudal to Nonfeudal Contract in Western Europe* (Cambridge: Harvard University Press, 1957), pp. 270–73. Reprinted by permission of the publisher.

60. Johannes Haller, *The Epochs of German History* (London: George Routledge & Sons Ltd., 1930), pp. 30–35. Reprinted by permission of Routledge & Kegan Paul Ltd.

61. Geoffrey Barraclough, *The Origins of Modern Germany* (Oxford: Basil Blackwell, 1946), pp. 101–7. Reprinted by permission of the publisher.

62. James Westfall Thompson, *Feudal Germany* (Chicago: University of Chicago Press, 1928), pp. 125–28. Copyright 1928 by The University of Chicago. Reprinted by permission of the publisher.

63. David Knowles, *The Monastic Orders in England* (Cambridge: Cambridge University Press, 1940), pp. 191–97. Reprinted by permission of the author and the publisher.

64. Walter Ullmann, *The Growth of Papal Government in the Middle Ages* (London: Methuen & Company, Ltd., 1965), pp. 262–63, 271–72, 299. Reprinted by permission of the publisher.

65. Christopher Brooke, *Europe in the Central Middle Ages* (London: Longmans, Green and Co., Ltd., 1964), pp. 249–50, 252–56. Reprinted by permission of Longmans, Green and Co., Ltd., and Holt, Rinehart and Winston, Inc. All Rights Reserved.

66. Gerd Tellenbach, *Church, State and Christian Society at the Time of the Investiture Contest* (Oxford: Basil Blackwell, 1966), pp. 162–67. Reprinted by permission of the publisher.

67. J. P. Whitney, *Hildebrandine Essays* (Cambridge: Cambridge University Press, 1932), pp. 88–89, 91–92. Reprinted by permission of the author and the publisher.

68. R. W. Southern, *The Making of the Middle Ages* (New Haven: Yale University Press, 1965), pp. 139–43. Reprinted by permission of the publisher.

69. Henry C. Lea, *A History of the Inquisition of the Middle Ages*, 3 vols. (New York: Harper & Brothers, 1888), vol. I, 100–7; vol. II, 109–12; vol. III, 645–46.

70. Albert C. Shannon, *The Popes and Heresy in the Thirteenth Century* (Villanova, Pa.: Augustinian Press, 1949), pp. 3–10, 135–36. Reprinted by permission of the publisher.

71. Steven Runciman, *The Medieval Manichee* (Cambridge: Cambridge University Press, 1947), pp. 139–47. Reprinted by permission of the author and the publisher.

72. Zoé Oldenbourg, *Massacre at Montségur*, trans. Peter Green (New

Acknowledgments

York: Random House, Pantheon Books, 1961), pp. 225–28, 365–67. Copyright © 1961 by George Weidenfeld & Nicholson Ltd., and Pantheon Books, a division of Random House, Inc. Reprinted by permission of Pantheon Books, a division of Random House, Inc.

73. Friedrich Heer, *The Medieval World* (London: Weidenfeld & Nicolson Ltd., 1962), pp. 173–79. Copyright © 1961 by George Weidenfeld & Nicolson Ltd., English translation Copyright © 1962 by George Weidenfeld & Nicolson Ltd. Reprinted by permission of The World Publishing Company and George Weidenfeld & Nicolson Ltd.

74. Norman Cohn, *The Pursuit of the Millennium* (London: Secker & Warburg Ltd., 1957), pp. 29–32, 307–8. Reprinted by permission of Secker & Warburg Ltd., and Oxford University Press.

75. Gordon Leff, *Heresy in the Later Middle Ages*, 2 vols. (New York: Barnes & Noble, Inc., 1967; Manchester: Manchester University Press), vol. I, 1–3, 46–47. Reprinted by permission of Barnes & Noble, Inc., and University of Manchester Press.

76. William Stubbs, *The Constitutional History of England*, 3 vols. (Oxford: Clarendon Press, 1877), vol. II, 220–25, 239–43. Reprinted by permission of the Clarendon Press, Oxford.

77. Frederic William Maitland, *Records of the Parliament, 1305* (London: Eyre and Spottiswoode, 1893), pp. lxxx–lxxxv.

78. A. F. Pollard, *The Evolution of Parliament* (London: Longmans, Green and Co., Ltd., 1926; 2d rev. ed., New York: Russell & Russell, 1964), pp. 48–53. Reprinted by permission of Russell & Russell and Longmans, Green and Co., Ltd.

79. D. Pasquet, *An Essay on the Origins of the House of Commons* (Cambridge: Cambridge University Press, 1925), pp. 173–80, 194, 196–97, 225–26. Reprinted by permission of the publisher.

80. G. O. Sayles, *The Medieval Foundations of England* (London: Methuen & Co., Ltd., 1948), pp. 448, 453–56. Reprinted by permission of the publisher.

81. Theodore Plucknett, "Parliament," in *The English Government at Work, 1327–1336*, ed. William Morris and James F. Willard, 3 vols. (Cambridge, Mass.: The Medieval Academy of America, 1940), vol. I, 112–14. Reprinted by permission of the publisher.

82. Bertie Wilkinson, *Constitutional History of Medieval England, 1216–1399* (London: Longmans, Green and Co., Ltd., 1958), pp. 265–73. Reprinted by permission of the publisher.

PREFACE

We have sought in these three volumes to make the most important views of historians on the central issues and questions in European history easily available to college students. We have provided introductory information to establish the contours of the problems and identify the assumptions of the particular scholars, without prejudging the issues. We have tried to present all significant views on each problem.

We hope that these volumes will whet students' appetites to make further inquiries on their own and particularly to read the important works excerpted in these volumes.

We are grateful to the publishers who have given us permission to republish selections from a large number of works. We are also grateful to our students whose eager pursuit of historical knowledge inspired us to undertake the considerable labor involved in editing these volumes.

N.F.C.
S.B.

CONTENTS

INTRODUCTION

Part 1
THE FORMATION OF JUDAISM   7

    1. HEINRICH GRAETZ, 10
    2. JULIUS WELLHAUSEN, 13
    3. WILLIAM F. ALBRIGHT, 18
    4. WILLIAM F. ALBRIGHT, 20
    5. YEHEZKEL KAUFMANN, 22
    6. WILLIAM C. GRAHAM, 24
    7. H. H. ROWLEY, 25
    8. JOHN BRIGHT, 28
    9. R. B. Y. SCOTT, 31
   10. SIGMUND FREUD, 35

Part 2
THE MAKING OF GREEK CIVILIZATION   39

    1. GEORGE GROTE, 44
    2. MIKHAIL ROSTOVTZEFF, 45

3. VICTOR EHRENBERG, 51
4. C. M. BOWRA, 55
5. ARNOLD J. TOYNBEE, 66
6. WERNER JAEGER, 70
7. BRUNO SNELL, 77
8. CHESTER G. STARR, 81
9. H. D. F. KITTO, 85
10. FINLEY HOOPER, 87

Part 3
THE END OF THE ROMAN REPUBLIC 89

1. THEODOR MOMMSEN, 93
2. RONALD SYME, 100
3. LÉON HOMO, 105
4. H. H. SCULLARD, 109
5. F. R. COWELL, 115
6. RICHARD E. SMITH, 122
7. MIKHAIL ROSTOVTZEFF, 124

Part 4
THE HISTORICAL JESUS AND THE BEGINNINGS OF CHRISTIANITY 129

1. ERNEST RENAN, 133
2. ALBERT SCHWEITZER, 137
3. ADOLF HARNACK, 142
4. SHIRLEY JACKSON CASE, 147
5. JULES LEBRETON AND JACQUES ZEILLER, 149
6. JOSEPH KLAUSNER, 157
7. CHARLES GUIGNEBERT, 160
8. RUDOLF BULTMANN, 163

Part 5
THE DECLINE OF ROME 173

1. EDWARD GIBBON, 177
2. TENNEY FRANK, 182
3. MIKHAIL ROSTOVTZEFF, 184
4. CHARLES NORRIS COCHRANE, 188
5. FRANK W. WALBANK, 194
6. JOSEPH VOGT, 196
7. A. H. M. JONES, 203
8. F. OERTEL, 214

Part 6
THE IMPACT OF THE GERMAN INVASIONS 227

1. JAMES BRYCE, 231
2. R. R. BOLGAR, 238
3. HENRI PIRENNE, 243
4. ROBERT LATOUCHE, 248
5. ALFONS DOPSCH, 254
6. FERDINAND LOT, 262
7. HEINRICH FICHTENAU, 268
8. C. DELISLE BURNS, 273
9. O. M. DALTON, 280

Part 7
THE NATURE OF FEUDALISM 285

1. RUSHTON COULBURN, 289
2. CARL STEPHENSON, 294

3. FRANÇOIS L. GANSHOF, 298
4. MARC BLOCH, 307
5. JOSEPH R. STRAYER, 318
6. GEORGES DUBY AND ROBERT MANDROU, 320
7. BRYCE D. LYON, 325

Part 8
THE GREGORIAN REFORM 329

1. JOHANNES HALLER, 333
2. GEOFFREY BARRACLOUGH, 338
3. JAMES WESTFALL THOMPSON, 343
4. DAVID KNOWLES, 345
5. WALTER ULLMANN, 351
6. CHRISTOPHER BROOKE, 354
7. GERD TELLENBACH, 357
8. J. P. WHITNEY, 362
9. R. W. SOUTHERN, 363

Part 9
CHURCH AND HERESY 367

1. HENRY C. LEA, 372
2. ALBERT C. SHANNON, 380
3. STEVEN RUNCIMAN, 384
4. ZOÉ OLDENBOURG, 390
5. FRIEDRICH HEER, 395
6. NORMAN COHN, 402
7. GORDON LEFF, 406

Part 10

THE ORIGINS OF PARLIAMENT 411

1. WILLIAM STUBBS, 415
2. FREDERIC WILLIAM MAITLAND, 420
3. A. F. POLLARD, 424
4. D. PASQUET, 427
5. G. O. SAYLES, 432
6. THEODORE PLUCKNETT, 436
7. BERTIE WILKINSON, 438

INTRODUCTION

In accordance with traditional practice, the ten Parts of this volume have been arranged in chronological order. However, the student will acquire a more comprehensive idea of history if he also tries to relate the individual selections to recurrent and universal themes. It is clear, for example, that the Parts on "The Formation of Judaism," "The Historical Jesus and the Beginnings of Christianity," "The Gregorian Reform," and "Church and Heresy" are quite closely connected. The first ones mentioned deal with two sources of patterns of thought so enduring and so profoundly influential that our civilization has been characterized as "Judeo-Christian." Christianity drew much of its inspiration from Judaism and for many centuries it was a unifying force transcending all other affiliations. It cohered and defined a civilization when nationalism, even the idea of Europe itself, did not exist; Christianity made it possible for an Irish monk and an Italian merchant to feel they shared a common culture.

The institutional and ideological dominance of Christianity was not undisputed; the Gregorian Reform and heresy presented the major challenges. It is easier to understand the struggle between Pope Gregory VII and Emperor Henry IV—and also the threat posed by heresy—in terms of the confused situation which existed in the Christian world at that time. Both the Papacy and the Empire were universal institutions; unfortunately, the distinction between them was not explicitly clear. Their jurisdictional borders had never been mapped out, and vague borders are always a source of conflict, especially when they separate powerful neighbors. Vagueness was also partially responsible for the growth of heresy. Heresy—deviation from orthodox dogma and practice—was part of the Christian story from the first because the fundamental tenets of Christianity were never spelled out in detail. Catholicism as we know it today is post-Tridentine, that is, it dates from the latter half of the sixteenth century. Before then, in the medieval centuries, it was much less structured, more subject to a variety of interpretation and practice. Heresy was an extreme response to this lack of coherence.

Part 2 is concerned with the making of Greek civilization. The modern student of this civilization encounters two initial difficulties. First, the ancient Greeks have been the object of unrestrained adulation. One scholar, in a dithyrambic vein, has gone so far as to say that "They contributed in less than a millennium more to the human treasury of civilization than all the rest of the world put together throughout all of its known history"! A realistic assessment of the Greeks will have to dispense with such excessive veneration. The Greeks, who had a wonderful sense of proportion, would themselves be appalled. They certainly had their share of pride and egotism, but at the same time they were realists.

The other difficulty is that today, when classical studies no longer occupy a central place in the educational curriculum, it is hard for us to see what we really owe to the Greeks. We have come far from the time when Shelley could declare that "we are all Greeks"; we are also far from a statement like the one which appeared in the introduction to Fustel de Coulanges' *The Ancient City* in 1864:

> In our system of education we live from infancy in the midst of the Greeks and the Romans, and become accustomed continually to compare them with ourselves, to judge of their history by our own, and to explain our revolutions by theirs. What we have received from them leads us to believe that we resemble them. We have some difficulty in considering them as foreign nations; it is almost always ourselves that we see in them.

But even today the Greek influence, though much less explicit, is still there and it often emerges unexpectedly. Thus when the members of a Communist-sponsored peace committee in France wanted to reach the French intelligentsia, they decided to call their propaganda tract "Trygaeus," after the hero of Aristophanes' play "The Peace." And the big surprise of the paperback book industry was that Homer became a best seller.

The thematic unity of the Parts dealing with "The End of the Roman Republic," "The Decline of Rome," and "The Impact of the German Invasions" needs no elaboration. At least three fascinating questions are introduced in these sections, and the ways historians have attempted to resolve them are extremely instructive. The expansion of Rome began in the republican era and may have been one of the chief contributing causes for the demise of the Republic. The first question, then, is whether expansion necessarily brings about internal change. In other words, how far can the body politic stretch and still retain its essential character? The figure of

Caesar (or Moses, Christ, Paul, or Pope Gregory) suggests the next question: What is the role of "great men" in history? Or, conversely, how large a role do individuals have in shaping their own destinies? The transition from Republic to Empire and the decline of the Empire—in effect the decline of a good part of ancient civilization—present the third and perhaps most difficult question. Among other things, history is the study of change; how do we measure change and how do we gauge the relationship between continuity and change? These are all difficult problems. But when they are considered in relation to specific phenomena, they invariably lead to a more profound understanding of the whole subject.

The most satisfying discussions of feudalism are precisely those in which the special relationship between lord and vassal is used to illuminate the structure of the entire society. Studying this helps us to understand feudalism, one of the fundamental organizing principles in European society before the advent of the territorial state. But the significance of feudalism reaches well beyond the Middle Ages. The late Professor Sidney Painter wrote that "Long after the disappearance of feudalism as a living political system, its traditions deeply affected the accepted political ideas of [Western Civilization] and inhibited the development of both absolutist government and nationalism. In it lay the foundations of the Anglo-American conception of government which has played so important a part in the modern world."

Finally, Part 10, "The Origins of Parliament," deals with one institution in one country. The subject is not at all narrow and no apology need be made for its inclusion in view of its intrinsic interest and its impact on the subsequent history of the Anglo-Saxon world, to which most of the readers of this volume belong.

These, then, are the major themes under consideration here. The historical literature on this vast chronological span is varied and complex. However, all students of this period face the same problem—the availability and reliability of sources. History is essentially a dialogue between the historian and his sources, between the student of the past and the materials surviving from that past. In the first place, then, the problem of sources concerns their availability. As Professor G. R. Elton has written, "questions for whose answer no material exists are strictly non-questions"; in the shadow of this sobering reality, historical scholarship goes about its task. Further, one must evaluate the reliability of the sources we do possess. The remainder of this introduction is devoted to these two problems.

The study of the ancient and medieval world often rests on a precarious factual foundation. Throughout this volume such expressions as "we may suppose," "we may guess," "probably," and "perhaps" appear. There is much we simply do not know. What is remarkable, however—and a tribute to the industry and ingenuity of countless scholars—is how many of the secrets of the ancient and medieval world have been uncovered. It is especially gratifying to contemplate the historiography of the last one hundred years in this field because one can believe, momentarily, in the idea of progress.

In no other area of historical inquiry has our craft been so aided and enriched by allied disciplines. Anthropologists have helped us understand the content of "primitive" religions. The archaeologists have uncovered all manner of buildings and artifacts that reveal so much about ancient Egypt, Greece, and Rome. The study of numismatics has shed considerable light on the political and social life of Greece and Rome. Linguists have deciphered previously unintelligible alphabets, opening up new areas for investigation.

By and large, this incremental growth in our knowledge has been steady and slow. On occasion, however, dramatic discoveries have accelerated this process suddenly. The most famous example of recent years is the Dead Sea Scrolls. The late 1940's and early 1950's witnessed a series of archaeological discoveries near the Dead Sea. In one instance, a Bedouin boy entered a cave and found several leather scrolls. These turned out to be a copy of the Book of Isaiah a thousand years older than what was then considered to be the oldest Hebrew manuscript in existence.

Much material has been uncovered and more is being found all the time. How reliable is this material? How much do these sources really tell us? The nature of this critical problem might well be illustrated with reference to any of the subjects treated in this volume. We will limit our discussion to one particular area—the sources for the life of Christ.

In two specific ways Christianity is permeated by a sense of history. First, it possesses a comprehensive vision of all of human history. Christians believe that history has a point of departure and an ultimate goal toward which it is moving inexorably; the beginning is the creation of the world, the goal the day of judgment, and there is a lineal progression from one to the other. Furthermore, within this progression there are certain crucial events: Paradise, the fall of man, the incarnation of Christ. Specific historical acts reveal God's intervention in human affairs. The most important of these, of course, is the life of Christ, which poses some perplexing problems for the historian. The historian cannot treat Christianity in terms of divine intervention. An "act of God" is a matter of faith, not an explanation. Religious convictions notwithstanding, when he turns to study the evidence on the life of Christ, the historian must assume a secular posture.

We know that Christ lived because the Bible tells us much about him. But for the historian the Bible is simply another historical source; he exercises the same degree of care and skepticism here as in dealing with any

Introduction

other document. Our main sources for the life of Christ are the Gospels. Other historical sources, including the rest of the New Testament, make almost no mention of Jesus. But the Gospels present a number of difficulties as historical sources. First, they are not contemporary documents. The earliest, Mark, was written about A.D. 60—some three decades after the death of Christ. The others were composed between A.D. 60 and 150. Accurate human memory is short; myths develop overnight and thirty years is a long way away from the events described. How reliable are the Gospels? Another difficulty arises from the fact that the Gospels were revised again and again during the first centuries after Christ. Were they altered? If so, how? Also, because the Gospels are compilations by several authors, their reliability is even more suspect. Finally, we should remember that the Gospels are a religious text designed to reinforce and perpetuate a particular faith. Symbolism and ambiguity are salient characteristics of such texts, and religious "truth" is not always commensurate with what the historian understands by the term.

This book has been assembled with four related goals in mind. First, the student will be exposed to some of the most important historians who have written on each area under consideration here. Second, the essays help to analyze the ingredients which make up such complex subjects as the decline of Rome or medieval heresy. Third, since each theme has sparked controversy, the selections will draw the student toward differing interpretations and encourage the formation of independent conclusions. In this connection we urge the student not to assume that, given two extreme views, the "truth" necessarily lies somewhere in the middle. It often does. But it may, instead, be found outside the two extremes. Lastly, the selections should stimulate thought and discussion about some fundamental problems in the study of history.

In a collection of readings on a far different subject, the Industrial Revolution, Professor Philip Taylor of the University of Birmingham, England, makes a statement which applies as well to this volume:

> It is for you to decide which of these ways of studying history is the most defensible. It is for you to decide whether the facts presented in these readings are adequate to support the generalizations, and whether the authors' reasoning is cogent. It is for you to decide, even, whether these long controversies have been fruitful. Certainly it will now be clear that history, as thought about by scholars, is not only a body of agreed fact—which is what 'history' as a subject at school commonly amounts to—but it is also a complex of doubts, interpretations, and judgements which may vary from time to time, and from one honest and learned man to another.

Part 1

THE FORMATION OF JUDAISM

The study of the formation of Judaism has not been characterized by the detached and disinterested exchange of views that ideally should prevail in a community of scholars. Much of the acrimony which accompanies this debate springs from the intrinsic delicacy of the subject matter, as well as from the latent tension between the assumptions underlying the work of the Jewish and Christian theologian-scholars, on the one hand, and secular historiography on the other. The first two selections in this Part clearly and sharply delineate the salient features of these two traditions.

At the outset, we must make it clear that these two traditions are not necessarily antithetical or in conflict at all points. Profound learning, careful attention to the texts, and an attempt at an objective assessment of the subject are found in both schools. The *History of the Jews* by Heinrich Graetz is a case in point. The multi-volume work was a labor of love to which this nineteenth-century Jewish historian devoted twenty-two years. A sympathetic critic has written of Graetz, "He often permits subjective views to obtrude themselves too much, and in stating his hypotheses he is apt to clothe them in terms too positive and incisive." This is certainly a fair judgment, but it should also be noted that in 1888 the Spanish government elected Graetz an honorary member of the Spanish academy of Madrid in recognition of the "fair" treatment he accorded the Spanish people in his history.

The same critic quoted above has succinctly described Graetz's role in the historiography of the formation of Judaism: "his greatest achievement, one that cannot be rated sufficiently high, is that of having procured a hearing with all the strata of his coreligionists by means of his charming, easy style. He revived the consciousness of an illustrious past, glorious in spite of persecution and degradation, and the belief in a future of spiritual triumph for Israel." The *History of the Jews* is, then, a distinctly Jewish work designed to inculcate a sense of pride in the past. Until very recently, it was—in the original German or in the Hebrew, Russian, English, or French translation—a permanent feature in the library of every Jewish home.

The immense popularity of the *History of the Jews* can only be explained in terms of its artistic power. Graetz—like Gibbon, Macaulay, and Burckhardt—was extremely successful, not because of his scholarship but because he made the study of the past so palatable, so dramatic. A careful reading of the selection will reveal some of the ingredients that went into this artistry.

In Egypt, the Jews lived in a state of sin; they "became devoid of all human dignity" because the "repulsive idolatry then prevailing in Egypt" insinuated itself into the very heart of the Jewish religion. This was a critical test for the Jews. "Would [they] conform to their hereditary law, or follow strange gods?" In other words, would the Jews survive? Almost all succumbed and the stage was skillfully set for the "exalted mission" of Moses who saved and formed the Jews. Like Christ, Moses was "the meekest of men." But the "prophetic spirit" touched him and prepared him for the audacious, heroic acts he was to perform. When faced with this "prophetic spirit," this inspiration, Graetz waxes mystical, leaving the senses for the domain of the "undisclosed faculty of the soul" to seek a clue to its meaning. He connects Moses with the later prophets but declares Moses the greatest of them. The essentials of high drama are all here; near catastrophe is averted by the hero and a whole people pass from a state of sin and corruption to salvation.

The second selection is taken from the important work of the Protestant scholar Julius Wellhausen (1844–1918). He was one of the principal practitioners of what came to be known as the "higher criticism" of the Bible, a scholarly movement which aroused intense, often vitriolic opposition when it appeared. Indeed, Wellhausen's views made him so many enemies that he was forced to resign his academic post. Fundamental to the "higher criticism" was Wellhausen's conviction that "Our science lags behind the other historical sciences because it has been almost monopolised by theologians."

Two related methodological procedures were employed by the "higher critics" to place biblical studies once again, in their view, on a sound basis. First, they sought to establish accurate texts. Second, they were convinced that these texts had to be understood in relation to their historical setting. Thus, many of the Jewish holy writings were found to be historically inaccurate and the Old Testament emerged as a composite of legends, myths, and genealogies edited at a later date by Hebrew scholars who were far from disinterested.

Some of the conclusions reached by the "higher criticism" were accepted by both Jewish and Christian scholars. But in the past few decades an interesting reversal has been taking place. The most recent work, greatly enriched by archaeological findings, is rather critical of the "higher critics." The accuracy of the Bible, so confidently assumed by the theologians and so vigorously attacked by the "higher critics," has now to a considerable extent been confirmed. The distinguished American scholar W. F. Albright observes that "Aside from a few die-hards among the older scholars, there is scarcely a biblical historian who has not been impressed by the rapid accumulation of data supporting the substantial historicity of patriarchical tradition."

The remaining selections in this Part are all taken from the work of contemporary or near-contemporary scholars. What emerges from these selections is the key position of three closely related themes that may serve as a structure for the study of the formation of Judaism. They are 1) Moses and his role in shaping the destiny of the Jews, 2) the uniqueness of the Jews and their relation to Egypt, and 3) the role of the prophets and, by implication, the relation of Israel to later Christianity. In addition to these specific themes there is an overriding question implicit in any phase of the study of Hebrew history: How can one explain the enduring self-identity of this people in the face of geographical dispersal and their "alien" status throughout European history?

1. HEINRICH GRAETZ

FROM Heinrich Graetz, *History of the Jews*, 6 vols. (Philadelphia: The Jewish Publication Society of America, 1891), vol. I, 10–15.

Egypt, in fact, was not peopled by an independent nation, but by bondmen. Hundreds of thousands were forced to take part in compulsory labour for the erection of the colossal temples and pyramids. The Egyptian priests were worthy of such kings and gods. Cruelly as the Pharaohs harassed their subjects with hard labour, the priests continued to declare that the kings were demi-gods. Under the weight of this oppression the people became devoid of all human dignity, and submitted to the vilest bondage without ever attempting to relieve themselves from the galling yoke. The repulsive idolatry then prevailing in Egypt had yet further pernicious consequences. The people lost the idea of chastity, after they had placed the brute creation on an equality with their deities. Unspeakable offences in the use of animals had become of daily occurrence, and entailed neither punishment nor disgrace. The gods being depicted in unchaste positions, there appeared to be no need for human beings to be better than the gods. No example is more contagious and seductive than folly and sin. The Israelites, especially those who were brought into closer contact with the Egyptians, gradually adopted idolatrous perversions, and abandoned themselves to unbridled license. This state of things was aggravated by a new system of persecution. During a long period, the Israelites residing in the Land of Goshen had been left unmolested, they having been looked upon as roving shepherds who would not permanently settle in Egypt. But when decades and even a century had passed by, and they still remained in the land and continued to increase in numbers, the council of the king begrudged them the state of freedom which was denied to the Egyptians themselves. The court now feared that these shepherd tribes, which had become so numerous in Goshen, might assume a warlike attitude towards Egypt. To avoid this danger, the Israelites were declared to be bondmen, and were compelled to perform forced labour. To effect a rapid decrease in their numbers, the king commanded that the male infants of the Israelites should be drowned in the Nile or in some of the canals, and that only the female infants should be spared. The Israelites, formerly free in the Land of Goshen, were now kept "in a house of bondage," "in an iron furnace"; here it was to be proved whether they would conform to their hereditary law, or follow strange gods.

The greater part of the tribes could not stand this trial. They had a dim knowledge that the God of their fathers was a being very different from the Egyptian idols; but even this knowledge seemed to decrease from day to day. Love of imitation, sore oppression, and daily misery made them obtuse, and obscured the faint light of their hereditary law. The enslaved labourers did not know what to think of an unseen God who only lived in their memories. Like their masters, the Egyptians, they now lifted their eyes to the visible gods who showed themselves so merciful and propitious to Israel's tormentors. They directed their prayers to the bovine god Apis, whom they called *Abir*, and they also offered to the he-goats. The daughter of Israel, growing up to womanhood, sacrificed her virtue, and abandoned herself to the Egyptians. It was probably thought that, in the images of the grass-eating animal, honour was paid to the god of the patriarchs. When the intellect is on a wrong track, where are the limits for its imaginings? The Israelites would have succumbed to coarse sensual idolatry and to Egyptian vice, like many other nations who had come under the influence of the people of the land of Ham had not two brothers and their sister—the instruments of a higher Spirit—aroused them and drawn them out of their lethargy. These were Moses, Aaron and Miriam. In what did the greatness of this triad consist? What intellectual powers led them to undertake their work of redemption, the elevating and liberating effect of which was intended to extend far beyond their own times? Past ages have left but few characteristic traits of Moses, and barely any of his brother and sister, which could enable us to comprehend, from a human point of view, how their vision rose step by step from the faint dawn of primitive ideas to the bright sunlight of prophetic foresight, and by what means they rendered themselves worthy of their exalted mission. The prophetic trio belonged to that tribe which, through its superior knowledge, was regarded as the sacerdotal tribe, namely, the tribe of Levi. This tribe, or at least this one family, had doubtless preserved the memory of the patriarchs and the belief in the God of their fathers, and had accordingly kept itself aloof from Egyptian idolatry and its abominations.

Thus it was that Aaron, the elder brother, as also Moses and Miriam, had grown up in an atmosphere of greater moral and religious purity. Of Moses the historical records relate that after his birth his mother kept him concealed during three months, to evade the royal command, and protect him from death in the waters of the Nile. There is no doubt that the youthful Moses was well acquainted with Pharaoh's court at Memphis or Tanis (Zoan). Gifted with an active intellect, he had an opportunity of acquiring the knowledge that was to be learnt in Egypt, and by his personal and intellectual qualities he won the affections of all hearts. But even more than by these qualities, he was distinguished by his gentleness and modesty. "Moses was the meekest of men," is the only praise which the historical records have bestowed upon him. He is not praised for heroism or warlike deeds, but for unselfishness and self-abnegation.

Influenced by the ancient teaching, that the God of Abraham loved righteousness, he must have been repelled by the baseless idolatry of animal worship and by the social and moral wrongs which then were rife. Shameless vice, the bondage of a whole people under kings and priests, the inequality of castes, the treatment of human beings as though they were beasts or inferior to beasts, the spirit of slavery,—all these evils he recognised in their full destructive force, and he perceived that the prevailing debasement had defiled his brethren. Moses was the open antagonist of injustice. It grieved him sorely that Israel's sons were subjected to slavery, and were daily exposed to ill-treatment by the lowest of the Egyptians. One day when he saw an Egyptian unjustly beating a Hebrew, his passion overcame his self-control, and he punished the offender. Fearing discovery, he fled from Egypt into the desert, and halted at an oasis in the neighbourhood of Mount Sinai, where the Kenites, an offshoot of the tribe of Midianites, were dwelling. Here, as in Egypt, he witnessed oppression and wrong-doing, and here also he opposed it with zeal. He gave his aid to feeble shepherdesses. By such action he came into contact with their grateful father, the priest or elder of the tribe of the Midianites, and he married Zipporah, the daughter of that priest.

His employment in Midian was that of a shepherd. He selected fertile grazing plots for the herds of Reuel, his father-in-law, between the Red Sea and the mountain lands. In this solitude the prophetic spirit came upon him.

What is the meaning of this prophetic spirit? Even those who have searched the secrets of the world, or the secrets of the soul in its grasp of the universe, can give only a faint notion and no distinct account of its nature. The inner life of man has depths which have remained inscrutable to the keenest investigator. It is, however, undeniable that the human mind can, without help from the senses, cast a far-seeing glance into the enigmatic concatenation of events and the complex play of forces. By means of an undisclosed faculty of the soul, man has discovered truths which are not within the reach of the senses. The organs of the senses can only confirm or rectify the truths already elicited. They cannot discover them. By means of the truths brought to light by that inexplicable power of the soul, man has learned to know nature and to make its forces subservient to his will. These facts attest that the power of the soul owns properties which go beyond the ken of the senses, and transcend the skilled faculties of human reason. Such properties lift the veil of the dim future, and lead to the discovery of higher truths concerning the moral conduct of man; they are even capable of beholding a something of that mysterious Being who has formed and who maintains the universe and the combined action of all its forces. A soul devoted to mundane matters and to selfishness can never attain to this degree of perfection. But should not a soul which is untouched by selfishness, undisturbed by low desires and passions, unsoiled by profanity and the stains of everyday life,—a soul which is completely merged in the Deity and in a longing for moral superiority,—should not such a soul be capable of beholding a revelation of religious and moral truths?

During successive centuries of Israel's history there arose pure-minded men, who unquestionably could look far into the future, and who received and imparted revelations concerning God and the holiness of life. This is an historical fact which will stand any test. A succession of prophets predicted the future destiny of the Israelites and of other nations, and these predictions have been verified by fulfilment. These prophets placed the son of Amram as first on the list of men to whom a revelation was vouchsafed, and high above themselves, because his predictions were clearer and more positive. They recognized in Moses not only the first, but also the greatest of prophets; and they considered their own prophetic spirit as a mere reflection of his mind. If ever the soul of a mortal was endowed with luminous prophetic foresight, this was the case with the pure, unselfish, and sublime soul of Moses. In the desert of Sinai, says the ancient record, at the foot of Horeb, where the flock of his father-in-law was grazing, he received the first divine revelation, which agitated his whole being. Moved and elated—humble, yet confident, Moses returned after this vision to his flock and his home. He had been changed into another being; he felt himself impelled by the spirit of God to redeem his tribal brethren from bondage, and to educate them for a higher moral life. ✻

2. JULIUS WELLHAUSEN

FROM Julius Wellhausen, *Sketch of the History of Israel and Judah* (London: Adam & Charles Black, 1891), pp. 17–23, 108–9, 114–16.

In the preceding sketch the attempt has been made to exhibit Mosaism as it must be supposed to have existed on the assumption that the history of Israel commenced with it, and that for centuries it continued to be the ideal root out of which that history continued to grow. This being assumed, we cannot treat the legislative portion of the Pentateuch as a source from which our knowledge of what Mosaism really was can be derived; for it cannot in any sense be regarded as the starting-point of the subsequent development. If it was the work of Moses, then we must suppose it to have remained a dead letter for centuries, and only through King Josiah and Ezra the scribe to have become operative in the national history. The historical tradition which has reached us relating to the period of the judges and of the kings of Israel is the main source, though only of course in an indirect way, of our knowledge of Mosaism. But within the Pentateuch itself also the *historical* tradition about Moses (which admits of being distinguished, and must carefully be separated, from the *legislative*, although the latter often clothes itself in narrative form) is in its main features manifestly trustworthy, and can only be explained as resting on actual facts.

From the historical tradition, then, it is certain that Moses was the founder of the Torah. But the legislative tradition cannot tell us what were the positive contents of his Torah. In fact it can be shown that throughout the whole of the older period the Torah was no finished legislative code, but consisted entirely of the oral decisions and instructions of the priests; as a whole it was potential only; what actually existed were the individual sentences given by the priesthood as they were asked for. Thus Moses was not regarded as the promulgator once for all of a national constitution, but rather as the first to call into activity the actual sense for law and justice, and to begin the series of oral decisions which were continued after him by the priests. He was the founder of the nation out of which the Torah and prophecy came as later growths. He laid the basis of Israel's subsequent peculiar individuality, not by any one formal act, but in virtue of his having throughout the whole of his long life been the people's leader, judge, and centre of union.

A correct conception of the manner in which the Torah was made by him can be derived from the narrative contained in Exod. xviii., but not from the long section which follows, relating to the Sinaitic covenant. The giving of the law at Sinai has only a formal, not to say dramatic, significance. It is the product of the poetic necessity for such a representation of the manner in which the people was constituted Jehovah's people as should appeal directly and graphically to the imagination. Only so can we justly interpret those expressions according to which Jehovah with His own mouth thundered the ten commandments down from the mountain to the people below, and afterwards for forty days held a confidential conference with Moses alone on the summit. For the sake of producing a solemn and vivid impression that is represented as having taken place in a single thrilling moment, which in reality occurred slowly and almost unobserved. Why Sinai should have been chosen as the scene admits of ready explanation. It was the Olympus of the Hebrew peoples, the earthly seat of the Godhead, and as such it continued to be regarded by the Israelites even after their settlement in Palestine . . . This immemorial sanctity of Sinai it was that led to its being selected as the ideal scene of the giving of the law, not conversely. If we eliminate from the historical narrative the long Sinaitic section which has but a loose connection with it, the wilderness of Kadesh becomes the locality of the preceding and subsequent events. It was during the sojourn of many years here that the organisation of the nation, in any historical sense, took place. "There He made for them statute and ordinance, and there He proved them," as we read in Exod. xv. 25 in a dislocated poetical fragment. "Judgment and trial," "Massa and Meribah," point to Kadesh as the place referred to; there at all events is the scene of the narrative immediately following (Exod. xvii.=Num. xx.), and doubtless also of Exod. xviii.

If the legislation of the Pentateuch cease as a whole to be regarded as an authentic source for our knowledge of what Mosaism was, it becomes a somewhat precarious matter to make any exception in favour of the Decalogue. In particular, the following arguments against its authenticity must be taken into account:—(1) According to Exod. xxxiv. the commandments which stood upon the two tables were quite different. (2) The prohibition of images was during the older period quite unknown; Moses himself is said to have made a brazen serpent which, down to Hezekiah's time, continued to be worshipped at Jerusalem as an image of Jehovah. (3) The essentially and necessarily national character of the older phases of the religion of Jehovah completely disappears in the quite universal code of morals, which is given in the Decalogue as the fundamental law of Israel; but the entire series of religious personalities throughout the period of the judges and the kings—from Deborah, who praised Jael's treacherous act of murder, to David, who treated his prisoners of war with the utmost cruelty—make it very difficult to believe that the religion of Israel was, from the outset, one of a specifically moral character. The true spirit of the old religion may be gathered much more truly from Judg. v. than from Exod. xx. (4) It is extremely doubtful whether the actual monotheism, which is undoubtedly presupposed in the universal moral precepts of the Decalogue, could have formed the foundation of a national religion. It was first developed out of the national religion at the downfall of the nation, and thereupon kept its hold upon the people in an artificial manner by means of the idea of a covenant formed by the God of the universe with, in the first instance, Israel alone.

As for the question regarding the historical presuppositions of Mosaism, there generally underlies it a misunderstanding arising out of theological intellectualism—an attribute found with special frequency among non-theologians. Moses gave no new idea of God to his people. The question whence he could have derived it therefore need not be raised. It could not possibly be worse answered, however, than by a reference to his relations with the priestly caste of Egypt and their wisdom. It is not to be believed that an Egyptian deity could inspire the Hebrews of Goshen with courage for the struggle against the Egyptians, or that an abstraction of esoteric speculation could become the national deity of Israel. It is not inconceivable indeed, although at the same time quite incapable of proof, that Moses was indebted to the Egyptian priests for certain advantages of personal culture, or that he borrowed from them on all hands in external details of organisation or in matters of ritual. But the origin of the germ which developed into Israel is not to be sought for in Egypt, and Jehovah has nothing in common with the colourless divinity of Penta-ur. That monotheism must have been a foreign importation, because it is contrary to that sexual dualism of Godhead which is said to be the fundamental characteristic of Semitic religion, is an untenable exaggeration which has recently become popular out of opposition to the familiar thesis about the monotheistic instinct of the Semites. Moab, Ammon, and Edom, Israel's nearest kinsfolk and neighbours, were monotheists in precisely the same sense in which Israel itself was; but it would be foolish surely in their case to think of foreign importation.

Manetho's statements about the Israelites are for the most part to be regarded as malicious inventions: whether any genuine tradition underlies them at all is a point much needing to be investigated. The story of Exod. ii. 1 *seq.* is a mythus which recurs elsewhere, to which no further significance is attached, for that Moses was trained in all the wisdom of the Egyptians is vouched for by no earlier authorities than Philo and the New Testament. According to the Old Testament tradition his connection is with Jethro's priesthood or with that of the Kenites. This historical presupposition of Mosaism has external evidence in its favour, and is inherently quite probable. . . .

Isaiah was so completely a prophet that even his wife was called the prophetess after him. No such title could have been bestowed on the wife of either Amos or Hosea. But what distinguished him more than anything else from those predecessors was that his position was not, like theirs, apart from the government; he sat close to the helm, and took a very real part in directing the course of the vessel. He was more positive and practical than they; he wished to make his influence felt, and when for the moment he was unsuccessful in this so far as the great whole of the state was concerned, he busied himself in gathering round him a small circle of like-minded persons on whom his hope for the future rested. Now that

Israel had been destroyed, he wished at all events to save Judah. The lofty ideality of his faith did not hinder him from calling in the aid of practical means for this end. But the current of his activities was by the circumstances of the case directed into a channel in which after his death they continued to flow towards a goal which had hardly been contemplated by himself. . . .

. . . In the year 621 (the eighteenth of Josiah) Deuteronomy was discovered, accepted, and carried into effect.

The Deuteronomic legislation is designed for the reformation, by no means of the cultus alone, but at least quite as much of the civil relations of life. The social interest is placed above the cultus, inasmuch as everywhere humane ends are assigned for the rites and offerings. In this it is plainly seen that Deuteronomy is the progeny of the prophetic spirit. Still more plainly does this appear in the *motifs* of the legislation; according to these, Jehovah is the only God, whose service demands the whole heart and every energy; He has entered into a covenant with Israel, but upon fundamental conditions that, as contained in the Decalogue, are purely moral and of absolute universality. Nowhere does the fundamental religious thought of prophecy find clearer expression than in Deuteronomy,— the thought that Jehovah asks nothing for Himself, but asks it as a religious duty that man should render to man what is right, that His will lies not in any unknown height, but in the moral sphere which is known and understood by all.

But the result of the innovation did not correspond exactly to its prophetic origin. Prophecy died when its precepts attained to the force of laws; the prophetic ideas lost their purity when they became practical. Whatever may have been contemplated, only provisional regulations actually admitted of being carried, and even these only in co-operation with the king and the priests, and with due regard to the capacity of the masses. The final outcome of the Deuteronomic reformation was principally that the cultus of Jehovah was limited to Jerusalem and abolished everywhere else,—such was the popular and practical form of prophetic monotheism. The importance of the Solomonic temple was thereby increased in the highest degree, and so also the influence of the priests of Jerusalem, the sons of Zadok, who now in point of fact got rid entirely of their rivals, the priests of the country districts. ✻

3. WILLIAM F. ALBRIGHT

FROM William F. Albright, "The Biblical Period," in *The Jews: Their History, Culture, and Religion*, ed. Louis Finkelstein, 2 vols., 3d ed. (New York: Harper & Row, 1960), vol. I, 11–12.

As against the decadence of contemporary Egyptian and Canaanite religion, Moses drew inspiration from the simple traditions of his own Hebrew people and the stern moral code of the nomads of Midian, among whom he spent much of his early manhood before the Exodus. Rejecting all mythology (in accordance with the example of Amarna and doubtless of other abortive efforts to reform religion of which we have no direct information), Moses kept a few traditional appellations of deity, which he applied to the new figure of YHWH, which may possibly be older than he but cannot have had any prior significance. Among these names, which we know from the earliest religious poetry of Israel, such as the Oracles of Balaam, were *El* ("The Powerful One"), *Elyon* or *Eli* ("The Exalted One," used by the Canaanites as an appellation of Baal, the great storm-god, king of the gods), and *Shaddai* . . . Just as the Canaanites had sometimes used the plural of *el*, "god," to indicate "totality of the gods" (as, for instance, in the Canaanite Amarna letters) so the Israelites used *Elohim* to stress the unity and universality of God.

In the Torah we have, carefully collected and arranged, a considerable body of civil and cultic legislation. These laws and regulations are couched in different wording, showing complex sources. They have been preserved for us in documents of different ages—all relatively early. Yet there is a basic similarity about their cultural and religious background which makes it impossible not to attribute their origin to the beginnings of organized Israelite monotheism—in other words, to Moses. The cultic laws never mention the Temple, while the civil laws reflect a period before the institution of the Monarchy and the appointment of magistrates by the king. Moreover, in recent decades it has become certain that the Book of the Covenant in Ex. 21–23 is part of a once much longer Hebrew analogue to the Code of Hammurabi, the Assyrian and Hittite legal codes, and similar legislation, all belonging to the period between 2000 and 1100 B.C.E. The Book of the Covenant reflects an agricultural society of patriarchal type and simple mores; it is very different in these respects from both

Babylonian and Hittite aristocratic feudalism, in which payments of money replace corporal punishment, especially where superiors are convicted of crimes against inferiors. It is at the same time, however, much more humane than the Draconic Middle Assyrian laws, which reflect a singularly harsh attempt to maintain traditional mores in a highly organized urban civilization. It is, in any case, incredible that the Book of the Covenant should reflect Canaanite jurisprudence in either spirit or details, though we may freely concede strong Canaanite influence on formulation and legal terminology.

If we turn to the Priestly Code, a similar situation develops; in it we have substantially the sacrificial and ritual practice of the Tabernacle as transmitted by tradition from the period before Solomon's Temple, just as in corresponding sections of the Mishna we possess a traditional account of the practice of Herod's Temple. Just how much of this ritual goes back to Moses himself would be idle to conjecture in the present state of our knowledge; the spirit and much of the detail may be considered as antedating the Conquest of Canaan—in other words, as going back to Mosaic origins.

To Albrecht Alt we owe recognition of an extremely important fact: that there is an element in both civil and cultic legislation of the Torah which was specifically Israelite and which went back to the beginnings of Israel —in other words, it was specifically Mosaic. This element is the apodictic legislation which we know best from the Ten Commandments, consisting of short injunctions, mostly couched in imperative form: "Thou shalt (not)!" The apodictic laws of the Torah reflect a monotheistic system with very lofty ethical standards. It is not necessary to insist that all this legislation goes back to the Mosaic period in its present form; it was long transmitted orally, and wording must have been modified in the course of the centuries, while relatively primitive injunctions were replaced by others which were better suited to a more advanced society.

The figure of Moses completely dominates the tradition of the Exodus and the Wanderings. It is, accordingly, impossible to picture the movements in question as though they were normal displacements of nomadic tribes. On the contrary, it took both Moses's unusual qualities of leadership and a sequence of extraordinary events, vividly portrayed for us by tradition, to induce his followers to flee from their Egyptian oppressors into the desert. After many generations in the northeastern Delta the Hebrew peasants and shepherds were resigned to submit to the odious corvée and to endure the treatment by which Sethos I and his son evidently hoped to reduce the preponderance of Semites in the region around their new capital without losing the advantage of a rich source of slave labor for the state; the alternative of risking all in a desperate break for freedom and even more perilous trek through the wild desert of the Sinai Peninsula did not appeal to them. Fortunately Moses prevailed, and his mob of serfs and slaves of every possible origin (Heb. *asafsuf* and *erebrab*) became crystallized around the tribal nucleus of Israel into a new people, with a new faith and an unparalleled mission in world history. ✳

4. WILLIAM F. ALBRIGHT

FROM William F. Albright, *From the Stone Age to Christianity* (Baltimore: Johns Hopkins Press, 1946), pp. 196, 205–7.

. . . It is absurd to deny that Moses was actually the founder of the Israelite commonwealth and the framer of Israel's religious system. This fact is emphasized so unanimously by tradition that it may be regarded as absolutely certain. Nowhere is there the slightest breath of doubt cast on this irrefragable fact by Israelite tradition. If we regard Zoroaster, Buddha, and Confucius as the founders of nomistic religions we cannot deny this right to Moses. In this case we are no more justified in insisting that the religion introduced by Moses was radically different from that of the Book of Exodus than we should be in trying to divorce the other higher religions which we have named from their founders. The Pentateuch reflects a series of traditions coming from circles in which the "law of Moses" was the ultimate standard. . . .

Having sketched the certain or probable content of the Mosaic system, let us consider possible sources of its teaching. That it was a true "teaching" (*doctrina*, in the empirical, not in the philosophical sense, of course) may be considered as virtually certain, in view of its traditional name *tôrah*, its traditional content, and the fact that the slightly earlier system of Akhenaten was also known as the "teaching" (*sbâyet*). Since Moses bore an Egyptian name and according to tradition had reached a place of considerable social importance in Egypt in his early life, his original *tôrah* may well have contained Egyptian elements which later disappeared before the impact of native Hebrew conceptions. Some of these elements seem still to persist, though we cannot be absolutely sure of any one case, owing to the absence of direct documentation or of complex borrowings from Egyptian sources. Among such possible Egyptian influences may be mentioned: 1. The concept of the god who is sole creator of everything and the formula from which his name, *Yahweh*, was derived (cf. Amun-Reʿ and his litany in the New Empire); 2. The concept of a single god and the establishment of a doctrine based on monotheism (cf. the Aten); 3. Recognition of the necessarily international, cosmic dominion of the reigning deity (cf. Sutekh-Baal under the early Ramessides). On the negative side it is clear that the religion of Israel revolted against virtually every external aspect of Egyptian religion, including the complex and grotesque iconography, the dominion of daily life in the Nineteenth Dynasty by magic, the materialistic absorption in preparing for a selfish existence in the hereafter.

Turning to assess the influence exerted by native Hebrew religion on Moses, we are faced with the difficulty of determining just what the latter accepted and what was introduced into Yahwism after his death from the older Hebrew stock. Leaving the second alternative aside for the moment, since it has been partly stressed above and will be emphasized again in other respects below, we can distinguish a number of clear Hebrew factors —and they are what gave Yahwism much of its vital power over the hearts and minds of Israel: 1. The close association between god and worshipper(s), illustrated by the giving of personal names and by sacrificial rites; 2. The contractual relationship between the deity of a tribe and his people, as illustrated by the constant use of the word *berîth*, "covenant," in early Israel (specific forms of this contractual relationship may be later); 3. The association of terrestrial manifestations of deity with storms and mountains, and the identification of Yahweh with Shaddai, "The One of the Mountain(s)"; the adoption of the stories of the Fathers as part of Israel's inheritance, and the identification of Yahweh with the God of the Fathers; specific appellations of deity and perhaps the nucleus of the cosmogony of Genesis, though the latter may again have been developed later from the native stock of myths and legends.

There is no clear trace of any West-Semitic influence of characteristically Canaanite type on the earliest religion of Israel. After the occupation of Palestine, however, this influence became more and more significant, as we shall see below. How remote early Hebrew tradition was from Canaanite influences may be illustrated by the total absence from it of any story of the conflict between the creator and the dragon at the beginning of world-history. After the seventh century B.C. we find such references becoming more and more frequent and the myth of the victory of Yahweh over Leviathan ultimately obtained wide popularity in rabbinic literature.

In bringing this chapter to a close we have yet one question to answer: Was Moses a true monotheist? If by "monotheist" is meant a thinker with views specifically like those of Philo Judaeus or Rabbi Aqiba, of St. Paul or St. Augustine, of Mohammed or Maimonides, of St. Thomas or Calvin, of Mordecai Kaplan or H. N. Wieman, Moses was not one. If, on the other hand, the term "monotheist" means one who teaches the existence of only one God, the creator of everything, the source of justice, who is equally powerful in Egypt, in the desert, and in Palestine, who has no sexuality and no mythology, who is human in form but cannot be seen by human eye and cannot be represented in any form—then the founder of Yahwism was certainly a monotheist. ✻

5. YEHEZKEL KAUFMANN

FROM Yehezkel Kaufmann, *The Religion of Israel* (Chicago: University of Chicago Press, 1960), pp. 223–25.

The Torah is . . . a folk literature, and it is pervaded by the monotheistic idea. The quest for origins cannot, therefore, concern itself merely with the author of the monotheistic idea; equally pressing is the question of the origin of that environment within which the popular monotheistic legends found in the Bible could have been created. The birth of the idea was not sufficient to produce such an environment; the idea might well have remained the private property of a spiritual elite. Only by uprooting the pagan popular religion could it have become the property of a people. And only men of the people, not philosophers or sages, could have succeeded in such an enterprise. The problem of origins, then, is this: When was the battle against the pagan folk religion joined, out of which a monotheistic people emerged?

The Torah literature testifies that this battle took place not only before the time of the literary prophets, but even before the formation of the Torah literature itself. This is the meaning of the fact that every level of the Bible, even the very earliest, views the pagan world as godless. That no story of a battle with paganism is recorded before the age of Moses suggests a terminus *a quo*. Only with Moses does the contrast between the faith of YHWH and paganism appear. Needless to say, it was not the intention of the biblical writers to make this distinction between the pre-Mosaic age and all that followed; nor, indeed, do they ever indicate that they are aware of such a distinction. The difference between the ages is, then, a historical one; the struggle with paganism began with Moses.

The Historical Testimony to Moses

The historicity of Moses is vouched for by trustworthy historical facts. It is a historical fact that while Israel, from its beginnings, regarded itself as the people of YHWH, this tie between people and YHWH did not exist in patriarchal times. It is a fact that apostolic prophecy is formative for the history of Israel from its beginnings. The political organization of the period of the judges is founded on belief in this institution. It is a fact that in early Israel a struggle was waged on behalf of YHWH, the jealous God. The setting of this struggle is a monotheistic people; its heroes are the apostolic prophets. When and where did belief in the jealous god YHWH, whose cause is championed by apostolic prophets, arise? Inasmuch as neither Babylon, Egypt, nor Canaan know of these phenomena, their origin must be sought within Israel itself. Moreover, the spiritual revolution, that gave historic moment to these ideas, must have been, like all similar events in history, the working of a creative genius and leader of men. Following the biblical saga, we call this pioneer creative spirit by the name Moses.

Every feature of the biblical Moses bespeaks a pioneer. The beginning of his activity is related in the legend of the burning bush (Exod. 3–4:17). Here, for the first time in history, a prophet is commissioned by a god to redeem men. The theophany takes place in the desert, at a site without cultic significance before or after. Neither the patriarchs nor later generations build altars or temples to YHWH at Sinai or Kadesh. The desert has prophetic sanctity only, and this originates in the theophany to Moses. Moses comes to the place ignorant of its holiness. He beholds something for which he was totally unprepared. He was not informed by Jethro either of the sanctity of the place, or of the name of the God who revealed himself there. The theophany of the bush has no roots in any existent cult, Kenite or Midianite, nor does the Hebrew people know of the sanctity of the place or the name of the God who manifested himself there. Moses is the first to discover both. He is called upon to proclaim a God heretofore known only to individuals to an entire people. The first prophet with a mission to a people was Moses.

The legend of the bush is the first in which signs play a part; Moses is given signs to confirm his mission. The Egyptian technical wonder is fundamentally recast; Israel's prophet performs miracles by the word of God. Moses learns YHWH's name, but not for magical purposes. This is typical of the entire saga; Moses never acts as an independent magician. On the contrary, he is helpless until the word of God comes to him. Moses is the archetype of the wonder-working prophet.

The redemption of Israel creates a clash between Moses and the heathen empire of Egypt. Pharaoh does not acknowledge YHWH, and so YHWH acts to glorify his name in the sight of Egypt. For the first time, the line is drawn between the people of YHWH and a heathen world that is ignorant of him. Moses is the one who draws the line.

There can be no doubt that there is a connection between the rise of that popular monotheistic environment within which the early biblical legends grew and the life of Moses. The religious transformation of Israel is the lifework of that colossus of the spirit.

Biblical tradition connects the commandment "You shall have no other gods before me" with the Sinaitic theophany, the climax of YHWH's revelation to Israel. And doubtless it was at Sinai that pagan beliefs were dealt their final blow and belief in YHWH was confirmed in the hearts of the people forever. But that battle must have started in Egypt; indeed, it must have occurred at the very outset. In the account of Moses' activity in Egypt the front against idolatry faces Egypt. The battle is already at full tilt, having as its presupposition the faith of Israel in YHWH and his prophet. The millennial-long contrast between Israel and the nations is already full blown in these stories. The struggle ends with the fall of the pagan king and his magicians. Egypt is not converted to belief in YHWH, but Israel's faith is confirmed. This was the ultimate purpose of all the signs given Moses at the bush (Exod. 4:1–31). The narrative of the wonders closes with: "The people feared YHWH and believed in YHWH and in Moses, his servant" (14:31). The legends of Moses in Egypt do not tell explicitly of his battle with Israelite paganism, but the testimony to this battle is implicit in these stories throughout. The revelation of the name YHWH at the bush opens the battle with paganism and establishes the contrast between Israel and Egypt. It is the beginning of the monotheistic revolution in Israel. ✽

6. WILLIAM C. GRAHAM

FROM William C. Graham, *The Prophets and Israel's Culture* (Chicago: University of Chicago Press, 1934), pp. 95–96.

. . . Through the prophets, the Hebrew people, as a people, developed the faculty of self-criticism which, whether in an individual or in a society, is always a necessary step in cultural progress.

At the outset it was stated that the prophets did not produce single-handed the distinctive religion-culture out of which both Judaism and Christianity later emerged. The system which prevailed in their days, and which had been inherited from hoary antiquity, remained in social control long after the prophetic movement here considered had petered out in frustration. But that system which survived the attack of the prophets became itself their enduring monument. There is no single aspect of it, whether its ideal, or its philosophy, or its institutions, or its literature, which does not testify for the prophetic contribution to progress, for the part they played in making the Hebrew spirit inherently influential and in setting it amarch down the centuries.

Through the impetus they gave, the cultus of the dominant system was gradually purged of sympathetic magic, until the very rituals and myths were made the vehicle of the expression of a higher philosophy, a different way of interpreting the meaning of life. Through the drive of their social ideals the place held by the common man in the brotherhood of Israel was gradually enlarged. Through the influence of their respect for human intelligence there developed, in the course of centuries, a passion for learning and education, for the part thought and meditation play in culture, which comes to a most noble expression in the first psalm, where "the law of the Lord" is not a mere instrument of social control, but a window that opens on the universe, a door into a larger life.

In much of that which is noble in the Jewish and Christian cultures, as they stand today, the prophetic influence lives. And one may be sure that the nobler cultures which may spring from these in the future will never so far advance as to escape from the aura of the spirit of Israel's prophets. For the prophetic way is a way that is bound up with life. It is of that eternal stuff which does not die. ✻

7. H. H. ROWLEY

FROM H. H. Rowley, *The Faith of Israel* (London: Student Christian Movement Press, Ltd., 1956), pp. 71–73; H. H. Rowley, *Men of God* (London: Thomas Nelson & Sons, 1963), pp. 35–36.

It should . . . be clear that the belief that there was worship of Yahweh in the world before the time of Moses, as the Bible states clearly and unequivocally, does not diminish the stature of Moses in the least, and does not lessen the greatness of his mission to men. Nothing can be farther from the truth than to suppose that all that Moses did was to introduce Israel to Kenite worship. He gave an altogether new quality and character to the religion, established it in Israel on a basis that was unique amongst men, and set a new standard before his people. The originality of his work—or, as I should prefer to say, of the work wrought by God through him—remains unaffected, and of the unmatched significance of his work for the world, and of the fact that before the days of our Lord no other of equal stature arose, I am fully persuaded. Not the least significant element of his work was his giving to men this short code of conduct which is still enshrined in men's hearts, and which still soars high above the attainment of the vast majority of mankind. For the genius of Moses was shown not alone in the new which he set before men, but in the old which he picked up and retained, and men do not conform to the Ten Commandments when they refrain from adultery and from stealing, unless they also have no other gods before the Lord—and that involves their loyalty to Him—and honour His name and His day. Here, it should be added, it is not without significance that in both Exodus and Deuteronomy the spirit of the law is expressed not alone by the prohibition of work on the Sabbath, but by the injunction to keep it holy. To Moses, the man of God, we are indebted, and to God, through him, for this high standard which is set before men, and for all that it has wrought for the enrichment of life by its inspiration and its summons down all the ages. . . .

It is often said that monotheism is characteristic of the three religions which derive in various ways from the Old Testament, Judaism, Christianity, and Islam, and that it is found nowhere else. Such unity as is found in other faiths is different from the personal unity of the Godhead found in these religions. How far it is legitimate to describe the faith of Israel as monotheistic, however, is a question that calls for some consideration. By many writers Israelite monotheism is thought to have had its beginnings in the eighth century prophets and to have been attained only by Deutero-Isaiah, and to have marked the later religion of the post-exilic period, but not to have been a feature of the faith of the Old Testament as a whole. By others it is maintained that full monotheism was achieved in the teaching of Moses. It seems more probable that the truth lies between these two positions, and that the seeds of monotheism are to be found in the work of Moses though not its full achievement. If this is so, we have here one more example of the rich significance of the revelation given through the Exodus and through Moses, where, as with the other elements of the character of God there revealed, we have a revelation which is only incipient, but which became clearer and fuller through the inspired work of the prophets.

It is hard to find any evidence that Moses either believed or taught that Yahweh was the only existing God, and that he was therefore not alone the God of Israel but of all men. On the other hand, it does not seem sufficient to note that at Sinai it was affirmed that Yahweh was alone the legitimate object of Israelite worship, and that there was no denial of the existence of other gods. For there were in the story the seeds of monotheism. The bringing out of Israel is not represented as a contest between Yahweh and the gods of Egypt. Those gods are ignored as negligible. Yahweh's will alone counted, and his power could not be challenged, while all the forces of Nature were obedient to his will. He could choose for himself what people he would. Whether other gods exist is neither affirmed nor denied. But that they mattered is implicitly denied.

Yet whatever degree of monotheism was attained then was lost later, when in the popular worship other gods were not alone recognized as legitimate for other peoples, but were actually worshipped in Israel. Hence we find the need for the teaching of the great pre-exilic prophets, in which there is a clear but implicit monotheism, and that of Deutero-Isaiah, in which speculative monotheism is explicitly set forth. Repeatedly it is here declared that Yahweh alone is God, and that all other gods are non-existent and their idols symbols of unreality. Moreover, the same prophet taught the corollary of monotheism in universalism. If there is but one God, then he must be the God of all men. Here again is something which finds its seeds in earlier teaching, and which meets us in many forms in the pre-exilic writers. Suffice it to mention the familiar passage attributed to both Isaiah and Micah, in which the age of universal peace, when men will no longer need swords and spears, is declared to be the age when all men will first go up to the house of Israel's God and will learn his way.

It is indeed surprising, and not easily to be accounted for on simple evolutionary lines, that Israel attained a monotheistic faith. She was never a powerful nation, and her monotheism was in no sense the reflection of the prestige of the nation in the prestige of its God. Assyria imposed the recognition of her gods as the suzerains of the gods of conquered peoples, and the prowess of her armies was thought to reflect the power of her gods, whose prestige in turn was enhanced by their exploits. But in Israel it was not so, and the prophet who most specifically formulates a monotheistic faith was the spokesman of a people living in exile. Her monotheism is not the expression of national pride, since the prophets were the spokesmen of judgement rather than of a superficial patriotism. It is the gift of revelation, begun in Moses and continued in the prophets, whereby God was making himself known, first to the people of his choice, and then through them to all his creatures. ✷

8. JOHN BRIGHT

FROM John Bright, *A History of Israel* (Philadelphia: The Westminster Press, 1959), pp. 92–93, 317–19.

As the patriarchal clans passed into the blood stream of Israel, and as their cults were subsumed under that of Yahweh—a procedure theologically quite legitimate—we may not doubt that Israel's structure and faith was shaped thereby more profoundly than we know. We have already suggested that Israel's legal tradition must have been transmitted to her by her own seminomadic forebears, many of whom had been settled in Palestine since early in the second millennium, rather than through strictly Canaanite mediation. The same was no doubt true of her traditions of primeval antiquity, to say nothing of those of the ancestral migrations themselves which, shaped in the spirit of Yahwism, became vehicles of her distinctive theology of history. Above all, there was in Israel's heritage a feeling of tribal solidarity, of solidarity between people and God, that must have contributed more than we can guess to that intensely strong sense of peoplehood so characteristic of her for all time to come.

Beyond this, the pattern of promise and covenant embedded itself in the Israelite mind. We may suppose that as certain elements, later to be incorporated in Israel, settled in Palestine and began to multiply, the promise of land and seed was regarded by them as fulfilled; the ancestral cults, now carried on in local shrines, gained thereby an enormous prestige. Other elements, however, likewise later to be a part of Israel, did not settle so early, but continued their seminomadic existence, while still others— the very nucleus of the later Israel—found their way into Egypt. The promise inherent in their type of religion remained, therefore, without fulfillment; since it was given none until the invasion of Palestine under the aegis of Yahwism, normative Hebrew faith—with justification—viewed this last event as the fulfillment of the promise made to the fathers. Even then the notion of a covenant supported by the unconditional promises of God lived on, for good and ill, in the Hebrew mind, powerfully shaping the national hope, as we shall see.

We must bring our discussion to a close. Although many gaps remain, enough has been said to establish confidence that the Bible's picture of the patriarchs is deeply rooted in history. Abraham, Isaac, and Jacob stand in the truest sense at the beginning of Israel's history and faith. Not only do they represent that movement which brought the components of Israel to Palestine, but their peculiar beliefs helped to shape the faith of Israel as it was later to be. With them, too, there began that restless search for the fulfillment of promise which, though realized in the giving of land and seed, could never be satisfied with that gift; but, like a pointing finger through all the Old Testament, must guide to a city "whose builder and maker is God" (Heb. 11:10). Abraham began far more than he knew. It is, therefore, not without sound historical reason that Christian and Jew alike hail him as the father of all faith (Gen. 15:6; Rom. 4:3; Heb. 11:8–10). . . .

Though heeded by few in their lifetime, these prophets perhaps did more than all others to save Israel from extinction. By ruthlessly demolishing false hope, by announcing the calamity as Yahweh's sovereign and righteous judgment, they gave the tragedy explanation in advance in terms of faith, and thereby prevented it from destroying faith. Though it certainly swept many from their religious moorings, and plunged others into numb despair, sincere Israelites were driven to the searching of their own hearts, and to penitence. More than this, the prophetic message, though addressed to the nation, had also been a summons to all who would hear to stand for Yahweh's word against the national policy and the national institutions. It therefore facilitated the formation of a new community, based on individual decision, which could survive the wreckage of the old. To be sure, to speak of Jeremiah and Ezekiel as discoverers of individualism, as handbooks often do, is misleading. For all its strongly corporate nature, Israel's faith had never been unaware of the rights and responsibilities of the individual under Yahweh's covenant law. Nor did either Jeremiah or Ezekiel proclaim an individual, as over against a corporate, religion, for both looked forward precisely to the formation of a new *community*. Yet the old national-cultic community to which every citizen automatically belonged was ending; a new community based on individual decision would have to replace it if Israel was to survive as a people. For this community the prophetic preaching prepared.

Jeremiah's religion was intensely individual in good part because the national cult was to him an abomination in which he could not participate. The fact that he not only censured it, but declared that its sacrificial ritual had never been more than peripheral to Yahweh's demands (Jer. 6:16–21; 7:21–23), together with his incessant stress on the necessity of internal cleansing (Jer. 4:3 f., 14, etc.), surely prepared for the day when religion would have to go on without external cult at all—a thing to the ancient mind impossible. Ezekiel too, through his famous individualizing of the problem of the divine justice (Ezek., ch. 18), seemingly mechanical and easily driven to absurdity though it is, helped to release men from the shackles of corporate guilt (v. 19) and the fatalistic feeling (Ezek. 33:10; 37:11) that they were forever condemned for the sins of the past: each generation, each individual, has his fair chance before the bar of God's justice. Both prophets thus encouraged individual Jews, lost and in despair, to be loyal to the calling of Yahweh, who was still, even in this, Sovereign Lord; and both assured them that Yahweh would meet them, without temple and without cult, in the land of their captivity if they sought him with their whole heart (Jer. 29:11–14; Ezek. 11:16; cf. Deut. 4:27–31). Men who received these words were not left hopeless.

Moreover, Jeremiah and Ezekiel, the demolishers of false hope, themselves offered positive hope, for both regarded the exile as an interim (Jer. 29:11–14; Ezek. 11:16–21) beyond which lay God's future. So unexpected is hope in Jeremiah that some have doubted that he had any. But he did! Even as Jerusalem was falling he attested his belief in the future of his people—and on the soil of Palestine!—by buying real estate (Jer. 32:6–15), declaring that "houses and fields and vineyards shall again be bought in this land." True, this was scarcely hope, but a sheer triumph of faith in Yahweh's purposes over Jeremiah's own hopelessness (Jer. 32:16–17a, 24 f.). Nor was it based in any expected resurgence of the nation, or in any human effort whatsoever, but in a new redemptive act (Jer. 31:31–34): Yahweh would again call his people, as he once had from Egypt, and, forgiving their sins, would make with them a new covenant, inscribing its law on their hearts. The awful chasm between the demands of Yahweh's covenant, by which the nation had been judged, and his sure promises, which faith could not surrender, was bridged from the side of the divine grace. The very exodus theology that had condemned the nation became the foundation of its hope.

After 587, Ezekiel likewise addressed to his fellow exiles words of comfort and hope. He spoke of a new exodus deliverance, a new wilderness discipline in which Yahweh would purge his people before leading them home (Ezek. 20:33–38). Though he looked for the restoration of a united Israel under Davidic rule (chs. 34:23 f.; 37:15–28), he expected Yahweh, who is himself the good shepherd of his sheep (ch. 34), to accomplish this: Yahweh would breathe his spirit upon the bones of the defunct nation, causing it to rise again "an exceedingly great host" (ch. 37:1–14) and, giving his people a new heart and a new spirit to serve him (v. 14; cf. chs. 11:19; 36:25–27; etc.), would lead them back to their land, establish with them his eternal covenant of peace (chs. 34:25; 37:26–28) and place his sanctuary forever in their midst. The old national hope was thus retained, but pushed into the future, awarded to a new and transformed nation, and made wholly dependent upon a new divine saving act. These were hopes of the sort around which the nucleus of a new community of Israel could rally, heartened to wait through the darkness—for God's future. �֎

9. R. B. Y. SCOTT

FROM R. B. Y. Scott, *The Relevance of the Prophets* (New York: The Macmillan Company, 1954), pp. 40–41, 59–62, 105–6.

Hebrew prophecy is the supreme element in what differentiated Israelite religion from other contemporary religions, and gave it a survival value they did not possess. Prophecy lies also at the heart of the Christian faith, for—whatever more one may say of Jesus—he was first of all a *prophet*, "the prophet from Nazareth of Galilee."

What is prophecy? The question cannot be answered simply in terms of cause and effect, of antecedents and environment; though prophecy when it came to its height retained features connecting it with antecedents which were something less than prophecy. But Amos and Hosea, Isaiah and Jeremiah cannot be adequately explained in terms of development from these antecedents. Something new emerged in such men—a manifestation of spiritual power which brought them to an altogether different plane of religious experience and insight, and which gives them unique significance.

It is to these men that we must turn if we would know what prophecy is, to the traditions and writings in which their mind and spirit have been enshrined, and to the story of the people whose life and thought and faith they moulded. They were, as we have seen, not merely foretellers, though they did express upon occasion their moral certainty of what God was about to do. They were not moral philosophers, for they had no systematized scheme of the world, and their apprehension of reality was intuitive rather than rational. They might be called preachers, but not preachers "like the scribes" who were exponents of a revelation received from tradition; they themselves were media of a divine self-disclosure. They were mystics (in the best sense), but men of action and of the world as well; moralists as well as poets; social radicals because (again, in the best sense) they were religious conservatives; markedly individual, but representative of and identified with their people. They were spokesmen of God to their nation, and to men of all ages who will listen to their words. In very truth they were the servants and envoys of the Living God, instruments of his creative purpose in the realm of spirit. Many will be satisfied to describe them as men of unusual spiritual genius. But they themselves insisted that they were men upon whom Yahweh had laid his hand, and to "whom he had spoken in the ear."

But, for all its uniqueness of character and importance, Hebrew prophecy appeared under the actual conditions of human life and development. It had its real connections with a religious present and a religious past. God did not create it out of nothing. Prophecy was the answer of something at the heart of Israelite religion to the clamant call of humanity for a divine utterance. But within the Hebrew tradition there had been, and were, other ways of obtaining a divine response, ways that were common to many religions of that time and since. The gods were believed to speak through the priests or the priest-king, the augurs or the "holy men," the astrologers or the necromancers. Such ways of ascertaining the divine will were found also in the earlier stages and on the persisting lower levels of Israelite religion. . . .

We may classify under five heads the literature produced, directly or indirectly, by the prophetic impulse before it died out about the end of the Persian period, under the growing pressure of the normative Law. (The vital spark of prophecy was then passed on to apocalyptic on the one hand, and to psalmody and the "Wisdom" literature on the other.) It must be emphasized that this five-fold classification is a classification primarily of the *literature* through which we trace the story of prophecy, rather than a definition of stages in the developments behind the literature. But, roughly speaking, these five kinds of literary records are successive, and correspond to successive epochs of the prophetic movement.

1. There is first of all *the traditional and partly legendary literature relating to the Founder, Moses,* preserved mainly in the several documents of the Pentateuch. These documents incorporate a few fragments of the old national saga, of which they are prose versions influenced by late prophetic teaching. To these may be added the several versions in which the Decalogue of Moses was preserved at various sanctuaries; versions whose common elements witness to their descent from a single original, and whose differences point to its antiquity. Though Moses is an authentic historic figure, his influence is felt rather than clearly seen in the literature relating to him and written centuries after his time.

2. The second body of material is the *narratives* in Judges, Samuel and Kings *in which individuals called "prophets" appear as actors in the national drama,* but in no sense are the center of it; (except for Samuel, whose prophetic office is really subordinate to his work as national leader). Nathan and Gad, Shemaiah, Ahijah and Jehu ben Hanani only flit across

the stage. But they are important as maintaining the continuity of the prophetic succession.

3. Thirdly, we have the *biographical and legendary material* that gathered around the names of *the pre-literary prophets Elijah and Elisha*, and which was inserted in blocks of narrative into the history of the monarchies in I and II Kings. Here the *acts and incidental sayings* of the prophets are the chief interest of the narrator; there is no extended discourse, and the historical circumstances recede into the background.

4. The fourth body of Biblical material, and by far the most important for the understanding of Hebrew prophecy, is the *classical literature of the Golden Age* of prophecy, the eighth, seventh and early sixth centuries B.C. This consists chiefly of *collections of oracles written down after having been spoken*. There is certain additional narrative matter, descriptive of the prophet's acts, or of the circumstances of his preaching—and also of his spiritual experiences—but in the main these records of the great days of prophecy comprise the *substance of the prophets' oracular utterances*. The speakers are known; a large proportion of the oracles attributed to them can be regarded as authentic; the collections are dated in general terms, and particular oracles sometimes are dated exactly; the historical circumstances are reasonably clear.

This material comprises most of the Books of Amos, Hosea, Jeremiah, Zephaniah and Nahum; and a substantial part of the Books of Isaiah, Micah and Habakkuk. The balance of the material in these books is to be classified either under heading (5) as anonymous written prophecy, or as oracular utterance from nameless prophets whose messages have been included with that of the well-known figures mentioned above. The brief revival of spoken prophecy, in the late sixth and early fifth centuries, which has left its record in Haggai, Zechariah 1–8 and Malachi may be called a Silver Age.

5. Finally, there is the most extensive of the bodies of literature relating to the prophetic movement, *post-classical written prophecy, anonymous and of uncertain date*. The collections of oracles of the known prophets of the eighth and seventh centuries appear to have been put together by their immediate disciples, and these collections were treasured and enlarged by later members of the prophetic school or party. The process went on for centuries, with the result that these anonymous supplements now comprise more than half (some would say, considerably more than half), of the prophetic canon of Scripture. The material which has been added includes some new major contributions such as II Isaiah and the semi-apocalyptic chapters 24–27 of Isaiah, in addition to briefer editorial insertions and additions by unknown minor prophetic writers. The result is that only one-quarter to one-third of a book like "Isaiah" can be attrib-

uted to the prophet of that name, the whole having gathered gradually around brief original collections of his work. More than half of the "Book of the Twelve" Minor Prophets is post-exilic and of unknown authorship and uncertain date. With respect to the Book of Ezekiel, such widely divergent views are held among scholars that one hesitates to estimate how much (if any) of its contents is authentic prophecy from the classical period.

It will be evident that when we ask who were the prophets, and what was their teaching, the answer is beset with critical difficulties, and cannot be given by indiscriminate quotation from the prophetic canon. If we agree to trace the line of prophetic succession back to Moses, it covers a thousand years and has left, as we have seen, a series of literary records of various kinds and differing value. The best procedure would appear to be to concentrate attention upon the materials under (4) above, the recorded spoken oracles of the period. We can come to grips with these prophets of the eighth and seventh centuries better than with any others, because their literary remains are fairly extensive and are usually comprehensible in the light of known historical and religious conditions. Moreover, with some significant exceptions such as the Servant Songs and II Isaiah, there is little elsewhere in our records to compare in importance and value with these prophetic masterpieces. Yet even these cannot be viewed in isolation from the great succession in which they stood. . . .

The prophets shared with other Israelites a belief in Yahweh as God of the nation. Yahweh had entered into a distinctive relationship with this people at a definite time in the past, his mighty acts had given direction and meaning to its subsequent history, and he still was universally acknowledged as the one peculiarly Israelite deity. There is consequently no argument in the prophets for the existence of Yahweh, nor as to his attributes of might and justice, mercy and truth. These were part of a common religious tradition, although they had never been made so clear before. And other things had entered into the tradition which were not native to it and which the prophets were the first to realize were incompatible with it. Yet the prophets did appeal to this common tradition in their denunciations and in their pleadings. Israel *knew about* Yahweh well enough. She acknowledged his part in her historical past, and she professed to serve him now in the cultus of the various sanctuaries. But she did not really know him as a child knows his father, and a wife her husband, in the constant awareness of an intimate relationship, where she could respond freely and naturally to his guidance. She did not know him in the present as she knew *of* him in the past. Yahweh had become a figure of tradition rather than a factor in life, a theological postulate rather than a divine reality.

Thus what we find in the prophets is both new and fuller teaching about the nature of God, and a new witness to the tremendous unrecognized reality of his presence and active participation in the affairs of men. The divine attributes are restated in dynamic terms. Yahweh is still the God of the fathers, known by his name, the Rock and Holy One of Israel. He is a God of transcendent glory and of awful power in natural phenomena and over mankind; of inscrutable and determinate purpose, all-seeing, wise and just; true and faithful, and eager to be gracious to the people chosen as the sphere of his revelation; watchful and active in the crucial moments of their social history. His demand for obedience and loyalty is peremptory, and he is terrible in his reaction to the obstruction of his will. Though his presence continues to be linked in a special way with Zion and even with Sinai, he is not any more a localized or territorial deity but one who might show himself to his people anywhere, and whose ethical concern and power extended to other nations. ✳

10. SIGMUND FREUD

FROM Sigmund Freud, *Moses and Monotheism,* trans. Katharine Jones (New York: Alfred A. Knopf, Vintage Books, 1955), pp. 133–36, 171–73.

If we are quite clear in our minds that a procedure like the present one—to take from the traditional material what seems useful and to reject what is unsuitable, and then to put the individual pieces together according to their psychological probability—does not afford any security for finding the truth, then one is quite right to ask why such an attempt was undertaken. In answer to this I must cite the result. If we substantially reduce the severe demands usually made on a historical and psychological investigation, then it might be possible to clear up problems that have always seemed worthy of attention and that, in consequence of recent events, force themselves again on our observation. We know that of all the peoples who lived in antiquity in the basin of the Mediterranean the Jewish people is perhaps the only one that still exists in name and probably also in nature. With an unexampled power of resistance it has defied misfortune and ill-treatment, developed special character traits, and, incidentally, earned the hearty dislike of all other peoples. Whence comes this resistance of the Jew and how his character is connected with his fate are things one would like to understand better.

We may start from one character trait of the Jews which governs their relationship to other people. There is no doubt that they have a very good opinion of themselves, think themselves nobler, on a higher level, superior to the others, from whom they are also separated by many of their customs. With this they are animated by a special trust in life, such as is bestowed by the secret possession of a precious gift; it is a kind of optimism. Religious people would call it trust in God.

We know the reason for this attitude of theirs and what their precious treasure is. They really believe themselves to be God's chosen people; they hold themselves to be specially near to him, and this is what makes them proud and confident. According to trustworthy accounts, they behaved in Hellenistic times as they do today. The Jewish character, therefore, even then was what it is now, and the Greeks, among whom and alongside whom they lived, reacted to the Jewish qualities in the same way as their "hosts" do today. They reacted, one might think, as if they too believed in the preference which the Israelites claimed for themselves. When one is the declared favourite of the dreaded father one need not be surprised that the other brothers and sisters are jealous. What this jealousy can lead to is exquisitely shown in the Jewish legend of Joseph and his brethren. The subsequent course of world history seemed to justify this Jewish arrogance, for when, later on, God consented to send mankind a Messiah and Redeemer, he again chose him from among the Jewish people. The other peoples would then have had reason to say: "Indeed, they were right; they are God's chosen people." Instead of which it happened that the salvation through Jesus Christ brought on the Jews nothing but a stronger hatred, while the Jews themselves derived no advantage from this second proof of being favoured, because they did not recognize the Redeemer.

On the strength of my previous remarks we may say that it was the man Moses who stamped the Jewish people with this trait, one which became so significant to them for all time. He enhanced their self-confidence by assuring them that they were the chosen people of God; he declared them to be holy and laid on them the duty to keep apart from others. Not that the other peoples on their part lacked self-confidence. Then, just as now, each nation thought itself superior to all the others. The self-confidence of the Jews, however, became through Moses anchored in religion; it became a part of their religious belief. By the particularly close relationship to their God they acquired a part of his grandeur. And since we know that behind the God who chose the Jews and delivered them from Egypt stood the man Moses, who achieved that deed, ostensibly at God's command, I venture to say this: it was one man, the man Moses, who created the Jews. To him this people owes its tenacity in supporting life; to him, however, also much of the hostility which it has met with and is meeting still. . . .

The return of the repressed proceeds slowly; it certainly does not occur spontaneously, but under the influence of all the changes in the conditions of life that abound throughout the history of civilization. I can give here neither a survey of the conditions on which it depends nor any more than a scanty enumeration of the stages in which the return proceeds. The father became again the head of the family, but he was no longer omnipotent as the father of the primeval horde had been. In clearly recognizable transitional stages the totem animal was ousted by the god. The god, in human form, still carried at first the head of an animal; later on he was wont to assume the guise of the same animal. Still later the animal became sacred to him and his favourite companion or else he was reputed to have slain the animal, when he added its name to his own. Between the totem animal and the god the hero made his appearance; this was often an early stage of deification. The idea of a Highest Being seems to have appeared early; at first it was shadowy and devoid of any connection with the daily interests of mankind. As the tribes and peoples were knit together into larger unities, the gods also became organized into families and hierarchies. Often one of them was elevated to be the overlord of gods and men. The next step, to worship only one god, was taken hesitatingly, and at long last the decision was made to concede all power to one God only and not to suffer any other gods beside him. Only then was the grandeur of the primeval father restored; the emotions belonging to him could now be repeated.

The first effect of the reunion with what men had long missed and yearned for was overwhelming and exactly as the tradition of the lawgiving on Mount Sinai depicts it. There was admiration, awe, and gratitude that the people had found favour in his eyes; the religion of Moses knows of only these positive feelings towards the Father God. The conviction that his power was irresistible, the subjection to his will, could not have been more absolute with the helpless, intimidated son of the father of the horde than they were here; indeed, they become fully comprehensible only by transformation into the primitive and infantile milieu. Infantile feelings are far more intense and inexhaustibly deep than are those of adults; only religious ecstasy can bring back that intensity. Thus a transport of devotion to God is the first response to the return of the Great Father.

The direction of this Father religion was thus fixed for all time, but its development was not thereby finished. Ambivalency belongs to the essence of the father-son relationship; it had to happen that in the course of time the hostility should be stirred up which in ancient times had spurred the sons to slay their admired and dreaded father. In the religion of Moses itself there was no room for direct expression of the murderous father-hate. Only a powerful reaction to it could make its appearance: the consciousness of guilt because of that hostility, the bad conscience because one had sinned against God and continued so to sin. This feeling of guiltiness, which the Prophets incessantly kept alive and which soon became an integral part of the religious system itself, had another, superficial motivation which cleverly veiled the true origin of the feeling. The people met with hard times; the hopes based on the favour of God were slow in being fulfilled; it became not easy to adhere to the illusion, cherished above all else, that they were God's chosen people. If they wished to keep happiness, then the consciousness of guilt because they themselves were such sinners offered a welcome excuse for God's severity. They deserved nothing better than to be punished by him, because they did not observe the laws; the need for satisfying this feeling of guilt, which, coming from a much deeper source, was insatiable, made them render their religious precepts ever and ever more strict, more exacting, but also more petty. In a new transport of moral asceticism the Jews imposed on themselves constantly increasing instinctual renunciation, and thereby reached—at least in doctrine and precepts—ethical heights that had remained inaccessible to the other peoples of antiquity. Many Jews regard these aspirations as the second main characteristic, and the second great achievement, of their religion. Our investigation is intended to show how it is connected with the first one, the conception of the one and only God. The origin, however, of this ethics in feelings of guilt, due to the repressed hostility to God, cannot be gainsaid. It bears the characteristic of being never concluded and never able to be concluded with which we are familiar in the reaction-formations of obsessional neurosis. ✣

Part 2

THE MAKING OF GREEK CIVILIZATION

This Part is designed to circumvent the traditional treatment accorded the study of Greek civilization in introductory history courses, a treatment characterized by chronological restriction, spatial or geographical limitation, and the attempt to form a rigidly unified and coherent synthesis. Far too often the study of ancient Greece has been confined to its "Golden Age"—the age of Pericles, Thucydides, Plato, Aristotle, the great poets and tragedians. It is perfectly natural that historians, who are certainly not insensitive to aesthetic considerations, should indulge themselves in thinking and writing about such an astonishingly fruitful period. And yet, this narrow concentration really violates one of the cardinal dimensions of history—the temporal dimension, change and process and development through time. The "Golden Age" was a product of what came before; it was not born overnight, and its roots, roots which conditioned the ultimate growth, must be sought in the previous history of Greece. For that reason, we are going to focus here on the period preceding the "Golden Age."

In the traditional, geographically limited approach, Athens is often mistakenly equated with the whole of Greek history. Although we have some knowledge of more than 250 Greek city-states, these lesser cities play little part in shaping our vision of what the Greeks were, how they formed political communities, how they traded, educated their youth, conceived of their gods and the world around them. Athens continues to occupy center stage. Yet, Greek tragedy should warn us that the chorus is often critically important: it reflects and illuminates the central action and frequently forms the substance of the drama. By turning to the period before Athenian dominance we can gain a more balanced perspective.

A second characteristic of the traditional approach to Greek history is a failure to consider Sparta's contribution. This omission is regrettable since there are at least three good reasons why the student of ancient Greece should not ignore the Spartan achievement. In the first place the Spartans were admired by their contemporaries for living up to certain standards, even by those who found these standards repugnant. Second, we should not think of Sparta as an anomaly in the Western tradition. The Spartan ethos represents a deeply rooted strain in our culture. It is the chief historical source of the ascetic ideal developed in Plato's *Republic* and later institutionalized and solidified by Christianity. Finally, and most important of all, it was probably the Spartans who saved Greece during the Persian invasions.

The third significant feature of the traditional approach may be described as its "classical symmetry." According to this view, the quintessence of Greek civilization is embodied in its art and architecture, where calm, clean lines prevail, where order and reason, logic and restraint are so manifest. There is much truth in this, but it fails to capture the crosscurrents, the contradictions and strains, above all the paradoxes. A more exact approximation of Greek history must take these erratic elements into account. In fact, Greek civilization may be studied in terms of a series of converging and interrelated paradoxes, an approach requiring some elaboration.

Paradox is the coexistence of qualities assumed to be antithetical and contradictory to one another; they abound in the Greek experience. Here, in schematic form, are some of the most intriguing and suggestive paradoxes in Greek history.

1. When he moves to the level of explicit generalization, the historian draws upon a series of adjectives designed to capture the essence of his subject. Thus, in any general discussion of Greek culture we might expect to encounter such words as "symmetrical," "coherent," "unified," "restrained," "ordered," and the like. But, the adjectives associated with the study of Greek politics stand in striking opposition; they include words such as "volatile," "internecine," and "centrifugal." Is this paradox more apparent than real? In any case, what do these contradictory tendencies in the realms of culture and politics tell us about the Greeks?

2. Arnold Hauser, the art historian, has written that "Greek classical art faces us with a difficult sociological problem: the liberalism and individualism of democracy would seem to be incompatible with the severity and regularity of the classical style." Can we reconcile this problem?

3. The selections by Mikhail Rostovtzeff, Victor Ehrenberg, and C. M. Bowra are organized dialectically. In them, the authors balance the ele-

The Making of Greek Civilization

ments of individuality and collectivity, geographical fragmentation and racial and cultural unity, centripetal and centrifugal forces—all elements which appear in Greek history. Is this approach more rewarding than the one that ignores contradiction and paradox?

The first selection in this Part is taken from the work of that remarkable English scholar George Grote (1794–1871). Grote, a banker, member of Parliament, friend of Bentham, Ricardo, and James Mill, produced a twelve-volume history of Greece between 1846 and 1856. The distinguished English historian G. P. Gooch has written that "A century of research and discussion . . . have overthrown or modified many of his conclusions, but whatever else is read, parts of Grote must be read also." Another reason why a selection from Grote is such an appropriate opening for this Part is his critical attitude toward the sources for the period preceding the "Golden Age." Grote was deeply interested in the "mythological" age of Greek history, but the real history of Greece began for him in 776 B.C., the first Olympiad, because "the truth is, that historical records, properly so called, do not begin until long after this date." Thus we are forewarned that much of the discussion in this Part rests on a rather tenuous factual base and that we must exercise great caution in formulating our generalizations.

To say that a source is not historically accurate is not to argue that it has no value and provides no key to the past. Grote recognized that Greek art and mythology were clues to the Greek mentality; they generated modes of thought and perception that survived in a more "scientific" age and helped unify the peoples of the disparate states into a common culture. Mikhail Rostovtzeff, professor of Latin and Roman history at St. Petersburg until the revolution of 1918 and then professor of history at Yale, had a similar view of the making of Greek civilization. The Homeric poems became the Greek Bible; "the Greeks gained a clear conception of their national unity and realized the racial peculiarities of their life and religion." There is, however, an added element in the Rostovtzeff selection—a discussion of what the Greeks owed to the East.

The selections which follow represent the work of two outstanding contemporary historians of Greece. Professor Ehrenberg was educated at the universities of Göttingen, Berlin, and Tübingen and then emigrated to England in 1939; C. M. Bowra has spent most of his productive scholarly life at Oxford. These selections lead to a consideration of the relation between geography and historical development, one of the most fascinating and complex problems in historiography. The great French historian Lucien Febvre asked: " 'What are the influences which the geographical environment exercises on the different ways in which human societies manifest themselves?' That is an immense question. It can be broken up into a multitude of secondary questions all of which belong to quite distinct sciences." His caveat is certainly not intended to discourage students from exploring the implications of this problem and evaluating the logic of what Ehrenberg and Bowra have to say. An initial sense of complexity prevents facile generalization and encourages sustained and rewarding thought.

Next we turn to a selection by the English historian Arnold Toynbee. Professor Toynbee is best known for his far-ranging and erudite work *The Study of History,* but he is also, among other things, a distinguished classical scholar. This is not the place to comment on his much debated philosophy of history. However, it is necessary to point out that Toynbee is an extremely controversial figure and that most historians, notwithstanding their admiration for his scholarship, have serious reservations about his approach to the past.

The selection included here contains two specific instances of the kind of conceptualization which other historians criticize in Toynbee's work. In the fourth paragraph he writes: "Humanism is the religion that appeals to man during the stage of his history when he has already become conscious of having won a mastery over non-human Nature but has not yet been forced, by bitter experience, to face the truth that he is still not master of himself." The distinguishing characteristic of this paragraph is its generality. Historians write about the Greeks, the Romans, the Russians, or the Japanese at a particular stage in their history. They do not write about "man" in general or posit formulas about man's conduct at a certain vaguely defined juncture. E. H. Carr has succinctly expressed the prevailing view among historians: "That elusive entity 'human nature' has varied so much from country to country and from century to century that it is difficult not to regard it as a historical phenomenon shaped by prevailing social conditions and conventions." Further on in this selection Toynbee mentions "a relatively short transitional stage that is known as the Neolithic Age." Perhaps for the geologist this period is "relatively short," but for the historian 3,000 years, the approximate length of the Neolithic Age, is a rather long time! In short, though Toynbee is always stimulating, his perspective is not that of the ordinary historian who anchors his study to specific phenomena.

For Toynbee, the essentials of Greek civilization are to be found in an all-embracing humanism. Werner Jaeger who wrote *Paideia,* one of the classics of twentieth-century Greek scholarship, emphasizes the importance of the early aristocracy in shaping Greek character. Bruno Snell focuses on Greek religion; Chester Starr discusses oriental stimuli and the great watershed of the eleventh century; and the English historian

H. D. F. Kitto concentrates on the consuming intellectualism of the Greeks. Finally, Finley Hooper reminds us—and we should keep this constantly in mind in studying Greek culture—that the culture we admire so much was limited to a few.

1. GEORGE GROTE

FROM George Grote, *Greece*, 12 vols. (New York: Peter Fenelon Collier, 1899), vol. I, 463; vol. IV, 100–1.

. . . The transition of the Greek mind from its poetical to its comparatively positive state was self-operated, accomplished by its own inherent and expansive force—aided indeed, but by no means either impressed or provoked, from without. From the poetry of Homer, to the history of Thucydidês and the philosophy of Plato and Aristotle, was a prodigious step, but it was the native growth of the Hellenic youth into an Hellenic man; and what is of still greater moment, it was brought about without breaking the thread either of religious or patriotic tradition—without any coercive innovation or violent change in the mental feelings. The legendary world, though the ethical judgments and rational criticisms of superior men had outgrown it, still retained its hold upon their feelings as an object of affectionate and reverential retrospect. . . .

The immense development of Grecian art . . . and the great perfection of Grecian artists, are facts of great importance in the history of the human race. And in regard to the Greeks themselves, they not only acted powerfully on the taste of the people, but were also valuable indirectly as the common boast of Hellenism, and as supplying one bond of fraternal sympathy as well as of mutual pride, among its widely-dispersed sections. It is the paucity and weakness of these bonds which renders the history of Greece, prior to 560 B.C., little better than a series of parallel, but isolated threads, each attached to a separate city; and that increased range of joint Hellenic feeling and action, upon which we shall presently enter, though arising doubtless in great measure from new and common dangers threatening many cities at once,—also springs in part from those other causes which have been enumerated in this chapter as acting on the Grecian mind. It proceeds from the stimulus applied to all the common feelings in religion, art, and recreation,—from the gradual formation of national festivals, appealing in various ways to tastes and sentiments which animated every Hellenic bosom,—from the inspirations of men of genius, poets, musicians, sculptors, architects, who supplied more or less in every Grecian city, education for the youth, training for the chorus, and ornament for the locality,—from the gradual expansion of science, philosophy, and rhetoric, during the coming period of this history, which rendered one city the intellectual capital of Greece, and brought to Isokratês and Plato pupils from the most distant parts of the Grecian world. It was this fund of common tastes, tendencies, and aptitudes, which caused the social atoms of Hellas to gravitate towards each other, and which enabled the Greeks to become something better and greater than an aggregate of petty disunited communities like the Thracians or Phrygians. And the creation of such common, extra-political Hellenism, is the most interesting phenomenon which the historian has to point out in the early period now under our notice. He is called upon to dwell upon it the more forcibly, because the modern reader has generally no idea of national union without political union,—an association foreign to the Greek mind. Strange as it may seem to find a songwriter put forward as an active instrument of union among his fellow-Hellens, it is not the less true, that those poets, whom we have briefly passed in review, by enriching the common language, and by circulating from town to town either in person or in their compositions, contributed to fan the flame of Pan-Hellenic patriotism at a time when there were few circumstances to coöperate with them, and when the causes tending to perpetuate isolation seemed in the ascendant. ✻

2. MIKHAIL ROSTOVTZEFF

FROM Mikhail Rostovtzeff, *A History of the Ancient World*, 2 vols. (Oxford: Clarendon Press, 1926), vol. I, 229–41.

The seventh and sixth centuries B.C. were a great creative epoch in the history of human civilization. Those laws of thought, political organization, and art, which mark out European civilization generally and distinguish it in many important respects from the civilizations of the East, began to take shape at this time. The chief peculiarities of Greek culture, both then and later, were its individual, personal character and its boldness—the unbounded hardihood, one might say, with which it stopped at nothing, and its entire independence of religion, though the latter maintained a separate existence beside it.

But together with this bent towards individualism, we observe another trait which is easily reconcilable with it. Throughout Greek history we find among all Greeks an increasing consciousness that they belong to one nation and form one body; and this unity was indicated, not only by a common religion and a common language, but also by a common civilization, more or less identical among them all. This national feeling was powerfully promoted by colonization and the trade which kept pace with colonization. The tie that bound a colony to the Greek world was never broken: the colony always felt herself the true daughter of her mother city and resembled her almost exactly in all respects. On the other hand, the deep gulf that separated the Greek view of life from that of their new neighbours was realized with exceptional clearness by the colonists.

Let us begin by dwelling for a little on the second of these traits, the feeling of nationality. In the dawn of Greek history it showed itself in religion. The primitive religious beliefs of the Greeks were the same as those of other peoples, the same as in the East—animism, or the belief that there exists in living beings an immortal part which is not identical with matter, the belief in a future life being derived from this; fetishism, or the belief in a mysterious power residing in certain inanimate objects, such as trees and stones; totemism, or the belief in the divinity of certain animals; and polytheism, which believes in an infinite number of gods and in the divinity of such natural phenomena as the sun and moon, thunder and lightning, rivers, springs, and forests. There was no national religion and could not be, because there was no nation. Each stock, each *gens*, each brotherhood (*phratria*), and each family had its own gods and its own rites.

It was the appearance of the so-called Homeric poems, during their first spontaneous expansion over the Aegean islands and Asia Minor, which first made the Greeks conscious that they were a nation. Through these poems and through their mighty culmination in the *Iliad* and *Odyssey*—a culmination which touched religion also and endeavoured to single out the common element in the religious ideas of all Hellas—the Greeks gained a clear conception of their national unity and realized the racial peculiarities of their life and religion. These poems set the figures of the chief gods before the eyes of the Greeks, gave to each of them a distinct form, forced men to believe in their nearness to humanity, and equipped them with attributes which every Greek recognized in himself.

Homer united the gods in one comprehensive family; the great monarch Zeus the Thunderer was the head of this family and governed it just as the Graeco-Aegean kings governed their households. At the same time Homer exalted the gods and Zeus in particular to a height beyond human attainment, placing them on the summit of Mount Olympus and illuminating them with the light of ineffable beauty. Homer became the Bible of the Greeks—the source from which they drew their conceptions of divinity, and which fixed for ever the divine images so familiar even to us. Supreme Zeus, ruler of gods and men; queenly Hera, his divine consort; Poseidon, lord of the sea; Ares, the terrible warrior; Hermes, the messenger of the gods; Aphrodite, born of the sea foam, ever young and lovely in her divine beauty; Hephaestus, the halting smith; the radiant Apollo—all these were clothed once for all in permanent forms of ineffable poetic loveliness.

Yet among these gods there was one in particular who became especially near and dear to every Greek, and with whom they connected their new conceptions of divinity and its part in human life. This was Apollo. Originally the god of light in particular, but also the god of agriculture and stock-raising, he assumed by degrees new attributes. Like Heracles, a champion of humanity against the dark forces of nature, he comes forth as a defender and saviour. He overcame with his arrows the formidable Python, the serpent which personified the dark and dangerous forces of the underworld; and men, in gratitude for this exploit, built him his bright temple at Delphi, where all nature proclaimed the power of light to conquer darkness. Together with Heracles he was builder of cities and their protector, and the patron of Greek civilization, especially of music. His first paean or song of victory he sang over the body of the slain Python. His oracles guided men along the path of truth and justice and advised them in their public and private affairs.

Still more important is the fact that, with the figure of Apollo, morality makes its first appearance as a part of religion. The god himself undergoes a humiliating penance for the slaughter of the Python, and feeds the flocks of Admetus. From his shrine at Delphi he holds forth a helping hand to others who have stained themselves with blood; by repentance and purification they are reconciled with their own consciences and with society; the god absolves them from their sins; for the matricide only there is no absolution. The religion of Apollo had a very great influence on Greece. The temple of Zeus at Olympia was not the only shrine where all Greeks worshipped: Apollo had two such temples—one at Delphi, the centre of an alliance, one of the most ancient in Greece, between several communities, and the other in Delos, where the religious life of all the Ionians was concentrated. In Asia Minor the place of Delphi was taken by the temple of Apollo at Didyma near Miletus, a shrine familiar to all Greeks. Pindar, one of the greatest Greek poets, claims to be a prophet who reveals the religion of Apollo and glorifies the god of light.

The worship of Demeter in her temple at Eleusis also became universal among Greeks. Demeter, the Great Mother, had been worshipped earlier by others; but the Greeks raised this cult to a high point of poetic symbolism and moralized it. Whereas Apollo was a god of all Greece, revered in every city and, as the 'god of our fathers', in every family, Demeter was more exclusive. She admitted to her mysteries only a chosen band of believers, only those who were pure in a ritual and moral sense. Yet there was no distinction of sex or station: even slaves were included; but no foreigner was admitted. To the initiated she promised complete regeneration, or rather, a new birth during this life and bliss hereafter. At the solemn ceremony of initiation, her worshipper, cleansed from earthly taint, drew near to the deity and was united with her.

A third cult, which spread by degrees over all the Greek world, was that of Dionysus. It reached Greece in the seventh century, coming probably from Thrace, and was quickly diffused through Greece, Asia Minor, and Italy. By Thracians and Greeks Dionysus was conceived as a suffering god: he personified the vegetation which dies in winter and is renewed in spring. In his youth he was torn to pieces by the Titans, the dark forces of earth, but is born again from himself, as young and beautiful as before. His worshippers, women especially, held nightly revels in his honour by torch-light on the mountain-tops. Dancing in ecstasy to the sound of cymbals and drums, they tore in pieces a sacrificed animal, whose blood they drank with wine, and so participated in the being and eternal life of their god. A group of religious reformers, who traced their descent to the Thracian minstrel, Orpheus, and called themselves 'Orphics', purified this worship of its rude primitive features and spiritualized it. The sacred writings of the Orphics taught that the soul, imprisoned in the body as a punishment for sin, is capable of purification. This purity is attained by a life of strict morality, even of asceticism, by participation in the great secret of Dionysus, the suffering god, and by initiation into his mysteries. To the initiated an endless life of happiness after death was promised. This doctrine gradually became united with the kindred mysteries of Eleusis. Dionysus-Iacchus was united to Demeter and her daughter, Kore; and this trinity became the object of the Eleusinian rites. The Orphic cult of Dionysus was propagated outside Greece by a succession of missionaries who founded everywhere communities of believers, of which the most important and long-lived belonged to the Greek cities in south Italy. Among them were many thinkers of a religious turn, notably Pythagoras, one of the founders of scientific mathematics and astronomy, and the head of an Orphic community which at one time governed the wealthy city of Croton.

These shrines, most of which were also oracular seats, were resorted to by all Greeks and served as a symbol of national unity. I have mentioned already the temple of Zeus at Olympia and those of Apollo at Delphi, Delos, and Didyma. Other oracular shrines were those of Poseidon near Corinth and of Zeus at Dodona in Epirus. The temples of the healing god, Asclepius, were national also. The sick and suffering flocked thither from all Greece, and schools of medicine were formed there by physicians, the pupils of the divine healer.

In connexion with some of these holy places competitions in honour of the god were instituted in athletic games, music, and poetry, and were open to all Greeks. From time immemorial the gods had been worshipped, not in Greece alone, with dance and song and competitions of various kinds. In these contests the youth of Greece sang hymns of praise in the god's honour; or reproduced scenes from his life in rhythmic choral dances, accompanied by music and singing; or vied with one another in running, jumping, wrestling, and the throwing of the discus and the javelin; or appeared as drivers of chariots drawn by the swiftest horses.

In these games and in the very nature of the Panhellenic shrines the two characteristics of the Greek genius and of Greek life are conspicuous. The god was glorified by all Greeks: during the games thousands of Greeks from Greece proper and the colonies gathered at Olympia or Corinth met, conversed, discussed questions of interest to a section or to them all, and united in combined rites and offerings. But, on the other hand, almost every community in Greece or the colonies prided itself on its 'treasury', a beautiful chapel-like building within the temple precinct, where its great deeds were told in painting and sculpture; each community brought thither its best artists and best athletes, and coveted the honour of raising a statue of their victorious townsman on the open space in front of the temple. Not only did each city in this way assert its individuality, but the competitors did the same with equal emphasis. These youths were eager to excel, to thrust themselves forward, to display to all Greece their personal superiority. They strove with persistent toil to attain perfection of mind and body, and to wrest the prize from rivals like themselves, who had submitted to the same training for the same object. Their highest reward was gained when all Greece, in the person of the chosen judges, acknowledged them as national and public heroes, crowned them with a wreath of twigs from the sacred tree, and permitted their statues to be placed beside those of the gods.

The Greek, however strongly he felt himself a part of the Greek nation, was, first and foremost, a citizen of his own community and would sink his individuality for it, and for it alone. The interests of that community touched him nearly and often blinded him to the interests of Greece as a whole. Throughout Greek history the forces of disruption were stronger and more active than those of centralization; rivalry and separation, which found vent in wars between the states, were stronger than the tendency to agreement and coalition—a tendency which showed itself in treaties, alliances, and national arbitration, and laid the foundations of European international law. To the Athenian the temple of his native goddess, Athena, on the Acropolis, the symbol of a united community and kingdom, was dearer than the temple of Poseidon in Calauria, the centre of a religious alliance between several communities akin to Athens, and dearer than the shrine of Apollo at Delos, the religious centre of all who used the

Ionic dialect. Nevertheless, Attica, united round Athens, Boeotia, rallying round Thebes, Argolis, concentrating round Argos, and Sparta, ruling a number of Dorian communities and clans—each of these powers sought to become the centre of a still more extensive union; but each of them regarded such a union as a point scored in the competition between states, and treated the members of the union not as allies with equal rights but as inferiors.

The individual character of the national genius is seen with special clearness in the region of thought and of art, where local patriotism, far from hindering the development of personality, in many cases even encouraged it. The communities were just as proud of their great thinkers and artists as of their champions who won prizes at Olympia, and strove as eagerly for pre-eminence in culture as in politics. Discovery and invention, which in the East had been impersonal things, lose that character in Greece and are closely connected for all time with the personality of the discoverer. It is significant that all the earliest discoveries of the prehistoric past were attributed by the lively imagination of Greece to a definite inventor, who was, in many cases, not even a Greek. Thus the Greeks could tell at once that Prometheus had taught mankind the use of fire, and that Daedalus was the father of sculpture; they knew who invented the potter's wheel, and who was the first to forge weapons of copper and iron. Much more did they make mention of those who created their own civilization—that civilization which distinguished them from all 'barbarians' who spoke no Greek. Greece was proud of them, and with good reason: they laid the foundation of all our modern civilization, which is as individual as that of Greece.

In matters of science, technical skill, and art the Greeks were, in many respects, pupils of the East, and they never forgot this. It was in Asia Minor, where they were in constant connexion with the East, that they started on the path of progress themselves. But, while drawing freely from the stores of Eastern civilization, they refashioned all they received, and stamped a fresh character upon it. Their genius recognized no tradition, no unalterable rules. They approached each fresh problem as a matter for investigation. If the problem was solved, the next investigator treated the solution as merely a starting-point for further inquiry. Nature, the world, and man became at once for them matter for this kind of reflection and investigation. They were not content to register what they saw and accept its mythological explanation. They felt the rule of law in nature and tried to make it clear. Their first question was not 'How?' but 'Why?' When foreign travel made them acquainted with new countries and strange seas, they perpetuated their knowledge by drawing maps, and also at once began asking: 'What is the whole world? what is its shape, and what its relation to other worlds, the sun, moon, and stars?' And having raised such questions, they suggested answers—answers which were at first childishly simple, no doubt, but scientific and not mythological. Thus they became the creators of scientific geography, cosmology, and astronomy. Before the end of the sixth century Pythagoras in Italy knew that the earth and the stars were of spherical shape.

In their study of the world, the Ionian inquirers and thinkers—or philosophers, as they called themselves—endeavoured to separate the chief and fundamental element in the creation. That a single substance underlies all matter was held first by Thales; and the question was discussed further by Anaximander and Anaximenes. All these three were Milesians. Thales found the primary substance of matter in water; Anaximenes found it in air; Anaximander, the creator of scientific prose and the first to publish his theory in a book, insisted on the infinity of the world, or rather worlds, and their perpetual interchanges. He also was the first to make a map of the world known to him. Still more profound were the views of Xenophanes, who migrated to Elea in south Italy and there founded the Eleatic school of philosophy. The unity of the world was his chief dogma. He believed one god to be the directing force of the world. 'He is all eye, mind, ear; he directs all things without effort by the power of his reason.' Polytheism and the legends told of the gods he treated as mere inventions of human imagination. God was perceived by reason, and reason led men to the knowledge of things. God is also moral force, and men should pray to God, in order to attain the ideal of justice. This is not the place to dwell on the beginnings of European science; but it is proper to repeat, that in Greece for the first time humanity treated nature and man as a problem that could be solved by reason. ✻

3. VICTOR EHRENBERG

FROM Victor Ehrenberg, *The Greek State* (Oxford: Basil Blackwell, 1940), pp. 5–9.

I base the remarks that follow on the recognized fact that geography and history stand to one another in a relation of mutual influence, equally important whether we are thinking in terms of geography or of history. Of these two related elements one is essentially constant, the other essentially changing; the facts of space and nature remain constant through all the changes of time and history, yet vary in their significance and their effects. The history of the area first occupied by the Greeks, from the Helladic period down through Hellenic, Hellenistic and Roman times into the Turkish period and the development of modern Greece, supplies unmistakable evidence both of changelessness and of change.

The region in which the Greek state had its original home embraces not only the peninsula that we call Greece, but also the islands and coasts of the Aegean Sea—the Aegean, as we call it for short. Sharply separated from the outside world by the open sea south of Crete and in the west, by the Balkan mountains in the north, and by the western edge of the plateau of Asia Minor in the east, this region may be regarded as a true geographical unit, with its base in its geological prehistory. In the course of history, the Ionic migration (late in the second millennium?) and the ensuing movements from west to east over the Aegean Sea made this geographical unit a Greek unit, and thus formed, beyond all inner political frontiers, an area entirely Greek, the motherland of the multitude of Greek states. Its centre is the sea, but this sea is so thickly sown with islands, and the shores of Greece and the western coasts of Asia Minor are so broken up by the sea, that land and sea appear to be indissolubly connected; thus, the whole region is closely bound together by nature. Though it belongs to two continents, the Aegean is still a unit, for it is 'thalassocentric', centred on the sea and situated around the sea and its parts. A people that had no name for the sea when they first entered the Aegean area, learnt there to think of the sea as central, and never quite lost the habit.

The same geographical factors worked together to create a multitude of units and a great variety of forms. The fact that land and sea were so broken up led also to the erection of innumerable barriers. The land was torn in pieces by the bays, gulfs and arms of the sea, and not less by the mountains which belong to a number of systems, created by mighty geological convulsions. Thus the Greek area displays an interlocked pattern of land and sea, mountains and mountainous districts, plains and valleys, islands and peninsulas, and the result is a wealth of small, sharply separated regions: nature sets an example of fragmentation that was followed and even surpassed by the political world. It was hard to find a place that offered any possibility for larger developments of power; even where (as for example, in Asia Minor) extensive river plains might have served as a basis for it, the political and historical requirements were lacking.

We have indicated in the last paragraph the small extent of the natural and, even more, of the political districts. The whole area of the Aegean is very narrow in its scope; but the full meaning of this narrowness was only felt and realized when it was broken up internally into small and ever smaller divisions. For the sailor the sea never vanishes into infinity and, even where islands are scarce, some high peak like that of Athos or the Cretan Ida is always there as a landmark; so too on land there is never a plain that is not soon bounded by a mountain or an inlet of the sea. This among other things forced the political units to renounce expansion and led to a swift and complete seizure of the space available and to the early development of numerous political bodies. Painfully recoiling from its narrow boundaries and concentrated on itself, the state preserved a unity which displayed the features of a human community rather than of a political organization. The narrow space, admitting of little variation, produced a marked unification of the civic type and a very distinct political consciousness, limited though it was by its small scale. Neither power nor expansion could be the true aim of the growing state, but from the narrowness of space sprang high tensions that stimulated the creativeness of the community.

The limited space of the single political unit was again the main cause of Greek colonization and was responsible for the wide extent of the area of Greek settlements and the great number of their cities. The reason for the foundation of most colonies was the insufficiency of the homeland for housing and feeding a growing population. Even where it was trade and warlike energy that led states to colonize, it was, in the last instance, the lack of a territory that could be exploited economically that drove men to the sea and created markets abroad. The age of colonization meant the spread of the Greeks of the Aegean over the whole of the Mediterranean and the Black Sea as well. A map, containing not only the Aegean, but the sea to the south of Crete, south Italy, east Sicily, the interior of the Balkans and the coasts of Asia Minor, or, better still, a map stretching from Massilia to Sinope and from Cyrene to Olbia, will help us to realize that the Aegean is in the centre of an area, knit into one by the bonds of the sea and both limited and defended by the surrounding mountains, steppes and deserts.

The sea, then, served as a safety valve for tensions within the narrow space, and so the exact position in relation to the sea was of decisive importance for political development. In the Aegean, in particular, the shores with their wealth of harbours called for trade and commercial intercourse and created economic prosperity and intellectual vitality, with a city state as their living centre. Lands as close to one another as Argolis and Laconia, or Attica and Boeotia, illustrate the difference between regions that turn their faces or their backs to the sea. As the city developed, there emerged two characteristic forms of settlement—the settlement round a citadel, which was based on Mycenaean traditions, and the 'Phoenician' pattern, especially popular with the colonies, on a jutting peninsula or an island lying off the coast. A city's situation within the Aegean was no less important. The Aegean was a much frequented market between two continents; it was therefore of the highest importance for the individual state to be near the routes of traffic and points of intersection. A map will show that favourable position usually coincided with a favourable configuration of the coast. In general, it is the coasts that face the Aegean which are moulded into peninsulas and bays. It was here, then —in a historical movement from east to west—that those Greeks lived who held the political and cultural leadership; the western countries of the homeland were far behind and had hardly woken out of their sleep outside history when a new Greece, intensely alive, had arisen still farther in the west. The slowing down of the pace of historical development in the Aegean world from Asia Minor to the islands, then to the east coast of Greece and finally to her central and western districts played an important part in the manifold variety of the Greek world of states.

If we disregard some fertile plains, mostly small, Greece was always a poor country, poor in water—springs were especially important in determining settlement—poor in arable land, poor in mineral wealth. The land trained the Greek peasant not so much to hard work and intensified methods as to frugality. The limitation and poor quality of the soil meant an early decline of grain crops in many districts and their replacement by vines and olive trees. The import of corn became necessary, while of wine and oil there usually was more than enough for the producer; the basic conditions of agriculture, remaining everywhere more or less the same, drove the peasant to the city market and, in time, increasingly to trade and seafaring.

The economic and political effects of the conditions innate in the soil were reinforced by the influence of the climate, the mild heat, the low rainfall and the short winter. The climate took life out into the open. House and family were far less important for daily life and social meetings than the market and the wrestling-school. A man's profession too came to matter less. Public life was almost the sole environment of the citizen. Man proved himself to be indeed a ζῶον πολιτικόν, a creature bound to the Polis, the community both urban and political.

Natural conditions in the Aegean thus led to the creation of numerous self-contained communities, characterized as much by their rich variety and mutual rivalries as by narrow space and inner coherence. In the colonies, too, the type of state, developed in the Aegean, was in all essentials retained. Colonization depended entirely on the sea—in contrast to Rome which colonized by land—and was almost exclusively confined to settlements on the shore. Difficulties of navigation, lack of harbours or of suitable land along the coast, occasionally discouraged the colonists. In other cases there were historical difficulties that made Greek colonization impossible, as, for example, in the south-east and on the north-west coast of Africa, where Phoenicians, the Assyrian power, or Carthage stood in the way. Conditions varied widely in the different areas of colonization. What the colonists sought chiefly were good harbours, fertile soil and protection against pirates and hostile natives. Here, too, the life of the state was strongly directed inwards rather than outwards. The natural requirements were in all important points the same, and that despite the larger territories of the Greek cities in Italy and Sicily. Out of the character of the Mediterranean world, both in east and west, grew the Greek state that at once shaped and revealed the Greek character. The close packing of states inside the Greek world, and of men inside the states, was the essential cause of the universal urge towards the *agon*, the passion to compete with your neighbour. ✣

4. C. M. BOWRA

FROM C. M. Bowra, *The Greek Experience* (Cleveland: The World Publishing Company, 1957), pp. 3–13, 20–21, 40–41.

A people lives by its geography. What nature provides as a home and a background is the most enduring element in any national history. Physical type may be altered beyond recognition by new strains and crossbreeding; languages may disintegrate before the political pressure or social attractions of new tongues; habits, which seem to be indestructible, collapse before unprecedented menaces or intoxicating novelties. But nature remains in the end what it was in the beginning, a school which by its prizes and its penalties fashions its children to a special pattern. In Greece the configuration and the character of the landscape have been a primary influence in shaping the destiny of its people ever since the first Greek tribes moved down from the north into the lands which still belong to their descendants. There have indeed been a few changes. The mountains, which were once covered with forests, are now for the most part denuded, largely because the omnivorous goat gobbles saplings before they have time to grow, and wintry rains wash away the scanty soil which has nothing to hold it, but the process is at least as old as Plato, who complained that, in comparison with earlier times, there remained 'only the bones of the wasted body'; at a few places, as at Thermopylae, the sea has receded before the silt of swollen torrents and changed the coastline; wolves and boars, lions and bears, no longer rove the mountains and wild places; here and there, as in Boeotia, marshes have been drained to make fields and orchards. But on the whole Greece is physically much the same today as it was four thousand years ago: a land of mountains, which are not huddled together in ungainly lumps but flaunt their peaks in proud independence, and of islands, which are themselves mountains with roots engulfed in the sea. It presents dramatic contrasts between barren marble or limestone masses and watered valleys, between rain and snow in winter and unbroken sunshine in summer, between an unequalled magnificence of wild flowers and blossoming trees in March and April and parched, crumbling earth from June to October. Though Greece begins where the mountainous Balkan mass narrows and projects into the midland sea, it is not Balkan, but emphatically itself in its configuration, its climate, its eternal intimacy with the sea.

Greece is a land of contrasts, but not of extremes. Even in winter there is abundant sunshine; the heat is intense in summer, but lacks the humidity which saps energy and effort; districts, near enough to each other as the crow flies, may be separated by almost impassable mountains, but often have easy communications by sea; though most Greek rivers become barren, stony gullies in summer, in winter they are hurtling torrents, whose water is stored in pools and wells; even the rudest shores may have safe harbours or sandy reaches on which boats can be moored. Greece is indeed a hard land, capable of maintaining only a small population, but if this population faces its tasks with decision, it will reap its rewards. The country is still incapable of feeding flocks or herds on any large scale. Olive-oil takes the place of butter, preservatives, and cooking fats. Fruit and vegetables can be grown only in a few fertile plains or in terraces and holes carved in hill-sides and held by stone embankments; fish is not nearly so common or so various as in northern seas; meat is rare and more likely to be kid than beef or mutton. Yet the Greek larder has its compensations. Wine is abundant; in a land of many flowers honey yields an ample supply of sugar; the goat gives milk and cheese; the mountains have their hares and wild birds, the sea its mullets, lobsters, and squids. Scarcity of food has never prevented the Greeks from being healthy and vigorous; and the very difficulties which attend its supply have stimulated their efforts and their ingenuity.

Such a land demands that its inhabitants should be tough, active, enterprising, and intelligent. When the Greeks exposed unwanted children at birth, they showed how seriously they interpreted the exacting conditions of their existence, and followed the example of nature, which exerts its own selection and control by allowing only the strongest to survive. The physical capacity of the Greeks is clear enough from their many male statues, whose sturdy, muscular frames and limbs are combined with slim waists and competent hands. Men living in such circumstances needed more than the usual qualities of workers in fields, since much of their labour lay on mountain-slopes and in rocky hollows. They must be able to climb easily, to carry heavy loads up and down hill, to be handy with the shifting and shaping of stones, to travel long distances on foot, to drive ploughs through obstinate, stony soil, to tame horses and mules, to repel the onslaughts of wild animals, and to endure alike sun and storm. This physical equipment must be supplemented by unflagging industry, careful foresight, skill in essential handicrafts, and all the age-old virtues of the farmer who works on difficult land. As labour in the fields promotes endurance and strength of body, so the handling of ships demands quickness of eye and hand, agility and lightness of movement, unresting vigilance, and rapidity of decision. Geographical circumstances formed the Greek character by forcing it to make the most of its natural aptitudes in a hard struggle with the earth and the elements.

The peculiar position of Greece in the south-eastern corner of Europe has determined much in the course of its history. It is physically a blind alley, and once immigrants have moved in, they are not likely to move out except by sea. It is moreover not easy to enter by land. There is no royal road from the Balkan mass into northern Greece, and any penetration must be slow, over mountains where passes are not indeed uncommon but not often easy, and the sparse river-valleys usually lead in the wrong direction. Nature protects Greece from any swift, overwhelming conquest by land; it is difficult even for mechanized, modern armies to control the whole country effectively. On the other hand, Greece lends itself to gradual, piecemeal penetration. It offers many convenient refuges where bands of immigrants can consolidate before making their next move and collect their forces without interference or even notice. Though its first inhabitants were akin to the 'Mediterranean' figures whom we see on the frescoes of Minoan Crete, the Greeks who supplanted them came from the north, probably in intermittent waves. They brought with them their language, which revealed its northern and inland limitations by having to take from the indigenous speech words for sea, olive-tree, bean, fig, cypress, hyacinth, wine, tin, and bath. They absorbed the original inhabitants, of whom only vague memories survived on the mainland under the name of 'Pelasgian', which may have had the same kind of connotation as 'Welsh'. From them the Greeks took a number of place-names, religious rites, and even divinities. But these different elements were at an early date fused into a whole, except in some islands, notably Crete, where in the fifth century BC there was a corner where the old Aegean or 'Minoan' language was still spoken. The Greeks of historical times were physically a mixed people, and advocates of 'purity' of breed will find in them no support for their views. If their sculpture and painting present a recognizably standard type, that is probably because climatic conditions exert their own control and not only give preference in survival to a type which has long been adapted to them but make acclimatization slow and difficult. The Greeks were not the blond giants of Teutonic fancy. The majority of them seem to have been, as they are today, dark-haired and olive-skinned, but among them, then as now, there were a few whose fair hair marked them out for admiring comment, like Homer's Menelaus, who is called *xanthos* and looks as if he had brown hair. Since the same adjective is given not only to some other heroes but to goddesses like Demeter, we can hardly doubt that it was to mark their exceptional appearance. Zeus, who embodies the masculine spirit of the Greeks, is said to have eyebrows of dark blue, and though we must make some allowance for poetical fancy, we recognize him at once as a type commonly to be seen in Greece today.

Though Greece is not easy to invade by land, it presents many promising openings to anyone who has control of the sea. From the sea it can be attacked at many points, and it is not difficult to establish beach-heads from which inland regions can be invaded and to some extent controlled. The possibilities of this situation were seen by Minos, king of Crete some two generations before the Trojan War. With his navy he ruled the Aegean and conquered the Cyclades; in which he put his sons to rule. The absence of fortifications at his capital of Cnossus betrays his confidence that no sea-raiders could attack it, and six different places, all on the islands or the coast of the mainland, called Minoa, indicate where he established control-points. It is unlikely that he actually conquered the mainland, even though he exacted tribute from some places. But he had grasped an essential feature of Greek political geography, and soon after 1200 BC the first serious conquest of Greece, as opposed to gradual infiltration, came, from the north-west, with the arrival of a related Greek people known to posterity as the Dorians. We can hardly doubt that they came by sea, and it is significant that among the last documents to be written in the palace of Pylos before its destruction is one which records the movement of oarsmen to Pleuron at the mouth of the Gulf of Patras. The conquest that followed was indeed devastating. It gave a death-blow to the Mycenaean civilization, which may already have been enfeebled by over-exertion abroad and by intestine struggles at home, and it plunged Greece into a Dark Age, from which the Greece that we know emerged into history some four centuries later. A similar menace came with the two Persian invasions of 490 and 480 BC. In these a powerful army was sent overland by the eastern coastal route, but it was supported at almost every point by a fleet, manned largely by Phoenician sailors, which not only secured supplies but was also on occasion able to transport troops. The Greeks defeated the Persians first at sea and then on land, but the victory at Plataea in 479 would hardly have been final if the Persians had not been heavily handicapped by the previous destruction of their fleet and the reduction in supplies which this meant. Greece was indeed at the mercy of the sea, and in the fifth century it took steps to command it. The Greeks became a people because they lived in an enclosed space with marked natural frontiers, and so long as they were not attacked from the sea, they were relatively free to develop on their own lines without foreign interference.

The presence of the sea and a knowledge of seamanship which goes back to early in the second millennium turned the eyes and the appetites of the Greeks to what lay beyond it. In the Mycenaean age they had already planted settlements on the western and southern shores of Asia Minor, in Cyprus, and even in Syria. The Dorian conquest drove other colonists over the Aegean, where the regions known as Aeolis and Ionia maintained the ancient traditions of the great past and developed their own distinguished and indubitably Hellenic civilization. From the eighth century onwards adventurous parties sailed farther afield, and Greek cities were built and maintained so far west as Marseilles and so far north as the Crimea. But the most favoured and most promising field for exploitation was Sicily and South Italy. Despite the hostility of the natives and the armed menace of powerful competitors like the Etruscans and the Carthaginians, the Greeks in 'Magna Graecia', or 'Great Greece', took full advantage of territories broader and richer than they had known at home to develop a varied and brilliant life. Despite the barrier of the sea, they kept in touch with the homeland, worshipped the same gods, took part in the same festivals, maintained the same customs, and spoke the same language. If they intermarried with the local inhabitants, it did not interfere with their conviction that they were full-blooded Greeks. Their law-givers were among the first and the most famous. When the first strong tide of Persian invasion drove Greeks from Ionia to seek new homes, they found a ready welcome in the West, where philosophy and mathematics took some of their most momentous forms. The western Greeks insisted on their Hellenism, and were right to do so, since they cherished it with unwavering devotion and knew from their acquaintance with more than one kind of 'barbarian' how much it meant to be a Greek. In remoter colonies, like the Crimea with its Scythian neighbours, the Greeks were probably in closer touch with native populations. But they gave more than they got, and the remarkable gold-work found in Scythian graves testifies to the power of their example. Indeed, Greek colonies did much to spread the fame of Greek crafts by their exportation of fine objects to distant places. A signal example is the great bronze crater found at Vix in the middle of

France, which is Peloponnesian work of the sixth century BC . . . We do not know how or why it reached this destination, but it shows the high esteem in which Greek handicrafts were held and how the Greeks met local demands without making concessions to local methods or tastes. The Greek colonies were indeed outposts for trade, but through trade for civilization, and their way of life was all the more consciously Greek because they were on the limits of the known world. The sea, which might have broken the Greek system into scattered and separate fragments, held it together and gave it a special unity in which far-severed communities kept in touch with the homeland and felt that in every sense they still belonged to it.

In Greece itself geography shaped the pattern of political life. If, as is probable, the Greeks in the thirteenth century BC were united in a loose confederacy under the king of Mycenae, they were never again united until Alexander of Macedon led them against Persia. The most marked feature of Greek politics is the division of the country into a number of small states, each with its own independent government and its own local character. This was imposed by a landscape in which men lived in valleys divided from one another by mountains, or on uplands which presented few entrances to the outer world, or on islands which were largely self-sufficient and self-contained. Each district developed its own life and customs and local pride, because it was separate, complete, and difficult to control from without. Mountainous barriers were not enough to prevent invasion, but they were enough to prevent one state from being merged into another. From time to time states might fall under the dominion of aggressive and powerful neighbours or be forced into union with one another, but they still maintained something of their political independence and many of their own institutions.

It is customary to speak of the units of Greek polity as city-states, and the phrase is apt enough if we recognize that such a state consisted of a good deal more than a city. If the city, usually walled, was the centre of government and justice and of many handicrafts and trades, other activities went on outside. If there were fertile plains, people would live in villages near their work. Beyond the plains was rising land, usually covered by scrub, hard to cultivate except in patches and pockets, and useful chiefly for pasturing goats. Beyond this, and still higher up, were the rough slopes of the mountains, perhaps here and there enclosing some isolated hamlet, but for the most part desolate, the haunt of hunters in summer and snow-covered in winter. Since many Greek cities lay close to the sea, there would be ports where ships could be built and harboured and a maritime population could have its home. In general, the inhabitants of a city-state would be formed of farmers, craftsmen, and sailors, and

many would combine two or even three of the roles. Because all members
of a city-state lived in close proximity within a more or less enclosed space,
they had a strong sense of unity and kinship. This did not save them from
internecine struggles or from class-war, but it meant that respect for local
tradition made them look on the men of other cities as somehow different
from themselves. Though the leading parts in Greek history were played
by a few states, we can even today see from the remains of many almost
forgotten places how distinctive their lives must have been. In obedience
to their natural surroundings they found their own characteristics, developed their own individuality, and, without making much impression on
the rest of Greece, conformed almost unconsciously to the general pattern
of its habits.

By its very nature the city-state created its own special kind of social
life. Governments might vary from the rule of the one to the rule of the
many, but when conditions were fundamentally simple and homogeneous,
differences in manners and outlook must have been more in degree than in
kind, according to the size and powers of the wealthier classes. No city
concealed divine monarchs in mysterious isolation or maintained privileged priests as a separate caste. Most men shared the same interests and
the same pursuits. Even those who lived in cities and engaged in manufac-
tures and handicrafts, or those who sought a livelihood on the sea, were
brought up close to the soil and knew its ways. Such men tended to behave
to each other as equals, because they had common concerns and back-
grounds, and, despite differences of wealth, lived in much the same
manner. Brought perpetually into contact with one another and knowing
their neighbours' foibles and follies, they developed a remarkable forth-
rightness in their social relations. Even if they respected birth and breed-
ing, there seem to have been few such formal restraints between men of
different position as exist in more highly organized societies, where professional pursuits promote isolated groups of specialists. As in most Mediterranean countries, the centre of activity, at least for men, is the street or
the public square, where all topics, and especially politics, are discussed
with eloquence, frankness, and some degree of knowledge. If such circumstances foster a reasonable measure of decorum and courtesy, they also
foster passionate quarrels, lewd banter, and scurrilous abuse. Hierarchical
stiffness and commercial servility tend alike to be lacking. Such conditions
encourage a lively curiosity about personal idiosyncrasies, with the result
that a man cannot shelter behind any delusive disguise conferred by office
or pedigree, and though good manners may be usual, they do not prevent
men from saying frankly what they think of one another. Such a situation
produces men who are fully aware of their surroundings, extrovert, and
civically minded. The city-state did not by any means always promote

democracy, but it fostered a freedom of intercourse, a sense of personality, and a social frame in which men were exposed to the full observation of their fellows but not prevented from being themselves.

No less powerful was the influence which the Greek scene had on the Greek eye and the Greek mind. The traveller who comes from the west or the north to Greece for the first time may feel a slight twinge of disappointment at the nakedness of its outline and its lack of exuberant colour, but he will soon see that he is faced by a commanding beauty which makes no ready concessions to his appreciation but forces itself slowly and unforgettably on him. What matters above all is the quality of the light. Not only in the cloudless days of summer but even in winter the light is unlike that of any other European country, brighter, cleaner, and stronger. It sharpens the edges of the mountains against the sky, as they rise from valleys or sea; it gives an ever-changing design to the folds and hollows as the shadows shift on or off them; it turns the sea to opal at dawn, to sapphire at midday, and in succession to gold, silver, and lead before nightfall; it outlines the dark green of the olive-trees in contrast to the rusty or ochre soil; it starts innumerable variations of colour and shape in unhewn rock and hewn stonework. The beauty of the Greek landscape depends primarily on the light, and this had a powerful influence on the Greek vision of the world. Just because by its very strength and sharpness the light forbids the shifting, melting, diaphanous effects which give so delicate a charm to the French or the Italian scene, it stimulates a vision which belongs to the sculptor more than to the painter, which depends not so much on an intricate combination or contrast of colours passing into each other as on a clearness of outline and a sense of mass, of bodies emphatically placed in space, of strength and solidity behind natural curves and protuberances. Such a landscape and such a light impose their secret discipline on the eye, and make it see things in contour and relief rather than in mysterious perspective or in flat spatial relations. They explain why the Greeks produced great sculptors and architects, and why even in their painting the foundation of any design is the exact and confident line.

Nor is it perhaps fanciful to think that the Greek light played a part in the formation of Greek thought. Just as the cloudy skies of northern Europe have nursed the huge, amorphous progeny of Norse mythology or German metaphysics, so the Greek light surely influenced the clear-cut conceptions of Greek philosophy. If the Greeks were the world's first true philosophers in that they formed a consistent and straightforward vocabulary for abstract ideas, it was largely because their minds, like their eyes, sought naturally what is lucid and well defined. Their senses were kept lively by the force of the light, and when the senses are keenly at work, the mind follows no less keenly and seeks to put in order what they give it. Just as Plato, in his search for transcendental principles behind the mass of phenomena, tended to see them as individual objects and compared his central principle to the sun which illuminates all things in the visible world and reveals their shapes and colours, so no Greek philosophy is happy until it can pin down an idea with a limpid definition and make its outline firm and intelligible. That the Greeks were moved by some such consideration may be seen from their use of the words *eidos* and *ideâ* to mean 'notion' or 'idea'. Originally they meant no more than 'form' and were applied to such obvious forms as the human body. The transference of the word from concrete to abstract, from visible to invisible, shows how the Greek mind worked when it moved from the gifts of the senses to the principles behind them.

If the light is the first element in the Greek scene, the second is the sea. Its 'watery ways', as Homer calls them, bind most districts in Greece, whether mainland or islands, to one another. It plays a larger part there than in any other European country because for most places it is the best, and for many the only, means of communication. There are few districts from which it is not somewhere visible. Often in isolated solitudes among the mountains a man will feel that he has lost sight of it, only to see it again round the next corner. Mastery of it was indispensable to survival, and once mastery was gained, new vistas inspired to adventure. The Greeks were sailors from the dawn of their history, and, because they were bred to ships, they were saved from sinking into the narrow, parochial round which would otherwise have been the lot of dwellers in small city-states. The sea drew alike those who wanted profit and those who wanted excitement, and was the chief means by which the Greeks expanded their knowledge of men and manners. But it was more than this. Its special enchantment, 'the multitudinous laughter of the sea-waves', of which Aeschylus speaks, took hold of the Greek consciousness and helped to shape some of its most characteristic convictions. At times no sea can be more alluring than the Aegean with its rippling waves or its halcyon calm, and then indeed it presents an image of that celestial radiance which the Greeks regarded as the most desirable state of man. But even when it seems to be most welcoming, it suddenly changes its temper and menaces with ruin on hidden reefs from merciless winds and mounting waves. By its unpredictable moods and its violent vagaries it provides a lesson on the precarious state of human life, which in the very moment when all seems to be lapped in golden calm is overwhelmed in unforeseen disaster. It is not surprising that when Sophocles sang of the unique achievements of man, he put seafaring first in his list:

> He makes the winter wind carry him
> Across the grey sea
> Through the trough of towering waves.

Command of the sea was indeed something of which to be proud, and it left an indelible mark on the Greek character. . . .

Though the new Greek world which emerged from the Dark Age was different indeed from that of the Mycenaean kings, it cherished legends of that resplendent past, and, with the longing admiration which men feel for a greatness which they cannot recover or rival, the Greeks saw in this lost society something heroic and superhuman, which embodied an ideal of what men should be and do and suffer. Their imaginations, inflamed by ancient stories of vast undertakings and incomparable heroes, of gods walking on the earth as the friends of men, of a noble splendour in external circumstances and in courtly manners, formed a vision of a heroic world which they cherished as one of their most precious possessions. From it they derived the notion that a man should live for honour and renown and play his part with style and proper pride among men as notable as himself. They knew of all this through a long tradition of poetry which derived its stories and its characters, no less than much of its technique and its language, from Mycenaean times and was passed from generation to generation by an oral tradition on the lips of men. For us this tradition survives in the Homeric poems, which came indeed towards its end but kept its authentic spirit in their generous outlook and strong sense of human worth. Since they were from an early time the staple of Greek education, they encouraged a conception of manhood in which personal worth held pride of place, and strengthened an ideal favoured already by other circumstances. The smallness and self-sufficiency of city-states promoted a degree of independence which was impossible in the centralized theocracies of Egypt and Asia. A nation of seafarers had opportunities for enterprise which would have been denied to mere workers on the land. The individualism, which conditions imposed on Greek life, suited its inherited cult of heroic manhood and endured in historical times as one of the most striking elements in its beliefs and its behaviour.

The essence of the heroic outlook is the pursuit of honour through action. The great man is he who, being endowed with superior qualities of body and mind, uses them to the utmost and wins the applause of his fellows because he spares no effort and shirks no risk in his desire to make the most of his gifts and to surpass other men in his exercise of them. His honour is the centre of his being, and any affront to it calls for immediate amends. He courts danger gladly because it gives him the best opportunity of showing of what stuff he is made. Such a conviction and its system of behaviour are built on a man's conception of himself and of what he owes to it, and if it has any further sanctions, they are to be found in what other men like himself think of him. By prowess and renown he gains an enlarged sense of personality and well-being; through them he has a second existence on the lips of men, which assures him that he has not failed in what matters most. Fame is the reward of honour, and the hero seeks it before everything else. This outlook runs through Greek history from Homer's Achilles to the historical Alexander. It is countered and modified and altered, but it persists and even extends its field from an individual to a national outlook. It is a creed suited to men of action, and through it the Greeks justified their passionate desire to vary the pattern of their lives by resourceful and unflagging enterprise. Though in its early stages, as we see it in Homer, it has much in common with similar ideals in other heroic societies, it is more resilient in Greece than elsewhere and endures with unexpected vitality when the city-state is established with all its demands and obligations on its members, and when the new conception of the citizen might seem to exclude an ideal which sets so high a value on the single man and his notion of what is due to him. . . .

. . . The heroic outlook, which the Greeks inherited from a distant past, shaped much of their thinking and their action. They fitted it into the frame of the city-state and its demands, and, when occasion called, into the larger pattern of Hellenism, of which they were never quite oblivious. When they claimed that they were superior to barbarians because they pursued a higher type of virtue, they were not wrong. In comparison with the herded multitudes of Egypt and Asia, or with the more primitive peoples on their own frontiers, the Greeks had found a principle which gave meaning to life and inspired them to astonishing achievements. Because they felt that they were different from other men, that they must always excel and surpass them, that a man wins his manhood through unflagging effort and unflinching risk, they broke away from the static patterns of society which elsewhere dominated their age, and inaugurated a way of life in which the prizes went to the eager and the bold, and action in all its forms was sought and honoured as the natural end of man. ✷

5. ARNOLD J. TOYNBEE

FROM Arnold J. Toynbee, *Hellenism: The History of a Civilization* (New York: Oxford University Press, 1959), pp. 9–15.

. . . The mere institution of city-states is not, in itself, the distinctive mark of the Hellenic way of life. What is distinctive of Hellenism is the use that it made of this institution as a means of giving practical expression to a particular outlook on the Universe. In the fifth century B.C. the Hellenic philosopher Protagoras of Abdera expressed this in his celebrated dictum that 'man is the measure of all things'. In traditional Jewish-Christian-Muslim language we should say that the Hellenes saw in Man 'the Lord of Creation' and worshipped him as an idol in the place of God.

Man-worship or Humanism is not an exclusively Hellenic form of idolatry. There is a sense in which it has been the characteristic religion of man in process of civilization at all times and places. It is, for instance, manifestly the dominant religion, in fact though not avowedly, in the Western World today. Westerners are enthusiastic worshippers of man's collective power, particularly of his power over non-human Nature through the practical application of the discoveries made by modern Western physical scientists. The eighteenth-century Western rationalists and the fifteenth-century Western humanists were also man-worshippers in their own ways. What distinguishes the Hellenic experiment in Humanism is that it was the most whole-hearted and uncompromising practice of man-worship that is on record up to date. This is the distinctive mark of Hellenic history, and it raises an interesting question: What was the connexion between the Hellenes' worship of man and Hellenism's rise, achievements, breakdown, and eventual fall?

That is the subject of this book. But, before embarking on the story and trying to read its meaning, we have to ask ourselves why Hellenism should have been the first of the civilizations to put its treasure in Humanism unreservedly and also have been the only one to do this up to date—for no later civilization, not even our own, has ever again committed itself to Humanism so completely. Here are some considerations that may help us to find an answer to this preliminary question.

Humanism is the religion that appeals to man during the stage of his history when he has already become conscious of having won a mastery over non-human Nature but has not yet been forced, by bitter experience, to face the truth that he is still not master of himself.

Man's mastery over non-human Nature was achieved by the civilizations of the first generation: the Sumerian civilization in the lower basin of the Rivers Tigris and Euphrates, the Indus civilization in Western Pakistan, the Shang civilization in the lower valley of the Yellow River, the Egyptian civilization in the lower valley of the Nile, the Minoan-Mycenaean civilization in the Aegean Archipelago. Before the rise of the Hellenic civilization and of its contemporary and sister in Canaan, the older civilizations had already made or inherited technical inventions—agriculture, the domestication of animals, the wheel, the boat—which, in point of creative genius, imaginativeness, and daring, surpass all previous inventions except primitive man's mastery of the use of fire, as well as all subsequent inventions, for which these have provided the basis. Yet, though these primary civilizations asserted man's victory over non-human Nature so triumphantly in their achievements, they were not tempted to worship man's power. Springing, as they did, out of primitive life, after a relatively short transitional stage that is known as the Neolithic Age, the primary civilizations were still living under the spell of previous aeons during which primitive man—in spite of his command of fire and his gift of speech—had not been master of Nature and had therefore worshipped her because he was conscious that she was his mistress. In particular, the primary civilizations had not mastered one element in Nature which concerns man more intimately than any other because it is the root, in Nature, to which individual human personalities are attached. They had not mastered the family: human beings were left still in bondage to it.

Primitive Nature-worship was the stuff out of which the primary civilizations made the higher religions that were their response to the experience of social breakdown and disintegration. Primitive man's worship of Nature embodied in the family and Nature embodied in the crops gave a means of expression to primary civilizations that were the first of their kind to taste the bitterness of failure. It gave them a symbol both for the tragic vein in human life and for life's miraculous victory that springs, so unexpectedly, out of life's defeat. These experiences were expressed in the image of the seed that dies and is buried in the womb of Mother Earth and then rises again in next year's crop or in the next generation of a human family. The image went into action in the worship of the sorrowing mother or wife and her suffering son or husband who has met a violent death and achieved a glorious resurrection. This religion radiated out of the Land of Sumer to the ends of the Earth. The Sumerian goddess Inanna (better known under her Akkadian name Ishtar) and her consort Tammuz reappear in Egypt as Isis and Osiris, in Canaan as Astarte and Adonis, in the

Hittite World as Cybele and Attis, and in distant Scandinavia as Nana and Balder—the goddess here still bearing her original Sumerian name, while the god, in Scandinavia as in Canaan, becomes an anonymous 'Our Lord'.

The most famous Hellenic seat of this almost world-wide cult of the sorrowing goddess and her male associate who dies and rises again was Eleusis, the shrine of Demeter ('Mother Earth'), her daughter Persephone, and the grain god Triptolemus. We may guess that the Eleusinian mysteries were a legacy to the Hellenic civilization from the Minoan-Mycenaean civilization that had preceded it. But, in the Hellenic World, it was exceptional for the worship of Nature to be the paramount religion, as it had continued to be at Eleusis. Nature-worship had not been eradicated. It was still the religion of the women and the peasantry; and these, together, constituted a large majority of the population. But they were a depressed majority, and their religion had gone underground with them.

This had happened because, in contrast to the relative continuity of civilization in the valleys of the Nile and of the Tigris and Euphrates, there had been a sharp and violent break, in the basin of the Aegean Sea, between the fall of the Minoan-Mycenaean civilization there and the rise of its Hellenic successor. The debris of the fallen society had been submerged under a flood of barbarian invasion; and the traces of the past had been effaced so thoroughly that, in Hellenic folk-memory, hardly any recollection of the antecedent civilization had survived. The Hellenic civilization had had to start life by living on two legacies from the barbarians: the epic poems ascribed to the poet Homer, which became for the Hellenes the equivalent of what the Bible is for Christians and the Qur'an for Muslims, and a pantheon of gods who were not symbols of the mysterious vicissitudes of Nature, but were made in the image of man, and of barbarian man, of all men.

These Olympian gods were life-like reproductions of their human prototype; and this was unfortunate, because barbarian human nature is peculiarly unedifying. The barbarian is a primitive man who has had the ill-luck to be drawn into an encounter with the last representatives of a decadent civilization. This historical accident has suddenly shattered the framework of the barbarian's traditional manners and customs and has thus released him from restraint before he has become ripe for freedom. The barbarian is, in fact, an adolescent who has lost the innocence of a child without having acquired the self-control of an adult. The upstart gods who had imposed their paramountcy upon the ancient Nature gods during the social interregnum in which the Minoan-Mycenaean civilization had foundered and the Hellenic civilization had emerged were a war-band of superhumanly potent but characteristically disreputable barbarians. They had established themselves on Mount Olympus and were domineering over the Universe from this magnificent brigands' eyrie.

The barbarian human nature that was reflected in the Olympian pantheon with painful realism was such an unworthy object of worship for a society in process of civilization that it quickly fell into disrepute in the Hellenic World. Even in the Homeric poems, in the final recension in which these became canonical, the Olympians are beginning to be discredited and derided. By the sixth century B.C. they were being indignantly denounced by the philosopher Xenophanes of Colophon. The Hellenes were driven to look for some alternative object of worship, and this quest went on until Hellenism itself passed out of existence; but the Hellenes, who achieved such prodigies in the fields of art and thought, never succeeded in breaking away, unaided, from the man-worship that they had inherited from their barbarian sires. They merely oscillated between two forms of man-worship that were less repugnant than the worship of deified barbarian warriors and viragos. One of these two alternatives was the worship of collective human power as manifested, first, in local city-states and finally in a single empire which seemed to its subjects to embrace the whole World and which did, in fact, embrace all the Hellenic city-states round the shores of the Mediterranean Sea. The second alternative was the worship of an individual human being who was deified because he appeared to be a saviour. There was the Sicilian despot or Macedonian king or Roman emperor who presented himself as a saviour of society; and there was the Stoic or Epicurean sage who seemed able to save other individuals by his chilly example because he had apparently saved himself by his own austere exertions.

The Hellenes never felt at ease in the practice of man-worship, even in its less ignoble forms. The measure of their uneasiness was their dread of becoming guilty of 'hybris', the overweening pride that draws down upon a human being who gives way to it the resentment and retribution of the gods. The Hellenes recognized that man cannot deify himself with impunity.

In the end, the Hellenes came to find the penalties of hybris so crushing, and the practice of man-worship in any form so unsatisfying, that they surrendered to two eastern religions that had arisen, under the impact of Hellenism, in Asian societies that the Hellenes had conquered by force of arms. In India and Central Asia the Hellenes became converts to Buddhism in the younger form of it that is known among its followers as 'the Great Career' (Mahayana); in the Mediterranean basin they became converts to Christianity.

6. WERNER JAEGER

FROM Werner Jaeger, *Paideia: The Ideals of Greek Culture*, 3 vols., 2d ed. (New York: Oxford University Press, 1945), vol. I, 5–14.

. . . The history of the idea of *areté* . . . goes back to the earliest times. There is no complete equivalent for the word areté in modern English: its oldest meaning is a combination of proud and courtly morality with warlike valour. But the idea of areté is the quintessence of early Greek aristocratic education.

The aristocracies of early Greece are first described by Homer—if we may use that name for the two great epics, the *Iliad* and the *Odyssey*. In Homer we find both the historical evidence for the life of that epoch and the permanent poetic expression of its ideals. We must study him from both points of view. We shall first use him to build up our picture of the aristocratic world, and then examine the ideals of that world as they are embodied in his heroes. For in the great figures of the epic the ideals of aristocracy attain a cultural significance which is far wider than their first narrow sphere of validity. We cannot, in fact, follow the history of culture unless we fix our attention on the ebb and flow of historical development, and at the same time on the artistic struggle to perpetuate the ideal which is the highest expression of every creative epoch.

In Homer, as elsewhere, the word areté is frequently used in a wide sense, to describe not only human merit but the excellence of non-human things—the power of the gods, the spirit and speed of noble horses. But ordinary men have no areté; and whenever slavery lays hold of the son of a noble race, Zeus takes away half of his areté—he is no longer the same man as he was. Areté is the real attribute of the nobleman. The Greeks always believed that surpassing strength and prowess were the natural basis of leadership: it was impossible to dissociate leadership and areté. The root of the word is the same as that of ἄριστος, the word which shows superlative ability and superiority; and ἄριστος was constantly used in the plural to denote the nobility. It was natural for the Greeks, who ranked every man according to his ability, to use the same standard for the world in general. That is why they could apply the word areté to things and beings which were not human, and that is why the content of the word grew richer in later times. For a man's ability can be appraised by different standards, varying according to the duties he has to perform. Only now and then, in later books, does Homer use areté for moral or spiritual qualities. Everywhere else (in conformity with the ideas of primitive Greece) it denotes the strength and skill of a warrior or athlete, and above all his heroic valour. But such valour is not considered as a moral quality distinct from strength, in the modern sense; it is always closely bound up with physical power.

It is not probable that in living speech the word areté had only the narrow Homeric sense, at the time when the two poems came into being. The epics themselves recognise standards other than areté. The *Odyssey* constantly exalts intellectual ability—especially in its hero, whose courage is usually ranked lower than his cleverness and cunning. In Homer's time merits different from valour and strength may well have been contained in the notion of areté: apart from the above exceptions, we find such extensions elsewhere in early poetry. It is clear that the new meaning given to the word by everyday speech was then forcing its way into the language of poetry. But areté as a special description of heroic strength and courage was by then fast rooted in the traditional speech of heroic poetry, and was to remain as such for a long period. It was natural that, in the warlike age of the great migrations, men should be valued chiefly for their prowess in battle: there are analogies for this in other countries. Again, the adjective ἀγαθός, which corresponds to the noun areté though it derives from a different root, came to imply the combination of nobility and valour in war. It meant sometimes 'noble' and sometimes 'brave' or 'capable'; but it seldom meant 'good' in the later sense, any more than areté meant 'moral virtue'. This old meaning long survived, in such formalised expressions as 'he died like a brave hero'; and is often found in sepulchral inscriptions and accounts of battles.

Now, although the military connotation of these words predominates in Homer, they have also a more general ethical sense. Both meanings were derived from the same root: both denote the gentlemen who possess (both in war and in private life) standards which are not valid for the common people. Thus the code of the nobility had a twofold influence on Greek education. In the first place, the city-state inherited from it one of the finest elements in its ethical system—the obligation to be brave. (In the city-state courage was called manliness, a clear reminiscence of the Homeric identification of courage with manly areté.) And, secondly, the higher social standards of the polis were derived from aristocratic practice; as is shown not so much in any particular precepts of bourgeois morality as in the general ideas of liberality and a certain magnificence in the conduct of life.

In Homer, the real mark of the nobleman is his sense of duty. He is judged, and is proud to be judged, by a severe standard. And the nobleman educates others by presenting to them an eternal ideal, to which they have a duty to conform. His sense of duty is *aidos*. Anyone is free to appeal to aidos; and if it is slighted the slight awakes in others the kindred emotion of *nemesis*. Both aidos and nemesis are essential parts of Homer's ideal of aristocracy. The nobleman's pride in high race and ancient achievement is partnered by his knowledge that his pre-eminence can be guaranteed only by the virtues which won it. The aristoi are distinguished by that name from the mass of the common people: and though there are many aristoi, they are always striving with one another for the prize of areté. The Greek nobles believed that the real test of manly virtue was victory in battle—a victory which was not merely the physical conquest of an enemy, but the proof of hard-won areté. This idea is exactly suited by the word *aristeia*, which was later used for the single-handed adventures of an epic hero. The hero's whole life and effort are a race for the first prize, an unceasing strife for supremacy over his peers. (Hence the eternal delight in poetic accounts of these aristeiai.) In peace-time too, the warriors match their aretai against one another in war-games: in the *Iliad* we see them in competition even in a brief pause in the war, at the funeral games of Patroclus. It was that chivalrous rivalry which struck out the motto of knighthood throughout the centuries:

αἰὲν ἀριστεύειν καὶ ὑπείροχον ἔμμεναι ἄλλων.*

(This motto, which teachers of all ages have quoted to their pupils, modern educational 'levellers' have now, for the first time, abandoned.) Into that one sentence the poet has condensed the whole educational outlook of the nobility. When Glaucus meets Diomede on the battlefield, and wishes to prove himself a worthy opponent, he first (in the Homeric manner) names his illustrious ancestors, and then continues: 'Hippolochus begat me, and I claim to be his son. He sent me to Troy, and often gave me this command, to strive always for the highest areté, and to excel all others.' It is the finest possible expression of the inspiration of heroic strife: and it was familiar to the author of the eleventh book of the *Iliad*, who makes Peleus give the same counsel to his son Achilles.

There is another way in which the *Iliad* bears witness to the high educational ideals of the early Greek aristocracy. It shows that the old conception of areté as warlike prowess could not satisfy the poets of a new age: their new ideal of human perfection was that character which united nobility of action with nobility of mind. And it is important to notice that the new concept is expressed by Phoenix, who is the old counsellor and teacher of Achilles, the pattern-hero of Greece. At a crisis in the action, he reminds his pupil of the ideal on which he has been moulded: 'to be both a

* "Always to excel and to be superior to all others."—ED.

speaker of words and a doer of deeds'. The later Greeks were right in believing this verse to be the earliest formulation of the Greek educational ideal, of its effort to express the whole of human potentialities. It was often quoted in the later ages of rhetoric and sophistication to set off the departed heroic world of action against the wordy and inactive present; but it can be interpreted in another way, for it shows the whole mental outlook of the aristocracy. They believed that mastery of words meant intellectual sovereignty. Phoenix speaks this line to Achilles when he has just received the envoys of the Greek chiefs with sullen anger. The poet presents the eloquent Odysseus and Ajax the laconic man of action as contrasts to Achilles himself. By this contrast he emphasises the highest ideal of developed humanity as personified in the greatest of the heroes—Achilles—who has been trained to it by the third envoy Phoenix. The word areté had originally meant warlike prowess; but it is clear from this passage that a later age found no difficulty in transforming the concept of nobility to suit its own higher ideals, and that the word itself was to acquire a broader meaning to suit this developing ideal.

An essential concomitant of areté is honour. In a primitive community it is inseparable from merit and ability. Aristotle has well described it as a natural standard for man's half-realised efforts to attain areté. 'Men,' he says, 'seem to pursue honour in order to assure themselves of their own worth—their areté. They strive to be honoured for it, by men who know them and who are judicious. It is therefore clear that they recognise areté as superior.' The philosophy of later times then bade man obey an inner standard: it taught him to regard honour as the external image of his inner value, reflected in the criticism of his fellows. But the Homeric man estimated his own worth exclusively by the standards of the society to which he belonged. He was a creature of his class: he measured his own areté by the opinion which others held of him. Yet the philosophic man of later times could dispense with such external recognition, although (as Aristotle says) he might not be entirely indifferent to it.

Homer and the aristocracy of his time believed that the denial of honour due was the greatest of human tragedies. The heroes treat one another with constant respect, since their whole social system depends on such respect. They have all an insatiable thirst for honour, a thirst which is itself a moral quality of individual heroes. It is natural for the great hero or the powerful prince to demand high and higher honour. When the Homeric man does a great deed, he never hesitates to claim the honour which is its fit reward. It is not chiefly the question of payment for services rendered which occupies him. The sources of honour and dishonour are praise and blame (ἔπαινος and ψόγος). But praise and blame were considered by the philosophic morality of later times to be the foundations of social life, the expression of objective social standards. Nowadays we must find it difficult to imagine how entirely *public* was the conscience of a Greek. (In fact, the early Greeks never conceived anything like the personal conscience of modern times.) Yet we must strive to recognise that fact, before we can comprehend what they meant by honour. Christian sentiment will regard any claim to honour, any self-advancement, as an expression of sinful vanity. The Greeks, however, believed such ambition to be the aspiration of the individual towards that ideal and supra-personal sphere in which alone he can have real value. Thus it is true in some sense to say that the areté of a hero is completed only in his death. Areté exists in mortal man. Areté *is* mortal man. But it survives the mortal, and lives on in his glory, in that very ideal of his areté which accompanied and directed him throughout his life. The gods themselves claim their due honour. They jealously avenge any infringement of it, and pride themselves on the praise which their worshippers give to their deeds. Homer's gods are an immortal aristocracy. And the essence of Greek worship and piety lay in giving honour to godhead: to be pious is 'to honour the divinity'. To honour both gods and men for their areté is a primitive instinct.

On this basis, we can comprehend the tragic conflict of Achilles in the *Iliad*. His indignation at his comrades and his refusal to help them do not spring from an exaggerated individual ambition. A great ambition is, for Greek sentiment, the quality of a great hero. When the hero's honour is offended, the very foundations of the alliance of the Achaean warriors against Troy are shaken. The man who infringes another's honour ends by losing sight of true areté itself. Such a difficulty would now be mitigated by feelings of patriotism; but patriotism is strange to the old aristocratic world. Agamemnon can only make a despotic appeal to his own sovereign power; and such an appeal is equally foreign to aristocratic sentiment, which recognises the leader only as *primus inter pares*. Achilles, when he is refused the honour which he has earned, feels that he is an aristocrat confronted by a despot. But that is not the chief issue. The head and front of the offence is that a pre-eminent areté has been denied its honour. The death of Ajax, the mightiest Greek hero after Achilles, is the second great tragedy of offended honour. The weapons of the dead Achilles are awarded to Odysseus, although Ajax has done more to earn them. The tragedy of Ajax ends in madness and death; the wrath of Achilles brings the Greek army to the edge of the abyss. Homer can scarcely say whether it is possible to repair honour once it has been injured. Phoenix advises Achilles not to bend the bow too far, and to accept Agamemnon's gift as an atonement—for the sake of his comrades in their affliction. But it is not only from obstinacy that Achilles in the original saga refuses the offers of atonement: as is shown once more by the parallel example of Ajax, who returns no answer to the sympathetic words of his former enemy Odysseus when they meet in the underworld, but silently turns away 'to the other souls, into the dark kingdom of the dead'. Thetis entreats Zeus thus: 'Honour my son, who must die sooner than all others. Agamemnon has robbed him of his honour; do you honour him, Olympian!' And the highest of the gods is gracious to Achilles, by allowing the Achaeans, deprived of his help, to be defeated; so that they see how unjustly they have acted in cheating their greatest hero of his honour.

In later ages, love of honour was not considered as a merit by the Greeks: it came to correspond to ambition as we know it. But even in the age of democracy we can see that love of honour was often held to be justifiable in the intercourse of both individuals and states. We can best understand the moral nobility of this idea by considering Aristotle's description of the *megalo-psychos*, the proud or high-minded man. In many details, the ethical doctrines of Plato and Aristotle were founded on the aristocratic morality of early Greece: in fact, there is much need for a historical investigation (from that point of view) of the origin, development, and transmission of the ideas which we know as Platonic and Aristotelian. The class limitations of the old ideals were removed when they were sublimated and universalised by philosophy: while their permanent truth and their indestructible ideality were confirmed and strengthened by that process. Of course the thought of the fourth century is more highly detailed and elaborated than that of Homeric times. We cannot expect to find its ideas, or even their exact equivalents, in Homer. But in many respects Aristotle, like the Greeks of all ages, has his gaze fixed on Homer's characters, and he develops his ideals after the heroic patterns. That is enough to show that he was far better able to understand early Greek ideas than we are.

It is initially surprising for us to find that pride or high-mindedness is considered as a virtue. And it is also notable that Aristotle does not believe it to be an independent virtue like the others, but one which presupposes them and is 'in a way an ornament to them'. We cannot understand this unless we recognise that Aristotle is here trying to assign the correct place in his analysis of the moral consciousness to the high-minded areté of old aristocratic morality. In another connexion he says that he considers Achilles and Ajax to be the ideal patterns of this quality. High-mindedness is in itself morally worthless, and even ridiculous, unless it is backed by full areté, the highest unity of all excellences, which neither Aristotle nor Plato shrinks from describing as *kalokagathia*. The great Athenian thinkers bear witness to the aristocratic origin of their philosophy, by holding that areté cannot reach true perfection except in the high-minded man. Both Aristotle and Homer justify their belief that high-mindedness is the finest expression of spiritual and moral personality, by basing it on areté as worthy of honour. 'For honour is the prize of areté; it is the tribute paid to men of ability.' Hence pride is an enhancement of areté. But it is also laid down that to attain true pride, true magnanimity is the most difficult of all human tasks.

Here, then, we can grasp the vital significance of early aristocratic morality for the shaping of the Greek character. It is immediately clear that the Greek conception of man and his areté developed along an unbroken line throughout Greek history. Although it was transformed and enriched in succeeding centuries, it retained the shape which it had taken in the moral code of the nobility. The aristocratic character of the Greek ideal of culture was always based on this conception of areté.

Under the guidance of Aristotle, we may here investigate some of its further implications. He explains that human effort after complete areté is the product of an ennobled self-love, φιλαυτία . This doctrine is not a mere caprice of abstract speculation—if it were, it would be misleading to compare it with early conceptions of areté. Aristotle is defending the ideal of fully justified self-love as against the current beliefs of his own enlightened and 'altruistic' age; and in doing so he has laid bare one of the foundations of Greek ethical thought. In fact, he admires self-love, just as he prizes high-mindedness and the desire for honour, because his philosophy is deeply rooted in the old aristocratic code of morality. We must understand that the Self is not the physical self, but the ideal which inspires us, the ideal which every nobleman strives to realise in his own life. If we grasp that, we shall see that it is the highest kind of self-love which makes man reach out towards the highest areté: through which he 'takes possession of the beautiful'. The last phrase is so entirely Greek that it is hard to translate. For the Greeks, beauty meant nobility also. To lay claim to the beautiful, to take possession of it, means to overlook no opportunity of winning the prize of the highest areté.

But what did Aristotle mean by the beautiful? Our thoughts turn at once to the sophisticated views of later ages—the cult of the individual, the humanism of the eighteenth century, with its aspirations towards aesthetic and spiritual self-development. But Aristotle's own words are quite clear. They show that he was thinking chiefly of acts of moral heroism. A man who loves himself will (he thought) always be ready to sacrifice himself for his friends or his country, to abandon possessions and honours in order to 'take possession of the beautiful'. The strange phrase is repeated: and we can now see why Aristotle should think that the utmost sacrifice to an ideal is a proof of a highly developed self-love. 'For,' he says, 'such a man would prefer short intense pleasures to long quiet ones; would choose to live nobly for a year rather than to pass many years of ordinary life; would rather do one great and noble deed than many small ones'.

These sentences reveal the very heart of the Greek view of life—the sense of heroism through which we feel them most closely akin to ourselves. By this clue we can understand the whole of Hellenic history—it is the psychological explanation of the short but glorious aristeia of the Greek spirit. The basic motive of Greek areté is contained in the words 'to take possession of the beautiful'. The courage of a Homeric nobleman is superior to a mad berserk contempt of death in this—that he subordinates his physical self to the demands of a higher aim, the beautiful. And so the man who gives up his life to win the beautiful will find that his natural instinct for self-assertion finds its highest expression in self-sacrifice. The speech of Diotima in Plato's *Symposium* draws a parallel between the struggles of law-giver and poet to build their spiritual monuments, and the willingness of the great heroes of antiquity to sacrifice their all and to bear hardship, struggle, and death, in order to win the prize of imperishable fame. Both these efforts are explained in the speech as examples of the powerful instinct which drives mortal man to wish for self-perpetuation. That instinct is described as the metaphysical ground of the paradoxes of human ambition. Aristotle himself wrote a hymn to the immortal areté of his friend Hermias, the prince of Atarneus, who died to keep faith with his philosophical and moral ideals; and in that hymn he expressly connects his own philosophical conception of areté with that found in Homer, and with its Homeric ideals Achilles and Ajax. And it is clear that many features in his description of self-love are drawn from the character of Achilles. The Homeric poems and the great Athenian philosophers are bound together by the continuing life of the old Hellenic ideal of areté.

7. BRUNO SNELL

FROM Bruno Snell, *The Discovery of the Mind* (New York: Harper & Row, 1960), pp. 39–42.

Hegel once said: 'Religion is the sphere in which a nation gives itself a definition of that which it regards as the True.' Plato, by defining the true as the perfect, the 'idea of the good', merely rings a change upon the basic concept of the Olympian religion. With equal force the plastic art of the Greeks seems to say that the beauty and perfection of this world of appearances ought to be evident to any one who probes deeply enough. And, most important of all, the sciences sprang up from this same belief that our world is reasonable and open to human intellection. Thus the Olympian gods have made us the Europeans we are.

This is not to say that the Homeric creed involves the kind of optimism which we associate with an era of enlightenment. The contrast between optimism and pessimism is too banal to have any bearing on our problem. Actually the Greeks might well be called pessimists. With deep sorrow they confront this life which sees human beings perish miserably like leaves in the autumn; and beyond life the suffering is even greater. But, let the world be happy or sad, it still contains all that is fair within it, and the gods are its children, its most perfect, most beautiful, most real products. The early Greeks justify their own misery on earth by pointing to the ease and the splendour which characterizes the life of the gods. In a similar fashion, the Greek of a later period will derive a vindication of his earthly existence from his admiring contemplation of the fixed courses of the stars. Even Plato and Aristotle who value the theoretical or 'contemplative' life above the practical life because it leads men beyond the material world, infuse their theory with traces of a religious emotion which ultimately stems from the Homeric *thaumazein*. True enough, this progress of thinking towards philosophy was effected at the sacrifice of the gods themselves. They lost their natural and immediate function in proportion as man became aware of his own spiritual potential. Whereas Achilles had interpreted his decision as an intercession of the goddess, fifth century man, proudly convinced of his personal freedom, took upon himself the responsibility for his choice. The deity whose guidance and authority he recognized with ever increasing assurance was formulated as the concept of justice, or the good, or honesty, or whatever else the norm of action be called. Such formulation actually helps to enhance the sublimity of the deity, but at the same time the gods are stripped of their former abundant vitality. The trials of Socrates and other philosophers occurred during this period, and they show how acutely this change was perceived and lamented. Socrates could be justly accused of having discarded the old gods; but in a deeper sense he continued to be a servant of the Olympian gods who had first opened the eyes of the Greeks. It would be absurd to suppose that Apollo or Athena could have regarded the intellect as their enemy, and Aristotle speaks as a true Greek when he says . . . that the god does not begrudge man his knowledge. A foe of the intellect who wishes to cite Greek views in corroboration of his stand must base himself upon the gloomy concepts of chthonic powers; he may point to some cult celebrated with ecstatic abandon; but he may not call to witness the great works of the Greek genius: the epics, Pindar's poems, or tragedy.

The Olympian gods were laid low by philosophy, but they lived on in the arts. They remained one of the most important themes for artistic production even after people had ceased to believe in them wholeheartedly. In fact they did not attain their perfect form, the form which was to be decisive for all times, until the days of Pericles when we may be sure that the artists were no longer believers in the old sense. Ancient poetry also continues to cull its more important material from the myths of the Olympian gods, and even the triumph of Christianity did not halt this trend. Finally, the rejuvenation which the gods experienced in the Renaissance also lay in the realm of the arts.

The Olympian gods prove that they are meaningful and natural, not only through their intercession in human affairs—to which we have so far given almost all our attention—but through their very existence; through it they furnish a meaningful and natural picture of the world, and it is this aspect of them which has left its imprint on later developments. It is through the gods that the Greeks approach the secret of existence. In their persons the Olympians give clear expression to all that is great and vital in this world. Nothing is concealed; all the forces operating in body and mind are drawn into the portrait of the gods. The resulting picture, far from being sombre and painful, is one of serenity, detachment and pure perfection. No single factor is extolled or placed in a ruling position; everything has its destined place and conspires to make for a purposeful cosmos. But this order is not an impersonal system, devoid of warmth and vitality. On the contrary, the world of the gods teems with a full measure of life, as is shown by the following example. Among the ladies of Mount Olympus Hera, Athena, Artemis and Aphrodite are supreme. We might divide them into two groups: Hera and Aphrodite representing woman in her capacity as mother and loved one; Artemis and Athena typifying the virgin, one lonely and close to nature, the other intellectual and active in the community. It may fairly be said that these four women signalize the four aspects of all womanhood. The four goddesses help to bring out the spiritual peculiarities of the female sex; more than that, they are instrumental in making the notion of femininity intelligible. Four goddesses who stem from totally different cults have effected this notion by merging their interests and permitting cross-reference between them. They are the products of men's meditation on the various manifestations of the divine; we find in them the first sketch of a logical system, a prelude to the eventual hypostatization of the typical and the universal.

The idealizing strain of their theology guards the Greeks against the danger of viewing the characteristic in the oblique light of caricature. The Greek goddesses, in spite of their one-sidedness, are faultless and attractive creatures. With no effort at all they possess the noble simplicity and quiet grandeur which Winckelmann regarded as the essence of the classical spirit. But the original Greek temper surpasses this classicistic ideal.

The Olympians have their full share of the passions, without however sacrificing an iota of their beauty; they are so assured of their status that they can safely indulge in their rather insolent moods towards one another. We find it difficult to understand how the gods of one's faith could be subjected to Aristophanic jests. But laughter is part of the meaning, the fruitfulness, the positive side of life, and it is therefore, in the eyes of the Greeks, more godlike than the sour solemnity which we associate with piety. Thus the Olympian gods combine in their persons three things: vitality, beauty, and lucidity. As the belief in these gods becomes more questionable—the end of this process is reached with the Roman poets who transmitted the gods to the Western world—the gulf between their life, ever serene and fair, and the reality of man begins to widen. In Homer the affairs of men are given their full meaning by the gods, but Ovid conveys to us that everything on earth is at bottom without rhyme or reason, and that we cannot look upward and spy the divine splendour save with a touch of nostalgia. Ovid escapes into that perfect world of yore as if it were a haven of solace and salvation. The Olympian gods of his *Metamorphoses* are already 'pagan' in the sense that their unfettered vitality is no longer pictured with a simple and unaffected heart. In Ovid, and even before him, robust strength and hearty buffoonery are replaced by bawdiness and frivolity. Nevertheless the Ovidian gods are the legitimate successors of Homer's Olympians, for like them they compel admiration, for their limpid beauty and their lively spirit. Perhaps, instead of spirit, we should use the word *esprit*, for the Ovidian deity is clever and ingenious as Homer's was not. But Ovid's wit is so pure, his alertness and charm so persuasive, that the Olympian gods could not really be angry with him. Take his account of how Apollo pursued Daphne, the wild and unwilling maiden: running behind her he offers her his love—he, the god with the beautiful locks, sees her tresses streaming in the wind before him—*et, quid si comantur ait*—and he says: imagine her with her hair done! On another occasion, Ovid tells the mournful tale of Orpheus who had to leave Eurydice behind in Hades. Thereupon, he continues, Orpheus invented pederasty, perhaps because his experiences with women had been so unfortunate, or again, because he wanted to remain loyal to his wife.

It is this world of the ancient gods, somewhat cynical but clever and brilliant, which the Renaissance came to know, and, as was to be expected, its specifically pagan flavour became immensely popular: the lighthearted gods stood out against the foil of an ascetic Christianity. The lords of Olympus and the classical myths were not among the least means to help the Renaissance once more to perceive and admire the beauty and the grandeur of the universe. In antiquity the failure of this perspective, the decline of the spirit of wonder, set in long before Ovid; not improbably it also was a natural consequence of the enlightenment which had carried men all the way from the primitive terror in the face of the unknown, to a free admiration of the divine. Democritus already praises *athaumastia* and *athambia,* the absence of wonder; the Stoic sages regard it as their highest aim not to lose their composure, and Cicero as well as Horace commends the *nil admirari.* But for an expression of the genuine Greek tradition we must go to the old Goethe: 'The highest to which man may aspire is wonder.' ✽

8. CHESTER G. STARR

FROM Chester G. Starr, *The Origins of Greek Civilization* (New York: Alfred A. Knopf, 1961), pp. 381–85.

During the century from 750 to 650—or, to hazard greater precision, principally in the brief decades from 720 to 680—the Greek world was galvanized into an interlocked revolution which affected every aspect of its structure. Nowhere, true, were the new patterns fully fashioned by 680; but by that date their basic outline was clearly visible.

The revolution was of many parts, but all expressed a common intellectual change. Accordingly the same major forces appear whether we turn to the arts, to letters, to religion, or to political, social, and economic institutions. This fact is fortunate, for often the evidence for a single aspect is weak. The period lies on the first fringe of historic times; but the hints which emerge in any field bear striking resemblances to those in adjacent areas.

The underlying event was a crystallization of the still inchoate promise of Greek culture in the Dark ages. This event took place on simple lines. Archaic Greece was still not far removed from barbarism, and in any case its geographical endowment was not one of material riches; but would the miracle have occurred amid opulence? In literature, in the arts, even in politics, the Greeks refined very limited forms which their genius selected as vehicles for almost limitless achievements. Selection and refinement were now virtually conscious processes.

The men who achieved so much were clear and logical in thought, but they were not passionless monsters. Only by imposing upon themselves the tyranny of form and type and by restricting individual license for the communal good were the Greeks able to master the threats of anarchy.

The victory was barely won. Whether we turn to the physical testimony of Proto-attic pottery or open our ears to the outcries against aristocratic exploitation, we can see that men came close to shattering all the bounds of earlier customs. Had they done so, the capabilities of Aegean civilization would have been blasted.

The achievement of the age of revolution, measured in the deepest historical terms, was twofold. On the one side the Greeks evolved a sense of individual, conscious meditation; and there emerged a concept of the political importance of the individual, which was safeguarded by the justice of the political system. Yet also men agreed to subordinate individual passions and aims within a commonly accepted structure of life and thought. Greece was deeply fortunate in that its greatest revolution took place, first, in a period when its internal system was still simple; and, secondly, at a time when the Aegean was not yet under severe external pressures.

Wherever we turn in the age, we must sense its decisive importance in spurring the Greeks to enduring creativity; yet more, the achievements of the era were a firm foundation for many basic qualities of Western civilization. One example may suffice, which has been admirably sketched in Sir Kenneth Clark's *The Nude: A Study in Ideal Form;* the Greek artistic concept of the nude human figure which was created in the seventh century B.C. has dominated European artistic thought down to the present generation. When even a sober historian generalizes about the age of revolution, his pen unconsciously moves into a range of forceful terms not always approved in Clio's trade—"genius," "miracle," and "achievement" have inevitably crept into the preceding paragraphs.

For their use I do not apologize—the significance of the age of revolution in human history requires no less—and yet such words can be dangerous. Too often they have been used to mask an unwillingness, or inability, to penetrate to the hidden springs which drove the Greek world. These springs, nonetheless, can be found; or, at the least, the search conducted in this volume has been devoted to that end.

In explaining the age of revolution one must pay due attention to Oriental stimuli. By the eighth century the East, no less than the western Mediterranean or Hellas itself, had progressed far beyond the level of the Late Bronze age; development there had been far greater, partly because civilization was more deeply rooted and had bent rather than broken in the upheavals of the late second millennium. The lure of Oriental culture, always tempting to less civilized areas, had been much enhanced by the cosmopolitan, graceful form it had assumed in the ninth and eighth centuries. That Eastern influences actually had a continuing effect on the Greek world from 800 onward is abundantly testified in the history of the alphabet, the appearance of Oriental-type monsters and mythical creatures, and many other artistic changes during the eighth and seventh centuries.

These forces, however, are not primary. Change was already under way in the Aegean before Eastern contacts were resumed on a significant scale. This basic point can be shown both from the Dipylon pottery and from the *Iliad;* Oriental stimuli can at best be used to account for the degree of speed with which development took place and for some of the avenues in which native enthusiasm spilled out. The Aegean down to this point had been an enclave, which turned outward to the Orient and gained inspiration thence because *it* so desired. Never again was the situation to be true in Greek civilization. After the resumption of ties with the Orient and the sowing of colonies over the western Mediterranean and Black seas the Aegean homeland was inextricably bound up with the rest of the ancient world and endured now Persian, now Roman onslaughts. The favorable stars which shone down on Greece at the end of the eighth century were a unique constellation. And the Greeks were amazingly able to use their light.

The sources of Greek progress lay within Hellas itself. By the latter decades of the eighth century these forces had gathered enough momentum to break forth in a volcanic, awe-inspiring rush; but before this event lay centuries of slow evolution, which have here been called the Dark ages. These years, like many dim eras, must exercise one's imagination—what mighty energies must have lain, coiled in outward sloth, in the men of the early Greek world! Later centuries, indeed, made of this age a period of mythical fantasy, and so it still often appears in historical works. But myths and folklore are poor tools to employ in the search for the true quality of the Dark ages; we are now, at last, fortunate in having surer guides in the outwardly dull pages of archaeological reports. Vases themselves can feed that imagination which must be part of the historian's equipment, provided always that we make use of the ceramic evidence with judicious understanding.

In the second section of this volume an attempt has been made to elicit the meaning of the physical material which has survived from the era 1100–750 and, secondarily, to fit within this framework whatever evidence of value may be drawn from the survivals of religious, social, and political customs and from the Homeric *Iliad*. The historian must consider everything else first and only then may venture to form tentative deductions from the timeless world of the epic.

The picture which results for the Dark ages is one of very slow change after the terrific upheaval at the end of the Late Bronze era. In the evolution of Protogeometric and then Geometric pottery we have the surest guide to the tempo of development and can detect the drawing together of the Aegean basin into a common frame of culture, albeit marked by local differentiations which became ever more clear. Linguistic and traditional evidence, however, tends to corroborate the general picture presented by the pottery.

In studying the Dark ages I have drawn attention not only to the main lines of evolution but also to the highly interesting problems involved in the tempo of development and its sources. Periodization is always a difficult problem in history, for the men of any age do not suddenly and casually decide that they will live in different fashion from their fathers. Yet there are true watersheds.

The greatest of these was the deeply significant change which can be dated approximately to the eleventh century. Then Protogeometric pottery appeared, rather suddenly and rather broadly over several mainland districts of Greece. More was involved in the change of potters' outlooks than might appear at first sight: this is the point at which Greek civilization emerged. The men who took the crucial steps did so largely out of the sheer necessity of establishing a new order of life, if their society was to continue to exist as a viable form. They drew almost entirely on the past in doing so; there are no signs of external influence at this point of time. But let us be perfectly clear: neither the Mycenaean world nor the earlier stages, which were sketched in the first two chapters, are in themselves Greek, in the sense in which we apply that term to historic Aegean culture. When we probe back from classic and archaic aspects of that culture, we find uninterrupted continuity as far as the beginnings of Protogeometric style, but no further; the turning point was the eleventh century. What then occurred was a veritable "jump," unpredictable in one sense, yet explicable in rational terms once it had occurred.

The historian who studies the progress of early Greece may justly feel that it is a story which makes sense and that it can now be surveyed in its main lines. Much remains to be discovered; and the efforts which may be made today on the basis of evidence now at hand will prove faulty ere long. Still, the student may hope to put his fingers on some of the basic forces which directed the story, or in the search to stimulate others to think more deeply. The emergence of Greek civilization is a subject which will endlessly fascinate its modern heirs who live within the stream of Western culture; an outlook which could already by the eighth century produce the *Iliad* or so marvelous a vase as the Dipylon amphora . . . was one of amazing potentialities. Anyone who is aware of the difficulties involved in its rise may justly marvel the more at its results.

9. H. D. F. KITTO

FROM H. D. F. Kitto, *The Greeks* (Baltimore: Penguin Books, 1960), pp. 26–28.

. . . If we compare the art of Classical Greece with Minoan or Aegean art, we find a significant difference. The best of Minoan art has all the qualities that art can have—except this consuming intellectualism. It is difficult to imagine Greek architects evolving, even by accident or under pain of death, a building so chaotic in plan as the palace at Cnossos. Greek art won some of its most brilliant victories in the hardest and most serious of all the arts, big-scale sculpture: it can be no accident, at this time of day, that no Minoan sculpture has been found other than quite small works. It is of course true that all art worthy of the name must be serious—and reflective: nevertheless, there is a sense in which one would attribute these qualities to Greek art and not to the Minoan: brilliant, sensitive, elegant, gay—these are the adjectives which one instinctively uses of the Minoan —but not 'intellectual'.

For the intellectual strain in Classical Greek art we must turn to the Hellenes—and not without evidence. When they descended from the northern mountains they brought no art with them, but they did bring a language, and in the Greek language—in its very structure—are to be found that clarity and control, that command of structure, which we see pre-eminently in Classical Greek art and miss in the earlier. In the first place, Greek, like its cousin Latin, is a highly-inflected language, with a most elaborate and delicate syntax, and the further back one can go in the history of the language, the more elaborate are the inflections, and (in many ways) the more delicate is the syntax. Greek syntax is much more varied, much less rigid, than Latin—as the young student of Classics soon discovers, to his joy or his sorrow, according to temperament. Consequently, it is the nature of Greek to express with extreme accuracy not only the relation between ideas, but also shades of meaning and emotion. But closer to our present point is a consequence of this—unless indeed it is a cause—the periodic style. Both in Greek and in Latin, if a statement happens to be complex, consisting of one or more leading ideas accompanied by any number of explanatory or qualifying ideas, the whole complex can be set out, and normally is, with perfect clarity in a single sentence. That is to say, both languages have a markedly architectural quality. But there is a significant difference between them. The Romans seem to have achieved the periodic style by sheer determination and courage: the Greeks were born with it. Not only has Greek many more ways of slipping in a subordinate clause—for example, the regular Greek verb has ten participles (if I have counted correctly), the Latin only three —but also Greek is well stocked with little words, conjunctions that hunt in couples or in packs, whose sole function is to make the structure clear. They act, as it were, as signposts. The reader must often have had the following embarrassing experience: reading aloud, he has embarked on an English sentence, and at a certain point has dropped his voice, under the impression that the sentence was coming to an end: but at the critical point he has found not a full-stop but only a semi-colon or a comma, so that he has had to retrace his steps for a word or two, hitch up his voice, and continue. This could never happen to him in Greek, because the Greek writer would have put at the very beginning the word which I must write as 'te' meaning 'This sentence (or clause or phrase) is going to have at least two co-ordinate members, and the second (and subsequent ones, if any) is going to be a simple addition to the first', or the word 'men', meaning precisely the same thing, except that this time the second (and subsequent) members will be not a continuation but a contrast. English of course can do this: an English sentence can begin 'While, on the one hand . . .'. But Greek does it with much more ease, by instinct, and always. We have indeed no direct transcripts of Ancient Greek conversation, but we have passages, in the dramatists and in Plato, in which the writer is striving to give the effect of unpremeditated speech, and in these a fairly elaborate periodic structure is not uncommon, but even if we do not find this we always find a perfectly limpid and unambiguous ordering of the sentence, as if the speaker saw the ground-plan of his idea, and therefore of his sentence, in a flash, before he began to put it into words. It is the nature of the Greek language to be exact, subtle and clear. The imprecision and the lack of immediate perspicuity into which English occasionally deviates and from which German occasionally emerges, is quite foreign to Greek. I do not mean that it is impossible to talk nonsense in Greek: it is quite possible —but the fact that it is nonsense is at once patent. The Greek vice in language is not vagueness or woolliness but a kind of bogus clarity, a firm drawing of distinctions which are not there.

The mind of a people is expressed perhaps more immediately in the structure of its language than in anything else it makes, but in all Greek work we shall find this firm grasp of the idea, and its expression in clear and economical form. With this clarity and constructive power and seriousness we shall find a quick sensitiveness and an unfailing elegance. This is the secret of what has been called 'the Greek miracle', and the explanation—or an important part of it—lies in the fusion of cultures, if not of peoples too. �֎

10. FINLEY HOOPER

FROM Finley Hooper, *Greek Realities* (New York: Charles Scribner's Sons, 1967), pp. 124–25.

A frequently repeated exaggeration about the ancient Greeks is the statement that they made a religion out of reason. If so, the Greeks as a people altered their mental processes in a way no people had before their time or have since. The statement is dangerously misleading because it fails to emphasize two points which may be of interest in the continuing debate over the role of the intellectual in a popular democracy. To begin with, only a small minority of Greeks ever abandoned the magical, mythological and supernatural common beliefs in favor of a speculative approach toward the universe around them or their own behavior in it. Speculation about the origin of all that exists, the conflict between being and becoming and the essence of virtue, is not a popular pastime. The vast majority of human beings in all places at all times have spent most of their existence in the honorable but routine process of making a living. The majority of the Greeks were no exception and they never gave up their belief in a god of the winds or a god of the sea. They lived, as do most Greeks in the modern world, by instinct, habit and faith. The assistance of the saints today replaces the assistance of the gods of yesterday. It is no misfortune that such help and comfort are always available.

Secondly, the minority, insofar as it gave expression to views contrary to accepted beliefs, was no more popular in Greece than such a minority has ever been anywhere. At the height of the Periclean democracy in the fifth century, the philosopher Anaxagoras was driven from the city on the charge of atheism. There may have been some politics involved, but even if the charge of atheism was a smoke-screen for the real reason, it was apparently calculated to win popular support.

Much more agreeable to the popular viewpoint were the comedies of Aristophanes, which pictured the sophistic intellectuals of the fifth century as undermining the moral structure of society by their persistent doubts and endless quibbling. Aristophanes in his play the *Clouds* presented Socrates as just such a man and his caricature of Socrates is thought to have contributed to the downfall of history's best known freethinker.

The impression of Athens in the fifth century as a haven of freedom where strangers were welcome and no man spied on his neighbor was enshrined by Pericles in his famed *Funeral Oration*. It is true that an extraordinary amount of free and open discussion took place on matters of politics . . . This achievement of a public forum on any subject was truly a remarkable advance over all previous societies—so remarkable indeed that there is no need to exaggerate the point in order to credit the Greeks with progress.

However, the average Greek considered politics a subject more open to discussion than he did religion. When has this ever been different? Respect for the gods was a very serious matter. It was believed that they could help or hinder a city and so any man who offended them was not only putting himself in jeopardy; he was risking the welfare of everybody else as well. The worship of Athena at Athens was not a matter of religious choice. It was an act of patriotism. The great democrat Pericles, who entertained non-conformists like Anaxagoras in his home, may have had his own doubts about the gods but he never expressed them in public. He was the most successful politician in the history of the Athenian democracy and he did not win his place by making mistakes.

So the Greeks as a people never did make a religion out of reason. For a brief time in certain cities, Athens especially, an atmosphere was provided wherein a tolerated minority of men were free to pursue their doubts and speculations and to keep alert the minds of other men. That they were generally tolerated does not mean that they were liked. Nor were they disliked only for their ideas. Their own persistent quarrelsomeness and frequent obnoxiousness had something to do with it.

This emphasis on the correlation between individual expression and the variety of thought is not intended to suggest that Greek creative works were only produced by those who broke with established convictions. The great dramatic poets, Aeschylus and Sophocles, treated the traditional themes in a respectful and meaningful manner. The building of temples, theaters, and much Greek statuary was a reflection of the desire to honor and offer worship to the gods. Their beauty was inspired by a faith common to a whole people. Yet the traditional and accepted does not of itself admit the diversity which is best gained through tolerance of the experimental, the unusual and the unorthodox. The history of rationalism in Greece is an intellectual tradition and not a popular one. Some men did find an opportunity to doubt and speculate and write what they would. The result was the best argument for why they should. �֎

Part 3

THE END OF THE ROMAN REPUBLIC

The subject of this Part does not immediately capture the imagination; it does not possess the inherent fascination of developments like the rise of Christianity, the decline of Rome, or the passing of the ancient world. The initial response might well be that this phase of Roman history had no far-reaching consequences, but greater familiarity with the subject should dispel such an impression quickly. In fact, what emerges is one of the most fascinating and suggestive problems in all of ancient history.

It is thus no accident that great historians from Tacitus to Mommsen have focused on the transition from Republic to Principate and that dramatists from Shakespeare to Shaw have built plays around some of the principal characters involved. The story is dramatic, the protagonists violent, shrewd, often enigmatic, and the problem highly complex. It is precisely because the subject raises so many questions, some of them immediately relevant to the modern world, that it continues to engage our attention.

The multifarious nature of this theme and the way it leads naturally to other problems of interest is well illustrated in the following selections. Let us take the Rostovtzeff selection as an example. In the very first sentence the author introduces three issues involved in the Republic's decline: the struggle between the oligarchy and revolutionary politicians who wanted a "popular assembly"; the issue of the redistribution of landed property; and the question of the extension of the franchise. Clearly these problems are not uniquely Roman, but ones which appear with striking regularity in the study of European history.

In reading the Rostovtzeff selection the richness of the subject unfolds. We encounter such fundamental issues as provincial administration, the social composition of the judiciary and the fairness with which justice was administered, interest rates and their implications. Then there is the crucial issue of the Roman army. Both "the democratic leaders and their opponents were alike absolutely dependent upon the army" which had only its own interests at heart. This was the spring for an imperialism which "unceasingly" extended the limits of the state. Thus, Rome was faced with "the problem of government for a world-wide state." Rostovtzeff has set the stage for his proposition that monarchy was "inevitable." That the transition from relative heterogeneity and local independence, from the concept of "a family of free and independent states" to "the ancient Eastern notion of a single world-wide state, possessing a uniform culture and ruled over by one man" was inexorable may be disputed. But there is no doubt that in the span of a few pages Rostovtzeff has given us much to think about.

The first selection in this Part is by the great nineteenth-century German historian Theodor Mommsen (1817–1903). Mommsen's scholarly career was characterized by profound erudition and breath-taking productivity. Furthermore, he was determined to reach a wider public and at the same time make specialized contributions. Mommsen was not simply an accomplished historian; he was a master of at least five other disciplines—epigraphy, numismatics, law, archaeology, and early Italian philology. There is considerable justification for speaking of his "breathtaking" productivity. In the three-year period between 1844 and 1847 he published ninety articles and, in his lifetime, some 1,500 titles.

Mommsen was more than a scholar's scholar. Of his *History of Rome* he said: "I wanted to bring down the ancients from their fantastic pedestal into the real world." He certainly succeeded in accomplishing this. What Grote did for Greece and Macaulay did for England, Mommsen did for Rome. His wide appeal and profound influence were due not only to his originality and learning but also to the fact that *The History of Rome* bears the unmistakable stamp of a passionate and lively intellect. Like all really great historians, Mommsen did not hesitate to state his own point of view explicitly. He had little patience with the timidity so characteristic of historical literature: "Those who have lived through historical events, as I have, begin to see that history is neither written nor made without love or hate."

Mommsen's vivid portrait of Caesar raises a problem of considerable interest to the student of history—that of the "great man" in history. Nineteenth-century historians were fascinated by "the mighty ones of the earth." The classic statement and the one that best reveals this attitude comes from the British philosopher-historian Thomas Carlyle (1795–1881):

> For, as I take it, Universal History, the history of what man has accomplished in this world, is at bottom the History of the Great Men who have worked here. They were the leaders of men, these great ones; the modelers, patterns, and in a wide sense creators, of whatsoever the general mass of men contrived to do or to attain; all things that we see standing accomplished in the world are properly the outer material result, the practical realisation and embodiment, of Thoughts that dwelt in the Great Men sent into the world: the soul of the whole world's history, it may justly be considered, were the history of these.

Unlike other Romantics, Carlyle was also fascinated by, and indeed embraced, the Industrial Revolution. And as Professor George Mosse has written, "this acceptance of the new industrial age turned the image of the romantic genius toward a stress on power." Because he was a Romantic, Carlyle identified power with the individual. Other forces were probably at work in shaping Mommsen's vision of the role played by "great men." But Bismarckian Germany certainly afforded him the opportunity to view the naked exercise of power at close range. Indeed, as E. H. Carr argues—perhaps too strongly—"Writing in the 1850's—the decade which saw the birth of the name and concept Realpolitik—Mommsen was imbued with the sense of need for a strong man to clear up the mess left by the failure of the German people to realize its political aspirations; and we shall never appreciate his history at its true value unless we realize that his well-known idealization of Caesar is the product of this yearning for the strong man to save Germany from ruin. . . ."

To pass from Mommsen to Syme is in some measure to pass from nineteenth- to twentieth-century historiography. Ronald Syme, an Oxford scholar, is universally recognized as an exceptionally gifted modern student of classical Rome, and his book *The Roman Revolution* is well on its way to becoming a classic. Most historians would agree that "In the quarter of a century since [its publication] . . . his book has withstood the test of subsequent research and criticism and he appears to have penetrated into the realities of government and society in a convincing and realistic manner achieved by no previous writer who tried to understand the significance of the great Roman drama of the first century B.C." Like all students of the subject, Syme was compelled to examine the nature of political power at this juncture of Roman history. But he looked beyond Caesar for an explanation for the transition from Republic to Principate.

Eight years before *The Roman Revolution* appeared, Sir Lewis Namier published his seminal work, *The Structure of Politics at the Accession of*

George III. Namier's study was the first complete example of a novel historical methodology which has since become known as "Namierism." This approach, consisting of detailed biographical study usually of politicians, has a wide following. It is designed to uncover the material, social, and familial framework in which political individuals move on the assumption that these factors structure and determine behavior. A tough-minded "realism" prevails; ideology and propaganda count for little. Syme's astringency, his acerbic wit, and vigorous, naked prose (consciously modeled on Tacitus) were probably also shaped by the events of the 1920's and 1930's. The age of Hitler, Mussolini, and Stalin called attention to the gap between rhetoric and reality. These modern Caesars created a climate which could imbue the mind of a young historian with bitter realism.

The following selections, all taken from modern studies, enrich the causal mixture. Léon Homo argues that personal government was the natural outcome of the expansion, the imperialism of the Republic. This brings up another fascinating problem: at what stage of expansion is the body politic stretched so that it can no longer retain its internal structure? In other words, what is the relation between foreign policy and internal development? Professor H. H. Scullard points to the Roman provinces as the key to understanding the transition from Republic to Empire, while F. R. Cowell explains it in terms of a vacuum created by internal dissension and chaos, which only the army could fill. And what finally emerges is a variegated pattern that lends verisimilitude to Richard E. Smith's assessment: "The Republic's crisis and failure . . . were a crisis and failure of society."

1. THEODOR MOMMSEN

FROM Theodor Mommsen, *The History of Rome*, 5 vols. (New York: Charles Scribner's Sons, 1911), vol. V, 305–15.

The new monarch of Rome, the first ruler over the whole domain of Romano-Hellenic civilization, Gaius Julius Caesar, was in his fifty-sixth year . . . when the battle at Thapsus, the last link in a long chain of momentous victories, placed the decision as to the future of the world in his hands. Few men have had their elasticity so thoroughly put to the proof as Caesar—the sole creative genius produced by Rome, and the last produced by the ancient world, which accordingly moved on in the path that he marked out for it until its sun went down. Sprung from one of the oldest noble families of Latium—which traced back its lineage to the heroes of the Iliad and the kings of Rome, and in fact to the Venus-Aphrodite common to both nations—he spent the years of his boyhood and early manhood as the genteel youth of that epoch were wont to spend them. He had tasted the sweetness as well as the bitterness of the cup of fashionable life, had recited and declaimed, had practised literature and made verses in his idle hours, had prosecuted love-intrigues of every sort, and got himself initiated into all the mysteries of shaving, curls, and ruffles pertaining to the toilette-wisdom of the day, as well as into the still more mysterious art of always borrowing and never paying. But the flexible steel of that nature was proof against even these dissipated and flighty courses; Caesar retained both his bodily vigour and his elasticity of mind and of heart unimpaired. In fencing and in riding he was a match for any of his soldiers, and his swimming saved his life at Alexandria; the incredible rapidity of his journeys, which usually for the sake of gaining time were performed by night—a thorough contrast to the procession-like slowness with which Pompeius moved from one place to another—was the astonishment of his contemporaries and not the least among the causes of his success. The mind was like the body. His remarkable power of intuition revealed itself in the precision and practicability of all his arrangements, even where he gave orders without having seen with his own eyes. His memory was matchless, and it was easy for him to carry on several occupations simultaneously with equal self-possession. Although a gentleman, a man of genius, and a monarch, he had still a heart. So long as he lived, he cherished the purest veneration for his worthy mother Aurelia (his father having died early); to his wives and above all to his daughter Julia he devoted an honourable affection, which was not without reflex influence even on political affairs. With the ablest and most excellent men of his time, of high and of humbler rank, he maintained noble relations of mutual fidelity, with each after his kind. As he himself never abandoned any of his partisans after the pusillanimous and unfeeling manner of Pompeius, but adhered to his friends—and that not merely from calculation—through good and bad times without wavering, several of these, such as Aulus Hirtius and Gaius Matius, gave, even after his death, noble testimonies of their attachment to him.

If in a nature so harmoniously organized any one aspect of it may be singled out as characteristic, it is this—that he stood aloof from all ideology and everything fanciful. As a matter of course, Caesar was a man of passion, for without passion there is no genius; but his passion was never stronger than he could control. He had had his season of youth, and song, love, and wine had taken lively possession of his spirit; but with him they did not penetrate to the inmost core of his nature. Literature occupied him long and earnestly; but, while Alexander could not sleep for thinking of the Homeric Achilles, Caesar in his sleepless hours mused on the inflections of the Latin nouns and verbs. He made verses, as everybody then did, but they were weak; on the other hand he was interested in subjects of astronomy and natural science. While wine was and continued to be with Alexander the destroyer of care, the temperate Roman, after the revels of his youth were over, avoided it entirely. Around him, as around all those whom the full lustre of woman's love has dazzled in youth, fainter gleams of it continued imperishably to linger; even in later years he had love-adventures and successes with women, and he retained a certain foppishness in his outward appearance, or, to speak more correctly, the pleasing consciousness of his own manly beauty. He carefully covered the baldness, which he keenly felt, with the laurel chaplet that he wore in public in his later years, and he would doubtless have surrendered some of his victories, if he could thereby have brought back his youthful locks. But, however much even when monarch he enjoyed the society of women, he only amused himself with them, and allowed them no manner of influence over him; even his much-censured relation to queen Cleopatra was only contrived to mask a weak point in his political position . . .

Caesar was thoroughly a realist and a man of sense; and whatever he undertook and achieved was pervaded and guided by the cool sobriety which constitutes the most marked peculiarity of his genius. To this he owed the power of living energetically in the present, undisturbed either by recollection or by expectation; to this he owed the capacity of acting at any moment with collected vigour, and of applying his whole genius even to the smallest and most incidental enterprise; to this he owed the many-sided power with which he grasped and mastered whatever understanding can comprehend and will can compel; to this he owed the self-possessed ease with which he arranged his periods as well as projected his campaigns; to this he owed the "marvellous serenity" which remained steadily with him through good and evil days; to this he owed the complete independence, which admitted of no control by favourite or by mistress, or even by friend. It resulted, moreover, from this clearness of judgment that Caesar never formed to himself illusions regarding the power of fate and the ability of man; in his case the friendly veil was lifted up, which conceals from man the inadequacy of his working. Prudently as he laid his plans and considered all possibilities, the feeling was never absent from his breast that in all things fortune, that is to say accident, must bestow success; and with this may be connected the circumstance that he so often played a desperate game with destiny, and in particular again and again hazarded his person with daring indifference. As indeed occasionally men of predominant sagacity betake themselves to a pure game of hazard, so there was in Caesar's rationalism a point at which it came in some measure into contact with mysticism.

Gifts such as these could not fail to produce a statesman. From early youth, accordingly, Caesar was a statesman in the deepest sense of the term, and his aim was the highest which man is allowed to propose to himself—the political, military, intellectual, and moral regeneration of his own deeply decayed nation, and of the still more deeply decayed Hellenic nation intimately akin to his own. The hard school of thirty years' experience changed his views as to the means by which this aim was to be reached; his aim itself remained the same in the times of his hopeless humiliation and of his unlimited plenitude of power, in the times when as demagogue and conspirator he stole towards it by paths of darkness, and in those when, as joint possessor of the supreme power and then as monarch, he worked at his task in the full light of day before the eyes of the world. All the measures of a permanent kind that proceeded from him at the most various times assume their appropriate places in the great building-plan. We cannot therefore properly speak of isolated achievements of Caesar; he did nothing isolated. With justice men commend Caesar the orator for his masculine eloquence, which, scorning all the arts of the advocate, like a clear flame at once enlightened and warmed. With justice men admire in Caesar the author the inimitable simplicity of the composition, the unique purity and beauty of the language. With justice the greatest masters of war of all times have praised Caesar the general, who, in a singular degree disregarding routine and tradition, knew always how to find out the mode of warfare by which in the given case the enemy was conquered, and which was thus in the given case the right one; who with the certainty of divination found the proper means for every end; who after defeat stood ready for battle like William of Orange, and ended the campaign invariably with victory; who managed that element of warfare, the treatment of which serves to distinguish military genius from the mere ordinary ability of an officer—the rapid movement of masses—with unsurpassed perfection, and found the guarantee of victory not in the massiveness of his forces but in the celerity of their movements, not in long preparation but in rapid and daring action even with inadequate means. But all these were with Caesar mere secondary matters; he was no doubt a great orator, author, and general, but he became each of these merely because he was a consummate statesman. The soldier more especially played in him altogether an accessory part, and it is one of the principal peculiarities by which he is distinguished from Alexander, Hannibal, and Napoleon, that he began his political activity not as an officer, but as a demagogue. According to his original plan he had purposed to reach his object, like Pericles and Gaius Gracchus, without force of arms, and throughout eighteen years he had as leader of the popular party moved exclusively amid political plans and intrigues—until, reluctantly convinced of the necessity for a military support, he, when already forty years of age, put himself at the head of an army. It was natural that he should even afterwards remain still more statesman than general—just like Cromwell, who also transformed himself from a leader of opposition into a military chief and democratic king, and who in general, little as the prince of Puritans seems to resemble the dissolute Roman, is yet in his development as well as in the objects which he aimed at and the results which he achieved of all statesmen perhaps the most akin to Caesar. Even in his mode of warfare this improvised generalship may still be recognized; the enterprises of Napoleon against Egypt and against England do not more clearly exhibit the artillery-lieutenant who had risen by service to command than the similar enterprises of Caesar exhibit the demagogue metamorphosed into a general. A regularly trained officer would hardly have been prepared, through political considerations of a not altogether stringent nature, to set aside the best-founded military scruples in the way in which Caesar did on several occasions, most strikingly in the case of his landing in Epirus. Several of his acts are therefore censurable from a military point of view; but what the general loses, the statesman gains. The task of the statesman is universal in its nature like Caesar's genius; if he undertook things the most varied and most remote one from another, they had all without exception a bearing on the one great object to which with infinite fidelity and consistency he devoted himself; and of the manifold aspects and directions of his great activity he never preferred one to another. Although a master of the art of war, he yet from statesmanly considerations did his utmost to avert civil strife and, when it nevertheless began, to earn laurels stained as little as possible by blood. Although the founder of a military monarchy, he yet, with an energy unexampled in history, allowed no hierarchy of marshals or government of praetorians to come into existence. If he had a preference for any one form of services rendered to the state, it was for the sciences and arts of peace rather than for those of war.

The most remarkable peculiarity of his action as a statesman was its perfect harmony. In reality all the conditions for this most difficult of all human functions were united in Caesar. A thorough realist, he never allowed the images of the past or venerable tradition to disturb him; for him nothing was of value in politics but the living present and the law of reason, just as in his character of grammarian he set aside historical and antiquarian research and recognized nothing but on the one hand the living *usus loquendi* and on the other hand the rule of symmetry. A born ruler, he governed the minds of men as the wind drives the clouds, and compelled the most heterogeneous natures to place themselves at his service—the plain citizen and the rough subaltern, the genteel matrons of Rome and the fair princesses of Egypt and Mauretania, the brilliant cavalry-officer and the calculating banker. His talent for organization was marvellous; no statesman has ever compelled alliances, no general has ever collected an army out of unyielding and refractory elements with such decision, and kept them together with such firmness, as Caesar displayed in constraining and upholding his coalitions and his legions; never did regent judge his instruments and assign each to the place appropriate for him with so acute an eye.

He was monarch; but he never played the king. Even when absolute lord of Rome, he retained the deportment of the party-leader; perfectly pliant and smooth, easy and charming in conversation, complaisant towards every one, it seemed as if he wished to be nothing but the first among his peers. Caesar entirely avoided the blunder into which so many men otherwise on an equality with him have fallen, of carrying into politics the military tone of command; however much occasion his disagreeable relations with the senate gave for it, he never resorted to outrages such as was that of the eighteenth Brumaire. Caesar was monarch; but he was never seized with the giddiness of the tyrant. He is perhaps the only one among the mighty ones of the earth, who in great matters and little never acted according to inclination or caprice, but always without exception according to his duty as ruler, and who, when he looked back on his life, found doubtless erroneous calculations to deplore, but no false step of passion to regret. There is nothing in the history of Caesar's life, which even on a small scale can be compared with those poetico-sensual ebullitions—such as the murder of Kleitos or the burning of Persepolis—which the history of his great predecessor in the east records. He is, in fine, perhaps the only one of those mighty ones, who has preserved to the end of his career the statesman's tact of discriminating between the possible and the impossible, and has not broken down in the task which for greatly gifted natures is the most difficult of all—the task of recognizing, when on the pinnacle of success, its natural limits. What was possible he performed, and never left the possible good undone for the sake of the impossible better, never disdained at least to mitigate by palliatives evils that were incurable. But where he recognized that fate had spoken, he always obeyed. Alexander on the Hypanis, Napoleon at Moscow, turned back because they were compelled to do so, and were indignant at destiny for bestowing even on its favourites merely limited successes; Caesar turned back voluntarily on the Thames and on the Rhine; and thought of carrying into effect even at the Danube and the Euphrates not unbounded plans of world-conquest, but merely well-considered frontier-regulations.

Such was this unique man, whom it seems so easy and yet is so infinitely difficult to describe. His whole nature is transparent clearness; and tradition preserves more copious and more vivid information about him than about any of his peers in the ancient world. Of such a personage our conceptions may well vary in point of shallowness or depth, but they cannot be, strictly speaking, different; to every not utterly perverted inquirer the grand figure has exhibited the same essential features, and yet no one has succeeded in reproducing it to the life. The secret lies in its perfection. In his character as a man as well as in his place in history, Caesar occupies a position where the great contrasts of existence meet and balance each other. Of mighty creative power and yet at the same time of the most penetrating judgment; no longer a youth and not yet an old man; of the highest energy of will and the highest capacity of execution; filled with republican ideals and at the same time born to be a king; a Roman in the deepest essence of his nature, and yet called to reconcile and combine in himself as well as in the outer world the Roman and the Hellenic types of culture—Caesar was the entire and perfect man. Accordingly we miss in him more than in any other historical personage what are called characteristic features, which are in reality nothing else than deviations from the natural course of human development. What in Caesar passes for such at the first superficial glance is, when more closely observed, seen to be the peculiarity not of the individual, but of the epoch of culture or of the nation; his youthful adventures, for instance, were common to him with all his more gifted contemporaries of like position, his unpoetical but strongly logical temperament was the temperament of Romans in general. It formed part also of Caesar's full humanity that he was in the highest degree influenced by the conditions of time and place; for there is no abstract humanity—

the living man cannot but occupy a place in a given nationality and in a definite line of culture. Caesar was a perfect man just because he more than any other placed himself amidst the currents of his time, and because he more than any other possessed the essential peculiarity of the Roman nation—practical aptitude as a citizen—in perfection: for his Hellenism in fact was only the Hellenism which had been long intimately blended with the Italian nationality. But in this very circumstance lies the difficulty, we may perhaps say the impossibility, of depicting Caesar to the life. As the artist can paint everything save only consummate beauty, so the historian, when once in a thousand years he encounters the perfect, can only be silent regarding it. For normality admits doubtless of being expressed, but it gives us only the negative notion of the absence of defect; the secret of nature, whereby in her most finished manifestations normality and individuality are combined, is beyond expression. Nothing is left for us but to deem those fortunate who beheld this perfection, and to gain some faint conception of it from the reflected lustre which rests imperishably on the works that were the creation of this great nature. These also, it is true, bear the stamp of the time. The Roman hero himself stood by the side of his youthful Greek predecessor not merely as an equal, but as a superior; but the world had meanwhile become old and its youthful lustre had faded. The action of Caesar was no longer, like that of Alexander, a joyous marching onward towards a goal indefinitely remote; he built on, and out of, ruins, and was content to establish himself as tolerably and as securely as possible within the ample but yet definite bounds once assigned to him. With reason therefore the delicate poetic tact of the nations has not troubled itself about the unpoetical Roman, and on the other hand has invested the son of Philip with all the golden lustre of poetry, with all the rainbow hues of legend. But with equal reason the political life of the nations has during thousands of years again and again reverted to the lines which Caesar drew; and the fact, that the peoples to whom the world belongs still at the present day designate the highest of their monarchs by his name, conveys a warning deeply significant and, unhappily, fraught with shame. ✳

2. RONALD SYME

FROM Ronald Syme, *The Roman Revolution* (Oxford: Clarendon Press, 1939), pp. 12–18.

The *nobiles*, by their ambition and their feuds, had not merely destroyed their spurious Republic: they had ruined the Roman People.

There is something more important than political liberty; and political rights are a means, not an end in themselves. That end is security of life and property: it could not be guaranteed by the constitution of Republican Rome. Worn and broken by civil war and disorder, the Roman People was ready to surrender the ruinous privilege of freedom and submit to strict government as in the beginning of time . . .

So order came to Rome. 'Acriora ex eo vincula', as Tacitus observes. The New State might be called monarchy, or by any other name. That did not matter. Personal rights and private status need not depend upon the form of government. And even though hereditary succession was sternly banished from the theory of the Principate, every effort was made to apply it in practice, for fear of something worse: sober men might well ponder on the apparent ridicule and solid advantages of hereditary monarchy. . . .

Though concealed by craft or convention, the *arcana imperii* of the *nobilitas* cannot evade detection. Three weapons the *nobiles* held and wielded, the family, money and the political alliance (*amicitia* or *factio*, as it was variously labelled). The wide and remembered ramifications of the Roman noble clan won concentrated support for the rising politician. The *nobiles* were dynasts, their daughters princesses. Marriage with a well-connected heiress therefore became an act of policy and an alliance of powers, more important than a magistracy, more binding than any compact of oath or interest. Not that women were merely the instruments of masculine policy. Far from it: the daughters of the great houses commanded political influence in their own right, exercising a power beyond the reach of many a senator. Of such dominating forces behind the phrases and the façade of constitutional government the most remarkable was Servilia, Cato's half-sister, Brutus' mother—and Caesar's mistress.

The noble was a landed proprietor, great or small. But money was scarce and he did not wish to sell his estates: yet he required ready cash at every turn, to support the dignity of his station, to flatter the populace with magnificence of games and shows, to bribe voters and jurors, to subsidize friends and allies. Hence debts, corruption and venality at Rome, oppression and extortion in the provinces. Crassus was in the habit of observing that nobody should be called rich who was not able to maintain an army on his income. Crassus should have known.

The competition was fierce and incessant. Family influence and wealth did not alone suffice. From ambition or for safety, politicians formed compacts. *Amicitia* was a weapon of politics, not a sentiment based on congeniality. Individuals capture attention and engross history, but the most revolutionary changes in Roman politics were the work of families or of a few men. A small party, zealous for reform—or rather, perhaps, from hostility to Scipio Aemilianus—put up the tribune Ti. Sempronius Gracchus. The Metelli backed Sulla. The last dynastic compact in 60 B.C. heralded the end of the Free State; and a re-alignment of forces precipitated war and revolution ten years later.

Amicitia presupposes *inimicitia*, inherited or acquired: a statesman could not win power and influence without making many enemies. The *novus homo* had to tread warily. Anxious not to offend a great family, he must shun where possible the role of prosecutor in the law-courts and win gratitude by the defence even of notorious malefactors. The *nobilis*, however, would take pride in his feuds. Yet he had ever to be on the alert, jealous to guard his *dignitas*, that is, rank, prestige and honour, against the attacks of his personal enemies. The plea of security and self-defence against aggression was often invoked by a politician when he embarked upon a course of unconstitutional action.

The dynast required allies and supporters, not from his own class only. The sovran people of a free republic conferred its favours on whom it pleased. Popularity with the plebs was therefore essential. It was possessed in abundance both by Caesar and by his bitter enemy, L. Domitius Ahenobarbus. To win a following at elections, to manage bribery, intimidation or rioting, the friendly offices of lowly agents such as influential freedmen were not despised. Above all, it was necessary to conciliate the second order in state and society, the Roman knights, converted into a ruinous political force by the tribune C. Gracchus when he set them in control of the law-courts and in opposition to the Senate. The *Equites* belonged, it is true, to the same social class as the great bulk of the senators: the contrast lay in rank and prestige.

The knights preferred comfort, secret power and solid profit to the burdens, the dangers and the extravagant display of a senator's life. Cicero, a knight's son from a small town, succumbed to his talents and his ambition. Not so T. Pomponius Atticus, the great banker. Had Atticus so chosen, wealth, repute and influence could easily have procured a seat in the Senate. But Atticus did not wish to waste his money on senseless luxury or electoral corruption, to risk station, fortune and life in futile political contests. Averse from ambition and wedded to quiet, the knights could claim no title of civic virtue, no share in the splendour and pride of the governing class. For that surrender they were scorned by senators. They did not mind. Some lived remote and secure in the enjoyment of hereditary estates, content with the petty dignity of municipal office in the towns of Italy. Others, however, grasped at the spoils of empire, as *publicani* in powerful companies farming the taxes of the provinces and as bankers dominating finance, commerce and industry. The *publicani* were the fine flower of the equestrian order, the ornament and bulwark of the Roman State. Cicero never spoke against these 'homines honestissimi' and never let them down: they were in the habit of requiting his services by loans or legacies.

The gains of finance went into land. Men of substance and repute grew yet richer from the spoils of the provinces, bought the farms of small peasants, encroached upon public land, seized through mortgages the ancestral property of senators, and thus built up large estates in Italy. Among senators were great holders of property like Pompeius and Ahenobarbus with whole armies of tenants or slaves, and financial magnates like Crassus. But the wealth of knights often outstripped many an ancient senatorial family, giving them a greater power than the nominal holders of dignity and office.

Equestrian or senatorial, the possessing classes stood for the existing order and were suitably designated as *boni*. The mainstay of this sacred army of the wealthy was clearly the financiers. Many senators were their partners, allies or advocates. Concord and firm alliance between Senate and knights would therefore arrest revolution—or even reform, for these men could not be expected to have a personal interest in redistributing property or changing the value of money. The financiers were strong enough to ruin any politician or general who sought to secure fair treatment for provincials or reform in the Roman State through the re-establishment of the peasant farmer. Among the victims of their enmity will be reckoned Lucullus, Catilina and Gabinius.

It was no accident, no mere manifestation of Roman conservatism or snobbery, that the leaders of revolution in Rome were usually impoverished or idealistic nobles, that they found support in the higher ranks of the aristocracy rather than in the power. It is all too easy to tax the Roman nobility in the last epoch of its rule with vice and corruption, obscurantism and oppression. The knights must not be left out of the indictment. Among the old nobility persisted a tradition of service to the State that could transcend material interests and combine class-loyalty with a high ideal of

Roman patriotism and imperial responsibility. Not so among the financiers.

The Roman constitution was a screen and a sham. Of the forces that lay behind or beyond it, next to the noble families the knights were the most important. Through alliance with groups of financiers, through patronage exercised in the law-courts and ties of personal allegiance contracted in every walk of life, the political dynast might win influence not merely in Rome but in the country-towns of Italy and in regions not directly concerned with Roman political life. Whether he held authority from the State or not, he could thus raise an army on his own initiative and resources.

The soldiers, now recruited from the poorest classes in Italy, were ceasing to feel allegiance to the State; military service was for livelihood, or from constraint, not a natural and normal part of a citizen's duty. The necessities of a world-empire and the ambition of generals led to the creation of extraordinary commands in the provinces. The general had to be a politician, for his legionaries were a host of clients, looking to their leader for spoil in war and estates in Italy when their campaigns were over. But not veterans only were attached to his cause—from his provincial commands the dynast won to his allegiance and personal following (*clientela*) towns and whole regions, provinces and nations, kings and tetrarchs.

Such were the resources which ambition required to win power in Rome and direct the policy of the imperial Republic as consul or as one of the *principes*. Cicero lacked the full equipment. He imagined that oratory and intrigue would suffice. A programme, it is true, he developed, negative but by no means despicable. It was an alliance of interest and sentiment to combat the forces of dissolution represented by the army-commanders and their political agents. It took shape at first in his consulate as *concordia ordinum* between Senate and knights against the *improbi*, but later widened to a *consensus omnium bonorum* and embraced *tota Italia*. But it was an ideal rather than a programme: there was no Ciceronian party. The Roman politician had to be the leader of a faction. Cicero fell short of that eminence both when a consul and when a consular, or senior statesman, through lack of family-connexions and *clientela*.

Within the framework of the Roman constitution, beside the consulate, was another instrument of power, the tribunate, an anomalous historical survival given new life by the party of the Gracchi and converted into a means of direct political action, negative with the veto, positive with the initiation of laws. The use of this weapon in the interests of reform or of personal ambition became a mark of the politicians who arrogated to themselves the name of *populares*—often sinister and fraudulent, no better than their rivals, the men in power, who naturally invoked the specious and venerable authority of the Senate. But there were to be found in their ranks a few sincere reformers, enemies of misrule and corruption, liberal in outlook and policy. Moreover, the tribunate could be employed for conservative ends by aristocratic demagogues.

With the Gracchi all the consequences of empire—social, economic and political—broke loose in the Roman State, inaugurating a century of revolution. The traditional contests of the noble families were complicated, but not abolished, by the strife of parties largely based on economic interest, of classes even, and of military leaders. Before long the Italian allies were dragged into Roman dissensions. The tribune M. Livius Drusus hoped to enlist them on the side of the dominant oligarchy. He failed, and they rose against Rome in the name of freedom and justice. On the *Bellum Italicum* supervened civil war. The party led by Marius, Cinna and Carbo was defeated. L. Cornelius Sulla prevailed and settled order at Rome again through violence and bloodshed. Sulla decimated the knights, muzzled the tribunate, and curbed the consuls. But even Sulla could not abolish his own example and preclude a successor to his domination.

Sulla resigned power after a brief tenure. Another year and he was dead (78 B.C.). The government which he established lasted for nearly twenty years. Its rule was threatened at the outset by a turbulent and ambitious consul, M. Aemilius Lepidus, claiming to restore the rights of the tribunes and supported by a resurgence of the defeated causes in Italy. The tribunes were only a pretext, but the Marian party—the proscribed and the dispossessed—was a permanent menace. The long and complicated war in Italy had barely ended. The Samnites, Sulla's enemy and Rome's, had been extirpated; and the other Sabellic peoples of the Apennine were broken and reduced. But Etruria, despoiled and resentful, rose again for Lepidus against the Roman oligarchy.

Lepidus was suppressed. But disorders continued, even to a rising of the slaves in southern Italy. Then a *coup d'état* of two generals (70 B.C.), restoring the tribunate, destroyed Sulla's system but left the *nobiles* nominally in power. They were able to repel and crush the attempt of the patrician demagogue L. Sergius Catilina to raise a revolution in Italy—for Catilina attacked property as well as privilege. The government of the *nobiles*, supported by a sacred union of the possessing classes, by the influence of their *clientela* among the plebs and by due subservience towards the financial interests, might have perpetuated in Rome and Italy its harsh and hopeless rule. The Empire broke it.

The repercussions of the ten years' war in Italy echoed over all the world. The Senate was confronted by continuous warfare in the provinces and on the frontiers of its wide and cumbersome dominion—against Sertorius and the last survivors of the Marian faction in Spain, against the great Mithridates and against the Pirates. Lack of capacity among the principal members of the ruling group, or, more properly, personal ambition and political intrigue, constrained them, in mastering these manifold dangers, to derogate from oligarchic practice and confer exorbitant military power on a single general, to the salvation of Rome's empire and to their own ruin.

As an oligarchy is not a figment of political theory, a specious fraud, or a mere term of abuse, but very precisely a collection of individuals, its shape and character, so far from fading away on close scrutiny, at once stands out, solid and manifest. In any age of the history of Republican Rome about twenty or thirty men, drawn from a dozen dominant families, hold a monopoly of office and power. From time to time, families rise and fall: as Rome's rule extends in Italy, the circle widens from which the nobility is recruited and renewed. None the less, though the composition of the oligarchy is slowly transformed with the transformation of the Roman State, the manner and fashion of dynastic politics changes but little; and though noble houses suffered defeat in the struggle for power, and long eclipse, they were saved from extinction by the primitive tenacity of the Roman family and the pride of their own traditions. They waited in patience to assert their ancient predominance. ✳

3. LÉON HOMO

FROM Léon Homo, *Roman Political Institutions* (London: Kegan Paul, Trench, Trubner & Co., Ltd., 1929), pp. 147–56, 202–4.

The decline of the Roman constitution, in the century which extends from the Gracchi to the final establishment of personal government (133–131 B.C.), and the constitutional crisis which was the immediate result of it, is manifested by three fundamental, parallel symptoms:—

(1) There was no longer a majority for the government.
(2) The constitution was perverted by the exclusive preponderance of the Comitia Tributa.
(3) Public morals broke down.

On this triple phenomenon we must dwell for a moment.

The old government majority of the third century, based mainly on the aristocracy and the middle class, had been gradually destroyed by the split between the Senatorial and Equestrian orders and by the gradual disappearance of the middle classes. Caius Gracchus put the finishing touch to the work of time, and the traditional majority, receiving its death-blow, would soon be a distant memory. . . .

The decline of the traditional constitution, officially represented by the oligarchical system, was due, as we have seen, to two fundamental causes —the split of the ruling aristocracy into two classes, Senatorial and Equestrian, henceforth distinct and presently actively opposed, and the disappearance of the middle class, the essential element of equilibrium and the backbone of the army and Comitia. The only possible cure for this situation was a return to the harmony of the classes which was so characteristic of public life in the third century, and which seemed to have been destroyed for ever by the conquest of the Mediterranean world. That return to the past seemed both desirable and necessary from the constitutional point of view; but could it be brought about, or must it be relegated to the realm of vain dreams? . . .

These two were the only solutions which might have saved the Roman constitution, if it could be saved, and, by widening it, have restored the admirable equilibrium of the past. The first, the agrarian solution, was successfully knocked on the head by the ruling oligarchy after the fall of the Gracchi; and all parties in Rome, in spite of the outcome of the Social War, combined to nullify the second, the Italian solution, and to rob it of all practical effectiveness. The old constitution had failed to scrap its obsolete machinery when the time came, to abandon the antiquated system of the City, and to accept in its laws, as it already did in fact, the unescapable formula of the future, the formula of the State. From that moment republican government was doomed irretrievably and the way lay open to monarchy. Rome would proceed along it at a full speed, but she would only enter port after a half-century of bloody trials and frightful anarchy.

The failure, one after the other, of the great agrarian and Italian reforms sealed the fate of republican government. The political life of a nation lies essentially in the conflict of parties within the framework of the constitution. Now, in the middle of the first century B.C., the old constitution was evidently quite worn out and decaying fast. We have seen this in the case of the organs of government. The same was true of the two great historical parties, the *optimates*, or government, and the *populares*, or opposition. When Sulla placed the oligarchy back in the saddle, it was dazed by its triumph and could not ride; it lacked both men and political sense. A few years later military power, the new force rising on the horizon, would deal it its death-blow.

The opposition showed itself even more powerless, for many and various reasons. The oligarchy, which controlled the Senate, the only permanent organ of the Roman constitution, like the Conservative party in the

British House of Lords, did not fight the democratic opposition on equal terms. The Comitia and the magistrates, the only legal weapons at the disposal of the opposition, were powerless against the action, or, still more, the inertia of the Senate, in consequence of the irregular manner in which the Comitia were held and the fact that the magistrates were hampered by the two fundamental restrictions, the principles of the college and annual tenure, to which their office was subject. The democratic magistrate came up against the right of intervention (*par potestas*) of his colleagues, and, since under the existing laws he could not hold office for a long continuous period, he had to bring off his reforms in a very short time—with a rush, as it were—and often, therefore, in a revolutionary manner. The failure of the Gracchi, in particular, made this quite plain. Moreover, the democratic party, since the disappearance of the old agrarian element which was its backbone and the vain efforts of the Gracchi to restore it, had been without cohesion, programme, or leaders. The urban proletariate which was henceforward the most active nucleus of it, being without convictions or patriotism, ready to answer the call of money or of an ambitious general, had made the political fortune of the big capitalist and was now about to forge military dictatorship with its own hands.

This state of political and social decomposition, the final result of the Roman conquest, which attacked organs and parties alike, found concrete expression in two phenomena which went together and were equally symptomatic—conspiracy and street-fighting. Contemporaries, with Sallust and Cicero at their head, give us full information about both.

The governmental machine seemed worn out beyond repair. The constitutional development of the Republic ended in complete shipwreck, by which government and opposition suffered equally. Restored by Sulla and provided with powerful weapons, the Senatorial oligarchy, lacking men and political sense, collapsed less than ten years after the Dictator had gone. The democratic opposition, having no exact object or definite programme, drained by the disappearance of the country middle class, reduced to an unorganized, poverty-stricken urban proletariate, and bound, since the time of the Gracchi, to the service of the big capitalists, whose humble servant and passive tool it had become, could create nothing but disorder, and surrendered to the military power, which made use of it without reserve or scruple in its advance to personal government. . . .

Personal government was the result of distant causes and deep-seated necessities. They may all be summed up in one word—the conquest. A time came when Rome, the city which, by a unique destiny, had conquered a world, had to choose between maintaining her traditional institutions and keeping her empire. It was one of those problems before which peoples never hesitate; on the day when the question was asked—and that was early—the Republic was doomed and the constitutional crisis had potentially begun. But such complete changes take a long time, and, though the development was inevitable, the solution was only reached after a century of civil war.

The idea which was to give birth to the Imperial system was slow to emerge. It was a product of facts much more than a source of them, as was natural in a people whose dominant quality was not imagination, and which always looked to experience for the guiding principles of its action. The Gracchi, Marius, Sulla, the forerunners of the new age, had felt much more than reasoned out how the Roman State would develop. Pompey, between 52 and 49, had obtained a supremacy in fact, but had not succeeded in finding an exact formula to express the constitutional problem which Rome had to solve at all costs. The lucid genius of Caesar was the first to pierce the mists of the future and to discover in the Hellenistic type of monarchy the inevitable end of an evolution which had been going on for three hundred years.

Late though the idea may have developed, the instrument by which it was put into effect had been made ready at an early date. The Romans, with their will-power and their capacity for realizing their ideas, had always had a very high conception of the executive power, in the successive forms of the Kingship and the Consulship. The development of the policy of conquest, with the practical institutions—extension of office and provincial governorships—which inevitably followed from it, still further reinforced that traditional principle. But they had not been blind to the dangers to which such a state of affairs might expose Republican institutions, and law and custom had set up against the holders of the public authority powerful barriers, which should support them in their functions and also confine them to their constitutional position.

The appointment of the Dictator for six months only, with a Master of Horse attached to him, and the appointment of the Consul for one year only, with a colleague, were precautions intended to hold difficult men in check. Provincial governors, in addition to the fact that their very numbers were a great safeguard for Republican institutions, were closely dependent on the Senate, in other words, the aristocracy, for the provinces allotted to them, the resources placed at their disposal, and the period for which they held their office. Last but not least, military leaders found an obstacle in the army serving under them, a citizen army which would have allowed no antics at any price, and would still less have favoured ambitious projects.

The dissolution of the city system, which began in the third century B.C. and ended with the establishment of the Empire, was the result of a double evolution—the gradual decline of the traditional political institutions and the steady development of military power. Even at the time of the Punic Wars, the Golden Age of the Roman constitution, Scipio Africanus had thrown over citizen equality and claimed to set himself up above the laws. A century later, the exception which had created an outcry had become the rule, and the barriers erected against military power fell one after another under the assaults of generals, each more powerful than the last. In 108, when the Senate, in virtue of its traditional prerogatives, gave Metellus an extension of his governorship of Numidia, the Consul Marius appealed to the Comitia, which passed a plebiscite in his favour overruling the Senate's decision.

The precedent was established. Pompey and Caesar obtained by the vote of the people (the Plebiscites of Gabinius, 67; of Manilius, 66; of Vatinius, 59) the great military commands which set them on the path to power. It was the people, too, in its complete sovereignty, which determined the length of the command, and granted the military and financial resources needed for the work in hand—two more blows at the rights of the Senate, two more barriers down. At the same time, the army underwent a great change. The reform of Marius turned it into a professional army, a faithful instrument in the hands of leaders who could or would use it.

In the last century of the Republic, the long evolution was completed. Sulla, during his Dictatorship, and Pompey, in 67 and 66, were really emperors. Only the rivalry of the great military leaders delayed the inevitable fall of the Republic and the final establishment of personal rule. The elimination of Crassus and Pompey created the monarchy of Caesar. The example had been given and the method found; Octavian had only to follow the one and apply the other. ✼

4. H. H. SCULLARD

FROM H. H. Scullard, *From the Gracchi to Nero* (New York: Barnes & Noble, Inc., 1964), pp. 13–16, 19–22.

The countries of the eastern Mediterranean provided Rome with material goods in addition to ideas, and in this traffic the western provinces also took their part. Though Rome had not acquired any of her provinces for commercial purposes, nevertheless their products began to enrich both state and individuals: war-booty, war-indemnities and the profits of administration, tax-collecting and trade all poured in. With these material aids the lives of many Roman nobles became more luxurious, and sumptuary laws were passed to check extravagance, though to little purpose. For the first few decades of the second century the deterioration was probably slight, but the annalist Calpurnius Piso, who was consul in 133, dates the overthrow of Roman modesty to the year 154 ('a quo tempore pudicitiam subversam') and another contemporary witness, Polybius, attests the general extravagance and dissoluteness of the young Roman nobles when Scipio Aemliianus was growing up. This decline was probably confined mainly to Rome itself and affected the nobility in the first instance, but there lay the danger: if the governing class became rotten, there would be little hope for the Republic. One way in which wealth was seriously misused was in the increasing bribery of the urban population at elections. Not unconnected with this was the growing elaboration of public festivals, games and gladiatorial shows with which the people demanded to be entertained. Other social changes included the greater emancipation of women, greater freedom of divorce, the increase of celibacy, a decline in family life and above all the increase of slavery.

Before the third century slavery had existed at Rome, but on a small scale, and since emancipation was frequent a considerable body of freedmen had come into existence. With the Punic and overseas wars, however, and the consequent influx of large numbers of war captives, slavery began to bulk much larger in Roman life. It took two forms: while the more barbarian captives would be sent by their Roman masters to work on their lands, the more cultivated Greek slaves were kept in their town houses and employed as secretaries, teachers and doctors. Though subject to the arbitrary whims and possible cruelty of their masters, these domestic slaves were often well treated and they had a good chance of saving up sufficient pocket-money (*peculium*) to buy their freedom before they were too old to enjoy it. Some alleviated their lot by pandering to the luxurious tastes of their masters, others more usefully helped to acquaint them with Greek culture, while yet others were employed in the manual trades and were often, after emancipation, set up by their former masters in small businesses of their own. The fate of the rougher slaves who were put to work on their masters' estates, often under the control of slave-bailiffs, was much more pitiful; they were often treated as mere beasts with revolting callousness; the lot of those who worked in the state mines in Spain or Macedon was still more wretched.

Such conditions led to insecurity even in Italy: runaway slaves naturally turned to brigandage and conspiracies became frequent. Most serious was a rising of the slaves in Sicily against their Greek and Roman masters in 135; from small beginnings soon no less than 70,000 slaves were organized into a disciplined fighting force by their leaders, a Syrian named Eunus and the Sicilian Cleon. This revolt was accompanied by sporadic outbreaks elsewhere, in Italy at Minturnae and Sinuessa, in Attica and Delos (this island being a main centre of the slave-trade) and in Asia Minor under Aristonicus: though there is little evidence to suggest that this development was due to concerted action or an 'international' organization, it at least shows the widespread nature of the evil of slavery. Though King Antiochus, as Eunus called himself, began to consolidate his power in central Sicily at Enna and gained control of Agrigentum, Tauromenium and Catana, the Romans' first reply was half-hearted: the forces that they sent were at first defeated, including those led by a consul of 134. L. Calpurnius Piso, consul of 133, however, improved discipline among the Roman troops and reached Enna; his successor, P. Rupilius in 132, who had more soldiers at his disposal after Rome's final victory in Spain at Numantia, brought the war to an end, reorganized the province of Sicily and, with ten senatorial commissioners, drafted a charter for its administration (*lex Rupilia*). The insurrection was thus crushed, but it vividly indicated the need for reform.

The fighting in Sicily demonstrated another widening chink in Rome's armour: her standards of military conduct were declining. Though the prospect of spoils may have rendered campaigning in the East not unattractive, harsher conditions of service in Spain made both officers and men unwilling to serve there. Cases of mutiny or insubordination are reported as far back as the 190s; generals, in pursuit of booty or triumphs, sometimes conducted campaigns in defiance of the wishes of the Senate; the management of the wars in Spain was marked by increasing treachery and bad faith; difficulties in raising the levies reached such a pitch that some tribunes in 151 arrested one of the consuls and others again in 138 threatened similar action. To meet this changing mood, conditions of service were ameliorated: Roman citizens on military service were first granted immunity from scourging and then allowed the right of appeal, like civilians; their period of service was reduced to six years; their rations were improved. But despite concessions, discipline deteriorated. When Scipio Aemilianus arrived in Spain in 134 he took over a demoralized army: he had to rid the camp of traders and women and put his men through some toughening drill before he could turn to fighting, and even then he could not think of trying to storm Numantia by assault but had to reduce it by blockade. Things had come to such a pass that campaigns tended to open with defeats before victories could be won.

The standard of provincial administration was threatened by the selfishness of individual governors and by the growing pressure of Roman business interests in their provinces. As a body the Senate no doubt wished to maintain high standards, if not for moral reasons, at least for practical ones: they would not want to see either individual governors gaining undue personal independence and power or members of the equestrian order becoming richer and so potentially more threatening to the Senate's own predominance. Thus in 149 a tribune, L. Calpurnius Piso (the future consul of 133), proposed a measure to set up in Rome a permanent court to try cases of extortion (*quaestio de rebus repetundis*); this court was to consist of senators and its judgements were subject neither to appeal to the People nor to the tribune's veto. Its establishment gave senators greater control over provincial governors, but at the same time its existence would not tend to improve relations with the Equites, since if some of them hoped to work hand-in-glove with corruptible governors, such governors would clearly be more chary of condoning their exactions in the future. On the other hand if a governor, himself a senator, had sufficient friends in the jury court, he could hope that his peers might be ready on occasion to judge his misdemeanours more lightly. On the whole, however, the establishment of the court must be reckoned as an honest recognition of a growing evil and a deliberate attempt to check it. Further, though abuses existed, and later reached an unparalleled pitch of shame in Verres' governorship in Sicily . . . the standard of provincial administration in the main was still high: Polybius paid a glowing tribute to the uprightness of Roman magistrates, and even Verres' prosecutor admitted that hitherto Roman rule in Sicily had been popular. . . .

Many Italians and Romans alike were suffering from changing economic conditions. The changes arose partly from the upheaval caused by the Hannibalic War, but chiefly from the influx of wealth from the provinces: this upset the older economy which was based on the peasant farmers who also formed the main bulk of the Roman army. Hannibal's invasion of Italy had caused widespread devastation so that in some parts of Italy farms and land were neglected and abandoned, but hard work would have restored this deterioration if it had not been accompanied by other difficulties. One complication that faced the small independent farmer who was still trying to make both ends meet was that more corn was being imported into Italy from the provinces, especially Sicily and Sardinia. This competition from abroad is often alleged to have ruined Italian farmers, but until 167 and perhaps until 146 most of this foreign corn was used by the Roman armies fighting overseas and did not reach the home market. By the time of the Gracchi, however, the pinch may have been felt by many farmers in the relatively limited area around Rome which had hitherto supplied the capital with corn and around some of the coastal towns (transport by sea was cheap, by land extremely dear); Italy as a whole was less affected. Further, conscription fell heavily upon the peasant when overseas wars demanded long periods of service: the rich could ensure that their farms were looked after during their absence, but the poorer man might often return to a ruined homestead.

Two other factors depressed the small farmer's prospects still further: wealth and slaves. War and provincial administration filled the pockets of senators and Equites, who often returned to Italy and looked around for safe investments. Land attracted most of their capital and it so happened that as a result of the Hannibalic War the State had much *ager publicus* of which to dispose: when unable to attract the peasant-farmer back to it, the State was ready to lease it out in large assignments to anyone who had the capital and vision to undertake the venture. Thus a slow revolution took place: land now became an object of speculation to be exploited as a regular source of profit. The owner might no longer live on his estate or take any personal interest in it, but would entrust its management to a steward (*vilicus*) while he himself joined the ranks of the aristocracy in Rome or some other city. At the same time the foreign wars had flooded the Italian slave-markets, so that servile labour, being abundant, began to oust free labour on the bigger estates. In many parts of Italy, especially in Etruria and the South, peasant husbandry, devoted to arable farming and cereal cultivation, gave place to a capitalist system of large estates (*latifundia*) worked by slaves and given over to pasturage and stock-rearing or to the cultivation of the vine and olive. Mixed farming could be quite profitable in Campania and Latium, and Cato in his handbook *De Agri Cultura* wrote for men, senatorial nobles or others, who would invest in a mixed estate of 100–300 *iugera* (66–200 acres), worked by slaves and with grazing on public land. These mixed farms could supply the towns with oil, wine, fruit, vegetables, meat and wool; together with the larger ranches, they might in fact represent the best use to which the land could be put in some parts of Italy. But few of the small farmers would have the capital or skill to switch over from corn-growing to other forms of production. The result was therefore disastrous: free men began to abandon their land to the larger proprietors. Forced off the land, some were absorbed by commercial enterprise abroad, since the number of Italians trading in the eastern Mediterranean greatly increased; some may have moved northwards to the Po valley, but most drifted to Rome and the other cities. Since no new industries were developed to absorb their labour and since the number of slaves was increasing in the cities as well as in the country, they soon became a useless mass of unemployed, whose presence would lead to social and political unrest.

A symptom of this economic decline is seen in the surviving census figures, which probably represent all adult male Roman citizens. After the great losses in man-power during the Hannibalic War, the figures steadily rose until 164 B.C., but thereafter they declined with equal regularity and had dropped by nearly 20,000 in 136 B.C. Nor was the fall in the population confined to the Romans themselves. The Latin authorities had on occasion to try to counter the drift of their population to Rome, while all the Italians found it increasingly difficult to meet the military demands of Rome. Both Appian and Plutarch stress the plight of the Italians at this time.

The development of the *latifundia* was accelerated not only by the plight of the small farmer, who was compelled to abandon his land, but also by the way in which the State had disposed of the public domain in the past. The *ager publicus populi Romani* was the land that Rome had acquired during her expansion in Italy: after a victorious war she normally confiscated about a third of the enemy's territory, leaving him in possession of the rest. This *ager publicus* had been used in various ways: for founding colonies, for distribution in allotments to individual Roman citizens, while some had been sold. The rest was leased out by the censors. The more fertile districts, as the *ager Campanus* in Campania, brought in a good revenue to the State, but large tracts were poor ground and the censors in Rome lacked an adequate staff to deal with all this in a careful manner. In fact any Roman citizens (and, if there was enough land available, probably Italian allies as well) could occupy this land as squatters (*possessores*) in return for payment of a rent (*vectigal*): this was a poll-tax for graziers, but a fluctuating amount for others (a tithe on ploughland, and a fifth on vineyards and orchards). But to have enforced strict payment clearly would have involved creating a large fiscal machine which would not have justified itself financially. Instead, the rent was often overlooked and the squatters came to regard the land as their own, which they might even bequeath to their children.

There was, however, one proviso: the amount of *ager publicus* that any individual could hold was limited by law. This limitation had probably been imposed in 367 B.C., and two hundred years later the maximum amount that anyone could hold (Cato refers to it in a speech of 167 B.C.) was 500 *iugera* (some 300 acres). But in practice this limitation had often been disregarded, and the State had turned a blind eye, partly perhaps because the senators themselves, as large landowners, would benefit, and partly because it was better that the land should be occupied rather than remain idle, while the rich would be able to develop it to better purpose. Thus the growth of large estates had gone on apace, though in so far as many men held public land in excess of the legal limit, it was always possible strictly to enforce the law and reclaim the excess land for the *populus Romanus*, its legal owners. ✣

5. F. R. COWELL

FROM F. R. Cowell, *Cicero and the Roman Republic* (London: Pitman & Sons, Ltd., 1948), pp. 288–94.

Government, in short, means directed activity towards certain approved ends and it implies the possession of the means of action. In the Roman Republic the sole effective means of executive action by the State in a time of crisis was provided by the army. In a very real sense therefore military dictatorship was able to supply the first essential of government. It had no rival. We may say that the army should have been subordinated to the civil power. But there was no civil power. There were Senators squabbling among themselves and businessmen making life difficult for Senators. There were individuals playing their own hand who grew reckless as the stakes mounted and the gamble became more hazardous and more exciting. "The Republic is merely a sham". The man who destroyed it wrote its epitaph. He was correct and the people seem to have realised the fact. They gave their support to any man who would get something done. The Senators did not qualify for their support, because they were more interested in trying to find ways of tripping up and removing the demagogues and agitators—as they would call them—than in looking for remedies for the discontents and evils upon which the power of the agitators was nourished. The troubles continued. The agitators grew louder and the prestige and influence of the Senate steadily declined.

There was no help for it. All alike seemed driven by some desperate necessity to their fate. Cicero at least, one of the wisest and most intelligent Senators, would not have known what to do had some miracle suddenly put him in the place of that enlightened ruler for whom he longed. Despite his inadequacy, he was on the side of the angels, for in comparison with his contemporaries, Julius Caesar included, he stood out as a great advocate of the eternal values of the human spirit.

Yet those Romans who, like Cicero, had read the works of Plato and Aristotle must have known that Rome's troubles were not new in the ancient world. Aristotle, who died over two hundred years before Cicero was born, describes in his writings called *The Politics* the causes of political troubles very like those of Rome. There was, he said, a form of democracy "in which not the law but the multitude have the supreme power and supersede the law by their decrees. This is a state of affairs brought about by the demagogues". It needed but a short step for a demagogue to set himself up as a tyrant or dictator. History had already proved to Aristotle that "almost all tyrants have been demagogues who gained the favour of the people by their accusation of the notables".

He preferred to see social justice established otherwise than through a revolution caused by economic discontents. Everything possible should of course be done to relieve the troubles of the poor. They should, he thought, be helped by being given an opportunity to help themselves. Let them be set up in trade or agriculture by being enabled to buy a small farm. He was against free doles because then "the poor are always receiving and always wanting more and more. Such help is like water poured into a leaky cask". Cicero must have thought of Caesar's creature Clodius and his free corn dole to almost every family in Rome when he read those words. Aristotle knew that political and social problems cannot be solved merely by economic action. Much more than the struggle for wealth and possessions is involved. Economic activities are driven forward by acquisitive desires and "it is of the nature of desire not to be satisfied" although "most men live only for the gratification of it". It is true that the aim should be to produce a State "composed as far as possible of equals and similars and these are generally the middle classes", for "great is the good fortune of a State in which the citizens have a moderate and sufficient property". Beyond that he was not interested to go because he believed that the mere pursuit of wealth is no worthy purpose for any man wishing to lead a good life.

The contrary notion that a State in which no man possesses more than his neighbours might provide a short way to salvation for society did not deceive him. He admitted that a law to equalise everyone's income had "a specious appearance of benevolence . . . men readily listen to it and are easily induced to believe that in some wonderful manner everybody will become everybody's friend". But he was under no illusion that men will begin to love their neighbours as soon as those neighbours prevent them from becoming rich. Not money or possessions, but "a very different cause, the wickedness of human nature" was for Aristotle the root of all evil.

With deeper insight, he saw that "it is not the possessions but the desires of mankind that require to be equalised". Consequently he held that the moral reformation of man through education alone offered much hope of realising that political and social progress he believed to be possible. The diverse elements composing a State should, said Aristotle, "be united into a community by education". For him "the adaptation of education to the form of government" was the influence above all others to which he looked to "contribute to the permanence of constitutions". Such education, he thought, should be the same for all because "women and children must be trained by education with an eye to the State . . . for the children grow up to be citizens and half the persons in the State are women". Slaves should have nothing to do with it. The aim should be to establish good moral values without losing sight of the fact that "the first principle of all action is leisure": leisure in which the good life is to be lived.

In his analysis of the causes of revolutions and the manner in which dictatorships are established and maintained, Aristotle used language which any free Roman might have regarded as sentence of doom upon his liberties and as a compelling incitement to kill any man by whom they were threatened. He sought further to show how constitutional governments should be preserved and how they should be administered. Here he laid great stress upon "the administration of justice . . . the principle of order in political society". "There is nothing", he said, "which should be more jealously maintained than the spirit of obedience to law, more especially in small matters; for transgression creeps in unperceived and at last ruins the State, just as the constant recurrence of small expenses in time eats up a fortune". On this great theme Cicero certainly followed Aristotle, whose words upon the supreme importance of the Rule of Law may well have inspired his own emphasis upon it . . . "He who bids the law rule", said Aristotle, "may be deemed to bid God and Reason alone rule, but he who bids man rule adds an element of the beast, for desire is a wild beast, and passion perverts the minds of rulers, even where they are the best of men. The law is reason unaffected by desire".

The Romans, who suffered a Clodius to make war upon them for five years, shamefully ignored this first principle of government. Aristotle's teaching contained plain warnings on other matters the Romans had begun to neglect, such as the rule against allowing the same persons always to rule or the same men to hold many offices, the danger of allowing men to buy their way into public office, as wealthy Romans did by providing free gladiatorial contests and other ruinously expensive displays. "Those who have been at the expense of purchasing their places will be in the habit of repaying themselves", he said. The Romans and still more their dependent peoples had good cause to agree with his caution that "special precautions" should be taken to ensure that "above all every State should be so administered and so regulated by law that its magistrates cannot make money".

There was therefore no lack of sound wisdom and good advice on how to manage a State in Cicero's day. But the traditional wisdom of the Greeks helped the Romans no more than the far longer experience of mankind has aided our own contemporaries. For in our own day we too have seen the bankruptcy of government on a scale far more vast and more disastrous than that of the catastrophe by which the Roman Republic was engulfed. We have seen self-appointed leaders, a Duce and a Führer, allowed to create and to develop a private force to such an extent that by luck, by bluff and by an extravagant combination of propaganda and intimidation, they succeeded in overawing and replacing the government of their countries amid the rejoicings of a large number, if not indeed a vast majority, of their fellow citizens who apparently despaired of relief or salvation from other quarters. What we witnessed was the surrender of liberty by millions of Italians and Germans. They gave up one right after another, accepted new laws and consented to new restrictions until they were reduced to political slavery in which any attempt to resist was so brutally repressed that none save men of the greatest resolution dared to disobey. We have seen how these same Nazi gangsters proceeded to apply the same tactics to their neighbours and by how narrow a margin and at what frightful cost they were withstood in order that civilisation and humanity might be rescued from the rule of the jack-boot and the revolver. We too have been forced to realise that "when periods of barbarism and violence are approaching it is only for the vile and the foolish that the ideal becomes unfreedom and slavery". Cicero would have been able to say, "That is what I also believed."

Today more than ever before, it is important to get the story right. How many people, misled by thoughtless praise of Caesar's genius, have in succeeding centuries right down to our own time been blinded to the danger of one-man rule? Not merely in Italy but in other parts of the world Mussolini's propaganda successfully suggested the notion of a revived Caesarism as a cure for the blunders of democracy. Cicero's example and his teaching were unfortunately then forgotten. He may not have been alert to discover and repair the imperfections in the Republican constitution but he did not make the mistake of thinking that abject surrender to an autocrat was their cure.

The quarrel between Cicero and Caesar has been perpetuated down the ages. Each has had his loyal partisans and equally bitter critics. But attitudes of praise and of blame, if they are to be assumed, must rest upon deep reflection and upon a scale of values which cannot be extracted from the bare narrative of events alone. History is a Muse, not a hanging judge, and what we should seek from her inspiration is understanding before verdicts. The temptation to continue the battle between these two great men is naturally strong because their fight seems to have been renewed in our own time on a grand scale in the struggle between the rule of law on the one hand and dictatorship by Italy, Germany and Japan on the other.

Cicero has the enduring honour of having been one of the very early champions of social harmony and of the rule of law. Indeed, to many of his countrymen he must have appeared as one preaching a new doctrine. The tragedy of Rome lay in that fact. The Romans of Cicero's day were unable to advance rapidly enough from the traditional morality, manners and customs of their grandfathers so as to be able and ready to give it up in favour of the new loyalty, preached by Cicero to an abstract ideal of a body politic governed by the rule of law. The more compelling urges of hunger and personal frustrations blinded them to the grand principles of political life and drove them, as such primitive urges always will, to seek short cuts to ease and happiness. How, in consequence, their government broke down, has been the theme of much of this work. The separate forces in it, particularly the elected magistrates, the sole and annually renewed legal source of executive authority in the Republic, were in Cicero's day no longer sustained in their sense of duty and kept in their proper place by the almost instinctive obedience their predecessors of the heroic age had unquestionably rendered to the tradition of Republican government handed down to them by their forefathers.

Without having had a schooling in the philosophy of civil polity such as that which Cicero himself so enthusiastically absorbed from Plato, Aristotle and their successors, and not being interested in the forthright Roman form in which he tried so hard to pass it on to them, his fellow citizens had for the most part no other guide in the desperate confusion of their times than the promptings of their own desires and their own short-sighted self-seeking.

Whatever may have been Caesar's defects, he was not as short-sighted as the selfish politicians of Rome. Did he not choose to sacrifice ten of the best years of his life to endure the boredom and hardships of camp life and campaigning in Gaul? He saw more clearly than Cicero that the old traditions of the Republic no longer had the power to activate the political and administrative machinery by which Rome rose to greatness. Yet the first necessity of the State was that the government should be strong. With the sure instinct of the born administrator and statesman, Caesar set about restoring, or rather creating for the first time as a permanent feature in the government of Rome, that unified line of command which had hitherto existed spasmodically when a Dictator had been created to deal with a special crisis in the country's fortunes. There can be no question but that Caesar was right in his strenuous and momentarily successful effort to vitalise the executive power of the Republic. All that we have since learned about the principles of public administration confirms that without a line of responsibility, authority, or unified command, executive and administrative action is lame or paralysed.

But government is more than administration and executive action. These activities supply the means of government. The ends of action, the purposes which government and administration are to achieve, have their source elsewhere. In the heroic age of the Republic, men were content to have traditional morality as their guide and as the source of their executive and administrative purposes and authority. When the men around Cicero no longer looked to tradition they ought, as he urged them to do, to have enthroned social harmony, social justice and the rule of law in its place. But his doctrine was too new, the law insufficiently developed, and the penalties of ignoring it not sufficiently appreciated, for many to be likely to listen to him.

Perhaps loyalty to an undoubted leader of men should have been a sufficient substitute for law or tradition as the guide and source of authority in the State? Caesar had nothing else to offer. At a high cost in Roman bloodshed and ruin he was prepared to prove that the State could be made to work on his basis of one-man personal leadership and for a time he succeeded. It was not enough. Caesar's genius could not discover, declare and pursue the purposes and the welfare of the millions of human beings inescapably united and bound together in the great society known as the Roman Republic. A state runs a desperate hazard when its fate hangs upon the slender thread of one man's insight, life and health. If Caesar had lived would he not have saddled Rome with the burden of an absolute monarchy on Oriental despotic lines? These were the fears which turned Cicero's early admiration for Caesar into mistrust and aversion. For all his energy and far-sighted practical measures of reform Caesar had no recipe for reviving the poor and deflated morale of his subjects. Caesar perished and instead of a statesman and military genius the Romans had Caesar's sword to rule them. Mere military dictatorship had still smaller chances of survival than rule by genius.

Caesar, in contrast to Cicero, has often been praised for his creative vision and ability to see in advance the shape of things to come, as though, of the men of Roman antiquity, he alone was clear-headed with his eyes upon the future, while Cicero has been dismissed as a muddler chained to the past and unable to see a future different in any essential way from that past. The matter is not so easily settled. Cicero was not muddled upon the question whether the rule of law is preferable to rule by gangsters.

The world-shattering events of our own time have enabled us to see more clearly the desperate calamity with which Cicero and Caesar were forced to grapple. We may admire Cicero's resolute stand for the grand principles of political freedom which alone make life tolerable for men of spirit. We may equally admire Caesar's stronger and more resolute determination to have done with drift and flabby lack of purpose; to hack his way through the appalling confusion in Rome and at all costs to make the machinery of government work so that administrative energies might begin to achieve worthy purposes in society. We may admire both points of view, and without pretending that the question between the two men is completely exhausted by the distinction implied, take our stand upon it at this particular epoch in world history. We may then say that the predominantly reflective genius of Cicero and the predominantly practical genius of Caesar were of different orders of excellence; that both were needed then as they are needed in government everywhere; that their tragic story should be given a broader setting than that merely of their own characters, ability, performance, and fate because it deserves to be regarded as part of the great loom of human destiny upon which all men work out their lives.

To see Caesar and Cicero, their friends and enemies and the millions of Romans whom they never knew, against this broad background of developing human history will be to get as near as it is yet given to mankind to that vision of men *sub specie aeternitatis;* that godlike, unattainable comprehension which finds a place for all the relevant facts, which at the same time makes clear their explanation, their meaning and their message, and so guides and directs our footsteps as we, like Cicero and Caesar before us, wrestle with our own difficulties and encounter our own fate.

Fifteen years after Caesar perished, when peace came again at last to the troubled city of Rome, it was achieved partly because many of the actors in the great drama of Cicero's age had died, committed suicide, been killed or had exhausted themselves and their countrymen in the miseries of a civil war too long drawn out. The young men in the rising generation at Rome hardly knew the meaning of political liberty, neither had they had any experience of stable, orderly government. The new peace was also partly due to the skill of that most unlikely young man, Octavianus, born in the year of Cicero's consulship, whom Cicero flattered but in whom he detected little sign of greatness. He was Caesar's great-nephew and adopted son. His was the great advantage of fighting under Caesar's colours and becoming the heir therefore to a mighty name and to the following it inspired amongst thousands of Romans. He was a young man. He had learned much from the failures of the elder generation of Roman statesmen, of Crassus, Pompey, Cicero, Antony and of the great Julius Caesar. He was helped too by the desperate desire of millions for peace and security at almost any price. He had a free field. Patiently, persistently and firmly he devised and dressed up a more plausible source of State authority so that the executive and administrative power of government could be more intelligently directed to serve public purposes and so to win acceptance by the majority of the peoples dependent on Rome. If he also is regarded as a political gangster on the grand scale, he was a successful one for he eliminated all his rivals. Thereafter he had a lifetime in which to make his experiments in ruling, backed by overwhelming power as a virtual dictator.

So the edifice which Octavianus, as Augustus Caesar, the first Roman Emperor, erected upon the ruins which the bankrupt Republicans had pulled down upon themselves as they slaughtered Julius Caesar, was a more subtle and more complicated construction than Caesar could have devised or would have had the patience to build. Pompey might perhaps have recognised it as a solution he had fumbled to find. It would probably have made less appeal to Cicero despite his wish for an enlightened ruler, but neither Caesar nor Cicero could have welcomed it wholeheartedly because it was designed for a new age and for a different race of men.

6. RICHARD E. SMITH

FROM Richard E. Smith, *The Failure of the Roman Republic* (Cambridge: Cambridge University Press, 1955), pp. 163–66.

. . . The Age of Augustus gave back to men the opportunity—for the wish had long been there—to live once again in conformity with their former moral code, to take up again the ideas and ideals of their happier past and give them life and purpose in an even greater future.

The Republic's crisis and failure have an interest for others than the specialist; for they were a crisis and a failure of society, and hence their interest extends to all societies and all students of society in every age. A society is more than the individuals that compose it, though it has no existence independently of them. 'What is a city without men?' asked Sophocles; it is equally pertinent to ask what are men without a city, i.e. a society; for only in a society does man find the opportunity to live a full life, to give full expression to all his talents, be they great or small, and to realize the best that is in him by living not merely among, but for, others. In a society he is able to give a loyalty and devotion to certain ideals which embody his faith and aspirations; and it is the sharing of those ideals by all its members which gives life to the society. Societies take long to come to being; it is not at once that the material circumstances of men's lives mould and are moulded until they and the men who live with and by them come to know each other and be welded into one; and in this process the ideals of the people are slowly fashioned, until at last there emerges a society with its own values, its own aspirations and its own faith.

But society is a sensitive organism; remove or destroy the unifying element, and it breaks into a thousand pieces; men still live together, but the cement which bound them into one is gone. And there is much in man that is selfish and disruptive; he lives largely by his instincts and emotions, and when the highest of these instincts loses its object, he is left only with those more animal ones by which to live. Live he does, at a lower level, harnessing his powers to attain his baser ends, conspiring and combining with some the better to accomplish his purpose against others. This happens in any society when its ideals are shattered, as it did in Rome; but once the faith is shaken and destroyed, it cannot be replaced to order; it can only be won again by suffering and experience. For a time things can seem to be well, until the last of the spiritual capital is spent; but when the final cheque has been drawn, society is bankrupt, and the consequences must ensue; before the society can come together once again, fresh capital must be created.

This was what happened at Rome as a result of what the Gracchi did. Tiberius' challenge to the Senate, made in the way in which it was, involved a challenge to the harmony of Rome's society, of which the Senate was so important a part; for inevitably the question must arise whether the Senate should be governing the Roman world; and the mob is not the best arbiter on so grave a matter. Yet to the mob Tiberius went, supposing that nothing but his legislation was at stake; his shrewder brother, and hence more culpable, of deliberate intent set his face against the Senate, and thought it clever to have raised the Equites against that body; what his shrewdness did not tell him—or so at least, in his defence, we hope—was that he had provoked a question which must now be solved before all others; and the answer to that question took a hundred years to find. The clash of groups came into being, and nothing could heal the wound the body politic had sustained; the contest for the power at Rome made it impossible for Rome to be in harmony, and the longer it continued, the worse became the disintegration, the lower the depths to which persons were prepared to go in their own or their group's interest. The ideals which had made of Rome a society evaporated into near-nothingness, and Rome was a society only in name. What is surprising is the essential vitality of the Roman spirit, which after more than fifty years of strife and civil war emerged again as tough and strong as ever, like an acorn from beneath a concrete slab, to create the Augustan Age and make possible the Roman Empire.

Yet Rome could not sever herself from her past; what had been had been; the present was the child of the past, and Cicero's Republic could never more come into being. Facts and sentiments were to be constantly at war; with Augustus as the personal saviour of society they might seem to have agreed like lamb and wolf to live together; but the deep opposition between the two could not be obscured or denied for ever; as time passed, the antagonism became ever more open until in Tacitus we see the fatalistic acquiescence in the facts against which the spirit revolted—in vain. This was the final consequence of what the Gracchi did—the death of the Republic. No society can break with its past and start again; if it changes— and change there must assuredly be—it must remain the same thing. England was more fortunate than Rome; in its greatest crises and convulsions its leading men knew this instinctively, and the more violent the break with the past, the more anxious were they to unite themselves with that past by spiritual bonds.

The Romans, too, had that instinct; the Gracchi unfortunately did not; once the disaster had begun, it had to run its course; and when the Roman spirit had its chance to show itself once more, it did its best, but the body was maimed. It is a measure of the gravity of what the Gracchi did that the Roman spirit was unable to react in time; if Scipio's humanism was provoked to bless Tiberius' murder and call down a curse on any that should imitate him, we may be sure that what Tiberius had done seemed a far more terrible thing than many historians suppose. But Scipio's curse proved only to be part of the greater Gracchan curse; Caius died as Scipio's curse required; but bloodshed and strife only multiplied themselves to bring destruction on the Republic Scipio's curse was invoked to save; and once begun there was no staying it. The Roman spirit, conservative, instinctive, emerged from the carnage of the civil wars to regain itself, and though it could not exorcise the past, it tried to link itself to the further past to create a better future; no new written constitution, no theory to justify or limit Augustus' power, but a feeling with the sensitive antennae of the spirit after what was best and Roman; and their efforts, though only in part did they succeed, gave us the Roman Empire and our Western civilization. ✻

7. MIKHAIL ROSTOVTZEFF

FROM Mikhail Rostovtzeff, *A History of the Ancient World*, 2 vols. (Oxford: Clarendon Press, 1927), vol. II, 158–61, 363–64.

The senatorial system of government was attacked by a succession of revolutionary politicians with a definite programme, which was, to transfer all power to the popular assembly, to redistribute the land, and to extend the limits of the franchise. Of this programme the last item only was realized to some extent, and that after a cruel war: the whole of Italy was admitted to the body of Roman citizens. The other two points led to a long political conflict, in the heat of which their real meaning was forgotten. Rome was divided into two camps—the partisans of the Senate, and its enemies. Meantime the need of constitutional reform grew with the growth of the state. The cautious foreign policy of the Senate, which shrank from the annexation of more provinces, gave place first, in the second century B.C., to the selfish policy of the great landowners, and then, in the next century, to a frankly imperialistic policy, which was carried out both by the Senate and by the enemies of the Senate, including the class of business men who were known as 'knights'.

The two highest classes of Roman society, the senators and knights, were supreme in the provinces. The former governed the provinces with almost unlimited powers and were sometimes guilty of scandalous misconduct. The speeches of Cicero against Verres, the governor of Sicily, describe such a case in vivid colours. The knights' chief business in the provinces was to collect the taxes and dues, which the Senate had let out to them through the agency of the censors. By collusion with the governor, by bribing him, by presenting him with shares in the joint-stock companies which were formed for the collection of taxes, the knights found it feasible to oppress the provincials and squeeze the last drop of juice out of them. It was useless to send complaints to Rome. Occasionally, as in the case of Verres, a skillful advocate was willing to plead for the provincials, if he could thereby crush a political adversary or improve his own prospects of advancement. But in most cases the juries, being composed of senators or knights or both together, returned a verdict in favour of those who paid them most.

Another scandal of provincial government consisted in the extensive financial operations of capitalists who lent money, often at usurious rates of interest. The loans were advanced chiefly to the cities of the East, which needed them in order to satisfy the greed of tax-farmers and governors. At the beginning of the civil wars these cities were already hopelessly involved, and each aspirant to supremacy at Rome laid them under contributions which they could not pay. Their difficulties were taken advantage of by the Roman bankers and capitalists, both senators and knights. They were ready to find money but demanded exorbitant interest and all the property of the city as security. If the city was unable to pay, the creditor was backed up by the power of Rome and demanded his money with the help of armed force. The tributary kings were treated no better. The real purpose of many military operations carried out by the Romans in Asia Minor was to enforce the payment of debt. To take a share in the business of tax-farmers and moneylenders was so much a matter of course, that men of the highest character, Cicero, for instance, a man of unstained reputation and an excellent provincial governor, did not scruple to engage in it. Brutus, the murderer of Caesar, invested his money in loans to cities and charged interest at 48 per cent.

The scandalous condition of the provinces provided the democratic leaders and also all ambitious aspirants to power with an effective weapon against the Senate and senatorial government. Nevertheless, neither the triumph of the democratic party, nor the temporary success of individual political leaders, brought about any real change. The democratic leaders and their opponents were alike absolutely dependent upon the army; and the army now consisted of professional soldiers, who sought by military service to satisfy their greed, first for booty and plunder, and then, when their time of service had expired, for allotments of land. Experience proved that it was impossible to use the army in order to carry out a definite political programme. The army supported Marius the democrat, and it supported Sulla the aristocrat. About politics it cared little; but money and land it insisted on having. The two requirements could only be supplied by constant wars and the annexation of province after province. Thus Sulla and Pompey and Caesar and Antony and Octavian were all forced to carry on an imperialistic policy and to extend unceasingly the limits of the state; and they found support for this policy, without regard to their political objects, among the class of knights and among the senators themselves.

The enormous growth of the state further increased the importance of the army. Without the army the Roman state would have broken up at once. But the army would obey no leader, unless he made them sure of victory and allotments of land. This was clearly seen by all the chief actors on the political stage. Pompey alone tried to avoid this logical conclusion: he wished to make a compromise between the constitution and a monarchy; he wished to rule as the first Roman citizen, and yet to enjoy the confidence of the people. But he failed and became in the end a tool of the constitution against which he was fighting: he was forced to defend the Senate against Caesar, a more consistent aspirant to autocracy based upon the sword. Caesar frankly confessed that he owed his power to the army; and the army was the weapon with which Antony and Octavian struck down the last attempt of the Senate to reassert itself. Antony and Octavian alike founded their pretensions to supreme power on military force alone. The military weakness of Antony and his inability to get recruits from Italy settled the dispute for primacy in favour of Octavian.

This same growth of the state, with the annexation of ever new provinces and the increasing number of tributary kings, made it more and more obvious that the Senate was incapable of dealing with a problem which was now forcing itself to the front—the problem of government for a world-wide state. The material well-being of Rome depended on the prosperity of the provinces; and Italy, tax-free herself except for a small revenue derived from customs, looked to the provinces mainly for support. But the provinces, drained dry by senators and knights, and treated by the leaders of civil war merely as a source from which to draw money, became steadily less prosperous: the economic development of the West was stopped, and the East was beggared. All this was well known to the chief men at Rome. The central point of Sulla's reforms was this very question, how the state could be governed; and to Caesar the same problem was of primary importance. But the question was insoluble, if the old order and the ancient constitution of Rome as a city-state were preserved. Here, too, the only possible expedient was to adopt some new form of constitution; and the only possible form, owing partly to the excessive importance of the army and its leaders and partly to the unwillingness of Italy and the Roman citizens to resign their dominant position in the state, was a constitution based on the military power of an individual—in other words, a system of monarchy was inevitable.

Thus the first century B.C. was an epoch of transition, when the old city-state was breaking up and degenerating into the rule of two privileged classes, the senators and knights, and when a new system of monarchy was growing up. The conception of a family of free and independent states—the conception which the Greeks fought for and which lay at the root of the Roman constitution in the fourth and third centuries B.C.—now gradually gave way to the ancient Eastern notion of a single world-wide state, possessing a uniform culture and ruled over by one man.

. . . The Roman aristocracy caught the lamp of civilization from Greece, and carried on the mission of Greece along the same lines, adding, as they worked, the national qualities peculiar to themselves. But Rome was more than a city-state: she was a city ruling over an empire: for every citizen she had hundreds of subjects. In Rome itself the aristocracy who had created the new Italian civilization were forced to endure the domestic conflict by which Greece had been divided. But so long as Rome was fighting for political pre-eminence in the ancient world, the division of classes within the state remained in the background or at least did not cause bloodshed. As soon, however, as she became mistress of the world, the power of 'the best men', the *optimates* or aristocracy, was assailed by the citizens in general. Their war-cry was a better and juster distribution of property, and a more democratic form of government. For eighty years this bloody conflict lasted, and the aristocracy came out of it defeated and demoralized. Its place was taken by the Italian middle class; and it now became their duty to hold aloft the standard of civilization.

The middle class paid dear for their victory. Though the municipal constitution and the freedom of the citizens were preserved, at least in appearance and for the time, yet a new superstructure, in the shape of the imperial power, towered above the state. It turned out that freedom—not merely political freedom but that freedom of thought and creation which was prized most highly by the noblest spirits—grew steadily less; and the very conception of freedom was lowered till it meant the voluntary submission of all to one, even if that one was the best among the best, even if he was the *princeps*. And even this freedom belonged only to those who possessed the title of Roman citizens: to the millions scattered over the empire even this shadowy privilege was denied.

The establishment of the empire brought with it a fresh advance of creative genius. But . . . this advance lacked the enthusiasm and power which marked the accomplishment of the Greek cities and even that of republican Rome. From the beginning it bears the stamp of weariness and disappointment—the stamp characteristic of a post-revolutionary era . . .

Part 4

THE HISTORICAL JESUS AND THE BEGINNINGS OF CHRISTIANITY

The study of the historical Jesus and the beginnings of Christianity presents some initial difficulties. First, there is the problem of sources discussed in the introduction to this volume. Second, Christianity is so deeply and firmly embedded in all aspects of Western history that perspective—an essential aspect of genuine historical understanding—is extremely difficult to attain. We cannot easily detach ourselves because the Christian influence is everywhere. Moreover, Christianity has known a variety of forms and much of the scholarship on it has been ardently partisan, designed to defend, reinforce, or express a particular vision of the Christian experience. Third, the study of Christianity, even of its early stages, inevitably leads into many other areas.

None of these difficulties are insuperable. We can proceed with a study of the basic sources so long as we are aware of their provenance. Perspective and disinterestedness can be achieved if vigorously pursued. And finally, a careful delineation of the component parts of the study of Christianity will help to limit and define the subject so that it may be approached in a rational manner.

The study of early Christianity may be organized in the following sequence: 1) the historical Jesus, 2) the rise and spread of Christianity, and 3) the consolidation and triumph of Christianity. This is a very general framework; it will soon become clear that there are sub-categories within each theme and that each one of them must be related to the others. The selections in this Part only deal with the first two themes, but to give the student a comprehensive picture of the problem we will also touch on the triumph of Christianity further on in this discussion.

The historical Jesus must be sought in *The New Testament*, a book open to many interpretations:

> And Jesus went forth, and his disciples, into the villages of Caesarea Philippi: and on the way he asked his disciples, saying unto them, Who do men say that I am? And they told him, saying, John the Baptist; and others; Elijah; but others, One of the prophets. And he asked them, But who say ye that I am? Peter answereth and saith unto him, Thou are the Christ. And he charged them that they should tell no man of him.

Reticence, ambiguity, indeed confusion—no wonder that from earliest times men have not been able to answer concretely the question posed by Jesus.

Of the many lives of Jesus published in the past century, few have been so popular or so controversial as the one by the French historian Ernest Renan (1823–92). The publication of *The Life of Jesus* in 1863 raised such a violent storm that Renan was expelled from his position as professor of Hebrew, Chaldaic, and Syriac at the Collège de France. The real reasons for academic dismissal invariably go beyond those given officially. In Renan's case we may pick out three causes, and each reveals something about the man and the ambience in which biblical scholarship was carried on a century ago.

It was Renan who introduced France to the critical methods inaugurated by Wellhausen; the Collège de France, unfortunately, considered his attitude toward religion excessively rational. No doubt there was a measure of truth in the official explanation but we may be certain more was involved. Renan was not an hermetic scholar writing learned monographs for a select, small circle of fellow erudites. On the contrary, he achieved enormous notoriety; his influence was so great that one historian remarked, "All that the Frenchman of ordinary culture knows of the Ancient East, of comparative religion, of exegesis, comes directly or indirectly from Renan." This wide-ranging influence was due, above all, to the substance and style of *The Life of Jesus;* this, even more than its popularity (always frowned on in academic circles) was probably the fundamental reason why its publication became a *cause célèbre*.

Scholarly and learned as he was, Renan departed from traditional scholarship and attempted, with remarkable success, to get close to Jesus the man. According to G. P. Gooch, "Renan is convinced that tradition contains precious elements, if not of fact, at least of atmosphere." Renan made use of these elements in creating the poetic representation of Christ which replaced the atrophied Jesus typical of previous biographies. The general public was delighted. If Christ was to be graphically portrayed as a man, He must be stripped of His supernatural crust. There were dangers involved in such a daring enterprise. Imagine the reaction of staid French professors to this description of a naïve Christ: Jesus had "no knowledge of the general state of the world. . . . The charming impossibilities with which his parables abound, when he brings kings and the mighty ones upon the stage, prove that he never conceived of aristocratic society except as a young villager who sees the world through the prism of his simplicity." Renan was fascinated by and focused his highly developed imagination on Christ's personality rather than on Christian dogma.

The selection by Albert Schweitzer represents an entirely different approach to the life of Jesus. Schweitzer cannot accept Jesus as "a figure designed by rationalism, endowed with life by liberalism, and clothed by modern theology in an historical garb," as some nineteenth-century writers depicted Him. Schweitzer speaks of the "danger" of theologians offering a picture of Jesus "who was too small, because we had forced Him into conformity with our human standards and human psychology." This is, of course, precisely what Renan had attempted to do. In his quest for the historical Jesus, Schweitzer rejects history. "Jesus means something to our world because a mighty spiritual force streams forth from Him and flows through our time also. This fact can neither be shaken nor confirmed by any historical discovery." Theology has replaced history.

The next three selections return to the realm of history. Adolf Harnack depicts Jesus as one of the Jewish reformers who rose to protest what they regarded as a perversion of their religion. Jesus is thus placed within a Judaic context, and Harnack is careful to demonstrate the limited "universalism" of His mission. Shirley Jackson Case tells us that "From the very outset this new movement was socially conditioned in a much more emphatic way than is commonly appreciated." The "unconventional methods" Jesus used in challenging "the elaborate machinery for the cultivation and preservation of religious values" were responsible for the stiff resistance He encountered. Jesus thus emerges as a social revolutionary. Jules Lebreton and Jacques Zeiller regard the historical Jesus as a man who had a clear conception of His mission.

The selections which follow shift the emphasis; the spread of Christianity becomes the central theme. According to Joseph Klausner, four elements facilitated the process by which Christianity—at the time of the crucifixion only a Jewish sect—spread and moved toward its eventual triumph. These elements consisted of 1) certain tendencies in the Judaism of Jesus that made it non-Judaic, 2) the dispersal of the Jews outside of Palestine, 3) the spiritual conditions among the Gentiles, and 4) the Hellenistic Jewish culture of non-Palestinian Jews. This framework is useful and some of these themes are examined in detail in the last two selections by Charles Guignebert and Rudolf Bultmann.

The spread of Christianity, of course, was no guarantee of its triumph. A number of circumstances help explain the remarkable success of this Jewish sect. Christianity was set afoot within the context of the Roman Empire, a universal state which had successfully broken down many of the barriers separating the peoples of the Mediterranean world. Thus, a cohesive framework, an established universalism was available to any religion that could become coterminous with the state. This association of church and state came about in the reign of Constantine, a ruler whose ability and longevity did much for the Christian cause. Moreover, the Church developed an organizational structure unrivaled by any other sect at that time. Concurrently, it formulated its dogma, the essentials of its faith and vision of the world. This dogma was characterized by inclusiveness and a subtle compound of rigidity and flexibility. By the time the disintegration of the Roman Empire was well advanced, Christianity was mature enough to provide a new European unity.

1. ERNEST RENAN

FROM Ernest Renan, *The Life of Jesus* (London: Trubner & Company, 1864), pp. 300–7.

Jesus, it will be seen, limited his action entirely to the Jews. Although his sympathy for those despised by orthodoxy led him to admit pagans into the kingdom of God,—although he had resided more than once in a pagan country, and once or twice we surprise him in kindly relations with unbelievers,—it may be said that his life was passed entirely in the very restricted world in which he was born. He was never heard of in Greek or Roman countries; his name appears only in profane authors of a hundred years later, and then in an indirect manner, in connexion with seditious movements provoked by his doctrine, or persecutions of which his disciples were the object. Even on Judaism, Jesus made no very durable impression. Philo, who died about the year 50, had not the slightest knowledge of him. Josephus, born in the year 37, and writing in the last years of the century, mentions his execution in a few lines, as an event of secondary importance, and in the enumeration of the sects of his time, he omits the Christians altogether. In the *Mishnah*, also, there is no trace of the new school; the passages in the two Gemaras in which the founder of Christianity is named, do not go further back than the fourth or fifth century. The essential work of Jesus was to create around him a circle of disciples, whom he inspired with boundless affection, and amongst whom he deposited the germ of his doctrine. To have made himself beloved, "to the degree that after his death they ceased not to love him," was the great work of Jesus, and that which most struck his contemporaries. His doctrine was so little dogmatic, that he never thought of writing it or of causing it to be written. Men did not become his disciples by believing this thing or that thing, but in being attached to his person and in loving him. A few sentences collected from memory, and especially the type of character he set forth, and the impression it had left, were what remained of him. Jesus was not a founder of dogmas, or a maker of creeds; he infused into the world a new spirit. The least Christian men were, on the one hand, the doctors of the Greek Church, who, beginning from the fourth century, entangled Christianity in a path of puerile metaphysical discussions, and, on the other, the scholastics of the Latin Middle Ages, who wished to draw from the Gospel the thousands of articles of a colossal system. To follow Jesus in expectation of the kingdom of God, was all that at first was implied by being Christian.

It will thus be understood how, by an exceptional destiny, pure Christianity still preserves, after eighteen centuries, the character of a universal and eternal religion. It is, in fact, because the religion of Jesus is in some respects the final religion. Produced by a perfectly spontaneous movement of souls, freed at its birth from all dogmatic restraint, having struggled three hundred years for liberty of conscience, Christianity, in spite of its failures, still reaps the results of its glorious origin. To renew itself, it has but to return to the Gospel. The kingdom of God, as we conceive it, differs notably from the supernatural apparition which the first Christians hoped to see appear in the clouds. But the sentiment introduced by Jesus into the world is indeed ours. His perfect idealism is the highest rule of the unblemished and virtuous life. He has created the heaven of pure souls, where is found what we ask for in vain on earth, the perfect nobility of the children of God, absolute purity, the total removal of the stains of the world; in fine, liberty, which society excludes as an impossibility, and which exists in all its amplitude only in the domain of thought. The great Master of those who take refuge in this ideal kingdom of God is still Jesus. He was the first to proclaim the royalty of the mind; the first to say, at least by his actions, "My kingdom is not of this world." The foundation of true religion is indeed his work: after him, all that remains is to develop it and render it fruitful.

"Christianity" has thus become almost a synonym of "religion." All that is done outside of this great and good Christian tradition is barren. Jesus gave religion to humanity, as Socrates gave it philosophy, and Aristotle science. There was philosophy before Socrates and science before Aristotle. Since Socrates and since Aristotle, philosophy and science have made immense progress; but all has been built upon the foundation which they laid. In the same way, before Jesus, religious thought had passed through many revolutions; since Jesus, it has made great conquests: but no one has improved, and no one will improve upon the essential principle Jesus has created; he has fixed for ever the idea of pure worship. The religion of Jesus in this sense is not limited. The Church has had its epochs and its phases; it has shut itself up in creeds which are, or will be but temporary: but Jesus has founded the absolute religion, excluding nothing, and determining nothing unless it be the spirit. His creeds are not fixed dogmas, but images susceptible of indefinite interpretations. We should seek in vain for a theological proposition in the Gospel. All confessions of faith are travesties of the idea of Jesus, just as the scholasticism of the middle ages, in proclaiming Aristotle the sole master of a completed science, perverted the thought of Aristotle. Aristotle, if he had been present in the debates of the schools, would have repudiated this narrow doctrine; he would have been of the party of progressive science against the routine which shielded itself under his authority; he would have applauded his opponents. In the same way, if Jesus were to return among us, he would recognise as disciples, not those who pretend to enclose him entirely in a few catechismal phrases, but those who labour to carry on his work. The eternal glory, in all great things, is to have laid the first stone. It may be that in the "Physics," and in the "Meteorology" of modern times, we may not discover a word of the treatises of Aristotle which bear these titles; but Aristotle remains no less the founder of natural science. Whatever may be the transformations of dogma, Jesus will ever be the creator of the pure spirit of religion; the Sermon on the Mount will never be surpassed. Whatever revolution takes place will not prevent us attaching ourselves in religion to the grand intellectual and moral line at the head of which shines the name of Jesus. In this sense we are Christians, even when we separate ourselves on almost all points from the Christian tradition which has preceded us.

And this great foundation was indeed the personal work of Jesus. In order to make himself adored to this degree, he must have been adorable. Love is not enkindled except by an object worthy of it, and we should know nothing of Jesus, if it were not for the passion he inspired in those about him, which compels us still to affirm that he was great and pure. The faith, the enthusiasm, the constancy of the first Christian generation is not explicable, except by supposing at the origin of the whole movement, a man of surpassing greatness. At the sight of the marvellous creations of the ages of faith, two impressions equally fatal to good historical criticism arise in the mind. On the one hand we are led to think these creations too impersonal; we attribute to a collective action, that which has often been the work of one powerful will, and of one superior mind. On the other hand, we refuse to see men like ourselves in the authors of those extraordinary movements which have decided the fate of humanity. Let us have a larger idea of the powers which nature conceals in her bosom. Our civilisations, governed by minute restrictions, cannot give us any idea of the power of man at periods in which the originality of each one had a freer field wherein to develop itself. Let us imagine a recluse dwelling in the mountains near our capitals, coming out from time to time in order to present himself at the palaces of sovereigns, compelling the sentinels to stand aside, and, with an imperious tone, announcing to kings the approach of revolutions of which he had been the promoter. The very idea provokes a smile. Such, however, was Elias; but Elias the Tishbite, in our days, would not be able to pass the gate of the Tuileries. The preaching of Jesus, and his free activity in Galilee, do not deviate less completely from the social conditions to which we are accustomed. Free from our polished conventionalities, exempt from the uniform education which refines us, but which so greatly dwarfs our individuality, these mighty souls carried a surprising energy into action. They appear to us like the giants of an heroic age, which could not have been real. Profound error! Those men were our brothers; they were of our stature, felt and thought as we do. But the breath of God was free in them; with us, it is restrained by the iron bonds of a mean society, and condemned to an irremediable mediocrity.

Let us place, then, the person of Jesus at the highest summit of human greatness. Let us not be misled by exaggerated doubts in the presence of a legend which keeps us always in a superhuman world. The life of Francis d'Assisi is also but a tissue of miracles. Has any one, however, doubted of the existence of Francis d'Assisi, and of the part played by him? Let us say no more that the glory of the foundation of Christianity belongs to the multitude of the first Christians, and not to him whom legend has deified. The inequality of men is much more marked in the East than with us. It is not rare to see arise there, in the midst of a general atmosphere of wickedness, characters whose greatness astonishes us. So far from Jesus having been created by his disciples, he appeared in everything as superior to his disciples. The latter, with the exception of St Paul and St John, were men without either invention or genius. St Paul himself bears no comparison with Jesus, and as to St John, I shall shew hereafter, that the part he played, though very elevated in one sense, was far from being in all respects irreproachable. Hence the immense superiority of the Gospels among the writings of the New Testament. Hence the painful fall we experience in passing from the history of Jesus to that of the apostles. The evangelists themselves, who have bequeathed us the image of Jesus, are so much beneath him of whom they speak, that they constantly disfigure him, from their inability to attain to his height. Their writings are full of errors and misconceptions. We feel in each line a discourse of divine beauty, transcribed by narrators who do not understand it, and who substitute their own ideas for those which they have only half understood. On the whole, the character of Jesus, far from having been embellished by his biographers, has been lowered by them. ✳

2. ALBERT SCHWEITZER

FROM Albert Schweitzer, *The Quest of the Historical Jesus* (New York: The Macmillan Company, 1959), pp. 398–403.

Those who are fond of talking about negative theology can find their account here. There is nothing more negative than the result of the critical study of the Life of Jesus.

The Jesus of Nazareth who came forward publicly as the Messiah, who preached the ethic of the Kingdom of God, who founded the Kingdom of Heaven upon earth, and died to give His work its final consecration, never had any existence. He is a figure designed by rationalism, endowed with life by liberalism, and clothed by modern theology in an historical garb.

This image has not been destroyed from without, it has fallen to pieces, cleft and disintegrated by the concrete historical problems which came to the surface one after another, and in spite of all the artifice, art, artificiality, and violence which was applied to them, refused to be planed down to fit the design on which the Jesus of the theology of the last hundred and thirty years had been constructed, and were no sooner covered over than they appeared again in a new form. The thoroughgoing sceptical and the thoroughgoing eschatological school have only completed the work of destruction by linking the problems into a system and so making an end of the *Divide et impera* of modern theology, which undertook to solve each of them separately, that is, in a less difficult form. Henceforth it is no longer permissible to take one problem out of the series and dispose of it by itself, since the weight of the whole hangs upon each.

Whatever the ultimate solution may be, the historical Jesus of whom the criticism of the future, taking as its starting-point the problems which have been recognised and admitted, will draw the portrait, can never render modern theology the services which it claimed from its own half-historical, half-modern, Jesus. He will be a Jesus, who was Messiah, and lived as such, either on the ground of a literary fiction of the earliest Evangelist, or on the ground of a purely eschatological Messianic conception.

In either case, He will not be a Jesus Christ to whom the religion of the present can ascribe, according to its long-cherished custom, its own thoughts and ideas, as it did with the Jesus of its own making. Nor will He be a figure which can be made by a popular historical treatment so sympathetic and universally intelligible to the multitude. The historical Jesus will be to our time a stranger and an enigma.

The study of the Life of Jesus has had a curious history. It set out in quest of the historical Jesus, believing that when it had found Him it could bring Him straight into our time as a Teacher and Saviour. It loosed the bands by which He had been riveted for centuries to the stony rocks of ecclesiastical doctrine, and rejoiced to see life and movement coming into the figure once more, and the historical Jesus advancing, as it seemed, to meet it. But He does not stay; He passes by our time and returns to His own. What surprised and dismayed the theology of the last forty years was that, despite all forced and arbitrary interpretations, it could not keep Him in our time, but had to let Him go. He returned to His own time, not owing to the application of any historical ingenuity, but by the same inevitable necessity by which the liberated pendulum returns to its original position.

The historical foundation of Christianity as built up by rationalistic, by liberal, and by modern theology no longer exists; but that does not mean that Christianity has lost its historical foundation. The work which historical theology thought itself bound to carry out, and which fell to pieces just as it was nearing completion, was only the brick facing of the real immovable historical foundation which is independent of any historical confirmation or justification.

Jesus means something to our world because a mighty spiritual force streams forth from Him and flows through our time also. This fact can neither be shaken nor confirmed by any historical discovery. It is the solid foundation of Christianity.

The mistake was to suppose that Jesus could come to mean more to our time by entering into it as a man like ourselves. That is not possible. First because such a Jesus never existed. Secondly because, although historical knowledge can no doubt introduce greater clearness into an existing spiritual life, it cannot call spiritual life into existence. History can destroy the present; it can reconcile the present with the past; can even to a certain extent transport the present into the past; but to contribute to the making of the present is not given unto it.

But it is impossible to over-estimate the value of what German research upon the Life of Jesus has accomplished. It is a uniquely great expression of sincerity, one of the most significant events in the whole mental and spiritual life of humanity. What has been done for the religious life of the present and the immediate future by scholars such as P. W. Schmidt, Bousset, Jülicher, Weinel, Wernle—and their pupil Frenssen—and the others who have been called to the task of bringing to the knowledge of wider circles, in a form which is popular without being superficial, the results of religious-historical study, only becomes evident when one examines the literature and social culture of the Latin nations, who have been scarcely if at all touched by the influence of these thinkers.

And yet the time of doubt was bound to come. We modern theologians are too proud of our historical method, too proud of our historical Jesus, too confident in our belief in the spiritual gains which our historical theology can bring to the world. The thought that we could build up by the increase of historical knowledge a new and vigorous Christianity and set free new spiritual forces, rules us like a fixed idea, and prevents us from seeing that the task which we have grappled with and in some measure discharged is only one of the intellectual preliminaries of the great religious task. We thought that it was for us to lead our time by a roundabout way through the historical Jesus, as we understood Him, in order to bring it to the Jesus who is a spiritual power in the present. This roundabout way has now been closed by genuine history.

There was a danger of our thrusting ourselves between men and the Gospels, and refusing to leave the individual man alone with the sayings of Jesus.

There was a danger that we should offer them a Jesus who was too small, because we had forced Him into conformity with our human standards and human psychology. To see that, one need only read the Lives of Jesus written since the 'sixties, and notice what they have made of the great imperious sayings of the Lord, how they have weakened down His imperative world-contemning demands upon individuals, that He might not come into conflict with our ethical ideals, and might tune His denial of the world to our acceptance of it. Many of the greatest sayings are found lying in a corner like explosive shells from which the charges have been removed. No small portion of elemental religious power needed to be drawn off from His sayings to prevent them from conflicting with our system of religious world-acceptance. We have made Jesus hold another language with our time from that which He really held.

In the process we ourselves have been enfeebled, and have robbed our own thoughts of their vigour in order to project them back into history and make them speak to us out of the past. It is nothing less than a misfortune for modern theology that it mixes history with everything and ends by being proud of the skill with which it finds its own thoughts—even to its beggarly pseudo-metaphysic with which it has banished genuine speculative metaphysic from the sphere of religion—in Jesus, and represents Him as expressing them. It had almost deserved the reproach: "he who putteth his hand to the plough, and looketh back, is not fit for the Kingdom of God."

It was no small matter; therefore, that in the course of the critical study of the Life of Jesus, after a resistance lasting for two generations, during which first one expedient was tried and then another, theology was forced by genuine history to begin to doubt the artificial history with which it had thought to give new life to our Christianity, and to yield to the facts, which, as Wrede strikingly said, are sometimes the most radical critics of all. History will force it to find a way to transcend history, and to fight for the lordship and rule of Jesus over this world with weapons tempered in a different forge.

We are experiencing what Paul experienced. In the very moment when we were coming nearer to the historical Jesus than men had ever come before, and were already stretching out our hands to draw Him into our own time, we have been obliged to give up the attempt and acknowledge our failure in that paradoxical saying: "If we have known Christ after the flesh yet henceforth know we Him no more." And further we must be prepared to find that the historical knowledge of the personality and life of Jesus will not be a help, but perhaps even an offence to religion.

But the truth is, it is not Jesus as historically known, but Jesus as spiritually arisen within men, who is significant for our time and can help it. Not the historical Jesus, but the spirit which goes forth from Him and in the spirits of men strives for new influence and rule, is that which overcomes the world.

It is not given to history to disengage that which is abiding and eternal in the being of Jesus from the historical forms in which it worked itself out, and to introduce it into our world as a living influence. It has toiled in vain at this undertaking. As a water-plant is beautiful so long as it is growing in the water, but once torn from its roots, withers and becomes unrecognisable, so it is with the historical Jesus when He is wrenched loose from the soil of eschatology, and the attempt is made to conceive Him "historically" as a Being not subject to temporal conditions. The abiding and eternal in Jesus is absolutely independent of historical knowledge and can only be understood by contact with His spirit which is still at work in the world. In proportion as we have the Spirit of Jesus we have the true knowledge of Jesus.

Jesus as a concrete historical personality remains a stranger to our time, but His spirit, which lies hidden in His words, is known in simplicity, and its influence is direct. Every saying contains in its own way the whole Jesus. The very strangeness and unconditionedness in which He stands before us makes it easier for individuals to find their own personal standpoint in regard to Him.

Men feared that to admit the claims of eschatology would abolish the significance of His words for our time; and hence there was a feverish eagerness to discover in them any elements that might be considered not eschatologically conditioned. When any sayings were found of which the wording did not absolutely imply an eschatological connexion there was a great jubilation—these at least had been saved uninjured from the coming *débâcle*.

But in reality that which is eternal in the words of Jesus is due to the very fact that they are based on an eschatological worldview, and contain the expression of a mind for which the contemporary world with its historical and social circumstances no longer had any existence. They are appropriate, therefore, to any world, for in every world they raise the man who dares to meet their challenge, and does not turn and twist them into meaninglessness, above his world and his time, making him inwardly free, so that he is fitted to be, in his own world and in his own time, a simple channel of the power of Jesus.

Modern Lives of Jesus are too general in their scope. They aim at influencing, by giving a complete impression of the life of Jesus, a whole community. But the historical Jesus, as He is depicted in the Gospels, influenced individuals by the individual word. They understood Him so far as it was necessary for them to understand, without forming any conception of His life as a whole, since this in its ultimate aims remained a mystery even for the disciples.

Because it is thus preoccupied with the general, the universal, modern theology is determined to find its world-accepting ethic in the teaching of Jesus. Therein lies its weakness. The world affirms itself automatically; the modern spirit cannot but affirm it. But why on that account abolish the conflict between modern life, with the world-affirming spirit which inspires it as a whole, and the world-negating spirit of Jesus? Why spare the spirit of the individual man its appointed task of fighting its way through the world-negation of Jesus, of contending with Him at every step over the value of material and intellectual goods—a conflict in which it may never rest? For the general, for the institutions of society, the rule is: affirmation of the world, in conscious opposition to the view of Jesus, on the ground that the world has affirmed itself! This general affirmation of the world, however, if it is to be Christian, must in the individual spirit be Christianised and transfigured by the personal rejection of the world which is preached in the sayings of Jesus. It is only by means of the tension thus set up that religious energy can be communicated to our time. There was a danger that modern theology, for the sake of peace, would deny the world-negation in the sayings of Jesus, with which Protestantism was out of sympathy, and thus unstring the bow and make Protestantism a mere sociological instead of a religious force. There was perhaps also a danger of inward insincerity, in the fact that it refused to admit to itself and others that it maintained its affirmation of the world in opposition to the sayings of Jesus, simply because it could not do otherwise.

For that reason it is a good thing that the true historical Jesus should overthrow the modern Jesus, should rise up against the modern spirit and send upon earth, not peace, but a sword. He was not teacher, not a casuist; He was an imperious ruler. It was because He was so in His inmost being that He could think of Himself as the Son of Man. That was only the temporally conditioned expression of the fact that He was an authoritative ruler. The names in which men expressed their recognition of Him as such, Messiah, Son of Man, Son of God, have become for us historical parables. We can find no designation which expresses what He is for us.

He comes to us as One unknown, without a name, as of old, by the lakeside, He came to those men who knew Him not. He speaks to us the same word: "Follow thou me!" and sets us to the tasks which He has to fulfil for our time. He commands. And to those who obey Him, whether they be wise or simple, He will reveal Himself in the toils, the conflicts, the sufferings which they shall pass through in His fellowship, and, as an ineffable mystery, they shall learn in their own experience Who He is. ✷

3. ADOLF HARNACK

FROM Adolf Harnack, *The Mission and Expansion of Christianity* (New York: Harper & Row, 1962), pp. 36–43.

Jesus addressed his gospel—his message of God's imminent kingdom and of judgment, of God's fatherly providence, of repentance, holiness, and love—to his fellow-countrymen. He preached only to Jews. Not a syllable shows that he detached this message from its national soil, or set aside the traditional religion as of no value. Upon the contrary, his preaching could be taken as the most powerful corroboration of that religion. He did not attach himself to any of the numerous "liberal" or syncretistic Jewish conventicles or schools. He did not accept their ideas. Rather he took his stand upon the soil of Jewish rights, *i.e.*, of the piety maintained by Pharisaism. But he showed that while the Pharisees preserved what was good in religion, they were perverting it none the less, and that the perversion amounted to the most heinous of sins. Jesus waged war against the selfish, self-righteous temper in which many of the Pharisees fulfilled and practised their piety—a temper, at bottom, both loveless and godless. This protest already involved a break with the national religion, for the Pharisaic position passed for that of the nation; indeed, it represented the national religion. But Jesus went further. He traversed the claim that the descendants of Abraham, in virtue of their descent, were sure of salvation, and based the idea of divine sonship exclusively upon repentance, humility, faith, and love. In so doing, he disentangled religion from its national setting. Men, not Jews, were to be its adherents. Then, as it became plainer than ever that the Jewish people as a whole, and through their representatives, were spurning his message, he announced with increasing emphasis that a judgment was coming upon "the children of the kingdom," and prophesied, as his forerunner had done already, that the table of his Father would not lack for guests, but that a crowd would pour in, morning, noon, and night, from the highways and the hedges. Finally, he predicted the rejection of the nation and the overthrow of the temple, but these were not to involve the downfall of his work; on the contrary, he saw in them, as in his own passion, the condition of his work's completion.

Such is the "universalism" of the preaching of Jesus. No other kind of universalism can be proved for him, and consequently he cannot have given any command upon the mission to the wide world. The gospels contain such a command, but it is easy to show that it is neither genuine nor a part of the primitive tradition. It would introduce an entirely strange feature into the preaching of Jesus, and at the same time render many of his genuine sayings unintelligible or empty. One might even argue that the universal mission was an inevitable issue of the religion and spirit of Jesus, and that its origin, not only apart from any direct word of Jesus, but in verbal contradiction to several of his sayings, is really a stronger testimony to the method, the strength, and the spirit of his preaching than if it were the outcome of a deliberate command. By the fruit we know the tree; but we must not look for the fruit in the root. With regard to the way in which he worked and gathered disciples, the distinctiveness of his person and his preaching comes out very clearly. He sought to found no sect or school. He laid down no rules for outward adhesion to himself. His aim was to bring men to God and to prepare them for God's kingdom. He chose disciples, indeed, giving them special instruction and a share in his work; but even here there were no regulations. There were an inner circle of three, an outer circle of twelve, and beyond that a few dozen men and women who accompanied him. In addition to that, he had intimate friends who remained in their homes and at their work. Wherever he went, he wakened or found children of God throughout the country. No rule or regulation bound them together. They simply sought and shared the supreme boon which came home to each and all, viz., the kingdom of their Father and of the individual soul. In the practice of this kind of mission Jesus has had but one follower, and he did not arise till a thousand years afterwards. He was St Francis of Assisi.

If we leave out of account the words put by our first evangelist into the lips of the risen Jesus (Matt. xxviii. 19 f.), with the similar expressions which occur in the unauthentic appendix to the second gospel (Mark xvi. 15, 20), and if we further set aside the story of the wise men from the East, as well as one or two Old Testament quotations which our first evangelist has woven into his tale (cp. Matt. iv. 13 f., xii. 18), we must admit that Mark and Matthew have almost consistently withstood the temptation to introduce the Gentile mission into the words and deeds of Jesus. Jesus called sinners to himself, ate with tax-gatherers, attacked the Pharisees and their legal observance, made everything turn upon mercy and justice, and predicted the downfall of the temple—such is the universalism of Mark and Matthew. The very choice and commission of the twelve is described without any mention of a mission to the world (Mark iii. 13 f., vi. 7 f., and Matt. x. 1 f.). In fact, Matthew expressly limits their mission to Palestine. "Go not on the road of the Gentiles, and enter no city of the Samaritans; rather go to the lost sheep of the house of Israel" (Matt. x. 5, 6). And so in x. 23: "Ye shall not have covered the cities of Israel, before the Son of man comes." The story of the Syro-Phoenician woman is almost of greater significance. Neither evangelist leaves it open to question that this incident represented *an exceptional case* for Jesus; and the exception proves the rule.

In Mark this section on the Syro-Phoenician woman is the only passage where the missionary efforts of Jesus appear positively restricted to the Jewish people in Palestine. Matthew, however, contains not merely the address on the disciples' mission, but a further saying (xix. 28), to the effect that the twelve are one day to judge the twelve tribes of Israel. No word here of the Gentile mission.

Only twice does Mark make Jesus allude to the gospel being preached in future throughout the world: in the eschatological address (xiii. 10, "The gospel must first be preached to all the nations," *i.e.*, before the end arrives), and in the story of the anointing at Bethany (xiv. 9), where we read: "Wherever this gospel shall be preached throughout the whole world, what this woman hath done shall be also told, in memory of her." The former passage puts into the life of Jesus an historical theologoumenon, which is hardly original. The latter excites strong suspicion, not with regard to what precedes it, but in connection with the saying of Jesus in verses 8–9. It is a *hysteron proteron*, and moreover the solemn assurance is striking. Some obscure controversy must underlie the words—a controversy which turned upon the preceding scene not only when it happened, but at a still later date. Was it ever suspected?

These two sayings are also given in Matthew (xxiv. 14, xxvi. 13), who preserves a further saying which has the Gentile world in view, yet whose prophetic manner arouses no suspicion of its authenticity. In viii. 11 we read: "I tell you, many shall come from east and west, and sit down with Abraham and Isaac and Jacob in the kingdom of heaven, but the sons of the kingdom shall be cast out." Why should not Jesus have said this? Even among the words of John the Baptist (iii. 9) do we not read: "Think not to say to yourselves, we have Abraham as our father; for I tell you, God is able to raise up children for Abraham out of these stones"?

We conclude, then, that both evangelists refrain from inserting any allusion to the Gentile mission into the framework of the public preaching of Jesus, apart from the eschatological address and the somewhat venturesome expression which occurs in the story of the anointing at Bethany. But while Matthew delimits the activity of Jesus positively and precisely, Mark adopts what we may term a neutral position, though for all that he does not suppress the story of the Syro-Phoenician woman.

All this throws into more brilliant relief than ever the words of the risen Jesus in Matt. xxviii. 19 f. Matthew must have been fully conscious of the disparity between these words and the earlier words of Jesus; nay, more, he must have deliberately chosen to give expression to that disparity. At the time when our gospels were written, a Lord and Saviour who had confined his preaching to the Jewish people without even issuing a single command to prosecute the universal mission, was an utter impossibility. If no such command had been issued before his death, it must have been imparted by him as the glorified One.

The conclusion, therefore, must be that Jesus never issued such a command at all, but that this version of his life was due to the historical developments of a later age, the words being appropriately put into the mouth of the risen Lord. Paul, too, knew nothing of such a general command.

Luke's standpoint, as a reporter of the words of Jesus, does not differ from that of the two previous evangelists, a fact which is perhaps most significant of all. He has delicately coloured the introductory history with universalism, while at the close, like Matthew, he makes the risen Jesus issue the command to preach the gospel to all nations. But in his treatment of the intervening material he follows Mark; that is, he preserves no sayings which expressly confine the activity of Jesus to the Jewish nation, but, on the other hand, he gives neither word nor incident which describes that activity as universal, and at no point does he deliberately correct the existing tradition.

In this connection the fourth gospel need not be considered at all. After the Gentile mission, which had been undertaken with such ample results during the first two Christian generations, the fourth gospel expands the horizon of Christ's preaching and even of John the Baptist's; corresponding to this, it makes the Jews a reprobate people from the very outset, despite the historical remark in iv. 22. Even setting aside the prologue, we at once come upon (i. 29) the words put into the mouth of the Baptist, "Behold the Lamb of God which taketh away the sin *of the world.*" And, as a whole, the gospel is saturated with statements of a directly universalistic character. Jesus is *the Saviour of the world,* and God so loved *the world* that he sent him. We may add passages like those upon the "other sheep" and the *one* flock (x. 16). But the most significant thing of all is that this gospel makes Greeks ask after Jesus (xii. 20 f.), the latter furnishing a formal explanation of the reasons why he could not satisfy the Greeks as yet. He must first of all die. It is as the exalted One that he will first succeed in drawing *all* men to himself. We can feel here the pressure of a serious problem.

It would be misleading to introduce here any sketch of the preaching of Jesus, or even of its essential principles, for it never became the missionary preaching of the later period even to the Jews. It was the *basis* of that preaching, for the gospels were written down in order to serve as a means of evangelization; but the mission preaching was occupied with the messiahship of Jesus, his speedy return, and his establishment of God's kingdom (if Jews were to be met), or with the unity of God, creation, the Son of God, and judgment (if Gentiles were to be reached). Alongside of this the words of Jesus of course exercised a silent and effective mission of their own, whilst the historical picture furnished by the gospels, together with faith in the exalted Christ, exerted a powerful influence over catechumens and believers.

Rightly and wisely, people no longer noticed the local and temporal traits either in this historical sketch or in these sayings. They found there a vital love of God and men, which may be described as implicit universalism; a discounting of everything external (position, personality, sex, outward worship, etc.), which made irresistibly for inwardness of character; and a protest against the entire doctrines of "the ancients," which gradually rendered antiquity valueless. One of the greatest revolutions in the history of religion was initiated in this way—initiated and effected, moreover, without any revolution! All that Jesus Christ promulgated was the overthrow of the temple, and the judgment impending upon the nation and its leaders. He shattered Judaism, and brought out the kernel of the religion of Israel. Thereby—*i.e.,* by his preaching of God as the Father, and by his own death—he founded the universal religion, which at the same time was the religion of the Son. ✻

4. SHIRLEY JACKSON CASE

FROM Shirley Jackson Case, *The Social Origins of Christianity* (Chicago: University of Chicago Press, 1923), pp. 38–39, 53–57.

Christianity first appeared in history as a religious movement among Palestinian Jews. Jesus was a Jew of Palestine, as were also his personal disciples. Contact with Gentiles during his lifetime was only occasional, and was so exceptional that its mention in the gospels usually calls forth special comment. It was also among the Jews of Palestine that the followers of Jesus assembled after his death when they constituted themselves into a distinct group bound together in loyalty to their crucified master.

From the very outset this new movement was socially conditioned in a much more emphatic way than is commonly appreciated. Its representatives retained a large body of heritages taken over from their ancestors, and carried on their activities in intimate contact with contemporary society. The main problems which they undertook to solve and the principal ends which they aimed to accomplish were furnished to them ready-made by the conditions amid which they lived. Also the dominating interests of the new communities were throughout socially motivated. The members were chiefly concerned with the hope of realizing a new status of society and they regarded it as their primary function to offer a new program for the attainment of this desire. The arid intellectualism of a subsequent age might find its own chief interests satisfied by attempts to define the content of early Christian dogma regarding the person of the Messiah, but the zeal of the first disciples easily overleaped all academic questions in its eager expectation of Jesus' speedy return to establish a new order that would be the "restoration of all things, whereof God spake by the mouth of his holy prophets" (Acts 3:19–21). . . .

The impression made by Jesus upon his contemporaries was so unusually forceful that it aroused a violent opposition which presently cut short his public career. While the main interests and aims which he and his friends represented were genuinely Jewish in character, the methods which they advocated for realizing their desires aroused vigorous hostility. The general content of Jesus' religious ideal of a kingdom of God, to be ushered in as a result of preparation on the part of the people through reconsecration and a heightening of their moral and spiritual sincerities, was not at all out of harmony with current Jewish interests. Rather it was the unconventional methods by which Jesus sought to bring these results to pass that constituted the real basis of opposition between him and his contemporaries. The problem at issue was not so much the question of what end was to be sought, as of the safe path to be pursued in order to arrive at the desired goal. It was on this problem of safe procedure that Jesus and his enemies came to deadly grips.

For centuries the religious leaders among the Jews of Palestine had been building up an elaborate machinery for the cultivation and preservation of religious values. As a result of these devoted efforts on the part of successive generations, society was equipped with a body of well-established institutions highly prized by the great majority of the people, who gave themselves zealously to the support of their religion, confident that their revered institutions had been divinely authenticated and were absolutely essential for the safety of society. Its duly appointed leaders had received a prescribed course of training and were thought to derive their wisdom from a sacred literature believed to contain all directions necessary for the safe conduct of life. One should not fail to appreciate the feeling of responsibility that rested upon these authenticated guardians of the common good and the sense of assurance resulting from devotion to their established institutions. As official protectors of the people's welfare, they undoubtedly felt in duty bound to preserve their institutions intact, while at the same time they entertained a very firm conviction that any other course of procedure would involve danger.

Jesus was not a member of the scribal profession and consequently did not share its psychology. While he had been laboring at the carpenter's bench, the rabbis had been devoting their time to study in the professional schools, and to the practice of their profession along regularly constituted lines. Their situation had been of just the proper sort to engender in them a feeling of sanctity for the established institutions as such. On the other hand, Jesus had been enveloped by conditions which, while not necessarily creating distrust, had not produced the same high estimate of inherent worth attaching to the traditional mechanisms of an established religion. Probably the fundamental ground of opposition between him and the contemporary religious leaders lay in the fact of his failure to appreciate their feeling toward the established social structure. He had not received that professional training necessary to produce the attitude of mind which emphasizes the importance of a traditional technique for the preservation of values.

When Jesus set himself up as a leader of the people, his direct and spontaneous procedure inevitably aroused the suspicion of those who had been trained by a different method, who had a different attitude, and who consequently held a different opinion regarding the way in which the values of life were to be secured. To the professional scribes Jesus cannot have seemed other than a menace to the welfare of Jewish society. His lack of deference toward methods which custom had decreed to be correct procedure in matters of religion must have been cause for deep anxiety on the part of those who felt themselves intrusted with the responsibilities of religious leadership. That they would be hostile to Jesus and make a very conscious and sincere effort to resist his work was, under the circumstances, a foregone conclusion. To them he must have appeared in the light of a dangerous non-conformist, who by unauthenticated modes of conduct was undermining the very foundation of the religious superstructure and thereby endangering the welfare of the whole Jewish race.

As Jesus persisted in his methods his opponents became more firm in their conviction of the danger involved in his activity. With the strengthening of their opposition, he and his group were placed more distinctly on the defensive and forced to assume the rôle of a discordant element in society. But the conflict was an unequal one. The sentiment of the majority naturally favored the preservation of the existing institutions and any individual or minor group that seemed to threaten the well-being of society by disregard for the customs, or even by an attitude of non-conformity, could appear only as a menace whose removal alone would insure safety.

5. JULES LEBRETON and JACQUES ZEILLER

FROM Jules Lebreton and Jacques Zeiller, *The History of the Primitive Church*, 2 vols. (New York: The Macmillan Company, 1949), vol. I, 83–86, 91–93, 105–9.

When St. Paul was a prisoner at Caesarea in the year A.D. 60 and expounded to King Agrippa the mission of Jesus and his own Apostolate, he was able to say: "The king knoweth of these things, to whom also I speak with confidence. For I am persuaded that none of these things are hidden from him. For neither was any of these things done in a corner" (*Acts* xxvi, 26). All historians share this assurance: the life and death of Jesus, the beginnings of the Church at Jerusalem, the travels and preaching of St. Paul —all this is clear to us in the full light of history.

Born "in the days of Herod the king," put to death, as Tacitus records, by the procurator Pontius Pilate, baptised by John, condemned by Annas and Caiphas, Jesus lived and preached in Judea in a period well known to us, and came up against those procurators, tetrarchs and high priests of whom we have written in the preceding chapter, utilising Josephus, Philo, and pagan historians. From the short life of Jesus the Church was born. Full of life and vigour, it flourished in Jerusalem, in Judea, then in Syria, and then in the whole Greco-Roman world. In A.D. 51, the proconsul of Achaia, Gallio, brother to Seneca, saw it spreading round him at Corinth; in A.D. 64 Nero's persecution at Rome affected, according to Tacitus, a "great multitude." That was only thirty-five years after the death of Jesus. All this has not the appearance of a dream, in an imaginary setting; all "takes its place in an historical setting of unquestioned continuity."

The Gospels

These great events live again for us in writings in which we hear the voice of the primitive church and its leaders—the *Gospels*, *Epistles*, and *Acts*. That becomes apparent to us on the threshold of this history in the study of the life of Jesus. The Gospels are not just literary works which have resulted from the initiative of a few writers; they are not books created by the authors whose names they bear, Matthew, Mark, Luke, or even John: they are catecheses taught for some time previously, and finally put in writing.

Certainly, these books bear the individual impress of the witnesses who have drawn them up or on whom they depend: in Matthew we recognise the Apostle of the Jews converted to Christianity, stressing the prophecies of the Old Testament, showing in the Gospel the fulfilment of the Law, warning the disciples against the leaven of the Pharisees. Mark is the interpreter of Peter, and this gives to his Gospel the freshness and charm of Galilean memories; Luke, the companion of St. Paul, did not know the Lord personally, but as a diligent historian he profited by his lengthy stay at Caesarea to question the disciples of Jesus and to gather recollections of His infancy from Mary. Of all the evangelists, John has most deeply impressed his own personality on his book. We shall describe it later on.

These individual characteristics give to the witness of the evangelists a character which makes them nearer to us, and more persuasive. But at the same time, the testimony which these books bring us is above all the testimony of the Church. From the very first, this witness is presented as a collective one: it is not a number of isolated individuals but the entire group of Apostles who narrate the life and teaching of the Master whom they followed during the whole course of His public life and even after His death, until His Ascension. In one of His last appearances, Jesus had said to them: "You shall be witnesses to me"; this testimony, given in all fidelity and freedom, was their first duty, and to the Jewish magistrates who sought to impose silence upon them, they replied through Peter, their head and spokesman, "We cannot but speak the things which we have seen and heard" (*Acts* iv, 20; cf., v. 29).

The Witness of the Church

It was from this daily preaching by the Church that the Gospel arose, and its character and guarantee come from the same source. Its aim was not to satisfy the curiosity of its readers, but to uphold the faith of the believers. Towards the end of his Gospel, St. John writes (xx, 30–31): "Many other signs also did Jesus in the sight of his disciples, which are not written in this book, but these are written that you may believe that Jesus is the Christ, the Son of God, and that believing you may have life in His name." The other evangelists have the same aim: the good news which they bring is salvation; their whole aim is to bring out the person of the Saviour, His teaching and His redemptive work.

The Church, then, did not aim at giving us a complete account of the life of Christ which would enable us to study and date all its development; in endeavouring to understand and interpret its testimony, we must respect its nature, and see in it a document of religious history rather than a biography of Jesus; its lacunae must not surprise us, nor the difficulty which we often find in localising the incidents, or marking their date or succession.

On the other hand, this religious character of the testimony provides us with the most certain guarantee of its fidelity. It was by contemplating the miracles of Jesus that the first disciples were converted (*John* ii, 11); it was by hearing them or reading their account that the new Christians came in their turn to the Faith. The office of an Apostle was thus that of a faithful witness, attesting what he had seen, heard, and touched, and by his testimony putting his catechumens in contact with Christ. If the facts which he reported were not true, his witness would be a lie, and the faith of his converts would be vain. . . .

Near the Jordan, Jesus called his first disciples, and it was then that He began to preach and to act. A problem here presents itself to the historian: did Jesus have a clearly defined plan, and did He follow this in his public ministry?

One feature of this plan is manifest, and very clearly marked: until His death, Jesus limited His ministry to the children of Israel; pressed by the

Canaanite woman, He put her off, saying: "I was not sent but to the sheep that are lost of the house of Israel" (*Matt.* xv, 24). He had already laid down the same limits when sending the Apostles on their mission: "Go ye not into the way of the Gentiles, and into the city of the Samaritans enter ye not. But go ye rather to the lost sheep of the house of Israel" (*Matt.* x, 5–6). We have already remarked when describing the state of Palestine in the time of Christ that these pagan and Samaritan towns were scattered all over the land of Israel, and if any did not enter them, it was because they intended to avoid them.

This reserve appears still more clearly in the exceptions which it allowed, and which were granted only for pressing reasons. The centurion of Capharnaum did not dare to go to Jesus himself, but had his request presented by Jews, who recommended him as a benefactor of their nation: "He is worthy that thou shouldst do this for him, for he loveth our nation, and he hath built us a synagogue" (*Luke* vii, 5).

The Canaanite woman, at first sent away by the Apostles and put off by Jesus, obtained only by her persistence the miracle which she sought (*Matt.* xv). The Greeks, who came to Jerusalem for the Pasch and who wanted to see Jesus, did not dare to accost him directly; they timidly expressed their desire to Philip, "who was of Bethsaida of Galilee"; Philip told Andrew, and the two presented the request to Jesus (*John* xii, 20–22).

Doubtless this reserve was not absolute or final. Jesus already made this understood in connection with the incidents we have just recalled. To the Greeks He replied by this prophecy: "The hour is come that the Son of man should be glorified. Amen, amen I say to you, unless the grain of wheat falling into the ground die, itself remaineth alone. But if it die, it bringeth forth much fruit. . . . And I, if I be lifted up from the world, will draw all men to myself." This universal fecundity was promised to Christ's ministry, but was gathered to Him only by His death. The grain of wheat had to fall to the ground and die; Jesus had to be lifted up on the cross. After His Passion, all the barriers fell down, and there was no limit to the mission of the Apostles: "All power is given to me in heaven and in earth. Going therefore teach ye all nations. . . ." (*Matt.* xxviii, 18–20).

This triumphant expansion will be set forth in the history of the Apostles. We shall then point out that it was the will of Jesus which sent them through the world, and that it was His death which secured the wonderful fruitfulness of their activity. But during the two and a half years of the Lord's ministry, the Jews alone, with a few very rare exceptions, were the hearers of His discourses and the beneficiaries of His miracles.

This feature of Christ's mission being understood, can we go further, and discover in His ministry to the Jews a plan drawn up in advance and followed out by Him? If we study the gospel narratives, and especially the earliest, this plan is not evident at first sight: we rather have the impression of a series of preachings and miracles, arising out of chance circumstances or rather Divine Providence, but not at all due to a deliberate plan, tracing out a path mapped out by Jesus from the beginning. The evangelisation of Galilee by Christ and His Apostles would rather resemble the preaching of the first disciples of St. Francis through Italy and the world.

But a more careful reading leads us to see that this first impression is due above all to the manner of composition of the early Christian catechesis, which cared little for chronology, and was much more attentive to the religious import of each episode than to the connection or progress of the different phases in the ministry of Jesus. We very soon note another cause of this apparent confusion: the plan foreseen and adopted by Jesus may indeed be little evident in the early narratives, but it was in Christ's own lifetime upset and broken by the constant opposition of His enemies. The reading of St. John enables us to reconstitute the original plan of the Master, at least in its main outline: He aimed at the conquest of Israel, and primarily of Jerusalem the capital, the Holy City, whose adhesion or opposition would be decisive. This plan, adopted at the beginning and returned to several times in spite of an obstinate opposition, finally collapsed before the irreducible hostility of the Jews and especially of their leaders. And then another plan appeared: Israel had not been won, and it would not be as a whole the missionary people it should have been, but from it Jesus would draw a faithful élite, the little group of Apostles and disciples which would form the hierarchy of the Church and would conquer the world. . . .

Next we have the fundamental question of the Old Law and the New. No case of conscience was graver or more pressing for the hearers of Christ. Nothing was more sacred to them than the Law, which was the Oracle of God. Nothing was dearer, for it was the privilege of Israel. And yet this law was heavy to bear, and Jesus more than once had given an example of a freer observance of the Sabbath, and of the distinction between pure and impure. In the presence of the scandalised Pharisees, he upheld this liberty, affirming that "the Sabbath was made for man, and not man for the Sabbath" (*Mark* ii, 27). He had also said that "no man seweth a piece of raw cloth to an old garment" or "putteth new wine into old bottles" (*ibid.*, 21–22). Soon afterwards he would say: "Not that which goeth into the mouth defileth a man, but what cometh out of the mouth" (*Matt.* xv, 11).

How strange this sounds when we remember that the distinction between pure and impure food was so sacred for the Jews that in order to uphold it the martyrs had laid down their lives in the days of the Machabees (*II Mach.*, vi–vii).

Of the principles laid down by Jesus the applications were to appear only progressively, in the light of the Holy Spirit, but already the Sermon on the Mount quietened the uneasiness of the Jews and showed them that the Gospel is not the abrogation but the accomplishment of the Law:

> "Do not think that I am come to destroy the law or the prophets. I am not come to destroy, but to fulfil. For amen I say unto you, till heaven and earth pass, one jot or one tittle shall not pass of the law, till all be fulfilled. He therefore that shall break one of these least commandments, and shall so teach men, shall be called the least in the kingdom of heaven. But he that shall do and teach, he shall be called great in the kingdom of heaven. For I tell you, that unless your justice abound more than that of the scribes and Pharisees, you shall not enter into the kingdom of heaven" (*Matt.* v, 17–20).

We see already what the Gospel is going to give to the Law: a greater perfection, more intimate requirements. The part of the sermon that follows enables us the better to understand this. It is not only murder that is forbidden, but also anger in thought and word; not only adultery, but also evil desires. Divorce was tolerated by Moses, this toleration is suppressed; no more vain oaths, but the simplicity of a speech which is always sincere; no more vengeance or even resistance to evil; no more narrowness in charity, but the love of enemies after the example of the heavenly Father, "who maketh his sun to shine upon the good and bad, and raineth upon the just and the unjust. . . . Be you therefore perfect, as also your heavenly Father is perfect."

Henceforth in the moral and religious life all is sincere, all is deep. This is indeed a new and more intimate requirement, but at the same time it is a deliverance. No more regulated attitude or correct appearance masking evil desires, or whited sepulchre concealing a corpse; virtue springs forth quite spontaneously fron the depths of life; it is this living water that Jesus promises to those who believe in Him. Hence as the soul becomes stronger, it can lay aside all those precepts which protected its infancy as a hedge protects a young crop; the Christian will be able to say with St. Paul: "Now that I have become a man, I have put away the things of a child." And if he gives himself up wholly and without reserve to the requirements of Christ, he will realise that the multiplicity of precepts are reduced to unity: the love of God and of one's neighbour is the whole law and the prophets (*Matt.* xxii, 36), and he will find that all the powers of his soul are carried along by the simplicity of the divine life which inspires it. Truly the yoke of Christ is easy, and His burden light (*Matt.* xi, 30).

It is above all when He promulgates this Christian moral teaching, so exigent and so beneficial, that Jesus speaks with full independence and authority: He recalls the imperfect laws which the Jews had received from Moses: "It was said to you"; and He adds: "But I say to you. . . ." All readers, even the most distant from our faith, have felt the force of these antitheses. Certainly no one who was not the author of the Law could treat it with at once more independence and more respect; the legislator had been able to give to a difficult people only a sketchy law; upon Christians, whom the Spirit is going to teach and fortify, the Master imposes, with His sovereign authority, a perfect law.

Interior Religion

Then He carries on the religious formation of His disciples, leading them on towards a wholly internal righteousness, in the secret of a life which is witnessed only by the heavenly Father (*Matt.* vi, 1–18). Here above all the example of Jesus is even more pressing than His teaching: "He that sent me is with me and He hath not left me alone," "I do always the things that please Him"; "my meat is to do the will of Him that sent me, that I may perfect His work." There is, of course, in the Father and the Son a unity of nature to which we cannot attain, and even in the human nature of Jesus there is the beatific vision which raises Him up irresistibly towards the Father and which we do not possess here below. But though all this surpasses us, it is, as it were, the ideal model to which we must unceasingly tend. The Master who has said to us: "Be ye perfect as your heavenly Father is perfect," has also said of us, addressing His Father: "That they may be one even as we are one, I in them and thou in me, that they may be made perfect in one."

In this teaching on internal religion and union with the heavenly Father, as in the preaching of the beatitudes, Jesus manifests Himself to us in and through His doctrine; more so than His first hearers, we who know Him better, realise that what He gives us here is the secret of His own life, and this life draws us more strongly still than His words. It is by this discreet revelation that He makes Himself henceforth known and loved. The imitation of Christ will be for all Christians from St. Paul onwards the supreme rule of morality; the Master, always anxious to efface Himself, will set forth this ideal model only towards the end of His life, and above all at the Last Supper, but already from the beginning of His ministry, His most faithful and clear-sighted disciples will be able to contemplate it in the transparency of His teaching.

Above all, there is the authority of His words: "It was said to them of old. . . . But I say to you. . . ." This sovereign dignity appears perhaps even better in the blessings attached to persecution: "Blessed are ye when they shall speak all that is evil against you, for my sake" (*Matt.* v, 11), and in the description of the Last Judgment: "Then will I profess unto them, 'I never knew you, depart from me, you that work iniquity'" (*Matt.* vii, 23). To sacrifice one's life for Jesus is eternal bliss; not to be recognised by Him is damnation.

It is thus that Jesus revealed Himself to the multitude of His disciples; the superhuman greatness of His mission and His nature is manifested discreetly but very efficaciously in the doctrine in which it is implied: whoever recognises in Jesus the supreme legislator, the unique revealer of the Father, the master whose cause deserves every sacrifice, and promises every reward, the judge who will decide the fate of all—such a one has only to confess, with St. Peter: "Thou art Christ, the Son of the living God."

But in order that this teaching may bear its fruit, it is not sufficient that the mind should understand it and be pleased with it: it is necessary that this doctrine should become the efficacious rule of our lives. That constitutes the concluding part of the sermon of Jesus:

> "Everyone therefore that heareth these my words, and doth them, shall be likened to a wise man that built his house upon a rock. And the rain fell, and the floods came, and the winds blew, and they beat upon that house, and it fell not, for it was founded on a rock.
>
> "And everyone that heareth these my words, and doth them not, shall be like a foolish man that built his house upon the sand. And the rain fell, and the floods came, and the winds blew, and they beat upon that house, and it fell, and great was the fall thereof" (*Matt.* vii, 24–27).

At the time of the great crisis, when, in presence of an almost universal defection, Jesus says to the Apostles: "Will you also go away?" Peter replies: "To whom shall we go? Thou hast the words of eternal life" (*John* vi, 68). Here we have the house built upon the rock, the rock against which the gates of hell shall not prevail, but what gives to this faith the firmness of a rock is the generous practice which has tested the words of Jesus and has recognised therein "the words of eternal life." Many admired the "words of grace" which proceeded from the mouth of Jesus (*Luke* iv, 22), many rejoiced in His light, but this admiration and joy were dissipated by the first storm. The most certain proof of the faith, and the one which gives it its unshakable firmness, is the fruits which it bears; but he only can taste these who has made his faith the rule of his life. ✺

6. JOSEPH KLAUSNER

FROM Joseph Klausner, *From Jesus to Paul* (New York: The Macmillan Company, 1943), pp. 3–6, 588–90.

"Jesus was not a Christian, he was a Jew"—this short and incisive sentence of Julius Wellhausen is a result of a hundred and fifty years of research. And this is also the principal conclusion of a Hebrew book of some hundreds of pages.

Jesus called upon the Jews to repent and do good works in order that they might become fit for the Days of the Messiah. Elijah the prophet, herald of the Messiah, had already come, and he himself, Jesus, was the Messiah. He said plainly to his disciples: "There are some here of them that stand by, who shall in no wise taste of death, till they see the Kingdom of God come with power," and ". . . verily I say unto you, Ye shall not have gone through the cities of Israel, till the Son of Man be come"; also he said, "This generation shall not pass away, until all these things be accomplished." There was only one condition necessary in order that the Kingdom of Heaven might come: to fulfill all that was written in the Law and the Prophets as the Pharisees demanded and even in greater measure than they demanded: "For I say unto you, that except your righteousness shall exceed the righteousness of the scribes and Pharisees, ye shall in no wise enter into the Kingdom of Heaven." The meaning was that the ceremonial laws, the laws of relations between man and God, cannot release man from carrying out the moral laws, the laws of relations between men and their fellows: ". . . these ye ought to have done, and not to have left the other undone." In spite of the opposition to this on the part of manifold scholars for various reasons, one must assert the view that Jesus saw himself sent, as Messiah, first of all and above all, "to the lost sheep of the house of Israel," and that he conceived of his relationship to the "Gentiles" as did every Jew of those days: the relationship of a son of the Chosen People (for whom the names "son of Abraham" and "daughter of Abraham" were appellations of love just as they are for the Talmud) to an errant and inferior mankind.

It is clear, then, that it did not even enter the mind of Jesus to form a new religion and proclaim it outside the Jewish nation. The Law and the Prophets—these were his faith and his religion; the people of Israel—this was the people to whom this religion had been given as an inheritance and who must establish it in its fulness—in its two parts: the ceremonial and the moral; as a result "the Days of the Messiah" and "the Kingdom of Heaven" would come, and then also the rest of the nations would be changed into worshippers of the One God and fulfillers of his Law, that is to say, they would become Jews.

By this two important questions are raised: *one*, How did it happen that from this completely Jewish, prophetic Pharisaic teaching there came forth a new religion?—and the *second*, How was there formed by this thorough Jew a faith which had such a particular appeal to pagans?

The first question I have attempted to answer in my book *Jesus of Nazareth*. In my opinion there were certain elements in the Judaism of Jesus that made it non-Judaism. When Jesus, for example, *overemphasized* that God was "*my* Father in heaven," he thereby brought it about that the disciples and their immediate followers found it possible, because of foreign influences in their environment, to take his words too literally and to make him only a little less than God, and finally—even to see in him the real Son of God. When Jesus, in his interpretation of prophetic Pharisaic Jewish ethics, went to extremes and forbade *all* swearing and the administration of justice *in general, completely* disregarded marriage and property relations, and did not recognize *at all* the importance of bettering existing conditions, since "the present world" is nothing but a state of transition to the Days of the Messiah and "the world to come"—by overfilling the measure of Judaism he caused his disciples and those that came after them to make from it non-Judaism. Specialists in optics know that there is a way of increasing light whereby the light is turned to darkness. Quantitative exaggeration of a thing sometimes turns it into a new quality, as many drops of water turn a brook into a river and a river into a sea, or as exaggerated resoluteness becomes impertinence and excessive humility, servility.

But this is only one of the answers to the first question: because of the extremism of Jesus with regard to the relations between himself and deity and because of his extreme emphasis on ethics, his disciples were able to attach the new religion to a good authority—to Jesus, who gave, although unconsciously, a certain impetus toward a new religion. One reason like this is not sufficient. By an impetus alone a new religion is not formed and spread with the speed and to the extent that characterized Christianity. There is need for still other reasons and causes.

This is the case also with regard to the solution of the second question: the departure of the new religion from the community of Israel and its spread among the Gentiles. Also here there are reasons and causes outside of Jesus.

The rise of Christianity and its spread among pagans were brought about by three other fundamental causes: first, *the dispersion of the Jews outside of Palestine;* second, *the spiritual conditions among the Gentiles at that time;* and third, *the Hellenistic Jewish culture of the non-Palestinian Jews in those days.* . . .

Jesus only *unwittingly* laid the foundation for a new religion by an *excessive* emphasis upon certain *radical* Jewish ideas—and no more; only by his unnatural death as a suffering Messiah did he become the authoritative source upon which depended a new religion. But the ideological and organizational structure of the Christian faith as a *religion* and as a *church* was built by Paul the Hellenistic Jew, born in Tarsus, educated in Jerusalem, a reader of the Septuagint, a writer of excellent Greek, and—a pupil of Rabban Gamaliel.

There is no doubt of the fact (although the proponents of Form Criticism attribute all this to "the necessities of preaching") that Jesus confined his mission "to the lost sheep of the house of Israel," and said that "it is not proper to take the children's bread and cast it to the little dogs." Nevertheless, because of the emphasis on the part of Jesus upon the higher value of ethics as compared with the ceremonial laws, it was possible for his disciples to find in his words the germ of the equalization of Gentiles with Jews in the Messianic Age (Days of the Messiah). This germ could also be found in Judaism, since according to it all the Gentiles would be saved in the Messianic Age, provided that they became proselytes and took upon themselves the yoke of Torah and ceremonial laws—as far as these laws might remain valid in the Age to Come. But the extreme conclusion that Torah and ceremonial laws must be set aside from the beginning for Gentiles, and afterwards for the Jews also, even before the realization of the Kingdom of Heaven (before the "Parousia" of Jesus as chief magistrate on the Day of Judgment)—this bold conclusion could have been reached only by Paul the Jew of the Diaspora, Paul who had lived among Gentiles and had been influenced more or less unconsciously by their doctrines and their mysteries. Without this, the faith in Jesus, retaining observance of the ceremonial laws as demanded by James the brother of Jesus and James' associates, the "Ebionite" Jewish Nazarenes, would have constituted *only a Jewish religious sect,* which after a time would have been absorbed into the main stock of Judaism, or else would have continually grown weaker, like the Samaritans and the Karaites.

So it was with the other matters common to Jesus and Paul. Jesus' belief, that as Messiah he would sit "at the right hand of Power" to judge the world and its peoples, became at the hands of Paul a belief in Jesus "the heavenly man," as opposed to the "earthly man" or the "first Adam." The *excessive* emphasis upon the words "*my* heavenly Father" on the part of Jesus was carried by Paul to the next to the last extreme (the last extreme being the doctrine of the Trinity), wherein God does everything through his "Son" Christ. From the emphasis upon the importance of the Holy Spirit in connexion with the Messiah and the Messianic Age, Paul created the theory of the radical difference between "flesh" and "spirit," and the theory of the spiritual ("pneumatic") man as distinguished from both the fleshly ("carnal") man and the natural ("psychical") man. From the customs of ritual ablution and the fellowship meal as practised by Jesus, Paul made "sacraments," that is to say, mystical acts by which man is joined in union with God or Christ. And from the impractical and pessimistic attitude of Jesus toward marriage and divorce, Paul made fixed rules for the new Church, of which, if he was not the creator, he certainly was the founder and the one who determined its characteristic form.

Thus it can be said with finality: *without Jesus no Paul and no Nazarenes;* but *without Paul no world Christianity.* And in this sense, Jesus was not the founder of Christianity as it was spread among the Gentiles, but Paul "the apostle of the Gentiles," in spite of the fact that Paul based himself on Jesus, and in spite of all that Paul received from the primitive church in Jerusalem. �֎

7. CHARLES GUIGNEBERT

FROM Charles Guignebert, *The Jewish World in the Time of Jesus* (London: Kegan Paul, Trench, Trubner & Co., Ltd., 1939), pp. 258–61.

As for the *Gospel*, it was in origin the book in which a sect, originally issuing out of Israel, had laid down the first principles of its hope and faith, but it was born outside of Israel, and the writers who have given us the three oldest versions of it, *viz.* the Gospel according to *Mark, Matthew* and *Luke*, and still more to the author and redactor of *John*, were already completely outside Judaism. Nevertheless, just as the elements which make up the oldest parts of the *Talmud* derived their origin from the Schools of the Scribes and the inspiration of the Pharisees, so the Jewish basis of the *Gospel* proceeds at one and the same time from the religion of the *'anavim* and from the piety, principles and hopes of Pharisaism. Moreover, these two sources alone do not exhaust the whole content of the complex soul and heterogeneous spirit of Israel, as it has been revealed to us.

Perhaps in course of time the discordant elements which we have met in

Palestinian Jewry might have been reconciled, and all the divergent tendencies co-ordinated in a single movement, but we cannot imagine what could have become the principle and actuating force of this happy harmonization. In the present confusion it is the Messianic hope alone which appears to have been sufficiently widespread and deeply rooted in the masses of the people to constitute such a force. It had within it the power, even if imperfectly realized, *i.e.* only on the human level and in the unstable form of the political emancipation of the people of God, to rally round it all the Jews of Palestine.

The final goal of the Messianic movement was, undoubtedly, the establishment of the Kingdom of God upon a regenerated earth. Nevertheless, from the ways and means by which its foundation was visualized, the forms under which its realization was envisaged, and from the dreams which its expectation aroused and the pictures it evoked in the hope of the Jews, it is clear that this vision of regeneration assumed an entirely nationalistic expression. In one sense, it presented itself as the final and overwhelming victory of those who had always been the conquered, and it was taken for granted that its natural prelude would be a revolt. "*God helps those who help themselves*" might well have served as the war-cry of the Zealots. It is precisely for this reason that the message brought by Jesus (if, indeed, it was such as the Synoptic Gospels represent it to have been), calling for the moral transformation of the individual and for a spirit of resignation whose only reward was the promise of supernatural bliss in "*the Coming Kingdom,*" had no chance of acceptance, and was not in fact accepted, by the prophet's fellow-countrymen.

The small band of the Nazarene's disciples continued in Jerusalem for some years after his death, in a state of arrested development, and only succeeded in making a very small number of converts. Statements to the contrary in the Acts of the Apostles will not bear the most superficial criticism.

On the other hand, the testimony of those whom we call the Apostles found more willing ears among certain Jews of the Dispersion whose religious duties brought them on pilgrimages to the Holy City. Such men, living outside Palestine, in a Gentile environment, no longer clung so firmly as did their brethren to the expectation of a warrior Messiah or the hope of a nationalistic revival of the Davidic Kingdom.

There came a day, probably not long after the death of Jesus, when certain of the Hellenistic Jews who had been converted to the Galilean hope began to vex the pure Jews of Jerusalem by entering the synagogues and advocating their faith with undue zeal. In consequence of this, they were all expelled from the city and scattered abroad, the greater part of them, no doubt, returning to their homelands. This was an event of cardinal importance, since the message which these men carried with them found on the soil of the Diaspora more favourable conditions of survival and of development than in Palestine, even among the genuine Jews whom constant intercourse with the Gentiles had broadened. Their nationalism had become blunted and their Messianism, gradually contaminated by the mixed environment of Greek thought and Oriental mysticism, evolved in time into a kind of universalist salvationism. Above all, their synagogues were surrounded by proselytes whose religious needs, interests and aspirations remained at root intensely personal, nay, individual, and who therefore evinced but little sympathy for the religious "totalitarianism" of orthodox Jewry and for its painful and uncomfortable demands. It was among these men that true Christianity, regarded as a religion, came to birth.

It was probably at Antioch that *"the brethren who called on the name of the Lord Jesus"* first became a conscious entity, and it was in that city that they received from the pagans the name by which they were to be noted through the ages, viz. *Christians*, or *believers in Christ*.

Behind the converts to Judaism there was the mass of pagans many of whom found themselves stirred by the same unrest as had led the Judaizers to the synagogue, and who were ready to be attracted to the Church. To them—and it may be said, through them also—the Jewish Messiah assumed the complexion and rôle of a *Soter* and rose inevitably to the status of absolute divinity.

We can well understand that Jesus of Nazareth should have been born in Galilee, and that the impulse behind his career should have been the expectation of the Messianic Kingdom; we can also understand that he should have drawn from the religion of the 'anavim and the piety of the Pharisees the fundamental elements of his spiritual development, the inspiration of his mission, and the substance of his teaching, welding together these various influences and stamping them with his own forceful personality. Indeed, as he appears behind the veil wherewith early Christian imagination has shrouded him, he is plainly inexplicable except as the product of this environment. It is, moreover, by no means impossible that there were other prophets of the same order, at present unknown to us, who arose in Palestine at the same time. If so, and if they really existed alongside of or in competition with the more warlike agitators, their obscure fate has been shrouded in oblivion, for lack of that apotheosis which martyrdom alone can earn. In any case, men of this type, to which Jesus himself belonged, could not possibly hope for success in Palestine. The prophet of Nazareth never gave voice to the sentiments necessary, if not to interest, then at least to attract and move the mass of his countrymen. It is, therefore, readily comprehensible that they did not follow him.

On the other hand, it is equally easy to understand how his personality and his utterances, when transplanted and adapted to the environment of the Diaspora, were found acceptable there, and, by the help of certain accommodations whose number and consequences were limited by no insurmountable obstacle, they there became the centre of a powerful and fruitful religion.

Developed to its logical extreme, Palestinian Judaism led perforce to the Great Rebellion, and hence to the downfall of the Jewish nation. Similarly, the spiritual evolution of the Judaism of the Diaspora would produce a religion, based on Israelitic monotheism and the ethic of the Mosaic Law, but based on the form and spirit of a universalist Salvationism, ready at all times to assimilate anything of religious vitality which came within its range.

Such a religion indeed saw the light of day, and it goes under the name of Christianity. To the historian, it might possibly appear as no more than the natural consequence of the appearance on Palestinian soil of a Messianic prophet of distinctively Jewish character. In reality, however, its true antecedents lie on Hellenistic soil, for it was in Hellenistic Judaism that it found its *raison d'être*, there it was born, nurtured and reared, and there it fulfilled its destiny. ✴

8. RUDOLF BULTMANN

FROM Rudolf Bultmann, *Primitive Christianity* (Cleveland: The World Publishing Company, 1956), pp. 86–93, 175–79.

The preaching of Jesus is controlled by an imminent expectation of the Reign of God. In this he stands in a line with Jewish eschatology in general, though clearly not in its nationalistic form. He never speaks of a political Messiah who will destroy the enemies of Israel, of the establishment of a Jewish world empire, the gathering of the twelve tribes, of peace and prosperity in the land, or anything of that kind. Instead, we find in his preaching the cosmic hopes of apocalyptic writers. True, he never indulges in learned or fantastic speculation such as we find in their works. He never looks back upon the past epochs of world history or attempts to date the End. He never invites his hearers to look for signs of the end in nature or history. Equally, he eschews all elaboration of detail as regards the judgement, resurrection and future glory. All these elements are absorbed in the single all-embracing thought that God will then reign. Only a few apocalyptic traits appear here and there in his teaching. Jesus clearly believes that the present age is ebbing out. Mark's summary of his preaching ('The time is fulfilled, and the Reign of God has drawn nigh', Mark 1.15) is a fair representation of numerous sayings of Jesus which point to a new future and characterize the present as the time of decision.

Jesus expects the coming of the 'Man' as the Judge and agent of redemption. He looks for the resurrection of the dead and the judgement. He describes the blessedness of the righteous simply as 'life'. True, he sometimes speaks of the heavenly banquet, when the righteous will sit down to meat with Abraham, Isaac and Jacob (Matt. 8.11; Luke 13.28f.), or of the prospect of drinking wine in the Reign of God (Mark 14.25). But it is difficult to be sure how far such sayings are meant to be taken literally, or only figuratively. In any case, when the Sadducees try to reduce the doctrine of the resurrection to an absurdity by a materialistic conception of life in the age of redemption, he counters their arguments by saying: 'When they rise from the dead, they neither marry, nor are given in marriage but are as the angels which are in heaven' (Mark 12.25).

If Jesus takes over the apocalyptic view of the future, he does so with considerable reductions. The unique feature in his teaching is the assurance with which he proclaims that *Now* has the time come. The Reign of God is breaking in. The time of the End is at hand.

> Blessed are the eyes which see the things that ye see:
> For I tell you,
> that many prophets and kings have desired to see the things which ye see,
> and have not seen them;
> and to hear those things which ye hear,
> and have not heard them (Luke 10.23f.; Matt. 13.16f.).

It is no time now to mourn or fast; the time for joy is breaking in. It is the time for the 'marriage' (Mark 2.18f.). Hence this word of encouragement for those who were waiting for God's Reign:

> Blessed are ye poor:
> for yours is the kingdom of God.
> Blessed are ye that hunger now:
> for ye shall be filled.
> Blessed are ye that weep now:
> for ye shall laugh (Luke 6.20f.).

There are, of course, signs of the times, though not the kind expected in apocalyptic fantasy: 'The kingdom of God cometh not with observation:

Neither shall they say, Lo here! or, lo there! for, behold, the Reign of God is (in a trice) in your midst' (Luke 17.20f.). 'For as the lightning, that lighteneth out of the one part under heaven, shineth unto the other part of heaven; so also must the Son of man be in his day' (Luke 17.24).

The people are blind to the true signs of the times:

> When ye see a cloud rise out of the west, straightway ye say, There cometh a shower; and so it is. And when ye see the south wind blow, ye say, There will be heat; and it cometh to pass. Ye hypocrites, ye can discern the face of the sky, and of the earth; but how is it that ye do not discern this time? (Luke 12.54–6).

> Now learn a parable of the fig tree:
> When her branch is yet tender, and putteth forth leaves,
> ye know that summer is near:
> So ye in like manner, when ye shall see these things come to pass,
> know that he is nigh, even at the doors (Mark 13.28f.).

Who is this 'he'? The 'Man'! But what is meant by 'when ye see these things come to pass'? What are the signs of the times? Jesus repudiates the Pharisees' demand for a sign: 'Why doth this generation seek after a sign? verily I say unto you, There shall be no sign given unto this generation' (Mark 8.11f.). God does not expose his doings to tangible criteria. They cannot be discerned by calculation, however ingenious, but only by an inner receptivity for Jesus' words and works. He himself, his appearance on the stage of history, his words, and his deeds—they are the signs of the times.

> The blind receive their sight, and the lame walk,
> the lepers are cleansed, and the deaf hear,
> the dead are raised up, and the poor have the gospel preached
>   unto them (Matt. 11.5; Luke 7.22).

The predictions of the prophets (for it is in their words that this saying is couched) are in process of fulfilment. Endowed with the power of the Spirit, Jesus is beginning to heal the sick and to cast out demons, to which, in common with his contemporaries, he attributed human suffering.

'If I by the finger of God cast out devils, no doubt the kingdom of God is come upon you' (Luke 11.20; Matt. 12.28). 'No man can enter into a strong man's house, and spoil his goods, except he first bind the strong man; and then he will spoil his goods' (Mark 3.27). In the flight of the demons men can discern already the overthrow of Satan. 'I beheld Satan as lightning fall from heaven. Behold, I give you power to tread on serpents and scorpions, and over all the power of the enemy and nothing shall by any means hurt you' (Luke 10.18f.).

There is no way of expediting the course of events God has determined —for instance, by a strict observance of the commandments and penitential exercises, as the Pharisees thought, or by force of arms, as the Zealots imagined.

> For so is the kingdom of God, as if a man should cast seed into the ground; And should sleep, and rise night and day, and the seed should spring and grow up, he knoweth not how. For the earth bringeth forth fruit of herself; first the blade, then the ear, after that the full corn in the ear. But when the fruit is brought forth, immediately he putteth in the sickle, because the harvest is come (Mark 4.26–9).

All man can do is to be ready, to 'turn'. Now is the time of decision. Jesus' preaching is a summons to decision.

'Blessed is he, whosoever shall not be offended in me' (Matt. 11.6; Luke 7.23). The 'Queen of the south' once came to hear the wisdom of Solomon: the Ninevites repented at the preaching of Jonah: 'and behold, a greater than Solomon is here . . . a greater than Jonah is here' (Luke 11.31f.; Matt. 12.41f.). 'Whosoever therefore shall be ashamed of me and of my words in this adulterous and sinful generation; of him shall the Son of man be ashamed, when he cometh in the glory of his Father with the holy angels' (Mark 8.38).

In the last analysis therefore Jesus himself in his person is the 'sign of the time'. This, however, does not mean that he invites men to believe in himself. He does not, for instance, proclaim himself as Messiah. In fact, he points to the Messiah, the 'Man', as the Coming One distinct from himself. He himself is the personal embodiment of the challenge to decision. His word invites men to decide for the Reign of God now breaking in. *Now* is the last hour. *Now* it is Either-Or. *Now* the question is: Do men really want God's Reign? Or is it the world they want? The decision they must make is a radical one.

'No man, having put his hand to the plough, and looking back, is fit for the kingdom of God' (Luke 9.62). 'Follow me, and let the dead bury their dead' (Matt. 8.22). 'If any man come to me, and hate not his father, and mother, and wife, and children, and brethren, and sisters, yea, and his own life also, he cannot be my disciple' (Luke 14.26; Matt. 10.37). 'Whosoever doth not bear his cross, and come after me, cannot be my disciple' (Luke 14.27; Matt. 10.38; Mark 8.34).

This is why Jesus himself left his own family: 'Whosoever shall do the will of God, the same is my brother, and my sister, and mother' (Mark 3.35). This is why he uprooted many others from home and trade and took them with him on his travels. Yet he did not establish a religious order or a sect (still less a church). Nor did he propose that everyone should leave his home and family. But all are challenged to a decision. All must make up their minds what they really want to set their hearts on, whether it is God, or the goods of this world. 'Lay not up for yourselves treasures upon earth . . . . For where your treasure is, there will your heart be also' (Matt. 6.19–21; Luke 12.33f.).

> No man can serve two masters:
> for either he will hate the one, and love the other;
> or else he will hold to the one,
> and despise the other.
> Ye cannot serve God and mammon (Matt. 6.24; Luke 13.13).

'How dangerous it is to be rich! It is easier for a camel to go through the eye of a needle than for a rich man to enter into the kingdom of God' (Mark 10.25). Most men cling to earthly possessions and anxieties; they certainly want to obtain the salvation God prepares for them, but when it comes to making up their minds, they refuse it, like guests who have accepted an invitation to a banquet. When the time arrives they are too preoccupied (Luke 14.15–21; Matt. 22.1–10). They must be quite sure what they really want, just as a man building a tower or going to war must count the cost beforehand (Luke 14.28–34). If men would enter the kingdom of God, they must be ready for any sacrifice, like the farmer who, having found a treasure, gives up everything to gain possession of it, or like the merchant who sells everything in order to acquire one precious pearl (Matt. 13.44–6).

> If thy right eye offend thee,
>   pluck it out and cast it from thee:
> for it is profitable for thee that one of thy members should perish,
> and not that thy whole body should be cast into hell.
> And if thy right hand offend thee,
>   cut it off and cast if from thee:
> for it is profitable for thee that one of thy members should perish,
> and not that thy whole body should be cast into hell (Matt. 5.29f.).

This renunciation of the world represents no escapism or asceticism, but an otherworldliness which is simply being ready for God's command, summoning men to abandon all earthly ties. On the positive side and complementary to it is the commandment of love, in which a man turns away from self and places himself at the disposal of others. In doing this, he has decided for God.

Of course, Jesus was mistaken in thinking that the world was destined soon to come to an end. His error was similar to that of the ancient prophets who believed that God's redemptive act was immediately impending, or like Deutero-Isaiah, who thought it was already dawning in the present. Does his message therefore stand or fall with that misconception? It would be better to reverse the proposition and say that this expectation springs from the conviction which lies at the root of his preaching. The prophets are so overwhelmed by their sense of the sovereign majesty of God and the absolute character of his will that they foreshorten the divine act of judgement. Contrasted with God and his will, the world seems such a trivial place that it is already as it were at an end. This sense of crisis in human destiny expresses itself in the conviction that the hour of decision has struck. So it is with Jesus. He is so convinced of God's will and determination, and that it is his business to proclaim it, that he feels himself to be standing on the frontiers of time. His eschatological preaching is not the outcome of wishful thinking or speculation, but of his sense of the utter nothingness of man before God. The understanding of human life implied thereby clearly does not stand or fall with his expectation of an imminent end of the world. It contains a definite judgement upon the world. In other words, it sees the world exclusively *sub specie Dei*.

His claim that the destiny of men is determined by their word to him and his word was taken up by the early Church and expressed in their proclamation of Jesus as 'Messiah'—particularly in their expectation that he was to come on the clouds of heaven as the 'Man', bringing judgement and salvation. His preaching was thus taken up in a new form, thus becoming specifically 'Christian' preaching. Jesus proclaimed the message. The Church proclaims *him*. . . .

Primitive Christianity arose from the band of Jesus' disciples, who, after their Master had been put to death by Pontius Pilate on the Cross, had seen him as one risen from the dead. Their belief that God had raised him from the dead gave them at the same time the assurance that Jesus had been exalted to heavenly glory and raised to the dignity of the 'Man' who would very shortly come on the clouds of heaven to set up the Reign of God. The growing company of those who awaited his coming was conscious of itself as the Church of the last age, as the community of the 'saints' and 'elect', as the true people of God, for whom the promises were now being fulfilled, as the goal and end of the redemptive history of Israel.

The eschatological community did not split off from Judaism as though it were conscious of itself as a new religious society. In the eyes of their contemporaries they must have looked like a Jewish sect, and for the historian they appear in that light too. For the resources they possessed— their traditions about Jesus, which were carefully preserved, and the latent resources of their own faith, led only gradually to a new form of organization and new philosophy of human life, the world and history.

The decisive step was taken when the good news of Jesus, crucified and risen, the coming Judge and agent of redemption, was carried beyond the confines of Palestinian Judaism, and Christian congregations sprang up in the Graeco-Roman world. These congregations consisted partly of Hellenistic Jewish Christians, partly of Gentiles, wherever the Christian mission sought its point of contact in the Hellenistic synagogues. For here, without going farther afield, it was possible to reach many of the Gentiles, who had joined the Jewish community, sometimes closely, sometimes more loosely. On other occasions the Christian missionaries went direct to the Gentile population, and then, in the first instance, to the lower classes in the cities. There were probably churches of Gentiles only, but few, if any, of the churches could have been purely Jewish. In any case Christianity found itself in a new spiritual environment: The Gospel had to be preached in terms intelligible to Hellenistic audiences and their mental outlook, while at the same time the audience themselves were bound to interpret the gospel message in their own way, in the light of their own spiritual needs. Hence the growth of divers types of Christianity.

By and large, the chief difference between Hellenistic Christianity and the original Palestinian version was that the former ceased to be dominated by the eschatological expectation and the philosophy of life which that implied. Instead, there was developed a new pattern of piety centred in the cultus. The Hellenistic Christians, it is true, continued to expect an imminent end of the world, the coming of the Judge and Saviour from heaven and the resurrection of the dead and the last judgement. But there were also Christians who became sceptical of the primitive Jewish Christian eschatology and rejected it. Indeed, some tried to get rid of it altogether. Above all, the Gentile Christians found the idea of a redemptive history foreign to them, and as a result they lost the sense of belonging to the community of the last days. They could no longer feel that they were standing at the culmination of redemptive history directed by the providence of God. This was the case wherever the tradition of the Synagogue and Christian catechetical instruction had failed to implant the idea of redemptive history. The speedy disappearance of the apocalyptic title 'Man' is symptomatic; even Paul himself refrains from using it. It was no longer understood that 'Christos' was a translation of 'Messiah', and meant that Jesus was the Lord of the age of redemption: the title simply became a proper name. Other titles took its place, such as 'Son of God' and 'Saviour', titles which were already current in the Gentile world to designate agents of redemption. It was however the title 'Kyrios' which became the most popular designation of Jesus. It characterizes him as the cult deity who works supernaturally in the worship of the Church as a cultic body. Hellenistic pneumatology, with ecstasy and speaking with tongues, find their way into the churches. The Kyrios Jesus Christos is conceived as a mystery deity, in whose death and Resurrection the faithful participate through the sacraments. Parallel with this sacramental cultus piety we very soon find Gnostic ideas of wisdom affecting the churches. Ideas originating from the Gnostic redemption myths are used to describe the person and work of Jesus Christ and the nature of the Church, and, accompanying these, ascetic and even libertinist tendencies.

At the same time, however, the Hellenistic Christians received the gospel tradition of the Palestinian churches. Admittedly, the importance attached to this tradition varied from place to place. Paul himself seldom refers to it. Yet almost everywhere the Old Testament asserts itself, being accepted as canonical scripture by all except extreme gnosticizing circles. This adoption of the Old Testament followed as a matter of course in those congregations which grew out of the Synagogue. The latter was also the medium by which Hellenistic Christianity adopted conceptions emanating from philosophical enlightenment, conceptions which the Synagogue itself had assimilated at an earlier stage. Christian missionary preaching was not only the proclamation of Christ, but, when addressed to a Gentile audience, a preaching of monotheism as well. For this, not only arguments derived from the Old Testament, but the natural theology of Stoicism was pressed into service. Quite early on the Christian churches adopted a system of morality, with its pattern of catechetical instruction derived in equal proportions from the Old Testament Jewish tradition and from the ethics of popular philosophical pedagogic, shortly to be enriched by the moral ideals of the Hellenistic bourgeoisie.

Thus Hellenistic Christianity is no unitary phenomenon, but, taken by and large, a remarkable product of syncretism. It is full of tendencies and contradictions, some of which were to be condemned later on by orthodox Christianity as heretical. Hence also the struggles between the various tendencies, of which the Pauline Epistles give such a vivid impression.

Yes, at first sight we are bound to agree that Hellenistic Christianity is the outcome of syncretism. The world is the creation of God, who cares for the birds and decks the grass of the field with its beauty (Matt. 6.26, 30). Yet at the same time it is the realm of Satan, the 'god of this world' (II Cor. 4.4), the 'prince of this world' (John 12.31). The earth is the Lord's and all the fulness thereof (I Cor. 10.26). Yet creation is subject to vanity and corruption ($\mu\alpha\tau\alpha\iota\acute{o}\tau\eta s$ and $\phi\theta o\rho\acute{a}$), yearning for the day of its deliverance (Rom. 8.19–22). The terms in which this deliverance is conceived are derived partly, and indeed mainly, from the Jewish tradition. The old age is already coming to an end, and the new age is about to dawn soon with the coming of the 'Man', the resurrection of the dead and the judgement. But side by side with these conceptions we get the eschatology of the Fourth Gospel, which uses not the Jewish dualism of the two ages but the Gnostic dualism of the two realms of light and darkness, truth and falsehood, above and below, and which asserts that the judgement and resurrection have already been realized, or at least have been inaugurated because 'the light is come into the world' (John 3.19). Now that Jesus has come, those who believe in him have already passed from death unto life (John 5.24f.). The person of Jesus is sometimes defined in terms of Jewish and apocalyptic categories, sometimes as the 'Lord' of the cultus, as a mystery deity, sometimes again as the Gnostic redeemer, the pre-existent being from the heavenly world, whose earthly body is only an outward garb. This explains why the 'rulers of this world' failed to recognize him, as only 'his own' can. The Christian community is sometimes described in Old Testament categories as the people of God, the true seed of Abraham, sometimes in Gnostic categories as the 'body of Christ', in which individuals are incorporated by means of the sacraments of baptism and the Lord's Supper. Of course, some of these concepts are confined to particular writings or groups of writings in the New Testament (which varies a great deal in its language and thought). But they are also to be found side by side or in combination in the same author, especially in Paul and the Epistle to the Hebrews.

Is Christianity then really a syncretistic religion? Or is there a fundamental unity behind all this diversity? A comparison of primitive Christianity with the various traditions and religious movements in which it was cradled and which influenced its growth should help us to answer this question. Does primitive Christianity contain a single, new and unique doctrine of human existence? The comparison may best be conducted by selecting certain main subjects as test cases. In doing this, we shall rely chiefly on the Pauline and Johannine writings, because they provide the clearest evidence for the Christian attitude to existence. ✻

Part 5

THE DECLINE OF ROME

"Among the historical questions which men have posed through the ages," writes Donald Kagan of Cornell University, "none has attracted more attention over a longer period of time than the one which asks, Why did the Roman Empire in the West collapse? It has remained a vital question because each age has seen in the tale of Rome's fall something significant and relevant to its own situation." Broadly speaking there have been two distinct stages in the conceptualization of the problem. The first stage appeared while the Empire was still in existence and lasted until the Italian Renaissance. We are presently in the second stage, which gives no indication of terminating.

From the first century A.D., articulate people within the Roman Empire seem to have been obsessed by a vague sense of deterioration. Seneca (*c.* 4 B.C.–A.D. 65), admittedly not a man prone to optimism, was convinced Rome had reached old age under the emperors, and death would soon follow. Dio Cassius, a third century commentator, thought that degeneration began sometime after A.D. 180: "Our history now descends from a kingdom of gold to one of iron and rust." With the rise of Christianity the decline of Rome became a central issue in philosophy and Christian polemic. In such apocalyptic writings as the Book of Revelations, the Empire was scorned and its end was predicted as the last stage before the coming of the millennium. When Christianity triumphed, when it became the official religion of the Roman state, the Church hierarchy presented a different vision: the Empire was God's instrument for the protection of the Christian world, it was thus worthy of support and loyalty for the fate of the universe depended on it. The medieval myth of the transfer of the Empire to Charlemagne meant that the idea of the Empire was very much alive long after the barbarian invasions. Thus the characteristic feature of this first stage of the conceptualization of the decline of Rome was that its decline lay in the future; it was a dreaded possibility but was not then considered an accomplished fact, subject to analysis.

All of this changed as the Italian humanists of the fourteenth and fifteenth centuries moved sharply away from the medieval conception of history. It is to these humanists, above all to Francesco Petrarch (1304–74), that we owe the modern tripartite division of Western history into "ancient," "medieval," and "modern" periods. What Giotto did for painting, Petrarch did for the study of history: he introduced the notion of perspective. The history of the classical world was conceived as a distinct and complete segment of European history. Rome had fallen and its fall was followed by a long medieval interlude preceding the dawn of the Renaissance. For the first time the decline of Rome became an historical problem.

Within this second stage there have been as many interpretations as there have been students of Rome's decline. But what one scholar has called "the forbidding difficulties standing in the way of consensus" need not dismay the student. The decline of Rome falls within a category of historical problems which involves issues so vast and all-embracing that consensus, even if desirable, could never be achieved. Historians who pose such questions show a certain hubris: they know, or should know, they cannot really answer such questions. When a scientist tackles problems like the origins of the universe or life itself, he is doing precisely the same thing. But in history, as in science, the research that yields results proceeds along different, more modest lines. The issues are more concrete and therefore more easily resolved: What was the social composition of the Roman army in the third century A.D.? How much support did Caesar have in the city of Rome? What evidence is there that Christianity penetrated the Roman educational system? This is not to say that the "big" questions are not worth asking. They certainly possess an intrinsic fascination and lead to a host of concrete problems; studying these specific problems helps us understand the civilization at issue. If the student keeps this in mind, he will not be "dismayed" by the conflicting interpretations of Rome's decline.

There are many ways to approach the decline of Rome. Clearly, we require some kind of framework in which to formulate questions and terminology so that we have an exact conception of what we are attempting to understand. Following is one suggested framework:

1. Again we quote Professor Kagan: "'The decline and fall of the Roman Empire' is a metaphorical usage in which the empire is compared with an edifice; like all metaphors it conveys general impressions but no

precise conceptions." These general impressions must be transformed into specific definitions.

2. What do we mean by the "Roman Empire" and its "fall"? It is necessary to start with a spatial or geographical delimitation of the problem. Most historians would agree that only the western Empire is at issue; Constantinople did not "fall" until 1453. A vaguely defined conception of the problem can readily lead to an easily demolished argument. As Professor A. H. M. Jones reminds us: "Many of the causes alleged for the fall of the west were common to the east, and therefore cannot be complete and self-sufficient causes." And consider this statement by Rostovtzeff: "The decline and fall of the Roman Empire, that is to say, of ancient civilization as a whole. . . ." In comparing the arguments of different historians be certain that they are indeed talking about the same thing.

3. Chronological delimitation follows geographical delimitation. Frank W. Walbank goes back to Greek times; Rostovtzeff tells us that "The decline began as early as the second century B.C."; and Gibbon makes the age of the Antonines (A.D. 96–180) his point of departure.

4. It is useful, though admittedly superficial, to separate "external" and "internal" developments. A further distinction—one separating material themes from spiritual or intellectual themes—is also in order. And throughout, as Rostovtzeff reminds us, "It is not easy to discriminate between causes and symptoms."

5. Finally, it has been suggested that most of the interpretive schemes fall into one of four categories: "death by accident, natural causes, murder and suicide."

No single system of classification does justice to the problem, and the student may very well formulate a more satisfactory alternative. Whatever the case, such a procedure is necessary.

As long as the decline of Rome remains a subject of historical interest, Edward Gibbon (1737–94) will continue to be the first historian consulted. *The Decline and Fall of the Roman Empire,* published between 1776 and 1788, is not only a great historical work but a masterpiece of English prose as well. A poetic, frequently quoted passage in his *Autobiography* reveals how Gibbon came to write his great book: "It was at Rome on the fifteenth of October, 1764, as I sat musing amidst the ruins of the Capitol, while the barefooted fryars were singing Vespers in the temple of Jupiter, that the idea of writing the decline and fall of the City first started to my mind." The scene—the juxtaposition of the Capitol, the heart of Roman civic life, and the friars singing Vespers in what once had been a pagan temple—suggests that even at its inception Gibbon's view of the problem centered on Christianity.

Gibbon's controversial thesis deserves several comments. Insofar as his explanation of the decline is monocausal, it is open to criticism. However, to lightly dismiss his argument, as some historians do, is to neglect one of the fundamental lessons of the modern social sciences—that religion does indeed shape economic, social, and political behavior and that to fully appreciate its significance one must go beyond the formal aspects of religion to the many and subtle ways it influences the whole range of human attitudes. Secondly, Gibbon is best understood as a product of the Enlightenment of the eighteenth century. Gibbon and his contemporaries attacked religion because to them it meant unreason and superstition; for men who worshipped reason, religion was the chief obstacle to human progress. When Gibbon uttered his famous maxim that history is "little more than the register of the crimes, follies and misfortunes of mankind," he was not giving vent to profound cynicism. In effect, he was saying that the past was so grim because men had not acted according to reason and rationality. When he wrote that the decline of Rome was "the natural and inevitable effect of immoderate greatness" he revealed his fundamental belief that order and moderation, such as prevailed in an eighteenth-century English garden, were the desired norms; deviation from this meant ruin. Gibbon's deep commitment to reason and logic prompted Carl Becker to declare, ". . . it was Gibbon after all who sought out the enemy in his stronghold and made the direct frontal attack on the Christian centuries."

The remaining seven selections are all taken from the works of distinguished modern historians writing in this field. They bear witness to the variety of issues brought into play when we ask why Rome declined, and the differing approaches and arguments represented should certainly provide ample basis for lively discussion and thought.

1. EDWARD GIBBON

FROM Edward Gibbon, *The Decline and Fall of the Roman Empire*, abridged by D. M. Low (New York: Harcourt, Brace & World, 1960), pp. 523–29.

The Greeks, after their country had been reduced into a province, imputed the triumphs of Rome, not to the merit, but to the FORTUNE, of the republic. The inconstant goddess, who so blindly distributes and resumes her favours, had *now* consented (such was the language of envious flattery) to resign her wings, to descend from her globe, and to fix her firm and immutable throne on the banks of the Tiber. A wiser Greek, who has composed, with a philosophic spirit, the memorable history of his own times, deprived his countrymen of this vain and delusive comfort, by opening to their view the deep foundations of the greatness of Rome. The fidelity of the citizens to each other and to the state was confirmed by the habits of education and the prejudices of religion. Honour, as well as virtue, was the principle of the republic; the ambitious citizens laboured to deserve the solemn glories of a triumph; and the ardour of the Roman youth was kindled into active emulation as often as they beheld the domestic images of their ancestors. The temperate struggles of the patricians and plebeians had finally established the firm and equal balance of the constitution, which united the freedom of popular assemblies with the authority and wisdom of a senate and the executive powers of a regal magistrate. When the consul displayed the standard of the republic, each citizen bound himself, by the obligation of an oath, to draw his sword in the cause of his country till he had discharged the sacred duty by a military service of ten years. This wise institution continually poured into the field the rising generations of freemen and soldiers; and their numbers were reinforced by the warlike and populous states of Italy, who, after a brave resistance, had yielded to the valour and embraced the alliance of the Romans. The sage historian, who excited the virtue of the younger Scipio and beheld the ruin of Carthage, has accurately described their military system; their levies, arms, exercises, subordination, marches, encampments; and the invincible legion, superior in active strength to the Macedonian phalanx of Philip and Alexander. From these institutions of peace and war Polybius has deduced the spirit and success of a people incapable of fear and impatient of repose. The ambitious design of conquest, which might have been defeated by the seasonable conspiracy of mankind, was attempted and achieved; and the perpetual violation of justice was maintained by the political virtues of prudence and courage. The arms of the republic, sometimes vanquished in battle, always victorious in war, advanced with rapid steps to the Euphrates, the Danube, the Rhine, and the Ocean; and the images of gold, or silver, or brass, that might serve to represent the nations and their kings, were successively broken by the *iron* monarchy of Rome.

The rise of a city, which swelled into an empire, may deserve, as a singular prodigy, the reflection of a philosophic mind. But the decline of Rome was the natural and inevitable effect of immoderate greatness. Prosperity ripened the principle of decay; the causes of destruction multiplied with the extent of conquest; and as soon as time or accident had removed the artificial supports, the stupendous fabric yielded to the pressure of its own weight. The story of its ruin is simple and obvious; and instead of inquiring *why* the Roman empire was destroyed, we should rather be surprised that it had subsisted so long. The victorious legions, who, in distant wars, acquired the vices of strangers and mercenaries, first oppressed the freedom of the republic, and afterwards violated the majesty of the purple. The emperors, anxious for their personal safety and the public peace, were reduced to the base expedient of corrupting the discipline which rendered them alike formidable to their sovereign and to the enemy; the vigour of the military government was relaxed and finally dissolved by the partial institutions of Constantine; and the Roman world was overwhelmed by a deluge of barbarians.

The decay of Rome has been frequently ascribed to the translation of the seat of empire; but this history has already shown that the powers of government were *divided*, rather than *removed*. The throne of Constantinople was erected in the East; while the West was still possessed by a series of emperors who held their residence in Italy, and claimed their equal inheritance of the legions and provinces. This dangerous novelty impaired the strength and fomented the vices of a double reign: the instruments of an oppressive and arbitrary system were multiplied; and a vain emulation of luxury, not of merit, was introduced and supported between the degenerate successors of Theodosius. Extreme distress, which unites the virtue of a free people, embitters the factions of a declining monarchy. The hostile favourites of Arcadius and Honorius betrayed the republic to its common enemies; and the Byzantine court beheld with indifference, perhaps with pleasure, the disgrace of Rome, the misfortunes of Italy, and the loss of the West. Under the succeeding reigns the alliance of the two empires was restored; but the aid of the Oriental Romans was tardy, doubtful, and ineffectual; and the national schism of the Greeks and Latins was enlarged by the perpetual difference of language and manners, of interests, and even of religion. Yet the salutary event approved in some measure the judgment of Constantine. During a long period of decay his impregnable city repelled the victorious armies of barbarism, protected the wealth of Asia, and commanded, both in peace and war, the important straits which connect the Euxine and Mediterranean seas. The foundation of Constantinople more essentially contributed to the preservation of the East than to the ruin of the West.

As the happiness of a *future* life is the great object of religion, we may hear without surprise or scandal that the introduction, or at least the abuse of Christianity, had some influence on the decline and fall of the Roman empire. The clergy successfully preached the doctrines of patience and pusillanimity; the active virtues of society were discouraged; and the last remains of military spirit were buried in the cloister; a large portion of public and private wealth was consecrated to the specious demands of charity and devotion; and the soldiers' pay was lavished on the useless multitudes of both sexes who could only plead the merits of abstinence and chastity. Faith, zeal, curiosity, and the more earthly passions of malice and ambition, kindled the flame of theological discord; the church, and even the state, were distracted by religious factions, whose conflicts were sometimes bloody and always implacable; the attention of the emperors was diverted from camps to synods; the Roman world was oppressed by a new species of tyranny; and the persecuted sects became the secret enemies of their country. Yet party-spirit, however pernicious or absurd, is a principle of union as well as of dissension. The bishops, from eighteen hundred pulpits, inculcated the duty of passive obedience to a lawful and orthodox sovereign; their frequent assemblies and perpetual correspondence maintained the communion of distant churches; and the benevolent temper of the Gospel was strengthened, though confined, by the spiritual alliance of the catholics. The sacred indolence of the monks was devoutly embraced by a servile and effeminate age; but if superstition had not afforded a decent retreat, the same vices would have tempted the unworthy Romans to desert, from baser motives, the standard of the republic. Religious precepts are easily obeyed which indulge and sanctify the natural inclinations of their votaries; but the pure and genuine influence of Christianity may be traced in its beneficial, though imperfect, effects on the barbarian proselytes of the North. If the decline of the Roman empire was hastened by the conversion of Constantine, his victorious religion broke the violence of the fall, and mollified the ferocious temper of the conquerors.

This awful revolution may be usefully applied to the instruction of the present age. It is the duty of a patriot to prefer and promote the exclusive interest and glory of his native country: but a philosopher may be permitted to enlarge his views, and to consider Europe as one great republic, whose various inhabitants have attained almost the same level of politeness and cultivation. The balance of power will continue to fluctuate, and the prosperity of our own or the neighbouring kingdoms may be alternately exalted or depressed; but these partial events cannot essentially injure our general state of happiness, the system of arts, and laws, and manners, which so advantageously distinguish, above the rest of mankind, the Europeans and their colonies. The savage nations of the globe are the common enemies of civilised society; and we may inquire, with anxious curiosity, whether Europe is still threatened with a repetition of those calamities which formerly oppressed the arms and institutions of Rome. Perhaps the same reflections will illustrate the fall of that mighty empire, and explain the probable causes of our actual security.

The Romans were ignorant of the extent of their danger and the number of their enemies. Beyond the Rhine and Danube the northern countries of Europe and Asia were filled with innumerable tribes of hunters and shepherds, poor, voracious, and turbulent; bold in arms, and impatient to ravish the fruits of industry. The barbarian world was agitated by the rapid impulse of war; and the peace of Gaul or Italy was shaken by the distant revolutions of China. The Huns, who fled before a victorious enemy, directed their march towards the West; and the torrent was swelled by the gradual accession of captives and allies. The flying tribes who yielded to the Huns assumed in *their* turn the spirit of conquest; the endless column of barbarians pressed on the Roman empire with accumulated weight; and, if the foremost were destroyed, the vacant space was instantly replenished by new assailants. Such formidable emigrations no longer issue from the North; and the long repose, which has been imputed to the decrease of population, is the happy consequence of the progress of arts and agriculture. Instead of some rude villages thinly scattered among its woods and morasses, Germany now produces a list of two thousand three hundred walled towns: the Christian kingdoms of Denmark, Sweden, and Poland have been successively established; and the Hanse merchants, with the Teutonic knights, have extended their colonies along the coast of the Baltic as far as the Gulf of Finland. From the Gulf of Finland to the Eastern Ocean, Russia now assumes the form of a powerful and civilised empire. The plough, the loom, and the forge are introduced on the banks of the Volga, the Ob, and the Lena; and the fiercest of the Tartar hordes have been taught to tremble and obey. The reign of independent barbarism is now contracted to a narrow span; and the remnant of Calmucks or Uzbecks, whose forces may be almost numbered, cannot seriously excite the apprehensions of the great republic of Europe. Yet this apparent security should not tempt us to forget that new enemies and unknown dangers may *possibly* arise from some obscure people, scarcely visible in the map of the world. The Arabs or Saracens, who spread their conquests from India to Spain, had languished in poverty and contempt till Mahomet breathed into those savage bodies the soul of enthusiasm.

The empire of Rome was firmly established by the singular and perfect coalition of its members. The subject nations, resigning the hope and even the wish of independence, embraced the character of Roman citizens; and the provinces of the West were reluctantly torn by the barbarians from the bosom of their mother country. But this union was purchased by the loss of national freedom and military spirit; and the servile provinces, destitute of life and motion, expected their safety from the mercenary troops and governors who were directed by the orders of a distant court. The happiness of an hundred millions depended on the personal merit of one or two men, perhaps children, whose minds were corrupted by education, luxury, and despotic power. The deepest wounds were inflicted on the empire during the minorities of the sons and grandsons of Theodosius; and, after those incapable princes seemed to attain the age of manhood, they abandoned the church to the bishops, the state to the eunuchs, and the provinces to the barbarians. Europe is now divided into twelve powerful, though unequal kingdoms, three respectable commonwealths, and a variety of smaller, though independent states: the chances of royal and ministerial talents are multiplied, at least, with the number of its rulers; and a Julian, or Semiramis, may reign in the North, while Arcadius and Honorius again slumber on the thrones of the South. The abuses of tyranny are restrained by the mutual influence of fear and shame; republics have acquired order and stability; monarchies have imbibed the principles of freedom, or, at least, of moderation; and some sense of honour and justice is introduced into the most defective constitutions by the general manners of the times. In peace, the progress of knowledge and industry is accelerated by the emulation of so many active rivals: in war, the European forces are exercised by temperate and undecisive contests. If a savage conqueror should issue from the deserts of Tartary, he must repeatedly vanquish the robust peasants of Russia, the numerous armies of Germany, the gallant nobles of France, and the intrepid freemen of Britain; who, perhaps, might confederate for their common defence. Should the victorious barbarians carry slavery and desolation as far as the Atlantic Ocean, ten thousand vessels would transport beyond their pursuit the remains of civilised society; and Europe would revive and flourish in the American world, which is already filled with her colonies and institutions.

Cold, poverty, and a life of danger and fatigue fortify the strength and courage of barbarians. In every age they have oppressed the polite and peaceful nations of China, India, and Persia, who neglected, and still neglect, to counterbalance these natural powers by the resources of military art. The warlike states of antiquity, Greece, Macedonia, and Rome, educated a race of soldiers; exercised their bodies, disciplined their courage, multiplied their forces by regular evolutions, and converted the iron which they possessed into strong and serviceable weapons. But this superiority insensibly declined with their laws and manners: and the feeble policy of Constantine and his successors armed and instructed, for the ruin of the empire, the rude valour of the barbarian mercenaries. The military art has been changed by the invention of gunpowder; which enables man to command the two most powerful agents of nature, air and fire. Mathematics, chemistry, mechanics, architecture, have been applied to the service of war; and the adverse parties oppose to each other the most elaborate modes of attack and of defence. Historians may indignantly observe that the preparations of a siege would found and maintain a flourishing colony; yet we cannot be displeased that the subversion of a city should be a work of cost and difficulty; or that an industrious people should be protected by those arts which survive and supply the decay of military virtue. Cannon and fortifications now form an impregnable barrier against the Tartar horse; and Europe is secure from any future irruption of barbarians; since, before they can conquer, they must cease to be barbarous. Their gradual advances in the science of war would always be accompanied as we may learn from the example of Russia, with a proportionable improvement in the arts of peace and civil policy; and they themselves must deserve a place among the polished nations whom they subdue.

2. TENNEY FRANK

FROM Tenney Frank, *A History of Rome* (New York: Henry Holt and Company, 1923), pp. 566–68, 574.

Closely connected with the political question is the "racial" one. We know as yet so little about race and racial inheritance that extreme caution is necessary in attempting to estimate this factor. Furthermore ease of communication has now so thoroughly mixed peoples of different parts of Europe that "pure races" hardly exist from which to draw safe illustrations. Yet biological study, advancing upon the work of Mendel, seems to have gone so far as to show that the historical theories of the 19th century, based upon Buckle's doctrine of environmental influences, were unsafe, and that in the future history must take into more generous account the mental and physical inheritance of the individuals that constitute a nation. The emphasis on racial inheritance is the more important in ancient history because the European folk groups of 3000 years ago were generally more homogeneous than those of to-day, for the reason that the migrating Indo-European hordes were landseekers who dispelled and scattered rather than assimilated the non-landholding savages which they found. This seems in general true of the early Latin, Celtic, and Germanic migrants.

Race-mixture may produce good results, but it has also been established that in the mixture of two excellent stocks of widely differing qualities an unstable fusion often results which perpetuates the poorer qualities of both. Applying this consideration to Rome, if we find that the Latin stock advanced consistently along certain lines so long as it was fairly unmixed, and that it gradually declined from about the time that racial fusion was marked, we may fairly attribute this new trend in some measure to the process of the "melting-pot."

Even a hasty survey of the Republic is enough to show how the original peoples were wasted in wars and scattered in migration and colonization, and how their places were filled chiefly by Eastern slaves. As early as 130 B.C. Scipio Aemilianus reminded the voters of Rome, in words pardonably exaggerated, that he had led many of them as captives to Rome. The assimilation of the foreign element was so rapid that the son of Marcus Aurelius seems to be the last emperor of Rome who could claim untainted descent from Italian parentage. That calm temper of the old state-builders, their love for law and order, their persistence in liberal and equitable dealings, in patient and untiring effort, their deliberation in reaching decisions, their distrust of emotions and intuitions, their unswerving devotion to liberty, their loyalty to tradition and to the state are the things one expects to find so long as the old Roman families are the dominant element in the Republic. By contrast the people of the Empire seem subservient and listless, caloric and unsteady, soft of fiber, weak of will, mentally fatigued, wont to abandon the guidance of reason for a crepuscular mysticism. The change is so marked that it is impossible to speak of the "spirit of Rome" or the "culture of Rome," without defining whether the reference is to the Rome of 200 B.C. or of 200 A.D. History must take cognizance of this change, and in doing so it is difficult to escape the conclusion that the change is primarily due to the fact that the Romans partly gave way before and partly merged their inheritance in a new brood which came largely from Asia Minor and Syria. According to this view the decline of Rome had begun in the last decades of the Republic.

There were also deficiencies of an economic nature which contributed to the decline; though the importance of this factor has probably been overrated in recent years owing to a tendency to project the phenomena of modern industrial states into ancient societies. The exhaustion of resources by undue taxation had created some havoc in the East even during the late Republic. But during the first two centuries of the Empire taxation was fair, and the East recovered till it was more prosperous financially than it had ever been. Distressing taxes were again imposed only after Caracalla's day when they doubtless helped choke an Empire already expiring. . . .

. . . By associating every kind of labor, not only physical but mental as well, with servility, the institution degraded all trades and crafts, and finally even the arts, till citizens of respectability found themselves deprived by caste-customs of all normal exercise. This was not only a great economic waste, but a calamity to the national morale. But doubtless its worst evil was the ethnological one, which we have discussed above under the race question. Slaves displaced the citizens of a race that had made Rome what it was. And however clever, however efficient they might be as individuals, they were Romans neither in tradition nor in temper, and they were all too apt to carry a slave's ideals of conduct into the performance of their new offices as citizens.

If from these many causes of Rome's decline we must select the more potent ones, we should be inclined to name first Rome's rapid and ill-considered expansion, the existence of slavery on a vast scale, and as an immediate consequence of these two, the thorough-going displacement of Romans by non-Romans.

3. MIKHAIL ROSTOVTZEFF

FROM Mikhail Rostovtzeff, *The Social and Economic History of the Roman Empire*, 2 vols. (Oxford: Clarendon Press, 1926), vol. I, 477–81, 486–87.

The social revolution of the third century, which destroyed the foundations of the economic, social, and intellectual life of the ancient world, could not produce any positive achievement. On the ruins of a prosperous and well-organized state, based on the age-old classical civilization and on the self-government of the cities, it built up a state which was based on general ignorance, on compulsion and violence, on slavery and servility, on bribery and dishonesty. Have we the right to accuse the emperors of the fourth century of having deliberately and of their own choice built up such a state, while they might have taken another path and have constructed, not the slave-state of the late Roman Empire, but one free from the mistakes of the early Empire and yet not enshrining the brutal practice of the revolutionary period? It is idle to ask such a question. The emperors of the fourth century, and above all Diocletian, grew up in the atmosphere of violence and compulsion. They never saw anything else, they never came across any other method. Their education was moderate, and their training exclusively military. They took their duties seriously, and they were animated by the sincerest love of their country. Their aim was to save the Roman Empire, and they achieved it. To this end they used, with the best intentions, the means which were familiar to them, violence and compulsion. They never asked whether it was worth while to save the Roman Empire in order to make it a vast prison for scores of millions of men.

Every reader of a volume devoted to the Roman Empire will expect the author to express his opinion on what is generally, since Gibbon, called the decline and fall of the Roman Empire, or rather of ancient civilization in general. I shall therefore briefly state my own view on this problem, after defining what I take the problem to be. The decline and fall of the Roman Empire, that is to say, of ancient civilization as a whole, has two aspects: the political, social, and economic on the one hand, and the intellectual and spiritual on the other. In the sphere of politics we witness a gradual barbarization of the Empire from within, especially in the West. The foreign, German, elements play the leading part both in the government and in the army, and settling in masses displace the Roman population, which disappear from the fields. A related phenomenon, which indeed was a necessary consequence of this barbarization from within was the gradual disintegration of the Western Roman Empire; the ruling classes in the former Roman provinces were replaced first by Germans and Sarmatians, and later by Germans alone, either through peaceful penetration or by conquest. In the East we observe a gradual Orientalization of the Byzantine Empire, which leads ultimately to the establishment, on the ruins of the Roman Empire, of strong half-Oriental and purely Oriental states, the Caliphate of Arabia, and the Persian and Turkish empires. From the social and economic point of view, we mean by decline the gradual relapse of the ancient world to very primitive forms of economic life, into an almost pure 'house-economy.' The cities, which had created and sustained the higher forms of economic life, gradually decayed, and the majority of them practically disappeared from the face of the earth. A few, especially those that had been great centres of commerce and industry, still lingered on. The complicated and refined social system of the ancient

Empire follows the same downward path and becomes reduced to its primitive elements: the King, his court and retinue, the big feudal landowners, the clergy, the mass of rural serfs, and small groups of artisans and merchants. Such is the political, social, and economic aspect of the problem.

From the intellectual and spiritual point of view the main phenomenon is the decline of ancient civilization, of the city civilization of the Greco-Roman world. The Oriental civilizations were more stable: blended with some elements of the Greek city civilization, they persisted and even witnessed a brilliant revival in the Caliphate of Arabia and in Persia, not to speak of India and China. Here again there are two aspects of the evolution. The first is the exhaustion of the creative forces of Greek civilization in the domains where its great triumphs had been achieved, in the exact sciences, in technique, in literature and art. The decline began as early as the second century B.C. There followed a temporary revival of creative forces in the cities of Italy, and later in those of the Eastern and Western provinces of the Empire. The progressive movement stopped almost completely in the second century A.D. and, after a period of stagnation, a steady and rapid decline set in again. Parallel to it, we notice a progressive weakening of the assimilative forces of Greco-Roman civilization. The cities no longer absorb—that is to say, no longer Hellenize or Romanize—the masses of the country population. The reverse is the case. The barbarism of the country begins to engulf the city population. Only small islands of civilized life are left, the senatorial aristocracy of the late Empire and the clergy; but both, save for a section of the clergy, are gradually swallowed up by the advancing tide of barbarism.

Another aspect of the same phenomenon is the development of a new mentality among the masses of the population. It was the mentality of the lower classes, based exclusively on religion and not only indifferent but hostile to the intellectual achievements of the higher classes. This new attitude of mind gradually dominates the upper classes, or at least the larger part of them. It is revealed by the spread among them of the various mystic religions, partly Oriental, partly Greek. The climax was reached in the triumph of Christianity. In this field the creative power of the ancient world was still alive, as is shown by such momentous achievements as the creation of the Christian church, the adaptation of Christian theology to the mental level of the higher classes, the creation of a powerful Christian literature and of a new Christian art. The new intellectual efforts aimed chiefly at influencing the mass of the population and therefore represented a lowering of the high standards of city civilization, at least from the point of view of literary forms.

We may say, then, that there is one prominent feature in the development of the ancient world during the imperial age, alike in the political, social, and economic and in the intellectual field. It is a gradual absorption of the higher classes by the lower, accompanied by a gradual levelling down of standards. This levelling was accomplished in many ways. There was a slow penetration of the lower classes into the higher, which were unable to assimilate the new elements. There were violent outbreaks of civil strife, the lead was taken by the Greek cities, and there followed the civil war of the first century B.C. which involved the whole civilized world. In these struggles the upper classes and the city civilization remained victorious on the whole. Two centuries later, a new outbreak of civil war ended in the victory of the lower classes and dealt a mortal blow to the Greco-Roman civilization of the cities. Finally, that civilization was completely engulfed by the inflow of barbarous elements from outside, partly by penetration, partly by conquest, and in its dying condition it was unable to assimilate even a small part of them. . . .

Christianity is very often made responsible for the decay of ancient civilization. This is, of course, a very narrow point of view. Christianity is but one side of the general change in the mentality of the ancient world. Can we say that this change is the ultimate cause of the decay of ancient civilization? It is not easy to discriminate between causes and symptoms, and one of the urgent tasks in the field of ancient history is a further investigation of this change of mentality. The change, no doubt, was one of the most potent factors in the gradual decay of the civilization of the city-state and in the rise of a new conception of the world and of a new civilization. But how are we to explain the change? Is it a problem of individual and mass psychology?

None of the existing theories fully explains the problem of the decay of ancient civilization, if we can apply the word 'decay' to the complex phenomenon which I have endeavoured to describe. Each of them, however, has contributed much to the clearing of the ground, and has helped us to perceive that the main phenomenon which underlies the process of decline is the gradual absorption of the educated classes by the masses and the consequent simplification of all the functions of political, social, economic, and intellectual life, which we call the barbarization of the ancient world.

The evolution of the ancient world has a lesson and a warning for us. Our civilization will not last unless it be a civilization not of one class, but of the masses. The Oriental civilizations were more stable and lasting than the Greco-Roman, because, being chiefly based on religion, they were nearer to the masses. Another lesson is that violent attempts at levelling have never helped to uplift the masses. They have destroyed the upper classes, and resulted in accelerating the process of barbarization. But the ultimate problem remains like a ghost, ever present and unlaid: Is it possible to extend a higher civilization to the lower classes without debasing its standard and diluting its quality to the vanishing point? Is not every civilization bound to decay as soon as it begins to penetrate the masses?

✻

4. CHARLES NORRIS COCHRANE

FROM Charles Norris Cochrane, *Christianity and Classical Culture*, 2d. ed. (New York: Oxford University Press, 1944), pp. 155–62.

The malady of *Romanitas*, in many ways still the most impressive secular system ever constructed by human hands, has inevitably excited much attention and, since the days of Cyprian himself, students of society have been concerned to diagnose its cause. To trace the history of their efforts would provide a fascinating comment on the development of social science, and even to catalogue the various explanations proposed is not without interest. There is, for example, the classical theory that the empire was suffering from the incurable disease of old age (*mundus senescens*)—a notion which, so far from having been invented by Gibbon, was part of the stock-in-trade of Graeco-Roman rhetoricians. A modern variant of this hypothesis is that empires, by the necessity of their constitution, expand until they burst; when, with the dissipation of the wealth which forms the basis of centralized power, they break up like a compound into its original elements, the agricultural village and the small local mart. Such explanations have their roots in the classical doctrine of cyclical evolution. For this reason they were already to come in for severe criticism at the hands of Christian apologists. And this criticism (whether the metaphor be chemical or biological) appears to be justified. For the validity of the latter depends upon the dubious assumption that societies, like individuals, fulfil the life-history of an organism; while the former is made plausible only by a Procrustean distortion of the material evidence.

Contemporary distrust of *a priori* reasoning has prompted historians, in general, to cast about for theories of a positive character. Thus, for example, the decline of Graeco-Roman culture has recently been connected with what is called the 'water-cycle of antiquity', according to which the grain-growers during the early centuries of our era were engaged in a losing battle with the Scythian nomads; though they were ignorant of this fact until, with the progressive desiccation of the Asiatic heartland, its inhabitants were forced outwards, thereby propelling the Germans in irresistible numbers upon the frontiers.

To those who prefer to look for an explanation within society itself rather than in any environmental condition such as drought, malaria, or the exhaustion of natural resources, a host of possibilities present themselves. Of these, one of the most obvious is dysgenic selection, the consequence of warfare and of social evils (like celibacy and vice) which bring about the extermination of the best; although, if this be taken to imply that certain stocks are 'bearers of culture', then to one mystery is simply added another. A second possibility is that of slavery, regarded as part and parcel of a fundamentally wasteful economy which, by distributing wealth in an arbitrary and illogical fashion, condemns the masses to perpetual subjection, hardship, and want. Or again, if to the purely economic be added a moral factor, it may be argued that 'Christianity, by preaching the gospel to the poor, unhinged the ancient world'. Finally, there remains the political explanation, Caesarism, with all its obvious weaknesses, including a failure to solve the problem of the succession. This theory has recently been restated by an eminent authority, and it will always carry weight with those who think in terms of political liberalism.

The *débâcle*, however, was not merely economic or social or political, or rather it was all of these because it was something more. For what here confronts us is, in the last analysis, a moral and intellectual failure, a failure of the Graeco-Roman mind. From this standpoint, we are not concerned to enter into a dispute as to the relative importance of the various theories proposed, but may freely admit that they all have a place within the complex tissue of material fact. If, however, the Romans themselves proved unable to come to grips with that fact, the reason must surely be supposed to lie in some radical defect of their thinking. In this defect we may find the ultimate explanation of the nemesis which was operating to bring about the decline and fall of ancient civilization.

Nor is it unreasonable to suggest that the defect in question was intimately connected with the classical *logos* of power. Classicism, as we have seen, resolved the concept of power into a subjective and an objective factor; the former, character (art and industry); the latter, circumstance (fate and fortune or the gods); tracing its genesis to a combination or, at least, a coincidence of the two. But, as must be evident, this solution was no solution at all. For, in this combination, no intelligible relationship could be established between the two component elements. That is to say, it involved a degree of obscurantism which classical reason strove in vain to eliminate, and, though reason did succeed in clearing a limited area into which the sunlight might penetrate, the forest remained in the background, ready and waiting to creep forward and resume its control. Accordingly, the doom which awaited *Romanitas* was that of a civilization which failed to understand itself and was, in consequence, dominated by a haunting fear of the unknown. The fear in question could by no possibility be exorcized; since it was a consequence of weaknesses which were, so to speak, built into the very foundations of the system. In this sense, however, it was not peculiar to *Romanitas;* it was merely the last and most spectacular illustration of the fate which, sooner or later, was to overtake the ideologists of classical antiquity.

In this fear we may see an explanation of many of the most characteristic phenomena of classical and post-classical times. To begin with, it serves to account for the steady and persistent growth of a belief in 'luck'. 'Throughout the whole world', declares Pliny, 'in every place, at all times, Fortune alone is named and invoked by the voices of all; she alone is accused and put in the dock, she is the sole object of our thought, our praise, and our abuse.' This belief Juvenal was to single out as one of the most significant aspects of contemporary 'vice'; and he denounced it in various satires, notably the fifteenth. But, in his attack on superstition, the satirist had no recourse other than to fall back on the prejudices of Ciceronian and Livian humanism, which he thus reaffirmed in the well-known lines:

> nullum numen habes si sit prudentia, nos te
> nos facimus, Fortuna, deam caeloque locamus.

A still more sinister development, if possible, was that of a belief in astrological and solar determinism, a faith which invaded the empire with the Chaldaeans or *mathematici*. For an account of this faith, we may refer to the summary statement of Censorinus:

> 'The Chaldaeans', he says, 'hold first and foremost that what happens to us in life is determined by the planets in conjunction with the fixed stars. It is the varied and complicated course of these bodies which governs the human race; but their own motion and arrangement are frequently modified by the sun; and, while the rising and setting of different constellations serve to affect us with their distinctive "temperature", this occurs through the power of the sun. Accordingly, it is the sun to whom we ultimately owe the spirit which controls us, since he moves the actual stars by which we are moved and, therefore, has the greatest influence over our existence and destiny.'

The evil of this superstition was, of course, that it utterly denied the reality of human freedom and responsibility, reducing men to the status of mere automata. The poem of Manilius indicates that it was already enjoying a considerable vogue in the early empire.

The acceptance of such beliefs involved a picture of nature in terms either of sheer fortuity or (alternatively) of inexorable fate. By so doing, it helped to provoke an increasingly frantic passion for some means of escape. This passion was to find expression in various types of supernaturalism, in which East and West joined hands to produce the most grotesque cosmologies as a basis for ethical systems not less grotesque. Of such manifestations, none was more characteristic than Gnosticism, 'the barbarous and orientalized Platonism' which resulted from an indiscriminate conflation of elements derived from Greek idealism with the metaphysical dualism of the Orient. Gnosticism began by identifying evil with the world of matter ($ὕλη$). It then proceeded to assert an absolute antithesis between matter and spirit. Human beings, it declared, are in the material world, the evil of which thus enters into their constitution. But, as spirits, they are not of that world and their one problem is to escape from it. This, it supposed, was to be effected through the communication of celestial revelation ($γνῶσις$). Such gnosis, conceived as 'illumination' rather than 'knowledge', laid emphasis upon outlandish and esoteric modes of apprehension. As such, it was thought to mark the culmination of an advance upon successive planes of experience in which the pilgrim made his way through a universe peopled by demons and hobgoblins, including the seven devils of Babylonian mythology. From this standpoint, Gnosticism admitted of the widest oscillations between exaltation and abasement, and it combined the most rigid asceticism with outbursts of unbridled libertinism. Thus, ethically, it stood at the opposite pole from the classical ideal of *sophrosyne;* just as, in its contempt for objective science, it registered the suicide of classical reason.

It does not lessen the tragic character of these developments that they were a logical outcome of moral and intellectual shortcomings inherent in the classical world. The effort of Classicism was, as we have seen, an effort to rescue mankind from the life and mentality of the jungle, and to secure for him the possibility of a good life. That is to say it was envisaged as a struggle for civilization against barbarism and superstition. In this secular conflict with the powers of darkness Augustus imagined himself to have scored a decisive victory. But, as events were to show, the Augustan system possessed no real immunity from disorders such as had threatened previous political experiments. On the contrary they were enshrined at the heart of the system itself in the worship of the divinized sovereign. In this sense the destiny of the empire was implicit in that of the Caesars.

We have tried to show how, according to Classicism, the power deemed necessary to protect civilization was supposed to depend upon a fortunate coincidence of character and circumstance, a coincidence thought to have been finally realized in the person of Augustus. From this standpoint the future of Rome appeared to be bound up with the cult of Augustan excellence which, together with *fortuna omnipotens et ineluctabile fatum*, was to constitute the guarantee and pledge of her eternity. But, if this was the Augustan hope, it was destined to disappointment. For, notwithstanding its pretension to finality, its basis in fact was merely pragmatic; and, though the emperor might seek to account for his success in terms of his 'virtues', there could be no certainty regarding the part which 'luck' had played in bringing it about. This meant in practice that those who accepted the system at its face-value found themselves committed to a hopeless battle against the forces of change—a battle in which 'order' was opposed to 'process' and identified with the maintenance of conventions established by the founder as norms for all time to come. The defect of this analysis was its failure to do justice to the sense of substantial growth or development. As a consequence it served to produce a sharp division between conservatives and innovationists, in which both sides were, no doubt, partially at fault. The tendency of the conservative was to regard all change as *ipso facto* evil or, at the very least, suspect as a dangerous leap in the dark. He was thus disposed to resist it, forcing everything into existing moulds of thought with the result that the moulds were ultimately bound to crack. On the other hand the weakness of the innovationist as such was that he lacked any adequate notion of direction. For this reason he was inclined to meet the demands of 'novelty' simply by letting himself go with the tide; and, by so doing, he exposed himself to the conventional charge of barbarism. The conflict had the effect of dividing the emperors into two opposing camps. It tended also to produce a 'heresy' of individual emperors, so to speak, against themselves, a heresy which may be detected even within the formal and superficial unity of what has been called the Hadrianic synthesis. In this way it prepared the ground for what was to materialize as the moral and intellectual crisis of the third century.

The heresy, which thus manifested itself in the realm of politics, was but one phase of a wider and deeper cleavage within the ranks of imperial society. Horace had prophesied that the greatness of Rome would continue so long as Jupiter and the Capitol remained unshaken, thereby advocating the conservation of strictly national ideals; and Vergil, while perhaps more generous and cosmopolitan in his outlook, was not less keenly alive to the perils of an indiscriminate internationalism. But now, under the nominal presidency of Jove, the Pantheon was steadily enlarged; and the national deities fraternized with a heterogeneous mob composed of all the Mediterranean gods except those which, like the Carthaginian Baal, were distinctly below civilization or those which, like the Jewish Jehovah, were above it. It thus became evident that, after all, the victory of Venus and Apollo over the forces of darkness had been incomplete.

The expansion of the Roman Pantheon, which has been taken to indicate a spirit of toleration, testifies in reality to the absence of anything like a genuine principle of discrimination within *Romanitas*. The imperial *pax deorum* concealed a mass of moral and intellectual incongruities; it was not a hierarchy but a hotchpotch, symbolizing, as has been said, the amazing congeries of races, customs, and traditions, not to speak of the profound economic and social distinctions which subsisted within the body-politic. The empire, indeed, was not so much a 'body without a soul' as an example of multiple personality. As such, it offers a grim comment on the Plutarchian doctrine of the 'mixing-bowl'. For, to begin with, the masses remained relatively untouched by culture, their role within the system being one of mere acquiescence. The widening divergence between the literary language and the vernacular is a measure of the gulf which separated the refined citizen of the *municipium* from the rough peasant or soldier of the township and the frontier. Moreover, while cultivation was thus restricted to the dominant classes, those to whom letters were accessible found themselves confronted by the claims of rival schools of opinion which, however well equipped as 'sects' to dispute control of the human mind, could provide no real basis for spiritual unity. Quite the contrary, they actually promoted tendencies towards disintegration which could be held in leash only by physical force. Vespasian, with shrewd peasant wit, had declared of the ideologues: 'I do not strike the dog that barks at me.' Nevertheless individuals vaguely designated 'philosophers' were, in general, suspect within the *regnum Caesaris* and, on more than one occasion, the government undertook to purge society of subversive influences by expelling them from the capital.

The activities of such men serve to illustrate the truth of the maxim that societies die at the top. Or, in the vigorous language of Tertullian: 'they come into the open and destroy your gods, attacking your superstitions amidst your applause. Some of them even dare with your support to snap and bark at your princes.' It is thus apparent that, through the very discipline she provided, *Romanitas* equipped her traducers with a weapon to dig her grave. The empire could indeed, afford to ignore the yelpings of a Commodian, which reflected merely the half-articulate hatred of the under-dog, buoyed up by some dim Messianic hope and giving vent to a Christian cynicism not unlike that of Diogenes himself. But the diffusion in intellectual circles of doctrines such as we have indicated helped to prepare for a revolt against civilization, by inculcating a widespread sense of failure and frustration, in striking contrast with the unshakable faith of Vergil in the mission of Eternal Rome. ✳

5. FRANK W. WALBANK

FROM Frank W. Walbank, *The Decline of the Roman Empire in the West* (New York: Abelard-Schuman Ltd., 1953), pp. 66–69.

To Gibbon the decline of Rome was something so natural as to require no explanation. 'The story of its ruin' he wrote 'is simple and obvious: and instead of enquiring why the Roman Empire was destroyed we should rather be surprised that it had subsisted for so long . . . The stupendous fabric yielded to the pressure of its own weight.' To-day that answer would no longer appear adequate. The stupendous fabric sinking beneath its own weight is after all a metaphor. The Roman Empire was not a building, but a State; and as Gibbon himself would have agreed, 'the pressure of its own weight' acquires meaning only when translated into a detailed analysis of various social and economic trends and forces within the Empire.

But in one respect Gibbon's formulation was of fundamental importance; quite simply and unequivocally it broke with all cyclical, mystical-biological and metaphysical theories of decline, and stated clearly the 'naturalistic' view. The cause of decay was to be sought inside the system itself; it was not something transcendental or apocalyptic, the fulfilment of a prophecy, or a link in a sequence, fated to recur throughout eternity; nor was it something fortuitous, like the barbarian attacks (though, as we saw, these were by no means fortuitous), or an error of judgement on the part of one or other of the Emperors or their respective assassins. To Gibbon the cause is something inherent, natural, and proportionate to the effect produced.

This view has been amply confirmed by our own analysis. For this has shown that the cause of the decline of the Roman Empire is not to be sought in any one feature—in the climate, the soil, the health of the population, or indeed in any of those social and political factors which played so important a part in the actual process of decay—but rather in the whole structure of ancient society. The date at which the contradictions, which were ultimately to prove fatal, first began to appear is not A.D. 200 nor yet the setting-up of the Principate by Augustus Caesar in 27 B.C., but rather the fifth century B.C. when Athens revealed her inability to keep and broaden the middle-class democracy she had created. The failure of Athens epitomised the failure of the City-State. Built on a foundation of slave labour, or on the exploitation of similar groups, including the peasantry, the City-State yielded a brilliant minority civilisation. But from the start it was top-heavy. Through no fault of its citizens, but as a result of the time and place when it arose, it was supported by a woefully low level of technique. To say this is to repeat a truism. The paradoxical contrast between the spiritual achievements of Athens and her scanty material goods has long been held up to the admiration of generations who had found that a rich material inheritance did not automatically ensure richness of cultural life. But it was precisely this low level of technique, relative to the tasks Greek and Roman society set itself, that made it impossible even to consider dispensing with slavery and led to its extension from the harmless sphere of domestic labour to the mines and workshops, where it grew stronger as the contradictions of society became more apparent.

As so often, we find ourselves discussing as cause and effect factors which were constantly interacting, so that in reality the distinction between the effective agent and the result it brought about is often quite arbitrary. But roughly speaking, the City-State, precisely because it was a minority culture, tended to be aggressive and predatory, its claim to autonomy sliding over insensibly, at every opportunity, into a claim to dominate others. This led to wars, which in turn took their place among the many sources of fresh slaves. Slavery grew, and as it invaded the various branches of production it led inevitably to the damping down of scientific interest, to the cleavage, already mentioned, between the classes that used their hands and the superior class that used—and later ceased using—its mind. This ideological cleavage thus reflects a genuine separation of the community into classes; and henceforward it becomes the supreme task of even the wisest sons of the City-State—a Plato and an Aristotle—to maintain this class society, whatsoever the cost.

That cost was indeed heavy. It says much for Plato's singlemindedness that he was willing to meet it. In the *Laws*, his last attempt to plan the just city, he produces a blue-print for implanting beliefs and attitudes convenient to authority through the medium of suggestion, by a strict and ruthless censorship, the substitution of myths and emotional ceremonies for factual knowledge, the isolation of the citizen from the outside world, the creation of types with standardised reactions, and, as a final guarantee, by the sanctions of the police-state, to be invoked against all who cannot or will not conform.

Such was the intellectual and spiritual fruit of this tree, whose roots had split upon the hard rock of technical inadequacy. Materially, the result of increasing slavery was the certainty that new productive forces would not be released on any scale sufficient for a radical transformation of society. Extremes of wealth and poverty became more marked, the internal market flagged, and ancient society suffered a decline of trade and population and, finally, the wastage of class warfare. Into this sequence the rise of the Roman Empire brought the new factor of a parasitical capital; and it spread the Hellenistic system to Italy, where agrarian pauperism went side by side with imperial expansion and domination on an unparalleled scale.

From all this arose the typical developments of the social life of the Empire—industrial dispersion and a reversion to agrarian self-sufficiency—and the final attempt to retrieve the crisis, or at least to salvage whatever could be salvaged from the ruins, by the unflinching use of oppression and the machinery of the bureaucratic State. These tendencies we have already analysed, and need not repeat them here. The important point is that they fall together into a sequence with its own logic, and that they follow—not of course in the specific details, which were determined by a thousand personal or fortuitous factors, but in their general outlines —from the premises upon which classical civilisation arose, namely an absolutely low technique and, to compensate for this, the institution of slavery. Herein lie the real causes of the decline and fall of the Roman Empire.

✣

6. JOSEPH VOGT

FROM Joseph Vogt, *The Decline of Rome* (New York: New American Library, 1967), pp. 50–51, 60–62, 183–84.

When Roman historians reflect on the historical role of the empire, when poets glorify Rome's eternal mission, they always point to the benefits Roman rule conferred on the subject peoples and the peace it brought to the whole world. Their view of what constituted the world was restricted to the lands ringing the Mediterranean, the sea they called 'our sea', the land complex they called 'our world'. Making a prudent assessment of Roman resources, Augustus had checked further expansion in the east and the north and set limits to the empire, on one side the three great rivers, Rhine, Danube and Euphrates, on the other the desert belt of

Africa and Arabia. Here and there some of his successors moved forward beyond these limits, but only in order to afford more secure protection to their frontiers by means of an advanced defensive zone. Such was the motive behind the conquest of Britain, of the Neckar region between the upper reaches of Rhine and Danube, and of Dacia north of the lower Danube; Septimius Severus eventually succeeded in creating a similar outpost across the upper Euphrates, the province of Mesopotamia. Where the natural frontiers of ocean, river or desert were lacking, the borders of the empire were protected by fortifications—palisades, forts, ditches and walls, depending on the terrain—so that the entire field of ancient civilization formed one vast enclosure.

In the third century a serious threat developed to several sectors of the imperial frontier as numerous tribes settled outside the empire went over to the attack. The Picts in Scotland were pressing on Hadrian's wall in the north of England, and from the middle of the third century the desert tribes of the Blemmyes were making raids on Egypt, thus threatening the empire at its southern extremity, the first cataract of the Nile. Desert peoples were now using dromedaries, whose value had long been proved in peaceful traffic, for military purposes. This innovation meant that long-distance forays were possible, so that Arabs could now direct their raids against Syria and Mesopotamia and it was not very long before the nomads south of the fortified frontier in Algeria also started to attack. The empire had two major enemies of long standing, both of whom profoundly influenced the fate of ancient civilization, the Persians and the Germans. Writing in the reign of Nero, the poet Lucan extolled the lands beyond the Tigris and the Rhine as retreats of freedom, regions unblemished by tyranny. It was from these very regions that the empire was now to be continuously attacked. . . .

When Egypt and China were declining they too enlisted foreign mercenaries and called on neighbouring peoples for military help. In Egypt and China foreigners also rose to high positions and ended by seizing power. These observations appear to yield a universal rule for the sequence of events in dissolving empires. But since the educated classes of the Graeco-Roman world knew all too little of the history of alien peoples, they were unable to draw much profit from these lessons. Even granted that their historical frame of reference was limited, one wonders how closely Romans from the time of the Marcomannic wars (in the reign of Marcus Aurelius) were observing the movements of their German neighbours; whether they were aware of the tribal incursions into the northeastern parts of their empire as part of a general process and whether they prepared their minds for meeting the onslaught. Tacitus, whose monograph on the Germans was written around the year AD 100, reveals an astonishing knowledge of the germanic world and an early presentiment of its vital energies, perhaps even of its future historic role. But in the century of crisis there was no-one of the stature of Tacitus to appraise and clarify the situation in which the empire found itself. The short lives of the emperors made long-term defence planning increasingly harder. The possibility that a pacific approach might reduce the antagonism between the old world and the new was apparently never canvassed. Official opinion remained true to its conviction that all peoples living outside the empire were to be classed as barbarians, a conviction which made it difficult for the ancient world to take a critical look at itself. The word barbarian was still used, as it had been a thousand years earlier when the Greeks first invented it, to designate all who spoke an outlandish tongue, all foreigners, despite the fact that constant experience had shown them as people possible to talk to, with ways of life worth imitating. The barbarians were still regarded as uncivilized children of nature, wild men; though at the same time, there were many Greeks and Romans who sensed that the pristine spontaneity of these peoples was brimful of promise and noble ideals. The Romans who used *barbari* (as also *gentes*) to cover all tribes innocent of urban institutions and the classical polis, were blind to the possibility that the social virtues of freedom, courage and loyalty were more secure among peoples whose communal life was founded on blood ties and personal allegiance than in the curias and corporations of the Roman empire, which were held together by force. Finally, there was a dangerous self-deception in treating the barbarians generally as robbers and aggressors while constantly calling on their support; so many of these alleged thugs were already serving in the Roman army that in ordinary speech the word *barbari* can on occasion simply mean 'soldiers'. Despite so many generations of actual contact with these foreigners, the illusion that a high degree of human civilization was attainable only within the Roman empire still remained unshattered and the expression barbarian retained its derogatory meaning. Pictorial representation of battles between Roman and non-Roman warriors show the latter as uncouth figures deserving to be beaten and crushed under foot, the primordial stuff of conquest (*materia vincendi*), as can be seen with great effect on the huge Ludovisi battle sarcophagus, which dates from the third century. But if we want to understand the folk migrations and the transformation of culture we shall do better to dispense with the word 'barbarian' altogether, especially in view of its equally depreciative effect in our modern usage, relegating what it describes beyond some moral pale. Where the term is met within the sources, the rendering chosen must fit the situation in question, so that the expression actually used—foreigners, enemies of the empire, aliens, new peoples—will depend on the context.

From the third century warfare on the Persian and German fronts was continuous, with only short interruptions. The army, on which the security of civilian life throughout the whole empire so manifestly depended, grew steadily in importance and staked out still higher claims. Units in the frontier provinces vied with one another in making emperors, and from the middle of the century civil wars and imperial assassinations were the order of the day. In this confused period parts of the empire were thrown back on their own resources, no longer receiving directives from the centre and economically isolated. The unity of the empire was severely tested by this crisis in the imperial régime. Some modern scholars claim to detect a political trend towards particularism, towards provincial autonomy, and even speak of a separatist movement within the ancient world. They point above all to those regions which were still not fully romanized, to peoples and nations (*gentes* and *nationes*) who had kept their own speech and in times of stress were an easy prey to the temptation of setting local patriotism above loyalty to the empire. It is true that there were many regions where local languages and traditional ways of life had been preserved; we have already noticed the Galatians and Phrygians of Asia Minor, the vitality of Syrian and Aramaic dialects and the role of Coptic in Egypt. Remnants of the Punic and Berber languages had survived in North Africa, in Gaul and in Britain there were areas exclusively inhabited by Celtic-speaking tribes. Some native tongues were actively supported by the Christian mission, which helped to promote Syriac and Coptic as literary languages. Altogether there was a notable divergence among the provincial cultures which grew from the soil of the empire, and this is most clearly illustrated from their artistic output. In figurative art, especially portraiture, the single cosmopolitan style splits up into local forms, so that soon we find a Roman, Greek and oriental style of portraiture. But whatever importance may attach to these distinctively regional forms of life and art, on the political plane they produced no national uprisings and no separatism. When emperors were being made in the provinces, the initiative lay neither with the tribes nor with the mass of the provincial population; the decisive voice was always that of the Roman frontier armies, stationed on the Rhine, the Danube and the south-east front. Admittedly, these army units already contained a substantial admixture of local elements, but the first concern of the legions and of the emperors they created was always the defence of the frontiers; they had no ambition to detach provinces from the empire.

The strength of the bond of unity, even at a period of supreme crisis, is apparent from the two lordships which came into being on the extremities of the empire in consequence of the Persian wars and the catastrophic defeat of Valerian, one in Gaul and the other on the borders of Syria. In 259 the army on the Rhine acclaimed its own commander, Postumus, as emperor. Although the new ruler drew his support from the population of Gaul, he still saw the defence of the Roman provinces against the Germans as his main task. When attempts at combining his rule in Gaul with allegiance to the central Roman government, which on Valerian's capture had passed to his son Gallienus, proved fruitless, Postumus set up a regional administration with its own senate and annually appointed magistrates; this *Imperium Galliarum*, in which the provinces of Britain and Spain also joined, continued for more than a decade. The emperor Gallienus was quite incapable of subduing this rival imperium; his successor Claudius was fully engaged in countering Gothic attacks on the Danube. The defeat of the Gallic emperor (Postumus' successor Tetricus) was finally accomplished in 273 by Aurelian, whose prodigious energy succeeded in restoring the central power of the empire. Although it existed for so long, the *Imperium Galliarum* was far from being a national Gallic state: the Roman administration continued everywhere in being and the government in Gaul knew no higher aim than to preserve the empire and its culture. . . .

Soon after the death of Theodosius, the initiative in the long, drawn-out contest between the empire and the hostile world outside, between the ancient world and the new peoples, passed to the close-knit leagues of German tribes; whether they were still outside the frontiers or had already advanced into Roman territory was immaterial. The elemental drive and will to freedom of these peoples now descended on the Romans in full spate. As we trace the advances made by the various groups down to the middle of the fifth century, our concern will not be with specific questions of warfare and policy but with the general aspects of German activity and the Roman reaction to it. The forefront of the picture will be occupied by the empire of the West, virtually the sole target of German attacks. For a number of reasons the eastern empire remained essentially unaffected by the Germans. In the first place, the geographical starting-point of the chain of aggression made it inevitable that tribes pressing in from eastern Europe would push against the Rhine and the Danube, that is to say the western empire. In addition, the diplomats of Constantinople repeatedly showed their skill by deflecting migrating tribes away from Thrace and sending them on to the West. But the decisive factor was that the political, military and economic systems of the eastern empire suffered no material damage. The capital city of Constantinople, a fortress protected by the sea, was impregnable, while the eastern government found ways of adapting the provincial government to the new situation and by its financial policy ensured that there was no fall in the value of money. The cities of Asia Minor and Syria continued to prosper from their industrial activity and active pursuit of trade. In view of their success in keeping the alien tribes at bay, it is no wonder that the men who ruled in Constantinople came to feel that whereas old Rome had abdicated her responsibilities they were the true representatives of Rome's world-wide mission.

Numerous references to the germanic peoples themselves in the first decades of the invasions are to be found in poems, sermons and lives of the saints; this literary history of the German migrations has been reconstructed for us by W. Capelle and P. Courcelle. But in these sources the Roman side of the picture overwhelmingly predominates. We hear much of the sufferings of inhabitants of the empire, of the atrocities committed by the barbarians—often deplored in the platitudes usual in ancient literature—and the plight of refugees who fled from Italy, Gaul and Spain to North Africa and the East. We hear something of the strong penetration of the Roman army by germanic elements and are told of the suspected or actual treachery perpetrated by individual officers and even by citizens of beleaguered towns. There are references to bishops who organized resistance to the foreigners and to churches used as places of asylum. In Christian writers, detached observation of the foreign invaders is often hindered by the author's excessive reliance on divine protection, secured through the intercession of the saints and the miraculous deeds of holy monks. Even military leaders could fall back on miracles, as for example the general named Jacobus whose cult of the saints inspired the poet Claudian to an ironic epigram. We thus cannot expect these contemporary witnesses to give us any definite information from the German side, even about matters of the first importance. The figures suggested for the numerical strength of the tribes are often pure fantasy; the results of modern scholarship suggest that in numbers the German fighting forces were far inferior to the Roman armies and that the total number of aliens introduced into the empire by tribal settlement was minute compared with its existing population. We are no better informed about the weapons available to the invaders. E. Salin and others who have investigated graves and their weapon deposits, using new archaeological techniques, have concluded that in this respect the Germans were superior to the Romans; it seems that their outstanding skill in making offensive weapons—lance, sword, javelin and throwing axe—was derived from the metal-working Celts of central Europe. If we ask how the tribes moved about, we discover that no author has described them on the trek, that no relief depicts their wagon trains or temporary encampments. Opinions vary as to the objectives of the invaders. It is often assumed they were in search of booty, but we know that these Germans were not strictly speaking nomads but dispossessed cultivators: in need of sustenance, they halted when they came to state granaries and had to move on again when the supply was exhausted; it was not long before they felt the urge to possess land for permanent cultivation. Often the political aims of the germanic princes also remain obscure. Many fought with dogged determination to achieve their ambition of high office under the empire; yet they shrank from seizing the imperial dignity itself—even at the height of his success, when he had won the emperor's daughter as his bride, the Visigothic king Athaulf preferred to set up an insignificant Roman rather than himself as rival emperor. At a certain juncture, though just when is often difficult to say, some chieftains were struck by the idea of achieving complete independence for their own peoples within the boundaries of the empire. There are many further questions we should like to ask: how was contact made between the strangers and the emperor and his emissaries, what relations did they have with the local urban and rural populations? Were there interpreters? We hear only seldom of Romans and Germans who could speak both languages. Our sources often allude to the conflict of religious belief, to tension between the Catholic inhabitants of the empire and the Arianized Germans. But these Greek and Roman writers make no comment on the way these tribes and peoples, uprooted as they were from their traditional way of life, endured the hardships of migrating with their wives and children, they tell us nothing of the poetry by which the Germans transfigured their heroic feats, nor of the religion which sustained them in their plight. When so much must remain obscure, it is all the more essential to bear constantly in mind that the phenomenon we are observing is a migration of peoples, not merely an invasion of 'barbarians'.

In describing the assault of the Germans on the Roman empire it is difficult to keep the various peoples sharply distinct, since the movements of Visigoths, Vandals and Burgundians were often closely interwoven, and other migrant groups were also involved. Unrest started among those Visigoths who had settled in Moesia following the treaty of 382. After the death of Theodosius, this tribe broke out in rebellion, led by Alaric, the chieftain who afterwards became their king. With their first onslaught (395–7) the Visigoths ravaged the whole Balkan peninsula and, being at the mercy of the rival governments of Constantinople and Milan, were first granted settlement land in Epirus. Having gathered strength for a new attack, the Visigoths directed their second onslaught against Italy (401–3) but were eventually expelled by Stilicho, who had summoned all available Roman forces including troops from the Rhine and Britain, and made to settle on the Save. It was during this war that the decision was made to transfer the imperial government, which had been besieged for a while in Milan, to Ravenna, a small town protected from surprise attack by its surrounding swamps. In earlier days the imperial fleet had been stationed here; the move to Ravenna gave Honorius' government an outlet to the sea, although the actual harbour, Classis, was silted up and much labour had to be expended before it could be re-opened for maritime traffic. Ravenna, difficult of access from the landward side but open to the sea, made a superb refuge for the imperial government in its hour of need. In the fifth book of his history Zosimus paints a vivid contrast between the land of Italy, for so many years an almost defenceless prey to its conquerors, and the court of Ravenna, pursuing its ceremonies and intrigues as though playing out some ghostly game. The many churches and tombs which came to adorn Ravenna over the years complement this impression of a cloistered monarchy, turned in on itself in anchorite seclusion. ✣

7. A. H. M. JONES

FROM A. H. M. Jones, *The Later Roman Empire*, 4 vols. (Oxford: Basil Blackwell, 1964), vol. II, 1026–31, 1062–68.

The Roman empire seems never to have evoked any active patriotism from the vast majority of its citizens. Most of them no doubt were indifferent but even those who admired the empire felt no call to devote themselves to its service. Their attitude was well expressed by Aelius Aristides' great panegyric on Rome, and symbolised by the official cult of Rome and Augustus. Rome was to them a mighty and beneficent power which excited their admiration and gratitude, but the empire was too immense to evoke the kind of loyalty which they felt to their own cities. They revered the emperor as a saviour and benefactor, who with his legions defended their cities against the barbarians, and by his wisdom, humanity and justice promoted their peace and prosperity, but they did not regard him as a leader whom they must serve. Rome was eternal, and the emperor was a god, who needed no assistance from his worshippers.

Under the later empire the same attitude persisted. The regular army was expected to defend the empire, and it was only in a most desperate emergency, when Radagaisus and his hordes had broken into Italy, that the government appealed to the provincials to join up as temporary volunteers 'for love of peace and country'. It was still in theory illegal for civilians to own or bear arms. Only when Gaiseric was threatening to invade Italy was this rule relaxed and the provincials urged to arm themselves in order to resist Vandal landings. Justinian tightened up the ban on arms by making their manufacture a strict imperial monopoly; but he did provide the cities with armouries, controlled by the *patres civitatum*. Nor did the fundamental attitude of the provincials to the empire change. The emperor was no longer a god, but he was the vicegerent of God, entrusted by him with the task of governing and defending the empire. His subjects were taught to render unto Caesar the things that are Caesar's, that is, to pay their taxes and obey the authorities; but they were not exhorted to devote themselves to the empire's service.

Christianity has been accused on the one hand of sapping the empire's morale by its otherworldly attitude, and on the other hand credited with giving the empire new spiritual energy and reforming it by its moral teaching. Neither allegation seems to have much substance. There is little to show that pagan worship promoted a patriotic spirit; the gods were, it is true, regarded as the patrons and protectors of the Roman state, so long as they were not offended by the breach of certain moral rules and were duly placated with sacrifices, but they do not seem to have inspired patriotic devotion. Constantine and his successors and their Christian subjects carried over the same attitude to the one God whom they worshipped. God in their eyes was the mighty power who would give victory and prosperity to the empire, provided that he was properly appeased by his worshippers. His demands were, it is true, more exacting than those of the old gods, since he required not only ritual acts, but correct belief about his own nature, and the standard of morality which he expected from his devotees was markedly higher. But for the vast majority of ordinary men Christianity caused no fundamental change of attitude.

To the ordinary man likewise the moral teaching and the otherworldly doctrine of Christianity seems to have made little practical difference. In some respects moral standards declined, and most people continued to devote their energies to the goods of this world. The average Christian does not seem to have worried greatly about the fate of his soul until he feared that death was near, and then hoped to win access to heaven by the rituals of baptism or penance. In the meanwhile he pursued his worldly ends with no more, and sometimes less, regard for moral principles than his pagan forebears.

There was, of course, a minority who took the Christian message seriously to heart, and regarding the things of the world as of no account, devoted themselves to achieving eternal life in the world to come. Many thousands withdrew into the desert or into monasteries and spent the rest of their lives striving by austerities and prayer to gain salvation; many were drawn, often against their will, into the service of the Church as priests and bishops.

Quantitatively the loss to the state was probably not significant. Numerous as the clergy, monks and hermits were, their withdrawal cannot have seriously accentuated the manpower shortage from which the empire suffered, nor can the fact that the majority of them were celibate have contributed much to the shrinkage of the population. Qualitatively the loss was more serious. It was men of high moral character who were most drawn to the spiritual life, and were thus lost to the service of the state. In the pagan empire such men had regarded the public service as one of the principal duties of the good man and citizen. Under the new dispensation they were taught that a public career was, if not sinful, so fraught with spiritual danger that it should be eschewed. The service of the state tended to be left to ambitious careerists, and Christianity thus paradoxically increased the corruption of the government.

It may be asked whether the Eastern parts suffered less from any of the weaknesses discussed above than did the West. In some respects the East was at a disadvantage. Christianity prevailed earlier in the Eastern parts and obtained a more thorough hold. Monks and clergy were more numerous and more richly endowed, and thus a heavier burden on the economy. Theological controversy was more widespread and more embittered, and the repression of heresy demanded a greater use of force and provoked more hostility. In so far as the otherworldly attitude which Christianity inculcated weakened public morale, the East should have been more gravely affected. In most matters no significant distinction can be traced. The most serious losses in the area of cultivation are recorded in Africa, but *agri deserti* were a problem common to both halves of the empire. The rules tying *coloni* to the soil and *curiales* to their cities were even more rigid in the East than in the West. The East was, it is true, more politically stable and dissipated less of its strength in civil wars, but as against this it was obliged on a number of occasions to waste its resources on suppressing Western usurpers.

In two ways, however, the East seems to have been stronger and healthier than the West. In the first place the Eastern provinces were probably initially richer and more populous than the Western. It is very difficult to substantiate this statement, but it must be remembered that Macedonia and Greece, Asia Minor, Syria and Egypt had been settled and civilised lands for many centuries when they were incorporated in the empire, while many parts of the West, Britain, northern Gaul, north-western Spain, and the Danubian provinces, had been barbarous and undeveloped even after their annexation. The resources of the Eastern lands had long been fully exploited and their population had swelled. In the north-western provinces much of the potentially best land was probably woodland and waste, forest or swamp. It is significant that Aquitania is more highly praised for its agricultural wealth by Salvian than northern Gaul, and that supplies had to be carted all the way from Aquitania to Châlons and even to Paris to feed Constantius II's and Julian's armies. It is even more significant that Sicily, Sardinia and above all Africa were still under the later empire regarded as the granaries of the Western empire. For these countries, with their mountainous terrain and scanty and irregular rainfall, can never have been highly productive, however intensively they were cultivated, and their yield would have been far exceeded by that of Britain, Gaul and the Danubian lands, had the resources of these regions been fully exploited. From the meagre figures available it would appear that the African diocese, the richest in the Western parts, produced only a third or a quarter of the revenue that Egypt, its richest diocese, yielded to the Eastern government.

This picture is rather difficult to believe when one looks at the present state of affairs, when north-western Europe is intensively cultivated and densely populated, and north Africa (with the exception of Egypt, whose natural wealth has in all ages remained indestructible), Syria, Anatolia and the Balkans are derelict after long centuries of neglect and misgovernment. Progressive denudation has by now reduced their water supplies and washed away much of their good soil, but even now they could produce far more than they do, and the archaeological remains show that they were far more extensively cultivated in Roman times.

A rough index to the geographical distribution of wealth under the Roman empire is provided by the ruins of ancient monuments; for under the Principate all cities expended as much as they could afford on public buildings. The survival of ancient buildings is of course largely a matter of chance, and their chances are far better in areas which have subsequently become derelict than in those which have remained in continuous occupation and prospered. Whole cities survive in the deserts of Africa and Syria and in the more desolate parts of Asia Minor, but virtually nothing at continuously occupied sites like Antioch or Alexandria. Nevertheless the distribution of ruins is suggestive. In all northern western Europe—Britain, northern Gaul, north-western Spain and the Danubian lands—no monumental buildings survive except at the imperial capital of Trier, and the buildings which excavation has revealed are mostly on a modest scale. By contrast Narbonensis, eastern and southern Spain, Italy, north Africa, Syria and Palestine, Asia Minor and the southern Balkans can boast of many, and the largest and most magnificent are in the Eastern parts. In these areas, furthermore, where the Roman buildings have disappeared, Roman columns, capitals and other architectural members have been freely reused in the medieval mosques and churches. It is hard to find a Roman column in north-western Europe, and it is likely the medieval builders found few.

The Eastern Empire was thus probably from the start richer than the Western, the greater part of which was still underdeveloped. The distribution of wealth was also probably more even in the East. This again is difficult to substantiate, but the few facts and figures that we possess strongly suggest that the senators of Rome were far wealthier than those of Constantinople and owned far more extensive estates. There were probably more medium landowners in the East, and fairly certainly more peasant proprietors, notably in Egypt, eastern Asia Minor, Thrace and Illyricum. The explanation of this appears to be historical. The Roman aristocracy in the West had begun to accumulate wealth far earlier, and in some Western lands, such as Gaul, there had already existed a landowning aristocracy before the Roman conquest. In the East an imperial aristocracy only began to accumulate wealth in the fourth century, and in some provinces, notably Egypt, the system of land tenure had protected the peasant proprietor.

The greater number of small freeholders, since taxes came to less than rent, meant that a higher proportion of the yield of agriculture remained in the hands of the cultivators in the East than in the West. By and large the peasantry were better fed and probably reared more children. It also meant that the state secured a higher proportion of the agricultural surplus, for peasant proprietors and small landowners paid full rate of tax, while the great senatorial landlords, apart from the legal exemptions which they enjoyed, could evade taxation.

The existence of an ancient wealthy aristocracy in the West also had important political effects. The Roman aristocracy from the reign of Constantine became ever more influential, and by the fifth century almost monopolised the higher administrative posts. These great noblemen were naturally tender to the interests of their own class, and were on the whole inefficient administrators. In the East, on the other hand, hereditary nobles did not dominate the administration, and the highest posts were often filled by men who had risen by ability, and being dependent on the emperor's favour, gave priority to the interests of the government. The result was that the fiscal privileges of the great owners were curbed, and also that there was less wastage in the administration: it is highly significant that the perquisites of the officials who collected the taxes were fifty or sixty times greater in the West than in the East.

The East then probably possessed greater economic resources, and could thus support with less strain a larger number of idle mouths. A smaller part of its resources went, it would seem, to maintain its aristocracy, and more was thus available for the army and other essential services. It also was probably more populous, and since the economic pressure on the peasantry was perhaps less severe, may have suffered less from population decline. If there is any substance in these arguments, the Eastern government should have been able to raise a larger revenue without overstraining its resources, and to levy more troops without depleting its labour force.

It is impossible to check this hypothesis for the crucial period, the fourth century, in which both halves of the empire were territorially intact. In the fifth and sixth centuries the Eastern government commanded a larger and more buoyant revenue than the Western. It could spend very large sums on lavish blackmail to the barbarians and on ambitious military operations without running into serious financial difficulties. Leo's expedition against the Vandals, followed by Zeno's reckless expenditure, did indeed temporarily exhaust the treasury, but Anastasius was quickly able to restore the empire's finances, and it was not until the reign of Maurice that the strain of the protracted Persian and Avar wars caused a serious financial crisis. It was also able to raise large armies from its own subjects and did not make excessive use of barbarian troops.

The Western government on the other hand was almost bankrupt by the end of Valentinian III's reign and had virtually abandoned conscription, relying almost entirely on barbarian federates. The collapse of the West was however by no means entirely attributable to its internal weaknesses, for the government had by now lost to the barbarians many of the provinces on which it had relied for revenue and recruits, and those which it still controlled had suffered so severely from the ravages of the barbarians that they had to be allowed remission of taxation.

Of the manifold weaknesses of the later Roman empire some, the increasing maldistribution of wealth, the corruption and extortion of the administration, the lack of public spirit and the general apathy of the population, were to a large extent due to internal causes. But some of the more serious of these weaknesses were the result, direct or indirect, of barbarian pressure. Above all the need to maintain a vastly increased army had far-reaching effects. It necessitated a rate of taxation so heavy as to cause a progressive decline in agriculture and indirectly a shrinkage of population. The effort to collect this heavy taxation required a great expansion of the civil service, and this expansion in turn imposed an additional burden on the economy and made administrative corruption and extortion more difficult to control. The oppressive weight of the taxation contributed to the general apathy.

The Western empire was poorer and less populous, and its social and economic structure more unhealthy. It was thus less able to withstand the tremendous strains imposed by its defensive effort, and the internal weaknesses which it developed undoubtedly contributed to its final collapse in the fifth century. But the major cause of its fall was that it was more exposed to barbarian onslaughts which in persistence and sheer weight of numbers far exceeded anything which the empire had previously had to face. The Eastern empire, owing to its greater wealth and population and sounder economy, was better able to carry the burden of defence, but its resources were overstrained and it developed the same weaknesses as the West, if perhaps in a less acute form. Despite these weaknesses it managed in the sixth century not only to hold its own against the Persians in the East but to reconquer parts of the West, and even when, in the seventh century, it was overrun by the onslaughts of the Persians and the Arabs and the Slavs, it succeeded despite heavy territorial losses in rallying and holding its own. The internal weaknesses of the empire cannot have been a major factor in its decline. . . .

In the eighteenth century the debate on the fall of the empire was resumed, and it has gone on ever since. Rationalists like Gibbon saw religion as a primary cause of its decline, but in a very different way from the pagan and Christian controversialists of the fifth century. Christianity in his view sapped the morale of the empire, deadened its intellectual life and by its embittered controversies undermined its unity. Other historians, according to the temper of their times, have emphasised the empire's military decline, its political or social weaknesses, or its economic decay.

All the historians who have discussed the decline and fall of the Roman empire have been Westerners. Their eyes have been fixed on the collapse of Roman authority in the Western parts and the evolution of the medieval Western European world. They have tended to forget, or to brush aside, one very important fact, that the Roman empire, though it may have declined, did not fall in the fifth century nor indeed for another thousand years. During the fifth century, while the Western parts were being parcelled out into a group of barbarian kingdoms, the empire of the East stood its ground. In the sixth it counter-attacked and reconquered Africa from the Vandals and Italy from the Ostrogoths, and part of Spain from the Visigoths. Before the end of the century, it is true, much of Italy and Spain had succumbed to renewed barbarian attacks, and in the seventh the onslaught of the Arabs robbed the empire of Syria, Egypt, and Africa, and the Slavs overran the Balkans. But in Asia Minor the empire lived on, and later, recovering its strength, reconquered much territory that it had lost in the dark days of the seventh century.

These facts are important, for they demonstrate that the empire did not, as some modern historians have suggested, totter into its grave from senile decay, impelled by a gentle push from the barbarians. Most of the internal weaknesses which these historians stress were common to both halves of the empire. The East was even more Christian than the West, its theological disputes far more embittered. The East, like the West, was administered by a corrupt and extortionate bureaucracy. The Eastern government strove as hard to enforce a rigid caste system, tying the *curiales* to their cities and the *coloni* to the soil. Land fell out of cultivation and was deserted in the East as well as in the West. It may be that some of these weaknesses were more accentuated in the West than in the East, but this is a question which needs investigation. It may be also that the initial strength of the Eastern empire in wealth and population was greater, and that it could afford more wastage; but this again must be demonstrated.

In one respect, however, the Eastern empire was demonstrably better placed than the Western. It was strategically less vulnerable, and was down to the end of the fifth century subjected to less pressure from external enemies. This suggests that the simple but rather unfashionable view that the barbarians played a considerable part in the decline and fall of the empire may have some truth in it. External pressures and internal weaknesses of course interacted. The enfeeblement of the empire no doubt encouraged the barbarians to win easy spoils. The devastations of the barbarians impoverished and depopulated the frontier provinces, and their unceasing pressure imposed on the empire a burden of defence which overstrained its administrative machinery and its economic resources. But directly or indirectly, it may be plausibly argued, barbarian attacks probably played a major part in the fall of the West.

During the first two centuries of the Principate the empire held its own against the barbarians with very little trouble. There was a serious crisis under Marcus Aurelius, and from the reign of Severus Alexander the imperial armies found increasing difficulty in beating off attacks across the frontier. How far was this due to increasing barbarian pressure? We know next to nothing of what was happening in the forests and marshes of Germany and the steppes of eastern Europe, but it is observable that in these areas there were long periods of relative stability, broken only by perennial border wars, and other periods of widespread restlessness. Trouble generally started when a tribe, whether because it had outgrown the means of subsistence in its homeland, or because it was hard pressed by aggressive neighbours, or lured by stories of richer lands far away which might be plundered or occupied, decided to abandon its home and start on trek. Such a movement had a snowball effect. Other tribes were excited and joined the adventure: others again were displaced and forced to migrate elsewhere; unless the movement was nipped in the bud, it tended to proliferate over a wider and wider area.

Some such movement probably produced the violent irruption of Gallic tribes into Italy in the fifth and fourth centuries B.C. and into the Balkans and Asia Minor in the third. The Cimbri and Teutones, whose migrations caused such turmoil at the end of the second century B.C., are certainly a case in point. Caesar was able to check a movement of the Helvetii before it gathered way. Then for two centuries northern Europe was quiescent.

We do not know what caused the disturbance of the Quadi and Marcomanni which gave Marcus Aurelius so much trouble, but in the third century we know from their national legends of the great trek of the Goths and other East German tribes from their homes round the Baltic. They and the tribes that they set in motion broke into the empire and were only beaten back after long struggles by the great Illyrian emperors of the late third century, and barbarian pressure on the Rhine and Danube remained heavy during the fourth.

From the third quarter of the fourth century there appears a new disturbing force, the Huns. Their advent produced panic and turmoil throughout the German tribes. Fleeing before them the Visigoths sought refuge within the empire and the Ostrogoths trekked westward. It was without doubt the pressure of the Huns, direct or indirect, that caused waves of Germanic tribes to flood into Italy under Radagaesus and to sweep over the Rhine a few years later. The Hunnic kingdom itself grievously afflicted the empire until it broke up in 454, and in the wake of the Huns came other Asiatic tribes, such as the Avars, who in their turn set in motion the Slavs.

It is impossible to measure numerically the strength of the attacking forces. Contemporaries certainly often grossly exaggerated the numbers of the barbarian hordes, and on the meagre and for the most part unreliable evidence available it would seem that a tribal group such as the Vandals or the Visigoths could not put into the field more than twenty or thirty thousand fighting men. To modern ears such figures seem negligible, but in relation to the size of the armies which the empire could muster at any given point they were formidable. Moreover it must be remembered that the empire had to defend itself against a considerable number of such groups, and that some major disasters, such as the great breakthrough on the Rhine in 407, were the result of a combined movement of several tribes. The difficulties of the defence were increased by the anarchic state of the barbarian world. The movements of the barbarians were entirely unpredictable; at any point along hundreds of miles of frontier there might at any moment flood a swarm of warriors which far outnumbered the troops immediately available. Moreover the gaps in the front line were always filled by newcomers; scarcely had the power of the Huns been broken when the Avars appeared in the West, and less than twenty years after Justinian's army had finally cleared the Ostrogoths out of Italy the Lombards swarmed in.

Though we cannot gauge the numbers involved, we can, if we compare the narratives of two historians who wrote on a similar scale—Tacitus and Ammianus—sense the change between the first and the fourth century A.D. In the Annals there are occasional border disturbances; but on the whole the frontier armies have very little to do except when an aggressive commander carries the war into enemy territory. In the pages of Ammianus we see Constantius II, Julian, Valentinian and Valens constantly engaged in repelling an attack here or conducting a punitive expedition there, and if for a moment their backs are turned, the barbarians forthwith break in. And except for the last book, Ammianus' history describes the period before the impact of the Huns pushed the German tribes westwards and redoubled the pressure on the Roman frontier.

The Persian empire under the Sassanid dynasty was certainly a more formidable enemy than had been the Parthian empire in the first two and a half centuries of the Principate. It was probably, when it put its full strength into play, more formidable than any but the largest concentrations of German tribes; the largest Roman armies on record were mustered against Persia.

On the other frontiers the barbarians were a nuisance rather than a menace, but everywhere the pressure seems to have increased. In the diocese of Africa, where we hear of very little fighting under the Principate after the annexation of Mauretania by Claudius, the Moorish tribes became increasingly aggressive from the end of the third century and by the sixth were a constant menace. Cyrenaica, which had been ungarrisoned under the early empire, suffered from heavy raids in the fifth century. In Upper Egypt, which had been adequately protected by half a dozen auxiliary units, a much larger garrison found it difficult to cope with growing activity of the Nobadae and Blemmyes. Even in the interior of the empire the Isaurian highlanders, who had given no trouble since the early first century, from the late third were a constant menace to the surrounding provinces.

The brunt of the barbarian attack fell for obvious reasons on the West. In the fourth century the Western emperor was generally responsible for the defence of the whole length of the Rhine and Danube frontier, except for the last 300 miles of the Danube's course. Even in the fifth century, when the Eastern emperor took over the Dacian and Macedonian dioceses, the Western emperor still had more than twice as long a frontier to guard. This put a constant heavy strain on the resources of the West, and moreover presented it with a very difficult strategic problem. It was beyond the resources of the Western empire to contain a simultaneous attack on the Rhine and the upper Danube, and when the front line was breached by such a double assault, as it was in the early fifth century, there was no satisfactory second line of defence. The Eastern emperor had less front to cover, and therefore less constant wear and tear on his resources, and if the lower Danube was breached, as it often was, could and did hold the enemy at the Straits. The defence of his capital, indeed, forced him to hold this line at all costs, and adequate forces were always kept in reserve to guard Constantinople. In the West the defence of Rome absorbed troops which might from a purely strategical point of view have been better employed guarding the Pyrenees or the straits of Gibraltar, and the result was that when the Rhine frontier was breached the barbarian invaders surged on almost unchecked into Spain, and a few years later were able to cross into Africa.

The Eastern emperor was, it is true, responsible for the defence of the empire against the Persians, and when Persia was aggressive this was a heavy burden. But the Persian kings had their own troubles, dynastic disputes, internal rebellions and the barbarian pressure on their own northern frontier, and they generally preferred to keep the peace with Rome. There was a brief Persian war under Diocletian in 297–8. There were prolonged, but not continuous, hostilities from the accession of Constantius II in 337 to the defeat of Julian's great expedition in 363. Thereafter, apart from some rather desultory fighting in Armenia under Valens and two brief wars under Theodosius II in 421–2 and 440–2, there was peace until in 502 Cavades attacked Anastasius.

In the 240 years which passed between the accession of Diocletian and that of Justinian there was thus a state of war between Rome and Persia for less than forty, and in most of those forty years there were no hostilities, but truces, official or unofficial, during which negotiations were pursued. Moreover when peace was arranged, there was genuine peace: Persia was a civilised power which normally kept its bond and could control its subjects. For most of the fourth century therefore and nearly all the fifth the empire did not have to worry about its Eastern frontier. From the beginning of the sixth century Persia, under a series of vigorous and aggressive kings, Cavades (488–531), Chosroes I (531–79) and Hormisdas IV (579–90) exercised heavy pressure on the empire, but there were long spells of peace, from 507 to 527, from 531 to 540, from 562 to 577 and from 590 to 602, and between 545 and 562 there were a series of truces, partial or complete, and little fighting of importance. Nevertheless the strain was severe, and partly accounts for the débâcle which followed the death of Maurice.

All things considered it would appear that on all fronts the empire was exposed to much greater pressure from the middle of the third century, and that this pressure became yet more intense with the advent of the Huns, and did not thereafter relax. It is also plain that the Western empire bore much more than its fair share of the burden and was much less favourably placed to make a recovery when its first line of defence was broken. Within twenty-five years of the great break-through on the Rhine, Italy was encircled by barbarian kingdoms in Gaul, Spain and Africa, and the struggle became hopeless. The Eastern emperors always had the resources of Asia Minor, Syria and Egypt on which to draw, and could always hold any tribes that crossed the Lower Danube at bay until they tired of ravaging Thrace and Illyricum and moved on to less devastated areas. In this way the strength of the East contributed to the troubles of the West. The Visigoths under Alaric moved West into Italy, having exhausted the possibilities of Illyricum, and so did the Ostrogoths under Theoderic. Even Attila tired of ravaging the Balkans and ultimately marched against the West. They all realised that Constantinople was too tough a nut to crack. ✳

8. F. OERTEL

FROM F. Oertel, "The Economic Life of the Empire," *The Cambridge Ancient History*, 12 vols. (Cambridge: Cambridge University Press, 1939), vol. XII, 249–55, 262–70.

The picture as a whole is one of a more lively and flourishing economic activity, reaching its zenith in the age of the Antonines, and finding its reflection in the widespread city prosperity of the times, a prosperity for which the *nouveaux riches*, naturally enough, claim most of the credit. The ruins of the cities, frequently still magnificent, and of the luxurious aristocratic residences in the country, the funeral monuments and the inscriptions in stone which record the munificence of wealthy citizens, and also the large and small farms in purely agricultural districts, all have the same clear tale to tell. Fortunes were made in a multitude of ways. Sometimes systematically organized agriculture brought wealth, as in Africa; where the tenants of the imperial domains, a numerous class since the Neronian confiscations, must be reckoned amongst the other large agriculturalists. Sometimes wealth had a mercantile origin, as in Palmyra, Doura, Petra, and also in Ostia. Sometimes its causes were both agricultural and mercantile activity, as in South Russia, sometimes mercantile, industrial, and agricultural, as in Gaul, Germany, and North Italy, or in the East. Prosperity grew not only in the cities of world-significance, but also in the thousands of medium-sized and small cities, such as Thamugadi and Lambaesis in Africa, Heddernheim in Germany east of the Rhine or Smyrna and Assos in Asia Minor, or Hermopolis Magna in Egypt. This wide diffusion of prosperity is, indeed, its characteristic feature; there is a decentralization of property corresponding to the economic decentralization. The huge fortunes concentrated more especially in Rome and Italy at the end of the Republican era and in the opening years of the Empire shrank or disappeared if we except the fortune of the emperor. The confiscations under emperors such as Nero and Vespasian indirectly assisted this process. Prosperity was now spread throughout the Empire—indeed, the change in the economic situation was mostly due to this one cause, namely a more equable distribution, and the middle class, under the direct encouragement of the emperor, shared to a considerable extent in the wealth of the Empire as a whole. This is but another aspect of the levelling process which manifested itself in very similar fashion in other spheres, such as those of nationality, of constitutional law, of defence policy, and of culture.

In view of this evidence it cannot be denied that an increase in economic activity took place, but on closer examination it appears that this increase was only in quantity not in quality. In other words, it was a matter of greater extension not of greater depth; the level of organization already reached in the Hellenistic age was not surpassed. There was merely a constant expansion of the existing economic system to embrace territories of the Empire newly opened to development. Hadrian marked a clear-cut break, as he was responsible for checking the expansion of the Empire, though by doing so he admittedly made it possible for the seed which had been previously sown to come to full maturity in the early years of the Antonines. A glance at the forms of production shows that there was no qualitative economic advance. In agriculture the *villa rustica* of Brioni Grande, and the luxury estates, the manors, and the farms of Gaul, Belgium, Germany, or Africa, surpass the Pompeian villas in size alone, not in organization, whereas the provincial villas, especially the larger ones, on the whole hardly approached the Pompeian standard, if, indeed, they had any desire to do so . . . In the industrial sphere it is true that in connection with the great estates of the emperors and of private citizens in Italy as in the provinces (Gaul, Germany, Belgium, Britain, Africa) new large-scale concerns producing for export on the model of the Egyptian *ousia*-manufacture did come into being, this process being encouraged by the fact that raw materials, such as clay and wool, could be processed by agricultural labourers during the winter. These forms of production, however, did not cause an advance in the essential character of industry, any more than did the large concerns run by specialists in some particular line of business (brickyards, potteries, builders' and glaziers' workshops), in the cities or the countryside of the new or old provinces. The step from the manufactory to the factory . . . and the machine as the fundamental means of production was still not made. In businesses the personal element predominates throughout. Often every imaginable form of business activity is united in one hand—industrial, commercial, agricultural, and banking. A crucial piece of evidence is that 'large-scale' industry practically never succeeded in exterminating, or even in markedly limiting, skilled craftsmanship, least of all in the West. The craftsman remained, not as a mere survival, but really independent and capable of competition, side by side with the rival form of production. It follows that even now there was no 'large-scale industry' in the technical sense of the word, in spite of all approximations to division of labour and specialized manufacture of the parts (which, however, are not inconsistent with skilled craftsmanship), but only highly organized production by skilled craftsmanship, a point to which we shortly return. The mining industry also introduced no new form of organization. So too, trade and banking provide no evidence which would point to an advance beyond the stage reached in the first century of our era or in the Hellenistic age. The arrangements at Doura, which we now know extremely well, are typical. Their subdivision, the limited scope of their transactions, their linking of shops for assorted commodities with pawnbroking all show a form of organization based on the small-scale unit. The 'trading companies' (*societates*) everywhere remain mere associations of dealers for business purposes, and do not lose their personal character. It is not surprising, therefore, that the economic picture appears fundamentally unchanged. Agriculture, not industry, is of prime importance, and has actually gained in relative significance . . . Fortunes are made either by the traditional means of a political career (emperor, favourites, senators, knights), or else by trade and speculation, rather than by industrial enterprise; and surplus profits from every type of undertaking, the industrial included, are still constantly invested in land.

What were the underlying causes of the absence of development in technique? The economy of the second and third centuries was a continuous organic development of the features observed in the first century, including both the actively progressive and the retarding elements . . . The actively progressive elements, whose ramifications continued into the third century and later and are exemplified at the close of that century in the planting of vineyards held on an emphyteutic tenure in the large Egyptian estates, have now been analysed. The retarding elements, where the old and the new are closely intertwined, now demand attention.

Among the old factors is the unstable character of ancient private economy, which is connected with the absence of extensive financial operations and of wide credit facilities for productive enterprises. In agriculture we may indeed call to mind the *alimenta* of Nerva and his successors (although considerations connected with the birth-rate and social reform rather than with economic policy were decisive here), the measures of relief for land-owners ascribed to Severus Alexander . . . , Hadrian's remission of rents, and the rebates in taxation on land held on emphyteutic tenure. There is nothing corresponding to this in industry. Indeed the financial resources brought into play by emperors (on the model of Hellenistic rulers) or by great landowners for their own industrial purposes constitute a movement away from the bourgeois system of economy, which is what we are considering here, and can thus be considered in another connection. State protection of industry is also absent.

A second retarding factor, also of long standing, which Rostovtzeff has emphasized, is that consumption remained low despite the progress made. The purchasing power of the very large lower class was small. The circle of buyers for wares of somewhat superior quality derived accordingly from the middle and upper classes, and from the army, which for this reason had unusual economic significance. So long as industry, keeping pace with the political expansion, could steadily enlarge and extend its field of custom from the buying capacity of the newly-acquired lands, there was no difficulty. When, however, the limits of the *oikoumene* were reached, and the external market in consequence grew weaker, industry should have exploited the internal market more actively, and should have extended its scope to include the lower classes. This, however, would have required a modification in the social structure of the Empire.

Here a third factor emerges, the legacy, from the Hellenistic era, of slave labour in manufacture as the most efficient form of industrial production. Although that era was the technical age of the ancient world, the evolution of the factory remained incomplete, not because of any technical or intellectual deficiency, but because the slave was a unit of labour which could be exploited to the full, so that the problem of economizing labour never became pressing. In Hellenistic, and even in early Imperial, times it was possible to manage tolerably well with a form of production that fell short of real intensity, first because the demand was still sufficiently large, secondly, because the nature of the ancient civilization, based on coastal and river communications, remained to some extent unaltered, so that the question of transport costs was not yet so acute, thirdly, above all because there were still sufficient slaves or substitutes for them. All three premises had now been more or less invalidated. Demand could not be increased under present methods. Slavery, on which the activity of even the smaller workshops was still chiefly dependent, diminished, and free labour gained in consequence, especially in the West. This necessarily implied greater emphasis on individual skilled craftsmanship, whereas the half-free labour of the East still remained as a factor favouring the larger type of organization, though at the same time perhaps favouring strikes of workmen. The question of transport costs became more difficult. The old system should have been jettisoned, the technical side perfected, and so the whole problem of communication, and, ultimately, the structure of society, would have been altered.

But the creative energy necessary for such a radical change was lacking. Instead, the problems at issue, including that of providing as cheap articles as possible for the lower classes, were solved by ever greater decentralization, in other words by retrogression instead of progress. Manufacture on the large estates is one of the symptoms of this decentralization. The striking provincialization and deterioration of industrial products, which constituted a bad, and at times a mechanical, copy of the material side of Mediterranean culture, is a consequence alike of decentralization and of the demand for cheaper articles. It was, however, inevitable that the constant attempts to eliminate or reduce the costs of transport would act as a deterrent to the development of large production into a genuine large-scale system, and would cut short approaches to this development, such as we encounter in the Fortis lamp-business or the Graufesenque potteries. A fourth new factor specially affecting agriculture should be mentioned. In the previous period Italian agriculture had become more intensive owing to a relative shortage of land. With the end of this shortage, and a shrinkage in the supply of labour (slaves), the change was made, as we saw, to a less intensive type of cultivation, which prepared the way for a revival of feudalism. In the provinces there was no land shortage for the ruling class. In view of the survival of the indigenous aristocracy down to this time (*e.g.*, in Gaul and Britain) intensive cultivation had, in any case, only advanced to a limited extent. It was accordingly possible for the Roman or romanized bourgeoisie to make a fortune through non-specialized agriculture, which involved far less trouble, and was the natural choice for the man who only resided partially on his estate, or for the absentee landlord. The system of small tenancies subject to the payment of a rent was in some cases simply the continuation of older conditions; elsewhere it arose since the native population was not forthwith enslaved but merely degraded to the condition of tenants or again native peasants who were heavily in debt were, it is true, deprived of their land but allowed to cultivate it on payment of a rent. Thus the approach was made to a system of cultivation which was securely based on the model of the working of the domains and on Italian prototypes. At any rate, sufficient forces were in operation to frustrate the methodical and intensive economy of the capitalistic system, and to prevent a more highly organized production even in agriculture.

A fifth factor, however, perhaps the most important of all, was the promotion of State-socialist tendencies that were opposed to the individualistic principle of economic theory. The gradual governing, whose interests were economic rather than political, and whose response to the demands of military service for defence and to the need of maintaining the numbers of the population was conditioned by the fatal consequences of over-civilization, resulted in a state of affairs terribly like conditions in Greece during the Hellenistic age. Thus after Vespasian, Italy slowly relinquishes the leadership, until under Septimius Severus and Caracalla she becomes politically insignificant. With the army drawing its recruits increasingly from the lower classes, especially of the peasant type, the centre of gravity shifts to these classes more and more, and in consequence to the provinces also. The old traditional culture of the ancient world had lost its power of resistance and could build no barrier against the irruption from the East and from the strange ('barbarian') North of foreign cultures and ideas, and of different forms of State and society. The situation was fraught with danger for the existing economic system, and the danger came from outside. The menace was magnified, however, by an internal danger arising out of stagnation. For life—including economic life—is movement. Every historical process from its earliest beginning carries within itself the counter-forces making for its own destruction. While progress is being made, they are kept under or even absorbed; but with stagnation they rise to the surface. Thus the economic system based on a private economy and tending to individualism and freedom concealed within itself the germ of the counter-movement in the sense of a controlled State-socialism which was now inevitably stimulated by the changed situation in the whole field of civilized life. . . .

The ordinary and extraordinary demands which this State made on its citizens were far greater even than those of the second century. The wars with their losses, the struggles between pretenders, and the extravagant outlay on soldiers and favourites cost vast sums. So did the expenditure on the army which numbered (at the time of Caracalla) some 400,000 men; and the soldiers' real wages had risen somewhat above their already high level. The menacing spectre of State bankruptcy drew ever nearer. The old remedy was prescribed: reduction in value of the currency and increased taxation. The aureus was reduced in size—in the years down to A.D. 256 to approximately a third of its original form—while the silver coins were reduced in purity and size. The denarius of the Severi retained only about half the silver content in comparison with the Neronian standard, and the double denarii under Caracalla and the later emperors (Antoniniani) were an overvalued fiduciary issue, which, in the same period of time, ultimately contained only about a third the silver content when compared with two Neronian denarii. These measures were to a large extent inflationary in character, and in the case of silver ended in disguising the true character of the coin; as they were not merely temporary measures, they caused a rise in prices, henceforth, after Commodus, to twice and almost three times their former level. The rise in taxation consisted for the time being . . . not in an increase in the normal items of taxation (land-taxes, poll-taxes, trade-taxes, etc.) corresponding to the devaluation of the currency—which such a step would have made plain to see—but in supplementary taxation. Thus there was levied a supplementary tax in gold, the *aurum coronarium* (originally a gold crown as a testimony of loyalty to the new ruler, but a regular exaction from Elagabalus' time onwards). Roman taxes were now levied on provincials and provincial taxes on Romans. Above all there were the requisitions in kind, and among those imposed on the landholder, so far as he did not substitute a money payment, was the provision of soldiers from among his *coloni*. It was just the financial and monetary difficulties that forced the State to raise the supplies it needed in kind instead of using for their purchase the declining revenue from taxation, and this change again favoured to some extent the establishment of a natural economy. The *annona*-corn was now demanded without payment offered, and the same applies to soldiers' clothing and to the wares which from about the beginning of the third century were extorted from the Egyptian producers, the *anabolicae species;* these were at first distributed among several of the chief cities of the Empire, but from Aurelian's time were set aside for the sole benefit of the city of Rome. The irregular impositions for troops on the march remained, and in view of prevailing conditions became heavier.

The State's demands were the more oppressive because the taxable resources had shrunk in the previous century, and from the time of the Severi onwards more and more land passed out of cultivation. Hence the claims of the State were fundamentally incapable of fulfilment. Yet the very existence of emperors and Empire alike depended on their being fulfilled. Thus began the fierce endeavour of the State to squeeze the population to the last drop. Since economic resources fell short of what was needed, the strong fought to secure the chief share for themselves with a violence and an unscrupulousness well in keeping with the origin of those in power and with a soldiery accustomed to plunder. The full rigour of the law was let loose on the population. Soldiers acted as bailiffs or wandered as secret police through the land. Those who suffered most were, of course, the propertied class. It was relatively easy to lay hands on their property, and in an emergency they were the class from whom something could be extorted most frequently and most quickly. Consequently, by the system already in force in the previous two centuries, they had been held ultimately responsible and liable for providing taxes and other impositions. For the same reason they were now the first to suffer from the exactions of the State. At the same time, quite apart from questions of finance, there was a purely political motive at work—the desire to shatter the privileged position of the bourgeoisie. A bitter resistance was put up by the bourgeoisie, supported as it was by some of the emperors, especially in lands such as Africa and Spain which were far removed from the war zone, and in which the bourgeoisie was economically still relatively intact. The civil wars of the third century and the frightful period of anarchy after Severus Alexander were the result, in the course of which the infuriated soldateska and its leaders indulged in orgies of brutality. We gain a vivid picture of the assassinations and confiscations, the terrorism and spying, and the sacking of cities from Herodian, the speech of pseudo-Aristides addressed to the Emperor Philip, and also from Cassius Dio, the *Historia Augusta*, and other sources.

There is no doubt that the inhumanity of the struggle was due in part to the hatred which the peasant soldiery, drawn from the lowest class, felt for the bourgeoisie, but it would be mistaken to over-stress this factor, to regard class hatred as the sole motive, and the civil war as a purely social revolution, which aimed at establishing the dictatorship of the proletariate. Such a view is disproved by the fact that not all the soldiers were members of the proletariate, some of them owned property; and moreover the poor suffered at least as much, perhaps more, than the rest from the general economic pressure resultant on unsettled conditions, and in particular from the violence of the soldiery. The petitions of Scaptopare (A.D. 238) and Araguë (A.D. 244–247) and above all Herodian's narrative in Book VII show this quite clearly. The proletariate may, it is true, look on with malice at attacks on the bourgeoisie, and the mob may join in plundering them, small folk who are oppressed by soldiers may appeal to soldiers who are their relatives or friends and beg for a kind of protection —but that does not provide any proof in social revolution from below. And if villagers in their appeals to the emperors declare that they cannot endure their present vexations and if the emperors confirm what they say, the conclusion cannot be drawn that the emperors had made the lower classes their one political support.

In connection with all this, compulsion and State-socialist regulation had established themselves more firmly. These had gradually come into being, their first beginnings dating back to the time of Trajan and Hadrian, when they had been applied with moderation, but now they had developed into an established system, and hence had been incorporated in the final synthesis devised by the new political theorists at the beginning of the third century . . . He who was not especially privileged, or who was not excepted for the performance of other services to the State— as imperial official and soldier, or, again, as lessee on a large or small scale of the emperor's estates and mines, as *navicularius, mercator, faber, cento-*

narius, etc.—had to undertake the municipal *munera* according to his powers, financial, intellectual or physical. Since the population had declined, and the number of those who might be called upon for services was still further reduced through privilege and exception, whereas more and more land had gone out of cultivation, the demands made successively on the remaining men of means were ever more quickly recurrent, the land remaining untilled was forcibly attached to the communities or the neighbouring landowners, and the financial guarantees of the *decaproti* and *curiales* were more and more frequently realized. Arrest, confiscation, and execution hung over their heads like a sword of Damocles. The proceedings of the city councils (which in the year 199 were set up also in the Egyptian *metropoleis* on the model of the rest of the Empire), councils which did not know how they were to meet the old and the newly imposed burdens, and whom they were to find to act as *archontes* and to undertake the liturgies of office, grimly illustrate the growing misery of the age. Even the *navicularii* complained and at times threatened to strike, as at Arelate in 201.

Yet the vicious circle, or rather spiral, could not be broken. If the propertied class buried their money, or sacrificed two-thirds of their estate to escape from a magistracy, or went so far as to give up their whole property in order to get free of the domains rent, and the non-propertied class ran away, the State replied by increasing the pressure. It demanded from the bodies liable . . . that they should produce and identify those who had to undertake liturgies, and enrolled on occasion (as in Egypt under Probus) the whole remaining population of the villages for extraordinary manual labour in helping to maintain the irrigation system. Moreover, in view of the steady drop of revenue from taxation, and the decline in the production and supply of gold and silver, the State resorted to repeated debasement and increase of the currency in circulation. The mints worked with feverish activity. The gold coinage remained pure, but the coins became smaller and smaller, and in the end they were only accepted by weight. After 256 the silver currency of the Empire in its chief denomination, the Antoninianus, lost 75 per cent, and ultimately 98 per cent, of its silver content; in other words it became silver-washed copper. The Egyptian provincial currency, which itself was of lower grade than the Imperial, followed suit though less drastically and rapidly. The mistrust of the 'new coinage' was general: in 260 the Egyptian money-changers of Oxyrhynchus refused to accept it at its official valuation, though the State itself seems to have made its demands in accordance with the old scale of values . . . In Egyptian contracts the parties preferred to reckon on the basis of the 'old Ptolemaic coinage.' Prices in Egypt rose after about 280 to from fourteen to twenty times their original level.

In these disturbed and catastrophic decades of the third century countless people, especially of the bourgeois middle-class, were ruined and impoverished, and these were precisely the men who had brought into being and maintained the economic prosperity of former times. The wasteful policy of the State, the constant interference with private economic life, and the inflations, amounted to a landslide beneath which a vast amount that was of value was crushed out of existence. How great a part was played by the spread of the system of liturgies is shown by the abundance of Egyptian papyri bearing on this theme. Admittedly conditions were not the same everywhere. Africa, the home of Septimius Severus, and Syria, the home of his wife, enjoyed a privileged position. So too did Germany and the Danubian regions because of the soldiers who came from them. And Britain, which lay far from the centre of things, and where city life was less of a determining factor than elsewhere in the Empire, actually enjoyed a relative prosperity in the third century . . . though here too after the middle of the century the cities declined. Moreover, it remains true that the bourgeoisie was not wholly destroyed; otherwise Diocletian could never have maintained the *curiales* as servants of the State with property to pledge, and the completion of the municipalization of Egypt at the beginning of the fourth century would have had no meaning. But the bourgeoisie, which had been the typical representative of a wholly different age, was broken; spiritually and materially it had received a mortal blow. The well-to-do bourgeois is now the exception, not the rule. The 'abundantia' on which the emperors had once prided themselves, which they had promised to maintain, and which they had proclaimed on their coinage, appears under Probus as a Utopian aspiration.

Yet although the bourgeoisie had lost incalculably, this does not mean that the position of the lower classes had in consequence improved. They too suffer and complain, strike and revolt; and this ill-will took highly dangerous forms on occasion, as is shown, for example, by the rising of the Bagaudae in Gaul in the second half of the third century, or the strike of the *monetarii* at Rome in Aurelian's time. Since, however, the masses turned upon the well-to-do alone as those who were squeezing them to the last drop—to turn upon the soldiery who did the same they were too weak—the ruin of the bourgeoisie was hastened in this way too. Thus the end of it all was discontent, depopulation, flight, and banditry among those who had been uprooted, and together with this a shortage of labour. It is estimated that the numbers of the population fell by approximately one third, from seventy to fifty millions. Pestilence and a growing reluctance to have children contributed to the decline. Documents from the Egyptian village of Theadelphia dating from the late third and early fourth centuries give appalling glimpses of the desertion of farms and depopulation. The State, which addressed its demands to the villagers as a body, by its own act drove them one after the other on to the streets. The resultant banditry, which the State in turn tried to meet by a special police force, took fantastic forms. In the petitions to the emperor the threat of flight is the 'ultimum refugium' and among the common questions which used to be put to an oracle in Egypt three standard types were: 'Am I to become a beggar?' 'Shall I take to flight?' and 'Is my flight to be stopped?'

When things had gone so far, it was impossible to turn back; all that remained was to follow the road to the end. This meant guarding against a general flight, announcing compulsory labour, and binding all classes—or at least all who did not belong to a privileged caste—to their professions, the peasant farmer to his land and forced labour, the State-employed worker . . . to his workshop, the trader, including the *navicularius*, to his business or his corporation, the small property-owner to his duties in connection with liturgies, the large property-owner to the *curia*, the soldier to his military service, and so on. By one means or another the development had to reach its conclusion in other respects also. Much was achieved in this direction, after Gallienus and the Illyrian emperors (Aurelian in particular) had shown the way, by the far-reaching reforms of Diocletian and Constantine. With these emperors we rightly begin a new era, even though much was not really completed until the fourth and fifth centuries.

The ancient world did not retire from the arena without a struggle; the history of the third century shows how it fought for what remained of political and spiritual freedom against the constraints of tyranny and dogma. But the same century shows how urgent was the need for peace, a need which ultimately led to acquiescence in Diocletian's régime, the more so since the external dangers continued undiminished. From the reign of Gallienus onwards the army had been re-organized; it had become less national, but readier for action, politically more trustworthy, and a more efficient instrument of power. The unity of the Empire was restored by Aurelian, the internal chaos became less pronounced. The organization of the corporations on a basis of compulsion goes back in essentials to Aurelian. The stabilization of the currency, which was in complete disorder, and hence of the revenue from taxation, was taken in hand. Aurelian, cautiously feeling his way, renewed the gold issues, and by some means or other (the details are controversial) fixed a value for the very debased billon coins . . . Diocletian began again to coin in pure silver, reviving the Neronian standard, even though the extent of this coinage was limited after the 'thorough discrediting' of the currency in the third century. He also organized a regular system, governed by the gold pound, with gold, silver, and large or small billon or copper issues. It is possible that on this occasion the Aurelian billon piece, which was continued in the Diocletian petty cash issues, was again devalued to correspond to its actual buying power, a reform whose immediate result was a further unsettlement of the market, which in its turn occasioned Diocletian's famous edict in 301 regulating prices and wages, though it may be admitted that as regards economic policy the value of this edict must have been very limited. At any rate, in spite of the new copper inflation of the fourth century, the currency was on the whole pretty well stabilized, especially after the solidus had been linked in A.D. 307 with the gold pound at a fixed ratio of seventy-two to one.

The price paid for the restoration of the Empire was twofold. First, the absolute State had come, catering for the population at large, schematic, appealing to mass-intelligence. Secondly, a complete State-socialism was in force, which with its terrorism by officials, its over-emphasized restrictions on the individual, its progressive State-interference, and its burdensome taxation and liturgies, previously not so clearly defined, and its methods of realizing its demands, acted very much as before, except in so far as the union with the Christian Church, from the time of Constantine, gave the system a religious veneer, and stamped subjection as resignation to the will of God. Those to whom this development does not appeal must reflect that, despite all the complaints and opposition, which still continued, this was the only way, under the circumstances, in which the Empire could survive, and remnants of the old bourgeois society, of the old culture, and incidentally of the old economic system could be saved. Finally, as we shall see, this was the only way in which a new culture could mature, though in a greatly changed form and realizing itself perhaps in opposition to the State rather than through it.

Part 6

THE IMPACT OF THE GERMAN INVASIONS

The impact of the German invasions has been described as "one of the central problems of European history." The theme raises some substantive issues of considerable interest. The German invasions are clearly related to the decline of Rome. A study of their impact necessarily involves the broad and fascinating question of the transition from the ancient to the medieval world. It also leads to a consideration of the origins and the periodization of medieval Europe.

Beyond these substantive concerns, the theme poses one of the most intractable and challenging methodological problems with which the historian must always be concerned: the relation between continuity and change. The poet who wrote that "history is one damn thing after another" was unkind, but he was correct in pointing to chronology as a basic element in the study of history. Among other things, history is the study of action through time, and this concern with chronology necessarily means a concern with continuity and change. Historians, unlike social scientists, are extremely wary of theory-building and few have attempted to construct models in which to measure change in a precise fashion. Thus the study of any problem involving continuity and change is not only open to differing interpretations because each historian brings his own point of view to the problem, but also because there is no agreement, no common measure, of what constitutes "significant" or "moderate" change. Professor Arthur J. Slavin of Bucknell University is right in saying that "The business of working toward an adequate historical language with which to describe the balance of continuity and change . . . looms as one of the great methodological challenges facing the next generation of historians."

The selections in this Part illustrate yet another dimension of the problem: historical change, however defined, is rarely uniform. Some aspects of human society seem to be especially resilient, at times almost impervious to change; others are fragile and given to rapid alteration. Language, religion, and family structure generally fall into the first category; artistic styles, political alliances, and historical interpretations into the second. These are, of course, broad generalizations, but they serve to illustrate the point.

The selections here deal with this relationship between continuity and change. And each historian, approaching the problem in his own way, comes to a different assessment of the impact of the Germanic invasions. In no small measure these various opinions stem from differing interests. Focusing on the history of ideas and values will lead an historian to measure change in a certain way; a concern with economics, however, will yield a different interpretation. The impact of the Germanic invasions is not one discrete and easily limited problem; in the following selections each historian undertakes to explain a segment of it. It is for the reader to compare the pieces and decide which interpretations seem to provide the most satisfactory explanation of the whole.

To write a book on so vast a subject as the Holy Roman Empire is difficult enough, but to do so at the age of twenty-six—as James Bryce did— and to have the product favorably compared to Jacob Burckhardt's classic essay, *The Civilization of the Renaissance in Italy*, is indeed a remarkable accomplishment. Bryce (1838–1922) was a Scottish-educated Oxford scholar. His book, *The Holy Roman Empire*, deals with the tenacious persistence of an idea in the face of historical change. The concept of Empire did not disappear with the physical dissolution of the Empire; it lived on, assuming a variety of forms which Bryce traced and explicated with great skill. His work is rich and suggestive. Certainly one of the fundamental lessons it conveys is that political ideology does not always reflect political reality. Moreover, Bryce brings up an intriguing question: can one really speak of the decline of Rome in view of the persistence of the idea of Rome?

For Bryce, whose interest was the history of an idea, the Germanic invasions of the Empire did not constitute a significant break, a watershed in European history. R. R. Bolgar, another distinguished student of the history of ideas, provides a different picture. While it is true that classical culture was not forgotten by Europeans—the Roman past "glittered in their traditions as a golden age"—it was nevertheless nurtured and then reintroduced to the West by peripheral countries like Ireland because the European heartland had suffered such devastation. "The ancient literatures could not become the principal avenue of approach to Graeco-Roman culture until the passage of time and the introduction of alien influences had brought about a clear break with the Graeco-Roman world." Bolgar thinks that this break occurred between the fourth and the sixth centuries, preparing the way for the Irish contribution.

The history of the early Middle Ages and the transition from ancient to medieval civilization has been the focus of much scholarly attention in the twentieth century; earlier theories—most of which viewed the Germanic invasions as catastrophic phenomena sharply differentiating the Roman Empire from the subsequent period—have undergone revision and modification. The great name in this process of revision is Henri Pirenne (1862–1935). Pirenne's bold conception of the early Middle Ages "upset the tranquility of the historian's world" and his influence has been so great that, explicitly or implicitly, much of the literature on this period now revolves around "the Pirenne thesis."

One colleague of Pirenne's said of him: "He is an architect, not a carpenter." Actually, Pirenne was both, and it is perhaps this dual role that explains his importance. His works of synthesis—*Medieval Cities, A History of Europe, Economic and Social History of Medieval Europe, The History of Belgium, Mohammed and Charlemagne*—are so compelling because Pirenne based his generalizations on detailed archival research to which he had also contributed a great deal. These detailed studies focused on such themes as municipal origins, popular uprisings, and the economic history of specific industries, and they paved the way for Pirenne's future work.

One of the essential characteristics of successful synthesis is clarity. Pirenne had adumbrated his thesis very early in his career and he returned to it a few months before his death when he completed the draft of *Mohammed and Charlemagne*. In the opening sentence of the selection, he boldly and clearly declares his position; his statement needs no further explanation. It would be helpful, however to consider the range of issues raised by Pirenne. Professor A. F. Havighurst has summarized the important points as follows:

1. What developments distinguish Antiquity from the Middle Ages? When do we properly cease to speak of the Roman world and begin to think in terms of the First Europe?

2. What was the impact of Islam and the Arabs on the West, and what was the impact of the Germans?

3. What is the relation between the Merovingian era (roughly 5th to 8th centuries) and the Carolingian era (the 8th and 9th centuries)? Do they present essential continuity or are they in sharp contrast?

4. What can historians say about trade and industry in the West, 400–1000?

The selections which follow Pirenne's are all concerned with the issues he raised. It is interesting that even when conclusions differ, the emphasis is on continuity. To be sure, there are gradations of disagreement. For example, the distinguished Austrian historian Alfons Dopsch tells us that "The Germans did not behave as enemies of culture, destroying or abolishing Roman civilization; on the contrary they preserved and developed it"; his French counterpart Ferdinand Lot vividly describes the "tragedy of the ancient world refusing to die." Do they express similar or subtly different points of view about the impact of the German invasions?

Professor Roberto Lopez has written that "It is a well-known law of historiography that every action provokes a reaction." The historians in this Part represent a reaction to the "cataclysmic" interpretation of the impact of the German invasions. There are signs that a reaction to their point of view is about to begin—but that is another story.

1. JAMES BRYCE

FROM James Bryce, *The Holy Roman Empire* (New York: The Macmillan Company, 1923), pp. 23–33, 68–75.

. . . the men of the fifth century, clinging to preconceived ideas, and filled with the belief, drawn from Jewish prophecy, that the great Fourth Kingdom was to last till the end of the world, refused to believe in that dissolution of the Empire which they saw with their own eyes. Because it could not die, it lived. And there was in the slowness of the change and its external aspect, as well as in the fortunes of the capital, something to favour the illusion. The Roman name was shared by every subject; the Roman city was no longer the seat of government, nor did her capture extinguish the imperial power, for the maxim was now accepted, Where the Emperor is, there is Rome. But her continued existence, not permanently occupied by any conqueror, striking the nations with an awe which the history or the external splendours of Constantinople, Milan, or Ravenna could nowise inspire, was an ever new assertion of the endurance of the Roman race and dominion. Dishonoured and defenceless, the spell of her name was still strong enough to arrest the conqueror in the moment of triumph. The irresistible impulse that drew Alarich was one of glory or revenge, not of destruction: the Hun turned back from Aquileia with a vague fear upon him: the Ostrogoth adorned and protected his splendid prize.

In the history of the last days of the Western Empire, two points deserve special remark: its continued union with the Eastern branch, and the way in which its ideal dignity was respected while its representatives were despised. Stilicho was the last statesman who could have saved it. After his death, and after the City had been captured by Alarich in A.D. 410, the fall of the Western throne, though delayed for two generations by traditional reverence, became practically certain. While one by one the provinces were abandoned by the central government, left either to be occupied by invading tribes or to maintain a precarious independence, like Britain and the Armorican cities, by means of municipal unions, Italy lay at the mercy of the barbarian auxiliaries and was governed by their leaders. The degenerate line of Theodosius might have seemed to reign by hereditary right, but after their extinction in Valentinian III it was from the haughty Ricimer, general of the barbarian troops, that each phantom Emperor—

Maximus, Avitus, Majorian, Anthemius, Olybrius—received the purple only to be stripped of it when he presumed to forget his dependence. Though the division between Arcadius and Honorius had definitely severed the two realms for administrative purposes, they were still deemed to constitute a single Empire, and the rulers of the East interfered more than once to raise to the Western throne princes they could not protect upon it. Ricimer's insolence quailed before the shadowy grandeur of the imperial title: his ambition, and that of Gundobald his successor, were bounded by the name of Patrician. The bolder genius of Odoacer, commander of the barbarian auxiliaries resolved to abolish an empty pageant, and extinguish the title and office of Emperor in the West. Yet over him too the spell had power; and as the Gaulish warrior had gazed on the silent majesty of the Senate in a deserted city, so the Herulian revered the power before which the world had bowed, and though there was no force to check or to affright him, shrank from grasping in his own barbarian hand the sceptre of the Caesars. When, at Odoacer's bidding, Romulus, nicknamed Augustulus, the boy whom a whim of fate had chosen to be the last native Caesar of Rome, had formally announced his resignation to the senate, a deputation from that body proceeded to the Eastern court to lay the insignia of royalty at the feet of the reigning Emperor Zeno. The West, they declared, no longer required an Emperor of its own; one monarch sufficed for the world; Odoacer was qualified by his wisdom and courage to be the protector of their state, and upon him Zeno was entreated to confer the title of Patrician and the administration of the Italian provinces. The Emperor, though he reminded the Senate that their request ought rather to have been made to the lately dispossessed Western Emperor Julius Nepos, granted what he could not refuse, and wrote to Odoacer, addressing him as Patrician. Assuming the title of King, Odoacer continued the consular office, respected the civil and ecclesiastical institutions of his subjects, and ruled for fourteen years under the nominal suzerainty of the Eastern Emperor. There was thus legally no extinction of the Western Empire at all, but only a reunion of East and West. In form, and to some extent also in the belief of men, things now reverted to their state during the first two centuries of the Empire, save that New Rome on the Bosphorus instead of Old Rome on the Tiber was the centre of the civil government. The joint tenancy which had been conceived by Diocletian, carried further by Constantine, renewed under Valentinian I and again at the death of Theodosius, had come to an end; once more did a single Emperor sway the sceptre of the world, and head an undivided Catholic Church. To those who lived at the time, this year (A.D. 476) was no such epoch as it has since become, nor was any impression made on men's minds commensurate with the real significance of the event. It is, indeed, one of the most striking instances in history of a change whose magnitude was not perceived until long after it occurred. For though the cessation of an Emperor reigning in the West did not destroy the Empire in idea, nor wholly even in fact, its consequences were from the first immense. It hastened the development of a Latin as opposed to Greek and Oriental forms of Christianity: it emancipated the Popes: it gave a new character to the projects and government of the Teutonic rulers of the Western countries. But the importance of remembering its formal aspect to those who witnessed it will be felt as we approach the era when the Empire was revived by Charles the Frank.

Odoacer's monarchy was not more oppressive than were those of the barbarian kings who were reigning in Gaul, Spain, and Africa. But the confederated mercenary troops who supported it were a loose swarm of predatory tribes: themselves without cohesion, they could take no firm root in Italy. Under his rule no progress seems to have been made towards the reorganization of society; and the first real attempt to blend the peoples and maintain the traditions of Roman wisdom in the hands of a new and vigorous race was reserved for a more famous chieftain, the greatest of all the barbarian conquerors, the forerunner of the first barbarian Emperor, Theodorich the Ostrogoth. The aim of his reign, though he professed deference to the Eastern court which had favoured the invasion in which he overthrew Odoacer, and whose titular supremacy he did not reject, was the establishment of what would have become a national monarchy in Italy. Brought up as a hostage in the court of Constantinople, he learned to know the advantages of an orderly and cultivated society and the principles by which it must be maintained; called in early manhood to roam as a warrior-chief over the plains of the Danube, he acquired along with the arts of command a sense of the superiority of his own people in valour and energy and truth. When the defeat and death of Odoacer had left both Italy and Sicily at his mercy, he sought no further conquest, easy as it would have been to tear away new provinces from the Eastern realm, but strove only to preserve and strengthen the ancient polity of Rome, to breathe into her decaying institutions the spirit of a fresh life, and without endangering the military supremacy of his own Goths, to conciliate by indulgence and gradually raise to the level of their masters the degenerate population of Italy. The Gothic nation appears from the first less cruel in war and more sage in council than any of their Germanic brethren: all that was noble among them shone forth now in the rule of the greatest of the Amals. From his palace at Verona, commemorated in the song of the Nibelungs, he issued equal laws for Roman and Goth, and bade the intruder, if he must occupy part of the lands, at least respect the goods and the person of his fellow subject. Jurisprudence and administration remained in native hands: two annual consuls, one named by Theodorich, the other by the Eastern monarch, presented an image of the ancient state; and while agriculture and the arts revived in the provinces, Rome herself celebrated the visits of a master who provided for the wants of her people and preserved with care the monuments of her former splendour. With peace and plenty men's minds took hope, and the study of letters revived. The last gleam of classical literature gilds the reign of the barbarian.

By the consolidation of the two races under one wise government, Italy might have been spared six hundred years of gloom and degradation. It was not so to be. Theodorich was tolerant, but toleration was itself an offence in the eyes of his orthodox subjects: the Arian Goths were and remained strangers and enemies among the Catholic Italians. Scarcely had the sceptre passed from the hands of Theodorich to his weaker offspring, when Justinian, who had viewed with jealousy the greatness of his nominal lieutenant, determined to assert his dormant rights over Italy and Sicily; its people welcomed Belisarius as a deliverer, and in the long struggle that followed the race and name of the Ostrogoths perished for ever. Thus again reunited in fact, as it had been all the while united in theory, to the Roman Empire, Italy was divided into counties and dukedoms, and obeyed the exarch of Ravenna, viceroy of the East Roman court, till the arrival of the Lombards in A.D. 568 drove him from some districts, and left him only a feeble authority over the Eastern and Southern parts of the peninsula.

Beyond the Alps, though the Roman population had by this time ceased to seek help from the Eastern sovereigns, the Empire's rights were still deemed to subsist, though as respects Gaul they were deemed to have been yielded by Justinian to the Franks. As has been said, those rights had been admitted by the conquerors themselves: by Athaulf, when he reigned in Aquitaine as the vicar of Honorius, and recovered Spain from the Suevi to restore it to its ancient masters; by the West Gothic kings of Spain, when they permitted the Mediterranean cities to send tribute to Constantinople; by Clovis, when, after the representatives of the old government, Syagrius and the Armorican cities, had been conquered or absorbed, and the West Gothic kingdom in Aquitaine had been overthrown, he received with delight from the Eastern emperor Anastasius the grant of a Roman dignity to confirm his possession. Arrayed like a Fabius or Valerius in the consul's purple robe and senatorial chlamys, the Sicambrian chieftain rode through the streets of Tours, while the shout of the provincials hailed him Augustus. They already obeyed him, but his power was now legalized in their eyes, and it was not without a melancholy pride that they saw the terrible conqueror himself yield to the spell of the Roman name, and do homage to the enduring majesty of their legitimate sovereign.

Yet the severed limbs of the Empire forgot by degrees their original unity. As in the breaking up of the old society, which we trace from the sixth to the eighth century, rudeness and ignorance grew apace, as language and manners were changed by the infiltration of Teutonic settlers, as men's thoughts and hopes and interests were narrowed by isolation from their fellows, as the organization of the Roman province and the Germanic tribe alike dissolved into a chaos whence the new order began to shape itself, dimly and doubtfully as yet, the memory of the old Empire, its symmetry, its sway, its civilization, must needs wane and fade. It might have perished altogether but for the two enduring witnesses Rome had left—her Church and her Law. The barbarians had at first associated Christianity with the Romans from whom they learned it: the Romans had used it as their only bulwark against oppression. The hierarchy were the natural leaders of the people, and the necessary councillors of the king. Their power grew with the decay of civil government and the spread of superstition; and when the Frank found it too valuable to be abandoned to the vanquished people, he insensibly acquired the feelings and policy of the order which he entered.

As the Empire fell to pieces, and the new kingdoms which the conquerors had founded began in their turn to dissolve, the Church clung more closely to her unity of faith and discipline, the common bond of all Christian men. That unity must have a centre, that centre was Rome. A succession of able and zealous pontiffs extended her influence—the sanctity and the writings of Gregory the Great were famous through all the West. Never permanently occupied by barbarians, she retained her peculiar character and customs, and laid the foundations of a power over men's souls more durable than that which she had lost over their bodies. Only second in importance to this influence was that which was exercised by the permanence of the old law, and of its creature the municipal organization of the cities. The barbarian invaders retained the customs of their ancestors, characteristic memorials of a rude people, as we see them in the Salic law or in the ordinances of Ini and Alfred. But the subject population and the clergy continued to be governed by that elaborate system which the genius and labour of many generations had raised to be the most lasting monument of Roman greatness.

The civil law had maintained itself in Spain and Southern Gaul, nor was it utterly forgotten even in the North, in Britain, on the borders of Germany. Revised collections of extracts from the Theodosian Code and other Roman law books were issued by the West Gothic and Burgundian princes. For some centuries it was the patrimony of the subject population everywhere, and in Aquitaine and Italy has outlived feudalism. The presumption that all men were to be judged by it who could not be proved to be subject to some other law continued to be accepted down to the end of the Middle Ages. Its phrases, its forms, its courts, its subtlety and precision, all recalled the strong and cultivated society which had produced it. Other motives, as well as those of kindness to their subjects, made the new kings favour it; for it exalted their prerogative, and the submission enjoined by it on one class of their subjects soon came to be demanded from the other, by their own Teutonic customs almost the equals of the prince. Considering attentively how many of the old institutions continued to subsist, and studying the ideas of that time, as they are faintly preserved in its scanty records, it seems hardly too much to say that in the eighth century the Roman Empire still existed in the West: existed in men's minds as a power weakened, delegated, suspended, but not destroyed. . . .

In civil affairs . . . Charles acquired, with the imperial title, a new position. Later jurists labour to distinguish his power as Roman Emperor from that which he held already as king of the Franks and their subject allies: they insist that his coronation gave him the capital only, that it is absurd to talk of a Roman Empire in regions whither the eagles had never flown. In such expressions there seems to lurk either confusion or misconception. It was not the actual government of the city that Charles obtained in A.D. 800; that his father had already held as Patrician, and he had himself exerted the rights which the title gave. It was far more than the titular sovereignty of Rome which had hitherto been supposed to be vested in the Emperor at Constantinople. It was nothing less than the headship of the world, believed to appertain of right to the lawful Roman Emperor, whether he reigned on the Bosphorus, the Tiber, or the Rhine. As that headship, although never denied, had been in abeyance in the West for several centuries, its bestowal on the king of so vast a realm was a change of the first moment, for it made the coronation not merely a transference of the seat of Empire, but a renewal of the Empire itself, a bringing back of it from faith to sight, from the world of belief and theory to the world of fact and reality. And since the powers it gave were autocratic and unlimited, it must swallow up all minor claims and dignities: the rights of Charles the Frankish king were merged in those of Charles the successor of Augustus, the lord of the world. That his imperial authority was theoretically irrespective of place is clear from his own words and acts, and from all the monuments of that time. He would not, indeed, have dreamed of treating the high-spirited Franks as Justinian had treated his half-Oriental subjects, nor would the warriors who followed his standard have brooked such an attempt. Yet even to German eyes his position must have been altered by the halo of vague splendour which now surrounded him; for all, even the Saxon and the Slav, had heard of Rome's glories, and revered the name of Caesar. And in his effort to weld discordant elements into one body, to introduce regular gradations of authority, to control the Teutonic tendency to localization by his *missi*—officials commissioned to traverse each some part of his dominions, reporting on and redressing the evils they found—as well as by his own oft-repeated personal progresses, Charles was guided by the traditions of the old Empire. His sway is the revival of order and culture, seeking to fuse the West into a compact whole, whose parts are never thenceforward to lose the marks of their connection and their half-Roman character, gathering up all that is left in Europe of intellect, knowledge and skill, hurling it with the new force of Christianity on the infidel of the South and the masses of untamed barbarism to the North and East. Ruling the world by the gift of God, and by the transmitted rights of the Romans and their Caesar whom God had chosen to conquer it, he renews the original aggressive movement of the Empire. The civilized world has subdued her invader, and now arms him against savagery and heathendom. Hence the wars, not more of the sword than of the cross, against Saxons, Avars, Slavs, Danes, Spanish Arabs, where monasteries are fortresses and baptism the badge of submission. The overthrow of the Irminsûl, in the first Saxon campaign, sums up the changes of seven centuries. The Romanized Teuton destroys the monument of his country's freedom, for it is also the emblem of paganism and barbarism. The work of the Cheruscan Arminius is undone by his successor.

This, however, is not the only side from which Charles's policy and character may be regarded. If the unity of the Church and the shadow of imperial prerogative was one pillar of his power, the other was the Frankish nation. The empire was still military, though in a sense strangely different from that of Julius or Severus. The warlike Franks had permeated Western Europe; their primacy was admitted by the kindred tribes of Bavarians, Lombards, Thuringians, Alemannians, and Burgundians; the Slavonic peoples on the borders trembled and paid tribute; the Spanish Alfonso of Asturias found in the Emperor a protector against the infidel foe. His influence, if not his exerted power, crossed the ocean: the kings of the Scots sent gifts and called him lord: the restoration of Eardulf to Northumbria, still more of Egbert to Wessex, might furnish a better ground for the claim of suzerainty than many to which his successors had afterwards recourse.

As it was by Frankish arms that this predominance in Europe which the imperial title adorned and legalized had been won, so was the government of Charles Roman in name rather than in fact. It was not by restoring the effete mechanism of the old Empire, but by his own vigorous personal action and that of his great officers, that he strove to administer and reform. With every effort for a strong central government, there is no despotism: each nation retains its laws, its hereditary chiefs, its free popular assemblies. The conditions granted to the Saxons after long and cruel warfare, conditions so favourable that in the next century their dukes hold the foremost place in Germany, shew how little he sought to make the Franks a dominant caste. One may think of him as a second Theodorich, trying to maintain the traditions of Rome and to breathe a new spirit into the ancient forms. The conception was magnificent; and it fitted the time better than it had done in the hands of Theodorich, not only because Charles was himself orthodox and pious, but also because the name and dominion of Rome were now more closely associated with Christianity than they had been in days when the recollection of heathen Emperors was still fresh in the memory of men. But two obstacles forbade success. The one was the ecclesiastical, especially the papal power, apparently subject to the temporal, but with a strong and undefined prerogative which only waited the occasion to trample on what it had helped to raise. The Pope might take away the crown he had bestowed, and turn against the Emperor the Church which now obeyed him. The other was to be found in the discordance of the component parts of the Empire. The nations were not ripe for settled life or extensive schemes of polity; the differences of race, language, manners, over vast and thinly-peopled lands baffled every attempt to maintain their cohesion: and when once the spell of the great mind was withdrawn, the mutually repellent forces began to work, and the mass dissolved into that chaos out of which it had been formed. Nevertheless, the parts separated not as they met, but having all of them undergone influences which continued to act when political connection had ceased. For the work of Charles—a genius pre-eminently creative—was not lost in the anarchy that followed: rather are we to regard his reign as the beginning of a new era, or as laying the foundations whereon men continued for many generations to build. ✻

2. R. R. BOLGAR

FROM R. R. Bolgar, *The Classical Heritage and Its Beneficiaries* (Cambridge: Cambridge University Press, 1954), pp. 91–92, 95, 116–17, 127–29.

. . . Conditions in the two halves of Europe were vastly different. In Byzantium we saw the shrinking nucleus of a superior civilisation, fearful of loss, constantly on the defensive, stereotyped in its institutions and culture. In the West we shall see by contrast evidences not of atrophy but of growth. The Western peoples were more anxious to acquire new blessings than to preserve the few they could already command. Their world had touched rock bottom, had been plunged into chaos and was now in mid-passage out. Unafraid of change, they were not desirous of barring its effects from any sector of their lives. The period of the Roman past glittered in their traditions as a golden age which having existed once could no doubt be restored; and that conviction in the midst of their ever-present discontents made them eager to throw as much as possible into the melting-pot.

Our proper starting-point is in time the sixth century and in space a remote island to which Roman power had never extended its latinising sway. The Ireland of St. Patrick was the first place to which the literary heritage of the classics came, as it was to come eventually to the whole of Western Europe, from the outside, a gift of the gods to be won through judicious learning, a gift possibly of forbidden fruit.

The ancient literatures could not become the principal avenue of approach to Graeco-Roman culture until the passage of time and the introduction of alien influences had brought about a clear break with the Graeco-Roman world. In the East that break had occurred when Islam had engulfed half the seminal area of Greek civilisation and the Iconoclast controversies had thrown the rest in turmoil. In the West, its incidence cannot be linked with such specific and spectacular events. The collapse of the Western Empire was due to a gradual disorganisation that followed the repeated barbarian inroads: and so occurred first in the areas furthest removed from the centre of Roman power. The forces of destruction worked inwards from the periphery. The Danube and Rhine frontiers were breached, Britain was abandoned, Spain became a Visigothic kingdom. But Gaul and Italy even when nominally conquered, still retained much of their old civilisation. Only with the passage of time, through the continual wars between the Frankish kingdoms and after the Lombard invasions, did they too sink reluctantly into barbarism. The new order which was to replace the Empire took shape first in localities far distant from Italy, and then worked inwards, through Britain and Gaul, to join hands in the end with the last faint survivals of Roman life that had managed to hold their own in what had once been the seat and nerve-centre of Roman power. . . .

Thus, the first epoch in the history of the classical education is associated primarily with Ireland, and the credit for having taken the first steps in that educational labyrinth where the classical writings were man's only guide belongs without question to the Irish. That epoch came to an end however with the seventh century. The torch of educational advance passed into other hands; and the work which the Irish had attempted, the training of Latin scholars in the monasteries of a barbarian people, was repeated more successfully among the Anglo-Saxons. The new learning was moving inwards from the periphery, one stage nearer to the old centre of Rome. After 668, the future lay with Canterbury and York. It is true that some of the most brilliant triumphs of Irish learning were still to come. But those triumphs—though they added to Western knowledge—did not contribute vitally to pedagogic technique; and they were to some extent dependent upon the work done by the Anglo-Saxons. History repeated itself. Ireland became educationally subordinate to England, as earlier Celtic Britain had fallen under the Irish spell. It is true that the extent of Anglo-Saxon influence on the Irish scholars from 668 onwards cannot be accurately estimated; and we cannot be sure of its impact in any particular case. But when we find that Muirchu's Life of St. Patrick contains a reminiscence of Virgil and another of Valerius Flaccus, when Adamnan of Iona refers to the *Aeneid* in his life of St. Columba and is mentioned as a commentator in a manuscript of the *Georgics,* we can no longer feel certain that their scholarship was the unaided product of the Irish tradition. The Anglo-Saxon scholars were already at work, and the future of the classical education was in their hands. . . .

We have looked at Alcuin's teaching in its detail. The evidence of its workings which has survived the obliterating forces of time, is fragmentary. But as we gaze upon the scattered fragments certain traits emerge of what must have been their general pattern. It becomes clear that we ought not to link Alcuin too closely with Petrarch and Erasmus, or see in him the founder of a premature Renaissance. The problems he set out to solve were such as allowed little scope for a cult of antiquity, and his mood was in any case Christian. He was asked to work out the means whereby the Frankish kingdom could be assured of a Latin-speaking priesthood, capable of performing its necessary tasks. So he produced his apparatus of simplified text-books and demonstrated their use in model schools. This part of his achievement, though of vast importance for the future acquisition of classical knowledge (for it made the Latin language a certain possession), did not involve him much in classical studies. He aimed at a level of attainment which fell below the point where the ecclesiastical and the pagan heritage separated. He was also asked to make some contribution to the higher advancement of knowledge. And in that field he followed strictly a somewhat narrow interpretation of Augustine's precepts. He concentrated on the impersonalities of technique: the definitions of logic, the rules and precepts of rhetoric, the facts of mathematics and astronomy. He was prepared to plunder the Egyptians. But how carefully he chose his booty! In the end he rejected more than he took. Though conscious of the value of the great pagan writers, as we can see from his account of the York

Library and prepared to countenance the intellectual fashions of the court, he remained distrustful. *Timuit Danaos et dona ferentes.*

The intellectual life of the Carolingian Age had a dual character. The main stream that watered its fields had its source in Alcuin and brought the calm waters of an ecclesiastically conceived Latin culture. The other stream, thinner but more spectacular, welled from the court and possibly from the teaching of Peter of Pisa. It was specifically classical, and to it we must attribute that flowering of imitative verse and unstinting appreciation of antiquity which we notice first in Charles's court and then a generation later among those who had been in personal touch with members of Charles's circle, in a Lupus of Ferrières, a Walafrid or a Hincmar.

Education does not stop today at the level set by the final degree examinations; and it did not stop in the ninth century at the level attained by the majority of pupils in the average school. That is, it did not come to a dead end. But its character changed. There were several reasons for this, the major one being a sharp fall in the number of students. The monastic schools were at no stage the crowded institutions which the cathedral schools afterwards became; moreover not every pupil in a monastery, who struggled through his grammar, had the ability to advance further, and most of those who did advance chose to concentrate their attention upon theology. Thus, in most schools the groups studying advanced grammar, rhetoric or literature must have been small; and the arrangements for their work must have been informal. Since custom did not demand that those who continued their training should do so without a break, they were likely too to be of different ages. They laboured at their own speed and quite often in their own spare time, having also some other job or study in hand. . . .

. . . The picture we form of Carolingian education must inevitably allow room for variety. Some students like Notker's young Salomo at St. Gallen left school with little knowledge outside of their grammar; others read anthologies; others again drank deeply of some Christian or even of some pagan author. The one common feature which emerges from this diversity is that between the time of Alcuin and that of Rémi, between the end of the eighth and the beginning of the tenth century, the general standard of educational attainment perceptibly increased, and the study of the classical heritage benefited from this advance. Alcuin having saved classical learning by his exertions, failed to smother its further growth by his example. The lingering survivals of the Roman world in Italy, the curiosity of the Irish, the patronage of enlightened monarchs like Charles the Bald combined to sustain the faltering course of ancient studies. The steady if slow labours of the copyists multiplied the available texts. The researches of individual scholars simplified their interpretation; and the greater knowledge of Latin among the clergy brought them within reach of an ever increasing number of readers. The man who could understand the Bible could also understand Virgil.

With the close of the Carolingian Age, the curtain sinks on the first act of the new Europe's assimilation to its past. We began with a state of ignorance which almost endangered the survival of the Latin-speaking Church. We saw this ignorance combated by the development of an education which necessarily utilised some of the traditional instruments of Roman pedagogy. That education spread from the Celtic to the Anglo-Saxon lands and then to France and Germany, increasing in efficiency at each remove. Its purpose was not the absorption of pagan knowledge, but more strictly the teaching of Latin so that monks could read the Bible and the Fathers, and so that a few men in each generation might be fitted to conduct the administrative business of the Church. But while the educated pursued these general aims, they also learnt to make better use of the classical heritage; and they made their own the greater part of what the ancients had discovered concerning the nature of language. Then with the ninth century the situation altered. It is true that the needs which had been responsible for the rise of monastic education still continued to operate. But they were needs which contemporary learning, having been adequately organised, now found easy to fulfil; and socially there was stagnation. There were no great changes of the sort which might have given rise to fresh educational demands. As a result, for a brief period, a situation existed in which human learning developed in response to its own interests independently of outside pressures.

It is a common belief among scholars that a disinterested curiosity has been the main force behind every advancement of learning. This theory, though it contains a measure of truth, is not altogether innocent of wishful thinking. That human curiosity has always existed and has always exercised its own dynamic admits of no doubt; but history suggests that the force of that dynamic cannot really be compared with the violent impulsions of the political and economic needs which are the main determinants of our destiny. Only at times when the action of those needs was temporarily suspended, when there was a certain favourable disproportion between the capabilities of an educational system and the calls which society made upon it, only that is to say, under quite exceptional circumstances, had curiosity more than a subsidiary role in deciding the direction, though it always contributed substantially to the vigour, of intellectual effort. But in the latter half of the Carolingian Age these exceptional circumstances did obtain, and the Walafrids, the Heirics, the Notkers were not seduced from following their particular bent by any feeling that there were more important problems to be solved. Nor were even the classicists among them seriously hampered by disapproval or active interference, since the nature of their work was as yet too elementary to represent a threat to the social or religious order.

It is true, however, that this halcyon state was not to be of long duration. By the middle of the tenth century the apparent standstill was at an end. The economic and social changes which the slow developments of the ninth century had imperceptibly prepared, were ready to burst upon Europe bringing their harvest of new intellectual and educational requirements. The study of the classical heritage which Walafrid could regard as a harmless pastime, was to impress Anselm of Bisate two hundred years later as a pursuit likely to bring an answer to all his intellectual problems; and Notker's gentle observation that pagan writings were useless was to give place to the diatribes of Peter Damian. For good or for ill the primary stage in the assimilation of classical culture, which had as its objects the elements common to both the pagan and the Christian traditions, was decisively over. What Europe now needed from the past in the shape of law, philosophy and science was more definitely secular and derived from those sectors of Roman civilisation that patristic Christianity had failed to make properly its own. Bede, Alcuin and Hraban had merely repeated the work of Isidore, as the similarity between the *Etymologiae* and the *de Universo* only too clearly shows. But now the time had come to carry the spoiling of the Egyptians one step—indeed several steps—further, in realms where the practice of the Fathers could offer no guidance. The self-styled pygmies of the Middle Ages were faced with the task of wresting from paganism a contribution to the City of God that the greatest of their authorities had been afraid to contemplate. ✳

3. HENRI PIRENNE

FROM Henri Pirenne, *Mohammed and Charlemagne* (London: George Allen & Unwin Ltd., 1958), pp. 140–44, 284–85.

From whatever standpoint we regard it . . . the period inaugurated by the establishment of the Barbarians within the Empire introduced no absolute historical innovation. What the Germans destroyed was not the Empire, but the Imperial government *in partibus occidentis*. They themselves acknowledged as much by installing themselves as *foederati*. Far from seeking to replace the Empire by anything new, they established themselves within it, and although their settlement was accompanied by a process of serious degradation, they did not introduce a new scheme of government; the ancient *palazzo,* so to speak, was divided up into apartments, but it still survived as a building. In short, the essential character of "Romania" still remained Mediterranean. The frontier territories, which remained Germanic, and England, played no part in it as yet; it is a mistake to regard them at this period as a point of departure. Considering matters as they actually were, we see that the great novelty of the epoch was a political fact: in the Occident a plurality of States had replaced the unity of the Roman State. And this, of course, was a very considerable novelty. The aspect of Europe was changing, but the fundamental character of its life remained the same. These States, which have been described as national States, were not really national at all, but were merely fragments of the great unity which they had replaced. There was no profound transformation except in Britain.

There the Emperor and the civilization of the Empire had disappeared. Nothing remained of the old tradition. A new world had made its appearance. The old law and language and institutions were replaced by those of the Germans. A civilization of a new type was manifesting itself, which we may call the Nordic or Germanic civilization. It was completely opposed to the Mediterranean civilization syncretized in the Late Empire, that last form of antiquity. Here was no trace of the Roman State with its legislative ideal, its civil population, and its Christian religion, but a society which had preserved the blood tie between its members; the family community, with all the consequences which it entailed in law and morality and economy; a paganism like that of the heroic poems; such were the things that constituted the originality of these Barbarians, who had thrust back the ancient world in order to take its place. In Britain a new age was beginning, which did not gravitate towards the South. The man of the North had conquered and taken for his own this extreme corner of that "Romania" of which he had no memories, whose majesty he repudiated, and to which he owed nothing. In every sense of the word he replaced it, and in replacing it he destroyed it.

The Anglo-Saxon invaders came into the Empire fresh from their Germanic environment, and had never been subjected to the influences of Rome. Further, the province of Britain, in which they had established themselves, was the least Romanized of all the provinces. In Britain, therefore, they remained themselves: the Germanic, Nordic, Barbarian soul of peoples whose culture might almost be called Homeric has been the essential factor in the history of this country.

But the spectacle presented by this Anglo-Saxon Britain was unique. We should seek in vain for anything like it on the Continent. There "Romania" still existed, except on the frontier, or along the Rhine, in the decumate lands, and along the Danube—that is to say, in the provinces of Germania, Raetia, Noricum and Pannonia, all close to that Germania whose inhabitants had overflowed into the Empire and driven it before them. But these border regions played no part of their own, since they were attached to States which had been established, like that of the Franks or the Ostrogoths, in the heart of "Romania." And there it is plain that the old state of affairs still existed. The invaders, too few in number, and also too long in contact with the Empire, were inevitably absorbed, and they asked nothing better. What may well surprise us is that there was so little Germanism in the new States, all of which were ruled by Germanic dynasties. Language, religion, institutions and art were entirely, or almost entirely, devoid of Germanism. We find some Germanic influences in the law of those countries situated to the north of the Seine and the Alps, but until the Lombards arrived in Italy these did not amount to very much. If some have held a contrary belief, it is because they have followed the Germanic school and have wrongly applied to Gaul, Italy, and Spain what they find in the *Leges Barbarorum* of the Salians, the Ripuarians and the Bavarians. They have also extended to the period which preceded the Carolingians what is true only of the latter. Moreover, they have exaggerated the role of Merovingian Gaul by allowing themselves to be governed by the thought of what it later became, but as yet was not.

What was Clovis as compared with Theodoric? And let it be noted that after Clovis the Frankish kings, despite all their efforts, could neither establish themselves in Italy, nor even recapture the Narbonnaise from the Visigoths. It is evident that they were tending towards the Mediterranean. The object of their conquest beyond the Rhine was to defend their kingdom against the Barbarians, and was far from having the effect of Germanizing it. But to admit that under the conditions of their establishment in the Empire, and with the small forces which they brought with them, the Visigoths, Burgundi, Ostrogoths, Vandals and Franks could have intended to Germanize the Empire is simply to admit the impossible. *Stat mole sua.*

Moreover, we must not forget the part played by the Church, within which Rome had taken refuge, and which, in imposing itself upon the Barbarians, was at the same time imposing Rome upon them. In the Occident, in the Roman world which had become so disordered as a State, the Germanic kings were, so to speak, points of political crystallization. But the old, or shall we say, the classic social equilibrium still existed in the world about them, though it had suffered inevitable losses.

In other words, the Mediterranean unity which was the essential feature of this ancient world was maintained in all its various manifestations.

The increasing Hellenization of the Orient did not prevent it from continuing to influence the Occident by its commerce, its art, and the vicissitudes of its religious life. To a certain extent, as we have seen, the Occident was becoming Byzantinized.

And this explains Justinian's impulse of reconquest, which almost restored the Mediterranean to the status of a Roman lake. And regarding it from our point of view, it is, of course, plainly apparent that this Empire could not last. But this was not the view of its contemporaries. The Lombard invasion was certainly less important than has been supposed. The striking thing about it is its tardiness.

Justinian's Mediterranean policy—and it really was a Mediterranean policy, since he sacrificed to this policy his conflicts with the Persians and the Slavs—was in tune with the Mediterranean spirit of European civilization as a whole from the 5th to the 7th century. It is on the shores of this *mare nostrum* that we find all the specific manifestations of the life of the epoch. Commerce gravitated toward the sea, as under the Empire; there the last representatives of the ancient literature—Boëtius, Cassiodorus—wrote their works; there, with Caesarius of Arles, and Gregory the Great, the new literature of the Church was born and began to develop; there writers like Isidore of Seville made the inventory of civilization from which the Middle Ages obtained their knowledge of antiquity; there, at Lérins, or at Monte Cassino, monasticism, coming from the Orient, was acclimatized to its Occidental environment; from the shores of the Mediterranean came the missionaries who converted England, and it was there that arose the characteristic monuments of that Hellenistico-Oriental art which seemed destined to become the art of the Occident, as it had remained that of the Orient.

There was as yet nothing, in the 7th century, that seemed to announce the end of the community of civilization established by the Roman Empire from the Pillars of Hercules to the Aegean Sea and from the shores of Egypt and Africa to those of Italy, Gaul, and Spain. The new world had not lost the Mediterranean character of the ancient world. All its activities were concentrated and nourished on the shores of the Mediterranean.

There was nothing to indicate that the millenary evolution of society was to be suddenly interrupted. No one was anticipating a catastrophe. Although the immediate successors of Justinian were unable to continue his work, they did not repudiate it. They refused to make any concession to the Lombards; they feverishly fortified Africa; they established their themes there as in Italy; their policies took account of the Franks and the Visigoths alike; their fleet controlled the sea; and the Pope of Rome regarded them as his Sovereigns. . . .

From the foregoing data, it seems, we may draw two essential conclusions:

1. The Germanic invasions destroyed neither the Mediterranean unity of the ancient world, nor what may be regarded as the truly essential features of the Roman culture as it still existed in the 5th century, at a time when there was no longer an Emperor in the West.

Despite the resulting turmoil and destruction, no new principles made their appearance; neither in the economic or social order, nor in the linguistic situation, nor in the existing institutions. What civilization survived was Mediterranean. It was in the regions by the sea that culture was preserved, and it was from them that the innovations of the age proceeded: monasticism, the conversion of the Anglo-Saxons, the *ars Barbarica*, etc.

The Orient was the fertilizing factor: Constantinople, the centre of the world. In 600 the physiognomy of the world was not different in quality from that which it had revealed in 400.

2. The cause of the break with the tradition of antiquity was the rapid and unexpected advance of Islam. The result of this advance was the final separation of East from West, and the end of the Mediterranean unity. Countries like Africa and Spain, which had always been parts of the Western community, gravitated henceforth in the orbit of Baghdad. In these countries another religion made its appearance, and an entirely different culture. The Western Mediterranean, having become a Musulman lake, was no longer the thoroughfare of commerce and of thought which it had always been.

The West was blockaded and forced to live upon its own resources. For the first time in history the axis of life was shifted northwards from the Mediterranean. The decadence into which the Merovingian monarchy lapsed as a result of this change gave birth to a new dynasty, the Carolingian, whose original home was in the Germanic North.

With this new dynasty the Pope allied himself, breaking with the Emperor, who, engrossed in his struggle against the Musulmans, could no longer protect him. And so the Church allied itself with the new order of things. In Rome, and in the Empire which it founded, it had no rival. And its power was all the greater inasmuch as the State, being incapable of maintaining its administration, allowed itself to be absorbed by the feudality, the inevitable sequel of the economic regression. All the consequences of this change became glaringly apparent after Charlemagne. Europe, dominated by the Church and the feudality, assumed a new physiognomy, differing slightly in different regions. The Middle Ages—to retain the traditional term—were beginning. The transitional phase was protracted. One may say that it lasted a whole century—from 650 to 750. It was during this period of anarchy that the tradition of antiquity disappeared, while the new elements came to the surface.

This development was completed in 800 by the constitution of the new Empire, which consecrated the break between the West and the East, inasmuch as it gave to the West a new Roman Empire—the manifest proof that it had broken with the old Empire, which continued to exist in Constantinople. ✻

4. ROBERT LATOUCHE

FROM Robert Latouche, *The Birth of Western Economy*, trans. E. M. Wilkinson (London: Methuen & Co., Ltd., 1961), pp. 117–25.

Henri Pirenne infused new life into the economic history of the Early Middle Ages by giving the Moslem conquest pride of place amongst the factors which transformed the structure of the ancient world. There is no need to summarize afresh a 'thesis' which was first presented to several historical congresses, which in 1922 and 1923 he condensed into two brilliant articles in the *Revue belge de philologie et d'histoire*, and which was fully and finally developed in a posthumously published work, *Mahomet et Charlemagne*. In actual fact, however, as one of his disciples has written, it is perhaps doing Pirenne an injustice to apply the word 'thesis' to a vast body of original ideas on the whole evolution of Europe from the third to the tenth century. It would be more accurate to say that new horizons have been opened up to those who are attempting to find out just how the transition from the ancient world to the Middle Ages was effected. The main contention of Pirenne, whose natural bent led him to place particular emphasis on economics, is that the ancient civilization, the *ordo romanus*, lived on even after the Germanic invasions, that the real destroyer of this *ordo* was Mahomet, whilst the creator, or at least the symbolic representative of the new order of things, was Charlemagne. Hence the title of the first memoir in which Pirenne expounded his views, a title which has been revived by the editors of his great posthumous book. These two evocative words have caught the imagination to an extraordinary degree, and though for the past thirty-two years the original ideas put forward by this great historian have been critically examined, hotly disputed, carefully sifted, they were still fresh enough to inspire in the *Revue historique* for November 1954 an article entitled: 'Encore Mahomet et Charlemagne'.

One of Pirenne's main theories is that in spite of the barbarian invasions the movement of trade through the Mediterranean continued throughout Merovingian times right up to the Moslem conquest, and that the Mediterranean way of life which was one of the characteristic features of the Late Empire persisted. Under the rule of the Ostrogoths Italy continued to get supplies of grain and oil from the opposite shore of the Mediterranean, and trade relations with Byzantium were maintained, as may be seen from many references in the correspondence of Theodoric edited by Cassiodorus. A first essential was the construction of light ships which Italy needed for the importation of foodstuffs, particularly of corn. The ships bringing food to Rome landed at the port of Ostia, where they were welcomed by the 'Count of the port of the city of Rome'. The orders given by the King to this high-ranking official show how anxious Theodoric was to maintain the volume of this traffic:

> It is a pleasant, rather than a heavy responsibility to hold the office of Count of the port of Rome. He supervises the arrival of innumerable ships. The sea, covered with sails, brings foreign peoples with merchandise from many different provinces. The task entrusted to you is therefore a privileged one; but it must be carried out with tact and good judgement. You are in a position to create prosperity by dealing fairly and justly with those who land there. An avaricious hand could close down the harbour altogether.

For a time, however, the occupation of North Africa by the Vandals was a threat to Mediterranean sea traffic, and Sidonius Apollinaris, who shortly before the fall of the Western Empire had assumed the grave responsibility of ensuring Rome's food supplies, has told in one of his letters how difficult his task was and with what breathless joy he sighted the ships bringing the *annona*.

This régime based on imports suited the indolent Romans to perfection, and Justinian's chief aim in reconquering North Africa from the Vandals was probably to regain for Italy a source of grain which had been partially lost to her for almost a century; yet in spite of the efficiency of the Byzantine merchant fleet, it is by no means certain that trade relations were fully restored. The Lombard invasion brought disorder, as well as poverty, to the peninsula. When Gregory the Great was elected Pope (590), an epidemic of the plague was raging in Rome, and when eventually it died down, famine threatened to descend upon the city. The letters written by the new Pontiff to the Praetor of Sicily urging him to speed up deliveries of corn seem to indicate that from the close of the sixth century Africa was no longer the great grain-provider.

Further concrete facts about the Mediterranean economy during the Merovingian period have also come to light, for instance the use of olive oil for food and lighting, replaced only at a later date by that of butter and wax, and the use of Egyptian papyrus for writing which persisted in Gaul until the middle of the eighth century. Coastal traffic along the shores of the Mediterranean was still relatively brisk in the sixth century in spite of the dangers involved. Pilgrims travelling from Central Gaul to Rome in the time of Gregory of Tours embarked at Marseilles and sailed along the coast of Provence and Italy. The island of Lérins was connected with the continent by a fairly regular service of boats. A hermit like St Hospice, who lived near Nice, fed on dates and herbs brought him by merchants from Egypt. The port of Marseilles was sufficiently busy for the Merovingian kings to quarrel for possession of it. At Fos, where the Rhône riverboats took over from seagoing ships, there was a warehouse belonging to the Treasury. A scholar who is also a skilled chemist has discovered that the glass factories in the Rhineland needed imports of Mediterranean natron, and that the garnet used in cloisonné enamelling up to the sixth century, but not later, came from markets in Asia Minor. Pirenne has listed other examples of this trade with the East which continued up to the Saracen invasion: ivory, silk, Syrian wines, spices such as pepper, cummin, cinnamon.

Such an accumulation of facts proves the existence of relations, uneasy perhaps but continuous, with the countries around the Mediterranean. We should not be deceived by their number. After the Germanic invasions the economy of Western Europe underwent a profound change, but without disputing the repercussions which followed the Moslem conquest it has to be admitted that it did not bring about the complete rupture, the clean-cut break, which has been attributed to it, since it was preceded by a long period of decay. The European economy was already in decline when the victorious Saracens closed, or tried to close, the Mediterranean to Christians. Pirenne never questioned, nor even minimized, the influence of the Germanic invasions, in describing which he coined the happy phrase 'barbarization'. Applied to economic life, it admirably epitomizes the muddled, spineless Merovingian world of the sixth century. There was, it was true, no definitive break between East and West, and Gregory of Tours in his History of the Franks, so rich in informative anecdote, gives facts which prove this, but the continuance of these relations simply means that the easy-going Merovingians left things as they were, the more willingly since it was in their own interests to maintain the *status quo*. The miserly Chilperic I found *laissez-faire* the best policy when the Emperor Tiberius made a point of presenting him with beautiful gold medallions each one lb. in weight. Childebert II was no less devoted to the Byzantine alliance, since it brought him 50,000 gold *solidi*, the price of his army's support for the Empire against the Lombards. Yet no effort was made to revitalize trade with the East. The administration simply let things slide. The native nobility, the Gallo-Romans, who lived in the country, with certain very rare exceptions did not engage in trade, and the majority of Germans also seem to have been allergic to this calling, so that commerce passed almost wholly into the hands of foreigners.

It was chiefly the Syrians, whom St Jerome called the most avaricious of mortals, who seized upon it and acquired a monopoly. Large numbers made their way into Gaul, and in some cities such as Orleans they formed veritable colonies. They succeeded in infiltrating into the Rhineland, into Germany and even into Great Britain. They had other eastern competitors: Greeks and Jews. One of the latter named Priscus had put himself at the service of King Chilperic I, who entrusted him with the purchase of goods. At the beginning of the seventh century Dagobert also had his Jewish *negociator*, a certain Solomon. They were commission agents, who filled the gap left by the lack or scarcity of merchants owning permanent shops. Shops were very rare, and the few allusions which might conceivably refer to them are not very convincing. When Gregory of Tours speaks of *domus negociatorum*, it is not certain that he means shops; they are more likely to be the merchants' actual homes. This lack forced people of means to resort, as the Emperors and high officials of the Late Empire were already doing, to agents whom they sent to make purchases on the spot. The royal example was followed by the abbots of monasteries who, responsible for the food supplies of their communities, also had their abbey merchants, veritable quartermasters. . . .

It would give quite a false impression of the merchants and their many-sided activities, which have been recorded for us in Merovingian documents, to equate them to merchants of our own day. These men were adventurers, whether they were Orientals come to the West to sell the produce of their native countries, or inversely, a few rare inhabitants of Gaul who were genuine pirates, like Samo of Senon, a contemporary of Dagobert. He had set out for Esclavonia, in other words Bohemia, to engage in trade, and imposing himself on the inhabitants of the country, had eventually become King of the Wends. Amongst the Germanic barbarians one nation alone seems to have had a flair for trading—the Frisians. Inhabiting the strip of coast in the Low Countries between the mouth of the Scheldt and that of the Eider, they engaged in trade in the Merovingian period. The poverty of a country very little of which had been cleared for cultivation, and which was exposed to frequent inroads from the sea, doubtless impelled them to leave their own land to trade as hawkers abroad. Their chief stock-in-trade was cloth (*pallia frisonica*) and it is tempting to think of them as ancestors of the Flemish cloth-merchants, but the connexion remains problematical.

Trading, carried on in these various ways, was frequently a dangerous undertaking and the men engaged in it banded themselves together for protection. In the sixth century the merchants of Verdun formed an association, and it was probably their influence which enabled the bishop to obtain from King Theodebert a loan of 7,000 gold *solidi* for his town. Samo himself did not set out for Esclavonia alone, but in the company of other merchants. It is recorded that one merchant armed six ships in order to undertake a certain expedition.

After a study of the various documents (most of which tell us very little, and which in any case are few in number) dealing with the Merovingian merchants, it is singularly difficult to define their activities. It is an exaggeration to speak in terms of big business, '*grand commerce*', international trade, import and export trade. Such phrases are far too grandiose to describe the modest activities in which most of these traders engaged. On the other hand we should not yield to the temptation, great though it may be, and not altogether wide of the mark, to compare them to the North Africans of our own day who hawk carpets and other native products, pester passers-by in the streets and haunt the cafés of our modern cities. They too form colonies in our cities, exactly as did the Syrians in Merovingian times, and who as we have seen did not live by themselves when they were in Gaul. Such a comparison would, however, rate the medieval merchants too low, since they did at least fill a gap in the contemporary economy by selling eastern products, such as spices, which were both useful and valued.

We cannot quite agree with those who have interpreted the presence in Gaul of foreign, and particularly of eastern merchants, as proof that large-scale trade continued to flourish in the West. We regard it, on the contrary, as evidence of the inertia of the western peoples and of the stagnation of their economic life. It was the deterioration of commercial activity resulting from the Great Invasions which spread over Gaul and Italy industrious eastern traders who hoped to make a substantial profit from the bundle of wares they had brought with them. Their advent in such large numbers was not the mark of a sound economy. Moreover, the goods in which they dealt were not always respectable. Slaves were the most profitable of their wares, and the money to be made from them attracted the Gallo-Romans also, who, following their example, went into business on their own account. The Frank Samo was a slave trader, of that there can be no doubt, since Esclavonia fed the slave-markets from the Early Middle Ages. The Great Invasions, by pushing the Germanic peoples westward, created east of the Elbe a vacuum which was filled by the Slavs. Certain of these peoples became human merchandise and traffic in them became so widespread that in the Romance languages the word slave, originally a man of Slav nationality, supplanted the Latin words *mancipium* and *servus*, which had been used to denote a human being in a state of slavery. But these dealers in human flesh sought their merchandise from many other countries as well. They made frequent expeditions to Great Britain whence many slaves were drawn, since, as Ferdinand Lot wrote: 'The Anglo-Saxons used to sell their fellow-countrymen.' The Frisians, who traded on the other side of the Channel, certainly engaged in this traffic. Though it was so widespread and though slavery was not officially condemned by the Church, it shocked religious people, and the buying back of captives, wretched creatures who though endowed with a soul were herded about like cattle to be sold and dispersed, they regarded as a charitable duty. St Eloi, Dagobert's minister, who was very rich, practised this on a large scale, buying back in batches of fifty or even one hundred souls the very moment they set foot on Gallic soil the Britains and Saxons being brought in as slaves. The slave trade increased in volume after the Saracen conquest; large numbers were imported into Spain which became an important market for the traders. It has even been asserted that this export trade brought in a little Moslem gold, that first dinars then Abbasid dirhams, flowed into the West, but its importance has probably been overexaggerated. A black market—and the slave trade was in fact a kind of black market—rarely benefits the community and brings its monetary gains into general circulation.

One serious defect in the Merovingian economy prevented trade from establishing itself on solid foundations, namely the poor quality of the coinage . . . The points already discussed may perhaps serve to justify a sceptical approach to this so-called Merovingian economic activity which, so the theory runs, was inherited from the ancient world, continued to flourish until it was blocked by the Moslem conquest, went into rapid decline from the middle of the seventh century and finally petered out under the Carolingians. We believe the opposite to be the case . . . that the dawn of the Carolingian era marks a restoration or in any case a serious attempt to put the economy on a sound footing. The harm done to the western economy by the Saracen invasion was only moderate and localized, since this economy had been thrown out of gear and seriously crippled when the Moslems partially succeeded in closing the Mediterranean to Christians. We shall see that the havoc wrought by the invasions of the Northmen in the ninth century was far more serious, since it profoundly disturbed a healthy economy which had been well on the way to recovery.

5. ALFONS DOPSCH

FROM Alfons Dopsch, *The Economic and Social Foundations of European Civilization* (London: Kegan Paul, Trench, Trubner & Co., Ltd., 1937), pp. 384–90.

The general picture drawn in this book of the social and economic development of the pre-Carolingian period, from the age of the folk migrations onwards, differs considerably from that which has usually been given. The conventional picture was one of backward and very primitive conditions. But this is completely at variance with the conditions which were known (even before the great achievements of modern epigraphical and papyrological research) to have prevailed in late Roman times, and in equally strong contrast with what the Germans actually achieved later, in the course of their settlement in the Roman provinces. If the people had been so backward at this time, how could the great task of land division have been carried out by Ostrogoths and Visigoths, Lombards, and Burgundians, as it is described? The Germans would have been utterly incapable of maintaining in the same state of cultivation the wide acreage which had already been methodically and intensively tilled by the Romans; and had they depended on the latter to do the work their position would soon have deteriorated, to a degree which would have brought them into economic subjection to their Roman *consortes*.

Similarly, there was no necessity to win new territory for cultivation by a slow and laborious process of reclamation, nor to seek ground in the forests for a purely primitive husbandry. Quite apart from the wide extent of unforested land, the existence of which is established by modern geographical research, and on which evidence of prehistoric settlements of husbandmen has been discovered, the division of land with the Romans must have provided a rich supply of arable. Even where no regular division took place, the Germans acquired land which had long been under cultivation. And yet another consideration: in those places in which the Germans took two-thirds of the Roman arable, they took only half of the forest clearings and newly reclaimed land. Does not this tell clearly both against the theory of the predominance of forest economy and against the idea that the cultivated sites changed from place to place, or even (truly a bold conception!) moved about the forests? Moreover, any such view would be in direct conflict with the motive usually assigned to the so-called folk migrations. Was not one of their chief causes supposed to be the land hunger of the Germans? And how could land and forests have been exploited in this "extensive" fashion, if land were so scarce that the Roman authorities had had to give the barbarians definite areas for settlement? In any case the adoption of such procedure would have been impossible, in view of the devastating results which would have accompanied it from the point of view of agricultural technique. It is only necessary to recall the case of Bavaria, where districts which to-day are moorland and useless for crops, must have been under cultivation in the Celtic and Roman period, as the surviving *Hochäcker* and Roman remains prove. The change may be traced to an irrational method of reclamation, which brought about a diminished rainfall and consequently the desiccation of the soil and the disappearance of the fertilizing layer of vegetation, as a result of which arable cultivation was no longer possible in that district.

Similar reasons may be urged against the Mark-association theory. It is most unlikely that the German occupation was accompanied by a rationalization of land holdings which had originally been divided into private properties under the Romans. It would have been an enormous undertaking to bring together all these holdings into anything like a uniform whole. Archaeological research has shown that the best known "Marks" were on the sites of early pre-Roman settlements.

The extension of cultivation had gone much farther than used to be supposed. Some recent scholars go so far as to consider that it was practically complete before Carolingian times in North-West Germany and in Bavaria, not to mention the districts of Roman settlement, and that all that took place later was an intensive internal colonization, in which a substantial beginning had already been made.

It used to be thought that the main characteristic of this early period was the fact that it was a "closed economy", in which men lived and worked in almost complete isolation, in separate self-sufficing units. On the contrary, however, it has become clear that already in Roman times the scattered plots of land belonging to a number of landowners were interspersed, even in small areas, and in single villages.

The highly developed network of roads and ways of communication, created by the Romans in the first centuries of the Christian era as far as, and in places even beyond, the *limes,* for military, commercial, and political reasons, was not destroyed; it was there to offer on all sides safe means of communication in early German times. We have seen that in the latter period new undertakings, such as the great colonization movement, were not only connected with the Roman settlements and proceeded from them, but actually advanced along the old Roman roads. The great migratory period brought the peoples closer to one another and did away with isolation. Recent research into the history of art has impressively developed this thesis by means of remains of industrial *objets d'art*, and the spread of late Roman technique.

The political expansion of Frankish rule, which was extended by King Theudebert in the first half of the sixth century to Pannonia and to the Adriatic, and in the North as far as the Saxons and Thuringians, first pointed a way out of the narrow limits of early tribal life, and must have banished the seclusion of former times. To this we must add the spread of Christianity and especially of Catholicism. As its name implies, it tends to cast a wide net and aims at distant results. In this period of early German culture, it was not only in religious life that its peculiarly international tendencies were at work; it had also a levelling and socialistic effect on material existence and on the law. It bridged over the special features of the various political institutions, and created over their heads a self-contained series of interests and efforts which were everywhere the same.

But what about the small individual farms? Were they not isolated? Scholars were led astray in this matter by the old interpretation of the *Hufe*, and still more perhaps by the descriptions of the social bases of German political life in that early age. If the German land occupation were imagined as taking place by means of settlements of free men with equal rights on a family basis, and if the single *Hufe* were the measure of private ownership, which fell equally to the lot of everyone, then it was easy to reach such a conclusion, in the light of Tacitus' description of the freedom of the Germans and of their characteristic tendency to isolated settlements. Have not certain scholars tried to make out that the *Einzelhof* in forest and uncultivated land was actually the original form of German settlement? But the single *Hufe* was certainly insufficient to maintain a freeman and his family. The truth, as shown by the records, is that free farmers possessed not one *Hufe* but several. We must not confuse the unit of measurement with the individual holding, nor imagine that the latter was always the same. No serious scholar to-day would support the old theory; it was born of eighteenth and nineteenth-century ideas concerning the freedom and equality of the Germans at the time of the occupation. It is certain not only that there were everywhere considerable inequalities of ownership, but that great estates existed from the beginning. But the Germans, under the influence of their characteristic law and social institutions (the *comitatus*), introduced important changes which sowed the seed of a vigorous new growth. And although we must assume a considerable measure of adoption of Roman institutions, the extraordinarily important part played by the Germans in the cultural development of the whole succeeding period consists in this, that after the conquest of the Roman Empire and the foundation of their new states on its soil, they were in a position to take over the Roman culture without further ado, to keep it alive and indeed to infuse new life into it; and that, as we learn from the fifth century Roman writer of Marseilles, they instituted better conditions of life, which actually influenced and attracted those in possession of the older Roman culture in favour of the barbarians.

The Germans did not behave as enemies of culture, destroying or abolishing Roman civilization; on the contrary they preserved and developed it. Even if they were at first rough and clumsy in their use of the Roman methods, there was no interruption or breach of cultural development, which might have compelled them, owing to their primitive incompetence, to build up a completely new edifice. The conquest of the Roman Empire took place on different lines from the conquest of other states in political history. The Germans did not overrun and destroy it in a savage onslaught, and then painfully build their primitive culture on its ruins. The Roman world was won by the Germans gradually from within, by a peaceful penetration which went on for centuries, during which they absorbed its culture and even, to a considerable extent, took over its administration. Thus the abolition of its political sway was only the last consequence of a long process of change, the readjustment (so to speak) of a firm, whose old name has for long ceased to describe the actual head of the business. The Gothic King Athaulf could boast with truth that he had not destroyed Roman civilization, but had restored and magnified the fame of Rome by means of German strength. It is for this reason that the abolition of the western Roman Empire in 476 was not felt by contemporaries to be the fall of Rome, and indeed was hardly considered to be a really important event. "The Roman Empire in the West fell asleep without any convulsion."

The attitude of the Germans to Roman organizations, as conquerors after the fall of Roman rule, was conservative in their own interests, and they continued to develop their rich inheritance. But it was not as if this inheritance had stayed unchanged, to serve as a pattern for the new structure; the Roman world was dissolving, and a process of disintegration, both economic and social, was taking place. The new rulers first of all determined the political organization. Even during the migrations the old tribal existence had changed considerably and had been forced into a unity, which was crystallized in the tribal constitution after the final settlements. Side by side with this, encouraged by the wars against the Romans, went the concentration of political power in the tribal kingship. The institution of monarchy emerged out of the military importance of the old German army leadership and dukedom, and a monarchical form of constitution was introduced after the final settlements. As a consequence there came about a change in the traditional democratic institutions. The authority which had formerly been vested in the people, in the assembly of common freemen, passed to the monarch; and the new system was decisively influenced by him. The control of the rural organizations (*pagi, civitates*), taken from Celts and Romans, was subject to royal authority and entrusted to royal officials (counts). A similar change occurred in the towns. Military authority was at first still in the foreground. Civil administration was then joined to it, and the old Roman communal autonomy, expressed in the municipal constitution, was replaced by a seigneurial organization. The heavy social and economic oppression of late Roman times, due to the peculiar fact that the fiscal interests of the state coincided with those of the great private landlords, who farmed the taxes, was done away with, and a political solicitude for the welfare of the mass of the free population was substituted. It was regulated by consideration of their public services (army and justice) and aimed at protecting the poorer men. For the unequal distribution of land in these new German states had already caused an economic differentiation, which brought with it a change in social status. Side by side with the ancient German nobility, the service of the king came also to mean ennoblement, while the acquisition of large estates divided the mass of freemen into different classes.

The upward movement of the lower classes (semi-free and unfree) was strongly encouraged by the Church, which, because of its philanthropic duties (care for the poor, manumission of slaves, etc.) attracted these strata of society to itself. Its administration, which had developed in a monarchical direction through the power given to the episcopate, met with the same tendency in the kingship, especially among the Franks. With the conversion of Clovis to Catholicism, a step prompted by internal politics, it placed itself under the protection of the monarchy, and, in its own interests, co-operated in developing the centralization of the royal power. This co-operation led not only to a rich economic endowment of the increasing number of ecclesiastical institutions, both bishoprics and monasteries, but also to the development of the political power of the episcopate, when the royal power declined, owing to the partition of the Frankish kingdom and the long civil wars. The secular and religious aristocracy, enriched by royal service and from royal property, was, as the Edict of Clothar II shows, more and more influential in feudalizing public authority, a process which went on side by side with the development of the great landlords (*potentes*). The development of the system of private churches (*Eigenkirchen*), which, like the great estates, derived from the Roman inheritance, is the economic side of this development, and typifies the great offensive campaign begun by the lay aristocracy in the seventh century against the rich property of the Church.

The subordination of the Frankish state Church to the authority of the crown, which made it a national church in opposition to the Roman Papacy, is not to be understood as an acceptance of Aryan tendencies, for the *Eigenkirchenrecht* does not seem to have been either denominational or national. Roman influences were doubtless encouraged by the Church; but it is not true that by its adherence to Roman law it reintroduced Roman culture to the Germans and familiarized them with it. The fact that the Merovingian national church was "free of Rome", and that the lay aristocracy came more and more to control and to disintegrate it, would certainly have tended rather to check such Romanization in the seventh and the beginning of the eighth centuries. The influence of the Roman Pope did not become important until after the great reform of the church, which took place under the first Carolingians. Here the co-operation of the new cultural factors is very plain, for though German civil law might be lastingly influenced by the Church in such institutions as the right of free division of property, freedom of testamentary disposal, and freedom of marriage, yet its German institutions, such as patronage and *mundium*, suited it well. Roman law did not always have the upper hand.

The subordination of the Church to the protection of the Frankish king and its rich endowments in land made it possible for the royal ruler to use ecclesiastical property for state purposes. As the lay lords had been doing on a small scale by virtue of their *patrocinium,* so now the King claimed Church property on a large scale and bestowed it on his followers and vassals; and thereby not only were the latter rendered capable of royal, especially military, service, but also this vast accumulation of Church lands became again economically useful to the laity. The rise of the beneficial system, beginning in the sixth century, was not decisively influenced by the Roman model, or by the ecclesiastical *beneficia*. As in other directions, formations of a similar type already existed in late Roman times, and parallel developments may also be observed in the East Roman Empire. Yet the beneficial system of the early Middle Ages emerged as an original and peculiar formation through the combination of the two new cultural factors, German civilization and the Church. It was aided by the internal political development of the Frankish kingdom from the middle of the sixth century, and was connected with the social and economic changes of the time, in the shape of the great estates. Charles Martel did not create the beneficial system, nor was there any reform of military organization at that period. The connection between *vassallitium* and *beneficia* was there from the beginning, and had its counterpart in the German right of maintaining a *comitatus.* Over and above its military purpose, the economic aims of the *beneficium* now for the first time became important.

The civilization of this pre-Carolingian period was not exclusively agrarian and non-urban. The Roman towns did not perish in the storms of the migrations, nor did the new German owners entirely avoid settling in them. In Italy, Spain, and Gaul they remained the administrative centres of the surrounding territory, and were of great economic importance as markets for trade and for the development of a free industry. Industry did not completely collapse or pass entirely into the hands of the omnipotent lords of the great estates, but only received a new character under the Germans. Here as in the country, in the place of the old autonomous administration by the community, there was some measure of control by the town itself, embodied in the city count (*Stadtgraf*) appointed by the king. Side by side with him the bishop rose to great power; after the collapse of Roman rule the episcopate had increasingly become the mainstay of the provincial Christian population, and in consequence of the wealth which it had acquired by gifts, it was a great economic force. Nor was it only a power among the proletarian masses, by reason of its care of the poor. On the foundation of the privileged position which it had obtained in the Roman period, a position which the new German conquerors acknowledged by means of royal privileges (immunities, freedom from taxation, and military service), its power incessantly grew until it came to vie with that of the count.

Roman urban life radiated its influence from the territory of the old *limes,* the Rhine, Main, and Danube, outwards over the Inner German lands. Even though such towns did not yet exist there, the seeds of urban development were already present, for the quasi-urban centres of the old folk- and Gau-communities (*vici*) were the centres of administration and of economic intercourse, with their markets, customs-houses, and mints, and also, often, of religious worship, with their Gau-temples. Like the folk-strongholds (*Volksburgen*) and strongholds of refuge (*Fluchtburgen*) and like the towns themselves, they were also places of shelter for the country folk in times of invasion, and were walled during the migrations. With their development into towns, the old tribal *territorium* became urban; the characteristic expression of this fact is seen in the transference of the tribal name to the town. After the conversion to Christianity these often populous places became very important, as sees of the newly founded bishoprics.

Above all, however, they fulfilled an important economic function. After the enormous eastward and northward expansion of Frankish territory, which under King Theudebert (534–548) reached Pannonia, the Adriatic, and Jutland, not only did the tribes of Inner Germany become linked up with the old lands, which were soaked in Roman culture, but also the new political relationships soon created economic relationships, accompanied by a revival of trade and commerce. Austrasia comes into the foreground.

The new annexations of Frisians and Saxons in the North, and of Thuringians and Baiuvari in the East, strengthen the German characteristics of the large and growing state; and a mixed culture comes into being, which derives a special stimulus from the formation of new relationships on the advancing northern, eastern, and southern boundaries, and new cultural tendencies appear from the North (Anglo-Saxons), from the eastern empire, and from Italy. Trade was by no means unimportant and undeveloped. It was not limited to luxuries and overseas products, such as spices and silk, brought by foreign merchants to central Europe. Orientals, Syrians, and Jews, and the maritime tribes, Frisians and Saxons, were not the only enterprising traders; so also were the Inner German tribes, Franks, Alemanni, and Baiuvari. There was already a class of professional merchants, who acted as middlemen between the original producers and the great mass of consumers, and harvested a rich profit thereby. The great estates did not take the lead here, any more than they did in industry. They did not provide for all their own needs in a closed domestic economy, but bought even ordinary necessaries in the market. Since in the more populous places, especially in the towns, a sufficient number of consumers was already present, a free industrial system was able to develop side by side with the manorial handicraft system, and this often employed wage labour. To this system we owe the artistic products of the gold, silver, and ivory industries of that time.

Commerce and trade were now able to develop into independent professions, because a freely working price mechanism made it possible to make high profits, and a brisk turnover secured sufficient gain even for the small retailer. Merchants were rich citizens, not only in Italy, where they were classed according to their wealth and might even perform military service in full armour, with sword and coat of mail, but also in the Frankish kingdom. This commercial intercourse was carried on not merely by barter but also with money, and the formularies show us that cash was frequently used in buying and selling. Even before the fall of the Roman Empire the Germans were familiar with the use of money; large sums were paid to them by Rome and Byzantium, so that from the fourth century it was necessary to make regulations to check the flow of gold and silver to the barbarians. In the newly founded German states, both for political and economic reasons coins were at first minted after the pattern of the coinage of the Eastern empire. As trade and commerce continued to develop even during King Theudebert's policy of expansion, a coinage of their own was minted by the German states. There was a double standard, which led in the seventh century to an issue of heavy silver *denarii* (12 = the old gold shilling = 40 lighter *denarii*), with the aim of removing the abuses which had arisen from this fact.

Like trade, the practice of moneylending was also widespread, so that not only professional merchants but also clergy were engaged in it. Even in the sixth and seventh centuries a great lust for gain had seized upon wide circles of the population; above all, the Jews, many of whom also farmed the mints, became rich through usury, a fact which led to their persecution, especially in Spain. The taxes in kind of agricultural produce mentioned in the folk-laws are no sign that a natural economy predominated; the alternative payments aimed rather at making more favourable conditions of payment for the poorer freemen and allowing them to profit by the state of the market.

Thus, this period of the fifth and sixth centuries is seen to be the organic and vital connecting link between late Roman and Carolingian times, and the so-called "Carolingian Renaissance" appears in a somewhat different light. Much which once seemed to be a new and deliberate creation is now seen, owing to our clearer knowledge of the period, never to have been lost at all, but to have persisted in those obscure, sparsely documented and twilight centuries of European cultural development. The later centuries did but complete and extend what had already been introduced and established in that earlier age. ✼

6. FERDINAND LOT

FROM Ferdinand Lot, *The End of the Ancient World* (New York: Barnes & Noble, Inc., 1953), pp. 183–86, 403–7.

The Roman Empire nearly perished in the great crisis which covers the period from 235 to 268. At last, the barbarians were repelled by the Illyrian Emperors, Claudius II, Aurelian and Probus, and political unity was restored. Nevertheless the situation remained precarious. The necessary changes were effected by two personalities of the highest calibre, Diocletian and Constantine. Some would have them idealists, visionaries and dreamers. This is an amazing misconception; they were practical minds, the former especially. They began by jettisoning what was necessary to save the ship. It was obvious that one man alone could not govern from the Euphrates to the Atlantic, and from the Sahara to Caledonia, two worlds, the Greek and the Latin, incapable of being welded together. To prevent any revolt on the part of a rival, Diocletian chose one and tried to turn him into both a colleague and a friend. The unity of the Empire, at least in theory, was thus maintained. Constantine made the separation of the two worlds final by changing aggrandized Byzantium into a new Rome (330). Thanks to its position, Byzantium could be saved from invasion; but for this inspiration of genius, Greek civilization would have disappeared, and like that of Chaldaea, it would be known to us only by some shapeless fragments.

A religious malady, Christianity, was threatening Roman society. Diocletian had not advanced beyond the old idea that the sect could be destroyed by force. Constantine in an apparent or real fit of madness saw in it a power to be utilized in the service of the Roman State. In the East, the Orthodox Church, Greek civilization and the State came to be so well fused that to be received into the bosom of the Church was *eo ipso* to become a Greek-speaking "Roman", at least for several centuries.

After capturing Christianity, the emperors next turned to the fiscal machinery which they strained to its utmost. To fight the barbarians and also to buy them off, and to keep the magnificent edifice of the Empire standing, great resources were needed.

But the Mediterranean world had suffered from a very serious economic upheaval. It was ruined and completely retrograde at the moment when the needs of the State were more pressing than ever. Fiscal ruthlessness ended by setting up a real caste system. The peasant was henceforth bound to the soil; this was not the only cause of the serfdom of the soil, the origins of which go back to a remote past, but the extension of this system to free labourers is one of the features of the Later Empire. Obliged to become a member of a *collegium*, the artisan was bound to his craft and the merchant to his calling. What shall we say of the workers in the mines and in the imperial factories who were branded with red-hot iron? They could not run away and their condition was hereditary. The middle classes were no less "regulated". The *curiales* formed a *consortium* responsible for the taxes and the putting of the land under cultivation; every avenue by which they might escape from the *curia* was closed.

The following was the result: the government broke all resistance, but also all independence; it completely changed the people into a herd of "rayahs", in the Turkish fashion.

Nevertheless we have not before us a purely selfish despotism, nor a long-matured, scientific and planned system. It was not with any deliberate purpose that the Emperors achieved centralization, unification and uniformity. A blind, unavoidable, irresistible necessity forced them to grind down everything so that the Empire might be able to exist.

These Emperors were busy with humanitarian schemes to which their legislation bears ample and frequent evidence, too frequent indeed for their decisions to have been effective. They wished to protect the lower and middle classes of the towns and they set up *defensores civitatis*. The *collegia* of tradesmen and artisans enjoyed privileges; they were allowed to make their own regulations and they were not harassed in their internal arrangements.

The Emperors wished to allow the complaints of their subjects to reach their own ears. They wished to put a check on the absolutism of their functionaries. Hence significant though at bottom fruitless institutions, such as the provincial councils, one of which, that of the Gauls, was to last until the end of the Western Empire. Lastly, individual measures, such as remissions of taxes, and the punishment of men in high places guilty of the betrayal of trust or of oppression, were not rare.

In spite of all, the State failed in its rôle of protector. It was ill served and betrayed by its own agents. The latter, the high functionaries, or, to speak more accurately, the "magistrates" and "judges", belonged to the class of large landowners. They shared its ideas, customs and interests. This aristocracy was disloyal in its service to the government, while cowering before it. It secretly thwarted it, not so much from hatred as from a spirit of opposition and from selfishness. Debarred from the army, confined to honorary functions, suspected and watched, the ruling class lost all spontaneity and initiative, and in its case also, character fell very low.

The fundamental cause of the decay and later of the breaking up of the Roman Empire appears to us to have been the following:

The Empire had become too vast, too cunning and too complicated a mechanism; the Mediterranean world, economically retrograde since the third century, could no longer support its weight. It split in two, the *pars Orientis* and *pars Occidentis*, from the end of this century. Even for the exercise of its authority, the State was under the necessity of narrowing its field of action. The same necessity was soon to force the West to break up into half-Roman, half-barbarian States. The latter in their turn would become subdivided, and the territorial splitting up was to go on increasingly without a stop for long centuries, until the twelfth century. This narrowing of political action was accompanied by a narrowing of public spirit, which was destined to go as far as the annihilation of the conception of public interest, and the disappearance of the notion of a State in the period of the barbarians.

Thus, under a still majestic appearance, the Roman Empire, at the end of the fourth century, was no longer anything but a hollow husk. It was powerless to withstand a violent shaking and soon it was to suffer a new and terrible attack from the barbarians. The East was destined to emerge from it as best it could, but the West was to be shivered in pieces.

There is something deeper and more stable than political forms, which are always ephemeral, and that is what is called civilization. In its highest reaches, literature, the arts, philosophy and religion, the changes are no less striking than in the political sphere. The old naïve nature deities, Greek or Latin, gave place to the Oriental "superstitions", Judaism, Christianity, Mithraism, Manicheism, etc., coming from Egypt, Syria and Persia. These foreign arrivals transformed the ethics and altered the psychology of the man of Antiquity. His art and literature felt the consequence of these great mutations. The blighting worship of the great models and certain defects inherent in the classical spirit, made an aesthetic renewal almost impossible. The triumph of Christianity and later of Islam were to detach men's souls from the ancient forms of beauty. Even before being condemned by religion, plastic art was to succumb, a victim to a revolution in taste originating in the East; line was sacrificed to colour and nobility of style to the fantastic and chimerical. Ancient literature was condemned by the Church. Wholly pagan, it ceased to be understood and to be loved. Unfortunately the twofold Christian literature, Greek and Latin, which sought to replace it, thought it would succeed in this by pouring itself into the same mould. But new thoughts and feelings need a new form. Christian literature, from the point of view of art, was still-born. Science and philosophy succumbed under the competition of Oriental mysticism which brought about a real transformation of values.

This transformation is as phenomenal as if a sleeper on waking should see other stars shining above his head. . . .

The Roman world had been able to endure only by means of a ruthless compression, and this compression by breaking every spring in the life of the peoples had made the Empire the prey of the barbarians, who by themselves were neither numerous nor very dangerous. When the bonds uniting peoples which were Romanized, but separated from each other by geography and differences of race, customs and aspirations, had been broken, would it not have been possible to turn to advantage this *fait accompli?* By putting an end to a decaying political form, the Empire, could not the barbarians have freed the peoples, and thus, without knowing or wishing it, have been indirectly beneficial to them?

Italy, Gaul, Great Britain and Northern Africa are geographical units. Each of these regions could and ought to have been the seat of an independent civilization. For a moment it had seemed that the great third-century crisis, by breaking the Roman world into fragments, might set up nationalities based on later civilization. But the peoples had lost all national and even particularist feeling. They were only fragments whose ambition was to be re-united and form once more the imposing whole of the Empire. Two centuries later the peoples formed only an amorphous mass without any initiative and fundamentally incapable of ruling their own destinies. By crystallizing round a barbarian dynasty what latent forces had been able to survive amongst the natives, it would have been possible to give back to these countries, which had been crushed under Roman uniformity, an individual character and original life.

This is in fact what took place in Spain, even in spite of the obstacle constituted by the Arianism of the ruling race. At the end of the seventh century, the fusion between Goths and Hispano-Romans was very far advanced, and, from every point of view, Spain was making for unity. This is what undoubtedly would have happened in Lesser Africa and in Italy with the Vandals and the Ostrogoths but for the thoughtless venture of Justinian, and in Gaul with the Visigoths but for the accident of Clovis.

Unfortunately these Romano-German States very soon proved to be frail. Roman civilization was not good for the barbarians. They aped without succeeding in assimilating it. The Southern climate certainly weakened them. They were not numerous and their armies remained very poor numerically, where, as in Africa and Italy, they continued to keep apart. The Visigoths in Gaul and Spain, who incorporated the natives, were undoubtedly swamped by the superior numbers of the latter. Lastly, these uprooted peoples brought no political institution apart from the monarchy. Their cohesion was due solely to the ascendancy of an illustrious chieftain or the prestige of a dynasty. When the old divine families of the Amalungs and the Baltungs amongst the Goths had disappeared, the throne was henceforth a prey to the continual strife of competitors. The Vandal State in Africa, the Gothic State of Toulouse, and the Gothic State of Toledo, fell in a single battle. If the Ostrogoths put up a long and glorious resistance, this was largely due to the fact that Justinian could bring against them only insignificant forces.

The States founded by the Franks and the Lombards did not, at the beginning at least, possess the mixed, amphibious character of the Gothic States. The Lombards were rude and ruthless conquerors, but the monarchy was, amongst them, almost immediately checkmated by the aristocracy. The kings failed to unite Italy under their authority not only because of the opposition of Byzantium and of the Papacy, but because their State scarcely included more than the Po Valley and part of Tuscany, the Lombard principalities of Central and Southern Italy being in reality independent. The Lombard nation had never been numerically a large people, either in Germany or Pannonia. When transported in its entirety to Italy, it must have been very soon swallowed up by the native population. In the eighth century, a Lombard was a man living under the authority of a king of barbarian origin and in conformity to German law, but in language and blood he was probably already an Italian. Two battles sufficed to put an end to the Kingdom of Pavia.

We have seen the peculiar nature of the Frankish State. It was founded by the ambition of one man. The Gallo-Roman population at once accepted the domination, or more correctly, the superior position of the Franks. The centre of power was very soon transferred to Roman territory. Nevertheless, it had behind it, what the Lombard State lacked, strong German reserves, on the Escaut, the lower Meuse, the Moselle and the Rhine. The Franks kept their individual character in the midst of the natives. They even imposed themselves on these by their prestige. From the beginning of the sixth century they formed the most formidable power in Western Europe, and they were destined to rule Gaul, almost the whole of Germany, and for a moment Northern Italy. But with them also the only institution was the Monarchy. The latter began to decay at the end of the sixth century. The Aristocracy prevailed in the seventh century. Only the institution of the Mayor of the Palace, a real Viceroy, prevented the breaking up of the State. A clever and ambitious family of Austrasia even succeeded in restoring the unity of the *Regnum Francorum* by removing its rivals in Neustria and Burgundy, and then by reigning under the name of the degenerate Merovingian. But at the beginning of the eighth century, it seemed that this house would, in its turn, also disappear. Failing the appearance of a new Clovis or Charles Martel, the Frankish State was being destroyed by the blows of the heathen Germans on one side and of the Moslems of Spain on the other.

In the eighth century, the bankruptcy was thus general. The more German States of the Franks and of the Lombards seemed to be crumbling as much as the Romano-German States of the Goths.

Hence the entry of the barbarians into the Roman world, under whatever form it took place, did not succeed in regenerating the ancient world or in replacing it by better political forms.

The regeneration by the barbarians is *a priori* a tempting thesis to maintain. But after we have had a glimpse, in our texts, of the terrible corruption of these times, it is impossible to see in it more than a theme for declamation. The Frankish, Visigothic, Ostrogothic and Lombard monarchies were only so many German Byzantiums, a combination of senility and barbarism. Such States, devoid of freshness and purifying virtue, could not live or could only drag on a miserable life. No vital force animated them, after the fighting days during which they took shape. The Catholic Church showed itself powerless to improve these new societies, howsoever little. Here too there was bankruptcy.

On the borders of these States, the Germans founded others, which were purely barbarian, on territories which had once been Roman, between the upper course of the Danube and the Alps and in Great Britain. We need not linger over them. The duchies of Alemannia and Bavaria came under the influence of the Franks and were an adjunct to their *Regnum*. In Great

Britain, Angles, Jutes and Saxons carried out the most ruthless of conquests and wiped out, as far as they could, all memory of Rome. The history of their petty kingdoms and their feuds contains nothing which deserves to detain us. The wholly German States do not, any more than the mixed Romano-German States, mark any appreciable progress in the march of humanity, in this period of history.

Meanwhile new forces had been or were being born, and it was for these that the future was reserved: Islam, whose prodigious success was of the nature of a miracle, the Papacy, which was about to seize the reins of the Church and to try to dominate civil society, and lastly Vassalage, the germ of the feudal system, in which was to be embodied the life of Western Europe for very many centuries.

With these forces, the Middle Ages really begin. ✳

7. HEINRICH FICHTENAU

FROM Heinrich Fichtenau, *The Carolingian Empire* (Oxford: Basil Blackwell, 1957), pp. 5–10, 46.

It is true that the Franks, at the time of their settlement in Gaul, did not think of the state as an abstract organism. They could not conceive the notion that the state had paid servants who collected the taxes. Among the Franks all public functions had originally been carried out by the king, the nobility and the assembled army, all of which were held together by the bond of personal fealty. But now the public domains passed to the conqueror, the king of the Franks. The administration of the provinces continued as before and the large sums which were collected as taxes and which had previously been handed over to the governor and the emperor, were paid to him. In addition, the loot of war and the confiscated property of political opponents, a veritable flood of gold, passed into the coffers of the Merovingian king whose power thus rose to unprecedented heights. To the Franks he was the master of the conquered land in which they had come to live. To the Romans, he took the place of the absolute monarch. No order but the king's was valid. The right of the assembled army to take part in the framing of policies and the influence of the magnates over public business was quickly extinguished. Similarly the old Germanic custom of electing the king disappeared. To coming generations it might well seem that the old Germanic institutions had been replaced by Roman forms of government and administration. At any rate, it had become quite clear that the old Germanic practices were hardly capable in the long run of coping with the problems of government in such a large and highly developed country as Gaul.

Members of the senatorial families became faithful followers of the Merovingian ruler. The majority of bishops were appointed from among their ranks. The people of Roman culture were granted equality before the law with the Franks, and soon after Clovis's death they also were expected to render military service. The *comes,* originally a Roman military commander, became the successor of the Roman governor. As such he was entrusted in each province with the highest civil authority and became the standard type of higher functionary. The Roman customs system, the tolls, the coinage, and the chancelleries of the higher organs of government, together with their *referendarii,* were all put at the disposal of the king. All these things had been unknown to the Germans.

The institutions themselves, of course, underwent a change. Members of the old senatorial families may have entered the royal service, but a large part of the public administration remained, nevertheless, reserved to the Frankish minority. At the same time, the sober, abstract character of the Roman bureaucracy was replaced more and more by a personal and emotionally conditioned conception of service. The practice of writing down all proceedings disappeared and the *comes* became more and more the count. His office was fused with that of the royal judge and of the commander of the army in the Germanic *pagus.*

Thus the centre of gravity in Clovis's kingdom was slowly shifted and the shift was emphasized by geographical factors. The real core of Frankish settlement was in the farthest north. But in Roman times it had been the south, with its flourishing towns, that had played the most important part. After the Frankish conquest the coast of Mediterranean Gaul was beyond the reach of Clovis's power. The western half of that coast formed the Visigothic province of Septimania and was destined to remain outside the Frankish kingdom proper. Cities like Arles, Narbonne and Marseilles and even the Burgundian towns of Lyons and Vienne, yielded pride of place to Paris, which Clovis had chosen to be his residence. The old merchant families continued to live in the metropolitan cities of the south. Since time out of mind they had controlled the overseas trade between Gaul and Italy, Egypt and Syria. These families consisted of Syrians, Romans, Jews and Greeks. By their origin and by their activities they were the people who maintained the contacts among the imperial lands along the shores of the Mediterranean. The Frankish conquest, however, gravely weakened their position, for there is no doubt that as the exponents of Roman civilization were being pushed into the background by

Frankish magnates, the import of luxury goods must have receded. Although these magnates soon learnt to appreciate Roman comfort and although much was spent on ornaments for churches, on reliquaries and clerical garments, overseas trade suffered from the 'barbarization' of daily customs. This decline of trade must have begun long before the Mediterranean had come to be dominated by Arab fleets.

In the north the king had rewarded his Frankish followers with the estates or *villæ* of Roman noblemen. The ordinary Frankish people, too, had exchanged their military occupations for the cultivation of the soil. The Franks had never known such an institution as a closed aristocratic caste. But as people began to feel the increasing importance of large estate-owners as against small peasant proprietors, social differentiation was bound to be accentuated. Moreover, this differentiation was not confined to the economic sphere. The same process began among the Franks as Salvian of Marseilles had already observed among the Romanized population of Gaul: the weaker men 'commend themselves to the magnates so that they may be protected by them. They become the clients (*dediticii*) of the wealthy and place themselves, so to speak, under their jurisdiction and orders'. Formally, the Franks who did this preserved their personal status at law; they had to remain freemen if they wanted to continue to belong to the nation of freemen (*franci*). But economically, socially, and legally a new situation had been created. Every man who had surrendered to a lord became, in fact, dependent in so far as he was subject to the lord's coercion and the lord's right to exact service from him. The distinction between wealthy and poor, between powerful men and small men in a dependent position, so characteristic of provincial Roman society, invaded the very nation which had been so proud of its aristocratic egalitarianism.

Clovis's successors not only continued his well-nigh absolute government but also divided the kingdom, according to Salian law, as they were wont to divide family property. Unity was no longer represented by an all-pervading idea of an abstract state but by the fact that the rulers of the several sub-kingdoms were related to each other. In the old days the Germanic clan and the Germanic family, under the strict leadership of its head, had represented a closed community with a strong will. Clan and family continued to be looked upon as a unit. But the old family discipline of the Merovingians, as well as of other families, was no longer preserved. According to the calculations of one historian, there were twenty-nine feuds between members of the royal family during the single century after Clovis's death. Again and again murders were committed in the closest family circles, and large stretches of land were devastated by armies consisting of vassals of the men concerned. Nevertheless, at least in the beginning, a common line of foreign policy continued to be pursued. Expansion was continued until the majority of the Germanic tribes dwelling in central Europe were united under the dominion of the Merovingian house.

The Alamans, Bavarians, Thuringians, Frisians and Saxons who thus came to be partially or wholly, temporarily or permanently, subject to the Frankish kingdom, created conditions favourable to yet a further removal of the centre of gravity of Frankish dominion. A stable centre, of course, could not be found while the members of the ruling family continued their feuds. But by the side of Neustria, the core of Clovis's power with Paris in its centre, there emerged Austrasia, the home of the Ripuarian Franks. It included the lands along the Moselle, and Alemannia and Hesse, and its 'capital' was Metz. This city was situated inside the borders of the old Roman empire, but it was even further removed from all Mediterranean contacts than Paris had been. Neustria became more and more Romanized. But Austrasia, in spite of its fairly considerable non-Germanic population, remained a 'barbarous' country. The most important ruler of this country was Theudebert, a grandson of Clovis. His rule extended even over Bavaria and the lower Rhineland, and it seemed in his day that it might even be possible to establish a continental empire that would revive all the claims of the ancient Mediterranean *imperium*. Theudebert himself wrote to the Byzantine emperor that his rule extended, after the subjection of numerous tribes, from the frontiers of Pannonia to the northern seas. He assumed the imperial title of Augustus and replaced, on the Austrasian gold coins, the name and the portrait of the emperor by his own. He also followed the custom of the emperors in collecting taxes from all the citizens of the empire, that is, from his Frankish fellow-tribesmen as well as from his Roman subjects.

Thus we see a Merovingian king consciously removing the last traces that reminded people of Roman dominion. But these traces were now little more than historical memories, and in obliterating them Theudebert was merely following a development that was conditioned by the times. How distant, after all, was the *pax Romana* in those days of turmoil! Overseas trade was perilous, and scarcely a place was left in which the ancient heritage of learning could be peacefully cultivated. Compared with the general decay of education, especially among the secular nobility, it signified little that one of the Merovingian kings tried his hand at grammar and poetry or that in Toulouse and elsewhere there still existed something like an 'academy' of learned *literati*. Hand in hand with the autonomy of the provinces there grew up a new provincialism in the style of living. The gold which could no longer circulate freely throughout an empire, disappeared into private coffers. Real estate with peasants, houses and livestock became the most important property.

The counts, originally appointed as the representatives of the king in each province, were drawn more and more into the orbit and interests of the landed magnates of their provinces. The less effective the king's authority became, the more necessary it was for the counts to build up their personal resources and authority in the form of landed property and of manorial influence. In other words, a royal appointment was ineffective unless it was backed by the appointee's own power. The appointee had to be the most powerful man and the wealthiest landowner in the district. It became necessary to choose the count from among the nobility of the province in which he was to exercise his authority. This meant that he had to be chosen from among the ranks of the very people against whose interests he was often supposed to direct his activities. In this way the king's central administration lost its influence in the provinces. Its losses were the gains of the magnates. As early as 614 king Chlothar had been obliged to give legal sanction to the prevailing practice. He promised that henceforward the counts would be chosen only from among the ranks of the landed magnates of every province.

Thus the royal authority, once so powerful, was more and more dissipated. It was usurped partly by the magnates, partly by the half-conquered tribes of Austrasia, partly by the Romanized south. The Romanized elements also increased relatively in numbers and recovered a considerable part of the influence over culture and language which they had lost in northern Neustria. The king was no longer the sole source of authority; each province had its own circle of powerful magnates. And some of these magnates endeavoured to dominate the king himself in the royal palace in order to gain ascendancy over their rivals. . . .

All things considered, there is little difference between the picture we form of Charles's surroundings and the one we have of his ancestors and of other princes of the period. The only difference was that the imperial household, as in fact the empire itself, was greater, more splendid and therefore also more exposed to danger. As long as its power and splendour were increasing, the cracks in the structure remained concealed. It was the achievement of Charles's own powerful personality to have brought about this rise which, without him, might have taken generations to reach its zenith. His efforts were crowned with success because his whole personality was in tune with the progressive forces active among his people. If this had not been the case, no amount of power concentrated in the hands of the king would have sufficed to stamp his countenance upon the age. If this is remembered much of the illusion of well-nigh superhuman achievement, that has inspired both the mediaeval legend of Charlemagne and many modern narratives, is dispelled. What remains is quite enough justification for calling Charles historically great. ✻

8. C. DELISLE BURNS

FROM C. Delisle Burns, *The First Europe* (New York: W. W. Norton & Company, Inc., 1948), pp. 221–28, 609–11.

The general results of the creation of the first barbarian kingdoms in the West may be described in summary form as follows. Political, administrative and judicial authority as well as military force was decentralized. There were several independent and equal sources of governmental authority in place of dependent governorships under one military autocracy. The new kingdoms were the result of conquest by armed bands of ignorant, superstitious and treacherous barbarians, who subjected to their desire for wealth a more highly civilized population. The fact that different barbarians had succeeded in imposing their rule on different parts of the Roman Empire was generally regarded as the will of God. There was, no doubt, some disagreement in answering the question why God should have so willed; but no one at that date seems to have doubted that the greed and violence which were the real foundations of the barbarian kingdoms had results which should be accepted as decisions made by God. The bishops under the different barbarian kings usually accepted their authority so long as they did not actually persecute the Church. And although the Churches in all the different kingdoms retained the old Roman language and the sense of unity across the new frontiers, this did not seriously affect the division of political authority among many different kings. St. Augustine wrote that the division of the world into many different kingdoms was a result of sin, because he believed that the ideal form of government was that of a single Empire including all Christian peoples; and the same explanation of the existence of several States dominated the thought of the Middle Ages, as in the works of Aquinas and Dante. The existence, therefore, of several independent and equal kingdoms was regarded as a regrettable necessity and not as an improvement upon the imperial domination of a single dictator. But in practice the barbarian kingdoms were maintained, at least for some centuries, as the only possible form of government. The ruler in each kingdom was closer to his subjects than the Emperor had been; and his armed forces could operate more efficiently over a restricted area. The frontiers between the new kingdoms were not defined; and the balance of power between them was constantly changing, either because of internal disunion or as a result of warlike expeditions of one against the other. There was a centre of power and authority in each kingdom, but no clearly defined circumference to mark the limit of the efficacy of each Government. The very vagueness of the conception of a frontier in the new kingdoms has influenced political thought and practice ever since. The frontier of the Roman Empire had been clearly defined; but it was a military frontier, outside of which in the West was only barbarism. No one thought of the Roman Wall in Britain or of the *Limes* in Germany as anything but a system of exclusion. The frontiers in the Roman tradition, therefore, at least in the West, were not lines of contact between one State and another but divisions between civilization and barbarism. When, therefore, the new barbarian kingdoms came into existence as centres of authority and used, as far as their barbarism allowed, the Roman experience of law, government and public policy, they had neither a theory nor a practice of what would now be called international affairs, to rely upon. Each separate kingdom inherited the mistaken idea that a State was distinguished from what lay outside it, as civilization is distinguished from barbarism. There was no governmental system connecting the new States; and their relations, therefore, were what Hobbes called those of a "state of nature." Medieval and modern Europe inherited from these Dark Ages their intellectual and emotional darkness in what are now called international affairs.

Secondly, even to-day an obscure idea survives of distinction between the functions of Church and State, which is derived from the Middle Ages. The later medieval conception of two social organizations, one "spiritual," the other "temporal," one a "Church" and the other a "Kingdom" or "State," was not derived from any analysis of the nature of things or of human nature. Nor was it derived from texts of the Bible which were quoted in support of it. It arose out of the actual situation in western Europe after A.D. 400, when the bishops of the several Churches and the kings of the barbarian kingdoms had to find some way of living together. The organization of the Churches was in fact distinct from that of the old imperial regime. The Churches were in a very peculiar position of dependence upon the Emperor after Constantine had allowed Christianity its place as a recognized religion in Roman Law. Bishops did indeed rebuke Emperors; but they never wavered in their reverence for Roman Order. Roman civilization was obviously older than the Churches; and it embodied in law and administration a much fuller and more detailed system of organized social relations than the Churches. Also it was one system covering the whole known world; and the Churches until the fifth century were still separately organized and almost independent, one of another. The Roman Empire had a kind of divinity of its own, as the kingdom of the

Last Age, even if good Christians might find in it traces of the Devil. Thus at first the Church was inferior in prestige to the State.

But when the Roman Empire in western Europe disappeared, the barbarian kingdoms did not inherit directly the "divinity" of the old system of law and government. Such divine authority as could be acquired by the new kingdoms had to come, therefore, from the Church. It had been said that the Church lay within the Empire. And when that was said, the Empire was obviously more inclusive than the Church. But when the barbarian kingdoms took the place of the Empire, each kingdom obviously lay within a Church whose prestige and authority extended far beyond the frontiers of any State. This new situation changed, both in practice and in theory, the relationship of the spiritual and temporal Powers.

It follows also that under the new system at the end of the fifth century there was a much clearer distinction than ever before between force as an instrument of government and moral authority as the justification for the use of such force. The Churches in the different kingdoms might indeed submit to conquest and subjection under barbarian kings, as men acquiesce in the results of a flood or earthquake. But such acquiescence does not imply an admission of moral authority in a destructive force. Even successful revolutionaries have sooner or later to discover some other ground than their success for their claim to be obeyed. The barbarian kings of the fifth century, therefore, were compelled to look to the Christian Churches, and primarily therefore to the bishops, for the maintenance of their moral authority over their subjects. And this situation continued for centuries into the Middle Ages. The dependence of the newly-established kingdoms upon the older Roman tradition of moral authority, now represented by the bishops, is one of the most important sources of the medieval difficulty about the relations of State and Church. The Church became in one sense superior to the State, because its prestige was greater in western Europe, from the fifth to the ninth century, than the prestige of any single king, however powerful.

Again, in all the early barbarian kingdoms from the fifth until perhaps the seventh century, there were two quite distinct groups of subjects under the king. The barbarian warriors and their families, who were encamped as conquerors in the old Roman lands, had laws and customs of their own. Their rights and duties were decided in accordance with their tribal conditions. On the other hand, the conquered Roman population continued to be governed in accordance with Roman Law. Therefore law and custom in western Europe for many centuries after the fifth were "personal" and not local. That is to say, a person had rights and duties and was judged in disputed cases as a member of a particular race or as a member of a social community distinct from another community within the same State or even the same city. In a famous passage of a treatise by Agobard, bishop of Lyons, in the ninth century, it is said that five men might be together, each of whom would have to be judged according to a different legal system . . .

But besides the distinction between the barbarian conquerors and their Roman subjects, there was a distinction between the clergy of the Catholic Church and those who held political authority. From this point of view the great body of the Christian people was ruled by two distinct groups of men—the clergy, represented chiefly by bishops, and the warriors of the king's company. This is the origin in practice of the medieval contrast between the cleric (*clericus*) and the soldier (*miles*). The distinction is not one of sacred and secular within the lives of all men, but a distinction between two types of authority, both claiming to be divinely appointed. Of the two the clergy were the more democratic, in the modern sense of the word, both because of the Christian tradition of equality among all Christians and because of the survival of some form of popular election as the basis of the authority of priests and bishops. The clergy had indeed, by the beginning of the fifth century, become a caste; and the original meaning of the word "caste" itself (*castus*—pure) indicates the reason for their separation from other Christians. But bishops and priests remained in closer touch than kings and warriors with the majority of the inhabitants of the new kingdoms, partly because of a common language, Latin, and partly because they represented the tradition and customs of the old Roman civilization. The other authority, which in later times was called secular or temporal—the *miles* as contrasted with *clericus*—was alien, maintained by force of arms and suspicious of popular movements among its subjects. Here, then, is the origin of some aspects of the State in later times. When, for example, Ennodius called Theodoric "*status reipublicae*," he implied that "the State" was something external to the social system which the king controlled. The "State" was certainly not "the people." It was an external organization which cared for "the people" only as a good farmer cares for his cattle. The Germanic kings and their warriors were so ignorant and simple-minded, that they may have thought themselves superior to their subjects because they had a greater power to loot and to kill. But by all the standards of civilized life they were savages in control of a machine which they did not understand.

It follows from this contrast between the clergy and the political or military Authorities, combined perhaps with the conception of "personal" law, that the clergy could reasonably claim to be treated under a separate law of their own. In fact, synods and councils had for some centuries laid down canons which were rules, partly affecting all Christians, but mainly concerned with the organization and rights of the clergy. . . . For the purpose of the argument here it is necessary to note only that the canons of the different Churches were collected and enforced long before the barbarian kingdoms came into existence. Thus "Canon Law" in the new kingdoms had the prestige and authority of antiquity and of an older civilization, before the laws of the barbarian kingdoms were formulated. The rights of the clergy, which so disturbed kings in the Middle Ages, had their origin in this situation. The clergy of the Catholic Church, under barbarian kings who were at first all Arian heretics, claimed and were granted a distinct "personal" law, as the Roman population had a law which was distinct from that of the barbarians.

It is worth noting, finally, that in the new barbarian kingdoms, as contrasted with the later Roman Empire, the military forces upon which the rulers relied were not mercenaries. The barbarians had entered into the Roman Empire at first as instruments of imperial policy, paid for their services with loot or land. But now, in each barbarian kingdom, the barbarians fought and ruled for themselves under kings of their own choice. And the king, ruling in the midst of a subject population much more numerous than were his immediate barbarian followers, relied upon some form of personal loyalty to secure the support of his warriors. Some of these warriors were, in course of time, settled as holders of land within the barbarian kingdoms; but even before the new principle of service in payment for land-holding was established, a fundamental change had taken place in the organization of the military force under the control of a Government.

In the fifth and sixth centuries such thinking on social and political problems as remains, preserved in the documents of the time, was hampered by ideas and terminology drawn from the experience of the Roman Empire. The letters of bishops and kings in the sixth century, therefore, do not explicitly recognize the new situation. The actual relationship between kings and bishops, between political and ecclesiastical authority, had already begun to take the form which was familiar in the Middle Ages. But policy and the action of powerful personalities were far ahead of theory and doctrine. An experiment in social and political organization had begun in western Europe. An entirely new world was coming into existence. But those who thought at all on such matters still looked back and not forward for guidance.

It is clear from this description of the situation in western Europe at the beginning of the sixth century that two types of institution, the Church and the State, had developed in new forms since the disappearance of the Roman Empire in the West. The Churches in the West were not indeed yet united in one system so closely as they were in the Middle Ages; but already the tendency to unity was strong among them. And the tendency to division in law and administration was producing the many different

States and systems of government of medieval and modern times. Again, the Churches maintained education and public services in support of the poor, as well as a traditional jurisdiction—functions which had hitherto been performed by the Roman Empire. The "State," on the other hand, in each barbarian kingdom, was hardly more than an instrument of armed force and a means of maintaining barbarian customs and traditions in a more civilized world. . . .

If anything more were needed to show that Charles the Great did not establish an Empire, and was not in anything but name an Emperor, a brief review of the actual situation in which he left Europe would be conclusive. There was no capital or permanent centre of administration and law. The old barbarian custom continued of moving the king's officials and retinue from villa to villa. It made no difference in practice that a villa or country residence of a king might be called a "palace" (*palatium*). Indeed, this use of the word is merely another sign of make-believe by which the central offices of ancient Rome on the Palatine Hill gave their name to any of the scattered houses of a barbarian chieftain. Again there was no central administration. The king's agents (*missi dominici*) were quite unable to control the counts or other local landowners who had established themselves in almost independent power over different districts. Worse still, there was no permanent armed force, either for internal order or for defence against foreign enemies. Charles the Great followed the old practice of summoning for an expedition as many armed men as he could collect in the early summer, and of allowing them to return to their scattered homes in the autumn. He did, indeed, attempt to establish small permanent outposts on his north-eastern frontier, manned by counts and their armed retainers; but that there was no single defensive system is proved by the number of expeditions the king had to make, to help these outposts. Finally, in the system established or rather continued under Charles the Great, there was none of that "providence" (*providentia*) with which the Emperor was credited under the old Roman system. He made no roads. His system of government did not require them. He conceived a plan of a canal between the Main and Danube; but when the work was begun, it was abandoned because the sides fell in, owing to the lack of competent workers. He repaired the old Roman harbour at Boulogne, but seems never to have grasped the need for new harbours, as a protection against the raids of the Northmen. He did, indeed, give money and land for the building and maintenance of churches and monasteries—which may be taken to correspond to the building of temples and public baths by the Roman Emperors; but the administration of what would now be called "social services" was in the hands of the clergy and not of the king or his counts.

In short, Charles the Great, stripped of the romances which adorned "Charlemagne," was simply a barbarian warrior of great energy, limited intelligence, no education and great simplicity of mind. Like Clovis, three hundred years before him, he believed that he could promote Christianity in the form familiar to him by killing some of those who had never heard of it and compelling the others to be baptized. He was intelligent enough to appreciate the services of scholars and to support their efforts for the promotion of learning and music among the clergy. His ambitions and ideals were those of a barbarian chieftain; and his leisure was spent in hunting and swimming. He was frugal in food and drink and clothing, but somewhat expansive in his affections. The number of his concubines and illegitimate children is not known; and he enjoyed having about him all his daughters. But in an age in which savage cruelty and reckless treachery were not uncommon, even at the Court of the Roman Emperor, which claimed to be the centre of civilized life, Charles the Great was exceptional in attracting faithful supporters and in exciting admiration for the power of his personality.

He was a sincere Christian, in one of the many different meanings of that word. His correspondence shows that he was interested in the peculiar habits of the moon, in the status of the Holy Ghost, in the restriction of the use of religious pictures and in the correct method of administering Baptism. He was not interested in the more subtle moral issues which perhaps would have seemed important to Paulinus of Nola or to St. Boniface. He is said by Einhard to have listened with attention to the reading of St. Augustine's *City of God* and to have kept a writing tablet under his pillow at night, in order to practise writing the alphabet, which he never succeeded in doing. He spoke usually his own Germanic dialect but could speak Latin also fluently; and he understood Greek, although he could not speak it. He extended the dominions which Frankish warriors and churchmen controlled; but he left them so badly organized that soon after his death they were continually troubled by civil war and so badly defended that they were raided year after year by the Northmen and by the Saracens.

9. O. M. DALTON

FROM O. M. Dalton, *Gregory of Tours, The History of the Franks*, 2 vols. (Oxford: Clarendon Press, 1927), vol. I, 191–94, 237.

The principles on which a Frankish kingdom was governed after the time of Clovis differed profoundly from those followed by the old German tribes, as revealed in the *Germania* of Tacitus; the popular element was reduced to a shadow, the royal power grew in substance. Before the time of Clovis, we seem to recognize among the Franks an organization similar to that which long afterwards survived among their neighbours and obstinate enemies, the pagan Saxons. The Saxon system was based upon loose confederations of tribes or cantons, the tribes being led in peace by local chiefs, or petty kings, and only in war by a supreme ruler; on the outbreak of hostilities a commander of the whole confederacy was chosen to ensure national unity in the face of the common danger. Before the final victories of Clovis, the Franks are found under the leadership of petty kings, all of whom the conqueror proceeded to remove from his path in order to secure his position as permanent leader of the whole nation.

The Crown now ceased to be elective unless extraordinary circumstances interfered with regular succession. The old election of the king by the free Franks at the tribal assembly fell into desuetude after the time of Clovis in all cases where a king left a suitable male heir behind him; under normal conditions, royalty became hereditary. But the ancient principle of choice by an assembly was occasionally revived when there was no apparent heir, or when a succession was suddenly changed, as a result of war or even of usurpation. Thus Sigibert was invited to become king of Soissons after he had driven Chilperic out of that kingdom, whereupon he was raised on the shield, and carried round the assemblage at Vitry . . . In this case, the lawful king and his heir-male were both alive, and it was necessary to consecrate the election of a new king at Soissons by a ceremonial act. While, therefore, the government of the Church in the main followed old precedents in the appointment of new bishops, the element of choice had rarely a part in determining the succession to the throne. Hereditary kings found themselves absolute, but their absolutism was insecure, as all else in an unstable age. They were free from constitutional checks, but a landed aristocracy growing in power was first a latent, and soon an open menace. The notables had only to unite to enforce their will upon the Crown, but their dispersion through the country, their turbulence and their anarchic spirit gave the monarchy a respite which it was long suffered to misuse. Despotism was inevitable when the military leader of the Frankish people, after rapid victories, settled his followers in the promised land; equally certain was its danger when the strongest among them became territorial magnates surrounded by large numbers of personal dependents. There came a time when the royal power could only have been fully asserted by a standing army, which no Merovingian king possessed. But during the sixth century the sons and grandsons of Clovis were still absolute monarchs as long as they gave the great landholders the licence they desired. The sense of loyalty to the royal house was still a living force; only in Austrasia, where it was weakest, was the throne seriously threatened. To a man like Chilperic ruling in loyal Neustria, an almost unchecked despotism was possible, even in the other kingdoms the wearer of the crown held a position more uncontrolled than that of his remoter ancestors.

When the kings began to take alarm at the growing independence of their chief subjects, they naturally cast about for means to strengthen their own position. They gave ear to the counsel of astute Gallo-Romans, who suggested the adoption of Roman methods, by which Gallo-Roman and Frank might be placed on a more equal footing, especially with regard to taxation; this advice was first seriously considered by the Austrasian court, which was the most threatened by the rise of aristocratic power. The Crown to some extent secured itself by throwing open high offices to capable men of all classes, even the humblest. Such a policy was well advised; but by the middle of the sixth century the magnates were already powerful enough to neutralize any danger, even though they were not a hereditary nobility, had no permanent organization, and only combined when an emergency arose. Even Queen Brunhild, with all her superiority of intelligence, was beaten by them in the end—though she made a determined effort to gain supremacy.

But if the Crown did not succeed in depriving the aristocracy of their privileges, its own position in Gregory's time was still very strong. Although on serious questions the king would summon a council . . . yet he was far more free to please himself than the chiefs of the pagan Franks had ever been; by the great advantage of his religious orthodoxy he was not, like his Visigothic neighbours, estranged from his Romanized subjects and from the Church, whose rulers they obeyed. He had not to fear the sullen passive resistance which, until the time of Recared, so terribly weakened the position of the Crown in Spain . . . On the contrary, his Gallo-Roman subjects were a support to his ambition in so far as they were traditionally in favour of a strong centralized government, and opposed to the anarchic tendencies of the unruly Frankish magnates. The king was supreme head of the armies, when raised. He made war or peace, though he might ask the advice of a council of bishops and notables if he decided to summon one. He chose ministers and officers as he pleased, and enriched his treasury by taking bribes for an appointment. He held the Church under his control, convening episcopal councils and interfering with the elections to vacant sees . . . He was above justice, and had arbitrary power of life and death. He could change old laws and make new ones. His tribunal, over which he might preside in person if he so desired, was the final court of appeal. No individual, however strong, could prevail against him, for he was the greatest and wealthiest of landowners. He represented force, and by force he ruled. The one individual feared by him was the assassin. To himself he was something more than an ordinary mortal. When Lothar I, son of Clovis, lay on his deathbed he expressed peevish astonishment that his majesty must really perish: 'Well-a-day!' he cried, 'what think ye? What manner of ruler is that in heaven who in this wise causeth great kings such as we to die?'

In early Merovingian times there was nowhere any patriotism or love of country. The kings treated their kingdoms as private estates to be exploited to the full for their personal advantage. They were dangerously free, and if they could have established an absolutism according to Roman precedent Gaul might have been ruled by their line for a very long period. But their despotism was precarious. It only lasted as long as it did because the powers which were to destroy it were not yet able to unite. These powers were the Church and the aristocracy. Just over a century after the death of Clovis they joined forces and put an end to all royal dreams of permanent absolute rule . . . In after times the aristocracy grew strong enough to dispense with the aid of Church and stand alone. . . .

With a country devoid of general education and ruled by barbaric masters; with a faith prone to an excessive reliance upon miracles, which did little to help uprightness and the independent love of good; with examples in high places of cruelty, treachery, and indifference to bloodshed; with greed, roughness, and lack of finer feeling on all hands; with much oppression and little justice for the poor; with a civilization, in short, exposed to every influence adverse to right living, the conditions for true religion in sixth-century Gaul were as bad as they well might be. The Church strove to mitigate the ills of the time, but often by methods which aggravated the evil. And the Church herself encouraged the resort to miracle as the master remedy; she hindered by her very kindness the self-help which the cruelty of the state already made too hard. The Church fed the poor and set the prisoner free; hers was the one influence devoted to alleviation of distress. Yet she could but mend and patch a structure which needed building anew from the foundations. As the Franks grew more corrupt by contact with Gallo-Roman ways, the Gallo-Romans grew rougher and more lawless by the example of the Franks. There was a general degradation, a coarsening of life; the rulers of the kingdoms and the notables whom they failed to control often set the worst example; and the rulers of the Church, by association with the government in the interests of public order, had largely surrendered their power of free action. To illustrate the morality of the time, we may derive from Gregory's own works sufficient instances drawn from all classes of society to show how far violence and corruption had spread through the whole community.

At the time of Gregory's activity as bishop of Tours, Christianity had been implanted in Gaul for four hundred years. ✸

Part 7

THE NATURE OF FEUDALISM

Perhaps the best way to understand feudalism is in terms of an organic analogy—the cycle of birth, maturity, and death. The following selections are organized around this concept, starting with a consideration of the origins of feudalism, then feudalism at its height, and finally the decline of feudalism as it gave way to other forms of political and military organization. Because each segment of the cycle is closely related to and helps illuminate the others, the whole must always be kept in mind.

There is constant interplay between the three stages. Take, for example, the decline of feudalism. The passing of any institution immediately suggests at least two things. First, that the institution contains endemic weaknesses and lacks the capacity for growth and innovation. In other words, the decline can be understood in terms of the internal structure of the institution. Were such weaknesses present in feudalism? The second possibility is that the society is in a state of flux. Even the most vigorous and resilient institutions collapse in the face of transformations in the social structure. Is this what happened in the later Middle Ages? If so, how was the institution of feudalism affected and what do the changes in feudalism tell us about its roots, strengths, and essential character? Here, the study of one aspect of feudalism leads to other problems, widening our field of vision and leading us to see the whole question in a new light.

The nature of feudalism will unfold in the following selections, but one aspect of it should be mentioned at the outset. The term "feudalism" has often been used as an epithet to condemn the total structure of a society. Vituperation may be good for the soul, but it rarely aids understanding. What is really objectionable here, however, is the equation of feudalism with the totality of medieval life. To describe or analyze a phenomenon is in one sense to place it in perspective, to distinguish it from its surroundings and thus point to its uniqueness. Even such highly sophisticated social analysts as Marx and de Tocqueville fail to do this in discussing feudalism. For Marx, feudalism is an economic system of exploitation determining the total makeup of medieval society; a close reading of de Tocqueville's famous chapter in *The Old Regime,* "Why feudalism had come to be more detested in France than in any other country," will reveal that he conceives of it as an economic institution. To be sure, feudalism had significant economic implications and it did play a strategic role in linking the segments of society. But it was not an economic institution and it must be clearly distinguished from manorialism.

The term manorialism refers to the economic substructure on which feudalism later came to rest. It was an economic system; feudalism was a political and military system. Among students of manorialism there is substantial agreement on the following points: 1) manorialism seems to have taken root in the third century and remained vigorous until the twelfth; 2) the dramatic reintroduction of a money economy marked the beginning of the end of manorialism—but the rate of decline was by no means uniform throughout western Europe; 3) in the manorial system a landed aristocracy controlled most of the land and exercised economic, legal, and political authority commensurate with this ownership. The masses were unfree serfs bound to the land and their lord's will. Manorialism preceded feudalism, and it relied on an unfree peasantry. The participants in the feudal arrangement, on the other hand, were free men connected by mutual obligations and ties of honor.

Historians have long debated the origins of feudalism. In the welter of conflicting interpretations, it is possible to distinguish four distinct approaches to the problem. The argument for the first one runs somewhat as follows: The origins of feudalism must be sought in the late Roman Empire, more specifically in the Roman clientage system. This was a system in which a powerful individual attracted a group of clients who could furnish military, political, or economic services. In turn, the clients received land and protection (an especially compelling need in a period which saw the breakdown of law and order). Though this view may still have some supporters, it is not represented here because, as Bryce D. Lyon notes, those supporters "have not been able to prove that the relations and services were honorable like those of medieval feudalism."

The second approach is represented in a selection by Rushton Coulburn. He emphasizes the Germanic origins of feudalism, primarily because the element of honor is so unmistakably a part of the bond uniting the German military leaders and their warriors. The third view, exemplified by the American scholar Carl Stephenson, is essentially a slightly modified version of the second. Stephenson argues that the nature of feudal vassalage derives from the German comitatus but that the fief, the granting of land, is directly attributable to the eighth-century Carolingians. The distinguished Belgian historian François L. Ganshof is a prime exemplar of the fourth approach, the "eclectic" one, which regards feudalism as a compound of German and Roman ingredients that developed gradually in the late Roman Empire.

Among the many historians who have so enriched our understanding of the medieval world in this century, Marc Bloch occupies a special place. A pioneer in the application of the social sciences (particularly sociology and anthropology) to the study of history, a profoundly learned man whose contributions range from the minute study of a legal conflict involving the serfs in the village of Rosny-sous-Bois in the twelfth century to a synthesis of medieval history, a great teacher who trained and inspired a whole generation of scholars—Marc Bloch was all these things and more. In the dark days of World War II, Bloch was moved to reflect on the historian's craft "as a simple antidote by which, amid sorrows and anxieties both personal and collective, I seek a little peace of mind." He was unable to complete his work on the writing of history, but everything he had done before made it certain that his fellow historians would always regard him as one of the very best practitioners of their craft.

Bloch's delineation of mature feudalism is best appreciated if it is related to the previous historiography on the subject. In the early twentieth century, the dominant emphasis in medieval studies was on legal and constitutional history. More often than not, studies of feudalism were developed within extremely precise and legalistic boundaries. Bloch's view of feudalism marked a significant departure from this narrow approach, and the intrinsic fascination of the subject was given free play.

Bloch's characterization of feudalism was designed to embrace and shed light on the totality of medieval life. This aim was informed by an assumption he states clearly in the first sentence of the selection reprinted here: "The framework of institutions which governs a society can in the last resort be understood only through a knowledge of the whole human environment." This guiding concept led him directly to his formulation of the essential nature of feudalism.

> A subject peasantry; widespread use of the service tenement (i.e. the fief) instead of a salary, which was out of the question; the supremacy of a class of specialized warriors; ties of obedience and protection which bind man to man and, within the warrior class, assume the distinctive form called vassalage; fragmentation of authority—leading inevitably to disorder; and, in the midst of all

this, the survival of other forms of association, family and state, of which the latter, during the second feudal age, was to acquire renewed strength—such then seem to be the fundamental features of European feudalism.

This tendency away from the narrow legalism of the previous historiography, so evident in the sweep and suggestiveness of Bloch's conception of feudalism, is also apparent in the work of the Princeton University medievalist Joseph Strayer. Strayer is quite explicit about the ways in which "narrow definitions" can be imaginatively stretched and lead to a host of new problems and themes. The concept of "feudal society" is legitimate because of the wide-ranging and profound ramifications of the feudal system. For example, those in power, the feudal lords, "will naturally mold their society to fit their own needs. They will manipulate the economy so that they get the greatest share of production; they will develop a class structure which gives them the highest position; they will, as wealthy consumers, influence writers and artists; they will establish standards to which their society must conform." It is clear that the French historians Georges Duby and Robert Mandrou have accepted this broader concept of the function of feudalism in medieval society.

This new treatment of feudalism has made possible another revision in medieval studies. Professor Bryce D. Lyon of Brown University, a leading student of the later stages of feudalism, has described the conventional view thus: "Traditionally historians have equated the end of the Middle Ages and the beginning of the modern world with the death of feudalism in the fifteenth century. We have been told that the strong rulers of the early sixteenth century put feudal particularism and the feudal aristocracy to rout and then proceeded to construct the national state." Lyon and other modern historians have raised some serious objections to this traditional argument. There was, in fact, little left of feudalism in the fifteenth and sixteenth centuries. And it took on a variety of new forms, such as the *fief-rente* delineated by Lyon. Finally, and perhaps most important of all, everything we now know about the limitations of the emerging nation-states and the social policies pursued by their rulers suggests that the landed aristocracy, the class associated with feudalism, retained much of the power and influence well into the eighteenth century. All the more reason for us to try to understand the nature of feudalism.

1. RUSHTON COULBURN

FROM Rushton Coulburn, *Feudalism in History* (Princeton, N.J.: Princeton University Press, 1956), pp. 189–94.

The idea that feudalism originated with barbarians is as old as the concept of feudalism itself. True, it has been hotly disputed in its application to Western Europe—often from other than scientific motives—but leading opinion now is that the idea is sound. The particular opinion advocated here is that, while other characteristic events and conditions are necessary to the origin of feudalism, the barbarian is the key man. There will therefore be a description of the barbarian before the other events and conditions are outlined.

The Greek word *barbaros* meant alien, non-Greek. It did not matter whether the people in question were highly civilized Persians or Egyptians, or wild fellows from the tribal societies of central Europe and Russia. The word was most often applied to those the Greeks encountered most often, the peoples on their frontiers, who inevitably became affected in some degree by the attractive culture of Greece. The typical barbarian came more and more to be a frontiersman. In the time of the Roman Empire the frontier had become a very important political fact, and the frontier barbarian had become eligible to serve the empire as a fighting man. In fact, he had become one of the empire's best soldiers, and as such was admitted to the civilized world. It was this barbarian who contributed at a later time to the origin and growth of Western European feudalism, and what he contributed he first learned in the frontier world, the world of the heroic age, which was part Roman, part barbarian. That world had its own quite special characteristics:

> "Now it deserves to be remarked [says Chadwick] that these characteristics are in no sense primitive. In social organisation the distinguishing feature of the Heroic Age is in the nature of a revolt or emancipation from those tribal obligations and ideas by which the society of primitive peoples is everywhere governed. The same remark applies in principle to political organisation; the princes of the Heroic Age appear to have freed themselves to a large extent from any public control on the part of the tribe or community. . . . The force formerly exercised by the kindred is

now largely transferred to the comitatus, a body of chosen adherents pledged to personal loyalty to their chief. So also in government the council of the tribe or community has come to be nothing more than a comitatus or court. The result of the change is that the man who possesses a comitatus becomes largely free from the control of his kindred, while the chief similarly becomes free from control within his community."

It was the attachment of leader and follower in the comitatus, or war-band, which came to serve as the central ethic of feudal society in Western Europe. The attachment was extremely strong, close, and personal. If it was not primitive, it certainly reproduced the simplicity, fervor, and durability of primitive relationships. Loyalty, courage, and personal honor were thus brought to a jaded imperial world, to be worked in time into a new system of cohesion. We shall find that essentially the same ethic came to prevail in other feudal societies, but that in some the sharp institutional break between tribe and war-band, found by Chadwick for Western Europe, did not occur. A society moving in a feudal direction is one in which the personal relations of loyalty between leader and follower, or lord and vassal, come to serve as a political system and to take the place of the political system operating through officials serving the state. When (and if) the old state has become nothing but a vestige and its personnel converted into feudal magnates, the feudal polity may be said to have arrived. Just how small a vestige the old state must be, no authority has sought to define closely.

But many things must have happened in the rise of feudalism before the old state is superseded. The old state must first weaken, and go on weakening for a long time. At an early stage in its weakening great magnates arise—landlords, generals, officials, sometimes chieftains of tribes or clans—who take over some of the state's powers upon a local basis. The great magnates must acquire the character of leaders of barbarian war-bands; the enduring lord and vassal relation must become established between them and their followers. Tribal chieftains acquire that character fairly easily, since it is at first for them only the substitution of one set of personal relationships for another. Hence, where the society consists at all largely of tribes, the passage from tribal relations to war-band relations to feudal relations is likely to be continuous and uninterrupted, except by the vicissitudes of internecine warfare and of the break-up of the old state. Where the majority of magnates are officials of the old bureaucratic state or great noblemen or military officers of such a state, the barbarians in their war-bands come in as invaders from outside the society, having already made the break with their tribal organizations which Chadwick describes, and there follows a merging of the barbarian and the civilized types of magnate. In those societies which thereafter proceed to feudal conditions the barbarian type comes to predominate.

There may come a time in a society whose leadership is changing in this manner when political reformers seek to restore the disintegrating state by calling to its aid the personal vassalage relations which have come to permeate its upper ranks, thus tightening up or replacing the loosened relations within the official hierarchy. Wherever a movement of this sort occurs, it is a well-marked innovation. It occurs in every case of feudalization studied here, and I call it the "proto-feudal" stage of those movements. It would be incorrect, I think, to suppose that a society which reaches the proto-feudal stage must necessarily continue into a fully feudal stage, but a likelihood that it will do so must be admitted.

After the proto-feudal stage there follows the early feudal stage, dramatically described for Western Europe by Mr. Strayer. The transition between the two stages is probably the most disorderly and violent period in the whole development of feudalism. The disorders and violence continue into the early feudal stage for perhaps a century or two, but in a spasmodically diminishing extent. It would be an exaggeration, however, to describe conditions in that stage, or even at the transition before it, as anarchic. In the Introductory Essay the doctrine that anarchy is a normal feature of feudalism was called in question. Here the doctrine is rejected and we begin now to show in what way, to what extent, and when fighting and the lack of functioning political institutions really are a part of the feudal system. I rather suspect that real anarchy could inhibit, perhaps prevent, the formation of a feudal system.

The arrival of the early stage of feudalism is announced by the emergence of the elemental, small, strong fief, that immensely tough little political unit headed by a feudal lord with his band of personal retainers, and populated by the lord, his retainers, his other vassals scattered over the fief, some rear-vassals probably, and all the simple people tending to become praedial and menial dependents. The elemental, strong fief is the characteristic product of the disorders attendant upon the collapse of the proto-feudal regime and the beginning of the true feudal regime. The disorders are the price paid for the elemental, strong fief; it is indeed probably correct to say that they are the necessary milieu in which the fief arises. Perhaps that is the chief reason for the notion that feudalism is essentially violent and anarchic. Yet, apart from the fact that in most of its later stages feudalism is far more orderly, the elemental, strong fief is an area of peace internally, a small state which is the very opposite of anarchic, for it is characteristically well-governed, often even governed with the active consent and cooperation of its members.

The elemental, strong fief results from survival of the fittest; it is a true exemplar, I believe, of the Darwinian doctrine, which is a rare thing in the evolution of society. Historians do not appear to have noticed hitherto that the elemental, strong fief also exemplifies another famous doctrine: it is an "in-group" arrayed against all "out-groups" after the manner conceived by Sumner. Feudal society in its early stage, in fact, seems to approximate quite closely to primitive society, as Sumner describes it. Here are some of Sumner's remarks:

"The conception of 'primitive society' which we ought to form is that of small groups scattered over a territory. . . . A group of groups may have some relation to each other (kin, neighborhood, alliance, connubium and commercium) which draws them together and differentiates them from others. Thus a differentiation arises between ourselves, the we-group, or in-group, and everybody else, or the others-groups, out-groups. The insiders in a we-group are in a relation of peace, order, law, government, and industry, to each other. Their relation to all outsiders, or others-groups, is one of war and plunder, except so far as agreements have modified it. . . .

"The relation of comradeship and peace in the we-group and that of hostility and war towards others-groups are correlative to each other. The exigencies of war with outsiders are what make peace inside, lest internal discord should weaken the we-group for war. These exigencies also make government and law in the in-group, in order to prevent quarrels and enforce discipline. Thus war and peace have reacted on each other and developed each other, one within the group, the other in the inter-group relation. The closer the neighbors, and the stronger they are, the intenser is the warfare, and then the intenser is the internal organization and discipline of each. Sentiments are produced to correspond. Loyalty to the group, sacrifice for it, hatred and contempt for outsiders, brotherhood within, warlikeness without,—all grow together, common products of the same situation. These relations and sentiments constitute a social philosophy."

This is a strikingly accurate description also of a feudal society, especially in an early stage of its development, with the fiefs all struggling against one another and being hammered in the course of the struggle into tougher and tougher little associations. Is a feudal society a primitive society, then? The question seems easy to answer in the affirmative until we recollect Chadwick's opinion. The primitive society is broken up in the heroic age. If the barbarians, leaders in that age and key men in the rise of feudalism, are not primitives, how comes it that the feudal society they form seems so nearly primitive? We can answer this question, and find a useful guide to the place of feudalism in the rise of civilized societies if we call in anthropological and sociological authority.

Redfield and Tönnies offer the two most serviceable analytical distinctions for these purposes, and Durkheim has an important principle which may be applied. Redfield shifts the distinction between the two kinds of society away from the categories civilized and primitive, and contrasts instead the "folk society" and the "urban society." The new distinction first facilitates abstraction, offering a theoretical picture of a society composed purely of folk features. But then Redfield returns to fact, pointing out that actual societies are combinations of folk and urban features, and that there are many possible combinations. A feudal society, then, is perhaps one of the combinations of folk and urban, or primitive and civilized features—I prefer the latter terms for reasons which will shortly appear.

This sounds elementary, and it is so, but it leads to particulars of the feudal combination—if it is a combination—and for the historian it raises the question how the proposed combination came into existence, something which is not elementary. Tönnies' distinction between *Gemeinschaft* and *Gesellschaft* throws some light on the matter. A fief at its formation is unquestionably a *Gesellschaft*, an association consciously formed by men for a certain purpose, to wit, mutual defense. Such things are not unknown in primitive societies, but they are certainly rare there; they are usually, always perhaps, *ad hoc* arrangements made between different primitive societies for purposes they have in common. They may produce a rudimentary superstructure based upon a number of primitive societies. Certainly the *Gesellschaft* type of association is not the basis of a primitive society as it is of the feudal society. Redfield, again, says that relations in a folk society are not contractual; they are tacit and traditional. But relations in a feudal society are, precisely, contractual. A feudal society, therefore, is not a primitive society.

And yet a feudal society undeniably shares many characters with a primitive society. Not only are both of them constructed of alternate in-group out-group relations, but their entire mentalities are similar. Redfield, yet again, suggests that the men of the folk society, like medieval men, think in terms of association of symbols, not in terms of cause and effect. Behavior in a feudal society is largely spontaneous and uncritical. It is strongly patterned. What Bagehot called the "cake of custom" settles easily and strongly over a feudal society. A feudal society's power to meet crises effectively is dependent more upon common understanding of what is important than it is upon discipline exerted by force. The original *Gesellschaft* tends to turn into a *Gemeinschaft*, an association men enter by birth or by circumstance, accepting its purposes unthinkingly, as of the nature of things. A feudal society is the product of no theory; it happens. So does a primitive society, but the feudal society happens by human agency in a sense that the primitive society does not.

Durkheim has shown how the division of labor, as a principle in operation at various junctures in the development of a society, enters into the changes through which a society may pass. In the feudal society there is one very conspicuous division of labor which is almost completely missing in a primitive society. It is the division between fighting man and farming man, or between political man and economic man, in Western Europe between noble and simple. If we look for the sources of this division, it will lead us to the historic process whereby a feudal society gets its special compromise between primitive and civilized characters. In the particular societies Chadwick thought about there is little to help, for there the primitive is, seemingly at any rate, suddenly cut off. The fighter is the barbarian, and the farmer must be the civilized peasant the fighter brings under his authority. But we get to know more about the peasant and about the barbarian fighter too if we study them in the places where the transition from primitive conditions was not sudden. Such places are Japan, Central and Northern Europe which had not been in the Roman Empire and to which feudalism was brought slowly after it had germinated in France, probably large parts or even all of Chou China, and other places—if we knew enough about China and the other places to be sure. ✷

2. CARL STEPHENSON

FROM Carl Stephenson, *Mediaeval Institutions* (Ithaca, N.Y.: Cornell University Press, 1954), pp. 216–18, 224–30.

Turning . . . to the native land of feudalism, we have no trouble in finding the central institution from which our word is derived. It was the *feudum* or fief. Yet this is not the primary element to be examined. Feudalism, as acutely remarked by [Ferdinand] Lot, presupposes vassalage; for a fief could not exist apart from a vassal to hold it. "On est convenu de parler de 'féodalité' et non de 'vassalité' à partir du moment où il n'y a plus en fait, sauf de rares exceptions, de vassal sans fief." The status of vassal, we know from countless documents of the eleventh and twelfth centuries, could always be acquired, with or without the prospect of a fief, merely by performing homage and swearing fealty. And solely in this way could one become a vassal. Although fiefs might be declared hereditary, vassalage was never inherited. When a vassal died, his fief legally reverted to the lord, in whose hands it remained until such time as the heir performed homage and so qualified himself to receive investiture. Only a vassal could properly be a fief holder, and there can be no doubt that, in the feudal age proper, vassalage was restricted to mature men. The reason is clear: a vassal was supposed to be a warrior. Clergymen, it is true, often held fiefs while debarred from bloodshed by canon law. But the qualifications that came to be put on their homage and fealty were plainly the result of compromise. At one time ecclesiastical vassals had fought like the rest; it was the Hildebrandine papacy that finally compelled the making of exceptions in their favor. Feudal tenure, whatever its minor adaptations, was essentially military because the original vassalage was a military relationship.

Here, if I am not mistaken, is the key to the whole development of feudalism—the justification for the emphasis long placed on the problem of its origin. No amount of legalistic reasoning can obscure the fact that the feudal aristocracy of the eleventh century differed radically from the Roman aristocracy of the fourth in being thoroughly warlike. And this character, beyond all question, was a barbarian inheritance. Is it mere coincidence that the vassalage glorified in the *chansons de geste* is so close in spirit to the primitive *comitatus*? To derive vassalage from the Gallo-Roman *patrocinium*, one must somewhere, in the course of a devious argument, introduce a revolutionizing factor. . . .

The conclusion that Carolingian vassalage from first to last was essentially honorable finds support, I believe, in all the pertinent sources. Indirectly the capitularies tell us a good deal about the mutual obligations of lords and vassals. The vassal was bound by oath to maintain unswerving loyalty to his lord; to refuse to follow one's lord on a lawful expedition was to break one's plighted faith. In return the lord owed his vassal protection and respect; if he failed in such duty, the vassal was justified in renouncing him. This relationship was established by the ceremony of homage, the earliest clear reference to which is found in the familiar story of Tassilo, duke of Bavaria. Whether written in 757 or some thirty years later, the account in the royal annals is good evidence that "commendation in vassalage" was a well-known Frankish custom by the second half of the eighth century and one in which contemporaries saw no ignominy. For here, as in the long series of like episodes that followed, the ruler employed vassalage for the purpose not of disgracing a rival but of securing his fidelity. The policy was quite similar to that adopted with a view to controlling officials of church or state and even members of the royal family.

On the whole, I find it incredible that the vassalage which suddenly appears in the records of the eighth century was in any respect a new development. Nor can I believe that the resemblance between this traditional vassalage and the Germanic *comitatus* was a matter of sheer coincidence.

Yet, if the connection between the two is not provided by the *antrustiones*, where is it to be found? By reviving an older view with regard to the Merovingian *leudes* (or *leodes*), Alfons Dopsch has suggested a possible answer. Here, briefly, is the evidence. Gregory of Tours, who almost never uses a Germanic word, mentions *leudes* (i.e., *leute*) three times—clearly implying that such "people" of a king were his, not in the general sense of political subjects but in the special sense of military followers. Men of this kind seem also to be thought of in the peace of Guntram and Childebert II (587), who agree not to entice or to receive each other's *leudes*. And the vaguer references in other sources at least indicate that the persons styled *leudes* belonged to the warrior class, were likely to be politically and socially prominent, and often received grants of land from the royal fisc. Accordingly, the Merovingian oath of *fidelitas et leudesamio* may well be understood as having anticipated the oath demanded by Charlemagne of every free subject, that he would be faithful to the emperor "as a man rightly should be to his lord."

We now realize that the Merovingian state, far from being the noble Germanic structure imagined by Roth, was a pseudo-Roman sham that utterly collapsed under the degenerate successors of Clovis. With it disappeared many vestiges of the old imperial government, including apparently the Frankish imitation of the Roman *scholares*. Much more vigorous than any such vestiges was the native custom of the barbarian conquerors, especially that governing the life of the warlike aristocracy. Within this sphere the persistence of what we call vassalage must be considered a strong probability. Guilhiermoz, I think, has rightly insisted that the chivalrous *adoubement* of the Middle Ages, despite the utter silence of the Merovingian records, must be traced back to the formal arming of the German youth as described by Tacitus. He even suggests that the substitution of homage for the Roman exchange of documents in commendation was a consequence "of the recrudescence of Germanism that accompanied the rise to power of the Austrasian family of the Arnulfings." Why may we not attribute the whole Carolingian development of vassalage to this same factor, rather than to juristic necessity or to an imaginary Anglo-Saxon influence? At any rate, the little information to be gained from the wretched sources of the early Frankish age points to the military retainers styled *leudes*, in preference to the palace guards styled *antrustiones*, as the precursors of the Carolingian *vassi*.

If the foregoing argument is well grounded, there is no reason for supposing any great change in the institution of vassalage under the Carolingians except that now produced by close association with fief holding. Whether the military benefice was or was not an eighth-century invention is a matter of secondary importance. Our chief interest is rather the wide extension of feudal tenure that came in the ensuing period. To account for this extension we must, in my opinion, consider the following points. The basis of the new system, assuredly, was military need. The king gave fiefs to his vassals and encouraged subinfeudation on the part of the latter for the primary purpose of securing a better army; and, no matter what may be made of the Saracen danger, there was an increasing demand for mounted troops. The rapid introduction of heavy-armed cavalry, as Guilhiermoz has admirably shown, was of profound social significance. As the *miles* became exclusively a *caballarius*, the gulf between his status and that of the peasant grew wider. The profession of arms came to be governed by an aristocratic code of chivalry—a set of rules that had meaning only for the highborn. Thus in the later Middle Ages knight and noble were virtually synonymous terms. Land held for agrarian rent or service, whatever the nature of the original contract, was no fief; the tenant, however free in law, was no vassal.

The vassal's obligation, being military, was *ipso facto* political; so, according to Carolingian standards, it was proper for him to receive political privilege in return. The truth should never be overlooked that a fief brought to the holder not merely the rights of a landlord but also those of an immunist. Leading authorities are today agreed that the personal relationship of lord to vassal carried with it no power of jurisdiction. What we know as feudal justice could not be separated from the territorial immunity which every fief was construed to imply. And insofar as the feudal lord had the right to hold courts, to levy tolls and other imposts, to requisition labor and materials, to raise fortifications, and to muster the population for local defense, he was obviously a public official. It is, indeed, no mere form of words to assert that every fief was an office; for the rule of primogeniture evidently came to be incorporated in feudal law through recognition of this principle. Another phase of the same development may be seen in the fact that by the end of the ninth century the more important agents of the state had been brought within the category of royal vassals. The transition was an informal one, of which the capitularies tell us little, but that the result was quite in accord with Carolingian policy seems clear. If every feudal tenant was to some degree a count within his own territory, when a count became a vassal, would not the county be his fief?

The conclusion thus seems inevitable that to talk of "political feudalism," as distinguished from "economic feudalism," is misleading. All feudalism was political; and if we wish to refer to the agrarian economy presupposed by feudal tenure, we have the accurate and familiar expression, "manorial system." The original feudalism, as I understand the term, was a phase of government developed by the Frankish kings on the basis of a pre-existing barbarian custom of vassalage. It was not, therefore, an inevitable stage in economic evolution. Although it involved a system of rewarding soldiers with grants of land, it was by no means that alone. Nor was it the mere equivalent of provincial autonomy under a failing empire. To appraise its historical significance is, to say the least, not easy; for, as feudal custom was inherited and further developed by the states of later Europe, it became increasingly complex and variable. ✣

3. FRANÇOIS L. GANSHOF

FROM François L. Ganshof, *Feudalism*, trans. Philip Grierson (London: Longmans, Green & Co., Ltd., 1952), pp. xv–xvii, 3–4, 15, 52–56, 59–62.

The word 'feudalism' (Germ. *Lehnswesen* or *Feudalismus;* Fr. *féodalité*) is one to which many different meanings have been attached. During the French Revolution, it was virtually adopted as a generic description covering the many abuses of the *Ancien Régime*, and it is still in popular use in this sense today. Even if this quite illegitimate extension of its meaning be ignored, there exist many attempts at its analysis and definition which do not seem to be very closely related to one another. But if we limit ourselves to essentials and are prepared to overlook the subtle nuances of meaning which scholars, and particularly legal scholars, delight in, it will be found that the word is used by historians in two more or less distinct senses.

Feudalism may be conceived of as a form of society possessing well-marked features which can be defined without difficulty. They may be summarized as follows: a development pushed to extremes of the element of personal dependence in society, with a specialized military class occupying the higher levels in the social scale; an extreme subdivision of the rights of real property; a graded system of rights over land created by this subdivision and corresponding in broad outline to the grades of personal dependence just referred to; and a dispersal of political authority amongst a hierarchy of persons who exercise in their own interest powers normally attributed to the State and which are often, in fact, derived from its break-up.

This type of society, whether one calls it 'feudalism' or the 'feudal régime', was that of western Europe in the tenth, eleventh and twelfth centuries. It came into existence in France, Germany, the kingdom of

Burgundy-Arles and Italy, all of them states deriving from the Carolingian empire, and in other countries—England, certain of the Christian kingdoms of Spain, the Latin principalities of the Near East—which passed under their influence. In other places and at other times, types of society have existed which show many analogies with the feudalism which one finds in France, Germany, the kingdom of Burgundy-Arles and Italy during the Middle Ages, so that scholars have been led to speak of 'feudalism' in ancient Egypt, in India, in the Arab world, in the Turkish empire, in Russia, in Japan, and elsewhere. In making these comparisons, historians have sometimes drawn parallels which a closer examination of the sources has failed to justify, though in some instances, as in that of Japan, the parallelism is very close.

Professor Calmette and the late Marc Bloch, in writing on feudalism in this sense, preferred to speak of 'feudal society'. Such a practice, if it were generally accepted, would have the advantage of allowing one to use the word 'feudalism' only in the second sense that can be attached to it.

In this second sense of the word, 'feudalism' may be regarded as a body of institutions creating and regulating the obligations of obedience and service—mainly military service—on the part of a free man (the vassal) towards another free man (the lord), and the obligations of protection and maintenance on the part of the lord with regard to his vassal. The obligation of maintenance had usually as one of its effects the grant by the lord to his vassal of a unit of real property known as a fief. This sense of the word feudalism is obviously more restricted and more technical than the other. We can perhaps regard it as the legal sense of the word, while the first use covers mainly the social and political senses.

These two meanings of the word feudalism are not unrelated to each other, since the society which we have described above is known as feudal because in it the fief, if not the corner-stone, was at least the most important element in the graded system of rights over land which this type of society involved.

Feudalism in its narrow sense, meaning the system of feudal and vassal institutions, was also, and to an even greater degree than feudalism in its broad sense, proper to the states born of the break-up of the Carolingian empire and the countries influenced by them. Once again, however, we find in other historical environments certain institutions which bear a remarkable resemblance to those of the feudalism of the western middle ages. The 'daimios' and the 'bushi' or 'samurai' of Japan can be compared to vassals, and land which was granted to them is comparable to the fief. The same is true of the Arab and Turkish 'iqta'. Russia, between the thirteenth and sixteenth centuries, knew institutions very close to that of vassalage, and the 'conditional ownership' which is met with at the same period and which in the fifteenth century came to be known as 'pomestie' has many analogies with the fief. . . .

The origins of medieval feudalism must be looked for in the kingdom of the Merovingian Franks, and more particularly in the heart of the kingdom between the Loire and the Rhine.

Under the Merovingians, Gaul was rarely united or at peace, and it frequently lapsed into a state of almost complete anarchy. The main cause of this, a cause which was renewed every few years, lay in the family feuds occasioned by the custom which required that on the death of a king his inheritance should be divided between his sons. Later, after repeated partitions had given birth to the kingdoms of Austrasia, Neustria and Burgundy, there was added to this the bitter rivalries between the regional aristocracies. The quarrels between the sons and grandsons of Clovis in the sixth century resembled nothing so much as the fighting of wild beasts, and in the succeeding period the conflicts between the kings and the magnates increased steadily in violence and ferocity as the seventh century drew to its close. Even apart from the political struggle for power, the state was quite unable to maintain the public peace or secure the safety of its inhabitants. Its structure was too primitive, the officials in its service too few in number and too unreliable, for it to carry out successfully this elementary function of government.

Such a society formed an ideal medium for the growth of bodies of retainers, and particularly of bodies of armed retainers. Those who felt the need of protection would look for it to their more powerful neighbours, and such protection would involve in return the acceptance of some form of service. The magnates on their side, whether from a desire to play a conspicuous part in political affairs or from the hope of profiting by the political disorder and of establishing or increasing their own power and wealth, needed the services of men who were personally attached to them and whom they could use in private warfare. In extreme cases, free men might be prepared to become the slaves of powerful protectors, or the latter might create their own soldiery by arming their slaves. Neither of these proceedings, however, could be regarded as typical. A more general custom was that by which a free man placed himself under the protection and at the service of another free man, while maintaining his own free status. Contemporaries called such persons *ingenui in obsequio*, free men in dependence.

The phenomenon itself was not new; the novelty lay in its wider diffusion. Like other parts of the *Orbis Romanus*, Gaul under the later empire was accustomed to the existence of private bands of soldiers, often called *buccellarii*, who formed the bodyguards of prominent men. The practice survived the barbarian invasions, at least south of the Loire, as we learn from the laws of the Visigothic king Euric towards the end of the fifth century. The Franks on their side had the institution known as the *comitatus*, the *Gefolgschaft* of German historians, which is already described in a celebrated passage of Tacitus at the end of the first century. The *comitatus* consisted of a group of free warriors who had taken service of their own free will under a chieftain, and fought with him and on his behalf as a band of close comrades. The bodies of armed retainers whom we meet with during the Merovingian period had thus a double origin, and it is not possible to say whether they owed more to their Roman or to their Germanic predecessors. . . .

. . . vassalage, an institution involving relationships of subordination and service on the part of one person with regard to another, and the benefice, a form of tenement held for life on very easy terms by the tenant, existed together in Merovingian society. A lord could indeed grant a benefice to his vassal in order to provide the latter with the maintenance due to him in return for service, but such a union of the two institutions was quite exceptional. There is nothing to suggest that it was as yet a normal or widespread practice, and there is certainly no evidence of the 'government'—kings or mayors of the palace—granting such benefices to its vassals or *antrustiones*.

During the Carolingian period a change gradually came about. The two institutions of vassalage and benefice, which up to this time had been quite independent of each other, now began to combine so as to constitute a new system of institutions. It is this that justifies us in using such an expression as 'Carolingian feudalism'. The union of benefice and vassalage, however, and the interaction of these two institutions upon each other, are things which only develop by degrees. We must therefore distinguish, in what follows, two distinct periods: that of the first Carolingians, and that of Charlemagne and his successors. . . .

The policy followed by the Carolingians failed to produce the fruits they expected from it. The great extension of vassalage, its incorporation in the framework of the institutions of government, the distribution of benefices on a large scale, all ended by diminishing the authority of the king instead of increasing it.

Even before the end of the reign of Charlemagne, it had become apparent that the bonds which united a vassal to his lord, bonds which were direct and immediately appreciable by the senses, were stronger by far than those which bound the subject to the king. When there was a conflict between the two types of allegiance, the vassal would nearly always hold to that deriving from the fealty which he owed to the lord whose 'man' he was. Already in 810/11, in a capitulary relating to military service, it is stated that some of the emperor's subjects had failed to appear with the army, on the ground that their lord had not been summoned and that their duty forbade them to leave him. When the reign of the feeble Louis the Pious began the period of partitions and revolts, matters went much further. Either through sincere attachment to their duties as vassals, or because they found in them a convenient pretext, the vassals of the rebel chiefs gave in their thousands their support to their lords against their king. The consideration that service was not owed to a lord who was in arms against the king was too feeble a barrier to resist their passion or their greed.

In the case of those who may be termed higher vassals, direct agents of royal power like the counts, margraves and dukes, the appetite for benefices promised or granted by the heads of the warring parties was so great that in order to gratify it they were prepared to ignore not only their public duties but also those arising from their position as royal vassals. The very existence of benefices had here a detrimental effect on the structure of the state. Not only was the primitive strictness of the obligations of vassalage completely ignored, but the uselessness of the whole machinery of vassalage as an aid to government was thrown into sharp relief.

The development of feudal institutions did other and more serious injuries to the strength of the Frankish monarchy and the states which were its heirs.

The character of virtually hereditary benefices which public offices came to assume in the course of the ninth century involved, at least in West Francia, severe limitations in the power which the king could hope to exercise over his officials. Amongst the aristocracy, the class from which the agents of royal power were drawn, the spread of vassal engagements, created by what was in form a mutual contract, contributed to the extension of the idea that the royal power was itself only conditional. If subjects had their duties towards the king, the latter had duties towards his subjects, and by subjects, here, 'magnates' was of course to be understood. The loyalty of the king in carrying out his duties was a condition of the loyalty of the *populus*—and, here again, the 'magnates' must be understood—towards him. Charles the Bald was compelled to formulate this rule of public law in the most precise fashion at the assembly of Coulaines in 843, and thenceforward it remained as the basis of the system of government of West Francia. And we may be sure that this doctrine did nothing to increase the strength of the state.

Furthermore, it is beyond dispute that the spread of vassalage involved in fact the withdrawal of many free men from the immediate authority of the state. It is true that in law the entry of a free man into vassalage did not release him from his duties towards the state. He was still bound to perform his military service and to attend the *placita generalia;* the public courts were still fully competent to bring him before them. But in each of these public functions the lord now appeared at his vassal's side to aid and protect him; to some extent even the lord's person was actually interposed between the state and the vassal. The vassal served in the army under his lord's orders, and was helped or represented by the lord in the courts. When the state now wished to touch the vassal, and particularly the vassal who, because he was without benefice or held only a small one, was most closely dependent on his lord, it had more and more to address itself to the lord and invite him to apply compulsion to his vassal. . . .

It would be wrong . . . to attribute the collapse of the state solely to the disintegrative action of vassalage. The advance of feudalism was not the primary cause of the usurpations which in the late ninth and early tenth centuries led to the passing of so many of the attributes of government from the hands of the king into those of territorial princes in France and Italy and, though to a lesser degree, into those of the dukes in Germany. But we cannot doubt that the formation of these territorial principalities and duchies was strongly favoured by the paralysing action exercised by feudalism and vassalage over so many forms of royal activity . . . From yet another point of view, the feudal bond was a factor, a factor indeed of considerable importance, in preventing the total breakdown of the state.

The territorial princes who in the tenth century divided between them the greater part of the soil of France were all descendants or successors of some count, margrave or duke who had been a vassal of a Carolingian sovereign and held his *honor* in benefice from him. This state of things continued so far as the law was concerned: the territorial princes remained vassals of the king and held from him in benefice—or in fief, as it would soon be said—their county, marquisate or duchy.

In the tenth and eleventh centuries, these territorial princes were in reality quite independent. They recognized the king as their superior, but his supremacy was a purely theoretical one, and the only bond which continued—not very effectively—to bind them to the crown was the fact that they were its vassals. That the consequences of this vassalage were occasionally recognized is shown when from time to time we find the princes performing certain services on behalf of the king or refraining from certain acts in his despite. Slight as was this recognition, however, it was its survival in these centuries that prevented the complete fragmentation of France.

It seems also that vassalage played a similar rôle in Germany. That the kings there were able to resist the usurpations of the dukes at the beginning of the tenth century was in part a consequence of the fact that a certain number of counts were still their vassals. When Otto I became king in

936 and undertook the task of creating some bond between himself and the dukes, whose power had grown up outside and at the expense of the regular institutions of government, he realized that the most satisfactory proceeding would be to make all of them his vassals. This is made clear by the chronicler Widukind, who writes of the dukes that 'they placed their hands in his, and promised him their fealty and support against all his enemies' . . . In Germany, therefore, as in France, vassalage at this time did something to prevent the complete disintegration of the state. . . .

What one may call the classical age of feudalism is the period between the tenth and thirteenth centuries. It is true that during this period the ties of vassalage lost much of the binding force which they had had in the preceding age, and that the formation of these ties and the granting of benefices—or fiefs as they were now more generally called—no longer played as essential a part in social life in the thirteenth century as they had in the three preceding ones. (This is at least the case in France, England and Germany west of the Rhine.) It is also true that it is only towards the end of the twelfth century that feudal institutions came to occupy a predominant place in the political structure of Germany. None-the-less, as a broad generalization, we may say that it was in this period that the system of feudal institutions arrived at its completest development.

It is during this classical age that these institutions ceased to be peculiar to those states—France, Germany, the kingdom of Burgundy-Arles, Italy —which had grown up out of the ruins of the Frankish monarchy. The conquest of England by the duke of Normandy in 1066 introduced feudalism into England; the *reconquista* brought it, at least to a limited degree, to Spain; and the Crusades carried it overseas to the kingdom of Jerusalem and the ephemeral Latin empire of Constantinople. In the eastern states, however, it was feudalism with a difference. The feudalism of the Crusader states was something that has been aptly described as 'colonial', for it was created within a political framework set up by an army of lords and vassals which constituted a species of military 'command' particularly exposed to attack. It is therefore not surprising that it should have exhibited well-marked peculiarities of its own. The system of feudal relationships was generalized and codified to a degree never known in the west, and much stronger emphasis was laid on the rights and prerogatives of vassals. The texts which deal with the feudalism of the Latin states, and in particular the collections known as the Assizes of Jerusalem, do not therefore throw much real light on feudal institutions as they existed in western Europe.

Feudalism in Spain, save in the county of Barcelona, which was derived from the Spanish March of Carolingian times and remained in theory subject to the French king up to 1258, must also be regarded as a thing apart.

The historical circumstances which attended its formation gave birth to institutions differing in many respects from those found north of the Pyrenees.

Italy, strictly speaking, was one of the constituent states of the Carolingian monarchy, but the medieval Italian kingdom and the principalities which grew up within its boundaries developed many institutions peculiar to themselves, institutions in which the Frankish contribution represented only a single element. In northern and central Italy, other factors combined in the course of centuries to give to the feudalism of these regions a character quite distinct from that which one meets elsewhere, and one cannot use, for the study of Western feudalism, various legal compilations put together in Lombardy in the twelfth century, despite the fact that they are concerned with feudal relationships and were known under such names as *Libri Feudorum* or *Consuetudines Feudorum*. Still more remote from what one may regard as the norm were those features which characterized the feudalism of the Papal States. In the Norman principalities of southern Italy, and in the Norman kingdom of Sicily into which these were finally absorbed, the feudal institutions imported from France had to be imposed on a social and political system of extreme complexity. A central government of unusual strength succeeded in formulating a remarkably coherent system of feudal relationships, in which the rights and prerogatives of the lord, and in particular those of the head of the state, were strongly emphasized. But such a development cannot be regarded as in any way characteristic of Western feudalism as a whole.

There remain France and Germany, and the kingdom of Burgundy-Arles, which was attached by a political and personal union to Germany but which was much closer to France in its social development. There also remains England.

In France, in the kingdom of Burgundy-Arles, in western and—though more feebly—in southern Germany, feudal relations became in the tenth and eleventh centuries so much a matter of general custom that a freeman of military habits, accustomed to fighting on horseback and of some status in society, was nearly always the vassal of a lord, though this did not of course prevent him holding allodial land of his own in addition to such estates as he held as fiefs. This at least was the general rule, but there were exceptions to it, and it varied somewhat from one region to another. In some places the custom of vassalage was less common, and in others it only developed at a relatively late date. These regions were often those where manorial economy and the system of great estates had not become general, as for example Frisia and Saxony. The rebellions in Saxony against Henry IV in the second half of the eleventh century were in part rebellions against the extension of the manorial system and the feudalization of the upper classes. It is possible that a similar state of affairs existed in certain parts of the south of France.

Feudalism was introduced into England in its French form, and more particularly in the form which it had assumed in Normandy, which was one of those few territorial principalities in which by the second half of the eleventh century the ruler had succeeded in creating a strong central power. It was introduced, moreover, by a conqueror at the head of an army of vassals. These two features explain the fact that feudal relationships were more universal in England than they ever were in France or Germany, for in England allodial property was completely eliminated; all land was held either directly or indirectly of the king. Moreover, the English crown succeeded in mastering the feudal structure and submitting it entirely to its own authority. English feudalism therefore shows a certain number of characteristics which are quite peculiar to itself.

Inside each of these countries, the rules in which feudal relationships were embodied were largely a matter of regional or local custom. Despite the infinite variations which these entailed, however, it is possible to determine the general principles which regulated the relationship of vassal to lord and the custom of fiefs: we can disentangle the essential traits of the *ius militare*, the feudal law, the *Lehnrecht* of these various countries. It is even possible to go further; while recognizing the existence of these national varieties of feudal law, we can isolate those elements which were common to the whole of western Europe.

In studying feudal relationships under the Carolingians, the royal capitularies were one of our main sources. We cannot depend to the same extent on legislation in attempting to describe and analyse feudalism in its classical age, for except in England this type of material is rare before the thirteenth century; there is almost nothing apart from the *Statute* of Count William II for the county of Forcalquier in Provence (1162), the *Assise au Comte Geoffroy* (1185) for Brittany and the *Charte féodale* (1200) for Hainault. We are therefore forced to fall back on the narrative sources and the charters in which the practice of the time was embodied. In the twelfth century, however, a new type of evidence comes to hand in the form of legal treatises. They first appear in England at the beginning of the century, and in France and Germany towards its end. Although they are private compilations and relatively late in date, these *coutumiers* or *Rechtsbücher* may be used, with due caution, to complete our picture of classical feudalism. ✣

4. MARC BLOCH

FROM Marc Bloch, *Feudal Society* (Chicago: University of Chicago Press, 1961), pp. 59–61, 441–47, 450–52.

The framework of institutions which governs a society can in the last resort be understood only through a knowledge of the whole human environment. For though the artificial conception of man's activities which prompts us to carve up the creature of flesh and blood into the phantoms *homo oeconomicus, philosophicus, juridicus* is doubtless necessary, it is tolerable only if we refuse to be deceived by it. That is why, despite the existence of other works on the various aspects of medieval civilization, the descriptions thus attempted from points of view different from ours did not seem to us to obviate the necessity of recalling at this stage the fundamental characteristics of the historical climate in which European feudalism flourished. Need I add that in placing this account near the beginning of the book there was no thought of claiming any sort of illusory primacy for facts of this kind? When it is a question of comparing two particular phenomena belonging to separate series—a certain distribution of population, for example, with certain forms of legal groups—the delicate problem of cause and effect undoubtedly arises. On the other hand, to contrast two sets of dissimilar phenomena over a period of several centuries, and then say: 'Here on this side are all the causes; there on that are all the effects', would be to construct the most pointless of dichotomies. A society, like a mind, is woven of perpetual interaction. For other researches, differently oriented, the analysis of the economy or the mental climate are culminating points; for the historian of the social structure they are a starting-point.

In this preliminary picture, designedly limited in scope, it will be necessary to retain only what is essential and least open to doubt. One deliberate omission, in particular, deserves a word of explanation. The wonderful flowering of art in the feudal era, at least from the eleventh century on, is not merely the most lasting glory of that epoch in the eyes of posterity. It served in those times as a vehicle for the most exalted forms of religious sensibility as well as for that interpenetration of the sacred and profane so characteristic of the age, which has left no more spontaneous witness than the friezes and capitals of certain churches. It was also very often the refuge, as it were, of certain values which could not find expression elsewhere. The restraint of which the medieval epic was incapable must be sought in Romanesque architecture. The precision of mind which the notaries were unable to attain in their charters presided over the works of the builders of vaults. But the links that unite plastic expression to the other features of a civilization are still insufficiently understood; from the little that we know of them they appear so complex, so subject to delays and divergences that it has been necessary in this work to leave aside the problems posed by connections so delicate and contradictions that to us seem so astonishing.

It would, moreover, be a grave mistake to treat 'feudal civilization' as being all of one piece chronologically. Engendered no doubt or made possible by the cessation of the last invasions, but first manifesting themselves some generations later, a series of very profound and very widespread changes occurred towards the middle of the eleventh century. No definite break with the past occurred, but the change of direction which, despite inevitable variations in time according to the countries or the phenomena considered, affected in turn all the graphs of social activity. There were, in a word, two successive 'feudal' ages, very different from one another in their essential character. We shall endeavour in the following pages to do justice as much to the contrasts between these two phases as to the characteristics they shared.

It is and always will be impossible for us to calculate, even approximately, the population of Western countries during the first feudal age. Moreover, there undoubtedly existed marked regional variations, constantly intensified by the spasms of social disorder. Compared with the veritable desert of the Iberian plateaux, which gave the frontier regions of Christendom and Islam the desolate appearance of a vast 'no man's land' —desolate even in comparison with early Germany, where the destruction wrought by the migrations of the previous age was being slowly made good—the country districts of Flanders and Lombardy seemed relatively favoured regions. But whatever the importance of these contrasts and whatever their effect on all the aspects of civilization, the fundamental characteristic remains the great and universal decline in population. Over the whole of Europe, the population was immeasurably smaller than it has been since the eighteenth century or even since the twelfth. Even in the provinces formerly under Roman rule, human beings were much scarcer than they had been in the heyday of the Empire. The most important towns had no more than a few thousand inhabitants, and waste land, gardens, even fields and pastures encroached on all sides amongst the houses.

This lack of density was further aggravated by very unequal distribution. Doubtless physical conditions, as well as social habits, conspired to maintain in the country districts profound differences between systems of settlement. In some districts the families, or at least some of them, took up their residence a considerable distance apart, each in the middle of its own farmland, as was the case, for example, in Limousin. In others on the contrary, like the Ile-de-France, they mostly crowded together in villages. On the whole, however, both the pressure of the chiefs and, above all, the concern for security militated against too wide dispersal. The disorders of the early Middle Ages had in many cases induced men to draw nearer to each other, but these aggregations in which people lived cheek by jowl were separated by empty spaces. The arable land from which the village derived its sustenance was necessarily much larger in proportion to the number of inhabitants than it is today. For agriculture was a great devourer of space. In the tilled fields, incompletely ploughed and almost always inadequately manured, the ears of corn grew neither very heavy nor very dense. Above all, the harvests never covered the whole area of cultivation at once. The most advanced systems of crop-rotation known to the age required that every year half or a third of the cultivated soil should lie fallow. Often indeed, fallow and crops followed each other in irregular alternation, which always allowed more time for the growth of weeds than for that of the cultivated produce; the fields, in such cases, represented hardly more than a provisional and short-lived conquest of the waste land, and even in the heart of the agricultural regions nature tended constantly to regain the upper hand. Beyond them, enveloping them, thrusting into them, spread forests, scrub and dunes—immense wildernesses, seldom entirely uninhabited by man, though whoever dwelt there as charcoal-burner, shepherd, hermit or outlaw did so only at the cost of a long separation from his fellow men. . . .

In the eyes of Montesquieu, the establishment of 'feudal laws' was a phenomenon *sui generis*, 'an event which happened once in the world and which will perhaps never happen again'. Voltaire, less experienced, no doubt, in the precise formulation of legal definitions, but a man of wider outlook, demurred. 'Feudalism', he wrote, 'is not an event; it is a very old form which, with differences in its working, subsists in three-quarters of our hemisphere.' Modern scholarship has in general rallied to the side of Voltaire. Egyptian feudalism, Achaean feudalism, Chinese feudalism, Japanese feudalism—all these forms and more are now familiar concepts. The historian of the West must sometimes regard them with a certain amount of misgiving. For he cannot be unaware of the different definitions which have been given of this famous term, even on its native soil. The basis of feudal society, Benjamin Guérard has said, is land. No, it is the personal group, rejoins Jacques Flach. Do the various exotic versions of feudalism, which seem to abound in universal history today, conform to Guérard's definition or to Flach's? The only remedy for these uncertainties is to go back to the origins of the problem. Since it is obvious that all these societies, separated by time and space, have received the name 'feudal' only on account of their similarities, real or supposed, to Western feudalism, it is the characteristics of this basic type, to which all the others must be referred, that it is of primary importance to define. But first it is necessary to dispose of some obvious instances of the misuse of a term which has made too much noise in the world not to have undergone many perversions.

In the system which they christened 'feudalism' its first godfathers, as we know, were primarily conscious of those aspects of it which conflicted with the idea of a centralized state. Thence it was a short step to describing as feudal every fragmentation of political authority; so that a value judgment was normally combined with the simple statement of a fact. Because sovereignty was generally associated in the minds of these writers with fairly large states, every exception to the rule seemed to fall into the category of the abnormal. This alone would suffice to condemn a usage which, moreover, could scarcely fail to give rise to intolerable confusion. Occasionally, indeed, there are indications of a more precise notion. In 1783 a minor municipal official, the market-watchman of Valenciennes, denounced as responsible for the increase in the price of foodstuffs 'a feudality of great country landlords'. How many polemists since then have held up to public obloquy the 'feudalism' of bankers or industrialists! Charged with more or less vague historical associations, the word with certain writers seems to suggest no more than the brutal exercise of authority, though frequently it also conveys the slightly less elementary notion of an encroachment of economic powers on public life. It is in fact very true that the identification of wealth—then consisting mainly of land— with authority was one of the outstanding features of medieval feudalism. But this was less on account of the strictly feudal character of that society than because it was, at the same time, based on the manor.

Feudalism, manorial system—the identification here goes back much farther. It had first occurred in the use of the word 'vassal'. The aristocratic stamp which this term had received from what was, after all, a secondary development, was not strong enough to prevent it from being occasionally applied, even in the Middle Ages, to serfs (originally closely akin to vassals properly so called because of the personal nature of their dependence) and even to ordinary tenants. What was then only a kind of linguistic aberration, especially frequent in somewhat incompletely feudalized regions like Gascony or Leon, became a more and more widespread usage, as familiarity with genuine vassalage faded. 'Everyone knows', wrote Perreciot in 1786 'that in France the subjects of lords are commonly called their vassals.' Similarly it became customary, in spite of etymology, to describe as 'feudal rights' the burdens to which peasant holdings were subject. Thus when the men of the Revolution announced their intention to destroy feudalism, it was above all the manorial system that they meant to attack. But here again the historian must interpose. Though an essential element in feudal society, the manor was in itself an older institution, and was destined to last much longer. In the interests of sound terminology it is important that the two ideas should be kept clearly separate.

Let us therefore try to bring together in broad outline what we have learned about European feudalism, in the strict sense of the word, from its history.

The simplest way will be to begin by saying what feudal society was not. Although the obligations arising from blood-relationship played a very active part in it, it did not rely on kinship alone. More precisely, feudal ties proper were developed when those of kinship proved inadequate. Again, despite the persistence of the idea of a public authority superimposed on the multitude of petty powers, feudalism coincided with a profound weakening of the State, particularly in its protective capacity. But much as feudal society differed from societies based on kinship as well as from those dominated by the power of the State, it was their successor and bore their imprint. For while the characteristic relationships of personal subjection retained something of the quasi-family character of the original companionage, a considerable part of the political authority exercised by innumerable petty chiefs had the appearance of a usurpation of 'regalian' rights.

European feudalism should therefore be seen as the outcome of the violent dissolution of older societies. It would in fact be unintelligible without the great upheaval of the Germanic invasions which, by forcibly uniting two societies originally at very different stages of development, disrupted both of them and brought to the surface a great many modes of thought and social practices of an extremely primitive character. It finally developed in the atmosphere of the last barbarian raids. It involved a far-reaching restriction of social intercourse, a circulation of money too sluggish to admit of a salaried officialdom, and a mentality attached to things tangible and local. When these conditions began to change, feudalism began to wane.

It was an unequal society, rather than a hierarchical one—with chiefs rather than nobles; and with serfs, not slaves. If slavery had not played so small a part, there would have been no need for the characteristically feudal forms of dependence, as applied to the lower orders of society. In an age of disorder, the place of the adventurer was too important, the memory of men too short, the regularity of social classifications too uncertain, to admit of the strict formation of regular castes.

Nevertheless the feudal system meant the rigorous economic subjection of a host of humble folk to a few powerful men. Having received from earlier ages the Roman *villa* (which in some respects anticipated the manor) and the German village chiefdom, it extended and consolidated these methods whereby men exploited men, and combining inextricably the right to the revenues from the land with the right to exercise authority, it fashioned from all this the true manor of medieval times. And this it did partly for the benefit of an oligarchy of priests and monks whose task it was to propitiate Heaven, but chiefly for the benefit of an oligarchy of warriors.

As even the most perfunctory comparative study will show, one of the most distinctive characteristics of feudal societies was the virtual identity of the class of chiefs with the class of professional warriors serving in the only way that then seemed effective, that is as heavily armed horsemen. As we have seen, of the societies where an armed peasantry survived, some knew neither vassalage nor the manor, while others knew them only in very imperfect forms—as in Scandinavia for example, or the kingdoms of northwestern Spain. The case of the Byzantine Empire is perhaps even more significant because its institutions bore the stamp of a much more conscious directing thought. There, after the anti-aristocratic reaction of the eighth century, a government which had preserved the great administrative traditions of the Roman period, and which was furthermore concerned to provide itself with a strong army, created tenements charged with military obligations to the State—true fiefs in one sense, but differing from those of the West in that they were peasant fiefs, each consisting of a small farm. Thenceforth it was a paramount concern of the imperial government to protect these 'soldiers' properties', as well as small-holdings in general, against the encroachments of the rich and powerful. Nevertheless there came a time towards the end of the eleventh century when the Empire, overwhelmed by economic conditions which made independence more and more difficult for a peasantry constantly in debt, and further weakened by internal discords, ceased to extend any useful protection to the free farmers. In this way it not only lost precious fiscal resources, but found itself at the mercy of the magnates, who alone were capable thereafter of raising the necessary troops from among their own dependants.

In feudal society the characteristic human bond was the subordinate's link with a nearby chief. From one level to another the ties thus formed—like so many chains branching out indefinitely—joined the smallest to the greatest. Land itself was valued above all because it enabled a lord to provide himself with 'men' by supplying the remuneration for them. We want lands, said in effect the Norman lords who refused the gifts of jewels, arms, and horses offered by their duke. And they added among themselves: 'It will thus be possible for us to maintain many knights, and the duke will no longer be able to do so.'

It remained to devise a form of real property right suitable for the remuneration of services and coinciding in duration with the personal tie itself. From the solution which it found for this problem, Western feudalism derived one of its most original features. While the 'men of service' who surrounded the Slav princes continued to receive their estates as outright gifts, the fief of the Frankish vassal, after some fluctuations of policy, was in theory conceded to him only for the term of his life. For among the highest classes, distinguished by the honourable profession of arms, relationships of dependence had assumed, at the outset, the form of contracts freely entered into between two living men confronting one another. From this necessary personal contact the relationship derived the best part of its moral value. Nevertheless at an early date various factors tarnished the purity of the obligation: hereditary succession, natural in a society where the family remained so strong; the practice of enfeoffment which was imposed by economic conditions and ended by burdening the land with services rather than the man with fealty; finally and above all, the plurality of vassal engagements. The loyalty of the commended man remained, in many cases, a potent factor. But as a paramount social bond designed to unite the various groups at all levels, to prevent fragmentation and to arrest disorder, it showed itself decidedly ineffective.

Indeed in the immense range of these ties there had been from the first something artificial. Their general diffusion in feudal times was the legacy of a moribund State—that of the Carolingians—which had conceived the idea of combating social disintegration by means of one of the institutions born of that very condition. The system of superposed protective relationships was certainly not incapable of contributing to the cohesion of the State: witness, the Anglo-Norman monarchy. But for this it was necessary that there should be a central authority favoured, as in England, not only by the fact of conquest itself but even more by the circumstance that it coincided with new material and moral conditions. In the ninth century the forces making for disintegration were too strong.

In the area of Western civilization the map of feudalism reveals some large blank spaces—the Scandinavian peninsula, Frisia, Ireland. Perhaps it is more important still to note that feudal Europe was not all feudalized in the same degree or according to the same rhythm and, above all, that it was nowhere feudalized completely. In no country did the whole of the rural population fall into the bonds of personal and hereditary dependence. Almost everywhere—though the number varied greatly from region to region—there survived large or small allodial properties. The concept of the State never absolutely disappeared, and where it retained the most vitality men continued to call themselves 'free', in the old sense of the word, because they were dependent only on the head of the people or his representatives. Groups of peasant warriors remained in Normandy, in the Danelaw, and in Spain. The mutual oath, strongly contrasting with the oaths of subordination, survived in the peace associations and triumphed in the communes. No doubt it is the fate of every system of human institutions never to be more than imperfectly realized. Capitalism was unquestionably the dominant influence on the European economy at the beginning of the twentieth century; yet more than one undertaking continued to exist outside it.

Returning to our feudal map, we find between the Loire and the Rhine, and in Burgundy on both banks of the Saône, a heavily shaded area which, in the eleventh century, is suddenly enlarged by the Norman conquests of England and southern Italy. All round this central nucleus there is an almost regular shading-off till, in Saxony and especially in Leon and Castile, the stippling becomes very sparse indeed. Finally the entire shaded area is surrounded by blank spaces. In the most heavily shaded zone it is not difficult to recognize the regions where the regularizing influence of the Carolingians had been most far-reaching and where also the mingling of Romanized elements and Germanic elements—more pronounced here than elsewhere—had most completely disrupted the structure of the two societies and made possible the growth of very old seeds of territorial lordship and personal dependence.

A subject peasantry; widespread use of the service tenement (i.e. the fief) instead of a salary, which was out of the question; the supremacy of a class of specialized warriors; ties of obedience and protection which bind man to man and, within the warrior class, assume the distinctive form called vassalage; fragmentation of authority—leading inevitably to disorder; and, in the midst of all this, the survival of other forms of association, family and State, of which the latter, during the second feudal age, was to acquire renewed strength—such then seem to be the fundamental features of European feudalism. Like all the phenomena revealed by that science of eternal change which is history, the social structure thus characterized certainly bore the peculiar stamp of an age and an environment. Yet just as the matrilineal or agnatic clan or even certain types of economic enterprise are found in much the same forms in very different societies, it is by no means impossible that societies different from our own should have passed through a phase closely resembling that which has just been defined. If so, it is legitimate to call them feudal during that phase. But the work of comparison thus involved is clearly beyond the powers of one man, and I shall therefore confine myself to an example which will at least give an idea of what such research, conducted by surer hands, might yield. The task is facilitated by the existence of excellent studies which already bear the hall-mark of the soundest comparative method.

In the dark ages of Japanese history we dimly perceive a society based on kinship groups, real or fictitious. Then towards the end of the seventh century of our era, under Chinese influence a system of government is founded which strives (exactly as the Carolingians did) to maintain a kind of moral control over its subjects. Finally, about the eleventh century, the period begins which it has become customary to call feudal and whose advent seems (in accordance with a pattern with which we are now familiar) to have coincided with a certain slackening of commercial activity. Here, therefore, as in Europe, 'feudalism' seems to have been preceded by two very different forms of social organization; and, as with us, it was profoundly influenced by both. The monarchy, though it had less connection than in Europe with the feudal structure proper—since the chains of vassalage terminated before reaching the Emperor—subsisted, in law, as the theoretical source of all power; and there also the fragmentation of political authority, which was fostered by very old habits, was held to be a consequence of encroachments on the State.

Above the peasantry a class of professional warriors had arisen. It was in these circles that ties of personal dependence developed, on the model furnished by the relations of the armed retainer with his chief; they were thus, it appears, marked by a much more pronounced class character than European 'commendation'. They were hierarchically organized, just as in Europe; but Japanese vassalage was much more an act of submission than was European vassalage and much less a contract. It was also more strict, since it did not allow plurality of lords. As these warriors had to be supported they were granted tenements closely resembling the fiefs of the West. Sometimes even, on the pattern of our *fiefs de reprises*, the grant was purely fictitious and involved in fact lands which had originally belonged to the patrimony of the pretended recipient. These fighting-men were naturally less and less willing to cultivate the soil, though as in Europe there were to the end exceptional cases of peasant 'vavasours'. The vassals therefore lived mainly on the rents from their own tenants. There were too many of them, however—far more, apparently, than in Europe—to admit of the establishment for their benefit of real manors, with extensive powers over the people. Few manors were created, except by the baronage and the temples, and being widely scattered and having no demesne, they recalled the embryonic manors of Anglo-Saxon England rather than those of the really manorialized regions of the West. Furthermore, on this soil where irrigated rice-fields represented the prevailing form of agriculture, the technical conditions were so different from European practice that the subjection of the peasantry assumed correspondingly different forms.

Although far too brief, of course, and too absolute in its appraisal of the contrasts between the two societies, it seems to me that this outline nevertheless enables us to reach a fairly firm conclusion. Feudalism was not 'an event which happened once in the world'. Like Europe—though with inevitable and deep-seated differences—Japan went through this phase. Have other societies also passed through it? And if so, what were the causes, and were they perhaps common to all such societies? It is for future works to provide the answers. I should be happy if this book, by suggesting questions to students, were to prepare the way for an inquiry going far beyond it. . . .

To the societies which succeeded it the feudal era had bequeathed knighthood, which had become crystallized as nobility. From this origin the dominant class retained pride in its military calling, symbolized by the right to wear the sword, and clung to it with particular tenacity where, as in France, it derived from this calling the justification for valuable fiscal privileges. Nobles need not pay *taille*, explain two squires of Varennes-en-Argonne about 1380; for 'by their noble status, nobles are obliged to expose their bodies and belongings in wars'. Under the Ancien Régime, the nobility of ancient lineage, in contrast with the aristocracy of office, continued to call itself the nobility 'of the sword'. Even today, when to die for one's country has altogether ceased to be the monopoly of one class or one profession, the persistence of the feeling that a sort of moral supremacy attaches to the function of professional warrior—an attitude quite foreign to other societies, such as the Chinese—is a continual reminder of the separation which took place, towards the beginning of feudal times, between the peasant and the knight.

Vassal homage was a genuine contract and a bilateral one. If the lord failed to fulfil his engagements he lost his rights. Transferred, as was inevitable, to the political sphere—since the principal subjects of the king were at the same time his vassals—this idea was to have a far-reaching influence, all the more so because on this ground it was reinforced by the very ancient notions which held the king responsible in a mystical way for the welfare of his subjects and deserving of punishment in the event of public calamity. These old currents happened to unite on this point with another stream of thought which arose in the Church out of the Gregorian protest against the myth of sacred and supernatural kingship. It was the writers of this clerical group who first expressed, with a force long unequalled, the notion of a contract binding the sovereign to his people—'like the swineherd to the master who employs him', wrote an Alsatian monk about 1080.

The remark seems even more full of meaning when taken in the context of the indignant protest of a (moderate) partisan of monarchy: 'the Lord's anointed cannot be dismissed like a village reeve!' But these clerical theorists themselves did not fail to invoke, among the justifications for the deposition to which they condemned the bad prince, the universally recognized right of the vassal to abandon the bad lord.

It was above all the circles of the vassals which translated these ideas into practice, under the influence of the institutions which had formed their mentality. In this sense, there was a fruitful principle underlying many revolts which on a superficial view might appear as mere random uprisings: 'A man may resist his king and judge when he acts contrary to law and may even help to make war on him. . . . Thereby, he does not violate the duty of fealty.' These are the words of the *Sachsenspiegel*. This famous 'right of resistance', the germ of which was already present in the Oaths of Strasbourg (843) and in the pact between Charles the Bald and his vassals (856), resounded in the thirteenth and fourteenth centuries from one end of the Western world to the other, in a multitude of texts. Though most of these documents were inspired by reactionary tendencies among the nobility, or by the egoism of the bourgeoisie, they were of great significance for the future. They included the English Great Charter of 1215; the Hungarian 'Golden Bull' of 1222; the Assizes of the kingdom of Jerusalem; the Privilege of the Brandenburg nobles; the Aragonese Act of Union of 1287; the Brabantine charter of Cortenberg; the statute of Dauphiné of 1341; the declaration of the communes of Languedoc (1356). It was assuredly no accident that the representative system, in the very aristocratic form of the English Parliament, the French 'Estates', the *Stände* of Germany, and the Spanish *Cortés*, originated in states which were only just emerging from the feudal stage and still bore its imprint. Nor was it an accident that in Japan, where the vassal's submission was much more unilateral and where, moreover, the divine power of the Emperor remained outside the structure of vassal engagements, nothing of the kind emerged from a regime which was nevertheless in many respects closely akin to the feudalism of the West. The originality of the latter system consisted in the emphasis it placed on the idea of an agreement capable of binding the rulers; and in this way, oppressive as it may have been to the poor, it has in truth bequeathed to our Western civilization something with which we still desire to live.

5. JOSEPH R. STRAYER

FROM Joseph R. Strayer, *Feudalism* (Princeton, N.J.: D. Van Nostrand Co., Inc., 1965), pp. 11–14.

Feudalism is a difficult word. It was invented in the seventeenth century, at a time when the social phenomena it purported to describe had either vanished or were decaying rapidly. The men of the Middle Ages, who were deeply involved in what we call feudalism, never used the word, so that we cannot work out a definition from their statements. Modern scholars have long argued about the meaning of the term, without ever reaching agreement. Laymen have used it loosely, often as a way of condemning any political, economic, or social relationships they did not like. No definition will satisfy everyone, and yet we must have a tentative definition in order to know what we are talking about and what kind of behavior we are trying to describe.

Origin of the Term

We might start by remembering why the word was invented. The seventeenth-century lawyers and antiquarians who first used the term were either perplexed or fascinated by the survival of certain customs and institutions which were difficult to harmonize with prevailing legal and political theories. Restraints on royal power, the possession of public authority by private persons, peculiar rules about the use and transfer of real property, did not seem to fit with the concept of the sovereign state, the doctrine of divine right, or ideas about the sanctity of private property. It was also clear that these survivals did not go back to the classical period; they were just as repugnant to the spirit of Roman law as they were to the absolutism of the seventeenth century. They must, then, have originated in the Middle Ages, and most of them seemed to be connected with the medieval institution of the fief. Hence they were lumped together under the name of feudalism. And the antiquarians who tried to explain the term, or the lawyers who tried to justify the peculiar rights of their clients, knew perfectly well where to find the explanations or justifications they needed: they began to examine with greater and greater care the legal and administrative records of medieval governments.

The first descriptions of feudalism, then, were derived from a study of the medieval political structure. This is still the place to turn, for, as we shall see, it is here, and here alone, that we find the sharply defined characteristics which make it possible to distinguish feudalism from other patterns of social organization. Some other societies had some of these characteristics, and one other society, Japan from 1300 to 1600, had most of them. But feudalism appeared first and developed most completely in Western Europe between 800 and 1200.

Definition of Feudalism

When we look at the political situation in Western Europe in this period, there are three things that strike us. First, there is a fragmentation of political power. Over much of Western Europe the county is the largest effective political unit, and in some places even the county has splintered into small, autonomous lordships. Moreover, even in these small districts no single ruler has a monopoly of political authority. There are rights of jurisdiction and administration which are held as hereditary possessions by lesser lords. There may be enclaves within a county or a barony in which the count or baron has no authority at all.

Second, this fragmented political power is treated as a private possession. It can be divided among heirs, given as marriage portion, mortgaged, bought and sold. Private contracts and the rules of family law determine the possessors of judicial and administrative authority. Public power in private hands is accepted as a normal and inevitable arrangement; no one considers it peculiar or undesirable.

Third, a key element in the armed forces—heavy-armed cavalry—is secured through individual and private agreements. Knights render military service not because they are citizens of a state or subjects of a king, but because they or their ancestors have promised to give this service to a lord in return for certain benefits. These benefits may range from mere sustenance in the lord's household to the grant of estates, villages, and even some rights of government. Increasingly, the grant of land comes to be the normal way of securing the services of a knight, but other arrangements are always possible. The essential point is that military service is provided through a series of private contracts between the lord and his men.

To sum up, the basic characteristics of feudalism in Western Europe are a fragmentation of political authority, public power in private hands, and a military system in which an essential part of the armed forces is secured through private contracts. Feudalism is a method of government, and a way of securing the forces necessary to preserve that method of government.

This is not as narrow a definition as it seems. The possessors of political and military power will naturally mold their society to fit their own needs. They will manipulate the economy so that they get the greatest share of production; they will develop a class structure which gives them the highest position; they will, as wealthy consumers, influence writers and artists; they will establish standards to which their society must conform. Thus, it is perfectly legitimate to speak of feudal society, or a feudal age, if we remember that it was the political-military structure which made the society and the age feudal.

On the other hand, if we try a wider definition, feudalism becomes an amorphous term. The most usual attempt to broaden the definition of feudalism stresses social and economic factors; in its simplest form it would find the essence of feudalism in the exploitation of an agricultural population by a ruling group. That this occurred in the feudal society of Western Europe is certainly true; it is equally true that it occurred in many other societies as well, both before and after the Middle Ages. Nor can we say that this situation is typical of all pre-industrial societies, and that therefore the socioeconomic definition of feudalism is useful in marking a universal stage of economic development. Some pre-industrial societies were never feudal in any sense of the word; some highly industrialized societies can be called feudal if we use the socioeconomic definition of feudalism. The ruling class (or party) of the Soviet Union built up its heavy industries by exploiting the tillers of the soil, and the ruling class of Communist China has recently attempted to do the same thing. A definition which can include societies as disparate as those of the Ancient Middle East, the late Roman Empire, medieval Europe, the southern part of the United States in the nineteenth century, and the Soviet Union in the 1930's is not much use in historical analysis. ✻

6. GEORGES DUBY and ROBERT MANDROU

FROM Georges Duby and Robert Mandrou, *A History of French Civilization*, trans. James Blakeley Atkinson (New York: Random House, 1964), pp. 32–33, 38–41.

Although the use of the term "feudalism" may be criticized on the ground that the fief is only one aspect of the newly arranged relations among men, and not the most important one, it is an accepted term; let us retain it while trying, at the same time, to make its content more explicit. The visible forms of social relations have been altered during the course of the eleventh century, and their mutation is an important one: henceforth, for many centuries, French civilization is to evolve within new frameworks which, even when they cease to form the skeleton of the society, continue permanently to influence patterns of thought. "Nobility," "chivalry," "honor," "homage"—these key words have reverberated for so long that even today they are not entirely mute. But this revolution was not in the least abrupt; for a long time, scarcely perceptible underground changes were preparing for it. The decades around the year 1020 produced the collective mind's grasp of these changes, their legal ratification and, simultaneously, the fixing and the final definition of social relations, until now conducted in the wake of instinctive reaction. These last represented the final, belated adjustment to the milieu, the isolation of people in the clearings, the regressive economy, and that sinking into rural life characteristic of the tenth century.

"Feudal" society exhibits, actually, two fundamental features. First, power is divided into small, autonomous compartments; the abstract ideas that had once surrounded political relations are definitively obliterated. With the possible exception of a few clerics whose minds are better trained for thought, the ideas of sovereignty and public community no longer have any meaning; to command other men and to punish them is a personal attribute, sold and inherited like a piece of land, and those who are lucky enough to possess it, use it to their exclusive advantage without having to account to anyone for their acts. Further, if authority is to be recognized, it must appear concretely: no one obeys a lord whom he cannot see or whose voice he does not hear. Because the physical presence of the leader is indispensable, his power can be extended only over small groups of assembled men. The second feature of this society is the distinct dividing-line that now isolates the nobility from the bulk of mankind. This again is a simple solidification of awareness: the aristocracy, that class of well-born men provided with customary privileges, has existed for a long time; but from now on its rights and titles are openly acknowledged. Actually, the idea of the division of Christian society into "orders," rigidly delineated categories, is widely held by the end of the tenth century. These "orders" (classes) each have been entrusted by God with a particular mission and, by virtue of that call, each has the right to special treatment. Originally a concept of the learned, formulated long ago in educated Church circles, it was applied first to priests and monks to separate them from the laity; now, it subdivides the laity into two groups. On the one hand, there is the minority of the lords, the rich, the leisure class; in order to merit the material advantages Providence has accorded them, they are obliged to turn their entire attention to the art of war, and to the armed defense of the other social categories. On the other hand, there is the "order" (class) of laborers, the mass of little people—the poor, the rustics—who, according to divine plan, have the responsibility of supporting with their labor those specialists in prayer and combat, in exchange for the spiritual and temporal protection these latter provide them. . . .

In the ideas of Germanic origin that had fashioned the political behavior of the early Middle Ages, the "freeman" was first and foremost a warrior—and, because military service was their prime public duty, free men nowhere felt themselves more a part of the social community than in the army, gathered on the edge of the battlefield. By virtue of developments accelerated by the tenth-century invasions, fighting methods have been transformed: in the midst of the soldiers, the small group of horsemen, more heavily armed, already placed in a better position and relieved of the fatigue of long marches, had gradually taken the leading position in battle. Foot soldiers, reduced to a minor and soon negligible role, had ceased to be called up regularly; ultimately, they were entirely exempt from service and no longer participated in expeditions except in the case of serious local alerts. Therefore, at the beginning of the eleventh century, the full brunt, but also the full prestige, of military duty are the privilege of the mounted fighting-men: they alone are true soldiers. Documents written in Latin begin to give them the title *miles* to distinguish them from the others. Popular dialects are more explicit: *miles* is the translation of "horsemen," or in northern France, "knight" [*chevalier*]. In this way, as long as the idea persists that fighting is the special activity of free men, total freedom is confined to a small military élite.

It is an élite of people of means: to be a horseman, one must be rich. Fighting men during the early Middle Ages were obliged to equip themselves without any assistance from the commanding authority. Lacking the means, most of them appear to have been fitted with the most primitive equipment, and one of the Carolingian capitularies had to state explicitly that it did not suffice to bring along a club. In a time when livestock were poorly fed and, indeed, sadly lacking, a horse—by which we mean a fighting horse, capable of carrying an armed man and his military accoutrements—was a very rare item of equipment, one whose maintenance presupposed his owner's superabundance of provisions; hence, available only to possessors of considerable capital. Furthermore, leisure was an especial necessity, as well as sufficient means to have one's estates cultivated by others and to entrust the maintenance of one's house to numerous tenants and domestics—for these men had to be trained in the difficult techniques of mounted warfare, had to spend time garrisoned in fortresses, and had to join the expeditions regularly undertaken in spring and summer—just when the land required the most constant care. Consequently, in the eleventh century, military duty becomes the prerogative of those who, by virtue of a patron's "blessing" but more often by inheritance, control a large estate, rich in land, one of those fine manors, furnished with abundant personnel, yielding sufficient food and funds to improve one's equipment. Thus the line of division, incised more deeply every day, places the "peasants" and *vilains* (men who, born in a hamlet, never leave it) below the "warrior order"; it is the distinction that, even in antiquity, separated the small group of lazy, well-fed *hobereaux* from the laborers. In most of the French provinces, the militia or "knights" tend to become identical with the landed aristocracy—the rich, the lords, the nobles.

The knights, who erect their residences on the chatelain's land, are placed under the stronghold owner's authority. This is so clearly recognized that people call them *milites castri*, the "knights of the castle," because the fort is their assembly point, the chief area of the military activity that distinguishes them from the bulk of mankind. But the authority of the leader is exercised over them in a special way, for they are soldiers like him; he treats them as associates. It is usually the case that they are his "Men," so it is a question of an honorable dependence, a free and personal attachment producing that spirit of mutual camaraderie uniting the fighting groups—not a blind subordination. They are exempted from the usual constraints: no *coutumes* for them, nor any of the exploitation out of which the lord's *ban* materializes. In this way is formed the idea that lasts so long and has such extensive consequences: that the military vocation produces a special immunity, that a certain exemption is due to anyone who risks his life and gives his blood.

By contrast, the entire burden of the lords' power rests on those who are unarmed, on the *vilains*. For them, the entry into personal dependence, the state of "belonging" to another man, means obedience to all his orders, the retreat into a strict and, most important, an hereditary, subjection from which it is impossible henceforth to break away. These are the people whom the lord exploits, through the medium of his provosts, his foresters, and those auxiliaries who, though of low birth, pull themselves up upon their invested powers and, exceeding their rights, quickly make their fortune. These last are the real and immediate controllers of the *manants* whom they often tyrannize. It happens sometimes, in cases of great emergency, that the rustics are called into combat—or rather, into preparations for the real combat of the knights. At such times, they are despised cannon-fodder, armed only with ridiculous farm implements. Normally, their co-operation in the common defense takes forms that are deemed degrading: delivery of provisions for the castle garrison and in particular hay and oats for the maintenance of the horses; or even *corvées*, theoretically devoted to the periodic repair of the fortifications, but often diverted into farm labor for the chatelain. Over them prevails the manor lord's justice, all the more strict and ready in that it is so profitable: fines in *deniers* whose total amount is customarily determined by a barbaric and undifferentiated code (seven *sous* for any kind of blow, sixty if blood flows, whether or not the wound be serious) cause the few peasant savings to pass into the lord's coffers and his agent's purse. If the guilty person is unable to pay he is imprisoned; this is not a punishment, but a means for accelerating the adjustment of the monetary penalties. In the case of serious crimes, the perpetrators are at the mercy of the chatelain: he can confiscate all their property, inflict corporal punishments such as mutilation of the guilty hand, or even death—for the gallows is another symbol of lofty power. Finally, as a price for the protection accorded them, the peasants whom the lord shelters owe him material "aids." They offer him lodging when he needs it—and if the chatelain himself rarely comes to his *manants'* huts to eat the family gruel, his knights, men, and hunting dogs take advantage of this gratuitous allowance—a periodic and dreaded drain on family food reserves, although most of the time, in fact, it is limited by custom. On the other hand, the leader's right to take from the *vilain's* house whatever he needs, whenever he needs it—called the *taille* —is exercised arbitrarily.

Thus a heavier lordship, that of the controller of the *ban*, weighs on the eleventh-century peasantry. For the tenants carry this burden in addition to the services they owe the owners of the land they farm and, for parish members, it augments the tithes and other fees given to the altar of the sanctuary. It is this coercion that leads the rural population, in order better to defend itself, to gather within the framework of the parish, where different hamlets join forces in a closer community, the guardian of the *coutumes*. This collectivity of the village, that other unit basic to the French countryside, germ of the present-day *commune*, the organ of resistance to the lords' demands, acquires form and texture around the church, the place of refuge. The establishment of the manor, through the net of exactions that spares the fortunes of the nobility but transfers into the lord's hands a good part of the peasants' small profits, is another means of accentuating the differences in position within the economic hierarchy. It raises the lord of a castle even higher over the others and, more important, it isolates more than ever the small knightly élite from the mass of backward people. . . .

The knights . . . are a closed group: everything converged then to make knightly rank and its privileges a condition handed down from father to son, and to make that limited élite of rich people and warriors an inherited society. The first cause of this was the extreme shrinking of the economy, which made appreciable variations in individual fortunes impossible, except in very rare instances, and maintained, from one generation to the next, an equal distance among the various family inheritances. Secondly, the exactions of the chatelain placed a new obstacle in the way of the peasants' chances of enriching themselves. Third, the strength of blood ties and the intimate solidarity of kinship prohibited the very thought that, at the father's death, the son, even though impoverished, might lose the high rank he had shared during his father's lifetime. Fourth, the multiplicity of family alliances set up an extremely effective barrier to all surreptitious social advancement, in that milieu where lasting changes of position were rare and where everyone knew his neighbor's genealogy and situation. Fifth, class consciousness was formed early and aroused scorn for all those who were not members of the class by birth. And finally, there was the vigilance of those who held the coercive power and who were directly concerned that few newcomers share the privileges and exemptions of the *coutumes*. In contrast to England, for example, or the countries of the Empire, knighthood in France is, beginning in the eleventh century, a nobility in the strictest sense of the term—a normally hereditary condition. ✷

7. BRYCE D. LYON

FROM Bryce D. Lyon, *From Fief to Indenture* (Cambridge: Harvard University Press, 1957), pp. 270–73.

This study of the *fief-rente* in the heartland of feudalism—England and the lands between the Loire and the Rhine—has necessarily been of a comparative nature in that the records of France, England, Germany, and the Low Countries were involved. From the relevant chancery, financial, legal, and military records it has emerged as a prominent institution with a character clearly delineated. Mitteis concluded that it was a completely new institution. Sczaniecki, though recognizing certain deviations from the ordinary fief, nevertheless contended that it was devoid of any originality. It was, according to him, modeled in almost all respects upon the ordinary fief. The traditional type of fief was indeed the model, but the fact that money rather than land was the foundation of the *fief-rente* made of it a new institution. To say that a man held land in fief was customarily to imply heritability; with the *fief-rente* life and provisional tenures prevailed. From region to region the application of the feudal incidents to the *fief-rente* varied; in none can it be asserted that the customary aids were applied. A *fief-rente* could be terminated at a moment's notice; an ordinary fief had to be confiscated with perhaps a war necessary to enforce the sentence. With the *fief-rente* such action was rarely taken. From even these few instances of juridical differences it is obvious that money set the *fief-rente* apart from the ordinary fief in the realm of feudal law. Money also brought to the *fief-rente* a fluidity unknown with the ordinary fief. No matter how great the distance between the lord and the man whose services were required, feudal relations were readily effected by means of the *fief-rente*. It is without exaggeration to say that fully half of the recipients of *fiefs-rentes* never saw their lords. One has but to recall the geographical dispersion of the vassals performing the political, diplomatic, and military services to understand how easily the *fief-rente* inaugurated and stretched the fabric of feudal relations. Practically all the *fiefs-rentes* granted by the English kings were to men on the Continent. The French kings conceded *fiefs-rentes* to men throughout France, the Low Countries, and Germany. In the Low Countries the *fief-rente* knew no boundaries except the English Channel and the North Sea; it crisscrossed the borders of the Low Country states and spilled into Germany and France. The German emperors, princes, and towns likewise crossed over borders, granting *fiefs-rentes* to Low Country nobles. The lord was limited as to the number of vassals he might have only by the amount of money at his disposal; the amount of land and the geographical location of lord and vassal were no longer restricting forces. But not all the advantages of the *fief-rente* fell to the lord. For the vassal it was a new means of augmenting an income which progressively decreased as his revenues from land shrank in value. It also provided employment of all sorts not only to feudal aristocrat but to men of the other estates. Whoever could offer military, political, and diplomatic services was a likely candidate for receiving a *fief-rente;* it would link lord to vassal by feudal bond and often, especially where military service was involved, would bring to the vassal, in addition to his yearly fee, war wages and other financial perquisites. Men performing diplomatic and political services for *fiefs-rentes* frequently received bonuses such as *dona* and were extended other considerations. Just as the pensions of the sixteenth, seventeenth, and eighteenth centuries kept the feudal aristocrat from bankruptcy, so the *fief-rente* in the Middle Ages gave him employment and helped to save him from financial ruin. Between the rigidity of the ordinary land fief and the malleability of the *fief-rente* there was a sharp difference. By introducing a flexibility into feudal tenure and relations, as well as by greatly multiplying the number of men and type of services that could be obtained through feudal custom, the *fief-rente* injected new vigor into feudalism and helped it to withstand for a longer time the ever new demands and situations brought about by the money economy.

The *fief-rente* varied in its use from area to area. The continental princes used it for political purposes much more than the English kings. As a diplomatic tool it was always of greater value to the French and English kings than to the German and Low Country princes. Its use to obtain castle-guard was almost exclusively limited to the Continent and predominated in Germany where this was practically the only type of military service acquired by it. On the Continent alone was it a means to secure strategic rights to castles. But in all western Europe princes granted *fiefs-rentes* to obtain service in the field. Relying most heavily upon the *fief-rente* for this form of service were the French and English kings; not far behind them were the most powerful of the Low Country princes. In spite of the varying political, diplomatic, and military emphasis put upon the *fief-rente* in each area, its pattern was fundamentally the same everywhere; there was not an English, French, German, or Flemish *fief-rente* that was a captive of political barriers. Rather the *fief-rente* was a western European institution whose value lay in its military role. It is difficult to understand the position of Sczaniecki, Mitteis, and Kienast when in no area of western Europe does the political and diplomatic evidence compare in bulk to the military evidence. In the evolution from military service provided by the traditional fief of land to non-feudal contractual service and finally to standing armies, the *fief-rente* had a place; it was the link between traditional feudalism and contractual military service.

But it is not enough to have shown what the *fief-rente* was or that it was prominent. A prominent feudal institution, yes, but even more it was a microcosm of the economic, political, and military evolution in western Europe between the eleventh and the fifteenth century; in it can be discerned the slow decline of feudalism in the face of the onrushing money economy and the replacement of feudalism by the new political, military, and social institutions rooted in a money economy instead of a natural economy. Barely existing in the tenth century when there was little money in circulation, but gradually increasing in numbers during the eleventh and twelfth centuries as the money economy spread and gained in rigor throughout western Europe, the *fief-rente* attained its apogee in the thirteenth and fourteenth centuries—a period when the money economy prevailed but had not yet completely routed feudalism. By the fifteenth century money had so antiquated feudal custom that the *fief-rente* virtually melted away. Money created and destroyed the *fief-rente* but did not alone completely control its fate. The *fief-rente* only flourished where feudalism was strong and knew a long tradition, as in the lands between the Loire and the Rhine, or where it had been successfully transplanted, as in the Latin States of the Crusaders. In an area such as southern Italy and

Sicily, which had never completely lost touch with money and where feudalism never became strong, the *fief-rente* failed to establish a beachhead. Born from a combination of feudalism and the money economy, the *fief-rente* depended upon both for its existence. Admittedly there were *fiefs-rentes* in kind, but if limited to this type, it would never have become a significant institution. In western Europe the money economy made possible the practice of granting annual incomes of money, but the tradition of strong feudal custom dictated that for a long period the principles of feudal tenure should be superimposed upon these incomes. When money had completely destroyed the hold of feudalism over men, feudal tenure fell away from these incomes and they became simply a non-feudal *rente*, a pension, an annuity, or a retaining fee. But let us not forget that the very money economy which eventually destroyed the traditional feudalism, and after it the *fief-rente*, paradoxically enabled feudalism to survive by means of the *fief-rente* far beyond the time when based solely upon land it would have ceased to exist. It is true that the traditional feudalism of land was teetering in the thirteenth century and was practically a vestigial system in the fourteenth, but in this same period feudalism, as represented and sustained by the *fief-rente*, was extremely virile. It will not do to have feudalism in its grave by the fourteenth century and to explain all the surviving feudal terminology as so much façade; the terminology pertaining to the *fief-rente* was real and meaningful. In the fourteenth century men did homage and fealty for *fiefs-rentes* and performed their feudal obligations; only in the fifteenth century did this cease. Into the early fifteenth century, at least, the feudalism of money had a vitality that must be recognized. No longer is it acceptable to look upon the decline and fall of feudalism as completed in the fourteenth century. ✻

Part 8

THE GREGORIAN REFORM

Every segment of Western history seems to have one or two themes so all-embracing and suggestive that when we examine them we are, in effect, plunging directly into a study of the society itself. The decline of Rome, the Reformation of the sixteenth century, and the French and Industrial Revolutions are all themes of this sort. In the case of medieval history, no development is more certain to illuminate the quintessence of medievalism than the Gregorian Reform. Explicitly and implicitly, the Gregorian Reform brings into play the manifold tensions and dimensions of medieval civilization, casting a wide and powerful searchlight on its fundamental features.

These brief introductory essays do not claim to be exhaustive. At this point, however, it would probably be helpful to spell out some of the reasons why the Gregorian Reform is such a rich and complex theme. The relationship between history and literature is a much debated subject; most people would agree that the practitioners of both are, by definition, concerned with the human personality as manifested in concrete, distinguishable individuals. Perhaps, then, we can explain the first attraction of the Gregorian Reform by noting that it contains complex, articulate, and powerful personalities. The dramatis personae reveal the full range of human character and emotion. One by one they appear on the stage: Peter Damian (or, in Italian, Damiani), the moderate mystic whose writings have been described as "a sort of barometric indicator of eleventh century attitudes"; Cardinal Humbert, the stern and learned author of *The Three Books against the Simoniacs*, one of the most influential and characteristic products of the Gregorian Reform; Pope Gregory VII, aggressive, intransigent, a "daemonic" revolutionary; and the shrewd and calculating Emperor Henry IV.

The confrontation between Emperor Henry and Pope Gregory at Canossa, January 21, 1077, was certainly dramatic, but it involved much more than a clash between powerful individuals. Each represented a universal institution in a fragmented Europe. The line between the Empire and the Papacy had never been clearly drawn and because of this ambiguity concerning their proper spheres of jurisdiction, encroachments were inevitable. As long as one of them was weak and forced into subservience, a modus vivendi could be established. But when both institutions were headed by vigorous and ambitious men—which is what happened with Henry and Gregory—trouble could be expected. Movement on one side implied a response on the other. Canossa was just one highlight in the struggle between Empire and Papacy, a struggle made more dramatic by the fact that it is uncertain which one emerged the real victor.

Significant reforms within the Church led unavoidably to a conflict with the Emperor, and they also entailed a reexamination of the fundamental ideology of medieval Europe. In one sense, the issue in their quarrel was a traditional one in the Christian Church: broadly formulated it concerned the dichotomy between church and state, between the city of God and the city of man. However, the nature of the Church was such that ideological questions became involved in the struggle as well. A ubiquitous institution cannot alter part of its posture without generating a series of unexpected and perhaps undesirable reverberations. The contemporary example of the ecumenical movement launched by Pope John XXIII illustrates the truth of this principle.

Another reason why the Gregorian Reform is such a fascinating and intricate subject is that it coincided with other manifestations of change. There were three significant developments in eleventh-century Europe aside from the Gregorian Reform. First, there was the expansion of commerce and the rise of urban communes. These developments reshaped the texture of the medieval world in a variety of ways. Commercial expansion meant greater contact between the disparate and isolated parts of Europe, and it set in motion the long process of transforming this predominantly agricultural society. In their quest for autonomy, the new urban communes challenged the authority of the Church and created a climate which fostered intense anticlericalism.

It was also in the eleventh century that the Normans established in England the first really cohesive, centralized medieval monarchy. The growth of feudal monarchies was slow and halting, but eventually they would do battle with the imperial and papal monarchies in a confrontation which plays a large part in the history of later medieval Europe. Finally, this is

The Gregorian Reform

the century we associate with the beginnings of the Crusades, those aggressive expeditions which reveal a Europe on the move, a Europe breaking out of its bonds. The post-Gregorian Papacy was deeply involved in the Crusades, and it is legitimate to ask if this involvement was not yet another aspect of the Gregorian Reform.

However we explain the relationship between these phenomena and the Gregorian Reform, it is at least clear that the Gregorian Reform was not an isolated example of change and dynamism and that it must be anchored to its historical setting. Seen in this light, we can understand why the Gregorian Reform continues to intrigue all students of medieval Europe.

The following selections illustrate two broadly defined approaches to the Gregorian Reform, suggesting the varieties of opinion within each. The two views may be described as "contextual" and "personnelist." The "contextual" method seeks to understand the Gregorian Reform in terms of its historical setting. Though the context may be widely or narrowly defined, there is always the underlying assumption that this movement should be seen as something much more significant than a squabble over appointing ecclesiastics. The "personnelist" approach focuses on the great protagonists—usually Pope Gregory VII; it attempts to come to grips with this complex movement through a sensitive and detailed analysis of the key personalities. Needless to say, these two approaches are not mutually exclusive. What is involved here is simply a question of emphasis, but, as we have seen before in this book, emphasis is an extremely important ingredient in shaping historical interpretation.

The first seven selections show the range covered by the "contextual" method. Thus the Gregorian Reform is explicated in terms of politics (Johannes Haller and Geoffrey Barraclough), economic interests (James Westfall Thompson), monasticism (David Knowles), political thought (Walter Ullmann), and the state of the clergy (Christopher Brooke). Perhaps the most suggestive interpretation—certainly an extremely influential interpretation—is that advanced by the German historian Gerd Tellenbach; it warrants a closer look.

Tellenbach is one of the most distinguished representatives of a group of twentieth-century historians who have sought to transcend what they feel is a limiting provincialism in the previous historiography and to develop a view of the Gregorian Reform as something approximating a revolution, a reordering of the total structure of Christian society. This attempted revision is predicated on the widest possible view of European history. Christian history in the eleventh century is placed in the context of the previous ten centuries. Thus, Tellenbach, according to R. F. Bennett, "distinguishes three main [historic] attitudes on the part of the

Church: (i) the ascetic, based on withdrawal from the world; (ii) the sacerdotal, based on conversion of the world by the priestly hierarchy; (iii) the monarchic, based on the conversion of the world by the action of a divinely-instituted kingship. . . ." And it was precisely because he was intent on pursuing the sacerdotal approach to its logical extension that Pope Gregory generated profound changes in the Christian community, a community coterminous with the medieval world.

In the last two selections the emphasis is on personality. In the J. P. Whitney selection, Pope Gregory emerges as a pragmatist with principles. "The course he took was that which, given the circumstances and the men he dealt with, was the most likely to bring his principles into practice." The brilliant Oxford medievalist R. W. Southern, whose book *The Making of the Middle Ages* is one of the most exciting works on medieval history published in recent years, points to the impact of Rome on Gregory's character. Once again we come back to those eternal questions in the study of history: How does man influence the course of history? And how is man shaped by his history?

1. JOHANNES HALLER

FROM Johannes Haller, *The Epochs of German History* (London: George Routledge & Sons, Ltd., 1930), pp. 30–35.

But in the latter half of the eleventh century a movement of reform began to make itself felt, issuing primarily from eastern France and Lorraine. It reached its flood tide in Germany and Italy when Henry III (1030–1056) took it under his care. Personally he was stirred by the new religious conception; as a ruler he felt it his duty to purify the church. But he was not in the least disposed to sacrifice any part of his own power to secure that end. The very fact of his reforming the church was to show that he was its supreme ruler; the very purpose of the reform was to establish his dominance and to place the church, the whole Catholic Church, with all its great moral and material resources, at the service of the German Emperor. With this idea in his mind he was not content simply with local measures, with the reforms of individual bishoprics or monasteries often witnessed before; he struck straight at the source, Rome. He would reform the Papacy in the spirit of the new age, and the Papacy itself should then reform the entire church.

The conditions in Rome called aloud for intervention. Things had reached such a pass that three pretenders were contesting the Papal chair, and none of them could truly be said to be in possession when in 1046 Henry III appeared in Italy. He promptly set aside all three, and so completely did he control the situation that no one disputed his action. The clergy and the people of Rome actually conferred on him the right, whenever the Papal chair should fall vacant, to nominate the new occupant for their election, as had been done by Otto I and later by Otto III.

In the use which Henry made of this right he clearly revealed his intentions. He nominated a German bishop; on the death of this bishop shortly after he again nominated a German bishop, and again and yet again. Four times in succession on his injunction German bishops were made Popes.

The intention was unmistakable: the Roman Church was to be incorporated in the German Empire as thoroughly as any bishopric north of the Alps. There could be no better guarantee of the German Emperor's mastery of Rome. The system of Otto I had shown its weaknesses. Only too frequently had Roman citizens failed him as Popes, or the German party been defeated in the Papal elections, and then the German Emperor had had to resort to armed intervention. That was now no longer to be feared.

The German Pope, who actually owed his elevation to the Emperor, was a good guarantee for the submissiveness of the capital.

Yet more: a German Pope, who felt himself the friend and servant of the Emperor, if not actually his tool, since he was lost without Imperial protection, necessarily worked throughout the world in Germany's interests. If he reformed the western churches and subjected them to Rome's direct control, it could be depended on that German interests would not suffer. Through the Pope as his agent, almost his deputy, the Emperor controlled Italy as never before. Through the Pope he could make his influence felt in neighbouring countries, in France, Scandinavia, Poland, Hungary. A German Papacy as the keystone of the German Imperial power—that meant the final achievement of German hegemony in the west. It was a clear and well thought out system, as simple as it was effective.

But no long life was granted it. The premature death of the Emperor in 1056, at scarcely forty years of age, wrecked it. The incapable and unscrupulous men who governed during the minority of Henry IV allowed the creation of the great Emperor to fall to pieces and degenerate into its opposite.

The reform of the Roman Church had been embarked on under German Popes, but the largest share in it had been taken by French monks. In Germany it would scarcely have been possible to find men of the required calibre in sufficient numbers; they had to be summoned from the home of reform, from Lorraine and Burgundy. These men could not be expected to have anything but distaste for the other aspect of their mission, the buttressing of the German imperial power. Their dream was no longer merely of the purification of the church, but of its liberation from all secular domination. The weakness of the imperial regency gave them a welcome opportunity. It was unable even to offer protection against the attempts which the Romans did not fail to make to rid themselves of domineering foreign ecclesiastics. In Rome men soon ceased to trouble about the German king and his guardians; they looked for help from quarters nearer at hand, from the rulers of Italy.

First and foremost there was the Margrave of Tuscany, Godfrey, born a Duke of Lorraine, who had arrived at his Margraviate through his marriage with the heiress of Tuscany. He had been constantly at issue with Henry III, and since the Emperor's death had been the unchallenged master of Tuscany and the northern slopes of the Apennines as far as Mantua. He, his wife Beatrice, and later their daughter Matilda, placed all their resources at the service of the reformed Roman Church—a development in no way to the profit of the German Emperor. The Emperor's rule had rested on the support of the bishops; with it he had held the secular princes in subjection. Now a secular princely house had risen to be the controlling power in central Italy.

Another force struck in Lombardy at the basis of the German domination, a pietistic popular revolt in the towns against the way of life of the bishops. The town populations arose *en masse*, under the banner of church reform and with religious slogans directed against the immoral priests, but in reality against the domination of Frankish and Lombard nobles and of bishops who served the German king. The revolt had the support and blessing of Rome, and the Lombard bishops, instead of being, as formerly, pillars of the German rule, now called for the king's help in their struggle to maintain their position, which they could not hold unaided.

A rival princely power established in Tuscany, and in Lombardy the bishops who had been the support of the German throne tottering—the outlook was sombre. Yet a third opponent came on the scene, to become in time the most dangerous—the Normans in southern Italy. The Normans had been arriving in Italy since the beginning of the century as mercenaries, they had settled in it, their number had been rapidly increased by camp followers and partisans; they had become invaders and conquerors, and since about 1050 almost the whole of southern Italy had fallen piece by piece into their hands. Already it was clear that the whole south would ere long be definitely in their power. Unconquerable at arms, they were the plague of the land and a permanent menace to their neighbours, including the Papal State. Pope Leo IX, the Alsatian, had tasted their quality when he marched against them with German troops in 1053. He was routed and taken prisoner and had to accept the victors' terms in order to regain his freedom.

Then came a development of far-reaching significance, clearly indicating the new policy adopted by Rome after Henry III's death. The Pope not merely gave up the struggle against the Normans but allied himself with them. In 1059 the two principal Norman chiefs, Richard of Capua and Robert of Apulia, did homage as vassals to St. Peter, and held as their fiefs from him all their existing and future conquests—Apulia, Calabria, Sicily. The Pope thus became suzerain of the whole of southern Italy, and won for himself a personal bodyguard of the best troops of the time. With these new gains he turned against the German imperial power: he no longer needed it; he was independent. The Normans at his side were a better protection and support than the distant German king; if need were they could even be used against the latter. The new feudal overlordship of St. Peter also fitted ill with the circumstance that since Otto I and Charlemagne the interior of southern Italy, the old Lombard principality of Benevento, had recognized the overlordship of the Emperor. Here the interests and claims of Empire and church, Emperor and Pope, came from 1059 onwards plainly into conflict.

In another respect too the year 1059 marks an epoch in the relations between the two powers. In this year a synod was held in Rome. It was presided over by Pope Nicholas II, a Frenchman and a favourite of Godfrey of Tuscany. The Pope had successfully held his own in face of opposition from the Romans, not without a struggle, but without help from the Germans. Among other things the assembly adopted a resolution on the method of Papal elections, the provisions of which all reflected the change that had come. The assembly did not venture entirely to ignore the inherited right of Henry IV to nominate candidates for the Papacy, but this provision was relegated to a subsidiary clause as a purely formal reservation. It was intended that the controlling influence of the German crown over the Papal election should in actual fact come to an end, and this it did; never after 1059 did a German ruler successfully bring it to bear. The epoch of the German supremacy over Rome and the church was over.

Another resolution of the same synod cast its shadow over the future: it was resolved that it should be forbidden to receive a church from the hands of a layman. This, if it was carried out, meant a fundamental and universal revolution, for it denied the traditional and acknowledged right of the laity to dispose of churches which it had founded and built. So far as the German king was concerned, it struck at the basis of his power. If the king could no longer dispose of the bishoprics and monasteries in his realm, no longer invest his bishops and abbots with their office, he was reduced to the state of a man who has had his right arm and his right leg taken off. That was entirely unacceptable. Against this innovation the German crown could only fight to its last man; it was fighting for its existence.

The synodal decree of 1059, the first ban on "investiture by laymen," remained at first a dead letter; nowhere was it acted on. But its shadow lay over the future. Sooner or later there was bound to come open warfare between kingdom and church, Empire and Papacy.

It came when in 1073 Gregory VII was raised to the Papal chair. To the ideas which had obtained sway over the Roman Church before his time, the ideas of reform and liberation, he added a third: the dominion of the church over the world. Earth as well as heaven belonged literally to the apostolic princes. Theirs was the disposal of all earthly ownership and dominion; they gave and took away according to men's deserts; kings and princes were bound to obey them and their deputy on earth, the Pope, and were at law his vassals and liegemen. Gregory struggled with fierce energy, with passionate eagerness to establish these claims. When he demanded the universal recognition of the ban on investiture, even from the German king, the latent conflict became an open one.

Henry IV had now come to man's estate, and had set to work to restore his royal authority. He had just victoriously quelled a Saxon revolt (1075) when, in the exercise of his traditional right of investiture in the Archbishopric of Milan, he encountered the resistance of the Pope, who reproached him with disobedience and threatened him with the loss of his crown. Over-estimating the strength of his position, the king went so far as to secure the deposition of the Pope by a synod of the German bishops at Worms, at the end of January, 1076. Gregory answered by deposing the king in turn, and excommunicating him. It was soon revealed who was the stronger. Not merely did the Saxon revolt flare up again, but the German dukes saw their opportunity to bring down this monarch who was becoming all too powerful. They leagued themselves with the Pope. More than ever the issue lay with the bishops. A small section of them, imbued with French ideas, had sided with Gregory from the beginning; the majority had remained true to the king. But to fight an open war against the Pope, their ecclesiastical suzerain, was more than even the loyalists could venture on. Henry then decided, in order to split the hostile coalition and so to avert the danger of a rival monarch being declared, to make his submission to the church. At the end of January, 1077, he unexpectedly met the Pope at Canossa on his way to Germany. Here, at the gates of Canossa, Henry did penance in his own person. So he compelled Gregory to absolve him and readmit him to the church. Thus he was again competent to rule. His chief aim he had not realized; in March the rebellious princes produced a rival king. But their faction was sufficiently weakened to enable Henry to embark on the struggle for the crown with fair prospects. One claimant after another failed against him. Finally, in March, 1080, Gregory himself renewed hostilities against him, and for the second time pronounced Henry deposed and excommunicated. The king retorted by inducing the German and Lombard bishops to nominate a rival Pope, to whom he gave armed support. He laid repeated siege to Rome, and in 1084 captured the city and was crowned Emperor. The belated arrival of the Normans compelled him to retreat; but Gregory too failed to hold the city. The Pope went to the south in the train of his liberators, and here in the following year (1085), alone, abandoned, almost forgotten, he died at Salerno. He had failed. �֍

2. GEOFFREY BARRACLOUGH

FROM Geoffrey Barraclough, *The Origins of Modern Germany* (Oxford: Basil Blackwell, 1946), pp. 101–7.

The remarkable recovery of Germany under the Saxon and Salian emperors, achieved in large measure through the willing co-operation of kings and churchmen, had rescued the Church from the heavy hand of the lay princes and built up its power and wealth and influence. Rulers like Henry II and Henry III had unhesitatingly turned from the immediate task of preserving royal authority to the further tasks of reform and the propagation of Christian culture which were incumbent on a 'just king'. They had willingly used their royal authority for the benefit of the Church, never doubting that such a use of authority was, in the Church's eyes, 'just' and 'righteous'. They had called on bishops and abbots to assist them in their task, and the clergy, impelled not merely by a sense of the solidarity of its own interests with those of the crown, but also and still more by a belief in the 'justice' of the king's control of Church and State, had willingly co-operated. They had accepted the king as the divinely appointed 'ruler' of the Church, as the *rex et sacerdos*, marked out by the sacred oil of unction as God's vicar on earth; and they looked to the monarch for leadership, and found in him a leader in the task of eradicating abuse and establishing a Christian society.

Suddenly, in 1073, with the election of Gregory VII to the Holy See, this whole conception of the relationship of Church and State, and with it the whole existing scheme of society, was challenged. It was challenged in the name of reform by a papacy which set out (in the words of an Italian bishop of the period) to champion lost laws which should be revived, against customs which had become corruptions. Whether the needs of reform required a revolutionary attack on the existing social and political order is one of the eternally debatable questions of history. There were, even among the most ardent reformers, many sincere and distinguished churchmen who were prepared to deny it and to oppose Gregory VII and his programme; they held that the Church's task was moral regeneration, not a re-ordering of the fundamental laws and principles of society, and on a lower and more practical plane they were unwilling to forgo the help which the monarchy could give to the reforming party. They appreciated the positive benefits of a strong monarchy in a corrupt, materialist society, and perceived that a major political conflict would compromise the true objects of reform. But the tide was against them, and when their leader, the great Peter Damiani, cardinal-bishop of Ostia, died in 1072, the Gregorian party won the upper hand. From the very beginning of his pontificate—indeed, from the remote days when he accompanied Pope Gregory VI into exile and when, under Alexander II (1061–1073), he became a more influential figure at the papal Curia than the pope himself—Gregory was a determined opponent of the German emperors, and seems to have made up his mind that the only way to bring the work of reform to completion was to overturn the old order, in which abuse and disorder had grown rife, and to remodel society on principles derived from a study of the old law and canons of the Church. Before he became pope, he urged Deusdedit and Damiani (and doubtless others) to search the libraries and bring together all decretals, canons and passages from historians setting forth the powers of the Holy See: after he became pope he distilled what he considered the essence of this research into twenty-seven propositions, famous as the *Dictatus papae*. Like all revolutionaries he convinced himself that he was only restoring the old law; but the principles he enunciated fell like a bombshell on the traditional thought of the age, which they challenged at every turn. Every sentence of the *Dictatus papae*, drawn up by Gregory in 1075, implies a programme; but none is more astounding than the curt statement that the pope may lawfully depose emperors. Gregory—'the great innovator, who stood quite alone'—was setting out on new and perilous paths.

After 1073, therefore, the political wing of the reform party assumed control. Many factors contributed to give it predominance, and thus to bring about open conflict with the empire. In the first place, we may recall the work of Henry III in freeing the papacy from the control of Roman factions and thus enabling it to resume its functions as the head of an oecumenical church. The popes introduced by Henry restored the prestige of the papacy in Europe, and his support enabled them to extend their field of action. He deliberately made the papacy a fit instrument for carrying out the work of reform to which he was devoted, and through the popes appointed with his support he brought it into contact with the main currents of reform, which had sprung up, independent of the papacy, in the western fastnesses of his empire, in Burgundy and Lorraine. Through Leo IX (1049–1054) the reform movement of Cluny found its way to Rome—a movement which was already pursuing objects less exclusively religious than the regeneration of monastic life. The Cluniac aim of freeing the churches, particularly monastic churches, from direct lay control—an aim expressed in the programme of 'free election'—was soon merged in a policy of raising the standards of lay society itself, because it was evident that the freedom of religious houses from aristocratic exploitation and control could never be assured unless lay society itself were purified and the worst excesses of feudalism eradicated. Hence it was through the action of Cluniac abbots and bishops that the Truce of God, the 'peace movement', was introduced at the end of the tenth century as a means of combatting feudal disorder which was particularly rampant in the old lands of the Middle kingdom, in Burgundy and Lorraine, where (in contrast with Germany) imperial rule was little more than nominal. The object was to establish a new, more peaceful social order, in which the 'liberty' which the churches claimed would be secure; and in this sense there is at least an element of truth in the view that the Cluniac movement was, from its inception, a political movement. But these political objectives did not involve hostility to the empire, or to the principles of imperial government, and it was only when Cluniac ideas and principles were adopted by the papacy and remoulded in combination with other elements of papal policy that the Cluniac movement and its off-shoots, of which the most important was Hirsau in southern Germany, became a formidable political power directed against the German monarchy. Under Gregory VII, although the leaders of the Cluniac movement still maintained a mediating position between pope and emperor, the monks and disciples of Cluny and Hirsau were the shock-troops of the papal army, the executants of papal orders, the protagonists of papal authority.

It was the pontificate of Leo IX (1049–1054) which saw the first rapid advance in the reconstruction of papal authority. Three times crossing the Alps to France and Germany, and holding synod after synod at which he legislated against abuse, Leo made the papal headship a reality. Already in 1049 at the synod of Reims he insisted on the requirement of canonical election to ecclesiastical offices. Everywhere he went he received the homage of bishops, thus demonstrating papal primacy in spite of the opposition of metropolitans, who refused to admit that the bishop of Rome had any right to interfere in the administration of their provinces. At the same time he gave the Roman Curia an international complexion corresponding to its oecumenic claims, by elevating non-Italians—chiefly his fellow-countrymen from Lorraine—to the cardinalate. Continuous control of the provinces was inaugurated by the frequent dispatch of cardinal-legates to inspect and reform, while bishops were pressed to visit the Holy See. Thus the foundations of the papal monarchy were laid. But it was the radical change in the political situation after Henry III's death in 1056 which enabled the papacy to consolidate its position. The succession of a minor and the regency of the Empress Agnes immediately resulted in a disastrous weakening of German power in Italy, and although the papacy still had to contend with the Roman factions, which again began to raise their heads, and with Duke Godfrey of Lorraine, who threatened to enthral it, it was quick to profit from the change of circumstances. When the German pope, Victor II, the last of Henry III's candidates, died in 1057 and was replaced by Godfrey of Lorraine's brother, Stephen IX, the only acknowledgement of the old imperial right of confirmation was the dispatch to Germany of a belated embassy after the pope had already been consecrated. Two years later the procedure for papal elections was defined and remodelled, electoral rights being for practical purposes placed in the hands of the cardinals. This change was intended primarily to free the papacy from dependence on the Roman mob, which had intervened on the death of Stephen IX in 1058; but it could be, and was, used also against the emperor and the imperial government, whose rights were whittled away; for although a vague personal right of confirmation was reserved for Henry IV, it was rendered meaningless by a decision empowering the person elected to exercise all the prerogatives of pope from the moment of his election. Thus the choice of the pope was made the affair of the cardinals, who were already an international body with little sympathy for the German government. The danger was quickly perceived at the imperial court, and on the death of Pope Nicholas II in 1061 a last attempt was made to preserve imperial rights. Asked by the Roman nobles to nominate a successor, the empress designated Bishop Cadalus of Parma, who was elected by German and Lombard bishops at a synod at Basel; but in the meantime the reform party, without consulting the imperial government, had elected Bishop Anselm of Lucca, a protégé of Godfrey of Lorraine, as Alexander II. The result was a schism, which continued until Cadalus' death in 1072; but already by 1064 the course of events in Germany had broken imperial resistance. The abduction of Henry IV by the princes at Kaiserswert in 1062, and the collapse of the regency government brought new powers into the saddle: Anno of Cologne, the bitter opponent of Adalbert of Bremen and therefore of imperial policy, went over to the reform party and under his influence a synod held at Mantua in 1064 decided in favour of Alexander II.

Thus the minority of Henry IV and the weakness and embarrassments of the regency compromised German government to such a degree that the papacy was able to carry through a revolutionary reorganization almost without protest and to emancipate the Roman church from imperial and German influence. Deprived of effective imperial support the bishops of Germany and Lombardy were left to fight in isolation against the centralizing policy of the papacy which threatened to sweep away their privileges and independence. They saw themselves subjected to legates, who were sent out from Rome to enforce clerical celibacy and repress simony;

and many of the most distinguished prelates, including Anno of Cologne himself, were summoned to Rome to answer for their actions. The Lateran Council of 1059 had attacked lay investiture, and the radical wing of the reform party already condemned all forms of lay investiture as simony, thus laying an axe at the roots of the established connexion between Church and State and at the system by which the monarchy, in Germany and in Lombardy, governed by entrusting counties and jurisdictions to carefully selected bishops. But conditions during Henry IV's minority were manifestly exceptional, and it was obvious that the papacy had to expect an imperial attempt to recover its lost rights as soon as Henry IV was firmly established in the saddle. To meet this contingency it needed allies, just as it needed allies within the Church against the bishops, whom a very evident community of interests drove into the royal camp. The earliest, as we have seen, was Duke Godfrey of Lorraine, whose power in Tuscany was a constant though dangerous bulwark of the papacy, ever threatening to turn protection into domination. Equally dangerous was the alliance with the Normans, formed in 1059 at the very moment when Nicholas II's decree governing papal elections and the prohibition of lay investiture challenged the German monarchy. But both alliances helped the reform party to maintain its position, and it was the troops of Godfrey and the Normans which assured Alexander II's victory over his rival, Cadalus. In Germany, the papacy ever since the days of Leo IX had been in contact with the south German nobility, who saw in the reform programme—particularly in the demand for 'free election'—a useful vehicle for the assertion of their rights against the centralizing policy of the monarchy. The German nobility, particularly in the west and in the south, quickly realized the advantages to be gained from support of the reform movement, and with their backing Cluniac influence spread with amazing rapidity during the decade following the introduction of Cluniac monks at St. Blasien in the Black Forest in 1060 and the reform of Hirsau about 1066. The result was the rapid propagation in Germany of a religious movement which owed its progress to the papacy and the princes, not to the empire, and which was organized with a maximum of cohesion since all new and reformed foundations received the status of priories, over which the abbot of Cluny retained control, without episcopal interference; for the papacy had granted Cluny exemption from the authority of any bishop save the bishop of Rome. This close-knit organization was of enormous advantage to the papacy. Dependent on papal prerogative for its autonomy, Cluny led the way in effective centralization in the western Church, and its monks were the best propagandists and champions of papal supremacy, particularly against the bishops who regarded the autonomy of the reformed monasteries as an encroachment on their canonical rights. Against the Lombard bishops, on the other hand, the papacy did not hesitate to ally with the social classes whose opposition to the episcopacy had introduced a new element of discord into Italian life during the past fifty or sixty years—an alliance with the 'mob' which provoked violent disapproval. In Milan, in particular, the so-called 'Patarini' stood out as champions of 'free election', hoping to obtain the chief see of the north for one of their own number, and thus to secure greater power for the feudatories in the administration of Milanese fiefs and territories. Their alliance with and formal recognition by the papacy reached back to 1059, and the question of Milan, where a 'Patarine' and an imperial bishop faced each other in bitter hostility, was the major issue between Henry IV and Gregory VII, after the latter's election to the Holy See in 1073. It was the test case which led to the outbreak of the conflict between Church and State. ✲

3. JAMES WESTFALL THOMPSON

FROM James Westfall Thompson, *Feudal Germany* (Chicago: University of Chicago Press, 1928), pp. 125–28.

History affords few more striking examples of revolutionary change than the contrast between the relations of the German crown, the German church, and the papacy in Saxon (919–1024) and Salian (1024–1125) times. Under the Saxon emperors the church was the friend and ally of the dynasty. This good relation became somewhat strained under Conrad II and Henry III, the first Salians, and under the last two Salian rulers, Henry IV and Henry V, the German church in large part, and the papacy wholly, were the implacable foe of the emperors and strove with might and main to compass the destruction of the German crown.

The conflict between Henry IV and Gregory VII has usually been portrayed with the dramatic grandeur of a Greek tragedy. Dramatic qualities and dramatic personalities that struggle certainly possessed. But in general its history has been pitched upon too high a plane. The character of Hildebrand is one of the most complex and difficult to understand in all history. He was at once a superlative idealist imbued with the Augustinian dream of a world-church supreme over a world-state, and a shrewd politician. Such a man is rarely always consistent in his conduct. Depending upon mood or circumstance he sometimes responds to one motive or stimulus, sometimes to another. It is the endeavor of this chapter to show that the root of the struggle between Gregory VII and Henry IV was an economic one; that the immediate and fundamental, though carefully concealed, purpose of the papacy was to acquire complete proprietary control of the German church (indeed the church throughout all Europe); and that the Cluny reform was sedulously propagated as a means to that end. Karl Wilhelm Nitzsch (1818–80) in his *Geschichte des deutschen Volkes* was the first who discerned this factor in the war of investiture. Since his death other scholars, in many monographs, have widened the field which he first tilled, and the enormous influence of the proprietary interests of the German church upon the history of the medieval empire has been abundantly demonstrated.

One of the most certain achievements of modern historical research is the proof which precludes denial of the interrelation of all the facts and forces of an epoch. The war of investiture cannot be rightly understood except in the light of the economic and social history of Germany in the tenth and eleventh centuries. The root of the problem between church and state in the Middle Ages, and the chief root of the evil in the church, was its immense landed wealth. Between the alternative of renouncing her feudal revenues, her temporalities, her privileges, her political power, and so seeking deliverance from secular control, and the alternative of keeping her temporalities and yet securing freedom from the authority of the state by crushing the state, the church did not hesitate. She chose the latter course, and the identification of the Cluny reform with the papal power by Hildebrand went far toward making the aspiration a reality.

Henry IV, when he reached his majority, was not hostile to the reform. If the issue between him and Gregory VII had been one merely of traffic in church dignities and the celibacy of the priest class, the rupture between emperor and pope would probably never have come to pass. There is no reason to doubt Henry IV's sincerity when in 1082 at Milan he took an oath not to practice simony, and when, in 1083, his anti-pope Clement III urged the clergy to live in chastity—and that at the very moment when Gregory VII had begun to waver upon the question of celibacy owing to the adverse situation in which he found himself. All these issues were minor ones between emperor and pope. Much smoke was raised over them at times, but there was really little fire in them.

The real issue was otherwise: the aspiration of Gregory VII for universal rule over both church and state, his passion for wealth and power, his pretentions to the right to set up and dethrone kings—these were the marrow of the conflict. In giving a new and formidable connotation to the word "simony," in dissolving the tie of fidelity and investiture which bound the German clergy to the king, Gregory VII attempted to cut the very nerves of the Salian monarchy. It is true that much of the property of bishoprics and abbeys was considered as royal property; but the church derived enormous benefit from the possession of it nevertheless, in spite of heavy political, financial, and military burdens imposed upon its clergy. The benefits resulting from the arrangement were worth the price exacted, as most of the German bishops perceived, and accordingly advocated the king's cause instead of that of the pope.

The war of investiture was a maze of cross- and counter-currents. While the struggles between emperor and pope and between the German crown and the rebellious Saxons were the two main streams, the strife between the bishops and the abbots was no unimportant chapter. The feud between the "regulars" and the "seculars," as we have seen, was an old one. The monasteries for centuries had chafed under the superior jurisdiction of the bishops, and the papacy had developed a lucrative trade in selling them exemptions from episcopal authority. The German kings, too, had always sustained the bishops against the monks. Naturally most of the monasteries, except conservative ones like St. Gall and Lorsch, supported the Cluny reform as a means of emancipation from both the episcopate and the crown. �֍

4. DAVID KNOWLES

FROM David Knowles, *The Monastic Orders in England* (Cambridge: Cambridge University Press, 1940), pp. 191–97.

. . . Since the decline of the ancient civilization, the spiritual and intellectual revivals in the West had been regional in origin and scope; even that under Charlemagne is scarcely an exception to the rule. In England, the ages of Alfred and of Edgar are examples of such a rebirth, but the most striking of all is also the last in point of time, the intense development within the ring-fence of the Norman territories. This, indeed, which has too often been studied in isolation, could only have reached such a perfection because the minds of the men who moulded it belonged to a new age, and the very decades which witnessed the evolution of this last great self-sufficient, self-contained *Landeskirche* saw also the growth of a new culture which transcended the bounds of kingdoms and duchies, and of minds capable of grasping and applying principles of wide and unified government. In monastic history, as in the history of learning and of the papacy, this new life showed itself first in numberless isolated strivings towards an ideal imperfectly grasped, and next in a series of attempts, growing more and more successful, to embody this ideal in an institution whose influence should reach beyond the nation to all Christendom. Alike in its spiritual, intellectual and political manifestations, this renaissance is clearly distinguishable from the smaller movements that had gone before by two characteristics—an increased intensity and clarity of vision, and a new appreciation of the legacy of the distant past. Just as in dialectic and theology minds such as those of Anselm and Abelard were of a calibre and temper that had not been seen for centuries, and just as the civilians, canonists and philosophers went back to Justinian, Gelasius, Plato and Aristotle for foundations on which to build, so in the circles of monastic reform a Peter Damian, a Romuald and a Stephen Harding had a clarity of vision and a resolution of aim wholly different from those of Odilo, Dunstan or William of Dijon, and consciously turned back to the past, as seen either in the bare text of the Rule of St Benedict, or in the earlier doctrine of the deserts of Egypt and Syria.

Seen in a bird's-eye view the new monastic movement falls quite clearly into two great tides, each having its rise in Italy and flowing north, separated by an interval such that when the first is reaching northern France the second is in flood south of the Alps. In the first, individuals or small groups leave the world, or long-established monasteries, to live under conditions of extreme simplicity either as hermits or in groups under no supreme authority; in the second, a series of attempts is made to organize a new form of life, more solitary and more austere than contemporary monasticism, at first informally, under the authority of a single leader, later more definitively under a written rule and within a framework sanctioned by Rome. Logically regarded, the first tide should have merged into the second, and this did indeed often come to pass, but very often the individual ventures died away without fruit, and not infrequently, as it were in the gap between the tides, even the most earnest of the community ventures reverted to type after a period of life in isolation, and became new centres of normal black monk life. Such was the case at Cava in Italy; such, as we have seen, was the course taken by Bec in Normandy, and Jarrow, Whitby, Selby and Malvern in England.

The new monastic movement, considered as a historical phenomenon, had its origin in Italy a little before the year 1000. Italy always a land of many cities and of wild but habitable mountainous districts, had in the fifth and sixth centuries been a land of hermits. Existing before St Benedict and surviving the cenobite call of the Rule, the race had perhaps never wholly died out, even in the north and centre of the peninsula, and in the south, which still formed part of the Byzantine Empire, anchorites and Basilian monks continued to live in considerable numbers. At the end of the tenth century, a time of decadence in the social life of the cities of Lombardy and among the clergy high and low, preachers of penance and the eremitical life began to appear afresh. The revival which they heralded had a twofold current; there was the call to a solitary, penitential life, and the conscious recall to the spiritual legacy of the East.

One of the first who revived the memory of the past in central Italy was St Nilus (c. 910–1005). A Calabrian by birth, familiar with the Greek Fathers and monastic saints, and himself of austere life, he visited Cassino and Rome and ultimately founded the Basilian monastery of Grottaferrata, which still exists on the slopes of the Alban Hills within sight of the papal city. He was only one of many disseminators of Greek traditions at the time, for the Turkish invasion of Asia Minor sent large numbers of refugee bishops and monks to Europe, who settled in north Italy and southern France, especially near Dijon and Lyons, and even penetrated to England.

The other, more eremitical, movement may count as its first important figure St Romuald of Ravenna (c. 950–1027). Although we have the advantage of possessing a life of Romuald written within a few years of his death by his great disciple, Peter Damian, the chronology of his career is highly uncertain. He belongs to that large group of reformers, almost peculiar to the eleventh century, who after beginning the religious life in some old-established monastery, left the old ways in search of greater solitude and severity and passed many years of wandering in which they influenced several groups of disciples, dying at last without leaving any fixed or permanent institute of their creation to survive them. Such, in outline, was Romuald's story; and if the sequence of events is obscure, his main purpose is clear. Becoming after his conversion a monk of the Cluniac house of San Miniato at Ravenna, he steeped himself in the literature of the desert fathers, and wished to restore to the monastic life its earliest traditions of solitude and asceticism; at the same time, by what seems to us something of a paradox, he desired to preach the monastic vocation to all as the one haven of salvation. He left behind him, in embryo and far from the retreat in which he died, the institutes of Fonte Avellana, a congregation of hermits in the Apennines, and of Camaldoli, a community of monks near Arezzo living as hermits within a single group of buildings, but coming together for the liturgical prayer and on certain days for meals in a common refectory. In both communities silence was all but perpetual, and the fasts were of great severity. Fonte Avellana soon came under the influence of Peter Damian, but it was not for more than half a century after Romuald's death that the practices of Camaldoli were stabilized as a Rule, and that the order was made a double one by the addition of houses of cenobites following St Benedict's Rule interpreted literally and strictly.

A younger contemporary of Romuald, and one influenced by him, was St John Gualbert of Florence (*c.* 990–1073). After the striking and familiar episode which led to his becoming a monk at San Miniato, he left that monastery, desiring greater perfection, and stayed for a time at Camaldoli. Ultimately, however, he left the eremitical life and went to live at Vallombrosa near Florence, where he founded a cenobite monastery following the Rule of St Benedict but defining its scope very strictly and giving it precision and limits in favour of a purely contemplative life. Thus silence was perpetual, enclosure absolute and manual work forbidden. In order to secure quiet for the monks by taking business administration out of their hands he added to them a body of non-clerical *conversi*, and thus may probably be taken as the first to give formal sanction to a system which in one form or another was to influence so profoundly the future history of monasticism and of the religious life in general.

Neither Romuald nor John Gualbert wrote a Rule, still less did either found an order. Indeed, to attribute to any leader before the end of the eleventh century the conception of an order—that is, an articulated religious institute with a peculiar form of government and supra-regional extension—would be anachronistic, for such a body demands as a *sine qua non* a Church in which are functioning centralized powers of government and control, and such a state of things did not exist till the epoch of Gregory VII. But both Romuald and John Gualbert established bodies which later became orders, and though these both remained small and for all practical purposes cisalpine, the reputation and ideals of both travelled far and wide. At Camaldoli we can see present almost all the elements that reappear less than a century later north of the Alps at the Grande Chartreuse and later still at Grandmont; Vallombrosa, besides giving to almost all subsequent religious bodies the system of lay brethren, served also as an inspiration for those who wished a life of greater seclusion within the four corners of the Rule.

The greatest single influence, however, in what may be called the campaign of propaganda for a severely ascetical, quasi-eremitical monastic life was that of Peter Damian, who alike in writings, words and actions stands in something of the same prophetical relation to his age as does St Bernard to the age that followed a century later. Damian, at least until recent years, has probably been the object of less study and more misunderstanding than any other medieval figure of equal magnitude and significance. His fame has suffered both from the scantiness of records of the time, and from the reputation he acquired of an intransigence amounting to ferocity. When his activities and writings are regarded more closely, however, his mental and spiritual powers appear at better advantage; not only is his title of Doctor of the Church seen to be merited by his sane and central position in the controversy concerning simoniacal ordination, but his spiritual outlook while opening, so to say, in one direction upon the desert, can be recognized as including in its scope much of the devotional sentiment of the new age of which Anselm and Bernard were to be the masters.

Peter Damian, like Romuald and Gualbert, came from a city family of Ravenna. Unlike them, he had as a youth entered fully into the new intellectual life of the schools of Lombardy before his conversion and entry into the Romualdine hermitage of Fonte Avellana, and this circumstance probably explains, as in similar cases throughout the ages, his frequent harshness of tone and exaggeration when criticizing the career he had abandoned. He early became a vehement advocate of a monasticism at once more austere and more eremitical than that of St Benedict and, trained as he had been in the schools that were so soon to develop into the universities of law, did not hesitate to defend his position with every kind of argument. More than once he met the critics who referred him to the words of the Rule which praise the common life by asserting roundly that the cenobitical life was a *pis aller* and had been recognized as such by the great legislator himself.

Damian, like the Jerome to whom he bears some resemblance, wrote and acted with the fire of the moment rather than with the cold elaboration of logic, and in spite of his outspoken rejection of the traditional monastic life and his numerous controversies with abbots and monks, he retained a deep friendship and admiration for individuals and communities of the old model. One such was Monte Cassino itself, where in Damian's later life Desiderius, his colleague in the cardinalate, was abbot; another was Cluny, which he visited as papal legate in 1063, and to whose abbot and monks he wrote several letters of the warmest affection and praise. Besides these letters we have, in an account of the journey composed by his travelling companion, a still more detailed record of his appreciation of Cluny and its abbot, Hugh "the Great", but Damian was only at Cluny for a few days, and it was his nature to respond impetuously to a new impression; for all his generous appreciation, Cluny's way was not his, and there is evidence that even in his short visit he criticized some aspects of the life; certainly years had not brought a change of outlook, for in a letter to his nephew, written later than his visit to Cluny, we find all the old fiery exhortation to penance, and depreciation of the easy life of a community as compared with the strictness of a hermitage.

Damian, indeed, was not one of those spiritual teachers who build up a scheme for the soul's patient growth in perfection. His genius was to exhort and impel to the heroic, to praise striking achievements and to record edifying examples. Yet in him, as in Romuald, along with much that recalls past ages and other climates, the reader meets with many traces of the new intuitions and an intimacy of devotion to the mysteries of Christ's life on earth and of his Mother's. There are many sides to Peter Damian, as his hymns show—in particular the magnificent *Anglorum jam apostolus* to St Gregory the Great—and an extraordinary moral force burns in all that he wrote.

In monastic history Peter Damian's life and writings are of twofold significance. They show, first, a clear decision to return to the desert and its ways, not shrinking, if needs be, from the admission that the Rule of St Benedict is a mere propaedeutic or an easier way. Secondly, the hermit's life is held up to all souls of good will as the most perfect way of following Christ; no distinction is made or implied between different vocations, or between that to the active and that to the contemplative life. Few were found, in the age that followed, to hold these drastic opinions so fully and so explicitly. However individuals might act, the great monastic reformers north of the Alps were content to restore the cenobitical life to a supposed original purity, and the founders of the eremitical orders came to regard their institutes as meeting the needs of a peculiar and uncommon vocation.

Damian's direct influence north of the Alps was small. There is no evidence that his writings spread rapidly to a distance, and it is not to be supposed that he inspired all, or even any, of the numerous hermit bands of France, England and the Rhineland. These were commonly less logically consistent in their aims than the recluses of Camaldoli and Fonte Avellana. As in Italy itself, where the hermitage of Alferius at Cava near Sorrento became an abbey of the traditional type, so in France the hermit group under Robert of Chaise-dieu (*ob*. 1067), and even the Vallombrosan foundation of Chézal-Benoît near Bourges became in time normal black monk houses. In all these cases, and in many others, we see the fervent individual, dissatisfied with contemporary monasticism, beginning anew in simplicity and attracting others of a like mind; then follows the rapid growth of the house, until its founder, who had not desired the eremitical life as such, and who certainly had no theoretical quarrel with the Rule, adopts almost *en bloc* the customs of an existing monastery, Cluny or another, having given to the monastic life an infusion of new vigour but no change of direction. It is the story of Benedict of Aniane repeated a hundred times, but the hour was now at hand for a new chapter to be written.

Under Gregory VII the various movements of reform, which in all countries save the Norman dominions were also movements towards independence of secular control, had found an abiding centre and leadership in the papacy, and in the same decades the desire for a simpler form of the monastic life than was presented by the wealthy houses of southern and central France was becoming more articulate, together with the sense that some sort of organization was needed that should perpetuate the benefits of a new start. The time had in fact come when the Western mind, here as in all other spheres of mental activity, was able and anxious to replace custom and tradition by law, and to rise from a system of personal dependencies to one of articulated government. ✳

5. WALTER ULLMANN

FROM Walter Ullmann, *The Growth of Papal Government in the Middle Ages* (London: Methuen & Co., Ltd., 1965), pp. 262–63, 271–72, 299.

The designation of the papacy as Reform papacy from Leo IX onwards expresses the fallacious view that with the accession of this pope the era of "reform" begins. If indeed "reform" was what distinguished the Hildebrandine papacy, one may be forgiven for asking why this epitheton ornans is not bestowed upon the emperors immediately preceding this period. For, as we hoped to show, the Saxon and quite especially the early Salian emperors were indeed imbued with the spirit of reform and were successful to a not negligible extent. In a way one might say that whatever "reform" the post-Leonine popes carried out or tried to carry out, was largely conditioned by the previous imperial reform measures. This point of view which sees in the papacy a mere "Reform" papacy, would restrict its objectives to the removal of certain evils and abuses: did the papacy in the second half of the eleventh century really aim at nothing higher than this barren and negative end?

What the papacy attempted was the implementation of the hierocratic tenets, that is, the translation of abstract principles into concrete governmental actions. It is no doubt true and understandable that the first concrete application of these principles is apt to give a contemporary a somewhat severe jolt, but this sensation is a reaction, however natural, to the application of the idea, not to the idea itself. The unparalleled advantage which the papacy had over any other institution was its own storehouse of ideological memory, the papal archives. On the other hand, it would have been impossible for any power, including the papacy, to achieve so much within so short a time, had there not been a potent permeation of the contemporary mind with the very same ideas which were now applied in practice. Moreover, there were unobtrusive channels which preserved the hierocratic theme, such as the symbolism expressed in *Ordo C,* which was a faithful mirror of the advance which hierocratic ideas had made. To this must be added a number of institutionalized manifestations: these are effective carriers of ideas and are, so to speak, its conservators. It was in these incubators of its own theme that the papacy had always found great support. . . .

. . . The period from the fifties of the eleventh century onwards, is not a period which witnessed the evolution of a new doctrine, but a period which saw the application and implementation of a—by now—old ideology. This hierocratic doctrine by virtue of being applied became the governmental basis of the papacy. What pure doctrine declared ought to be done, is now being done. Hierocratic doctrine emerges in the shape of the hierocratic system, the essence of which is the conception of the universal Church as a body corporate and politic, comprising all Christians. This is the *societas christiana,* to use Gregory VII's distinctive terminology, in which the authority of the Roman pontiff holds sway; in which the pope's function as legislator and judge of appeal is effective; in which the mandate of the pope creates binding effects. For practical purposes this *societas christiana* is Western Europe, whose paternity can be traced back to Charlemagne and to the first Gregory's prophetic vision. This *societas christiana* is an entity which is to be governed on the monarchic principle: it is the *corpus* of the Christians over which the Roman Church exercises its monarchic *principatus* through the medium of the pope as the vicar of St Peter. This European society is technically a body politic, and despite its cementing bond, the spiritual element of the Christian faith, it is also earthy and has all the appurtenances and paraphernalia attendant upon civil society: its legislative, consultative, administrative, executive offices. Indeed, the *societas christiana* or what Cardinal Humbert called the *ecclesia,* is a *societas perfecta.* . . .

Some preliminary remarks on Gregory VII's premises may profitably precede the survey of his thought.

Firstly, it is axiomatic for him that the *ecclesia* is a body corporate and politic the constituent element of which is the spiritual element of the Christian faith. As such this society knows no territorial frontiers: it is literally universal. As a body politic it is territorially confined to Latin Christendom. But this society despite its constituent spiritual substance, is not by any means a pneumatic body, but has all the appurtenances of real earthiness. As such it must be governed and the substratum of this society necessitates its government by those who are uniquely qualified to function as the directing and governing organs, namely by the ordained members of the Church. The principle of functional qualification must be translated into a workable governmental machinery. The *sacerdotium* alone is qualified and entitled and bound to function as the governmental organ of the *societas christiana*. The correct application of this principle rests, on the one hand, on the delineation of the *ordo laicalis* and the *ordo sacerdotalis* and, on the other hand, entails strict hierarchical ordering within the functionally qualified part of the *ecclesia*.

Secondly, it is axiomatic for Gregory that order, that is, the neat demarcation between the two *ordines* must be preserved: order within the *societas christiana* is the second vital principle of Gregory VII. It means that each and every member must fulfil the functions allotted to him, functions, that is to say, which are determined by the nature of the body of the Christian society. The function of each member of this *societas* is orientated by the purposes of this society. When therefore everyone acts according to the function allotted to him, there will come about what Gregory VII calls *concordia* entailing *pax* within the *ecclesia*. Its opposite is *discordia*, which emerges when the individual members do not adhere to the functions which they are called upon to fulfil.

Thirdly, it is fundamental to Gregory VII that the basis of the allocation of the functions is *justitia*. *Justitia* is not a purely religious-ethical idea, nor is it a purely nomological idea: it partakes of both. It contains the totality of all those ideological principles which flow from the substratum of the *societas christiana*, namely the Christian faith. The substance of *justitia* is the right *norm of living*, and *justitia* answers the question: what is the appropriate norm of conduct in a Christian society? *Justitia* is the crystallized and most abstract expression of hierocratic doctrine. It is according to Gregory the Christian norm of conduct, a regulative principle which yields an applicable criterion for measurement. Just conduct is unquestioned acknowledgment and acceptance of the ideological principles constituting *justitia*. He who thus acts shows *humilitas;* he who refuses to acknowledge and to accept these principles shows *superbia*. *Superbia* is the deliberate setting aside of the norm of conduct as prescribed in and by *justitia*. *Justitia* is the canon of Christian world order, according to which the functions are allotted in Christian society and its life consequently regulated. *Justitia* shows what is right conduct, and what, therefore, ought to be the law—in a Christian society. . . .

An attempt has been made to set forth the main ideological principles of Gregory VII. It will have become sufficiently clear that Gregory's thought-pattern is hewn in one mould: he stands firmly on the old tenets and pursues their logical implications to the very utmost. To him, as we have repeatedly pointed out, the multitude of Christians forms one corporate entity, constituting the *societas christiana*, whose essence is the spiritual element of faith, but which has nevertheless all the appurtenances of real earthiness.

6. CHRISTOPHER BROOKE

FROM Christopher Brooke, *Europe in the Central Middle Ages* (London: Longmans, Green and Co., Ltd., 1964), pp. 249–50, 252–56.

Cluny has been the centre of two disputes among modern historians: one concerns its relations with Gorze and the other movements of monastic reform of the tenth and eleventh centuries; the other its relation to the papal reform. It used to be the convention to call the latter the 'Cluniac' reform, as if its inspiration stemmed from Cluny; in more recent times it has been called the 'Gregorian' reform, after Pope Gregory VII (1073–85), who was its most famous, though not its first leader. The title 'Cluniac reform' gravely exaggerates the importance of Cluny; 'Gregorian reform' somewhat exaggerates the influence of Gregory. For that reason I prefer the neutral 'papal reform'. The papacy was at the centre of reforming currents from the mid-eleventh century on; and although the reform of the papal Curia was only the centre of a much wider movement—so that even the colourless label 'papal' is not free from objection—reform at the centre was the process which made possible the drastic revolution in the Church's government and outlook.

The association of Cluny with the papal reform received its plausibility from three circumstances: the great fame of Cluny among historians of the period; the chronology of the movement—the revival of the papacy in the heyday of Cluny's influence; and the notion that Pope Gregory VII himself had been a monk of Cluny. Pope Gregory had been a monk; so had most of the leaders of the papal reform; so were most leading churchmen who had the leisure to think and to write in the tenth and early eleventh centuries. The monastic inspiration of the papal reform cannot be doubted. But it is unlikely that Gregory had been professed at Cluny. His friend Bishop Bonizo of Sutri tells us that he had, but he lends his story artistic verisimilitude by telling how the abbot of Cluny presented the young Hildebrand (as he then was called) to Pope Leo IX (1049–54) on his way from Germany to Italy to become Pope. With his genius for inaccuracy Bonizo has chosen the only month in the eleventh century when Cluny had no abbot; and there are grounds for thinking that Hildebrand was a monk, not at Cluny, but at Cologne. As for the other grounds for associating Cluny and papal reform, Cluny's fame no longer dominates the age as it once did; we see it more in perspective now, and we can observe that it was not from Cluny, but from Lorraine and from Italy that the monks whom Leo IX gathered round him came. The chronological relation survives: it was the movements of the tenth and early eleventh centuries which provided the atmosphere which made papal reform possible; these movements were mainly monastic or inspired by monks; and Cluny still holds a dignified place among them. . . .

The papal reform, whichever way one looks at it, was one of the most dramatic and startling events of the Middle Ages; the sudden emergence of the papacy, reformed, transformed, as a central organization for the direction and improvement of the Church. Many of its sources can be traced. Something has been said of the monastic reform which preceded it and there will be more to say in a later chapter of the intellectual revival which accompanied it; but these do not dim its dramatic quality, any more than listing the causes of the French Revolution abolishes the excitement of the event.

The reformers themselves were an oddly assorted group of men, with divergent ideas and often with divergent motives. But their impact on the contemporary world was that of a group of prophets come to make Europe live up to its spiritual vocation. It took time for this to be apparent, still longer for all the tensions they let loose to be felt; but the main ingredients were already present in the papal Curia before the death of Pope Leo IX. The second half of the eleventh century was in many ways the heroic age of papal history, the time when the medieval papacy was most evidently in touch with the roots of its inspiration. What the reformers achieved was no doubt less dramatic; but it was remarkable enough. Hitherto the papacy had been a venerable institution, the preserver of the tradition of St Peter in the Church, the custodian of his shrine and of an immeasurable treasury of relics. Rome had been a distant goal of pilgrimage, of immense prestige, to those who had lived at a distance; those who lived near had observed rather more of the difference between the Rome of legend and the papacy of present fact, the toy of local faction. The reformers brought the papacy to the notice of the whole of Europe; made an organized government out of it, which, like all effective governments, was respected, disliked, and sometimes obeyed. The reformers' work, however, went deeper than that; and its numerous ramifications appear in almost every chapter of this book.

I have purposely avoided any attempt to sketch the character of the Church at large in the tenth and early eleventh centuries. Historians of the papal reform have often repeated the rhetoric of contemporaries on the depravities of the clergy of their day. It is doubtless true that the secular clergy, especially those who served the parishes, were ignorant men, with no very lofty standards of life; it may also be true that marriage was a normal practice among them, in spite of the canons forbidding it. But both these generalizations were as true in the late twelfth as in the eleventh century, so far as the documents can inform us—and may have been largely true for centuries to come. The educated secular clergy were probably very few in number; monks were more numerous and, although the reforms of the tenth and eleventh centuries often lacked staying-power in individual monasteries, the monastic ideal was in higher repute than for many centuries before. The assimilation of clergy and laity was an abuse which stirred the reformers' anger. We have seen how the German kings treated clergy as royal officers, and blurred any distinction there might have been between the spiritual and the temporal. No doubt there were objections, on any Christian standard, to a bishop whose life was spent in warfare; though before we become too censorious, let us remember, first, how much effort for the welfare of their flock as well as for their kings many of the great administrator-bishops of tenth- and eleventh-century Germany made; let us remember too that Leo IX himself was a noted warrior as well as a reformer. In many ways we are very ignorant of the state of the Church in 1049; what we do know suggests that it deserves understanding as well as reproach; that it had its ideals, which were in many ways very different from those of the reformers; and yet that the reformers had taken on an immensely formidable task in trying to make it live up to its Christian vocation as they understood it. . . .

The human race has never been so savagely denounced as in St Peter Damian's *Book of Gomorrah*, save perhaps in the last book of *Gulliver's Travels*, which it somewhat resembles. An overwhelming sense of sin, and a sense that, under God's providence, the clergy had the vocation to attempt the superhuman task of lifting mankind from the appalling depravity of its ways, inspired Damian, and, in only a slightly less measure, his colleagues. They feared above all assimilation, since they held that if the clergy became wholly assimilated to the world, they would accept the whole gamut of the world's abominable standards. The grip of the world on a man was held to be especially symbolized by the influence of money and of the other sex. There was some humanity, but no chivalry among the reformers. At the high level, simony was part of the machinery by which bishoprics and abbeys had become largely secular offices in many parts of Europe; and if the emperor's treatment of the German Church, and of such parts of the Italian as he could control, had often been free from simony, it led no less to assimilation of the things of the world and of the Church; so that some reformers reckoned all lay interference as wicked as simony itself. At the lower level there was danger of an even more complete assimilation. The high offices of the Church were not hereditary, and it did not suit kings or princes that they should be; the higher clergy were commonly, though not invariably, celibate. Among the lower clergy the growth of the parish church which was also an *Eigenkirche* of the local lord had tended to encourage the growth of a class of clergy who were little different in manner of life from their secular neighbours. The lord of a village built a parish church on his domain; he was its owner; the priest who served it was his vassal, his servant; the lord could do what he liked with priest and altar. The system became exceedingly widespread in the century and a half after the break-up of the Carolingian Empire. These clergy seem (so far as we can tell) quite often to have married and passed their benefices from father to son like any other small vassal holding. Over these clerks the bishops could assert a little control, since they alone could ordain them; but because there were no seminaries or theological colleges and no means of training the ordinary parish clergy, and because many of the bishops were themselves essentially men of the world, there was little chance of new, different or higher standards passing through to the clergy. These factors encouraged the reformers to campaign for the abolition of simony and clerical marriage; and for the enforcement of the supremacy of the Holy See as the instrument for reform. They help to explain why it was these particular aspects of the law on which the reformers laid so much stress, why so much of their research into the authorities for canon law was concerned with these three points. ✤

7. GERD TELLENBACH

FROM Gerd Tellenbach, *Church, State and Christian Society at the Time of the Investiture Contest* (Oxford: Basil Blackwell, 1966), pp. 162–67.

The age of the Investiture Controversy may rightly be regarded as the culmination of medieval history; it was a turning-point, a time both of completion and of beginning. It was the fulfilment of the early middle ages, because in it the blending of the Western European peoples with Christian spirituality reached a decisive stage. On the other hand, the later middle ages grew directly out of the events and thoughts of the decades immediately before and after the year 1100; as early as this the general lines, the characteristic religious, spiritual and political views of later times had been laid down, and the chief impulses for subsequent development given.

The great struggle had a three-fold theme. On the basis of a deeper understanding of the nature of the Catholic Church, an attempt was made to remodel three things: first, the relations of clergy and laity with each other; secondly, the internal constitution of the Church, through the imposition of papal primacy; and thirdly, the relations of Church and World. The first of these disputed questions, in which lay investiture played the most important part, has given its name to the whole period. The old state-controlled constitution of the Church and the proprietary church system, both of them factors of the first importance in the conversion of the Western European peoples and in the building-up of Church organisation, had originated in pre-Christian times and were at bottom foreign to the Church's real nature. Only after long and wearisome struggles did the Church succeed in restricting them or incorporating them in the structure of the canon law. Lay investiture and the whole proprietary system were, however, burning questions only for a few centuries during the earlier part of the middle ages; but the battle between episcopalism and papalism has, in spite of periodic interruptions, intermittently disturbed the Church from the earliest Christian era down to the present time, and the relationship between Christianity and the secular state is, for Catholics and Protestants alike, still a deeply moving and not yet completely solved question. The best-known and most violent conflict to which it ever gave rise, the struggle in which Church and State met each other in the pride of their strength and fully-armed with their natural weapons, was the Investiture Controversy.

It will never be quite possible to discover what were the real causes of the great eleventh-century crisis in Christian history; many factors in the political life of the times which did in fact coalesce to form a developing situation the main lines of which are clear, might, it seems to us now, have operated very differently. It is just as difficult to explain why it was that men who were capable of great things came together in Rome at that particular time, and, above all, why at the critical moment the daemonic figure of the greatest of the popes occupied the throne of the Prince of the Apostles. Only a very wide-ranging view can make clear, even in part, the concurrence of events out of which the new age was born, for only thus will due influence be assigned to the advanced stage which the christianisation of the world had then reached. Ecclesiastical organisation had spread far and wide, monastic religion had taken a strong hold on men and made them more concerned for their souls' health, had spurred them on to greater conscientiousness and made them more anxious for the purity and right order of the Church. Thus a new and victorious strength was lent to the old belief in the saving grace of the sacraments and to the hierarchical conceptions based on their administration. Out of this arose the conviction that the Christian peoples of the West formed the true City of God, and as a result the leaders of the Church were able to abandon their ancient aversion from the wickedness of worldly men and to feel themselves called upon to re-order earthly life in accordance with divine precept. In the eleventh century the position had not yet been reached where the pope, the imperial Lord of the Church, appointed and confirmed the kings of the earth and watched over and judged their actions, but the enormous advance made by Gregory VII had opened the way for this, and he himself had already realised more of it in practice than any single one of his successors was able to do. Gregory stands at the greatest—from the spiritual point of view perhaps the only—turning-point in the history of Catholic Christendom; in his time the policy of converting the world gained once and for all the upper hand over the policy of withdrawing from it: the world was drawn into the Church, and the leading spirits of the new age made it their aim to establish the "right order" in this united Christian world. In their eyes, however, the most immediate task seemed to be that of successfully asserting the supremacy of the "Servant of the servants of God" over the kings of the earth.

Gregory VII was not particularly notable for his faithfulness to tradition. He was at heart a revolutionary; reform in the ordinary sense of the word, which implies little more than the modification and improvement of existing forms, could not really satisfy him. He desired a drastic change, and could be content with nothing short of the effective realisation on earth of justice, of the "right order" and of "that which ought to be." "The Lord hath not said 'I am Tradition,'" he once wrote, "but 'I am the Truth.'" And yet, in spite of this reaction against the merely traditional, Gregory himself embodied the essence of Catholic tradition in a peculiarly characteristic manner; this fact shows, therefore, how instinctive and unreasoning—in a sense, how primitive—his faith was. Catholicism was to him the directive principle of life itself. For him the age-old Catholic ideas of righteousness (*justitia*), a Christian hierarchy (*ordo*), and a proper standing for everyone before God and man (*libertas*), were the core of religious experience, and their realisation the purpose of life here on earth. It would be incorrect to treat these and related ideas as the personal discoveries of St Augustine or any other particular individual among the early Fathers, or to attempt to trace out exactly the stages by which Gregory is supposed to have inherited them; they are in reality an inseparable part of the Catholic faith, and can only be understood on that assumption. It is just as wide of the mark to suggest that ideas such as these were discovered for the first time by Gregory and his contemporaries, or that they were in any significant way remoulded during the Gregorian period; Gregory's real service was to leaven the earthly lump with the principles of Catholicism, and to make the latter, in a manner hitherto undreamed of, a really decisive force in politics. His aim was to bring the kingdom of God on earth, as he saw it in his mind, nearer to realisation, and to serve the cause of order, justice and "freedom." "He was indeed," writes Bernold of St Blasien, "a most zealous propagator (*institutor*) of the Catholic religion and a most determined defender of the freedom of the Church. For he did not wish the clergy to be subject to the power of the laity, but desired them to excel all laymen by their holiness and by the dignity of their order."

The unity of the Christian world, as Gregory and his contemporaries wished to see it, could never quite be established in practice; nevertheless, unity has always remained an idea of the greatest historical influence, though neither before nor after Gregory's time was it ever completely realised. Before the eleventh century, the principle of unity was represented by the kingship; but the persistence of the old Christian feeling of indifference towards the world, together with the remains of paganism, robbed the monarchy of full co-operation and hampered its action. Later on, the clerical claim to leadership was advanced with such intensity that it provoked resistance of another kind: belief in the Divine Right of kings and princes immediately made itself more strongly felt, and was never quite overcome wherever monarchy was the prevailing form of the state. But as Divine Right was no longer fully accepted by the Church, tension and some impairment of the principle of unity was often the result. The assertion of their own direct responsibility to God—put forward so forcefully by Henry IV—still remained for the kings of Europe their strongest argument against excessive claims on the part of the papacy, for the conception that the rule of one man over others can only be justified and made holy by direct divine intervention must always retain a certain moral value. It is further probable, as has often been pointed out recently, that the papacy's attacks on the Divine Right of Kings led directly to later attempts to set the state on new, and this time secular, foundations. Conclusions such as this, the truth of which is difficult to demonstrate, must however be handled with great caution. The "order" which Gregory introduced remained dominant for centuries, and showed an astounding ability to overcome all opposing forces or to turn them to its own service. A similar picture is presented by Gothic art, which combined numberless powerful elements fundamentally at variance with each other, and yet was able to create out of them a stylistic unity in spite of the resultant stress and strain.

The enormous strength of the ecclesiastical claim to world-domination is only to be explained if we recognise how profoundly religious were its roots; it grew directly out of the fundamental tenets of the Catholic faith, and failure to realise this is the reason why many earlier attempts at explanation must be rejected as mistaken or insufficient. To derive a demand for world-wide power from asceticism and the flight from the earthly life, as some historians have done, is to ascribe an improbable religious perversity to the Church; and there is equally little logic in the connected theory that the Church wished to reduce the world to subjection in order to be free from it. Nor is it possible to suppose that the emperor was deprived of the right of investiture simply in order that the clergy alone should represent the unity of the Church. Further, it is scarcely a half-truth to assert, as is sometimes done, that Gregory VII combated lay influence in order to increase his opportunities of carrying out moral reform and the internal reorganisation of the Church. This was only part of his purpose; as we have seen, the real reason for the action he took lies deeper: his moral principles were outraged by the mere fact that the laity were occupying a position which, according to the sacramental conception of the hierarchy, was not really theirs at all. A true understanding of the ideas of Gregory VII and of post-Gregorian Catholicism about the relation of the spiritual power to the world, and of the origins of these ideas themselves, can only be reached by going right back to the belief in the incarnation of God in Christ. This is the most fundamental of the Church's beliefs, for in the Church the saving grace of the incarnation has become an ever-present reality, and all the Church's institutions find in this belief their *raison d'être* and their ultimate justification. Mystical and hierarchical trains of thought arise naturally from the belief that God comes down from Heaven to man, and that the multitude of His priests serves as the steps by which He descends. If, therefore, the Church and the hierarchy of its servants have a part in the mediating office of Christ, if they exist in order to link Heaven and earth, then it is only just that the world should meekly accept their guidance and be subject to them. This demand forms a principle the validity of which Catholicism is always bound to assert; it is this principle which must ultimately decide its attitude towards the State, although in recent centuries it has been applied less in the purely political field than during the middle ages, and more as a claim to the care of souls and to moral leadership.

8. J. P. WHITNEY

FROM J. P. Whitney, *Hildebrandine Essays* (Cambridge: Cambridge University Press, 1932), pp. 88–89, 91–92.

As a man of affairs we see the Pope using the good offices of all likely people to bring him and the king into 'concord'. Here, as usual, Gregory was hopeful, and hopeful with some justification from his experience. He had a great power of managing men: it was not St Peter Damiani alone that he fascinated and bent to his will. He was a man of affairs, but he was something more. He was a man of principles. He has often been described as merely a man of politics and, perhaps, some modern statesmen have led us to regard politics and principles as too far apart. Gregory, all the same, had not a policy independent of men and of events. The course he took was that which, given the circumstances and the men he dealt with, was the most likely to bring his principles into practice. This is different from the commoner view which describes him as one who came to the papal throne bent upon carrying out a high papal policy: it is still more different from that which depicts him as an unscrupulous schemer. But the application of his principles depended upon circumstances, upon men, and upon localities. The differences which have been pointed out so often between the policy of Gregory in Germany, France, and England imply no lack of principle, no unscrupulous readiness to make the most for the Church or himself out of varying conditions. They arose from the application of his general principles to varying circumstances. . . .

It would be difficult, perhaps, to point to any part of Gregory's action which was markedly original. His peculiarity lay in the bold energy in the application of principles. In those business matters at Rome which were to be so important for the papacy and the world at large, his reign marks no epoch, even if he had possibly been trained for an official career, and had certainly been an official himself. But two characteristics of his mind gave to his papacy its vast importance: the first was his power of bringing together things which otherwise would have remained apart, and the second was the scope of his vision. His cares and his interests ranged over a wider field than many of his predecessors had known, and over this large field the practical business side of Roman diplomacy and administration was welded into a coherent system by a consistent theory of the Church and its administrative head the papacy. The well-known extension of the system of legates under him is one instance of what he did, of his development of what was already in use and of its employment on a larger scale, of its direction upon a more deliberate policy to further the effective unity of the Church and the papal control. And while at the centre, Rome, his papacy seemed to end in confusion and defeat, the threads by which he had connected the papacy with other lands, even remote, still remained. For Europe at large the results of Gregory's papacy stood firm.

One incident of his closing years is typical of what was the weakness of his power, as it had been indeed with Popes before. The desertion of 1084, when thirteen cardinals, three of them Gregory's own creation, and others left him, as Hugo Candidus, the leader in his election, had left him long ago, was a blow to his cause, and weakened it immensely on the side of administration: Peter the Chancellor; Theodinus his archdeacon; John, the head of the College of Cantors; Peter the Oblationarius with all his staff save one; Poppo, the head of the College of Regionarii with his whole staff; Cincius, the companion of his boyhood, head of the Judices, with all his subordinates; John, head of the school of Cantors, with all his staff; the Prior of the Scriniarii. It was a wholesale official desertion, the causes of which can only be conjectured, but the effect of which was certain. It meant defeat for the Pope at Rome. It was at Rome that the papacy was weakest, and most often suffered defeat. And yet no Pope had done more to make the papacy strong elsewhere. ✲

9. R. W. SOUTHERN

FROM R. W. Southern, *The Making of the Middle Ages* (New Haven: Yale University Press, 1965), pp. 139–43.

Gregory VII was a man about whom many anecdotes circulated. Most of them were told by his enemies and are not to be trusted. Nevertheless they cast a vivid light on the passionate animosities which rent Rome in the days of his pontificate and divided Christendom on a theoretical question as it had never been divided since the days of the great heresies. All of them bear witness to the dramatic intensity of Gregory's character. The abbot Hugh of Cluny had more opportunity than most to observe the Pope with a detached but not unfriendly eye, and a special interest attaches to a small group of stories which were current in his circle. One of them tells of an incident in Gregory's life before he became Pope, when he was a papal legate. He and Abbot Hugh were riding together in a large company. The abbot had fallen behind and was reflecting on the character of the legate, and on the strange command which this small man of obscure origin exercised in the world; mentally, he wrote him down as proud, and accused him of seeking his own glory. Suddenly the legate turned on him and broke out with—"It's a lie; I seek not my own glory, but that of the Holy Apostles." True or not—and there is no reason to doubt its substantial accuracy—the story reveals the man, explosive, filled with a dynamic power which brought on him accusations of dark practices, eaten up with the one burning passion to restore the glory of the Apostles.

The Apostles he was thinking of were St. Peter and St. Paul, under whose patronage he had lived since childhood. He was fond of recalling that he had been brought up from infancy under the shadow of St. Peter's. How far he was Roman by birth is difficult to determine, but certainly in feeling, in background and in his social milieu he was altogether Roman. In this he differed from most other members of the Reforming party: they were mostly foreigners from Lorraine, Burgundy or Northern Italy. Indeed Rome was the despair of the Reformers: however much they differed, they were all agreed in denouncing the corruptions of Rome, and especially of its aristocracy. All forward-looking policy for the last two hundred years had come from outside Rome, particularly from Germany. But Gregory had little use for all this. His eyes were fixed on a more distant past before there were German Emperors. The first recorded words of his we possess were a denunciation of the relaxation of the rule for Canons authorized by the German Emperor, Louis the Pious, in the ninth century—a ruler who, in the conditions of his time, had done more than anyone else to restore the regular canonical life. On another occasion, speaking of the practice of shortening matins to three Psalms and three Lessons, Gregory writes of the languor which has crept in "especially since the time when the government of our church passed to the Germans. . . . But we, having searched out the Roman Order and the ancient custom of our church, imitating the old Fathers, have ordered things to be restored as we have set out above."

Gregory VII found his strength in Rome. He was allied to the new urban families who were beginning to appear there, men who were making a name and fortune for themselves as financiers and men of business to the popes. Two of these families, the Pierleoni and Frangipani, were to have a great future in the history of the city and the papacy. It was at Gregory's instigation that the first of the Pierleoni used his wealth to support the fortunes of the reform party in the critical days of Alexander II. Cencius

Frangipane and Alberic Pierleone were Gregory's intimates—"men" as he affectionately said, "who have been brought up with us almost from adolescence in the Roman court." When the Countess Matilda made her will in 1102 she recalled that they were at the Pope's side during the first moves in that important transaction. Gregory was at home in Rome. He was the first Pope since the unregenerate days of the Tusculan Popes to make the city his normal place of residence. The constant perambulations of his immediate predecessors were discontinued; except for his one journey north to Canossa and its neighbourhood, he was rooted in Rome until he was driven out in the last months of his life. His last words "I have *loved righteousness and hated iniquity*—therefore I die in exile" show the bitterness for him of the loss of Rome. Other Popes had been, and were to be, driven from the city without experiencing any great diminution in their authority; but for Gregory VII it meant the end.

This concentration gives Gregory his intensity. But he was only the most intense to a group of men who had the same general purpose. It is usual to call them the 'Reforming Party,' but it would be truer—and more suggestive of their revolutionary purpose—to call them the 'Restoring Party.' They aimed at the restoration of ancient discipline, or what they believed to be ancient discipline. The names which they took when they became Popes show this more clearly than many words: they abandoned names such as John and Benedict, which had been common in the tenth and early eleventh centuries, and took those by preference which had not been used for many centuries—Clement, Damasus, Victor, and so on. These names contained a challenge.

In thus associating themselves with the first centuries of Christian history, they were going back to a past which in many ways seemed clearer to them than it does to us. They had a series of documents, stretching, as they believed, back to Clement I, the immediate successor of St. Peter, which proclaimed the rights and authority of the Roman see. Some of these, as we now know, were compositions of the eighth and ninth centuries; the most important of them was the Donation of Constantine, a document in which the first Christian Emperor purported to give extensive temporal rights over large parts of Italy and over all islands to the Pope Silvester I. This was a document to which Gregory VII and his successors attached great importance, and its authenticity was accepted (though its authority was not) by friends and foes alike. But the greatest treasury of documents which inspired the Reformers was of undoubted authenticity: it was the vast collection of letters of Gregory the Great. It was here that they found in its most practical form the lofty spirit of order and papal initiative in the affairs of all the churches of the West which they sought to renew. It was not an accident that Hildebrand (following his master Gregory VI) broke the sequence of popes who took names from the earliest centuries, and chose that of the greatest of his predecessors after St. Peter.

Gregory VII made no great innovations in the machinery of papal government, nor did he introduce into the papal service any body of new men to carry on his work. He took over the men who had been working with his predecessor, and the machinery which had been developed during the previous twenty years. But though he was not himself a great administrator, it is in his pontificate that the documents first become sufficiently abundant for us to see the papal administration at work. And though he almost broke the machine, he embodied more ardently and expressed more clearly than anybody else the impulses of the men who had built it. His pontificate was certainly not a success in any practical sense. Nothing that he did as Pope hastened the process of bringing business to Rome, or of giving the Pope a new place in the calculations of practical men. When he died he had been deserted by most of the cardinals on whom the work of government depended: for the timid he was too dangerous; too violent for moderate men; too autocratic for men of independence. Visionaries found him too much of a politician, and politicians found him too careless of consequences. For one reason or another the men fell away: the Councils of his later years (1080–4) are a shadow of the great manifestations of power which culminated in the Lateran Council of 1079; his staff deserted him and the secretarial work fell into arrears. Before the end of his life, his authority was denied or challenged over great parts of Europe. Everywhere there was bewilderment and confusion. But his failures, however one judges them, were only temporary set-backs. The "zeal not for my own glory but for that of the Holy Apostles" was winning adherents all over Europe to the new ordering of Church government under papal leadership; and pressing practical needs came in to reinforce the effects of this zeal. ✥

Part 9

CHURCH AND HERESY

The study of medieval heresy may be organized in a variety of ways, but whatever approach is taken it is essential to start off with a precise definition. Fortunately, Gordon Leff has formulated one:

> Heresy is defined by reference to orthodoxy. It does not exist alone. A doctrine or a sect or an individual becomes heretical when condemned as such by the church. For this, there has to be a body of accepted beliefs to violate and a recognized orthodoxy to enforce it. In their absence, to profess even the most outrageous opinions is to operate in a doctrinal—as opposed to a moral or legal—vacuum; the community may be scandalized; the law may be broken; but there will be no officially constituted outlook against which they offend.

Heresy is thus antisacerdotal; it is a rejection of the Christian sacraments, the quintessence of the faith, and of the clergy's role as the indispensable intermediary in the Christian drama. It strikes at the very heart of Christianity. Heresy should not be equated with anticlericalism, which does not necessarily constitute a challenge to the faith and which is a critical assault on the members of the clergy for not performing their duties and not living in a manner appropriate to their sacred calling.

In general terms, there are two conceptualizations of the problem of heresy. The first, which is rarely encountered, is discussed here as a complement to the second, more common one. According to this view, Christianity was not a rigidly structured and ideologically finished sect when it triumphed over its competitors and became the official religion of the Roman Empire. On the contrary, Christianity continued to grow and take on added features, and the process of self-definition was by no means complete in the twelfth century. From the early fourth century, the Church was engaged in the difficult task of turning nominal Christians into "real" Christians. Pagan Europe had to be brought into the fold and educated, and, at the same time the Church itself had to decide through trial and error, controversy and debate, just what this education should comprise—in other words, what it meant to be a Christian. This essential concern was not really dealt with until the Council of Trent met in the middle of the sixteenth century. Heresy was thus divergence from dogma and practice. And since dogma was vaguely defined, practice varied enormously from one part of isolated Europe to another. Heresy was endemic in medieval Christianity, and silent manifestations of it probably existed everywhere. To conceive of the medieval world as a homogeneous entity is to ignore the varieties of religious experience which prevailed. Orthodox Christianity was certainly dominant; it was not exclusive. Medieval Europe was much more complex than our limited historical terminology suggests.

The second approach, the one represented by selections here, is characterized by a tighter chronological scheme and an attempt to understand heresy with reference to particular phenomena such as the social, political, and economic milieu. This specificity extends to the very useful delineation of the basic differences between the various sects and to a discussion of particular regions and towns. The following selections amply testify to the richness of this approach, and they suggest at least six major questions or themes.

The first theme concerns the antecedents and long-term consequences of the heretical movements of the twelfth and thirteenth centuries; the aim is to see this period in a wider context. For example, Steven Runciman believes that the Cathari were direct spiritual descendants of the Manichees of the fourth century. Actually, the coincidence of belief between the two sects does not establish a direct connection between them, and a connection is difficult to prove because of the lack of documentation. It is interesting though that contemporaries implied there was a continuity between the two sects by referring to the Catharist heretics as "Manichaeans."

Or, on the other hand, we may explore the possibility of a link between the heretical sects of the twelfth and thirteenth centuries and the great heresies which held sway in the fourteenth century, especially in England and Bohemia. And can Hus and Wyclif be tied to the Reformation of the sixteenth century? Significantly, Protestantism was extremely strong in southern France about three hundred years after these particular heresies, and Lutherans appeared in areas where the Lollards had flourished. Are we, then, engaged in the study of phenomena limited to the twelfth and thirteenth centuries? If not, where is the logical place to begin and conclude the study of heresy.

In any event, we must still try to understand the threat that heresy posed. Why did Christian Europe respond so passionately to this challenge? Here are a few excerpts from a description of the Albigensians by an early fourteenth-century member of the Inquisition: "They usually say of themselves that they are good Christians . . . and that they are persecuted just as Christ and his apostles were by the Pharisees . . . they talk to the laity of the evil lives of the clerks and prelates of the Roman Church . . . they invoke, with their own interpretation and according to their abilities, the authority of the Gospels and the Epistles . . . they attack and vituperate . . . all the sacraments of the Church . . . they claim that confession made to the priests of the Roman Church is useless . . . they read from the Gospels and the Epistles in the vulgar tongue." Had the Albigensians merely confined themselves to bringing the "evil lives" of the clergy to the attention of the laity, that would have been but another manifestation of anticlericalism. However, they denied the validity of the most crucial principles of Christian orthodoxy: the sacraments and confession and the role of the clergy in interpreting the holy texts. To tolerate abuse of these basic elements of Christianity was to court eternal damnation.

Another factor which made these heretics so dangerous—and which helps to explain the intense hostility they aroused—was their astounding missionary zeal. This zeal was demonstrated most strikingly by their willingness to die for their faith. It is with some justice that Henry Lea wrote: "If the blood of the martyrs were really the seed of the Church, Manichaeism would now be the dominant religion of Europe." Given such energy even one heretic posed a real danger. A German mystic declared in all sincerity: "Had I a sister in a country wherein there were but one heretic, still that one heretic would keep me in fear for her."

The third theme to emerge from these selections concerns the Inquisition. This infamous, often misunderstood institution is certain to raise a variety of questions, but here we can touch on only two: the Inquisition and the secular polity; the Inquisition as a determining factor in creating an intellectually "closed" society. Because heresy was clearly a threat to society as a whole and because church and state were so closely interconnected, the Inquisition was supported by and its edicts enforced by the secular polity. In this sense it was a characteristically medieval institution. Paradoxically, it probably aided the formation of strong monarchies that were soon to challenge the Church. The connection between national or territorial unification and the Inquisition is seen most clearly in late fifteenth-century Spain. Here the Inquisition was revived after a long period of quiescence, and it became the only really all-Spanish institution.

Thus, the Inquisition, which originated as a means of fighting heresy, may also be studied as a late medieval political development.

Professor Cecil Roth has pointed out that "By an accident of lexicography, the English reader looks for Inquisition between Iniquity and Insincerity." And Friedrich Heer writes: "With its appearance on the scene, the Middle Ages ceased to be 'open,' and the closed society, closed Church and closed state of the later medieval and early modern periods had come unmistakably into being." In evaluating the Inquisition's role in shaping the intellectual life of late medieval Europe, one must consciously strive for objectivity; all too often the Inquisition has been maligned by historians who impose the values of their own age on the medieval past.

Three other issues are raised by the study of heresy: 1) What impact did the heretical movements have on the subsequent history of southern France, the center of European civilization in the early twelfth century? 2) What is known about the social composition of the sects, and how does this knowledge illuminate the origins, nature, and destiny of heresy? 3) What is the psychological content of medieval heresy?

Heresy gave birth to the Inquisition and to a crusading movement designed to eradicate it; according to Lea, these combined forces "left a ruined and impoverished country. . . . The precocious civilization which had promised to lead Europe in the path of culture was gone, and to Italy was transferred the honor of the Renaissance." This is probably an exaggeration but it is a provocative theory nonetheless. As Professor Runciman, among others, has shown, southern France was in a real sense fighting for its life. "The religious issue became blurred in the territorial issue." Again the study of heresy leads to some intriguing historical problems and the heretical movements emerge as a catalyst, a force generating change in the secular makeup of society.

Since heresy was a revolt against some of the fundamentals of established society, historians have tried to examine the social composition of the sects to see if perhaps this was basically a social or class struggle. The general consensus, however, seems to be that all segments of society were involved. Clearly, medieval heresy was an expression of diverse interests, tensions, hopes, and dreams, and we should be wary of facile generalizations about it.

In the past few decades, social psychology has become a powerful conceptual tool in trying to understand past and present societies. It has been especially illuminating when applied to mass movements and when based on a sound historical foundation. Professor Norman Cohn's *The Pursuit of the Millennium* has aroused heated controversy because Cohn identifies medieval messianism with modern revolutionary messianism. However, as an explanation of medieval hysteria and irrationality it has been almost universally praised, and even his severest critics will grant that he has made a substantial and exciting contribution to the application of psychological theory to historical research. He has opened a new approach to the study of medieval heresy, and his work is a testament to the vitality of the subject.

1. HENRY C. LEA

FROM Henry C. Lea, *A History of the Inquisition of the Middle Ages*, 3 vols. (New York: Harper & Brothers, 1888), vol. I, 100–7; vol. II, 109–12; vol. III, 645–46.

There was nothing in such a faith to attract the sensual and carnal-minded. In fact, it was far more repellant than attractive, and nothing but the discontent excited by the pervading corruption and oppression of the Church can explain its rapid diffusion and the deep hold which it obtained upon the veneration of its converts. Although the asceticism which it inculcated was beyond the reach of average humanity, its ethical teachings were admirable. As a rule they were reasonably obeyed, and the orthodox admitted with regret and shame the contrast between the heretics and the faithful. It is true that the exaggerated condemnation of marriage expressed in the formula, that relations with a wife were as sinful as incest with mother or sister, was naturally enough perverted into the statement that such incest was permissible and was practised. Wild stories, moreover, were told of the nightly orgies in which the lights were extinguished and promiscuous intercourse took place; and the stubbornness of heresy was explained by telling how, when a child was born of these foul excesses, it was tossed from hand to hand through a fire until it expired; and that from its body was made an infernal eucharist of such power that whoever partook of it was thereafter incapable of abandoning the sect. There is ample store of such tales, but however useful they might be in exciting a wholesome popular detestation of heresy, the candid and intelligent inquisitors who had the best means of knowing the truth admit that they have no foundation in fact; and in the many hundreds of examinations and sentences which I have read there is no allusion to anything of the kind, except in some proceedings of Frà Antonio Secco among the Alpine valleys in 1387. As a rule, the inquisitors wasted no time in searching for what they knew was non-existent. As St. Bernard says, "If you interrogate them, nothing can be more Christian; as to their conversation, nothing can be less reprehensible, and what they speak they prove by deeds. As for the morals of the heretic, he cheats no one, he oppresses no one, he strikes no one; his cheeks are pale with fasting, he eats not the bread of idleness, his hands labor for his livelihood." This last assertion is especially true, for they were mostly simple folk, industrious peasants and mechanics, who felt the evils around them and welcomed any change. The theologians who combated them ridiculed them as ignorant churls, and in France they were popularly known by the name of Texerant (Tisserands), on account of the prevalence of the heresy among the weavers, whose monotonous occupation doubtless gave ample opportunity for thought. Rude and ignorant they might be for the most part, but they had skilled theologians for teachers, and an extensive popular literature which has utterly perished, saving a Catharan version of the New Testament in Romance and a book of ritual. Their familiarity with Scripture is vouched for by the warning of Lucas, Bishop of Tuy, that the Christian should dread their conversation as he would a tempest, unless he is deeply skilled in the law of God, so that he can overcome them in argument. Their strict morality was never corrupted, and a hundred years after St. Bernard the same testimony is rendered to the virtues of those who were persecuted in Florence in the middle of the thirteenth century. In fact the formula of confession used in their assemblies shows how strict a guard was maintained over every idle thought and careless word.

Their proselyting zeal was especially dreaded. No labor was too severe, no risks too great to deter them from spreading the faith which they deemed essential to salvation. Missionaries wandered over Europe through strange lands to carry the glad tidings to benighted populations, regardless of hardship, and undeterred by the fate of their brethren, whom they saw expiate at the stake the hardihood of their revolt. Externally they professed to be Catholics, and were exemplary in the performance of their religious duties till they had won the confidence of their new neighbors, and could venture on the attempt of secret conversion whenever they saw opportunity. They scattered by the wayside writings in which the poison of their doctrine was skilfully conveyed without being obtrusive, and sometimes they had no scruple in calling to their aid the superstitions of orthodoxy, as when such writings would promise indulgences to those who would read them carefully and circulate them among their neighbors, or when they purported to come from Jesus Christ and be conveyed by angels. It does not say much for the intelligence of the clergy when we are told that many priests were corrupted by such papers, picked up by shepherds and carried to them to be deciphered. Even more reprehensible was the device of the Cathari of Moncoul in France, who made an image of the Virgin, deformed and ugly and one-eyed, saying that Christ, to show his humility, had selected such a woman for a mother. Then they proceeded to work miracles with it, feigning to be sick and to be cured by it, until it acquired such reputation that many similar ones were made and placed in churches or oratories, until the heretics divulged the secret, to the great confusion of the faithful. The same device was carried out with a crucifix having no upper arm, the feet of Christ crossed, and only three nails—an unconventional form which was imitated and caused great scandal when the mockery was discovered. Even bolder frauds were attempted in Leon, and not without success, as we shall see hereafter.

The zeal for the faith, which prompted these eccentric missionary efforts, manifested itself in a resolute adherence to the precepts enjoined on the neophyte when admitted into the circle of the Perfects. As in the case of the Waldenses, while the Inquisition complained bitterly of the difficulty of obtaining an avowal from the simple "credens," whose rustic astuteness eluded the practised skill of the interrogator, it was the general testimony that the perfected heretic refused to lie, or to take an oath; and one member of the Holy Office warns his brethren not to begin by asking "Are you truly a Catharan?" for the answer will simply be "Yes," and then nothing more can be extracted; but if the Perfect is exhorted by the God in whom he believes to tell all about his life, he will faithfully detail it without falsehood. When we consider that this frankness led inevitably to the torture of death by burning, it is curious to observe that the inquisitor seems utterly unconscious of the emphatic testimony which he renders to the superhuman conscientiousness of his victims.

It is not easy for us to realize what there was in the faith of the Cathari to inspire men with the enthusiastic zeal of martyrdom, but no religion can show a more unbroken roll of those who unshrinkingly and joyfully sought death in its most abhorrent form in preference to apostasy. If the blood of the martyrs were really the seed of the Church, Manichaeism would now be the dominant religion of Europe. It may be partially explained by the belief that a painful death for the faith insured the return of the soul to God; but human weakness does not often permit such habitual triumph of the spirit over the flesh as that which rendered the Cathari a proverb in their thirst for martyrdom. The hostile testimony to this effect is virtually unanimous. In the earliest persecution on record, at Orleans about 1017, out of fifteen, thirteen remained steadfast in the face of the fire kindled for their destruction; they refused to recant though pardon was offered, and their constancy was the wonderment of the spectators. When, about 1040, the heretics of Monforte were discovered, and Eriberto, Archbishop of Milan, sent for Gherardo, their leader, he came at once and voluntarily set forth his belief, rejoicing in the opportunity of sealing his faith with torment. Those who were burned at Cologne in 1163 produced a profound impression by the cheerful alacrity with which they endured their fearful punishment; and while they were in their agony it is related that their leader, Arnold, half roasted to death, placed a liberated arm on the heads of his disciples, calmly saying, "Be ye constant in your faith, for this day shall ye be with Lawrence!" Among this group of heretics was a beautiful girl whose modesty moved the compassion of even the brutal executioners. She was withdrawn from the flames and promises were made to find her a husband or place her in a convent. Seeming to assent, she remained quiet till the rest were dead, and then asked her guards to show her the seducer of souls. In pointing out the body of Arnold they loosened their hold, when she suddenly broke from them, and, covering her face with her dress, threw herself upon the remains of her teacher, and, burning to death, descended with him into hell for eternity. Those who about the same time were detected at Oxford, rejected all offers of mercy, with the words of Christ, "Blessed are they which are persecuted for righteousness' sake, for theirs is the kingdom of heaven"; and when they were led forth after a sentence which virtually consigned them to a shameful and lingering death, they went rejoicing to the punishment, their leader Gerhard preceding them, singing "Blessed are ye when men shall revile you." In the Albigensian Crusade, at the capture of the Castle of Minerve, the Crusaders piously offered their prisoners the alternative of recantation or the stake, and a hundred and eighty preferred the stake, when, as the monkish chronicler quietly remarks, "no doubt all these martyrs of the devil passed from temporal to eternal flames." An experienced inquisitor of the fourteenth century tells us that the Cathari usually were either truly converted by the efforts of the Holy Office or else were ready to die for their faith; while the Waldenses were apt to feign conversion in order to escape. This obdurate zeal, we are assured by the orthodox writers, had in it nothing of the constancy of Christian martyrdom, but was simply hardness of heart inspired by Satan; and Frederic II enumerated among their evil traits the obstinacy which led the survivors to be in no way dismayed or deterred by the ruthless example made of those who were punished.

It was, perhaps, natural that these Manichaeans should be accused of worshipping the devil. To men bred in the current orthodox practices of purchasing by prayer, or money, or other good works whatever blessings they desired, and expecting nothing without such payment, it seemed inevitable that the Manichaean, regarding all matter to be the work of Satan, should invoke him for worldly prosperity. The husbandman, for instance, could not pray to God for a plentiful harvest, but must do so to Satan, who was the creator of corn. It is true that there was a sect, known as Luciferani, who were said to worship Satan, regarding him as the brother of God, unjustly banished from heaven, and the dispenser of worldly good, but these, as we shall see hereafter, were a branch of the Brethren of the Free Spirit, probably descended from the Ortlibenses, and there is absolutely no evidence that the Cathari ever wavered in their trust in Christ or diverted their aspirations from the hope of reunion with God.

Such was the faith whose rapid spread throughout the south of Europe filled the Church with well-grounded dismay; and, however much we may deprecate the means used for its suppression and commiserate those who suffered for conscience' sake, we cannot but admit that the cause of orthodoxy was in this case the cause of progress and civilization. Had Catharism become dominant, or even had it been allowed to exist on equal terms, its influence could not have failed to prove disastrous. Its asceticism with regard to commerce between the sexes, if strictly enforced, could only have led to the extinction of the race, and as this involves a contradiction of nature, it would have probably resulted in lawless concubinage and the destruction of the institution of the family, rather than in the disappearance of the human race and the return of exiled souls to their Creator, which was the *summum bonum* of the true Catharan. Its condemnation of the visible universe and of matter in general as the work of Satan rendered sinful all striving after material improvement, and the conscientious belief in such a creed could only lead man back, in time, to his original condition of savagism. It was not only a revolt against the Church, but a renunciation of man's domination over nature. As such it was doomed from the start, and our only wonder must be that it maintained itself so long and so stubbornly even against a Church which had earned so much of popular detestation. Yet though the exaltation caused by persecution might keep it alive among the enthusiastic and the discontented, had it obtained the upper hand and maintained its purity it must surely have perished through its fundamental errors. Had it become a dominant faith, moreover, it would have bred a sacerdotal class as privileged as the Catholic priesthood, for the "veneration" offered to the consecrated ministers as the tabernacles of the Holy Ghost shows us what vantage ground they would have had when persecution had given place to power, and carnal human nature had asserted itself in the ambitious men who would have sought its high places.

The soil was probably prepared for its reception by remains of the older Manichaeism which, with strange pertinacity, long maintained itself in secret after its public manifestation had been completely suppressed. Muratori has printed a Latin anathema of its doctrines, probably dating about the year 800, which shows that even so late as the ninth century it was still an object of persecution. It was about 970 that John Zimiski transplanted the Paulicians to Thrace, whence they spread with great rapidity through the Balkan peninsula. When the Crusaders under Bohemond of Tarento, in 1097, arrived in Macedonia they learned that the city of Pelagonia was inhabited wholly by heretics, whereupon they paused in their pilgrimage to the Holy Sepulchre long enough to capture the town, to raze it to the earth, and to put all the citizens to the sword. In Dalmatia the Paulicians founded the seaport of Dugunthia (Trau), which became the seat of one of their leading episcopates; and in the time of Innocent III we find them in great numbers throughout the whole Slav territory, making extensive conversions with their customary missionary zeal, and giving that pontiff much concern, in unavailing efforts for their suppression. Numerous as the Cathari of Western Europe became, they always looked to the east of the Adriatic as to the headquarters of their sect. It was there that arose the form of modified Dualism known as Concorrezan, under the influence of the Bogomili, and religious questions were wont to be referred thither for solution. . . .

. . . The Inquisition triumphed, as force will generally do when it is sufficiently strong, skilfully applied, and systematically continued without interruption to the end. In the twelfth century the south of France had been the most civilized land of Europe. There commerce, industry, art, science, had been far in advance of the age. The cities had won virtual self-government, were proud of their wealth and strength, jealous of their liberties, and self-sacrificing in their patriotism. The nobles, for the most part, were cultivated men, poets themselves or patrons of poetry, who had learned that their prosperity depended on the prosperity of their subjects, and that municipal liberties were a safeguard, rather than a menace, to the wise ruler. The Crusaders came, and their unfinished work was taken up and executed to the bitter end by the Inquisition. It left a ruined and impoverished country, with shattered industry and failing commerce. The native nobles were broken by confiscation and replaced by strangers, who occupied the soil, introducing the harsh customs of Northern feudalism, or the despotic principles of the Roman law, in the extensive domains acquired by the crown. A people of rare natural gifts had been tortured, decimated, humiliated, despoiled, for a century and more. The precocious civilization which had promised to lead Europe in the path of culture was gone, and to Italy was transferred the honor of the Renaissance. In return for this was unity of faith and a Church which had been hardened and vitiated and secularized in the strife. Such was the work and such the outcome of the Inquisition in the field which afforded it the widest scope for its activity, and the fullest opportunity for developing its powers.

Yet in the very triumph of the Inquisition was the assurance of its decline. Supported by the State, it had earned and repaid the royal favor by the endless stream of confiscations which it poured into the royal coffers. Perhaps nothing contributed more to the consolidation of the royal supremacy than the change of ownership which threw into new hands so large a portion of the lands of the South. In the territories of the great vassals the right to the confiscations for heresy became recognized as an important portion of the *droits seigneuriaux*. In the domains of the crown they were granted to favorites or sold at moderate prices to those who thus became interested in the new order of things. The royal officials grasped everything on which they could lay their hands, whether on the excuse of treason or of heresy, with little regard to any rights; and although the integrity of Louis IX caused an inquest to be held in 1262 which restored a vast amount of property illegally held, this was but a small fraction of the whole. To assist his Parlement in settling the innumerable cases which arose, he ordered, in 1260, the charters and letters of greatest importance to be sent to Paris. Those of each of the six sénéchaussées filled a coffer, and the six coffers were deposited in the treasury of the Sainte-Chapelle. In this process of absorption the case of the extensive Viscounty of Fenouillèdes may be taken as an illustration of the zeal with which the Inquisition co-operated in securing the political results desired by the crown. Fenouillèdes had been seized during the Crusades and given to Nuñez Sancho of Roussillon, from whom it passed, through the King of Aragon, into the hands of St. Louis. In 1264 Beatrix, widow of Hugues, son of the former Viscount Pierre, applied to the Parlement for her rights and dower and those of her children. Immediately the inquisitor, Pons de Poyet, commenced a prosecution against the memory of Pierre, who had died more than twenty years previously in the bosom of the Church, and had been buried with the Templars of Mas Deu, after assuming the religious habit and receiving the last sacraments. He was condemned for having held relations with heretics, his bones were dug up and burned, and the Parlement rejected the claim of the daughter-in-law and grandchildren. Pierre, the eldest of these, in 1300, made a claim for the ancestral estates, and Boniface VIII espoused his quarrel with the object of giving trouble to Philippe le Bel; but, though the affair was pursued for some years, the inquisitorial sentence held good. It was not only the actual heretics and their descendants who were dispossessed. The land had been so deeply tinctured with heresy that there were few indeed whose ancestors could not be shown, by the records of the Inquisition, to have incurred the fatal taint of associating with them.

The rich bourgeoisie of the cities were ruined in the same way. Some inventories have been preserved of the goods and chattels sequestrated when the arrests were made at Albi in 1299 and 1300, which show how thoroughly everything was swept into the maelstrom. That of Raymond Calverie, a notary, gives us every detail of the plenishing of a well-to-do burgher's house—every pillow, sheet, and coverlet is enumerated, every article of kitchen gear, the salted provisions and grain, even his wife's little trinkets. His farm or bastide was subjected to the same minuteness of seizure. Then we have a similar insight into the stock and goods of Jean Baudier, a rich merchant. Every fragment of stuff is duly measured—cloths of Ghent, Ypres, Amiens, Cambray, St. Omer, Rouen, Montcornet, etc., with their valuation—pieces of miniver, and other articles of trade.

His town house and farm were inventoried with the same conscientious care. It is easy to see how prosperous cities were reduced to poverty, how industry languished, and how the independence of the municipalities was broken into subjection in the awful uncertainty which hung over the head of every man.

In this respect the Inquisition was building better than it knew. In thus aiding to establish the royal power over the newly acquired provinces, it was contributing to erect an authority which was destined in the end to reduce it to comparative insignificance. With the disappearance of Catharism, Languedoc became as much a part of the monarchy as l'Isle de France, and the career of its Inquisition merges into that of the rest of the kingdom. It need not, therefore, be pursued separately further. . . .

When we consider, however, the simple earnestness with which such multitudes of humble heretics endured the extremity of outrage and the most cruel of deaths, in the endeavor to ascertain and obey the will of God in the fashioning of their lives, we recognize what material existed for the development of true Christianity, and for the improvement of the race, far down in the obscurer ranks of society. We can see now how greatly advanced might be the condition of humanity had that leaven been allowed to penetrate the whole mass in place of being burned out with fire. Unorganized and unresisting, the heretics were unable to withstand the overwhelming forces arrayed against them. Power and place and wealth were threatened by their practical interpretation of the teachings of Christ. The pride of opinion in the vast and laboriously constructed theories of scholastic theology, the conscientious belief in the exclusive salvation obtainable through the Church alone, the recognized duty of exterminating the infected sheep and preserving the vineyard of the Lord from the ravages of heretical foxes, all united to form a conservatism against which even the heroic endurance of the sectaries was unavailing. Yet there are few pages in the history of humanity more touching, few records of self-sacrifice more inspiring, few examples more instructive of the height to which the soul can rise above the weaknesses of the flesh, than those which we may glean from the fragmentary documents of the Inquisition and the scanty references of the chroniclers to the abhorred heretics so industriously tracked and so pitilessly despatched. Ignorant and toiling men and women—peasants, mechanics, and the like—dimly conscious that the system of society was wrong, that the commands of God were perverted or neglected, that humanity was capable of higher development, if it could but find and follow the Divine Will; striving each in his humble sphere to solve the inscrutable and awful problems of existence, to secure in tribulation his own salvation, and to help his fellows in the arduous task—these forgotten martyrs of the truth drew from themselves alone the strength which enabled them to dare and to endure martyrdom. No prizes of ambition lay before them to tempt their departure from the safe and beaten track, no sympathizing crowds surrounded the piles of fagots and strengthened them in the fearful trial; but scorn and hatred and loathing were their portion to the last. Save in cases of relapse, life could always be saved by recantation and return to the bosom of the Church, which recognized that even from a worldly point of view a converted heretic was more valuable than a martyred one, yet the steadfast resolution, which the orthodox characterized as satanic hardening of the heart, was too common to excite surprise. ✳

2. ALBERT C. SHANNON

FROM Albert C. Shannon, *The Popes and Heresy in the Thirteenth Century* (Villanova, Pa.: Augustinian Press, 1949), pp. 3–10, 135–36.

Heresy, in its strictest meaning, was construed as a deliberate and intentional denial of some article or articles of the revealed truth of the Catholic faith, and a public and obstinate persistence in that error. A person was considered guilty of heresy who knew the doctrine of the Church and nevertheless denied it or believed something contrary to it, while a person would not be guilty of heresy who was ignorant of the true doctrine. In the latter case, however, when such a person was officially informed of the orthodox teaching but persisted in his error, then he was formally guilty of the crime of heresy. Moreover, it was required that the crime of heresy be externalized, for that is what gave it the character of a delict. Through the years the word "heretic" acquired a broader meaning and came to include *credentes*, persons who remained under excommunication for a year without seeking absolution, and in the reign of Boniface VIII even the obstreperous Colonnas were classed as "tamquam heretici." Jews since they were not baptized were not regarded as heretics, though they became subject to the inquisitorial tribunal if they attempted to proselytize Christians. Divination and sorcery did not fall within the competency of the inquisition unless manifest heresy was involved. Individual polemicists, canonists, and even inquisitors were inclined to extend and enlarge the concept of heresy to include various other crimes and delinquencies, but such gratuitous interpretations never received papal approbation.

Papal legislation recognized several categories of persons who came under the competency of the inquisition. It may be well to have these clearly before us at the outset of our discussion. Heretics properly so-called were those who had made a formal profession of heresy by being initiated into the sect and by performing all the duties which this involved. In the Albigensian sect, in strict terminology, the heretics were the *Perfecti. Credentes* or Believers were those who adhered to the doctrines of an heretical sect without submitting themselves to all its laws and practices. Before the law, however, they were equally guilty as formal heretics and subject to the same penalties. In addition to these two main divisions there were also other minor designations which were not mutually exclusive but designated activities contrary to the law rather than juridical classifications of heretics. Suspects were those who associated with heretics in more or less close familiarity by frequenting their sermons, bowing the knee before them, praying with them, asking their blessing, and proclaiming them to be good men. According to the frequency and ardor with which a person performed these acts he was considered lightly, vehemently, or violently suspected of heresy with proportionately graduated penalties. Concealers were those who at times saw and recognized heretics but who resolutely refused to denounce them to the proper authorities. Receivers were those who knowingly gave asylum to heretics on different occasions in order to protect them or to give them opportunity to carry on their religious functions. Defenders were those who defended heretics in any way or denied the right of the Church to prosecute them. Such defenders were termed *fautores* when they gave aid, counsel, or favor to the heretics. A relapsed heretic was one who had abjured his error and afterwards had fallen into the same heresy. The term *relapsus* was of special importance because a relapsed heretic came to be one who was without further trial handed over to the secular arm to receive the full penalty of the law. Hence any extension of its technical meaning had a vastly more real and practical significance than a mere elucidation of juridical terminology. In this regard the queries submitted to Alexander IV for solution by the Dominican and Franciscan inquisitors were of major consequence.

Is he to be considered a relapsed heretic who upon investigation is cleared of the charge of heresy and abjures it, yet afterwards is actually convicted of heresy? To this the pope replied that if the suspicion against the accused in the first case was violent and supported by certain and true grounds, then by a certain fiction of law such a one is to be held as a relapsed heretic. If, on the other hand, he was arrested in the previous instance on light suspicion the defendant is not now to be considered a relapsed heretic. Again, if a person abjures heresy and then afterwards favors heretics in any way Alexander IV declared that he is to be regarded as a relapsed heretic because his subsequent conduct would seem to be a consequence of the approval of his previous error. Finally, one who was found guilty of heresy on one point of doctrine and then after abjuration erred on a different article of faith fell within the category of a *relapsus*.

With perhaps one exception the papal registers provide few details concerning the teachings of the Albigensians. Innocent III, so far as can be ascertained, acquired most of his information on the spread of heresy from local prelates and legates dealing directly with the heretics, and from the records of the investigations sent to him. In general, he speaks of the Manicheans as now calling themselves Catharists or Patarins and teaching that corporal food was not created by God but by the devil, the principle of darkness who created all corporal and visible things. The pope further states that Mani held that marriage was forbidden, asserting that it was not a greater sin to violate one's mother or sister than a third party. He speaks of the heretics as perverting the Scriptures, simulating justice in order to seduce the innocent, and as claiming that they alone are just and holy. Finally the pope charges that they repudiate the sacraments, deny the efficacy of the sacraments in the hands of unworthy priests, advocate lay preaching, and make unauthorized translations of the Bible.

In regard to the Waldensians in particular, Innocent III evidently believed that they had departed far from the orthodox teaching as seen from the wide range of dogmas included in the profession of faith demanded of them. These doctrines concerned the nature of God, the Blessed Trinity, creation, the inspiration of the Old and New Testaments, the Incarnation, the institution of the Roman Catholic Church, the nature of the sacraments, the validity of the sacraments administered by unworthy ministers, the Mass, the necessity of jurisdiction for preaching, matrimony, the eating of meat, the taking of oaths, the existence of purgatory and the value of alms-giving and prayers for the dead, the resurrection of the body, and the precept of supporting the clergy. Such a profession was actually made by Durand of Huesca and his associates, a branch of the Waldensians, when they submitted to the Church and formed a new religious congregation called the Poor Catholics. But for the most part the Waldensians maintained their doctrines prohibiting lying, the taking of oaths, killing for any reason, and stressing anti-sacerdotal teachings. While it may be assumed that Innocent III possessed a fairly wide knowledge of the tenets of the heretics and their activities, he seemed to be more concerned with the antireligious aspects of their teaching, and the consequent contamination of the innocent than with carefully distinguishing individual groups and their peculiar teachings. It is this consideration that is the dominating factor in his attitude toward heresy. At the same time he insisted on the investigators finding out the truth in the matter of preaching the orthodox doctrine, refuting the errors, and reporting the full facts to him without delay.

Honorius III never once details the tenets of any particular heretical group beyond the fact of merely mentioning their names. The same is true of all the remaining pontiffs of the thirteenth century: condemn and excommunicate heretics they did, but without enumerating tenets which they evidently regarded as common knowledge. Clement IV when archbishop of Narbonne surely was in a position to know the heretics with some intimacy, but he wrote a treatise for the benefit of the local inquisitors without so much as alluding to particular sects or to their beliefs. Even Gregory IX contents himself with renewing the sentence of excommunication levied against the Catharists without specifying their errors. This readiness of the popes to speak in generalities contrasts strangely with Gregory's acceptance of the report that the Stedingers had perpetrated terrible cruelties and devastations, that they were devotees of black art, consulted witches and demons, and performed magical rites with waxen images. Even more extraordinary is the letter addressed to the archbishop of Mainz, the bishop of Hildesheim, and Conrad of Marburg in which Gregory IX described in detail the repulsive rites of the Luciferians as they had been reported to him. Waxing eloquent in castigating these malodorous ceremonies the pope declared that such practices were not only contrary to reason and disgusting to mankind, but were sufficient to provoke even nature to rise against them. Initiation into this sect reportedly involved obscene obeisance to toads and cats, reverence to a clammy ghoul symbolic of renunciation of the Catholic faith, and a banquet followed by frightful orgies. In addition adherents were to profane the Host every Eastertide in contempt of the Redeemer. In conformity with their devil worship the Luciferians maintained that God had unjustly cast Satan into hell, and that he would one day triumph over heaven; consequently they loved evil and hated good. Such excesses defy belief and savor rather of the wild imaginings and vile tales reminiscent of the rumors concocted about ancient mystery cults. And in fact the pope never again alludes to this sect; it is difficult to believe that his letter represents a reasoned and measured judgment, based on full information in regard to it.

Several other isolated groups of heretics receive passing notice by the popes during the course of the thirteenth century, including the followers of Arnold of Brescia, and the Humiliati who apparently separated into an heretical and an orthodox group, the former joining the Poor Men of Lyons while the latter gained official recognition and continued as an orthodox religious congregation.

With an understanding of the nature and compass of the crime of heresy and of the central doctrines of the predominant heretical sects of the thirteenth century the intention and activities of the papacy in suppressing heresy may be viewed in proper historical perspective. Certainly from the foregoing it is evident that the popes took it for granted that the individual doctrinal errors of the heretical groups were common knowledge, for they showed a remarkable disinclination to enumerate them, much less discuss them in detail. Apart from Innocent III none of the popes revealed in their correspondence a very precise acquaintanceship with the tenets of the dissident sects. A careful examination of the papal correspondence would seem to warrant the conclusion that the papacy was primarily concerned with discovering and suppressing heresy in general with only a subordinate interest in the intricacies of the exact errors involved....

With these limitations in mind an examination of the papal attitude toward the observance of prescribed legal processes by the inquisitors, of papal knowledge of their activities, and finally of the papal method of dealing with delinquent inquisitors would seem to justify the following conclusions: The papacy established several checks on the conduct of the inquisitors in office and paid careful attention to complaints reaching the Holy See of miscarriages of justice. Upon hearing of complaints against inquisitors the popes, so far as we know, followed the same procedure as in the case of appeals: a special legate or commission of high dignitaries was dispatched to investigate the charges. On the strength of the reports subsequently submitted the pope either dismissed the charges as unwarranted and unfounded or, in case they were verified, he removed the unworthy inquisitors from office. From the papal registers it appears that few such complaints were lodged against the inquisitors at Rome in the thirteenth century, and this lends support to the thesis that the inquisitors as a whole fulfilled the duties of their office with integrity and devotion. ✻

3. STEVEN RUNCIMAN

FROM Steven Runciman, *The Medieval Manichee* (Cambridge: Cambridge University Press, 1947), pp. 139–47.

The murder of Peter of Castelnau altered the situation. Moral indignation all over France supported the Pope. Philip Augustus might content himself with writing sympathetically to the Pope, saying that he too had reason to be displeased with the Count of Toulouse, whose conduct during the English Wars was far from satisfactory, but reminding him that the Count could not be deprived of his lands (which he held from the French King), unless heresy was definitely proved. The Pope's Crusade was, in fact, an infringement of the King's sovereignty. But the nobles of the North would no longer be restrained. They found their leader, rather surprisingly, in a petty noble of the Ile de France, Simon de Montfort, who had become Earl of Leicester as the husband of a great English heiress. Under his guidance, and inspired by the ceaseless preaching of the Pope's new legate, Arnald of Cîteaux, the Crusaders gathered together in the course of 1208, and in the autumn marched southwards. A series of wars was begun that would end at last in the suppression of heresy.

But the first war took twenty years; and even so the heretics' resistance was not over. They on their side had considerable material resources. Great nobles like Raymond of Toulouse or Raymond-Roger of Foix might only be *hereticales* and unreliable; but they would obviously oppose to their utmost the barbarians from the North. Other nobles, such as the Viscount of Béziers, and almost all the nobility of the second rank, were devoted to heresy. There were towns, such as Fanjeaux, Béziers, Duns, or Laurac, where, whatever the overlord might think, the population was so wholly heretic that they might count as heretic fortresses. There were castles that were admittedly heretic fortresses, for example Servian, by Béziers, or Minerve, above Narbonne. Above all, there was the impregnable city of Montségur, the Mountain of Safety, the Mount Thabor of the Cathars. This great castle stood on the territory of the Counts of Foix, and was, it seems, part of the dowry of the heretic princess Esclarmonde of Foix, from whom it was held by Raymond of Perelle. He was a fervent heretic and in effect handed the whole fortress over to the unrestricted use of the Cathar Church. Here the heretics found a safe asylum during their troubles, and here they kept up their best establishments of Perfects, over one of which Esclarmonde herself presided.

The story of the war known as the Albigensian Crusade is long and intricate. The religious issue became blurred in the territorial issue. Pope Innocent III and the Dominican Brothers were above all eager to extirpate heresy as quickly and efficiently as possible, by force and fire if need be but preferably by preaching and willing repentance. But their allies, the Northern barons under Simon de Montfort, though many of them were sincerely religious, were all of them anxious to enrich themselves at the expense of the wealthy Southern lords; and they were encouraged by the Papal legate, Arnald-Amaury of Cîteaux, and by the French bishops who saw in Raymond of Toulouse and his peers slippery renegades, the murderers of Peter of Castelnau, men whose power must be broken forever if heresy was to be eliminated. The Southern barons were in a difficult position. Many like Raymond himself were anxious to reconcile themselves with the Church, but they were temperamentally easy-going and they could not afford to persecute a sect that included half their subjects; and they naturally wished to retain their lands. Others, like Raymond-Roger of Béziers, felt that the best policy was an open support of heresy. Others again, like King Peter of Aragon, were steadfastly Catholic but deeply resented this Northern invasion into territory over parts of which (such as Carcassonne) he was suzerain. But, for all their hatred of the Northerners, the Southern lords would not join together. Raymond of Toulouse in vain approached Raymond-Roger, who was his nephew; in vain Raymond-Roger sought help from King Peter, who was his suzerain. Raymond of Toulouse made his submission to the Church and performed a humiliating penance at Saint-Gilles and for a campaign joined the Crusaders, and a little later went with his son on a weary journey to Rome to interview the Pope himself. Meanwhile Simon de Montfort, urged on by the Abbot of Cîteaux, annexed his lands and his titles. Raymond-Roger equally tried to submit in time; but his was the first territory to be attacked. The holocaust and massacres at Béziers in July 1209 were a foretaste of what the South might expect. After the capture of Carcassonne later in the year Raymond-Roger was declared to have forfeited his territory, which was annexed by Simon de Montfort. Atrocities grew in number, encouraged by the legate despite Innocent's disavowal. At the capitulation of Minerve in July 1210, when the heretics' lives were to be saved by the terms of the surrender, de Montfort's troops butchered them at his orders, and the legate did not interfere. Finally at the Council of Montpellier in 1211 Innocent III yielded to the extremist party; the Northern barons were established in the South with the fullest right and intention of persecution.

Then came the reaction. The Count of Toulouse returned from Rome and was welcomed as a deliverer. The King of Aragon came out openly against the Northerners, after the failure of his attempt to stop the Crusade with Innocent's help. Innocent's hand was forced again by his extremists; and Peter of Aragon joined his forces to those of Raymond of Toulouse, Raymond-Roger of Foix and the Count of Comminges. With the reaction, the heretics came out of hiding again, and preached openly in the Toulousain and Foix. But their revival was short-lived; the Southern lords met disaster by the castle of Muret in 1213. Their army was scattered by the knights of Simon de Montfort. The Counts of Toulouse and Foix fled to English territory, and Peter of Aragon lay dead on the battlefield.

The disaster at Muret was not so fatal as might have been expected. Innocent preached moderation and grudged Simon de Montfort the fruits of victory; and King Philip Augustus sent his son Louis to the South to see what was happening. At the Lateran Council of 1215 the Southern lords were reconciled again with the Church, promising again to persecute heresy. They returned to their battered lands; and Simon de Montfort's attempt to dislodge them once more was closed by his death before the walls of Toulouse in June 1218. The South was secure for a while, and by 1220 the heretics again worshipped freely. The Albigensian Crusade seemed to be over, having achieved nothing but material destruction. Heresy still was rampant.

Innocent III was dead by now, and Honorius III had committed the Church to Simon's support. With Simon's death his cause crumbled. His heirs and the Pope saved it by handing his rights over to the new King of France, Louis VIII. Raymond VI died in 1222. Raymond VII, his son, had a better record of orthodoxy. But it did not avail him. In 1226, after a comparatively peaceful interlude, too short for the country's recovery, Languedoc again was invaded by the enemy, a great army of Northern barons under King Louis VIII himself. In three years the royal army achieved its ends. Raymond VII was reduced to sign the treaty of Meaux in April 1227 with the young King Louis IX and his mother the Regent Blanche—Louis VIII had died in the previous year. Raymond performed a humiliating penance, agreed to pay an indemnity and a heavy tribute for five years, married his daughter and heiress Jeanne to the King's brother Alphonse, and undertook to persecute heresy. His allies, the Counts of Foix and of Comminges and the Viscounts of Béziers and Béarn, joined in the treaty, giving up castles as guarantees but refusing to promise a thorough repression of the Cathars.

For ten years an uneasy peace reigned in Languedoc. Raymond periodically tried to carry out his side of the bargain. The Dominicans were allowed to set up their Inquisition at Toulouse, at Albi and at Narbonne; large numbers of heretics were arrested and examined and the majority of them were burnt. But the town authorities, the Consuls and the *Capitouls*, resented the Inquisition as much as an infringement of their rights as from love of heresy. Many of the nobles, in particular the Count of Foix and the Viscount of Béziers, still openly gave the heretics protection. The heretic preachers again wandered through the countryside, avoiding now the bigger towns but preaching freely in many of the castles of the nobility; in the smaller towns communities of the Perfect were maintained undisguised. But they were nervous. In 1232 the heretic leaders negotiated with the Lord of Perelle to have his guarantee that Montségur should continue to be their asylum. He agreed, and henceforward it became the recognized centre of their power. Raymond of Perelle's alliance with the heresy was to be cemented in the blood of his daughter Esclarmonde. Periodically a concentrated attack of the Inquisitors would destroy for the time being a Cathar community; for example at Moissac in 1234 the leading

Cathars were burnt or forced to flee for refuge, some to Lombardy and some to Montségur. But so long as the native nobility survived, the heretics could still be hopeful.

For the native nobility, however, the situation was difficult. Pressed by the Church and by the French King, Raymond of Toulouse found himself steadily shorn of his power and unable to give legitimate protection to his subjects. Raymond Trencavel, Viscount of Béziers, belonging to a family long suspected by the Church, with his town of Carcassonne forfeited, felt even more desperate. In 1239 the two of them tried to recapture their freedom. But Raymond Trencavel's attempt was crushed before Carcassonne; and in two years Raymond of Toulouse was reduced to submission by the royal troops of France. Raymond Trencavel retired broken to his estates in Catalonia. The Count of Toulouse became once more a dutiful son of the Church.

His first duty was to deal with the castle of Montségur. So long as the Cathars had their City of Refuge, it would be impossible to stamp them out. But he was unwilling to act, till the heretics themselves gave provocation. They had had great hopes of the 1239 rising; and its failure had been a shock to them. Moreover in 1241 their friend Roger-Bernard of Foix died, reconciled on his deathbed to the Church. His son Roger IV was more anxious to preserve his lands than to protect his father's friends. In 1242 a band of desperate heretics from Montségur joined with the heretics of Avignonet to ambush the party of Inquisitors that was on its way to visit the latter town and massacred them all. The crime was disastrous in its effects. Public opinion, remembering the murder of Peter of Castelnau in his father's day, at once suspected Raymond of Toulouse. He, to disassociate himself from it, wrote letters of humble submission to the Queen-Regent Blanche and vowed vengeance on the murderers. His officers hastened to hand over large numbers of heretics to the Inquisitors. Throughout 1243 and 1244 the fires of the Inquisition burnt merrily. Many of the nobility perished in the flames: Peter Robert of Mirepoix, Arnalda of Massa, Peter of Navidals, the Dowager Lady of Fanjaux, and the young Esclarmonde of Perelle. The heretics fled to the mountain valleys of the Pyrenees or away to Lombardy or to Bosnia; their leaders congregated in Montségur. There on their mountain-top where no Catholic had set foot for a generation they carried on their rites and defied the Catholic world. Raymond saw clearly that to fulfil his obligations to the Church Montségur must be destroyed.

At Montségur the heretics prepared their resistance. They appealed to their overlord, the young Count of Foix, but he disowned them and left them to their fate. In 1238 they had easily withstood a siege attempted by Raymond; but Raymond had been only half-hearted then. This time he was in earnest with the royal troops backing him; and they had less hope. Men and women alike took part in the defence, led by the Lord of Perelle and by Guillebert of Castres, the most venerated of the Cathar bishops. But, hopelessly outnumbered, they could not for all their courage hold the fortress for ever. When the end seemed near, the greater part of the defenders received the Consolamentum, the final rite of their church, although by so becoming Perfects they condemned themselves to the fires of the Inquisitors. Then, one dark March night, four of the Perfect crept from the castle with the holiest books and the treasure of the Cathars, to carry them through to the Cathar communities in the high Pyrenees. Next day Montségur surrendered to the Count of Toulouse.

The fortress was destroyed. The Perfect, to the number of about two hundred, were burnt without trial. The rest of the defenders were imprisoned, to be released some months later on the payment of fines and penances.

The fall of their citadel was a blow from which the Cathars never recovered. They became an underground sect, without a centre, without a storehouse for their treasure and their lore. The Perfect with the holy books from Montségur reached the Pyrenean castle of So, but they could not stay in peace there. Wherever they rested, soon they had to move on; and their treasure and their writings gradually were scattered in the wandering. But still large Cathar communities remained. For another half-century the Inquisitors were fully occupied, perpetually discovering nests of heretics and destroying them. During these years there was a steady migration of the Cathars to the comparative safety of Lombardy; some went farther to the greater safety of Bosnia.

In 1249 after the death of Raymond VII, his successor, his son-in-law Alphonse of France, attempted an act of clemency, promising to restore confiscated goods to the repentant children of heretics. The Church forbade him. In the discouragement that followed, the native dynasty now extinct, the leading Cathars of Toulouse fled to Lombardy. About the same time St Louis destroyed the Cathar church of Languedoïl; and its remnants also fled across the Alps. By 1274 there were said to be no more Cathar bishops in the French King's lands. The heretic that wished to become a Perfect had to come to Italy to his old bishops that were settled there to receive the rite. In France the Consolamentum was administered only to the dying.

In 1277 and 1278 we find the Inquisition indulging in fresh activities. By 1290 its fierceness seems to have provoked a popular recrudescence of sympathy towards the Cathars. At Béziers and at Carcassonne in 1296 Inquisitors were driven out by the people and by the municipal authorities. Cathar bishops came back from Lombardy and held assemblies again in

Languedoc. But it was not for long. The great persecutions of Philip IV's reign, from 1304 to 1312, destroyed the new enthusiasm; and persecution went steadily on throughout the next decades. By 1330 it seems that the Cathar church in France was effectively crushed; henceforward it was negligible. ✻

4. ZOÉ OLDENBOURG

FROM Zoé Oldenbourg, *Massacre at Montségur*, trans. Peter Green (New York: Random House, Pantheon Books, 1961), pp. 225–28, 365–67.

Since the time of De Montfort's victories, the Church had benefited from the conqueror's protection, and had been enriched by a variety of gifts—in particular the goods of dispossessed heretics. But now she found herself in a more critical position even than before 1209; for the Counts and the *faidit* knights were not only trying to get back this confiscated property, but also to lay hands on those domains which Raymond VI had been compelled to give up to the Church. Encouraged by his military successes, Raymond VII had even repossessed himself of the County of Melgueil, which had been made a direct fief of the Papacy, and held by the Bishop of Maguelonne. Such bishops as were enthroned during the Crusade now had perforce to fly from their sees; Guy des Vaux de Cernay, Bishop of Carcassonne, had gone back to die in France, and was replaced by his predecessor, Bernard-Raymond de Roquefort, who had been evicted from office and was therefore a popular choice. Foulques, the excommunicate Bishop of Toulouse, did not dare show his face there, since he was held responsible for all the city's misfortunes. Thédise, Bishop of Agde (the former Legate and one of the principal instigators of the Crusade), together with the Bishops of Nîmes and Maguelonne and the Primate of All Languedoc (that aged figure Arnald-Amalric, Archbishop of Narbonne), had been forced to take refuge in Catholic Montpellier. Here, where the riotous populace could not touch them, they pursued a vigorous diplomatic campaign, in which excommunication notices alternated with appeals to the Pope. At times they tried to conciliate the Counts; at others they did their best to bring down royal or pontifical thunderbolts on their heads.

After a period spent backing Amaury de Montfort; the former Abbot of

Cîteaux was now betting on local nationalism; he seems at last to have grasped just how great a danger the French threat represented to his country—and perhaps for the very political independence of the Church in Languedoc. Having realized that the King would never undertake this Crusade except on condition of annexing the Midi provinces, Arnald-Amalric now definitely swung over to Raymond VII, and was working to get him recognized by the Church as legitimate *seigneur* of his own domains. It is an odd fact that this former Crusader general should have been practically alone among the Bishops of Languedoc in having some end in view beyond the extirpation of heresy and the Church's immediate material interests. At least, he may have done so. But this turbulent, bellicose prelate died in 1225, bequeathing to the Abbey of Fontfroide his books, his arms, and his warhorse. In him the nationalist movement lost an ally who may not have had much influence, but at least never lacked energy. Arnald-Amalric was replaced by Peter Amiel, a declared partisan both of the Crusade and the French Crown. The Occitan clergy was now identified with a political party as aggressive as it was unpopular, and all the more dangerous in that its every setback was regarded in Rome as a defeat for the Church.

That the Church *was* excessively unpopular in Languedoc is not at all surprising. By openly and wholeheartedly approving the Crusade, these bishops and abbots merely alienated confidence—even that of loyal Catholics. The troubadours bracketed Frenchmen and clerics as targets for their maledictions—*Francès et clergia*—and on several occasions the *Chanson* credits Occitan *seigneurs* with remarks such as: 'We should never have been defeated *if it had not been for the Church* . . .' The Church, even for those who invoked the Saints and venerated relics, was the enemy by definition. Must we assume from this that she had no local supporters at all?

Every major city had its Bishop, who was a most puissant *seigneur:* frequently co-suzerain of the community, and on occasion its sole overlord. Béziers and Toulouse both owed homage simultaneously to the Count (or Viscount) and the Bishop; and the pretensions of an Arnald-Amalric, *qua* Archbishop, to the Duchy of Narbonne were contestable but by no means extravagant. Even in a situation—such as that of Toulouse before Foulques' arrival—when episcopal authority was virtually in abeyance, the bishopric still disposed of a vast administrative organization, complete with fiscal and judiciary branches; this afforded employment to numerous persons, clerks for the most part, who served the Bishop and derived their livelihood from him. Before the Crusade, when the Church was both weakened and little regarded, there were plenty of powerful and prosperous abbeys in Languedoc; Cistercian reforms had produced a revival of

Catholicism, and Foulques of Marseilles the troubadour, far from turning Cathar, had become a monk at Fontfroide. The monasteries were not all mouldering or emptied by mass desertions. Abbeys such as Grandselve or Fontfroide were centres of deeply sincere religious life, and the monks who spent their days there in prayer and fasting rivalled the *perfecti* when it came to austerity. The number, and the great wealth, of these abbeys makes it plain that, despite the lamentations of Popes and bishops, the Church in Languedoc was very far from being reduced to a mere cypher. The very hatred she aroused bears witness to her relative power; and even if she had no other supporters apart from the clergy themselves, these constituted a permanent minority—small, indeed, but far from negligible—in the very heart of the community.

The mere fact that they led a comparatively easy life, and were in any case hardly ever bothered by real hardship, conferred a kind of superior status on them *ab initio*. They were also literate, and therefore very often indispensable adjuncts to the smooth functioning of civic life. They were secretaries, accountants, translators, notaries; and very often scholars, engineers, architects, economists, jurists, and heaven knows what else. Even in a country which was almost visibly acquiring a secular culture, they still formed an absolutely essential intellectual élite.

There can be no doubt that many such clerics, during the misfortunes which befell their country, must have thrown in their lot with the nationalist cause. But this was a dangerous choice to make: as Churchmen they could not break openly with the Church. It is true that before the Crusade we find cases of priests and even of abbots who favoured heresy (or at any rate, did not fanatically oppose it); it is equally true that later there were monasteries that sheltered heretics, and clerics who attended sermons by the *perfecti*. But such tolerant views cannot be representative of the majority; certainly not of the more active missionary element.

Besides, these abbots and bishops—apart from the ones appointed during the Crusade—had friends and relations in the country, not to mention all the persons bound to them by motives of self-interest—the merchants, whose best clients they were; the contractors who carried out commissions for them, and many others. Doubtless among all these adherents there must have been at least some loyal supporters. Finally, the Church's party could count on the allegiance of all those who had too openly favoured the occupying Power while the Crusade was being fought; those who had cemented bonds of marriage or friendship with the French; and also those sincere or fanatical Catholics of the sort who had formed Bishop Foulques' White Brotherhood in Toulouse. As we shall see, the Crusade bred a strong Catholic reform movement, which in a few years achieved international status; it won over the Church, and had hopes of winning the masses as well.

In a country where hatred of the foreign invader seems to have been well-nigh universal, these various elements could only form a minority; but the very violence of feeling unleashed by the war must have sharpened their desire for revenge. We should bear in mind that Southern patriotism was a relatively recent phenomenon, and that fifty years earlier the burghers of Toulouse had themselves called in the Kings of France and England to protect them against their own Count.

So despite the national coalition that formed in Languedoc after Simon's death and Amaury's withdrawal, the country had no chance of internal peace while the Church continued to hold the threat of its thunderbolts over such legitimate suzerains as had reconquered their own lands. Peace with the Church was vital to Raymond VII. Quite apart from considerations of foreign policy, it would help to stabilize the situation at home. We cannot tell whether he would have bargained over the fate of the heretics or not, since the Church never gave him a chance to furnish proof of his good intentions. By the time Raymond received her absolution, he was tied hand and foot. . . .

Five years after the fall of Montségur Raymond VII died at the age of fifty-two, still without a legitimate heir. The County of Toulouse passed into the hands of Alphonse of Poitiers, who was married to the Count's only daughter, the Countess Jeanne. Both of them died in the same year, 1271, without leaving any issue. These two deaths finally brought under the French Crown a country which for the past twenty years had been, *de facto*, a French province, in the ancient, traditional sense of that term: i.e., an area of secondary importance which is colonized, exploited, and dominated both intellectually and with regard to its administration by a powerful metropolis well aware of its own best interests.

In twenty-two years Alphonse of Poitiers only went to Toulouse twice: in 1251, on the day that he appeared there to receive homage from his new vassals, and in 1270, a year before his death. He was a good administrator, and chiefly concerned with the organization of a harshly efficient fiscal system, which would permit him to levy from his domains such monies as he needed for the achievement of his political ambitions—or rather, those of his brother: for St Louis the reconquest of the Holy Land remained the prime objective of French policy. It seems clear that Alphonse never took his position as Count of Toulouse at all seriously, and was only a faithful executor of his brother's wishes. The people who, in 1249, followed Raymond VII's coffin from Millau to Fontevrault, weeping as they went, knew that what they wept for was the end of their existence as a nation.

A few months before his death the Count had burnt at Agen some eighty heretics, or persons suspected of heresy, after a summary judgment that even the Inquisition might have disallowed. No doubt he thought to win back the Church's favour by this act of violence; but it is possible that he also wanted to make the heretics expiate the evils they had brought upon his country. It was, indeed, more than enough. Exhausted by persecution, humiliated, demoralized by the progressive stifling of all their living traditions, the people of Languedoc—or at least its privileged classes, those who had most to lose—abandoned the Catharist faith and ranged themselves, in bitter resignation, on the side of the conquerors.

Languedoc was incorporated into France; it is pointless to ask whether this unification, which after all was demanded by the country's geographical and political position, could not have been accomplished in a less brutal fashion. Did there really exist such incompatibilities of interests and beliefs between North and South that it took a most savage war of conquest to bring about a union in which both partners were Frenchmen? Before 1209 there may have been mutual lack of understanding, but no hatred. After Raymond VII's death his people grew weary of hatred and suffering; they gradually resigned themselves—though it came hard to them, and there were further rebellions still—to seeing their language degenerate into a mere *patois*.

Who has ever calculated what a people must lose with their independence? How can one draw a line between regional idiosyncrasies and legitimate national aspirations? We may say, as a rule, that might always appears to be right in the end, and that what *is* always has more immediate reality than what might have been.

The French monarchy emerged from this ordeal with added strength, more conscious than ever of its Divine Rights; very soon it was to defy the Papacy, which had both served and made use of it. In her desire to extirpate heresy, the Church had exposed herself to the danger of seeing her too-powerful ally trampling on her temporal authority.

The Catholic Church had certainly not been unaware of this danger. Her struggles against the Empire, and her recent experiences with Frederick II in particular, had enabled her to take its measure very clearly; but in her eyes the peril that heresy represented was something far more terrible still. Yet though, thanks to the Inquisition, the Papacy finally triumphed, first over Catharism, and then over numerous other heretical movements which arose during the thirteenth and fourteenth centuries, her victory was to cost her dear. The humiliation inflicted at Anagni did not compromise the Church in its basic dignity; it was simply one episode in that unending battle which the Church was forced to wage in order to safeguard her moral and material independence. But the repressive terrorism which the Inquisition for several centuries imposed, as a policy, on the nations of the West—this was to undermine the Church's edifice from the inside, and to bring about a terrible lowering of Christian morality and Catholic civilization.

Before the Albigensian Crusade and the Inquisition, bishops and abbots still raised their voices in protest against the burning of heretics, and preached compassion towards such strayed brethren. In the thirteenth century, however, St Thomas Aquinas justified such *autos-da-fé* in terms that are ill-suited to any Christian. Excesses that could previously be attributed to ignorance or the brutal *mores* of the period were now given the stamp of approval, consecrated *ex cathedra theologica* by one of the greatest philosophers of Christianity. This fact is too serious to be minimized. From the thirteenth century onwards we no longer find saint or doctor in the Catholic Church bold enough to assert (as for instance St Hildegarde had done in the twelfth century) that a man who errs in religious matters is still one of God's creatures, and that to deprive him of his life is a crime. The Church which so resolutely forgot this very simple truth no longer deserved the title of 'Catholic'; in this sense we may claim that heresy had dealt the Church a blow from which it never recovered.

The victory was bought at too great a price. Even if the Roman Church, by taking the strong line against heresy that she did, spared Western Christendom grave troubles which might have brought the whole social and cultural structure crashing down in ruins—and this is by no means certain—she only did so at the cost of a moral capitulation the consequences of which she is still suffering today. ✽

5. FRIEDRICH HEER

FROM Friedrich Heer, *The Medieval World* (London: Weidenfeld & Nicolson, Ltd., 1962), pp. 173–79.

The Inquisition was set up at Toulouse as soon as the Albigensians had been crushed in the field. All women over the age of twelve and all men over fourteen were required to abjure heresy. No one was to have in his possession either the Old or the New Testament, whether in Latin or the vernacular; the only books allowed, and they had to be in Latin, were the Psalter, the Breviary, and the Virgin's Book of Hours. The synod of Toulouse issued in 1229 the first of a long series of ecclesiastical prohibitions and restrictions on reading the Bible in the vernacular.

The papal university of Toulouse was also founded in 1229, the year of the great victory. It was planned as a centre of militant theology, to assist the Mendicant Orders, especially the Dominicans, in their task of running heretics to earth; once detected, heretics would be handed over to the secular arm for sentence. In Italy the Emperor Frederick II and the Pope vied with each other in evolving new codes of law against heretics, a singular form of rivalry. The Emperor, in typical fashion, took the lead: he was all for burning heretics, since he saw a heretic in every rebel against his rule. The Italian towns impartially resisted both laws, imperial and papal. The Pope decreed the introduction of his law into the papal territories in 1231, and in 1232 the burning of heretics became a law of the Empire. From 1233 the Pope made it his business to bring the Inquisition into the towns of Italy. The risings against the Inquisition which occurred in Italy, southern France and Germany throughout the later thirteenth century are evidence of popular opposition to this novel and unprecedented institution. With its appearance on the scene, the Middle Ages ceased to be 'open', and the closed society, closed Church and closed state of the later medieval and early modern periods had come unmistakably into being.

This is made plain by the maxim which governed the Inquisition: 'There must be no arguing with heretics. If a heretic believes, he should be received back, if he refuses to believe he must be condemned.' The Inquisition had no use for 'conversations between adversaries' of the kind which took place in the open world of the twelfth century; the Inquisition recognized nothing short of total surrender, the abject prostration of conscience and intellect.

All this had some serious side-effects: denunciation of heretics was imposed on orthodox believers as a duty, the identity of the person denouncing them was withheld from the accused, the estate and chattels of heretics were confiscated, to be divided in varying proportions among the monarchy, the informer and the Church. Resistance to the Inquisition was gradually broken only by some iron-willed Popes, particularly Innocent IV, who again and again intervened to protect his Inquisitors, and by the fanaticism of religious obsessed with their mission; the procedure was built up slowly, piece by piece, to the point where it became a merciless machine. The Cathars died serenely, indeed cheerfully, true to their text: 'Blessed is he who is persecuted for righteousness' sake.' 'There is no happier death than the death by fire.'

Despite the Albigensian Crusade, Catharism remained a power in southern France until about 1244. In northern France, starting from 1233, the Cathar underground was ruthlessly exterminated. Survivors fled to Italy, only to be hounded down by the Inquisition's secret police. Cathars fled from Provence not only into Italy but also into Catalonia, a region which had close links with their homeland. Once the Inquisition had been admitted to Spain, it became a country of 'two nations', a division which still exists: on the one hand there developed the freedom-loving, heterodox 'Franciscan' Spain, with its centre in Catalonia, which sheltered sizable groups of Cathars and also some Waldensians; on the other was Castilian Spain, the Spain of St Ferdinand (a great-grandson of Queen Eleanor, incidentally), who carried on his own shoulders timber to stoke the heretic bonfires. In Germany during the first third of the thirteenth century there were Cathars at Cologne, Strasbourg, Goslar, Erfurt and at places along the Danube. Bohemia received a number of Cathar and Waldensian refugees whose presence there prepared the way for Hus.

The office of Inquisitor in France was held by the sinister Robert le Bougre, whose name suggests that there was heresy in his family (Bougre = Bulgar = heretic); he died in a royal prison. In Germany between 1231 and 1233 Conrad of Marburg was chief Inquisitor, leaving a trail of havoc behind him. Conrad, who burned heretics in droves, was father-confessor and spiritual director to St Elizabeth of Hungary, a Hungarian princess who had lived in Germany since childhood, and one of the most appealing and tender-hearted of all medieval saints. For three years Conrad raged up and down Germany in search of heretics, accompanied by his two lieutenants, Conrad known as Dorso, and the one-handed, one-eyed John.

Contemporary German sources, mostly of ecclesiastical provenance, give a horrifying picture of the reign of terror of these three 'madmen', intent on their mission of purging the world of vile heretics: they had undertaken the purification of the 'pure'. For example, this is what the *Chronica regia Coloniensis* has to say: 'In various parts of Germany it has happened that many people, nobles and non-nobles, monks and nuns, townsmen and peasants, have been given to the flames by Brother Conrad because of their actual or suspected heresy after a trial which, if we may say so, was far too hasty. For a man may be sentenced without opportunity of appeal or defence and thrust into the fearful flames on the very same day on which he is accused; whether the accusation is justified or no makes no difference.' Conrad was assassinated on July 30, 1233, by the followers of some noblemen he had summoned to appear before his court. After his death Archbishop Siegfried III of Mainz and a Dominican named Bernard sent the Pope, Gregory IX, full details of Conrad's reign of terror, his intimidation of prisoners, his false judgments and his atrocities. The Archbishops of Cologne and Trier had earlier brought similar charges. The Pope, shocked and bewildered, expressed his surprise: 'We marvel that you allowed legal proceedings of this unprecedented nature to continue for so long among you without acquainting us of what was happening. It is our wish that such things should no longer be tolerated, and we declare these proceedings null and void. We cannot permit such misery as you have described.'

For Germany the death of Conrad was like the vanishing away of a spectre. Suddenly it seemed absurd that an entire people, great men and small, should have for so long remained in terror of this little man, riding about on his tiny mule, and of his two gloomy-looking assistants; people wondered how it had ever been possible. This raises a question of some interest, not only from our own contemporary point of view, but also because of the light it sheds on some frequently overlooked features of the later medieval Inquisition, which can only be understood in the context of mass and group psychoses (for example, an infection spread by the Mendicant Orders). It was very often the masses, spurred on to 'purge' themselves of all 'uncleanliness' by a fervour in which hysterical devotion was mingled with fear (of everything alien and of Hell), who were both the mainstay of the Inquisition and its driving force. The aristocracy and the episcopate were hostile and in some places continued their resistance over several centuries, for the Inquisition infringed on their own jurisdiction and even set itself up as a superior authority. One finds such opposition in Germany during the thirteenth century and in Spain in the fifteenth and sixteenth centuries. Conrad had started his career in Germany by preaching the Crusade, in 1214. His oratory was impassioned and skilful: he kindled the ardour of the masses and stoked his own fires afresh at the flames. As with other demagogues of later date, in the course of time he became poisoned by his own venom; intoxicated with the power he had so demonstrably achieved over the popular mind, infected by the greed, hatred and envy of the populace, always glad at the prospect of striking a blow at the mighty, Conrad fell under the spell of the very people he sought to lead. The leader had become the led, and led into temptation. Every town, castle and cloister had its malcontents, people with an account to settle. Conrad acted in Germany as a catalyst. His highly neurotic personality touched off the neuroses of the masses and of individuals, and recharged them with new dynamite.

Conrad was buried at Marburg close to St Elizabeth in the new cathedral. This is the first German cathedral to be built in the Gothic style, and a magnificent example of it. In the south of France Gothic only appeared after the conquest of the region by the French king. This 'assimilative' role of Gothic is one of the keys to its 'invention'.

In southern France, despite its occupation by the enemy and harsh repressive measures, a few embers still glowed, ready to flare up over and over again. The registers of the Inquisition are filled with the names of noblemen, clerks, monks, episcopal officials, lawyers, physicians and merchants, and some of the northern officials who had come south to combat heresy were won over to the Cathar cause. At Albi, Cordes and Limoux there was always a heretical party, though it might vary in strength. At Carcassonne two successful attempts were made on the archives of the Inquisition, in 1280 and 1291. The whole movement flared up again in the years following 1295, when Provençals who had fled to Como attempted the reconquest of their homeland. This revival was crushed by the Inquisition around 1310. But the 'red South' (as it was later called) remained unquiet; it was soon to become the refuge of persecuted 'left-wing' Franciscans, Joachimites and Fraticelli. Here and in Catalonia such refugees created an intellectual and spiritual climate sufficiently disturbed to make possible the Spanish revivalist movements of the fifteenth and early sixteenth centuries.

During the thirteenth and fourteenth centuries, however, the main stream flowed in the direction of Italy. There are some similarities between the Langue d'Oc and the language of Friuli, and between the Ligurian and Sicilian dialects; some modern philologists ascribe these resemblances to the wanderings of the Cathars, who as time went on pressed further and further into southern Italy. There were well-organized escape routes for the Perfects leading from France and Germany into all parts of Italy. The safety of the routes and of the refuges along it was secured by a network of middlemen and guides, who could find a way through wild and pathless regions. The most desirable havens were wealthy cities, often in conflict with their bishops and cathedral chapters, where heretics might be sheltered by respectable citizens or even by the nobility. The Cathars had powerful friends at Florence, the Cavalcanti, the Baroni, the Pulci and the Ciprani; at Rome there was the house of Senator Brancaleone. It was not uncommon for Cathars to find advocates among nobles supporting the Ghibelline cause, men such as Ezzelino da Romano and Uberto Pallavicini. Italy was the only place where Catharism survived the persecutions of the thirteenth century. After 1300 the Italian Cathars fled to Sicily, to the Aragonese king, Frederick III (1296–1337). As late as 1412 the corpses of fifteen Cathars were exhumed and burnt at Chieri near Turin, so great was the fear that this 'plague' might send out its poison even from the grave to putrefy the body of the Italian populace.

Some of the most energetic of the Italian Inquisitors had started out as convinced Cathars. There was the famous Raynier Sacconi, for example, and his colleague St Petrus Martyr, murdered by the Cathars. Petrus was a Dominican; his murder was plotted by a wide variety of enemies, including a Franciscan. His actual assassin, a man named Carino, made a saintly end in a Dominican priory at Forli, which was presided over by a brother of his victim. This episode illustrates the complexities of medieval animosities, the way the lives of adversaries so closely interlocked.

These complex situations could work the other way. During the later thirteenth century a certain Armanno Pungilupo was being venerated as a saint at the cathedral of Ferrara, where he was buried and where an altar had been raised in his honour. Proceedings for his beatification were set in train, only to end, in 1300, as a case for the Inquisition. The 'saint' was unmasked as a heresiarch. All his images were destroyed, and his altar and his corpse consigned to the flames.

Ecclesiastical sources even during the twelfth century are full of complaints about the 'hypocrisy' of the Cathars, their remarkable talent for dissembling. The people, it was said, took the Cathars for saints; they had such an air of being thoroughly pious and right-minded men, capable of conquering the world by their learning, their charity and their innate attraction. Nicodemism, to give it its later name, soon became a fine art in Italy; Nicodemism meant outward scrupulous conformity with the norms of orthodoxy, whilst at the same time pumping them dry of all their original content and substituting in their place a new spirit and a new creed. The poetry of the *dolce stil nuovo* and of courtly love is drenched in Nicodemism; so, too, is the work of Dante.

A French cleric writing in 1215 named Milan as the main heretical stronghold. Pope Innocent III threatened the city with the same fate as had befallen the Albigensians. This pious wish could not be fulfilled, since in Italy itself the Papacy was weak. The effects of interdict and excommunication, the Popes' sharpest weapons in their struggle with the towns and city-states, were soon blunted: for if, as happened during the thirteenth and fourteenth centuries, great cities like Milan and Florence were left for years to languish under the Church's ban, with the complete suspension of the sacraments and all Church services that this entailed, 'heretics' became all the more active in filling the vacuum. It was even possible for a declared heretic, Otto Visconti, to hold for a time the Archbishopric of Milan. There was scarcely a diocese whose bishop had not ranged himself politically against the Pope. Innocent III was acutely conscious of the deterioration among the clergy. In his *De Contemptu Mundi*, written before he became Pope, he complains of clerks who 'by night embrace Venus and next morning honour the Virgin Mary'. At the opening session of the Fourth Lateran Council, on November 11, 1215, Innocent painted a gloomy picture of Christianity and the Church in decay. 'It often happens that bishops, by reason of their manifold preoccupations, fleshly pleasures and bellicose leanings, and from other causes, not least the poverty of their spiritual training and lack of pastoral zeal, are unfitted to proclaim the word of God and govern the people.'

The country clergy were harshly oppressed by their noble landlords and patrons, and as poor as church mice. There were plenty of clerks who could not write and were scarcely able to read. Some priests kept alehouses to support their wives and children. Superstition, magical practices (still common today in the South), soothsaying and astrology all exerted their baleful and seductive influence. Until well after the time of the Renaissance daily life was a close-woven tissue of habits derived from very ancient ritual practices, the dredged-up treasure of old non-Christian religions. Some Italian sorcerers had their training in Spain, until Siena became the centre of Italian sorcery, the Italian Toledo. The resources of magic were freely invoked in daily living, as a defence against the omnipresent perils of town and countryside laid waste by hatred, envy, wickedness and war. It was particularly useful in killing enemies on the field of battle.

In this turbulent Italy nearly every town was at war with its neighbour, and within the towns the parties were always at each other's throats: while at Rome the factions continually wrangled over the papal succession. Taking all the thirteenth century vacancies together, the Papal See was unoccupied during this period for more than nine years. A vacancy arose when the electors failed to reach agreement. Between Celestine IV and Innocent IV there was a gap of nineteen months (1241–42), a gap of two years and nine months between Clement IV and Gregory X (1268–71), a gap of eleven months between Honorius IV and Nicholas IV (1287–88) and another of two years and three months between Nicholas IV and Celestine V (1292–94). There were also several other vacancies lasting between three and seven months.

The towns and the people of Italy had long ago learned to cope with each other and their own problems without recourse to external authority. It is hardly surprising that heresy should have flourished among them. In a few towns the heretical party even temporarily captured the government. At Orvieto (not so very far from Rome) heretics in 1199 murdered the Roman *podestà*, who had only been imposed on the town by the Catholic faction after much difficulty; with the support of Innocent III the *podestà* had been taking active steps against heresy. More than two hundred noblemen were implicated as 'heretics' in his murder. In 1204 the town of Assisi chose an excommunicate as *podestà*, and remained loyal to him despite papal objections. The town's resistance was broken only by an interdict.

And so we have come to Assisi, where, in 1204, the star of St Francis was already in the ascendant. This saint of the Catholic Church, venerated by his much-harried and devoted companions as the 'second Christ', has won friends and admirers far outside his own Church and time; the power radiating from the *Poverello* has touched many different kinds of men and women, including the reformers of Luther's day, non-conformists of the eighteenth and later centuries, and people right outside Europe and right outside Christendom. We may wonder whether it was merely by accident that the earliest writings about him, the testimony of his earliest and closest companions, were rediscovered only at the close of the nineteenth century. It may also be significant that they were found in the archives of Poor Clares, Franciscan nuns, where they had been deposited to save them from destruction. And is it an accident that it is only now that Franciscan studies are sufficiently advanced to permit us to strip away the layer upon layer of false piety and sentimentality, sometimes deliberately superimposed, as in many early Christian paintings in the catacombs, so that the features which begin to emerge at last bear some resemblance to the reality? ✷

6. NORMAN COHN

FROM Norman Cohn, *The Pursuit of the Millennium* (London: Secker & Warburg, 1957), pp. 29–32, 307–8.

In addition to poverty as great as that of any peasant, the masses of journeymen and casual labourers suffered disorientation such as could scarcely occur under the manorial *régime*. There was no immemorial body of custom which they could invoke in their defence, there was no shortage of labour to lend weight to their claims. Above all, they were not supported by any network of social relationships comparable to that which sustained a peasant. Although by modern standards the largest medieval towns seem small, there can be no doubt that in conglomerations of towns such as were to be found for instance in Flanders, in which each town had a population of from 20,000 to 50,000, the unfortunate could go under in a way which would not be possible in a village of perhaps fifty, perhaps a couple of hundred souls. And if in the upper strata of the urban population kinship-groups were still important, in the lower strata they dwindled away to the point of insignificance. The migrations from the overpopulated countryside into the industrial centres began by disrupting and ended by destroying the large peasant families. Amongst the industrial population on the other hand kinship-groups of any considerable size hardly had a chance to form—partly because, given the high death-rate, that population had largely to be recruited anew each generation; and partly because poor families were unable to acquire more than a small amount of living-space in any one quarter.

Journeymen and unskilled workers, peasants without land or with too little land to support them, beggars and vagabonds, the unemployed and those threatened with unemployment, the many who for one reason or another could find no assured and recognised place—such people, living in a state of chronic frustration and anxiety, formed the most impulsive and unstable elements in medieval society. Any disturbing, frightening or exciting event—any kind of revolt or revolution, a summons to a crusade, an interregnum, a plague or a famine, anything in fact which disrupted the normal routine of social life—acted on these people with peculiar sharpness and called forth reactions of peculiar violence. And the way in which they attempted to deal with their common plight was to form a salvationist group under the leadership of some man whom they regarded as extraordinarily holy.

In this they were following a very usual medieval practice, and one which obtained in the most diverse social strata; at least from the eleventh century down to the close of the Middle Ages the laity was constantly throwing up salvationist movements of one kind or another. To appreciate with what passionate fervour perfectly orthodox Catholics could throw themselves into such movements one has only to read the account given by the Norman abbot Aimo in the middle of the twelfth century. He describes how multitudes of both sexes and all ages, including some of noble birth and great wealth, helped in the building of a church. Having banded together in communities under the leadership either of a priest or of a layman noted for his piety, these people yoked themselves like oxen to wagons loaded with building-materials and dragged them across mountains and rivers to the site of the church. During halts the leaders, working themselves into a frenzy, called their followers to repentance; and the followers scourged themselves, weeping and crying to the Virgin for forgiveness of their sins. 'Hatreds were lulled to sleep, discord put away, debts forgiven, the union of minds restored. But if anyone refused to obey the priest and to put sin from him, his offering was thrown off the wagon as something unclean and he himself expelled with ignominy from the Holy People.' When the teams came to the mouth of a river, led by God they marched straight ahead and lo! the sea was held back for them as it had once been for the Children of Israel. And in their carts they carried sick and dumb and insane people, whom they cured by their prayers. A holy people indeed, chosen by God and endowed with superhuman, thaumaturgic powers.

In such descriptions as this there is a good deal that would apply equally well to the salvationist groups which proliferated amongst the poor in the over-populated, urbanised areas. For these groups too holiness was a quality which was to be attained through renunciation of the world and the flesh, through self-abnegation and even through self-torture. For them too the outward sign of holiness was the power to bring down divine blessing upon the world, and in particular the power to perform miracles. Yet from the point of view of the Church these groups were heretical sects; and it is easy enough to see wherein the heresy lay.

Amongst the surplus population living on the margin of society there was always a strong tendency to take as leader a layman, or maybe an apostate friar or monk, who imposed himself not simply as a holy man but as a prophet and saviour or even as a living god. On the strength of inspirations or revelations for which he claimed divine origin this leader would decree for his followers a communal mission of vast dimensions and world-shaking importance. The conviction of having such a mission, of being divinely appointed to carry out a prodigious task, provided the disoriented and the frustrated with new bearings and new hope. It gave them not simply a place in the world but a unique and resplendent place. To a far greater extent even than groups such as that described by Abbot Aimo a fraternity of this kind felt itself an *élite*, set infinitely apart from and above ordinary mortals, sharing in the extraordinary merits of its leader, sharing also in his miraculous powers. Moreover the mission which most attracted these masses from the neediest strata of the population was—naturally enough—a mission which was intended to culminate in a total transformation of society. In the eschatological phantasies which they had inherited from the distant past, the forgotten world of early Christianity, these people found a social myth most perfectly adapted to their needs.

This was the process which, after its first occurrence in the area between the Somme and the Rhine, was to recur in later centuries in southern and central Germany and, still later, in Holland and Westphalia. In each case it occurred under similar circumstances—when population was increasing, industrialisation was getting under way, traditional social bonds were being weakened or shattered and the gap between rich and poor was becoming a chasm. Then in each of these areas in turn a collective sense of impotence and anxiety and envy suddenly discharged itself in a frantic urge to smite the ungodly—and by doing so to bring into being, out of suffering inflicted and suffering endured, that final Kingdom where the Saints, clustered around the great sheltering figure of their Messiah, were to enjoy ease and riches, security and power for all eternity. . . .

In some major civilisations the general attitude to history has been unpropitious to revolutionary chiliasm. To find an example one does not have to look back to the old Indian civilisation as shaped by Hinduism. An equally striking example is offered by the civilisation, often but incorrectly called Western, which is at present flourishing—admittedly with considerable local variations—from Britain to New Zealand and from the United States to Scandinavia. Over vast areas of the world, history has been coming more and more to be seen as an immensely complex process of change which has no predetermined course, which is largely unpredictable and even fortuitous—and which nevertheless human beings can at certain times and in certain respects direct in such fashion as to enlarge the scope of human living and reduce the burden of human suffering. Such a view of history provides a very poor climate for revolutionary chiliasm: it is with good cause that Nazis and Communists alike have abominated all undogmatic, empirical meliorism and, whenever they could, have killed those who have upheld it by word or deed. For where revolutionary chiliasm thrives best is where history is imagined as having an inherent purpose which is preordained to be realised on this earth in a single, final consummation. It is such a view of history, at once teleological and cataclysmic, that has been presupposed and invoked alike by the medieval movements described in the present study and by the great totalitarian movements of our own day.

Between the revolutionary eschatology of the later Middle Ages and modern totalitarian 'ideologies' there is of course one obvious difference. Where the former borrowed the language of Judeo-Christian prophecy, the latter have drawn upon nineteenth-century speculations in the fields of history, biology and sociology. A naive and explicit supernaturalism has been replaced by an orientation which is secular and which moreover claims to be scientific. In reality however the racial theory adopted by National Socialism was wholly unscientific and the simplified version of Marx's teaching known as Marxism-Leninism (formerly Marxism-Leninism-Stalinism) is hardly less so. Beneath the pseudo-scientific terminology one can in each case recognise a phantasy of which almost every element is to be found in phantasies which were already current in medieval Europe. The final, decisive battle of the Elect (be they the 'Aryan race' or the 'proletariat') against the hosts of evil (be they the Jews or the 'bourgeoisie'); a dispensation in which the Elect are to be most amply compensated for all their sufferings by the joys of total domination or of total community or of both together; a world purified of all evil and in which history is to find its consummation—these ancient imaginings are with us still. ✺

7. GORDON LEFF

FROM Gordon Leff, *Heresy in the Later Middle Ages*, 2 vols. (New York: Barnes & Noble, Inc., 1967), vol. I, 1–3, 46–47.

Heresy is defined by reference to orthodoxy. It does not exist alone. A doctrine or a sect or an individual becomes heretical when condemned as such by the church. For this, there has to be a body of accepted beliefs to violate and a recognized authority to enforce it. In their absence, to profess even the most outrageous opinions is to operate in a doctrinal—as opposed to a moral or a legal—vacuum; the community may be scandalized; the law may be broken; but there will be no officially constituted outlook against which they offend.

Now it was precisely the existence of such a prevailing orthodoxy, defined by the church and jointly enforced with the lay power, that distinguished medieval society. In this sense it was a closed society. Every member belonged to the church, and his or her salvation depended upon living and dying within it. To be outside it, for whatever reason, was to be anathema, whether as an infidel—pagan, Jew, or Moslem—or as a heretic. But whereas the first category was a matter for lamentation, opprobrium or crusade, according to circumstances, a heretic was the church's immediate concern: either to be restored or punished. There could be no intermediate position. The church was God's communion; to reject it, or be rejected by it, was to reject God. It was to be excluded from society, which was by definition Christian, in its civil no less than its spiritual aspect.

In these conditions heresy was endemic, since to step outside the accepted framework was to be opposed to authority. But heresy was far from an automatic process in which error was inseparable from excommunication and burning. In the first place, as we shall have ample occasion to see, error was of various degrees, and far from uniformly heretical. Moreover, it often took generations to define, as in the disputes over the poverty of Christ within the Franciscan order. In the second place, heresy was not just a matter of doctrine but also one of discipline—pertinacious error. The heretic was one who persisted in his mistake, refusing correction after his fault had been shown to him. It was for obduracy that he was finally punished after all efforts to make him abjure had failed. Consequently the test of heresy was a moral and practical one—willingness to submit; and conviction for it was an admission of defeat. It meant failure to save a soul from certain damnation: in consigning a man to the flames he was being consigned to the devil. Hence the great—often tireless—efforts to gain a recantation; what was at stake was a man's eternal life and obedience to God's saving will on earth. The church, as the medium for both, was, in asserting its authority, affirming God's law. Only if this is grasped can the zeal with which heresy was combated be understood: the misconception that belief can be enforced, and the undoubted injustices and cruelties which accompanied efforts to do so, must not blind us to the very genuine concern to save souls and the conviction that it was done in the service of God. Even Hus's judges, certain though they were of his guilt, tried to the end to persuade him to abjure.

From this it follows that, initially at least, heresy was a deviation from accepted beliefs rather than something alien to them: it sprang from believing differently about the same things as opposed to holding a different belief. With the egregious exception of the Cathars—whose non-Christian origins exclude them from this discussion, even though their evolution followed parallel lines—heresy during the middle ages was an indigenous growth; its impulse was invariably the search for a fuller spiritual life, and it drew upon the common stock of religious concepts to implement it. Whatever its forms, medieval heresy differed from orthodoxy and mere heterodoxy less in assumptions than emphasis and conclusions. It became heresy from pressing these too far. From the eleventh to the fifteenth centuries, its aspirations were common to all religious reform: namely, the desire to emulate the life and teachings of Christ and his Apostles; and more particularly to seek a return to the precepts of the gospel through a life of poverty—or one of complete simplicity—and preaching. That it frequently became debased, or a subterfuge, as with the Free Spirit, and was rarely found in its pure form, should not blind us to the power of this desire. What ultimately turned it into heresy was the failure to gain ecclesiastical sanction. It was usually then, in a group's subsequent development as a proscribed sect, that its original impulse took on a directly anti-sacerdotal character. In doing so it inevitably changed. What —except for the heresy of the Free Spirit, which was not a sect but an outlook, the origins of which are not clearly known—began as an accentuation of a particular aspect of belief, or life, became a rival outlook; its adherents came to regard themselves as Christ's true apostles and their struggle against the church as part of the wider struggle between the forces of Christ and Antichrist. As such, even if it did not lead to the formation of an independent church, it meant the sect's transformation into an autonomous body with its own tenets. These, as we shall mention shortly, despite their diversity, had a number of features in common. Central to them all was the fact that they were under the ban of the church; hence in continuing to practise and propagate their beliefs they were acting in opposition to its authority. Inevitably, therefore, to be heretical was also to be anti-sacerdotal; for ultimately, whatever the circumstances, a heresy received its final stamp, as heresy, from the church. In that sense, heresy was born when heterodoxy became, or was branded, dissent; and more specifically when the appeal—common to the Waldensians, Franciscan sects, English Lollards and the Hussites—to the bible and to the evangelical virtues of poverty and humility, became, or were treated as, a challenge to the church. It was then that protest became uppermost, conceived henceforth in directly anti-sacerdotal terms. This point was the culmination in the conflict between a group and authority. There was, as we shall see, a regular progression from initially non-heretical belief to open heresy; all the main sects began by embracing the commonly accepted tenets; only subsequently, in the course of growing hostility between them and the church, did they take on a more extreme, and often debased, form. Excepting the Free Spirit—and, of course, the Cathars—their sources were the accepted sources, and often objects of universal veneration: the bible, the Apostles' church, St. Francis, and even Joachim of Fiore. Those who sought to follow them, in their own way, believed that they were the true Christians and the hierarchy, which persecuted them, the heretics. Even Wyclif—with Peter Valdes, the one really influential medieval heresiarch in the strict sense—would have rebutted his posthumous condemnation and recoiled from the actual consequences of his teaching. . . .

There was a wide range of punishments: perpetual imprisonment, either solitary and in irons and on diet of bread and water (*murus strictus*), or a less restricted confinement (*murus largus*); the wearing of crosses as a sign of infamy; the performance of major or minor pilgrimages, lasting up to three or four months; fines, which were supposed to defray the expense of the tribunal and be used for good works; confiscation of goods, total for those abandoned to the lay power, even if they afterwards repented and were imprisoned: in the case of France, the proceeds went to the king; elsewhere, in Italy and in Germany, they were shared, usually between the locality, the inquisition and the papal court. Finally houses in which heretics had sheltered were to be destroyed and the inquisitor could employ their materials on building new edifices such as hospitals. Heretics were deprived of all civil rights.

The extraordinary jurisdiction exercised by inquisitors also extended to remission and commutation; by their right of grace they could exempt anyone from the worst penalties if he should come forward and confess his own errors or reveal those of others within a prescribed period, usually a month. This so-called 'time of grace' was frequently used; nor, as Bernard

Gui pointed out, was it unprofitable since it usually led to the capture of more heretics.

The arbitrary nature of these procedures need hardly be stressed. Inevitably they led to cruelties and abuses; but they should not be exaggerated. It has been calculated that of a total of 930 condemnations by Bernard Gui, the inquisitor for Toulouse from 1307 to 1324, 307 were imprisoned, and 139 relaxed to the secular arm—a comparatively small number for nearly a generation of one of the most intensive phases of inquisitorial activity in the middle ages. No total estimate for the whole period is possible; but it is unlikely to have exceeded thousands. It is not however quantitatively that the importance of medieval heresy can be properly assessed. For this we must look to its significance for contemporaries. The fact that a whole elaborate machinery was created and extended to most parts of western Christendom is the best proof of it. From the time of Innocent III onwards heresy became one of the central preoccupations of church and secular power alike. It grew with the middle ages, just as heresy increasingly merged with criticism of the church and spiritual life.

Ultimately, medieval heresy must be measured by its impact upon society. From the later twelfth century until the sixteenth century, it was continually combated by an increasing array of forces. But it was never overcome: and in the heresy of the Hussites, and to a lesser degree the English Lollards and the Waldensians, passed into the Reformation. Such a progression in one form or another was inherent in medieval society: on the one hand, heresy was an inevitable accompaniment of dissent in a world of orthodoxy; yet the very process of defining one in relation to the other narrowed the area in which heterodoxy could remain uncondemned. In that sense heresy was the outlet of a society with no outlets. Their absence made tensions into explosions, and common aspirations the programme of sects. Only when the latter became independent churches did heresy lose its impact. Instrumental in the crisis of the later medieval Church, it waned with the waning of the Church's ecumenicalism. That was the paradox. Medieval heresy arose from within medieval society and declined with its supersession. It was a catholic phenomenon concerned with the universal issues confronting a catholic society. As such it must be treated.

Part 10

THE ORIGINS OF PARLIAMENT

The debate over the origins of the English Parliament is one of the classic historiographical battles of this century. To understand why such an ostensibly "dry" subject should have engaged the attention and passion of so many historians is, in some measure, to see how lively and relevant medieval studies can be. Two developments help explain the theme's continuing interest. For one thing, although representative institutions were common in thirteenth-century Europe, the English Parliament was the only one that survived the late Middle Ages and the era of territorial state-building in the sixteenth century. Historians have, then, naturally been intrigued by this resilient institution, recognizing that a similar dynamism in France, Spain, or Prussia might have significantly altered the development of European society and government. A study of the English Parliament also implies a fleeting glance at the failure of other representative institutions, and one is thus engaged in asking some fundamental questions about the political history of late medieval Europe. As we have seen throughout this volume, examining concrete situations almost invariably leads to more general conclusions; the English Parliament is no exception.

A second reason why the question of the origins of Parliament is so compelling has to do with the crucial role of Parliament in English history. The controversy began in the sixteenth and seventeenth centuries and went well beyond antiquarian interest or "pure" history. Whatever it was in the thirteenth century, Parliament was by no means the potent institution it was to become in the Tudor-Stuart period. The crystallization of Parliament's power was inextricably tied to the bitter political struggles that sprang from the desire of some to limit the rights and prerogatives of the monarchy. The crown responded energetically to this challenge, and

Parliament was redefined by its supporters, who sought legitimacy in the institution's medieval roots. History became a political tool. From then on, the debate over Parliament was on a highly sensitive political issue; since English "liberties" were so closely associated with this institution, the intensity of the argument was certain to last long after Parliament emerged the victor in its struggle with the crown. Parliament, the embodiment of English liberty, is—and perhaps always will be—a sacrosanct institution.

Every historical controversy seems to have a definite point of departure; in this case, the debate began with William Stubbs (1825-1901). On the basis of range and depth of learning, ability to express complex ideas lucidly, and extent of influence, Stubbs certainly ranks as the greatest of the English medievalists. G. P. Gooch has written that Stubbs "inaugurated the critical study of medieval sources in England" and that when *The Constitutional History of England* appeared it "was immediately recognized as one of the half-dozen major historical works in the English language." When this great work was completed in 1878, Englishmen possessed a "sacred depository of ultimate truth." J. R. Tanner provides a vivid picture of its effect:

> The subject was deposited in three sacred volumes, which were approached by the devout disciple in much the same spirit as that in which the youthful Brahmin draws near to the Vedas. To read the first volume of Stubbs was necessary to salvation; to read the second was greatly to be desired; the third was reserved for the ambitious student who sought to accumulate merit by unnatural austerities . . . The lecturer lectured on Stubbs; the commentator elucidated him; the crammer boiled him down. Within those covers was to be found the final word on every controversy, and in this faith the student moved serene.

Though he has accurately been described as "a natural Tory," Stubbs advanced a Whig interpretation of Parliament that gratified Victorian liberals. The Whig view of the past was, characteristically, colored by contemporary conceptions. For Stubbs, the thirteenth-century Parliament was an embryonic nineteenth-century Parliament, and he took great pride in the antiquity of English freedoms and rights. This interpretation was embraced not only because it suited the outlook of the day, but also because it was part of a comprehensive view of English history from Julius Caesar to the accession of the Tudors. In Stubbs' work, Parliament served as the centerpiece of a grand edifice which G. P. Gooch called "the first authoritative survey of our national life"; and, in this context, Parliament seemed all the more magnificent.

Stubbs reigned supreme for some three decades. Then, as is the fate of all influential interpretations, the reaction set in. The response to Stubbs has been complex and, as we shall shortly see, some scholars now defend him. However, the following statements provide a fair assessment of the situation today. Gaillard T. Lapsley remarked, "Stubbs' account of the early history of parliament resembles the opening chapters of the book of Genesis in two important respects—it describes an act of creation and it no longer commands general acceptance"; and Geoffrey Templeman has pointed out,

> Scholars are now much less disposed than formerly to find the true significance of medieval parliamentary history in the way it foreshadows, prepares or illuminates the development of parliamentary government in more recent times. They are less anxious than Stubbs was to show how much those who opposed the Stuarts owed to 'the heroes of the thirteenth century,' not to mention Parliament's lesser medieval pioneers. Much greater emphasis is now laid upon the necessity for interpreting the early history of Parliament in medieval terms and in the light of medieval conditions.

There is poetic justice in the fact that the attack on Stubbs, the greatest English historian of the nineteenth century, should have been launched by F. W. Maitland, the outstanding English historian to emerge in this century. Significant historical revisions are often submerged in learned articles. Because this was the case with Maitland, the revolutionary implications of his cautiously worded thesis were not immediately recognized by the historical profession. But once they were, no one could ever read Stubbs in the same way again.

Maitland noted that Parliament had several functions in the thirteenth century: it was a supreme tribunal, a deliberative assembly, and a royal council. His critical question was: "But when is it a court, when a council and when a parliament?" Maitland's answer, an answer which clearly overturns Stubbs' view, has been succinctly summarized by Professor Helen Cam: "Maitland suggested, only too cautiously, that Parliament was in essence royal, not popular; a court of justice before it was a legislature; an expansion of an aristocratic and bureaucratic council before it had any representative character." This realistic view of Parliament was commensurate with Maitland's legal training. A. F. Pollard dramatically popularized the Maitland interpretation. And D. Pasquet, the French scholar, has clearly been influenced by it.

Maitland had not only made it difficult to accept Stubbs' theory, he also opened up a new approach to the study of Parliament. Simply stated, he was a functionalist—that is, he tried to understand an institution in terms of what it did. Action defined being, and a host of fresh questions about the power, composition, duties, and privileges of Parliament emerged. The distinguished medievalist G. O. Sayles has carried on his valuable studies along this line.

The historiographical pendulum is perpetually in motion. The Canadian scholar Bertie Wilkinson, termed a "neo-Stubbsian," has explicitly accepted and defended some of Stubbs' main ideas about the representative nature of Parliament and the pervasiveness of the elements of consent and political liberty. Basic to Wilkinson's argument is the contention that we must go beyond the purely parliamentary sources. He believes the royal government was indeed influenced by the notion of cooperation between monarchy and people, and that Parliament was, above all, a political institution and not—as Maitland and his followers contend—a judicial institution.

1. WILLIAM STUBBS

FROM William Stubbs, *The Constitutional History of England*, 3 vols. (Oxford: Clarendon Press, 1877), vol. II, 220–25, 239–43.

We have now to link together very succinctly the several cases in which, before the year 1295, the representative principle entered into the composition of the parliaments . . . From the year 1215 onwards, in the total deficiency of historical evidence, we can only conjecture that the national council, when it contained members over and above those who were summoned by special writ as barons, comprised such minor members of the body of tenants in chief as found it convenient or necessary to obey the general summons which was prescribed, for the purpose of granting special aids, by the fourteenth article of the charter. These would be more or less numerous on occasion, but would have no right or title to represent the commons; they attended simply by virtue of their tenure.

The year 1254 then is the first date at which the royal writs direct the election and attendance in parliament of two knights from each shire: the occasion being the granting of an aid in money to be sent to the king in Gascony, and the parliament being called by the queen and the earl of Cornwall in the belief that, as the bishops had refused to grant money without consulting the beneficed clergy, the surest way to obtain it from the laity was to call an assembly on which the promise of a renewal of the charters would be likely to produce the effect desired. There is no reason to suppose that the counties were represented in the Oxford parliament of 1258, or that the knights who brought up the complaints of the shires to the October parliament were elected as representatives to take part in that parliament, or that the 'bacheleria,' which in 1259 took Edward for its spokesman, was the collective representation of the shires. The provisionary government which lasted from 1258 to 1264 restricted rather than extended the limits of the taxing and deliberative council. In the intervening struggle however both parties had recourse to the system of representation: in 1261 the baronial leaders summoned three knights of each shire to a conference at S. Alban's, and the king retaliated by directing the same knights to attend his parliament at Windsor. In 1264, immediately after the battle of Lewes, Simon summoned two knights of each shire to a parliament at London, and in the December of the same year he called together the more famous assembly, to which not only knights of the shire were summoned by writs addressed to the sheriffs, but two discreet and lawful representatives from the cities and boroughs were summoned by writs addressed to the magistrates of the several communities. It is not impossible that Henry III, or earl Simon, may have summoned representatives of the commons, when he summoned proctors for the cathedral chapters, to the parliament at Winchester which was to have been held in June 1265. The preamble to the statute of Marlborough in 1267 states that the king had called to parliament the more discreet men of the realm, 'tam de majoribus quam de minoribus,'—the discretion, which was the peculiar qualification of the knights of the shire, affording a presumption that they were present. In 1269, at the great court held for the translation of S. Edward the Confessor, attended by all the magnates, were present also the more powerful men of the cities and boroughs; but when the ceremony was over, the king proceeded to hold a parliament with the barons, and the citizens and burghers can only be supposed to have been invited guests, such as attended, by nomination of the sheriffs, at the coronations and other great occasions. In 1273 we find a more important illustration of the growth of the custom: at Hilary-tide a great convocation of the whole realm was held to take the oath of fealty to Edward I, and to maintain the peace of the realm: 'thither came archbishops and bishops, earls and barons, abbots and priors, and from each shire four knights and from each city four citizens.' This assembly was, in its essence if not in its form, a parliament, and acted as the common council of the kingdom. The preamble of the statute of Westminster of 1275 declares the assent of archbishops, bishops, abbots, priors, earls, barons and the community of the land thereto summoned; an assertion which distinctly implies, besides the magnates, the attendance of a body which can hardly have been other than the knights, though not necessarily elected representatives. In 1278 the statute of Gloucester was enacted with the assent of the most discreet, 'ausi bien les greindres cum les meindres.' In 1282 the two provincial councils of Northampton and York contained four knights of each shire and two representatives of each city and borough. In 1283 the parliament of Shrewsbury comprised representatives of twenty-one selected towns separately summoned as in 1265, and two knights of each shire. In 1290 two knights of each shire attended the Westminster parliament: in 1294 four; and in 1295 two knights from each shire, two citizens from each city, and two burghers from each borough.

The last date, 1295, may be accepted as fixing finally the right of shire and town representation, although for a few years the system admits of some modifications. The great councils of the baronage are sometimes, until the writs of summons are examined, almost indistinguishable from the parliaments; they are in fact a permanent survival from the earlier system. But even in the parliaments proper there were, as we shall see, a variety of minute irregularities, such for instance as the summoning to the parliament of Lincoln of the representatives who had sat in the preceding parliament, and in 1306 of one representative from the smaller boroughs; but such anomalies only illustrate the still tender growth of the new system. The parliament of 1295 differed, so far as we know, from all that had preceded it, and was a precedent for all time to come, worthy of the principle which the king had enunciated in the writ of summons. The writs for assembling the representatives are addressed to the sheriffs; they direct the election not only of the knights but of citizens and burghers; the return to the writ is not merely as in 1265 and 1283 the reply of the separate towns but of the county courts, in which the elective process is transacted; and the parliament that results contains a concentration of the persons and powers of the shiremoot. In that assembly, on great occasions, the towns had appeared by their twelve burghers, now they appear to make their return to the sheriff, who thereupon makes his report to the government.

In thus tracing the several links which connect the parliament of 1295 with those of 1265 and 1254, we must be content to understand by the name of parliament all meetings of the national council called together in the form that was usual at the particular time. We must not take our definition from the later legal practice and refuse the name to those assemblies which do not in all points answer to that definition. After 1295 it is otherwise; that year established the precedent, and although, in the early years that follow, exceptional practices may be found, it may be fairly questioned whether any assembly afterwards held is entitled to the name and authority of parliament, which does not in the minutest particulars of summons, constitution, and formal dispatch of business, answer to the model then established. This rule, however, was not at once recognised, and for many years both the terminal sessions of the king's ordinary council, and the occasional assemblies of the magnum concilium of prelates, barons and councillors, which we have noticed as a great survival of the older system, share with the constitutional assembly of estates the name of parliament.

Before proceeding to inquire into the powers of the body thus composed, we have to meet the natural question, who were the electors of the representative members? On any equitable theory of representation, the elected representatives represent those members of the body politic who have not the right of appearing personally in the assembly, and they are elected by the persons whom they represent. The knights of the shire represented the community of the shire which was intermediately represented by the county court; the representatives of the towns represented the community of the several towns intermediately represented by their agents in the county court. The two cases must be considered separately. . . .

The early years of Edward I saw all the privileges which had been really used or acquired under Henry III fully exercised. The parliament of prelates and barons had been asked for, and had granted aids, had given counsel and consent to legislation, had acted as a supreme court of justice, and had discussed questions of foreign policy and internal administration. The further steps gained by the constitutional assembly in this reign were gained by it in its new and complete organisation.

Two drawbacks materially affected the value of these rights: the recognition of certain power on the king's part to do by his own authority acts of the same class as those for which he asked counsel and consent; and the recognition of certain undefined rights of individual members to concede or refuse consent to the determinations of the whole body; the latter drawback was seriously increased by the incompleteness of the national representation before the 23rd of Edward I.

Although the national council had made out its right to be heard on all four points of administrative policy, it had not obtained an exclusive right to determine that policy. The taxes might be granted in parliament, but the king could still take the customary aids without reference to parliament; he could tallage his demesnes and could interpret the title of demesne so as to bring the chartered towns, or a large portion of them, under contribution; he could increase the customs by separate negotiations with the merchants, and at any time raise money by gifts negotiated with individual payers, and assessed by the officers of the exchequer. The laws again were issued with counsel and consent of the parliament, but legal enactments might, as before, in the shape of assizes or ordinances, be issued without any such assistance; and the theory of the enacting power of the king, as supreme legislator, grew rather than diminished during the period, probably in consequence of the legislative activity of Frederick II, Louis IX, and Alfonso the Wise. The king's court, the curia regis, might be influenced and used to defeat the right of the barons to be judged by their peers, and there was not in the article of the charter anything that so fixed the method of such judgment as to make it necessary to transact it in full council; and the political action of the crown, in matters both foreign and domestic, could, as it always can, be determined without reference to anything but the royal will. Nor, as we shall see, was the failure of the national council to secure exclusive enjoyment of these rights owing to their own weakness: both Henry III and Edward I possessed, in their personal inner council, a body of advisers organised so as to maintain the royal authority on these points, a council by whose advice they acted, judged, legislated, and taxed when they could, and the abuse of which was not yet prevented by any constitutional check. The opposition between the royal and the national councils, between the privy council and the parliament, is an important element in later national history.

The second, however, of these points, the uncertainty of the line dividing corporate and individual consent, and the consequent difficulty of adjusting national action with incomplete representation, bears more directly on the subject before us. The first question has already arisen: did the consent of a baron in council to grant a tax bind him individually only, or did it form part of such a general consent as would be held to bind those who refused consent? When Geoffrey of York, or Ranulf of Chester, refused to agree to a grant, was the refusal final or was it overborne by the consent of the majority? Did the baron who promised aid make a private promise or authorise a general tax? Was taxation the fulfilment of individual voluntary engagements or the legal result of a sovereign act? Secondly, how far could the consent, even if it were unanimous, of a national council composed of barons and superior clergy, bind the unrepresented classes, the commons, and the parochial clergy? The latter question is practically answered by the contrivances used to reconcile compulsion with equity. The writ of Edward I for the collection of the aid *pur fille marier* rehearses that it was granted in full parliament by certain bishops and barons, for themselves and for the community of the whole realm, so far as in them lay. As a parliamentary assembly, legally summoned, they authorised a tax which would bind all tenants of the crown, but they did it with an express limitation, a conscious hesitation, and the king did not at the time venture to collect it. This was on the very eve of the contest for the confirmation of the charters. The documentary history of the reign of Henry III illustrates the difficulty at an earlier stage. In 1224 the prelates granted a carucage of half a mark on their demesne lands and those of their immediate tenants, and two shillings on the lands of the under tenants of those tenants: the feudal lord thus represented all who held directly or mediately under him. In 1232 the writ for collecting the fortieth states that it was granted by the archbishops, bishops, abbots, priors, clergy, earls, barons, knights, freeholders, and villeins, implying that not only the national council but the county courts had been dealt with: but in 1237 a similar writ rehearses the consent of the prelates, barons, knights and freeholders for themselves and their villeins. Yet it is certain that in neither of the parliaments in which these taxes were granted were the villeins represented, and almost as certain that the commons were unrepresented also. The consent thus rehearsed must have been a simple fabrication, a legal fiction, on a theoretical view of parliament, or else the exacting process of the central assembly must have been supplemented by the consent of the county courts, in which alone, at the time, the liberi homines and villani assembled, that consent being either taken by the itinerant judges or presumed to follow on a proclamation by the sheriff. The expressions, however used, show a misgiving, and warrant the conclusion that the line between corporate and individual, general and local, consent was lightly drawn: the theory that the lord represented his vassal was too dangerous to be unreservedly admitted when all men were the king's vassals; the need of representation was felt. But the line continued uncertain until 1295; and even after that the variety of proportion in which the several estates taxed themselves shows that the distinction between a voluntary gift and an enacted tax was imperfectly realised.

The idea that the refusal of an individual baron to grant the tax absolved him from the necessity of paying it, although now and then broached by a too powerful subject, could be easily overborne by force: ordinarily the king would seize the lands of the contumacious, and take by way of fine or ransom what could not be extracted by way of gift. The claim of a particular community to refuse a tax which had not been assented to by its own representatives, such as was claimed by Ghent in the sixteenth century, was based on the same idea, and would be overcome in the same way. Such a hypothesis, however, could only arise in a community which had not realised the nature of sovereign rights or of national identity. The refusal of an estate of the realm to submit to taxation imposed in an assembly at which it had not been represented, or to which its representatives had not been summoned, rested on a different basis. Such was the plea of the clergy in 1254, and it was recognised by the spirit of the constitution.

The practice had long been to take the consent of the communities by special commission. The year 1295 marks the date at which the special commissions, as a rule, cease, and the communities appear by their representatives to join in the act of the sovereign body. The process of transition belongs to the years 1282 to 1295, and the transition implies the admission of the commons to a share of taxing power, together with the clergy and the baronage. ✳

2. FREDERIC WILLIAM MAITLAND

FROM Frederic William Maitland, *Records of the Parliament, 1305* (London: Eyre and Spottiswoode, 1893), pp. lxxx–lxxxv.

A court which is to stand above the king's bench is being evolved out of the old court held *coram rege;* its rolls are the 'parliament rolls.' But the process is slow. For a while this highest tribunal is hardly distinct from the king's bench. Every plea in the king's bench is in theory a plea *coram ipso domino rege,* and the rolls of the king's bench never cease to be the *coram rege* rolls. The superior tribunal is rather, if we may so speak, an afforced, an intensified form of the inferior tribunal than a separate court; a plea that is put upon the parliament roll may be put upon the king's bench roll also; the justices of the king's bench are members of the council, and a case heard at a full meeting, a parliament, of the council, is heard by, among others, the justices of the king's bench. A plea may be adjourned from a parliament to the king's bench or from the king's bench to a parliament without breach of continuity.

A new tribunal is evolved, or rather, two tribunals become three. We can see this development taking place in the pages of Bracton and Fleta. Bracton knows but two of those courts of which we are speaking: there are justices resident at the bench; there are yet more exalted justices attending the king's person. Fleta knows three: there are justices resident at the bench; there are other justices who fill the king's own place, but above even them there is another tribunal, 'for the king has his court in his coun- 'cil in his parliaments, in the presence of prelates, earls, barons, nobles, and 'other learned men, where judicial doubts are determined, and new rem- 'edies are established for new wrongs, and justice is done to every one ac- 'cording to his deserts.' Bracton has to account for two sets of rolls; Fleta for three. Whether we ought to say that the highest of the three tribunals is the new one, whether we ought to describe the process as the deposit of a middle tribunal between the lowest and the highest, whether both of these phrases are not too definite and too modern to describe the real facts— these are grave problems which must be left to others. Our imaginary archivist would perhaps say that he could not decide them until he had made up his mind on the humbler question whether many parliament rolls have been lost. Our present point must be that before the end of Edward's reign there are three courts each with its roll.

What is the nature of the highest of these three? Is it council, is it house of lords? Fleta will warn us that we are asking an almost unanswerable question. 'Habet enim Rex curiam suam in consilio suo in parliamentis 'suis, præsentibus prælatis, comitibus, baronibus, proceribus et aliis viris 'peritis,' that is all that we can safely say. The highest tribunal of the realm is the king in council; it is the king in his council in his parliaments, in the presence of prelates, barons, and other learned men. To deny that it is the king in council is impossible; to deny that it is the king in parliament, or rather that its sessions are parliaments, is impossible.

Events which were still in the future when the great Edward died, decided that the highest ordinary tribunal of the realm should be 'the king in parliament,' and that this term should mean the house of lords; they decided that this tribunal should become for the more part but a court of error, and during the rest of the middle ages and far into modern times should have exceedingly little to do; they decided also that the king in council should dispense an extraordinary justice and this on a very large scale. If asked to mark the difference between ordinary and extraordinary justice, we can hardly do better at the present moment than place ourselves once more in the archivist's room, and say that the court of ordinary jurisdiction keeps a proper Latin plea roll and that the council keeps none. This is no insignificant detail. When the time has come for abolishing that court of star chamber which is one of the forms that the council has assumed, this will be charged against it as one of its many irregularities—it has no proper Latin plea roll. In the eyes of the lawyers of the seventeenth century this want of a roll goes far to prove that the council board is an upstart tribunal. What has been its strength in time gone by when, having no stiff Latin record to draw up, it could modify its procedure to suit every new want, has become its weakness in the age of Coke and Prynne, an age which demands a parchment title for every unpopular institution.

Long ago the parliament roll has passed from the custody of the council. Long ago it has become the record of those meetings of the estates of the realm which have acquired an exclusive right to the name of parliaments, and more particularly it has become the record of the house of lords. Long ago the rule has been that those members of the council who are not peers of the realm, but yet are summoned to parliament, are to sit in the house of lords as 'mere assistants,' are not to vote, are not to speak unless their opinions are demanded. This being so, we are apt to approach the parliament rolls of Edward I's reign with a certain prejudice in our minds. They ought, so we think, to be the records of the estates of the realm; in so far as they are judicial records, they ought to be the records of the house of lords. It is hard to think away out of our heads a history which has long lain in a remote past but which once lay in the future; it is hard to be ever remembering that such ancient terms as *house of lords* and *peers of the realm* were once new terms; it is hard to look at the thirteenth century save by looking at it through the distorting medium of the fourteenth. And so we are apt to approach our earliest parliament rolls with a belief that they ought to be rolls of the house of lords and not rolls of the king's council, that the supreme tribunal of England ought to be the house of lords and not the king's council, that, whatever upon our record makes against this belief should be explained away as irregular or anomalous.

Even if he had settled opinions about debateable questions of constitutional history, it would be wrong for the editor of such a book as this is to thrust them forward. The most that he can legitimately do is to provide materials for the formation of opinions. In so doing, however, it may perhaps be lawful and desirable that he should remind his readers of some facts that are like to be forgotten. And in the present case he may be allowed to say once more that we have very few parliament rolls of Edward I's reign, to remark that his son's reign was filled with momentous events, and to plead that those events may not be suffered to cast their shadow over the past. We must judge the rolls of Edward I's reign on their own merits without reference to the parliament rolls of his grandson's, or of any later, reign. As regards the matter that is now before us, the jurisdictional competence of the parliaments, there seem to be some special reasons why this warning should not be neglected.

We are dealing with something that is new. However ancient may be the roots whence the jurisdiction of 'the king in his council in his parlia-'ments' draws its nourishment, it is a new thing that men should see three different tribunals rising one above the other; it is a new thing that they should see a yet higher court above that court which is held in theory *coram ipso domino rege*. The competence of this highest court is as yet indefinite. Fleta uses vague words about it. He has a fairly clear view of the competence of the king's bench; it hears criminal causes; it corrects the errors and false judgments of all justices, except when such matters are brought before the king himself and his council or before auditors specially assigned for the purpose. But of the justice that is done by the king 'in his council in his parliaments,' we must speak loosely:—Judicial doubts are there decided, new remedies are provided for new wrongs, and justice is done to every one according to his merits. We can see, however, that this tribunal is not solely a court of error; it has a far wider power than the house of lords will have in later days. This doctrine is fully borne out by the parliament rolls. The causes which come before the parliaments do not usually come there by writ of error. The jurisdiction that is exercised is more commonly than not a jurisdiction of first instance. If we ask why a case comes before a parliament rather than before the king's bench or the common bench, often we can give no certain answer. We may say perhaps —to take examples from our own roll—that Nicholas Segrave is tried in a parliament because he is a baron charged with treason; but why should the citizens of Winchester be haled before a parliament for suffering a prisoner to escape, and why should not the Bishop of Salisbury urge his claim to tallage the men of Salisbury before one of the two benches, or even before the exchequer? Seemingly all that we dare say is that the causes heard in parliament are important causes, important because they concern the king, or because they concern very great men, or because they involve grave questions of public law, or because they are unprecedented. We must not miss the 'equitableness' of this tribunal. When Fleta says that it provides new remedies for new wrongs, and that justice is done to every man according to his deserts, he means that this supreme court can look at 'the merits of the case' with some disregard for technicalities. We are dealing with a court that has large, indefinite powers.

3. A. F. POLLARD

FROM A. F. Pollard, *The Evolution of Parliament* (London: Longmans, Green and Co., Ltd., 1926), pp. 48–53.

What, then, were these "parliaments" of the "Rolls," and what was the nature of their business? An answer is suggested by a complaint and an ordinance made in 1280. The complaint is of the delay and inconvenience caused to the folk who come to "parliament" by the great number of petitions which might be dealt with by the chancellor and justices; and the ordinance is that only petitions that cannot otherwise be dealt with are to come before the king and his council in parliament. The business is legal, these parliaments are "parliaments of the council," their essence is royal and judicial, and there is little in common between them and the occasional gatherings of tenants-in-chief summoned by special and general writs in pursuance of Magna Carta to give counsel and consent to demands for aids. Their proceedings are naturally entered in "Rolls," the characteristic records of courts, and they deal with "petitions" and "placita." Their sessions are regular and not spasmodic; they do not depend upon the king's financial necessities; and they are held three times a year. The three parliaments of 1290 are followed by three in 1291, and there is little doubt that this was the normal practice.

Its antiquity is obscure, but there is no reason to suppose that Edward I invented it. The earliest proceedings recorded in the "Rolls" do not give the impression of novelty; the complaint of 1280 suggests inveterate growth; and the multiplication of forms of original writs during the reign of Henry III would lead us to infer a rapid increase in the number of petitioners at Westminster, and the provision of means to expedite their suits. In 1190 Philip Augustus had ordered the regents he left behind him to hold three judicial sessions a year; and the parlement of Paris, like the English "parliament" of the "Rolls," was a joint session of the several *chambres* or courts of the *curia regis*, to which the name of "parlement" was given as early as 1239. When the English barons in 1258 usurped the position of regents, they arranged for three "parliaments" a year, though their parliaments were to consist, not in joint sessions of royal judges, but in joint sessions of baronial councillors.

The distinction between judges and councillors must not, however, be pressed. Every councillor might partake in judicial proceedings; and these "parliaments" of the "Rolls" were joint sessions of the judges with the less professional members of the council. Prelates, magnates, *proceres*, and clerks were present as well as the justices, though probably no magnate or prelate who was not also a councillor; and in these parliaments the business, while mainly, was not exclusively, judicial. In the "post-paschal" parliament of 1290 the statute of Westminster III (*Quia Emptores*) was passed; the resolution to expel the Jews was adopted; and "so far as in them lay," the handful of magnates present granted *pro se et communitate totius regni* an aid for the marriage of Edward's sister. The need for further consent was probably the reason for the summons to the knights of the shire to meet on July 15. Moreover, there was no narrow definition of legal or judicial functions; a *pax* between the Cinque Ports and Yarmouth was *recitata et recordata*—"registered" in the French parliamentary sense—in this parliament, and so were similar agreements between the bishop of Lincoln and the university of Oxford, and between "town" and "gown" in the latter city. Even the taxation of those who were not represented was not yet regarded by Edward I, or by those whom the chroniclers describe as his evil counsellors, as being outside the competence of the "council in parliament"; and in the autumn of 1290 it was decided to levy a fifteenth of their moveable goods from *universi regnicolæ tam clerici quam laici, sæculares pariter et religiosi*, without the consent of any representative assembly. Such exactions were, however, denounced and resisted, for in the worst days of feudalism the crown had possessed no power to levy general taxation. The aids and scutages and even the danegeld and carucages levied on tenants-in-chief were in the nature of rent rather than taxes; they were part of the "consideration" which the tenants owed to their landlord, and the mesne tenants enforced similar claims on their vassals. Arbitrary tallage was an incident of villein tenure, which was due to the lord whether he was a king or a baron. But a general tax on personal property, like a fifteenth, levied on all irrespective of their position as tenants of the king or other lords was a novelty, indicating the supersession of the feudal by the national idea, and providing scope for the maxim *quod omnes tangit ab omnibus approbetur*.

This approbation had been the normal function of the assemblies promised in Magna Carta and frequently held in the thirteenth century. It was not the function of the terminal sessions of the council, whose business is recorded in the early "Rolls of Parliaments"; and so far we have had two kinds of meetings, widely differing in composition and character, but both described as "parliaments" by different authorities. One kind, which is so called by the chroniclers, is or may be a large and tumultuous gathering of tenants-in-chief summoned by special and general writs; and while its potential size is reduced by the practice of permitting from two to four knights to represent all the lesser tenants-in-chief of the shire, it is increased by the admission of representatives of cities and boroughs which are regarded as collective tenants-in-chief of the crown. The other kind of "parliament"—so called by the clerks—is a smaller, regular meeting of the king's council, consisting of some prelates and magnates, most of the judges, and a selection of clerks, and dealing mainly with judicial business. The two bodies are summoned by different methods, meet at different times, and discharge different functions.

But during the latter half of Edward I's reign there is a process of amalgamation, and it is this amalgamation between "estates" and "parlement," rather than his addition of burgesses to the meetings of tenants-in-chief, that constitutes Edward's claim to be the creator of a model English parliament. Not that Edward I completed the process; parliament remained for centuries after his time a composite body, in which judicial and representative elements, legal and political functions were curiously blended, and it still retains the marks of its original heterogeneity. The approximation made in the reign of Edward I was confined to summoning the two assemblies to the same place at the same time and establishing a common session for certain purposes. But inasmuch as this co-operation between "estates" and "parlement" was the main constitutional difference between England and the rest of Western Europe during the later middle ages, the achievement was great enough, and requires greater attention than it has yet received. It was not determined by any large principle or any single dominating cause, but by the cumulative force of a number of small considerations; and the process of adoption consisted of gradual and almost imperceptible changes.

The principal predisposing cause of union was the fact that the crown in council was always present at both kinds of parliament, in the one to lay before the assembled tenants-in-chief and burgesses the financial demands of the government and to explain the causes of their necessity, and in the other to hear petitions, move the courts, and decide cases about which the judges differed or doubted. It would clearly be a convenience that, when the council was gathered together for judicial business *in pleno parliamento*, it should at the same place and during the same period meet the larger assembly summoned for financial and political considerations. Further, it must be remembered that according to feudal theory every tenant-in-chief of the crown was liable to suit and service at the *curia regis;* and that not merely the joint session of the courts in parliament but each individual session *ad scaccarium, in banco,* or *coram rege* was a session of the *curia,* to which any tenant-in-chief might be summoned; and therefore, although this feudal theory was obsolescent in Edward's reign, the *personnel* from which both kinds of assemblies were drawn might be regarded as potentially identical. ✻

4. D. PASQUET

FROM D. Pasquet, *An Essay on the Origins of the House of Commons* (Cambridge: Cambridge University Press, 1925), pp. 173–80, 194, 196–97, 225–26.

If Edward I really entertained the designs attributed to him, he should not be compared, as he is by Stubbs, to Alfonso the Wise, to Philippe le Bel, or to Saint Louis, but to one of those great men of rare political genius, who have at intervals appeared in human history, to Julius Caesar or to Augustus. But such designs are so utterly opposed to the conceptions of Edward's time and to his own authoritarian temperament as not even to have an air of probability. In 1305 Edward obtained the pope's cancellation of the Great Charter and his own release from all his promises to his people. How can we believe that, in calling the representatives of the counties and towns to his parliament, he desired of his own free will to share his power with the nation? We may further observe that the phrase, which is held to summarize Edward's whole policy, does not appear in the writ ordering the sheriffs to proceed to elections, but only in that addressed to the prelates. If, therefore, we wish to give it any precise significance, it can only be applied to the representatives of the inferior clergy. But in reality the phrase seems to have been a commonplace of thirteenth century political literature, borrowed, as Stubbs himself points out, from Justinian's Code. It is but a part of that store of philosophical maxims and flowers of rhetoric, on which English chancery clerks loved to draw, especially when addressing the clergy, who seemed to them more capable than the laity of appreciating elegance of style. Edward was so little disposed to see that what concerned all should be approved by all, that after 1295, as before that date, he often reserved the most important questions for the consideration of his barons or merely of his council, without calling representatives of the commons to a parliament.

It is clear that Edward's object, in assembling deputies of the counties and towns, was not to make them participate in his legislative activities. Legislation was a royal prerogative, in which subjects took no part, except to give counsel, when the king demanded it of them. . . . A considerable number of ordinances or statutes—there was then no precise distinction between these two terms—were promulgated by the king alone and as concessions to his subjects. Others were promulgated by the king, on the advice of his council. Others were promulgated by the king, on the advice of the prelates and barons. So little importance was attached to the presence and the opinion of the commons that in 1290 the statute *Quia emptores*, although it affected the knights, was promulgated a week before the delegates of the counties arrived at the parliament. Even when the knights and burgesses were present, it was not considered necessary to mention the fact. The statute of merchants of 1283, whose object was to facilitate the recovery of debts and which was drawn up at the parliament of Shrewsbury probably after consultation with the burgesses, contains no allusion to any such participation. The *Articuli super cartas* were promulgated in 1300, at the close of a parliament, at which representatives of the counties and the towns had been present, but probably after their departure. Only prelates, earls and barons are mentioned. The only laws of Edward I, in which the consent of the community or communities of the realm is mentioned, are the first and the last of his reign, the statute of Westminster of 1275 and the statute of Carlisle of 1307. As regards the latter statute, the king did not wish to have trouble with the Roman curia and therefore no doubt thought it best to shelter himself behind the united opinion of the whole nation. He accordingly decided to add "the communities of the realm" to the list of those on whose counsel he had acted. It had been impossible to place the clergy on the list, but the mention of the communities gave increased authority to the decision taken. But too much importance should not be attached to this addition. In 1307, as in 1275, in the writs sent to officials for the execution of the law all mention of the communities of the realm has disappeared. The writs speak only of earls and barons.

Neither did Edward I summon the delegates of the commons in order to consult them on questions of general policy. This is so evident that it seems hardly necessary to waste time proving it. A few examples will suffice. In 1294 the decision to engage in war with France was taken in a parliament of barons in June; the knights of the shires were only summoned to the parliament of November. In 1301 the letter addressed to the pope, on the rival claims of the papacy and the English king on Scotland, bears only baronial names and seals and is dated the 12th February, thirteen days after the departure from parliament of the representatives of the counties and towns. In 1305 the parliament of February was specially summoned, according to the text of the writs, to consider the affairs of Scotland. The king ordered the bishop of Glasgow, the earl of Carrick and

John de Mowbray jointly to consider what steps should be taken to consult representatives of Scotland, who should appear at a subsequent parliament. On the 26th March the committee thus appointed presented a report submitting that two bishops, two abbots, two earls, two barons and *"deus pur la comune"* would be an adequate representation and that an assembly should be held to elect them. The king then acted in the matter and decided that the parliament, at which the organization of Scotland would be regulated, should be held on the 15th July in London. The assembly was subsequently postponed to the 15th September at Westminster, and, as we have seen above, it was then that the ordinance *Super stabilitate terre Scotie* was drawn up in the presence of the Scottish delegates and several members of the council. Now we have already shown that on the 21st March—five days before the discussion on these important matters began—the deputies of the counties and towns and those barons and clergy who were not of the council had received leave to depart.

Discussion of questions of general policy was long to remain reserved for the prelates and barons or even for the king's council alone.

The desire for financial support, on the contrary, has been considered by most historians to have been the principal cause for the convocation of deputies of the commons. Edward I, like his contemporary Philippe le Bel, was always short of money. The royal demesne was impoverished. The government of the kingdom was becoming more and more complex and more and more costly. The great undertakings of the reign, the conquest of Wales, the conquest of Scotland, the war with France, were very expensive. The king was thus forced by financial pressure to summon the representatives of his counties and good towns in order to obtain the necessary aids from them; and they used their financial power to diminish the royal prerogative by gaining ever-increasing concessions in matters of legislation and policy.

This theory is attractive. There is often a clear connection between the convocation of the knights and burgesses and the financial demands of the king. The concession made by them (or by the knights alone) is mentioned in the writs that order the collection of an aid in 1275, 1283, 1290, 1294, 1295, 1296, 1297 and 1301. A marginal note on the roll even tells us that the two assemblies of 1283, at Northampton and York, were expressly summoned *de subsidio petendo*. Unfortunately, we know that similar formulae are found in the writs of Henry III, although they were apparently not preceded by any convocation of representatives of the counties and towns. We are therefore forced to discount the value of the consent granted by the knights and burgesses. Further, Edward I, especially in the latter part of his reign, often assembled the delegates of the commons without apparently making any pecuniary demand from them. Such was the case in 1283 (at Shrewsbury), 1298, 1300, 1302, 1305 and 1307. The question is therefore not so simple as it might appear at first sight.

It seems even more complicated when we come to examine the circumstances in which the summons of the knights and burgesses to parliament were issued. In 1297 the barons showed their conviction that they could not rightfully be required to pay any aids but such as they had freely granted. Consent to aids was indeed an undoubted principle of feudal law, and, although the articles touching aids had been struck out of the Great Charter after John's death, we know that they had been observed in practice by the royal government at any rate in relation to the baronage. As an order, the clergy were as little disposed as the baronage to submit to what ecclesiastical writers called the "extortions" of kings, although they more than once had to yield to force. But it is far from certain that the mass of freemen were equally convinced that they possessed such rights or that they attached the same importance to the question. A very large proportion of the freemen were not the immediate tenants of the king. They could not, like the barons, invoke the principle of aids by consent; nor, like the clergy, plead the privileges of the church and the orders of the pope. Throughout the period during which aids were granted by the barons alone, we do not find that the freemen ever complained that such a practice was unlawful. In 1220, when the barons' stewards in the county court of Yorkshire refused to pay the aid demanded of them, they did so not in the name of the county, but on behalf of their lords, who had not been summoned to parliament. Even in 1297, when the county court of Worcestershire refused to pay an aid that had not been granted in parliament, it did so not because the aid had not been voted by its delegates, but for a wholly different reason. The king was demanding the aid in return for promises which no sanction compelled him to keep and which his father, Henry III, in similar circumstances, had not kept. "Therefore," concluded the members of the court, "when we are in enjoyment of these liberties, we will freely give the money mentioned." What really interested the lesser gentry of the countryside, much more than did constitutional machinery, was that the amount of the aid should not be too large and that an aid should remain, as in the past, an exceptional expedient of the crown. . . .

It is . . . inexact to say that the king assembled the delegates of the knights and burgesses in order that they might grant him aids. Aids had previously been collected without their views being asked and they had not claimed any right to sit in parliament with the prelates and barons. But, for greater facility in collecting the aid, it was to the king's interest that delegates of each county and town should undertake in advance that it should be paid. Edward had no thought of surrendering the rights of the crown, when he summoned the plenipotentiaries of the counties and towns before his council to demand this undertaking from them; any more than he believed that he was surrendering his rights by permitting his officials to argue with the magistrates of a town over the amount which they should pay for a tallage in common, as in 1304, or for an aid, as in 1282 and 1294. . . .

The documents published in the collection of *Rotuli Parliamentorum* and, for the parliament of 1305, in the *Memoranda* of Maitland show us that in these parliaments, as in nearly all the parliaments of Edward I, most of the work consisted of hearing the suits which the king had reserved for himself in parliament and examining the petitions presented to the king and his council. Important questions of policy and legislation might be dealt with in conferences between the king and the *fideles* whom he summoned, but suits and petitions were the normal business of parliamentary routine. Thus parliament, in its essential functions, appears as the continuation of the old *curia regis*, as the high court of justice of the realm, capable of redressing wrongs which could not be redressed by the common law. . . .

Edward I changed an occasional expedient into a regular custom, not in order to associate the whole nation with himself in the work of government, but in order to strengthen the royal power. He only summoned the representatives of the commons when such a course seemed to him to serve his own interests; and often the most important agenda were discussed in their absence. If in the end he made a practice of summoning them almost regularly, this was because he perceived that the previous consent of the knights and burgesses greatly facilitated the collection of aids and even enabled the government to collect rather more than would otherwise have been possible. Another reason was that the petitions, in which the delegates of the communities begged him to redress wrongs irremediable by the ordinary processes of the law, gave him full information on the condition of his kingdom and enabled him to make all aware of the strength of the royal arm. Every abuse of power by a great lord, every injustice by a servant of the crown, every invasion of the royal rights was denounced before the king's court; and thus the sessions of the full parliaments carried on the grand inquests of the beginning of the reign. Lastly, the assemblies of representatives from counties and towns embodied one of the fundamental ideas of Edward's policy. In parliament, as formed by him, the old feudal distinction between tenants-in-chief and sub-vassals was entirely abolished. The king had before him only subjects. Despite its feudal form, the summoning of the commons was an essentially anti-feudal measure, the object of which was to strengthen the central power and to subject all the inhabitants of the realm, of whatever rank in the feudal hierarchy, to the direct authority of the monarch. In this respect Edward continued the policy of Henry II and emulated Philippe le Bel.

But Edward's plans did not succeed; or rather they succeeded only in part. The assembly of representatives from counties and towns did indeed rapidly achieve the destruction of the feudal system of society. But it did not result in an increase of the royal power, as Edward had hoped.

About the middle of the fourteenth century the house of commons, which existed only in embryo in the model parliaments of Edward I, assumed the character of an established and clearly defined institution. ✳

5. G. O. SAYLES

FROM G. O. Sayles, *The Medieval Foundations of England* (London: Methuen & Co., Ltd., 1948), pp. 448, 453–56.

It is probable that England will be remembered *sub specie aeternitatis* for that experimentation in the art of government which ultimately produced the English parliament. Yet its history in the formative period of its growth is only now in process of being written. For its outline has been seriously distorted under the democratic and liberal bias of a modern age. The root cause of confusion has lain in the assumption that the history of parliament is identical with the history of popular representation, whereas it is the crux of the problem to understand why these two currents of development, once separate and separable, should have found their way eventually into a single channel. For at first they had little to do with one another: for example, between 1258 and 1300 some seventy parliaments were convoked, and only at nine of them were popular representatives summoned to be present, and we must accept the fact that during the thirteenth and early fourteenth centuries the presence of the commons was not regarded as essential to parliament, whose work was as effectively accomplished without them as with them.

What then is a parliament? When medieval men are permitted to supply their own answer, it is plain that all the emphasis is being placed upon the reform of administration and law and the dispensation of justice as the essential work of parliament, and that parliament was valued by the people at large because it provided a means of obtaining relief which for some reason or other could not be obtained elsewhere. The presence of the commons, the granting of taxes, the issue of legislation, are non-essentials:

parliament can exist and do its work irrespective of them. If they are found associated with it, that arises from the convenience of the moment and not from any obligation, for they are found associated equally well with other types of assemblies, which made no formal provision for the righting of wrongs and which were not termed parliaments by contemporaries.

We have already remarked that the English constitution was the product of three forces, represented by the king, the feudal barons and the subject people: long at work in the past, they combined to produce the parliament of the thirteenth century. . . .

The abundant records which exist for the reign of Edward I enable us to get a clear and detailed picture of parliament at that time. During the first half of his reign there was obviously a deliberate scheme for holding parliaments at Westminster twice a year, at Easter and at Michaelmas: thus eighteen parliaments were in session between 1275 and 1286. Between 1290 and 1307, when the king's time was greatly occupied with affairs in Scotland, Wales and Gascony, parliament had to meet when convenient opportunities arose, and it assembled on twenty-seven occasions. Since parliament was a court placed above other courts and devised to dispense the highest justice in the land, it was covered by the special peace which attached to all such institutions: the place in which it assembled was sacrosanct and no one must come there possessed of arms; those who attended must not be interfered with either in coming or departing, nor must their property or their household be molested during their absence; those responsible for the conduct of affairs, like councillors and clerks, were immune from the ordinary process of law for wrongdoing so long as parliament remained in session. Indeed, if we seek the origins of the parliamentary privileges of later times, like freedom of speech and freedom from arrest, it is in the peculiar sanctities, accruing to a court of law, that we must look for them.

We can classify the business of parliament under seven heads: (i) the discussion of affairs of state, more especially foreign affairs; (ii) legislation; (iii) taxation or supply; (iv) the audience of petitions; (v) judicial business, such as the determination of causes, criminal and civil; (vi) administrative matters of difficulty; (vii) feudal ceremonial, such as the taking of homage. Not all of these kinds of business were transacted at every parliament, and little of the time of parliament was taken up with politics—with debating state affairs or questions of supply or public grievances. The surviving parliament rolls of Edward I are in overwhelming measure occupied by entries about the hearing of large numbers of private petitions. Indeed, if we took out of these rolls all the passages relating to petitions and pleas and other legal processes, the remaining entries would be found to fill but a small space and to provide relatively little information. The history of parliament is not made up of great monuments of legislation or of dramatic political incidents: these have their place, but they take up little of parliament's time and are given little space upon its records. If the king so willed it, high politics could be, and very often were, transacted elsewhere than in parliament, and no one objected. What concerned the ordinary man was that his personal grievances and requests should receive attention, and to him it was parliament as the dispenser of the highest justice available to him that was most essential. For there was a general understanding that a petition, presented in parliament, should receive an answer before the session came to an end and, though this understanding was not always faithfully observed, a breach of it was resented. As for the subject-matter of parliamentary petitions, it fell into two broad categories: those which prayed for relief which the common law of the land did not for some reason or other afford, and those which solicited special favours not touching law at all, pure matters of grace.

The fact that parliament was an institution open to every man in the land inevitably determined the structure of the parliamentary machine. Parliament was an afforced council—that is to say, a council strengthened both in numbers and ability. But, sitting as a single body, it could not get through the vast amount of trivial business to be transacted, even if it had been proper to assemble so many important people in one place to do so much that was unimportant. So experiment after experiment was made to obtain workmanlike arrangements. The first business of the petitioners was with receivers of petitions, who performed a preliminary weeding-out and rejected such as need not have been brought to parliament. Those they accepted were then passed to a tribunal of auditors or triers, to whom the receivers acted as clerks. The auditors might deal with the matters out of hand: their directions would then be written briefly on the back of the petitions. But if they did not feel competent to give a final decision, the petition went to a yet higher tribunal, a body which was technically the council, though that might mean only a select number of its members. And there, if the subject-matter of the petition in some way affected the king's interests, it was reserved for the attention of persons who could act on the king's behalf and who perhaps received his personal instructions. Already by 1290 the tribunals of receivers and auditors were overburdened with work and had to be divided into panels so that one group of receivers and a corresponding group of auditors could concentrate on the English petitions, another on Irish petitions, and a third on Gascon petitions. In ascending scale, therefore, a petition might pass before four tribunals. The replies given were rarely final. There was no time during a parliamentary session for thorough investigations. But a favourable reply would secure a remedy or accelerate a decision in the appropriate court or government department. But this was not the end of refinements in organization. For, although the creation of special tribunals to deal with petitions relieved the council of much detailed work, although its time was carefully reserved for important matters, even then it was often found necessary to refer various items of council business, including litigation, to specially constituted committees. Only in this way could the work of parliament be dispatched. The occasions on which the full body of councillors met—ministers and magnates—were few and only for very solemn and formal business.

The men who arranged the business of each parliament and who composed its tribunals were mainly men in the service of the king: they were predominantly clerks, trained in the various branches of the king's administration, and justices employed on one of the benches or on eyre, though there were lesser barons and knights among them who were regularly employed by the king in positions of trust. It is rare to find barons, whose relationship to the king was essentially feudal and not ministerial, and whose appearance in parliament hinged upon their responsibility to do suit at the king's court, achieving anything of consequence save in quite unusual circumstances. And there are few signs of any activity on the part of popular representatives on the few occasions when they were summoned to be present. It is true that sometimes the assent of the magnates and the 'community' was required to taxation or legislation, or their support was wisely solicited in the prosecution of foreign policy; that homage was rendered or royal marriages discussed or services in war rewarded in parliament: parliament has sprung in part, as we have seen, from a feudal court and may bear the guise of a feudal court from time to time. But the important element of parliament was the official element, and the important aspect of the business of parliament was the dispensation of justice and the expedition of matters of administration. Under Edward I parliament was an institution staffed by men trained in English and even Roman or canon law, men who were in every way professionally competent to cope with the kind of business which took up nearly the whole time of parliament. Their contribution was immeasurably greater than that of any other body of men represented there regularly or intermittently—barons, knights, or burgesses. ✲

6. THEODORE PLUCKNETT

FROM Theodore Plucknett, "Parliament," in *The English Government at Work, 1327–1336*, ed. William Morris and James F. Willard, 3 vols. (Cambridge, Mass.: The Medieval Academy of America, 1940), vol. I, 112–14.

There is every cause for believing that, while parliament was sitting, the council regarded itself as part of parliament, and its acts might therefore be described as the acts of parliament. It is likewise important to remember that parliament was a convenient occasion, since several officials and judges were taken momentarily away from their posts and assembled in conference. In short, whether we examine parliament as a court or as an administrative body, it is for the most part only a reflection of the council, which exercised its powers in parliament, and was, in fact, the very core and heart of parliament. It is, however, to be noted that during our period we do get a few significant assertions of the dignity of parliamentary judicature: a decree of parliament ought not to be revoked save by a parliament; it is 'the highest place in the realm' and the tampering with its endorsement is a serious offence, although the chancellor seems unaware of it. Politically, too, parliament becomes more and more self-conscious and eventually will even oppose the policies of the court and council. We must therefore beware of over-simplifying the constitution of parliament, especially during this period. The growth of the idea of peerage and of the representative principle was certainly changing the political complexion of parliament so that finally parliament could consider itself as not only distinct from, but also as antagonistic to the council to some extent. But even when this development had been accomplished, it was still the council that organized parliament's work, and on many occasions spoke in parliament's name without causing thereby any constitutional scandal. This close intimacy between parliament and council was in fact essential if parliament was to serve any useful purpose. All this, however, must not lead us to the opposite extreme of denying the fact that there are broadly two different institutions. Thus the assertion that 'a meeting only of the king, council and the justices to try *placita* and hear petitions was perfectly a parliament' would be much better expressed in terms of functions rather than of institutions; we should prefer to say that the council, a small group of official experts surrounding the king and forming the heart and core of parliament, would often describe its decisions as those of parliament, especially in matters which did not raise important questions of politics. That is by no means the same as the assertion that institutionally council and parliament were one.

Taking all the evidence, we suggest that parliament was nominally, rather than actually, the crown of the judicial edifice, and as the fourteenth century advances, its position was hardly improved. The rise of the present appellate powers of the house of lords dates mainly from post-mediaeval times, when a thin stream of mediaeval authority was rapidly developed. If we seek an answer to the very pertinent question which Mr Richardson and Dr Sayles have posed, we may suggest that one of the principal reasons why our parliament did not go the way of the French *parlements* and become an assembly of jurists and administrators sitting as a court lies in the fact that the council was strong enough to dominate the situation; parliament's judicial powers are as yet indistinguishable from those of the council, and the council never parted with its own, but used them freely out of parliament as well as in. The council, moreover, was continuously available, although parliaments became less frequent soon after our period. The growing prominence of political, peerage, and representative elements in parliament was accompanied by a corresponding decline in the position of the conciliar and official group. These persons, judges and others, were reduced before the end of our century to the position of mere assessors to the peers. This turn of events must have contributed largely to the decline of parliament as a judicial body, and we need hardly be surprised that litigants addressed their complaints to the council, chancery, or exchequer, where they could be sure of their affairs coming before expert officials who were equally competent in administrative and in judicial matters. Above all, the council supervised the working of the common law side of chancery which handled the vast business arising out of the crown's feudal rights, and so parliament was likewise prevented from becoming a true feudal jurisdiction for practical purposes.

It is now time to turn to the petitions, which, as we have remarked, were the principal method by which parties could set in motion and direct the machinery of parliamentary judicature. It was not the primary duty of the commons to present petitions—even from their own constituents; the city of London will therefore send its officers, and not its representatives, to present its petitions. Still less was parliament at this time a body that could be petitioned. ✻

7. BERTIE WILKINSON

FROM Bertie Wilkinson, *Constitutional History of Medieval England, 1216–1399* (London: Longmans, Green and Co., Ltd., 1958), pp. 265–73.

Even in the cautious pages of Stubbs, G. T. Lapsley wrote, the works of the fourteenth-century parliaments (and presumably of the thirteenth) are often exhibited in the light reflected from the seventeenth century. Later writers, he observed with apparent approval, have departed strongly and properly from this view, and the tendency now is to minimize the importance of parliament and to bring forward the council and administrative machinery as dominating the constitutional struggle of the period. Against this latest tendency, however, it is possible to suggest that in relation to parliament, at least, historians may have departed too strongly from the views of Bishop Stubbs. It is true that Stubbs read too many notions derived from the seventeenth century into the fourteenth; yet he may be accused of underestimating rather than exaggerating the parliamentary radicalism of the earlier period; and there are very good arguments which may be adduced to defend the central position which he gave to parliament in the constitutional struggles of that age.

The essence of parliament in the Stubbsian tradition was that of a great political assembly, the "forum of the nation," in which according to a tradition of the greatest antiquity the king and his subjects foregathered to dispose of the nation's affairs. Since Stubbs, there have developed a multiplicity of views all departing more or less from this simple monolithic concept, and testifying by their variations to the vigour of recent thinking on this important point. The school of writers which has departed farthest from Stubbs is that which derives ultimately from his younger and some think even greater contemporary, F. W. Maitland. The departure, which was at first expressed in gentle and far from challenging terms, has since led to a wide cleavage of opinion. Instead of regarding parliament as being essentially a political assembly, the disciples of Maitland have regarded it as essentially a court of justice. Its history is to be explained in terms of this inner nature, as are its functions and personnel at various stages in the medieval period. The only essential part of the assembly was the council; its only indispensable function was the judicial work of the conciliar body. The decisive turning-point in its history was not the addition of representative estates, which were never completely necessary to its full existence during the medieval period (though custom tended to make them so), but the transformation of the early political gatherings into judicial and conciliar assemblies. This occurred, it is believed, roughly at the time of the Provisions of Oxford; by the reign of Edward I, parliament was a court placed above other courts and devised to dispense the highest justice in the land. According to this interpretation parliament served an altogether different and more limited purpose than that which had been claimed for it in the pages of Bishop Stubbs.

The consequences which flow from this fundamental divergence between the "schools" of Maitland and Stubbs extend to almost every problem of the medieval parliament; from its origin to its composition, from its relation to the monarch to its evolution into the High Court of the Realm. One view tends to make parliament the instrument of the ruler; the other makes it essentially a meeting between the king and the *universitas*, serving the purpose of both. There are many concepts of parliament which lie between these extremes. Some of these, for example, reject the notion that parliament was essentially a court, but nevertheless hold that it was a "conciliar" assembly. Sometimes it may be suspected that such compromises entail the combination of incompatible elements; and it seems probable that historians will have to make a choice between the two main lines of interpretation which cannot be reconciled. According to one, parliament was a political assembly; according to the other, it was a body whose essence is to be found in the judicial functions which it exercised in common with the council, and which expanded in due course into those of the High Court of the Realm.

Of the sources which throw light on this problem, the most obvious are the Rolls of Parliament. Unfortunately, they only begin in the reign of Edward I. At that time, they consist almost exclusively of a record of judicial proceedings—the unsystematic recordings of the activities of a court. The haphazard arrangement and fragmentary character of the records appear, not as something to be explained away, but rather as something to be expected from a body whose business mostly originated in written petitions to the king. Like the rolls of any court of law, those of parliament were at first merely a "putting together of odds and ends." Unfortunately it has not been possible to translate them below; for if we wished to give a true picture of their nature we should have to illustrate them at length. It must be emphasized, however, that no historian can properly deny their judicial nature: one reason for not translating them at length is that their nature is not in any way in doubt. It is only the conclusions which are to be drawn from them which are a matter of debate.

Despite the character of the early Rolls, it may still be doubted whether the activities they reflect provided the essential reason why parliament was summoned. Of course the different people who attended had different reasons for placing a high value upon it. Those who put forward petitions probably cherished their access to king and council; but petitions to the king could be made at any time, and did not need a session of parliament. Moreover, it seems likely that anybody, whether summoned to parliament or not, could petition the king during a parliamentary assembly. These facts seem to suggest that the judicial work which took place there, derived from petitions, was incidental. The main purpose for which "members" were summoned, and which was peculiar to them, was the weighty business of the realm and of foreign lands, referred to by Edward I in 1280. Finally, and this is of great importance, we know that in the early parliaments much political business was transacted which was never, or very rarely, recorded on the rolls of the parliaments of Edward I. The parliament of Edward I was becoming an institution with an entity and traditions of its own; but it had not developed so far as to have a record of its "corporate" activities, distinct from those of the king and council who acted in the assembly of parliament or who acted, as *Fleta* put it, in the presence of the magnates. It was the king and council in parliament who judged and heard petitions in the age of *Fleta*, not the High Court of Parliament.

Two other major sources of our knowledge of parliament before the death of Edward I are the chronicles, which contain frequent and important references to particular assemblies, and the writs of summons . . . which often indicate briefly the purpose for which individuals or representatives were commanded to attend. The former were no doubt inconsistent and lacking in precision in their references to parliament; and the latter probably tended to become conventional; but together they represent a formidable body of evidence. They tell us what purpose was seen in the actual assemblies by the educated opinion of the age, and also what the king and his ministers proclaimed to be the purpose of the parliamentary assembly. Matthew Paris in particular wrote in great detail and with a sensitive ear for significant formulae, and he has left a fine memorial to some of the great public assemblies which occurred between 1232 and 1258.

The first conclusion suggested by these documents is that the general concern of the early parliaments was with what we may call politics. The second is that the general assemblies which were summoned after 1242 were as much genuine parliaments as those which were later summoned by Edward I. The third, which will, indeed, only become fully apparent at a later stage, is that there was no real break in the early development of the parliamentary assembly. It follows from all this that parliament was already well established, and its problems were already very familiar, long before the end of the thirteenth century. The fourth and final conclusion is that there was a deep distinction between the council and parliament. In particular, the two bodies were summoned for different purposes, or at least in a different relationship to the king.

The last conclusion need not be further debated, though perhaps one fleeting reference should again be made to the Provisions of Oxford, where the council, though plainly exceptional in its attributes, was no less plainly distinguished from parliament whose essence was the community of the realm. One or two comments should be offered, however, on the great "public assemblies" of this age, now first coming to be called parliaments, and on one or two of the summonses which help us to understand their nature and the footing on which the knights first made there the tentative and uncertain beginning of what was destined to be a glorious career.

The gathering of 1237 was not called a parliament but it was summoned by a writ which closely resembled those used in connection with the parliamentary assemblies of Edward I. The earls and barons were gathered together to treat about royal business which concerned the whole realm. According to the king, the prelates and magnates had treaty with him concerning the state of the ruler and of the kingdom. It is quite certain that this formula was considered to be significant. The assembly of 1237 was, in fact, a meeting between the king and the *universitas;* its concern was the welfare of the *regnum;* and it shows a distinction between the magnates and the council, composed of the *secretarii,* one of whom acted as "mediator between the king and the magnates of the realm."

The assembly of 1242 produced what Stubbs called the first authorized account of a parliamentary debate. Matthew Paris both gave his own account and reproduced a record which had been drawn up, he said, lest the replies of the barons should be forgotten. The magnates were summoned, he said, to hear the wish of the king and the business for which he had called them. He did not record the terms of the writ, perhaps because they were not so striking; but we have the enrolment of the actual summons, maybe the first such to survive; and it strongly resembles the corresponding writs of Edward I's reign. Henry wanted the magnates to treat with him and with each other concerning arduous business of his foreign policy which especially touched the estate of his realm. The money which the king asked for was to be spent for the advantage of the king and the kingdom. It was thus for business which was both general and political, at least as far as this kind of evidence will take us, that parliament was summoned in 1242.

In 1254, the surviving writs summoning assemblies began to include those directed to the shires commanding the attendance of "representative" knights. The problem of the relationship of the Commons to parliament begins to be important; and enough writs have survived to suggest that this was the case even before the accession of Edward I. We do not yet understand, and maybe shall never quite understand, all the implications of the carefully worded summons of knights in 1254 . . . to be before a meeting of the council in the king's absence. The knights were not summoned to say "yes" or "no" to a request for aid to the king, but to say "what sort of aid they will give." But we should notice their summons on these terms was suggested by the magnates in England rather than by Henry overseas; and it was probably a recognition that the voice of the knights was something which, in regard to taxation or military service, could not be safely ignored.

Important summonses of knights and burgesses to parliament . . . were issued in the period of baronial control and experiment between 1258 and 1265. The magnates, who were controlling the king, summoned the knights in 1261 to "treat" about the common affairs of the kingdom, apparently on terms of equality with the magnates; but the king, who was at odds with his nobles, issued a countersummons in which he invited the knights merely to have a colloquy and to understand his honourable intentions. This seems to indicate that the significance of the terms of summons was well understood.

In the famous Montfortian parliament of June 1264, unmistakably expressing baronial and not royal views of such matters, knights were summoned to "treat" about the affairs of both the king and the kingdom; and it is possible but not certain that both knights and burgesses received a similar summons in January 1265.

Thus parliament was already well established by the age of Edward I, and the question of enlarging the *universitas* there had already arisen. If parliament was still an occasion or an event, it was rapidly clothing itself with the forms and procedures of an institution. The political activities of the earlier period continued to be fundamental. Justice soon began to overshadow other matters; but Edward I himself disapproved of this; he wanted to keep his hands free for the great business of his realm and of his "foreines" lands. The English parliament was a European phenomenon, the product of European conditions of political life; and it was marked by universal characteristics. "It is the custom," Humbert de Romans, Master General of the Dominican Order, wrote about the time of Edward I's accession, "for great kings to hold parliaments at appointed times every year, at which assemble many counsellors and many of the worldly great and many prelates. These parliaments are held for three great purposes: that the more important public affairs may be the more wisely resolved there after more searching considerations; that account may be rendered there by the ministers of the realm; and that order may be taken there for the good government of the realm." It is far more important to insist on the implications of such a description than on the many meanings of *parliamentum*, or the extent to which parliament was still not an institution but an event.